Existence, Truth, and Provability

Existence, Truth, and Provability

Hugues Leblanc

Department of Philosophy, Temple University

State University of New York Press   Albany

Published by State University of New York Press, Albany

© 1982 State University of New York

All rights reserved

Printed in the United States of America

No part of this book may be used or reproduced in any manner whatsoever without written permission except in the case of brief quotations embodied in critical articles and reviews.

For information, address State University of New York Press, State University Plaza, Albany, N.Y., 12246

Library of Congress Cataloging in Publication Data

Leblanc, Hugues, 1924-
  Existence, truth, and provability.
  Bibliography: p. 453
  Includes index.
  1. Logic—Addresses, essays, lectures.
  2. Philosophy—Addresses, essays, lectures.
  3. Truth—Addresses, essays, lectures.
  4. Evidence—Addresses, essays, lectures.
  5. Semantics (Philosophy)—Addresses, essays, lectures.
  I. Title.
  BC51.L42   160   79-12852
  ISBN 0-87395-380-0
  ISBN 0-87395-450-5 (pbk.)

To
N. D. Belnap, Jr., E. W. Beth, H. Goldberg,
T. Hailperin, K. Lambert, R. P. McArthur, R. K. Meyer,
R. H. Thomason, and G. Weaver
for their collaboration

Contents

Preface *ix*

Part 1   Existence

Introduction *3*
1. Non-Designating Singular Terms (T. Hailperin, coauthor) *17*
2. Completeness Theorems for Some Presupposition-free Logics (R. H. Thomason, coauthor) *22*
3. On Prefacing $(\forall X)A \supset A(Y/X)$ with $(\forall Y)$: A Free Quantification Theory without Identity (R. K. Meyer, coauthor) *58*
4. Truth-Value Semantics for a Logic of Existence *76*
5. Open Formulas and the Empty Domain (R. K. Meyer, coauthor) *91*
6. A Liberated Version of S5 (K. Lambert and R. K. Meyer, coauthors) *99*
7. On Dispensing with Things and Worlds *103*

Part 2   Truth

Introduction *123*
8. A Simplified Account of Validity and Implication for Quantificational Logic *139*
9. A Simplified Strong Completeness Proof for $QC_=$ *144*
10. Truth-Value Assignments and Their Cardinality *156*
11. Three Generalizations of a Theorem of Beth's *166*
12. Truth-Value Semantics for the Theory of Types (R. K. Meyer, coauthor) *177*
13. Wittgenstein and the Truth-Functionality Thesis *198*
14. Matters of Relevance *205*
15. Truth-Functionality and the Ramified Theory of Types (G. Weaver, coauthor) *220*

16. That *Principia Mathematica, First Edition*, Has a Predicative Interpretation After All   *236*
17. A Strong Completeness Theorem for Three-Valued Logic: Part I (H. Goldberg and G. Weaver, coauthors)   *240*
18. A Strong Completeness Theorem for Three-Valued Logic: Part II   *247*
19. A Completeness Result for Quantificational Tense Logic (R. P. McArthur, coauthor)   *258*
20. Semantic Deviations   *267*

Part 3   Provability

Introduction   *283*
21. Marginalia on Gentzen's Sequenzen-Kalkule   *293*
22. Structural Rules of Inference   *301*
23. Proof Routines for the Propositional Calculus   *306*
24. Two Separation Theorems for Natural Deduction   *328*
25. Two Shortcomings of Natural Deduction   *350*
26. Subformula Theorems for N-Sequents   *358*
27. A Note on the Intuitionist and the Classical Propositional Calculus (E. W. Beth, coauthor)   *382*
28. Intuitionism Reconsidered (N. D. Belnap, Jr., coauthor)   *385*
29. On *Not* Strengthening Intuitionist Logic (N. D. Belnap, Jr., and R. H. Thomason, coauthors)   *390*
30. The Demarcation Line Between Intuitionist Logic and Classical Logic (R. H. Thomason, coauthor)   *397*
31. Boolean Algebra and the Propositional Calculus   *404*
32. The Algebra of Logic and the Theory of Deduction   *408*
33. All or None: A Novel Choice of Primitives for Elementary Logic (R. H. Thomason, coauthor)   *414*
34. Matters of Separation (R. K. Meyer, coauthor)   *422*
35. Generalization in First-Order Logic   *431*

H. Leblanc: A Bibliography   *453*
Index of Proper Names   *457*
Index of Subject Matters   *461*

Preface

Reissued in this volume are thirty-five of my papers on logic and the philosophy thereof. The papers, published over the last twenty years, are assembled in three groups, respectively headed *Existence, Truth,* and *Provability*. The seven comprising the first group deal with non-designating terms and more generally "presupposition-free logic," a logic to which #1 (and a paper by Hintikka published like #1 in 1959) constituted one of the very first contributions. The thirteen papers comprising the second group deal with the substitution interpretation of the quantifiers and more generally "truth-value semantics," a semantics to which #8 (and a paper by Dunn and Belnap published like #8 in 1968) constituted an early contribution.* And the fifteen comprising the third group deal with natural deduction, Gentzen's sequents, the demarcation between intuitionist and classical logic, that between Boolean algebra and the sentential calculus, etc. For lack of space papers dealing with matters other than existence, truth, and provability were systematically left out. Hence the absence of studies in confirmation theory, probability theory, and *probabilistic semantics,* the last an outgrowth of truth-value semantics that is gaining attention. I hope to reissue some of these papers separately.

It has repeatedly been my good fortune to interest others in problems I was working on and secure their collaboration. So, of the thirty-five papers in this collection fifteen are coauthored, a figure which well underscores my debt to fellow logicians (N. D. Belnap, Jr., E. W. Beth†, T. Hailperin, K. Lambert, R. K. Meyer, R. H. Thomason, and G. Weaver) and to former students at Temple University (H. Goldberg and R. P. McArthur). Dedicating the book to them seemed the only fitting way of expressing my gratitude: much of the material is theirs, and credit for it should accordingly go to them. I further thank them for permission to amend the papers as I saw fit, a liberty of which I availed myself

---

*Not one of the first contributions, though. That distinction goes to Beth's *The Foundations of Mathematics* (1959) and to writings of Schütte's (1960 and 1962). Credit is also due to Ruth B. Marcus, who championed the substitution interpretation of the quantifiers throughout the sixties.

throughout the book. Numerous errors (some detected by readers and the rest by me as I edited the papers) had to be corrected; ill-written passages, also numerous, had to be revised; etc. Responsibility for these changes and the Introductions to the three parts of *Existence, Truth, and Provability* rests entirely with me.

Thanks are also due to the editors and publishers of eleven journals (*American Philosophical Quarterly, Archiv für mathematische Logik und Grundlagenforschung, Fundamenta Mathematicae, Journal of Philosophical Logic, The Journal of Philosophy, The Journal of Symbolic Logic,* Logique et Analyse, Mind, Philosophia, The Philosophical Review,* and *Zeitschrift für mathematische Logik und Grundlagen der Mathematik*), four collections of essays (*Contributions to Logic and Methodology in Honor of J. M. Bochenski, Philosophical Problems in Logic: Some Recent Developments, Logic and Ontology: Studies in Contemporary Philosophy,* and *Truth, Syntax and Modality*), and the proceedings of one congress (*Akten des xiv. Internationalen Kongresses für Philosophie*) for publishing the original papers and permitting me to reissue them here. The provenance of each paper, incidentally, is reported at the close of the book.

Finally, thanks are due to Temple University for awarding me in 1977 a Summer Research Fellowship; to Dean George W. Johnson of the College of Liberal Arts for his unfailing support and encouragement; to Raymond D. Gumb (California State University, Northridge) for his labors on behalf of free logic and nonstandard semantics; to Margaret A. Mirabelli who so efficiently and so patiently prepared the typescript for the printer; to Nancy Sharlet and Suellen Wenz of SUNY Press who saw the book through the press; and to all others who enabled me to complete this task.

September 7, 1981   Hugues Leblanc
                                                                                                             Temple University

---

*The Director of the American Mathematical Society requested inclusion of the following copyright statement regarding #8, #26, and #33: "Reprinted with permission of the publisher Association for Symbolic Logic from the *Journal of Symbolic Logic:* Copyright © 1968, Volume 33, pp. 231–235, Copyright © 1968, Volume 33, pp. 161–179, Copyright © 1967, Volume 32, pp. 345–351."

Part 1: Existence

Introduction

As the reader doubtless knows, formulations of QC (the first-order quantificational calculus), $QC_=$ (the first-order quantificational calculus with identity), etc., used to disavow the null set as a "domain." They thus presupposed that "something exists," a minimal presupposition, to be sure, but one purists objected to, feeling that the laws of logic should hold whether there be individuals or not, whether there be attributes (= properties and relations) or not, whether there be sets or not, etc. For instance, *Principia Mathematica* (1910 – 13) disavowed $\emptyset$ as a domain, but Russell himself came to deplore this, as he admits in *Introduction to Mathematical Philosophy* (1919). So from 1934 on *various* reformulations of QC (and of such extensions of QC as $QC_=$) have been devised which acknowledge $\emptyset$ as a domain and for that reason are sometimes known as *inclusive* quantificational logics.[1]

I deliberately italicized the word 'various': there are indeed quite a few ways of so editing, say, QC that it will accommodate the extra domain $\emptyset$. (i) Jaśkowski in his 1934 paper on natural deduction admits only closed formulas (or, as another terminology would have it, only closed wffs) as theorems; so does Hailperin in his 1953 paper on empty domains; and so does Quine in his 1954 rewrite of Hailperin's paper. Mostowski, on the other hand, has open as well as closed theorems in his 1951 paper, and so do most subsequent writers on the subject. (ii) Whether you admit only closed theorems or admit both open and closed ones, you may with Mostowski declare a vacuous quantification $(\forall X)A$ "true in" $\emptyset$ only if A is true in $\emptyset$, or as in Hailperin and Quine you may treat it true in $\emptyset$ no matter what. The latter way of doing things is simpler, and so usually preferred. (iii) When open as well as closed theorems are admitted, you may with Mostowski count any open formula automatically true in $\emptyset$, this on the grounds that (a) *any non-vacuous quantification should be true in* $\emptyset$[2] and (b) *in* $\emptyset$ *as in any other domain an open formula should be true if its universal closure is*. However, devotees of free logic (the logic to occupy us next) often take exception to (b), and in any event Modus Ponens fails under

3

Mostowski's account of open formulas. Another and far better way of doing things is to put '$p \supset p$' for all universal quantifications in an open formula, put '$\sim(p \supset p)$' for all existential ones, and ascertain the truth-value of the resulting formula by means of a truth-table. Meyer and I pursue the point in #5, the one paper in Part 1 to deal exclusively with $\emptyset$ as a domain.[3]

Standard formulations of QC (and of such extensions of QC as $QC_=$) also presupposed that the individual variables 'x', 'y', 'z', etc., each "have values," and hence that singular terms—which one is normally free to substitute for these variables—each designate something. The presupposition is of far greater concern than the one Russell deplored. However broad one's understanding of the verb 'to designate', there are certain expressions which just do not—in some cases, just cannot—designate anything, and yet are used as singular terms.[4] A case in point is 'the impossible', an expression which cannot possibly designate anything. Yet we use it in such sentences as 'The impossible can't be', 'You're undertaking the impossible', etc.

Repeatedly raised, the issue is often dodged. Logic primers, for example, advise one to use only designating terms. Non-designating ones, unfortunately, are often indispensable in everyday exchanges; and, in any event, whether a certain term designates or not (and, hence, may be substituted or not for 'x', 'y', 'z', etc.,) need not be known. Other times the issue is met head-on: Quine, for example, advises one to discard singular terms in favor of (definite) descriptions, and handle the latter as Russell did.[5] Since in *Principia Mathematica* you cannot substitute descriptions for 'x', 'y', 'z', etc., at will, the latter may have values without the former necessarily designating anything. The advice, however, leaves many uneasy: Russell's theory of descriptions has met with severe criticism, and using descriptions in lieu of singular terms is *quite* a departure from ordinary practice.

Dissatisfaction with these recommendations led from the late fifties on to the devising of "(presupposition-)free" logics, i.e., to formulations of QC, $QC_=$, etc., which are free of the present presupposition, and frequently of that on p. 3 as well.[6] Tentative, but nonetheless suggestive, essays were contributed by Leonard (1956), Nakhnikian and Salmon (1957), and Rescher (1957 and 1959). Then came papers by Leblanc and Hailperin (1959), Hintikka (1959), Lambert (1963 and 1967), van Fraassen (1966), Cocchiarella (1966), etc., and free logic was born.[7]

Now for some specifics. Suppose first that QC, $QC_=$, etc., have singular terms.[8] Then there are various formulas which on the face of it demand that these terms each designate something. Cases in point are

$$f(a) \supset (\exists x)f(x) \qquad (1)$$

and its dual

$$(\forall x)f(x) \supset f(a) \qquad (2),$$

where 'a' is to be understood as a singular term. Or suppose that QC, $QC_=$, etc., have no singular terms, but that the individual variables 'x', 'y', 'z', etc., serve as place-holders for such terms. Then there are various formulas which on the face of it demand that 'x', 'y', 'z', etc., each have a value. Cases in point are of course

$$f(y) \supset (\exists x)f(x) \qquad (3)$$

and its dual

$$(\forall x)f(x) \supset f(y) \qquad (4).$$

Free logicians, as a result, have two tasks:

(a) so amend the standard axioms and rules of inference to QC, QC$_=$, etc., as to block proof of (1), (2), and the like when the calculi in question have singular terms, otherwise of (3), (4), and the like, and

(b) so amend the standard notion of validity that all and only such formulas of QC, QC$_=$, etc., as are provable by the amended axioms and rules of QC, QC$_=$, etc., will qualify as valid.

Assignment (a) was tackled by Leblanc and Hailperin in their 1959 paper (#1 below) for a brand of QC$_=$ with singular terms. The axioms and rules proposed there block proof of (1)–(2) and of the corresponding inference forms

$$f(a) \qquad \text{and} \qquad (\forall x)f(x)$$
$$\therefore (\exists x)f(x) \qquad\qquad \therefore f(a).$$

However, they permit proof of (3)–(4). So Leblanc and Hailperin's individual variables cannot serve as place-holders for singular terms, a feature of the paper and of various post-1959 contributions to free logic which I for one now frown upon. The assignment was also tackled by Hintikka in his 1959 paper for a brand of QC$_=$ without singular terms. His axioms and rules of inference block proof of (3)–(4) and of the corresponding inference forms

$$f(y) \qquad \text{and} \qquad (\forall x)f(x)$$
$$\therefore (\exists x)f(x) \qquad\qquad \therefore f(y).[9]$$

As Leblanc and Hailperin knew, their axioms and rules of inference permit proof of

$$(\exists x)(f(x) \lor \sim f(x)) \qquad (5),$$

a formula which on the face of it demands something to exist. Their formulation of QC$_=$ is therefore not free of the presupposition on p. 3. Hintikka, on the other hand, meant to block proof of (5), but—further investigations of the matter reveal—failed in the attempt. The first formulation of QC$_=$ that is free of the presupposition on p. 3 as well as that on p. 4 may therefore be in Lambert's 1963 paper.

A feature of the Leblanc-Hailperin paper and the Hintikka one calls for comment.[10] Prior to 1934 the practice, when formulating such a calculus as QC$_=$, was to enlist formulas of QC$_=$ as axioms ((4), incidentally, was often

6   Part 1: Existence

one of them); enlist such metastatements as Modus Ponens, Generalization, etc., as rules of inference; pronounce certain columns of formulas derivations, more specifically, derivations of certain formulas from certain (sequences of) formulas; and say that formula B is derivable from (the sequence of) formulas $A_1, A_2, \ldots, A_n$—for short, $A_1, A_2, \ldots, A_n \vdash B$—*if there is a derivation of B from $A_1, A_2, \ldots, A_n$*.[11] In 1934 Gentzen and Jaśkowski showed (independently of each other) that '$\vdash$' can be defined in a totally different and far more natural way. In certain clauses of the definition, known as *the base clauses*, you declare certain formulas derivable from certain sequences of formulas; and in the remaining clauses, known as *the inductive clauses*, you declare certain formulas derivable from certain sequences of formulas if—to limit ourselves to the simplest case—certain other formulas are derivable from certain other sequences of formulas.

$$A \vdash A,$$

sometimes known as Reiteration, is a typical base clause; and

If $A_1, A_2, \ldots, A_{n+1} \vdash B$, then $A_1, A_2, \ldots, A_n \vdash A_{n+1} \supset B$,

sometimes known as Conditional Introduction, is a typical inductive clause.

The Leblanc-Hailperin account of '$\vdash$' is of the sort just described, their one axiom schema being a base clause and their rules of inference being inductive clauses. Hintikka's account is of a kindred sort. Instead of directly defining '$A \vdash B$', he first defines

$$A \leftrightarrow B,$$

a metastatement tantamount to '$A \vdash B$ and $B \vdash A$', and next defines his counterpart

$$A \rightarrow B$$

of '$A \vdash B$' as '$A \leftrightarrow A \& B$'. The more general '$A_1, A_2, \ldots, A_n \rightarrow B$' can then be defined as '$(\ldots (A_1 \& A_2) \& \ldots) \& A_n \rightarrow B$' when $n > 0$, and as '$B \vee {\sim}B \rightarrow B$' when $n = 0$. Hintikka's account of derivability is somewhat less perspicuous than its rivals, which may account for the difficulty over (5) reported on p. 5.

Formulas (1)–(2) would of course hold in free logic if prefaced by some such clause as

'a' designates something

or, equivalently,

a exists   (6);

and so would formulate (3)–(4) if prefaced by the matching clause

'y' has a value

or, equivalently,

Introduction 7

$$y \text{ exists} \tag{7}$$

In his 1956 paper Leonard offered a symbolic rendition of (7), to wit:

$$(\exists f)(f(y) \ \& \ \Diamond \sim f(y)) \tag{8}$$

and in his 1959 paper Rescher offered a revision of (8) which contains no modal operator, to wit:

$$(\exists f)(f(y) \ \& \ (\exists z)\sim f(z)) \tag{9}$$

But these renditions of (7), if at all proper, are of course of no help in such *first-order* calculi as QC, $QC_=$, etc.[12] Nakhnikian and Salmon suggested in their 1957 paper a rendition of (7) which uses but ' = ', to wit:

$$y = y \tag{10}$$

The proposal is reminiscent of Theorem *14.28 in *Principia Mathematica*:

$$E!(\imath x)\varphi(x) \equiv . \ (\imath x)\varphi(x) = (\imath x)\varphi(x),$$

and thus has venerable credentials. It unfortunately will not do in all those formulations of $QC_=$ (and they are a majority) which own (10) as a theorem.[13] Yet another rendition of (6) uses but ' = ', to wit:

$$(\exists x)(x = y) \tag{11}$$

Stemming from Theorem *14.204 in *Principia Mathematica*, to wit:

$$E!(\imath x)\varphi(x) \equiv (\exists b)((\imath x)\varphi(x) = b),$$

(11) suits formulations of $QC_=$ in which (10) is provable.

It is (11) which Hintikka uses in "Existential Presuppositions and Existential Commitments" as his way of saying (7), and the equivalent

$$(\exists x)(y = x)$$

which Leblanc and Hailperin use in "Non-Designating Singular Terms" as their way of saying (7). Proof is offered in the first paper of the "free" counterpart

$$(\exists x)(x = y) \supset (f(y) \supset (\exists x)f(x)) \tag{12}$$

of (3), and proof offered in the second of the "free" counterpart

$$(\exists x)(a = x) \supset (f(a) \supset (\exists x)f(x)) \tag{13}$$

of (1).[14] Leblanc and Hailperin go on to show that (1) is not provable in their formulation of $QC_=$; exactly the same argument would show that (3) is not provable in Hintikka's formulation of the calculus. These results, in my opinion, launched free logic on its course.

The reader will have noticed the existence predicate 'E!' in the foregoing quotations, *14.28 and *14.204, from *Principia Mathematica*. An extension of QC, occasionally referred to as QC! and first formulated in a paper by Lambert

8   Part 1: Existence

(1967) and one by Meyer and Lambert (1968), does boast 'E!' as a primitive sign. The "free" counterparts of (1) and (3) in QC! are of course

$$E!a \supset (f(a) \supset (\exists x)f(x))$$

and

$$E!y \supset (f(y) \supset (\exists x)f(x)),$$

two formulas readily had as theorems.

QC does not permit definition of '=' or of 'E!'. The closest analogues there of (12)−(13) are

$$(\exists x)(f(x) \equiv f(y)) \supset (f(y) \supset (\exists x)f(x))$$

and

$$(\exists x)(f(a) \equiv f(y)) \supset (f(a) \supset (\exists x)f(x)),$$

two formulas which by dint of Generalization, Distributivity of '∀' through '⊃', and Modus Ponens deliver

$$(\forall y)(\exists x)(f(y) \equiv f(x)) \supset (\forall y)(f(y) \supset (\exists x)f(x))[15] \qquad (14).$$

The consequent of (14) is of particular interest. Indeed,

$$(\forall y)(f(y) \supset (\exists x)f(x))$$

often does duty for (1) in free formulations of QC using '∃' as a primitive sign; and its dual

$$(\forall y)((\forall x)f(x) \supset f(y))$$

often does duty for (2) in those using '∀' in that capacity (see **A6** below).[16]

Axiom schemata and rules of inference for free QC, QC$_=$, QC!, and four modal extensions of QC will be found in five papers from Part 1 (#1–#4 and #7) and one paper from Part 3 (#35). In #3, #4, #7, and #35 I employ so-called *individual parameters*. These are individual signs that can be understood either as *free* individual variables (i.e., as individual variables which in a formula *occur free and free only*) or alternatively as singular terms. In the other two papers I employ *both free individual variables and singular terms, and—as suggested earlier— occasionally require that the former each have a value*.

(i)   In the case of QC I would recommend the following axiom schemata.[17]
    A1. $A \supset (B \supset A)$
    A2. $(A \supset (B \supset C)) \supset ((A \supset B) \supset (A \supset C))$
    A3. $(\sim A \supset \sim B) \supset (B \supset A)$
    A4. $A \supset (\forall X)A$, where X is foreign to A
    A5. $(\forall X)(A \supset B) \supset ((\forall X)A \supset (\forall X)B)$
    A6. $(\forall Y)((\forall X)A \supset A(Y/X))$
    A7. $(\forall X)(\forall Y)A \supset (\forall Y)(\forall X)A$,[18]

plus $(\forall X)A(X/P)$, where A is an axiom and P is an individual parameter. These axiom schemata are studied in #3, #7, and #35.

(ii) In the case of $QC_=$ I would recommend **A1 – A5**, *plus*
 B1. $(\forall Y)(\exists X)(X = Y)$
 B2. $P = P' \supset (A \supset A(P'/P))$, where P and P' are individual parameters and A is atomic
 B3. $P = P' \supset (A(P'/P) \supset A)$, where P, P', and A are as in **B2**,
 B4. $P = P$

plus $(\forall X)A(X/P)$, where A and P are as in (a). These axiom schemata are studied in #35.

(iii) In the case of QC! I would recommend **A1 – A5**, *plus*
 C1. $(\forall X)A \supset (E!P \supset A(P/X))$, where P is an individual parameter
 C2. $(\forall X)E!X$,

plus $(\forall X)A(X/P)$, where A and P are as in (a). These axioms schemata are studied in #4.

In all three cases only one rule of inference is needed: Modus Ponens; proof of (5) is blocked; and so is proof of any formula of either of the two sorts $(\forall X)A \supset A(P/X)$ and $A(P/X) \supset (\exists X)A$.

Another set of axiom schemata and rules of inference for free $QC_=$ will of course be found in #1, a paper which—as reported earlier—sports both free individual variables and singular terms and permits proof of (3) – (5). And fifteen additional sets can be found in #2, a paper which also sports both free individual variables and singular terms, and addresses various possibilities: free individual variables having no values, singular terms designating something not a value of a variable or designating nothing, and so on. Two rules of inference are needed in some of these fifteen cases, three in others.

To my knowledge no serious attempt was made until 1966 to tackle assignment (b) on p. 5. True, Mostowski had provided in 1951 an account of validity for his inclusive formulation of QC, and Hailperin had offered in 1953 his alternative (and now generally accepted) treatment of the matter. But seven years were to elapse between the publication of the Leblanc-Hailperin and Hintikka papers discussed on pp. 5–7 and that of van Fraassen's "Singular Terms, Truth-Value Gaps, and Free Logic," a paper which explicates validity for Lambert's 1963 free formulation of $QC_=$ and—after slight adjustments—for the Leblanc-Hailperin and Hintikka ones.

A sketch of van Fraassen's account may be welcome. Given a non-empty domain D and an interpretation over D, call it I_D, of the variables of QC and of zero or more of the singular terms of QC, van Fraassen introduces a first function—called a *classical valuation over the model* $<D,I_D>$—which assigns a truth-value to each closed formula of QC. He next introduces a second function—called a *supervaluation over the model* $<D,I_D>$—which assigns the truth-value **T** to the closed formulas of QC assigned **T** by all the classical valuations over $<D,I_D>$ and **F** to those assigned **F** by all the supervaluations in question. Valid then is any closed formula A of QC (1) which, no matter the model

$\langle D, I_D \rangle$, is assigned **T** by all the supervaluations over $\langle D, I_D \rangle$ and (2) which substitution of '$p \supset p$' for every universal quantification in A transforms into a tautology.[19] As the reader who glances back at p. 4 will realize, (2) is a way here of owning $\emptyset$ as a domain.

Van Fraassen then attends to '$=$' and winds up with an account of validity for free $QC_=$ as well as free QC. He does not trouble to show that a closed formula of $QC_=$ is valid in his sense if and only if provable by Lambert's axioms and rules of inference, but classical soundness and completeness proofs are readily adjusted to yield the result. Incidentally, if condition (2) in the previous paragraph were dropped, a closed formula of $QC_=$ would qualify as valid if and only if provable by the axioms and rules of inference in Leblanc and Hailperin's paper or those in Hintikka's.

Van Fraassen's account of (formula) validity for free $QC_=$ (and, by implication, free QC) does the job, and does it very neatly. His account of entailment, however, poses a problem. Heeding classical precedent, van Fraassen takes a set S of closed formulas of $QC_=$ to entail a closed formula A of $QC_=$ (or, to use his own terminology, van Fraassen takes the argument from S to A to be valid) if A is assigned **T** by all supervaluations that assign **T** to all members of S. Under this account, the formula '$(\exists x)f(x)$'—though not derivable from the set $\{f(a)\}$ by means of Lambert's axioms and rules of inference—is entailed by $\{f(a)\}$; and, similarly, the formula '$f(a)$'—though not derivable from the set $\{(\forall x)f(x)\}$ by means of Lambert's axioms and rules of inference—is entailed by $\{(\forall x)f(x)\}$. Van Fraassen concludes from this that Lambert's axioms and rules of inference do not suit entailment (or, as he puts it, argument validity) in free $QC_=$. I would rather conclude that van Fraassen's account of entailment is defective, indeed totally at variance with the intentions of Leonard, Leblanc and Hailperin, Hintikka, etc. A substitute account can fortunately be had, which to me is in the spirit of free logic and which the axioms and rules of inference in (i)–(iii) exactly suit: you take a finite set $\{A_1, A_2, \ldots, A_n\}$ ($n \geq 0$) of formulas to entail a formula B if the conditional $A_1 \supset (A_2 \supset (\ldots \supset (A_n \supset B) \ldots))$ is valid in van Fraassen's sense, and you take an infinite set S of formulas to entail B if some finite subset of S does.

A second paper by van Fraassen, entitled "The Completeness of Free Logic," appeared the same year as "Singular Terms, Truth-Value Gaps, and Free Logic." It supplied a fresh account of validity for free $QC_=$ and showed in all required details that any closed formula of $QC_=$ valid in this sense is provable by Lambert's axioms and rules of inference. A sequel to it, published in 1968, has a fresh account of entailment, equivalent by the way to the one I suggested above, and showed—again in all required details—that any closed formula of $QC_=$ entailed in this sense by a set of closed formulas of $QC_=$ is derivable from the set by Lambert's means.

The account of entailment in the 1968 paper is a familiar one, B being entailed by S if B is true in every model in which every member of S is true. However, the account of validity in the second 1966 paper is quite complicated, using as it does domains, interpretation functions, assignment functions, denotation functions, auxiliary valuation functions, and valuation functions; and van Fraassen's two completeness proofs (the weak or statement completeness proof in the second 1966 paper and the strong or argument one of 1968) are in my estimation somewhat arduous to follow, the 1966 proof using analogues of Beth's semantic tableaux (called *semantic sequences*) and the 1968 one borrowing from topology.

Alternative accounts of validity for free QC, free QC$_=$, free QC!, etc., may thus be welcome, and so may be alternative completeness proofs, in particular proofs in what is called *the Henkin style*. Samples will be found in #2 − #4. #2, the reader will recall, offers a superabundance of accounts and proofs: fifteen in all. Some are included just for completeness' sake, but others might well repay examination. I especially have in mind the accounts where two domains are used, a so-called *inner domain D* and a so-called *outer domain D'*. Individual variables, when they have values, draw these from D only; but singular terms, when designating something, may designate something from D' as well as D. (A prefiguration of this will be found in a 1963 paper of Kripke, where for each possible world W individual variables draw their values from the population of W, but a singular term may designate something from the population of *any* possible world, in some cases W itself, in others some possible world W' other than W.) The counterpart in #2 of Leblanc and Hailperin's formulation of QC$_=$ is shown complete by an adaptation (and simplification) of Henkin's 1949 argument; the result of owning $\emptyset$ as an inner domain in that calculus is shown complete by a further and more radical adaptation of the argument; and the completeness of the remaining thirteen calculi is then gotten in four corollaries of these two results.

Today I would fault #2 on several counts. Open formulas, i.e., formulas containing free individual variables, are held automatically true in $\emptyset$. So (3) − (4) turn up as theorems (though (1) − (2), of course, do not), and free individual variables as a result cannot serve as place-holders for singular terms, a shortcoming #2 shares with #1. Further, closed formulas containing non-designating singular terms are held either all false, a move inspired by Russell's theory of descriptions, or else all true, a move inspired by a 1954 paper of Hailperin's. After van Fraassen's papers Thomason (the coauthor of #2) and I saw no point in treating in detail the next possibility: holding some of the formulas in question true and the rest false. But that possibility is the most interesting of them all; and, as van Fraassen's treatment of it in "The Completeness of Free Logic" is somewhat unwieldly, we should have addressed it more fully.[20]

#3, written in collaboration with Meyer, makes up for the gap in #2. We provide an account of validity for free QC (a calculus we refer to as QC*) that is reminiscent of but simpler than van Fraassen's in "The Completeness of Free Logic." We show *in outline form* that every formula of QC provable by dint of the paper's axioms and Modus Ponens is valid in our sense. And we show *in nearly full detail* that every formula of QC valid in our sense is provable by dint of these axioms and Modus Ponens. Our completeness proof is in the Henkin style, but deviates at key points from Henkin's own proof, as indeed it must since the Axiom of Specification,

$$(\forall X)A \supset A(P/X),$$

is now available only in the weaker **A6** form

$$(\forall Y)((\forall X)A \supset A(Y/X)).$$

It is nonetheless simpler—in my estimation—than van Fraassen's 1966 proof. Our soundness proof, possibly the first such proof in print for free QC, is also quite elementary.

The reader will have noticed that 'in outline form' and 'in nearly full detail' are italicized. The change of font is not for emphasis only.

When attending to matters of completeness Meyer and I assumed that all formulas of the sort

$$(\forall X)(\forall Y)A \supset (\forall Y)(\forall X)A$$

were provable by dint of our axioms and Modus Ponens. However, in a paper published the same year as #3 Trew questioned a like assumption by Kripke,[21] and possibly with good reasons, as all attempts to prove those formulas by the means in question have so far failed. To be sure, attempts to prove the independence of the formulas have also failed, but in the meantime one must draft **A7** as an extra axiom schema, and I have done so in the versions of #3 and #7 below (#35 was written after I read Trew and so it featured **A7** all along).

When attending to matters of soundness Meyer and I *showed in full detail* that (i) axioms of the sort **A6** and (ii) axioms of the sort $(\forall X)A(X/P)$, where A is an axiom, are valid in our sense, but *assumed* that axioms of the sorts **A1 – A5** also were. We were right in the first four cases, but unfortunately wrong in the fifth. In his 1972 doctoral dissertation Shipley produced a formula of the sort **A4** which is not valid in our sense. In the version of #3 below I set things to right (or so I hope) by amending one truth-condition for vacuous quantifications.[22] Shipley himself devised a substitute account of validity for free QC, which I reproduce in an appendix to #3. Like van Fraassen's the account—in my estimation—is somewhat unwieldy, but it is demonstrably sound.

#3 contains a further result of interest, the so-called *Substitution Theorem*, according to which a formula is provable in free QC (as formulated in #3) if and only if it is provable in Quine's inclusive QC (as formulated in "Quantification and the Empty Domain") or is a "parametric instance" of a formula provable in Quine's inclusive QC. The result neatly ties together inclusive quantification theory (which merely owns ∅ as a domain) and free quantification theory (which owns ∅ as a domain and allows for non-designating terms).

#4 deals with free QC!, for which it provides a truth-value semantics. Thanks to 'E!' and the axioms governing that predicate, formulas of the sort

---

Added in proof: The independence of **A7** has just been established by Kit Fine.

A7 are provable without further ado. And because quantifiers are interpreted *substitutionally* rather than *model-theoretically* (or, as Quine would put it, *objectually*), a pellucid, concise, and handy account of validity can be had at long last. The completeness proof is again of the Henkin style, with only minor adjustments needed this time to accommodate non-designating singular terms. Truth-value semantics, the reader may recall, is the main concern of Part 2. But information on the subject can be found in #4, of course, and in #7, a paper which recapitulates some of Part 1 and foreshadows some of Part 2.

#6, written in collaboration with Lambert and Meyer, deals with Lewis's modal logic S5 and the counterpart there of (4), to wit:

$$\Box p \supset p.$$

Interpreted the Kripke way the formula demands that there be possible worlds, a presupposition which devotees of free logic have taken exception to. Borrowing from #5, we (i) weaken $\Box A \supset A$ (which does duty as an axiom schema in most formulations of S5) to read

$$\Diamond A \supset (\Box B \supset B);$$

(ii) allow Kripke's sets of possible worlds (called here *assignment classes*) to be empty; and (iii) go on to show that a formula of S5 is provable by dint of the resulting axioms and Modus Ponens if and only if it is valid in our sense. The result has since been extended by Morgan to various modal logics weaker than S5.

Quantified extensions of the modal logics M, B, S4, and S5 turn up in #7, where they are supplied with truth-value interpretations. I offer two formulations of each calculus, one having $(\forall X)A \supset A(P/X)$ as Specification Axiom and the other having the presupposition-free $(\forall Y)((\forall X)A \supset A(Y/X))$. As the reader may know, prefacing $(\forall X)A \supset A(Y/X)$ with $(\forall Y)$ blocks proof of the Barcan formula

$$(\forall x)\Box f(x) \supset \Box(\forall x)f(x)$$

and its converse, two conditionals whose existential presuppositions have been of concern to many.

Geared as it is to #1 – #7, the foregoing review of presupposition-free logic is perforce fragmentary. Additional information on the subject, a bibliography numbering more than two hundred entries, and translations of twenty-two key papers will be found in Bencivenga's *Le Logiche Libere*. Perusal of the book and of such texts as Haack's *Deviant Logic,* Schock's *Logics without Existential Assumptions,* and Woods's *The Logic of Fiction* would shed further light on the history of presupposition-free logic, the uses to which this new quantificational logic is currently put, and its prospects as an alternative to the older one.

Notes

1. The epithet 'inclusive' was suggested by Quine, who refers to standard formulations of QC as "exclusive," i.e., exclusive of $\emptyset$ as a domain.

14   Part 1: Existence

2. If you think of, say, '$(\forall x)f(x)$' as equivalent to (or, should '$\exists$' rather than '$\forall$' serve as primitive, short for '$\sim(\exists x)\sim f(x)$', then '$(\forall x)f(x)$' must clearly be held true in $\emptyset$.

3. The paper contains various sets of axiom schemata and rules of inference for inclusive QC (one set being of the so-called *natural deduction* kind), a strong completeness proof, and sundry historical notes. In these preliminary remarks, incidentally, I talk of *formulas*, but in the papers themselves will talk of *well-formed formulas*.

4. By a *singular term* (or *individual constant*) I understand *roughly* any expression in the singular that can serve as the subject or the object of a verb.

5. See, among texts of Quine's on the subject, "On What There Is" and pp. 227–34 of *Methods of Logic*. Russell's theory of descriptions is informally expounded in "On Denoting" and more formally in Section *14 of *Principia Mathematica*.

6. When free of the presupposition on p. 3 as well, presupposition-free logics are sometimes called *universally free*. I shall not use the label here.

7. Note the 'etc.' Among early contributors to free logic I list only those who influenced in any way the writing of #1 – #7. (Though favoring the label 'presupposition-free logic' over 'free logic' I frequently bow here and in the papers below to more general practice and drop the qualifier 'presupposition'.)

8. In which case such letters as 'f', 'g', 'h', etc., are best construed as abbreviations for predicates, and the calculi QC, QC$_=$, etc., are best construed as what Church calls *simple applied calculi*. Calculi that have individual variables and predicate ones make good sense: they are language forms. So do calculi that have singular terms and predicates (i.e., individual constants and predicate ones): they are languages. But calculi that have singular terms and predicate variables now strike me as oddities, and I urge the reader to read 'predicate' for 'predicate variable' throughout #2. (The original version of #1 talked of *predicate signs*; I have changed this to 'predicates'.)

9. As I eventually do in later papers, Hintikka uses two different runs of individual variables, one run ('x', 'y', 'z', etc.,) occurring exclusively *bound* and the other ('a', 'b', 'c', etc.,) occurring exclusively *free* in (well-formed) formulas. Having already used 'a' as a term, I cannot exactly mimic Hintikka's practice in the text. In papers where I use two runs of individual letters, two runs of predicate letters, etc., I save the appellation 'variables' for bound variables and refer to free ones as *parameters*.

10. The comment is a lengthy one, but it will prove highly pertinent in Part 3. So the reader should bear with me. The type of derivation credited lower in the text to Gentzen and Jaśkowski is what is known as *natural deduction*.

11. With the symbol '⊢' on hand, the inference forms two paragraphs back can be rendered as $f(a) \vdash (\exists x)f(x)$, $(\forall x)f(x) \vdash f(a)$, etc. In this context sets of formulas often do duty for sequences of formulas.

12. Rescher argues in his 1959 paper that (8) is conceptually objectionable as a rendition of (7). Some would argue that so is (9). The matter cannot be pursued here.

13. In #35 I consider a formulation of free QC$_=$ in which (10) and the next rendition of (6), to wit: '$(\exists x)(x = y)$', are equivalent (and neither is provable). But, as reported in the text, (10) almost invariably counts as (an axiom and hence) a theorem of free QC$_=$.

14. (12) appears in Hintikka under the guise '$(\exists x)(x = a)$ & $f(a/x) \rightarrow (\exists x)f$', and (13) in Leblanc and Hailperin under the guise $(\exists W)(W' = W)$, $A' \vdash (\exists W)A$, where W' is a singular term and A' contains W' wherever A contains free occurrences of W. (12)–(13) mimic *14.18 in *Principia Mathematica*. Hintikka remarks in a footnote that proof of '$(\exists x)(x = a)$ & $f(a/x) \rightarrow (\exists x)f$' can be retrieved from Montague and Kalish's "A Simplification of Tarski's Formulation of the Predicate Calculus" (1956). The paper was unknown to me when I hit upon proof of $(\exists W)(W' = W)$, $A' \vdash (\exists W)A$.

15. '$(\exists x)(f(x) \equiv f(y)) \supset (f(y) \supset (\exists x)f(x))$' (to be more exact, its dual '$(\exists x)(f(x) \equiv f(y)) \supset ((\forall x)f(x) \supset f(y))$') made its first appearance in the original version of #4.

16. The axiom first appeared in Lambert's 1963 paper, and its so-called *closure* was used the very same year by Kripke in his "Semantical Considerations on Modal Logic."

17. I implicitly assume in most of these introductory remarks that '$\sim$', '$\supset$', and '$\forall$' serve as

Introduction 15

sole primitive operators. '(∃X)' in the axiom schema **B1** of (ii) must therefore be interpreted as short for '~(∀X)~'.
18. I discuss further on the presence of axiom schema **A7** in (i).
19. Note that with A presumed closed the result of putting '$p \supset p$' for every universal quantification in A is a formula exhibiting just 'p', connectives, and parentheses.
20. The fourth major possibility, holding some of the formulas in question true, others false, and the rest truth-valueless is of course covered by van Fraassen's first 1966 paper. Note indeed that some formulas containing singular terms are neither assigned **T** by all valuations nor assigned **F** by all of them, and hence end up without a truth-value. Neglected for some years, the account has been revived (in modified form) by Bencivenga in his doctoral dissertation of 1977.
21. In his 1963 paper "Semantical Considerations on Modal Logic."
22. See note 12 of #3 for details on this matter.

References

[1] Bencivenga, E. 1976. *Le Logiche Libere*. Turin: Boringhieri.
[2] Beth, E. W. 1959. *The Foundations of Mathematics*. Amsterdam: North-Holland.
[3] Church, A. 1956. *Introduction to Mathematical Logic, Volume I*. Princeton: Princeton University Press.
[4] Cocchiarella, N. B. 1966. "A Logic of Possible and Actual Objects." *The Journal of Symbolic Logic* (hereafter *JSL*) 31: 688.
[5] Gentzen, G. 1934-35. "Untersuchungen über das logische Schliessen." *Mathematische Zeitschrift* 39: 176-210 and 405-31.
[6] Haack, S. 1975. *Deviant Logic*. Cambridge: Cambridge University Press.
[7] Hailperin, T. 1953. "Quantification and Empty Individual Domains." *JSL* 18: 138-42.
[8] _____. 1954. "Remark on Identity and Description in First-Order Axiom Systems." *JSL* 19: 14-20.
[9] Henkin, L. 1949. "The Completeness of the First-Order Functional Calculus." *JSL* 14: 159-66.
[10] Hintikka, J. 1959. "Existential Presuppositions and Existential Commitments." *The Journal of Philosophy* (hereafter *JP*) 56: 125-37.
[11] Jaśkowski, S. 1934. "On the Rules of Supposition in Formal Logic." *Studia Logica* 1: 5-32.
[12] Kripke, S. 1963. "Semantical Considerations on Modal Logic." *Modal and Many-Valued Logics*. Helsinki: Societas Philosophica 16: 83-94.
[13] Lambert, K. 1963. "Existential Import Revisited." *Notre Dame Journal of Formal Logic* (hereafter *NDJFL*) 4: 288-92.
[14] _____. 1967. "Free Logic and the Concept of Existence." *NDJFL* 8: 133-44.
[15] Leonard, H. S. 1956. "The Logic of Existence." *Philosophical Studies* (hereafter *PS*) 4: 49-64.
[16] Lewis, C. I. and Langford, C. H. 1932. *Symbolic Logic*. New York: The Century Co.
[17] Meyer, R. K., and Lambert, K. 1968. "Universally Free Logic and Standard Quantification Theory." *JSL* 33: 8-26.
[18] Montague, R., and Kalish, D. 1956. "A Simplification of Tarski's Formulation of the Predicate Calculus." *Bulletin of the American Mathematical Society* 62: 261.
[19] Morgan. C. G. 1970. "Weak Liberated Versions of **T** and S4." *JSL* 40: 25-36.
[20] Mostowski, A. 1951. "On the Rules of Proof in the Pure Functional Calculus of the First Order." *JSL* 16: 107-11.
[21] Nakhnikian, G., and Salmon, W. C. 1957. " 'Exists' as a Predicate." *The Philosophical Review* (hereafter *PR*) 66: 535-42.
[22] Quine, W. V. 1948. "On What There Is." *The Review of Metaphysics* 2: 21-38.
[23] _____. 1954. "Quantification and the Empty Domain." *JSL* 19: 177-79.
[24] _____. 1959. *Methods of Logic*, revised edition. New York: Holt.

[25] Rescher, N. 1957. "Definition of Existence." *PS* 7: 65–69.
[26] _____. 1959. "On the Logic of Existence and Denotation." *PR* 68: 157–80.
[27] Russell, B. 1905. "On Denoting." *Mind* 14: 479–93.
[28] _____. 1919. *Introduction to Mathematical Philosophy*. London: Allen & Unwin.
[29] Schock, R. 1968. *Logics without Existence Assumptions*. Stockholm: Almqvist & Wiksell.
[30] Shipley, C. T. 1972. "A Semantical Theory and Several Deductive Systems for Universally Free Logic." Ph.D. dissertation, The University of Nebraska.
[31] Trew, A. 1970. "Non-Standard Theories of Quantification and Identity." *JSL* 35: 378–418.
[32] Van Fraassen, B. C. 1966. "Singular Terms, Truth-Value Gaps, and Free Logic." *JP* 67: 481–95.
[33] _____. 1966. "The Completeness of Free Logic." *Zeitschrift für mathematische Logik und Grundlagen der Mathematik* (hereafter *ZMLGM*) 12: 219–34.
[34] _____. 1968. "A Topological Proof of the Löwenheim-Skolem, Compactness, and Strong Completeness Theorems for Free Logic." *ZMLGM* 14: 245–54.
[35] Whitehead, A. N., and Russell, B. 1910–13. *Principia Mathematica*. Cambridge: Cambridge University Press.
[36] Woods, J. 1974. *The Logic of Fiction*. The Hague: Mouton.

1
Non-Designating Singular Terms
T. Hailperin, coauthor

1. Exception has frequently been taken to the treatment of singular terms or individual constants in modern logic.[1] Consider indeed the standard introduction rule for '∃':

∃I: $A' \vdash (\exists W)A$, where A' is like A except for containing free occurrences of an individual constant *or* variable W' at all the places where A contains free occurrences of the individual variable W.

It permits us to infer the existence of something which is such and such from any true premise of the form 'a is such and such', where 'a' is an individual constant; to infer, for example, the existence of something which is not identical with anything from the true premise 'Pegasus is not identical with anything'.[2]

To block such inferences one may, of course, eliminate from one's language all individual constants like 'Pegasus' which fail to designate anything. Or, following W. V. Quine in [3], §37, one may replace in one's language all individual constants, whether or not they designate anything, by definite descriptions *à la* Russell; $(\exists W)A$ will then follow from A', where A' is like A except for containing free occurrences of a definite description of the form $(\imath X)B$ at all the places where A contains free occurrences of W, only if $E!(\imath X)B$ is true, an existence premise which may be defined as $(\exists Y)(Y = (\imath X)B)$.[3] Or, following H. S. Leonard in [2], one may retain in one's language individual constants of either kind, but insert to the left of '⊢' in ∃I an existence premise $E!W'$, which Leonard defines as $(\exists F)(F(W') \& \Diamond \sim F(W'))$, but which we may define more simply as $(\exists Y)(Y = W')$.[4]

It proves awkward, however, to deprive oneself entirely of non-designating individual constants. As for Quine's proposal, which uses the whole machinery of definite descriptions, and Leonard's original proposal, which drags quantified predicate variables and modal operators into elementary logic, they are rather costly. Our revision of Leonard's proposal, finally, has an unexpected drawback to be pointed out in Section 4. We accordingly take the liberty of submitting here new rules of singular inference. We intend them for languages of a very familiar sort, which we shall call *the languages L.*

2. The vocabulary and grammar of L may be outlined as follows. The primitive signs of L are to be: a list of predicates; an infinite list of individual variables and a list of individual constants, referred to here by the capital letters 'W', 'X', 'Y', and 'Z'; the two connectives '$\sim$' and '$\supset$'; the quantifier letter '$\exists$'; the identity sign '$=$'; and the two parentheses '(' and ')'. The formulas of L, referred to here by the capital letters 'A', 'B,' 'C,' and 'D,' are to be all the finite sequences of primitive signs of L. The well-formed formulas of L are to be: $F(W_1, W_2, \ldots, W_n)$, where F is an n-place ($n \geq 1$) predicate and $W_1, W_2, \ldots, W_n$ are individual constants or variables; $W = X$, where W and X are individual constants or variables; $\sim A$, where A is a well-formed formula; $(A \supset B)$, where A and B are well-formed formulas; and $(\exists W)A$, where W is an individual variable and A is a well-formed formula. An occurrence of an individual variable W in a well-formed formula A is to be bound in A if it occurs in a well-formed part $(\exists W)B$ of A; an occurrence of an individual variable W in a well-formed formula A is to be free in A if it is not bound in A; and every occurrence of an individual constant W in a well-formed formula A is to be free in A.

The standard rules of inference for L may be cast in the following form:

R (Reiteration) $A \vdash A$;

T (Thinning) If $A_1, A_2, \ldots, A_n \vdash B$, then $A_1, A_2, \ldots, A_{n+1} \vdash B$;

P (Permutation) If $A_1, A_2, \ldots, A_n \vdash B$, then $A_i, A_2, \ldots, A_{i-1}, A_1, A_{i+1}, \ldots, A_n \vdash B$;

C (Cut) If $A_1, A_2, \ldots, A_n \vdash A_{n+1}$ and $A_1, A_2, \ldots, A_{n+1} \vdash B$, then $A_1, A_2, \ldots, A_n \vdash B$;

NE (Negation Elimination) $\sim \sim A \vdash A$;

NI (Negation Introduction) If $A_1, A_2, \ldots, A_{n+1} \vdash B$ and $A_1, A_2, \ldots, A_{n+1} \vdash \sim B$, then $A_1, A_2, \ldots, A_n \vdash \sim A_{n+1}$;

CB (Conditional Elimination) $A, A \supset B \vdash B$;[5]

CI (Conditional Introduction) If $A_1, A_2, \ldots, A_{n+1} \vdash B$, then $A_1, A_2, \ldots, A_n \vdash A_{n+1} \supset B$;

∃E (Existential Elimination) If $A_1, A_2, \ldots, A_{n+1} \vdash B$ and no occurrence of the individual variable W is free in any A_i from A_1 through A_n or in B, then $A_1, A_2, \ldots, A_n, (\exists W)A_{n+1} \vdash B$;

∃I (Existential Introduction) $A' \vdash (\exists W)A$, where A' is like A except for containing free occurrences of an individual constant *or variable* W' at all the places where A contains free occurrences of the individual variable W;

IE (Identity Elimination) $W = W', A \vdash A'$, where W and W' are individual variables and A' is like A except for containing free occurrences of W' at zero or more places where A contains free occurrences of W;

II (Identity Introduction) $\vdash W = W$, where W is an individual variable.

These rules yield, as the reader may check, the following three derived rules of inference (in which $(\forall W)A$ is short for $\sim (\exists W) \sim A$):

L1. If $A_1, A_2, \ldots, A_n \vdash A_{n+1} \supset B$, then $A_1, A_2, \ldots, A_{n+1} \vdash B$;
L2. If $A_1, A_2, \ldots, A_n \vdash B$ and no occurrence of the individual variable W is free in any A_i, then $A_1, A_2, \ldots, A_n \vdash (\forall W)B$;
L3. If $A_1, A_2, \ldots, A_n \vdash (\forall W)B$, then $A_1, A_2, \ldots, A_n \vdash B'$, where B' stands to B as A' stands to A in $\exists$I.

With the aid of L1–L3 the following strengthened versions of **IE** and **II** are easily obtained:

IE* $W = W'$, $A \vdash A'$, where W and W' are individual *constants or* variables and A' is as in IE;
II* $\vdash W = W$, where W is an individual *constant or* variable.

II* follows from **II** by L2 and L3. As for **IE***, one case of it, where W is a variable and W' is a constant, can be proved as follows:

Let X be a new individual variable and let A'' be like A' except for containing occurrences of X at all the places where (a) A' contains free occurrences of W' and (b) A contains free occurrences of W.[6] Then:

1   $A, W = X \vdash A''$ (IE, P)
2   $A \vdash W = X \supset A''$ (CI, 1)
3   $A \vdash (\forall X)(W = X \supset A'')$ (L2, 2)
4   $A \vdash W = W' \supset A'$ (L3, 3)
5   $A, W = W' \vdash A'$ (L1, 4)
6   $W = W', A \vdash A'$ (P, 5)

3. We propose as a solution to the problem of singular inference that $\exists$I be weakened to read:

∃I* $A' \vdash (\exists W)A$, where A' is like A except for containing free occurrences of an individual variable W' at all the places where A contains free occurrences of the individual variable W;

and that **IE** and **II** be strengthened to read like the above **IE*** and **II***.
Our amended rules yield:

∃I** $(\forall W)(W' = W)$, $A' \vdash (\exists W)A$, where A' is like A except for containing free occurrences of the individual constant W' at all the places where A contains free occurrences of the individual variable W

and permits us to infer $(\exists W)A$ from A' whenever W' designates something. The proof of **∃I**** runs as follows:

20 Part 1: Existence

1 $A, W' = W, A' \vdash (\exists W)A$ $(\exists I^*, T, P)$
2 $W' = W, A', A \vdash (\exists W)A$ $(P, 1)$
3 $W' = W, A' \vdash A$ (IE^*)
4 $W' = W, A' \vdash (\exists W)A$ $(C, 2, 3)$
5 $A', W' = W \vdash (\exists W)A$ $(P, 4)$
6 $A', (\exists W)(W' = W) \vdash (\exists W)A$ $(\exists E, 5)$
7 $(\exists W)(W' = W), A' \vdash (\exists W)A$ $(P, 6)$

Our amended rules do not, however, yield $\exists I$, which permitted us to infer $(\exists W)A$ from A', whether or not W' designates anything. For let L include among its primitive signs an individual constant W_0 such that (1) $W_0 = W_0$ is true, (2) $W_0 = W$ is false for any other individual constant W of L, and (3) the individual designated by W_0 does not fall among the values of the individual variables of L. $\exists I$ does not hold under the present interpretation since

$$W_0 = W_0 \vdash (\exists W)(W_0 = W)$$

has a true premise and a false conclusion. The remaining rules of inference for L hold, however, under this interpretation.

A word on our primitive rules of inference IE^* and II^* may be in order. We allow W and W' in IE^* to be non-designating individual constants as well as designating ones. We feel indeed that if $W = W'$ is true and a statement A which exhibits the individual constant W is true, then the result A' of replacing W by the individual constant W' anywhere in A should also be true, whether or not W (and hence W') designates anything. We also allow W in II^* to be a non-designating individual constant as well as a designating one. We feel indeed that a statement of the form $W = X$ is true if and only if X designates whatever W designates. But W designates whatever W designates, whether or not W designates anything. Hence $W = W$ should be true, whether or not W designates anything.[7]

4. As an alternative solution one might consider adopting $\exists I^{**}$ as a primitive rule of inference and retaining IE and II in their original form. The burden of singular inference would then rest exclusively on $\exists I^{**}$. Attractive as the proposal would seem, it has a shortcoming. The resulting rules of inference do not yield IE^* and II^*, two rules which the reader will sorely miss when he undertakes to prove the standard laws of identity. For let L include among its primitive signs two individual constants W_0 and X_0 and a predicate F such that (1) $W_0 = X_0$ and $F(W_0)$ are true, (2) $X_0 = X_0$ and $F(X_0)$ are false, and (3) the individuals respectively designated by W_0 and X_0 do not fall among the values of the individual variables of L. II^* does not hold under the present interpretation since $X_0 = X_0$ is false. IE^* does not hold either since

$$W_0 = X_0, F(W_0) \vdash F(X_0)$$

has two true premises and a false conclusion. The remaining rules of inference

Non-Designating Singular Terms 21

for L hold, however, under this interpretation. $\exists I^{**}$, in particular, holds because $(\exists W)(W' = W)$ is false when W' is either W_0 or X_0.

Notes

1. See [2] among others.
2. The reader for whom 'Pegasus' designates something (i.e., a mythological entity) may mull over the following substitute inference: "The impossible can't be. So there exists something that can't be."
3. See [4], *14.
4. The definition stems of course from [4], *14.
5. The original version of this paper used a different rule of Conditional Elimination: $A \supset B$, $(A \supset C) \supset A \vdash B$. The rule, studied at great length in Part 3 of this volume, plays no special role here and is consequently dropped in favor of the handier **CE**.
6. The original version of this paper merely required that A'' be like A' except for containing occurrences of X wherever A' contains free occurrences of W'. However, condition (b) must also be met if A'' is to be like A except for containing free occurrences of X at zero or more places where A contains free occurrences of W, and line (1) below is to hold by **IE** and **P**. For let A be $F(W, W')$ and A' be $F(W', W')$ for some two-place predicate F of L. Then $F(X, X)$, though meeting condition (a), will *not* do as A'' in (1). The need for (b) was first noted by Professor Tatsuo Fujimura (Tokyo Suisan Daigaku).
7. For a different account of things, see [1], Note 30.

References

[1] Leblanc, H. 1979. "Generalization in First-Order Logic." *Notre Dame Journal of Formal Logic* 20: 835–57 (#35 in this volume).
[2] Leonard, H. S. 1956. "The Logic of Existence." *Philosophical Studies* 7: 49–64.
[3] Quine, W. V. 1950. *Methods of Logic*. New York: Holt.
[4] Whitehead, A. N., and Russell, B. 1910–13. *Principia Mathematica*. Cambridge: Cambridge University Press.

2
Completeness Theorems
for Some Presupposition-free Logics

R. H. Thomason, coauthor

1. Introduction. Contemporary logic has often been faulted for requiring (a) that its individual variables have values and (b) that its individual constants each designate a value of the individual variables. In recent years various modifications of $QC_=$, the first-order quantificational calculus with identity, have been designed, that eschew one, or the other, or both of these presuppositions;[1] and some, though not all, of the calculi in question have received a semantical interpretation.[2] Our purpose in this paper is to furnish a systematic account—both from a syntactical point of view and a semantical one—of such like *presupposition-free logics*. We shall study ten of them in the body of the paper, and prove the (semantical) completeness of each, in Henkin's sense of the word 'completeness' and in Gödel's.[3] Further presupposition-free logics are discussed in the notes and appendices; some may prove as interesting as the ten treated in the text, but for lack of space could not be accommodated therein.

When an individual constant is not required to designate any value of 'x', 'y', 'z', etc., it may designate something not a value of a variable, a possibility often overlooked. It may also fail to designate at all, i.e., serve as a *non-designating* constant. Various options are open as regards the truth of statements containing a non-designating constant: (i) the statements in question may be denied any truth-value whatsoever; (ii) they may all be assigned some truth-value other than the classical **T** and **F**; (iii) some may be assigned **T** or **F**, and the rest assigned no truth-value; (iv) they may all be assigned the truth-value **T**; (v) they may all be assigned the truth-value **F**; and (vi) some (but not all) may be assigned **T**, and the rest **F**. Perhaps the most interesting alternative under (vi) is the one, say, (vi'), in which all atomic statements containing a non-designating constant are arbitrarily assigned one of the two truth-values **T** and **F**, and the truth-value of non-atomic ones is determined by the standard semantical rules of truth. For lack of space we skip (ii), refer the reader to [18] for treatment of (i), and refer him to [17] for treatment of the major alternative under (iii), thus restricting ourselves in the main text to (iv), (v), and (vi').

Among our ten modifications of $QC_=$, five (namely, $QC\,\underline{\overset{2}{=}}$, $QC\,\underline{\overset{4}{=}}$, $QC\,\underline{\overset{6}{=}}$, $QC\,\underline{\overset{8}{=}}$, and $QC\,\underline{\overset{10}{=}}$), lift the classical restriction that variables must have values by acknowledging the empty set $\emptyset$ as a possible domain. The others do not. $QC\,\underline{\overset{3}{=}}$, $QC\,\underline{\overset{4}{=}}$, $QC\,\underline{\overset{7}{=}}$, and $QC\,\underline{\overset{8}{=}}$ allow for non-designating constants, yet require that designating ones each designate a value of a variable. $QC\,\underline{\overset{3}{=}}$ and $QC\,\underline{\overset{4}{=}}$ handle formulas that contain a non-designating constant in the spirit of (iv) above; $QC\,\underline{\overset{7}{=}}$ and $QC\,\underline{\overset{8}{=}}$ in the spirit of (v). $QC\,\underline{\overset{5}{=}}$ and $QC\,\underline{\overset{6}{=}}$ are like $QC\,\underline{\overset{3}{=}}$ and $QC\,\underline{\overset{4}{=}}$, respectively ($QC\,\underline{\overset{9}{=}}$ and $QC\,\underline{\overset{10}{=}}$ like $QC\,\underline{\overset{7}{=}}$ and $QC\,\underline{\overset{8}{=}}$, respectively), except for allowing designating constants to designate something not a value of a variable. This is accomplished by introducing, besides the domain D (or *inner* domain) serving as the range of values of the individual variables, an *outer* domain D' that is disjoint from D and whose members may also be assigned to the individual constants of $QC\,\underline{\overset{5}{=}}$, $QC\,\underline{\overset{6}{=}}$, $QC\,\underline{\overset{9}{=}}$, and $QC\,\underline{\overset{10}{=}}$.[4]

$QC\,\underline{\overset{1}{=}}$ and $QC\,\underline{\overset{2}{=}}$, possibly the most interesting of our ten calculi, are susceptible of various semantical accounts. The most general of these, call it *Account One*, (1) uses an outer as well as an inner domain, thus permitting an individual constant to designate something not the value of a variable, and also (2) allows for non-designating constants, formulas that contain such being handled in the spirit of (vi') above. It turns out, though, that as regards soundness and completeness,[5] (2) is dispensable in the presence of (1), and likewise (1) dispensable in the presence of (2).[6] Thus two further accounts yield completeness theorems for $QC\,\underline{\overset{1}{=}}$ and $QC\,\underline{\overset{2}{=}}$: one requiring every individual constant of $QC\,\underline{\overset{1}{=}}$ and $QC\,\underline{\overset{2}{=}}$ to designate (*Account Two*), the other requiring every such constant—when it designates—to designate a value of 'x', 'y', 'z', etc. (*Account Three*). For convenience (and novelty, since Account Three is close to van Fraassen's in [16]), we employ Account Two in the main text, and relegate Accounts One and Three to Appendix 2.

Anticipations of one of our results, Theorem 7(b) in Section 4, will be found in [14] for the case where A is a closed formula of $QC\,\underline{\overset{2}{=}}$ that contains no identity sign nor any individual constant, in [15] for the case where A is a formula of $QC\,\underline{\overset{2}{=}}$ that contains no individual constant, and in [16] for the case where A is a closed formula of $QC\,\underline{\overset{2}{=}}$ that contains no sentence variable.[7] To our knowledge the remaining results, though, are new.[8]

The argument whereby we deduce from the completeness in Henkin's sense of $QC\,\underline{\overset{5}{=}}$ and $QC\,\underline{\overset{6}{=}}$ that of $QC\,\underline{\overset{3}{=}}$ and $QC\,\underline{\overset{4}{=}}$, can be put to further use: deducing from the completeness in Henkin's sense of $QC\,\underline{\overset{1}{=}}$ that of $QC_=$ or, as we shall label that calculus here, $QC\,\underline{\overset{0}{=}}$.[9]

2. Syntax.

We attend in this section to the syntax of $QC\,\underline{\overset{0}{=}} - QC\,\underline{\overset{10}{=}}$ (calculi which of course all have the same signs and hence the same formulas), and that of $QC\,\underline{\overset{\infty}{=}}$, an auxiliary calculus that is like $QC\,\underline{\overset{1}{=}}$ except for having $\aleph_0$ extra

24 Part 1: Existence

individual constants of its own and hence extra formulas of its own. In the definitions and remarks that follow, the index i is meant—unless otherwise indicated—to run from 0 to 10.

Definition 1. *The signs of* $QC^i_=$ *are the two connectives* '$\sim$' *and* '$\supset$', *the one quantifier letter* '$\forall$', *the identity sign* '$=$', *the two parentheses* '(' *and* ')', *one or more sentence variables (among them* 'p'*), one or more monadic predicate variables (among them* 'f'*), for each m from 2 on zero or more m-adic predicate variables,* $\aleph_0$ *individual variables (among them* 'x' *and* 'y'*), and one or more individual constants.*

Definition 1^∞. *The signs of* $QC^\infty_=$ *are those of* $QC^1_=$, *together with* $\aleph_0$ *extra individual constants.*
Remarks. The individual variables and individual constants of QC^i [$QC^\infty_=$] will be collectively known as the *individual signs of* $QC^i_=$ [$QC^\infty_=$], and be presumed to be arranged in some fixed alphabetical order. We shall refer to the sentence variables of $QC^i_=$ [$QC^\infty_=$] by means of 'P', to its predicate variables by means of 'F', and to its individual signs by means of 'X', 'Y', and 'Z'.

Definition 2. *Let A be a finite sequence of signs of* $QC^i_=$.
(a) *If A is a sentence variable of* $QC_=$, *then A counts as a formula of* $QC^i_=$;
(b) *If A is of the kind* $F(X_1, X_2, \ldots, X_m)$, *where F is an m-adic (m $\geq$ 1) predicate variable of* $QC^i_=$, *then A counts as a formula of* $QC^i_=$;
(c) *If A is of the kind* $(X = Y)$, *then A counts as a formula of* $QC^i_=$;
(d) *If A is of the kind* $\sim B$ *and B counts as a formula of* $QC^i_=$, *then A counts as a formula of* $QC^i_=$;
(e) *If A is of the kind* $(B \supset C)$ *and both B and C count as formulas of* $QC^i_=$, *then A counts as a formula of* $QC^i_=$;
(f) *If A is of the kind* $(\forall X)B$, *where X is an individual variable of* $QC^i_=$, *and B counts as a formula of* $QC^i_=$, *then A counts as a formula of* $QC^i_=$;
(g) *A counts as a formula of* $QC^i_=$ *pursuant only to one or another of (a)–(f).*

Definition 2^∞. *Like D2, but with* '$QC^\infty_=$' *in place of* '$QC^i_=$'.
Remarks. Except D6–D8 and D10, every further definition in this section will be understood to carry along its analogue for $QC^\infty_=$. We shall refer to the formulas of $QC^i_=$ [$QC^i_=$] by means of 'A', 'B', and 'C', and to sets of such by means of 'S'. To abridge matters, we shall usually write '$(A \& B)$' for '$\sim(A \supset \sim B)$', '$(A \lor B)$' for '$(\sim A \supset B)$', '$(A \equiv B)$' for '$((A \supset B) \& (B \supset A))$', '$(\exists X)A$' for '$\sim(\forall X)\sim A$', and '$E!X$' for '$(\exists x)(x = X)$' when X is distinct from 'x', otherwise for '$(\exists y)(y = X)$'; and we shall usually omit outer parentheses. Lastly, we shall assume that the formulas of $QC^i_=$ [$QC^\infty_=$] are arranged in some fixed alphabetical order.

Definition 3. *Let A and B be formulas of* $QC^i_=$.
(a) *If A and B are the same, then B counts as a component of A;*

Completeness Theorems for Some Presupposition-free Logics   25

(b)   If A is of the kind $\sim C$ and B counts as a component of C, then B counts as a component of A;
(c)   If A is of the kind $C \supset C'$ and B counts as a component of C or of C', then B counts as a component of A;
(d)   If A is of the kind $(\forall X)C$ and B counts as a component of C, then B counts as a component of A;
(e) B counts as a component of A pursuant only to one another of (a)–(d).

Definition 4. Let X be an individual sign of $\mathrm{QC}^{i}_{=}$, and A be a formula of $\mathrm{QC}^{i}_{=}$.
(a)   An occurrence of X in A is said to be bound if it is in a component of A of the kind $(\forall X)B$, otherwise to be free.
(b) X is said to occur bound in A if at least one occurrence of X in A is bound, to occur free in A if at least one occurrence of X in A is free.
Remark. It follows from D2–D4 that every occurrence of an individual constant of $\mathrm{QC}^{i}_{=}$ [$\mathrm{QC}^{\infty}_{=}$] in a formula of $\mathrm{QC}^{i}_{=}$ [$\mathrm{QC}^{\infty}_{=}$] is free.

Convention. Let A be a formula of $\mathrm{QC}^{i}_{=}$ [$\mathrm{QC}^{\infty}_{=}$], and let X be an individual sign of $\mathrm{QC}^{i}_{=}$ [$\mathrm{QC}^{\infty}_{=}$].
(1)   Let Y be an individual variable of $\mathrm{QC}^{i}_{=}$ [$\mathrm{QC}^{\infty}_{=}$]. If X does not occur free in A or X occurs free in at least one component of A of the kind $(\forall Y)B$, we shall take both $A(Y/X)$ and $A(Y//X)$ to be A; otherwise, we shall take $A(Y/X)$ to be the result of replacing *every* free occurrence of X in A by an occurrence of Y, and $A(Y//X)$ to be any result of replacing *zero or more* free occurrences of X in A by an occurrence of Y.
(2)   Let Y be an individual constant of $\mathrm{QC}^{i}_{=}$ [$\mathrm{QC}^{\infty}_{=}$]. If X does not occur free in A, we shall take both $A(Y/X)$ and $A(Y//X)$ to be A. If X occurs free in A, we shall take $A(Y/X)$ to be the result of replacing every free occurrence of X in A by an occurrence of Y, and $A(Y//X)$ to be any result of replacing zero or more free occurrences of X in A by an occurrence of Y.

Definition 5. Let A be a formula of $\mathrm{QC}^{i}_{=}$.
(a)   If A is as in D2(a)–(c), then A is said to be *atomic*.
(b)   If no individual variable of $\mathrm{QC}^{i}_{=}$ occurs free in A, then A is said to be *closed*; otherwise, to be *open*.
(c)   If no individual constant of $\mathrm{QC}^{i}_{=}$ occurs in A, then A is said to be *constant-free*.
(d)   If '$\forall$' does not occur in A, then A is said to be *quantifier-free*.
Remark. In view of D5 a formula A of $\mathrm{QC}^{i}_{=}$ [$\mathrm{QC}^{\infty}_{=}$] is closed and quantifier-free if no individual variable of $\mathrm{QC}^{i}_{=}$ [$\mathrm{QC}^{\infty}_{=}$] occurs at all in A.

Definition 6. Let A be a formula of $\mathrm{QC}^{i}_{=}$, where $i = 2$ or 6.
Case 1: A is open. Then '$p \supset p$' counts as the $\varnothing$-associate of A.
Case 2: A is closed.
(a)   If A is atomic, then A counts as the $\varnothing$-associate of A;

(b) If A is of the kind ~B and B' is the ∅-associate of B, then ~B counts as the ∅-associate of A;
(c) If A is of the kind B ⊃ C, and B' and C' are the ∅-associates of B and C, respectively, then B' ⊃ C' counts as the ∅-associate of A;
(d) If A is of the kind (∀X)B, then 'p ⊃ p' counts as the ∅-associate of A.[10]
Remark. It follows from the above definitions that the ∅-associate of a closed formula of $QC_=^i$ ($i = 2$ or 6) is closed and quantifier-free.

Definition 7. (a) A formula of $QC_=^i$ counts as an axiom of $QC_=^0$, $QC_=^3$, and $QC_=^7$ if it is of one of the following eight kinds, where in the fourth case X is understood not to occur free in A:

$$A \supset (B \supset A),$$

$$(A \supset (B \supset C)) \supset ((A \supset B) \supset (A \supset C)),$$

$$(\sim A \supset \sim B) \supset (B \supset A),$$

$$A \supset (\forall X)A,$$

$$(\forall X)(A \supset B) \supset ((\forall X)A \supset (\forall X)B),$$

$$(\forall X)A \supset A(Y/X),$$

$$X = X,$$

and

$$X = Y \supset (A \supset A(Y/X)).$$

(b) A formula of $QC_=^i$ counts as an axiom of $QC_=^1$, $QC_=^5$, and $QC_=^9$ if it is of one of the eight kinds listed under (a), but with Y understood to be an individual variable (rather than an individual variable or an individual constant) of $QC_=^i$ when the formula is of the kind $(\forall X)A \supset A(Y/X)$.
(c) A formula of $QC_=^i$ counts as an axiom of $QC_=^2$, $QC_=^6$, and $QC_=^{10}$ if it is of one of the eight kinds listed under (a), but with Y understood to be an individual variable of $QC_=^i$, and with X understood to occur free in A, when the formula is of the kind $(\forall X)A \supset A(Y/X)$.
(d) A formula of $QC_=^i$ counts as an axiom of $QC_=^4$ and $QC_=^8$ if it is of one of the eight kinds listed under (a), but with X understood to occur free in A when the formula is of the kind $(\forall X)A \supset A(Y/X)$.

Definition 7^∞. A formula of $QC_=^\infty$ counts as an axiom of $QC_=^\infty$ if it is of one of the eight kinds listed under (a), but with Y understood to be an individual variable of $QC_=^\infty$ when the formula is of the kind $(\forall X)A \supset A(Y/X)$.

Definition 8. (a) Let A and B be formulas of $QC_=^i$.
(a1) B is said to follow from A and A ⊃ B by means of rule **R1**.
(a2) If A is closed or B is open, then B is said to follow from A and A ⊃ B by means of rule **R2**.[11]

Completeness Theorems for Some Presupposition-free Logics 27

(a3) *If every individual constant of* $QC_=^i$ *that occurs in A also occurs in B, then B is said to follow from A and* $A \supset B$ *by means of rule* **R3**.
(a4) *If A is closed or B is open, and every individual constant of* $QC_=^i$ *that occurs in A also occurs in B, then B is said to follow from A and* $A \supset B$ *by means of Rule* **R4**.
(a5) *B is said to follow from A and* $\sim A$ *by means of rule* **R5**.
(a6) *If A is closed or B is open, then B is said to follow from A and* $\sim A$ *by means of rule* **R6**.
(b) *Let* $(\forall X)A$ *be a formula of* $QC_=^i$, *and Y be an individual variable of* $QC_=^i$ *that does not occur free in* $(\forall X)A$. *Then* $(\forall X)A$ *is said to follow from* $A(Y/X)$ *by means of rule* **R7**.

Definition $D8^\infty$. (a) *Let A and B be formulas of* $QC_=^\infty$. *Then B is said to follow from A and* $A \supset B$ *by means of rule* **R1**.
(b) *Like D8(b), but with* '$QC_=^\infty$' *in place of* '$QC_=^i$'.

Definition 9. *Let K be a finite column of formulas of* $QC_=^i$; *let* $(\forall X)A$ *be any entry in K that follows from a previous one by means of rule* **R7**; *and let* $A(Y/X)$ *be the earliest entry in K that is previous to* $(\forall X)A$ *and from which* $(\forall X)A$ *follows by means of rule* **R7**. *If X and Y are the same, then Y is said to be generalized upon in K; otherwise, Y is said to be quasi-generalized upon in K.*

Definition 10. *Let A be a formula of* $QC_=^i$, *S be a finite set of formulas of* $QC_=^i$, *and K be a finite column of formulas of* $QC_=^i$ *such that (i) K closes with A and (ii) no individual variable of* $QC_=^i$ *that is generalized or quasi-generalized upon in K occurs free in any member of S.*
Case 1: $i = 0$ or 1. If every entry in K belongs to S, counts as an axiom of $QC_=^i$, *follows from two previous entries by means of rule* **R1**, *or follows from a previous entry by means of rule* **R7**, *then K counts as a derivation of A from S in* $QC_=^i$.[12]
Case 2: $i = 2$. If every entry in K belongs to S, counts as an axiom of $QC_=^i$, *follows from two previous entries by means of rule* **R2**, *or follows from a previous entry by means of rule* **R7**, *then K counts as a derivation of A from S in* $QC_=^i$.
Case 3: $i = 3$ or 5. If every entry in K belongs to S, counts as an axiom of $QC_=^i$, *follows from two previous entries by means of rule* **R3**, *or follows from a previous entry by means of rule* **R7**, *then K counts as a derivation of A from S in* $QC_=^i$.
Case 4: $i = 4$ or 6. If every entry in K belongs to S, counts as an axiom of $QC_=^i$, *follows two previous entries by means of rule* **R4**, *or follows from a previous entry by means of rule* **R7**, *then K counts as a derivation of A from S in* $QC_=^i$.
Case 5: $i = 7$ or 9. If (i) every entry in K belongs to S, counts as an axiom of $QC_=^i$, *follows from two previous entries by means of one of rules* **R1** *and* **R5**, *or follows from a previous entry by means of rule* **R7**, *and (ii) every individual*

28 Part 1: Existence

constant of $QC_=^i$ *occurring in any entry in K that counts as an axiom of* $QC_=^i$ *occurs in some member or other of S, then K counts as a derivation of A from S in* $QC_=^i$.
Case 6: $i = 8$ *or* 10. *If (i) every entry in K belongs to S, counts as an axiom of* $QC_=^i$, *follows from two previous entries by means of one of rules* **R2** *and* **R6**, *or follows from a previous entry by means of rule* **R7**, *and (ii) every individual constant of* $QC_=^i$, *occurring in any entry in K that counts as an axiom of* $QC_=^i$ *occurs in some member or other of S, then K counts as a derivation of A from S in* $QC_=^i$.

Definition 10$^\infty$. *Like D10, Case 1, but with* '$QC_=^\infty$' *in place of* '$QC_=^i$'.
Remark. The restrictions placed in $QC_=^0 - QC_=^{10}$ upon $(\forall X)A \supset A(Y/X)$, **R1**, and (when applicable) **R5**, can be tabulated as follows:

TABLE I[13]

	$(\forall X)A \supset A(Y/X)$	R1	R5
0	no restriction	no restriction	
1	Y a variable	no restriction	
2	X free in A & Y a variable	A closed or B open (= **R2**)	
3	no restriction	every constant in A occurring in B (= **R3**)	
4	X free in A	A closed or B open & every constant in A occurring in B (= **R4**)	
5	Y a variable	every constant in A occurring in B (= **R3**)	
6	X free in A & Y a variable	A closed or B open & every constant in A occurring in B (= **R4**)	
7	no restriction	no restriction	no restriction
8	X free in A	A closed B open (= **R2**)	A closed or B open (= **R6**)
9	Y a variable	no restriction	no restriction
10	X free in A & Y a variable	A closed or B open (= **R2**)	A closed or B (= **R6**)

Definition 11. Let A be a formula of $QC_=^i$; and S be a set of formulas of $QC_=^i$.
Case 1: S *is finite. Then A is said to be derivable from S in* $QC_=^i$ *if there is a derivation of A from S in* $QC_=^i$.
Case 2: S *is infinite. Then A is said to be derivable from S in* $QC_=^i$ *if there is a finite subset* S' *of S such that A is derivable from* S' *in* $QC_=^i$.[14]
Remarks: It follows from D10 – D11 that a formula A of $QC_=^i$ is not derivable

Completeness Theorems for Some Presupposition-free Logics 29

from $\emptyset$ in $QC_{=}^{i}$ for any i from 7 to 10 unless A is constant-free. To abridge matters, we shall write, e.g., '$S \vdash_1 A$', for 'A is derivable from S in $QC_{=}^{1}$', and '$S \vdash^\infty A$' for 'A is derivable from S in $QC_{=}^{\infty}$'; we shall further write, e.g., '$\vdash_1 A$' for '$\emptyset \vdash_1 A$', and '$\vdash^\infty A$' for '$\emptyset \vdash^\infty A$'; and we shall call a derivation in $QC_{=}^{i}$ of a formula A of $QC_{=}^{i}$ from a set S of formulas of $QC_{=}^{i}$ constant-free if every entry in the derivation is constant-free.

Definition 12. *A set S of formulas of $QC_{=}^{i}$ is said to be inconsistent in $QC_{=}^{i}$ if $S \vdash_i p$ & $\sim p$; otherwise to be consistent in $QC_{=}^{i}$.*

The following consequences of D1–D12 merit separate recording as lemmas.

Lemma 1. *Let S be a set of formulas of $QC_{=}^{\infty}$; A and B be formulas of $QC_{=}^{\infty}$; X and Y be individual variables of $QC_{=}^{\infty}$; and Z, Z', and Z'' be individual signs of $QC_{=}^{\infty}$.*
(a) *If $S \vdash^\infty A$, then there is a finite subset S' of S such that $S' \vdash^\infty A$.*
(b) *If A belongs to S or is an axiom of $QC_{=}^{\infty}$, then $S \vdash^\infty A$.*
(c) *If $S \vdash^\infty A$, then $S \cup S' \vdash^\infty A$ for every set S' of formulas of $QC_{=}^{\infty}$.*
(d) *Let every member of S be a formula of $QC_{=}^{1}$ and A be a formula of $QC_{=}^{1}$. Then $S \vdash^\infty A$ if and only if $S \vdash_1 A$.*
(e) *S is inconsistent in $QC_{=}^{\infty}$ if and only if some finite subset of S is inconsistent in $QC_{=}^{\infty}$.*
(f) *If $S \vdash^\infty A'$ and $S \vdash^\infty \sim A'$ for some formula A' of $QC_{=}^{\infty}$, then S is inconsistent in $QC_{=}^{\infty}$.*
(g) *If $S \cup \{A\}$ is inconsistent in $QC_{=}^{\infty}$, then $S \vdash^\infty \sim A$.*
(h) *If $S \cup \{A\} \vdash^\infty B$, then $S \vdash^\infty A \supset B$.*
(i) *If $S \vdash^\infty A$ and $S \vdash^\infty A \supset B$, then $S \vdash^\infty B$.*
(j) *If $S \vdash^\infty A$ or $S \vdash^\infty \sim A$, then $S \vdash^\infty A \supset B$ if and only if $S \vdash^\infty B$ or it is not the case that $S \vdash^\infty A$.*
(k) *If $S \vdash^\infty A(Y/X)$, then $S \vdash^\infty (\forall X)A$, so long as Y does not occur free in any member of S nor in $(\forall X)A$.*
(l) *If $S \vdash^\infty (\exists X)A$ and $S \cup \{A(Y/X)\} \vdash^\infty B$, then $S \vdash^\infty B$, so long as Y does not occur free in any member of S, nor in $(\exists X)A$, nor in B.*
(m) *If $S \vdash^\infty \sim(\forall X)A$, then $S \vdash^\infty (\exists X)\sim A$.*
(n) *$S \vdash^\infty E!X$.*
(o) *If $S \vdash^\infty (\exists X)A$ and $S \cup \{A(Z/X), E!Z\} \vdash^\infty B$, then $S \vdash^\infty B$, so long as Z does not occur free in any member of S, nor in $(\exists X)A$, nor in B.*
(p) *$S \vdash^\infty E!Z$ if and only if $S \vdash^\infty (\exists X)(X = Z)$.*
(q) *If $S \vdash^\infty (\forall X)A$, then $S \vdash^\infty E!Z \supset A(Z/X)$.*
(r) *$S \vdash^\infty (\exists X)((\exists X)A \supset A)$.*
(s) *$S \vdash^\infty Z = Z$.*
(t) *It $S \vdash^\infty Z = Z'$, then $S \vdash^\infty Z' = Z$.*
(u) *If $S \vdash^\infty Z = Z'$ and $S \vdash^\infty Z' = Z''$, then $S \vdash^\infty Z = Z''$.*
(v) *If $S \vdash^\infty Z = Z'$, then $S \vdash^\infty A$ if and only if $S \vdash^\infty A(Z'/Z)$.*

Lemma 2. Let S be a set of closed formulas of $QC_=^2$; A and B be closed formulas of $QC_=^2$; and X, Y, and Z be individual constants of $QC_=^2$.
(a)   S is inconsistent in $QC_=^2$ if and only if some finite subset of S is inconsistent in $QC_=^2$.
(b)   If $S \vdash_2 A'$ and $S \vdash_2 \sim A'$ for some closed formula A' of $QC_=^2$, then S is inconsistent in $QC_=^2$.
(c)   If $S \cup \{A\}$ is inconsistent in $QC_=$, then $S \vdash_2 \sim A$.
(d)   If $S \vdash_2 A$ or $S \vdash_2 \sim A$, then $S \vdash_2 A \supset B$ if and only if $S \vdash_2 B$ or it is not the case that $S \vdash_2 A$.
(e) $S \vdash_2 X = X$.
(f)   If $S \vdash_2 X = Y$, then $S \vdash_2 Y = X$.
(g)   If $S \vdash_2 X = Y$ and $S \vdash_2 Y = Z$, then $S \vdash_2 X = Z$.
(h)   If $S \vdash_2 X = Y$, then $S \vdash_2 A$ if and only if $S \vdash_2 A(Y/X)$.

Lemma 3. Let S be a set of formulas of $QC_=^i$; A, B, and C be formulas of $QC_=^i$; X and Y be individual variables of $QC_=^i$; and $0 \leq i \leq 6$.
(a) $S \vdash_i A$, then there is a finite subset S' of S such that $S' \vdash_i A$.
(b)   If A belongs to S or is an axiom of $QC_=^i$, then $S \vdash_i A$.
(c)   If $S \vdash_i A$, then $S \cup S' \vdash_i A$ for every set S' of formulas of $QC_=^i$.
(d)   If $S \cup \{\sim A\}$ is inconsistent in $QC_=^i$, then $S \vdash_i A$.
(e)   If $S \cup \{A\} \vdash_i B$ and $S \cup \{\sim A\} \vdash_i B$, then $S \vdash_i B$, so long as no individual sign of $QC_=^i$ occurs free in A.
(f)   If $S \cup \{A\} \vdash_i B$, then $S \vdash_i A \supset B$.
(g)   If $S \vdash_i A$ and $S \vdash_i A \supset B$, then $S \vdash_i B$, so long as (1) in case $i = 2, 4,$ or 6, A is closed or B is open, and (2) in case $3 \leq i \leq 6$, every individual constant of $QC_=^i$ that occurs in A also occurs in B.
(h)   If $S \vdash_i A$, then $S \vdash_i B \supset A$.
(i)   If $S \vdash_i A \supset (B \supset C)$, then $S \vdash_i (A \supset B) \supset (A \supset C)$.
(j)   If $S \vdash_i \sim A \supset \sim B$, then $S \vdash_i B \supset A$.
(k)   If $S \vdash_i A \supset B$, then $S \vdash_i \sim B \supset \sim A$.
(l)   If $S \vdash_i A$ and $S \vdash_i B$, then $S \vdash_i A \& B$.
(m)   If $S \vdash_i A(Y/X)$, then $S \vdash_i (\forall X)A$, so long as Y does not occur free in any member of S nor in $(\forall X)A$.
(n)   If $S \vdash_i (\exists X)A$, then $S \vdash_i A$, so long as X does not occur free in A.
(o)   If $S \vdash_i A \supset B(Y/X)$, then $S \vdash_i A \supset (\forall X)B$, so long as Y does not occur free in any member of S nor in $A \supset (\forall X)B$.
(p)   If $S \vdash_i (\forall X)(A \supset B)$ then $S \vdash_i (\forall X)A \supset (\forall X)B$.
(q)   If $S \vdash_i (\exists x)(f(x) \lor \sim f(x))$, then $S \vdash_i (\exists X)(f(X) \lor \sim f(X))$.

Lemma 4. Let $i = 2$ or 6.
(a)   Let S' consist of the $\emptyset$-associates of the members of S, and let A' be the $\emptyset$-associate of A. If $S' \vdash_i A'$, then $S \cup \{\sim(\exists x)(f(x) \lor \sim f(x))\} \vdash_i A$.
(b)   Let A be an open formula of $QC_=^i$. Then $\{\sim(\exists x)(f(x) \lor \sim f(x))\} \vdash_i A$.

Lemma 5. (a) Let X be an individual variable of $\mathrm{QC}_=^i$ that does not occur free in A, and $i = 2$ or 6. Then $\vdash_i (\exists x)(f(x) \lor \sim f(x)) \supset ((\forall X)A \supset A)$.
(b) If $S \vdash_1 A$, then $S \cup \{(\exists x)(f(x) \lor \sim f(x))\} \vdash_2 A$.
(c) If $S \vdash_5 A$, then $S \cup \{(\exists x)(f(x) \lor \sim f(x))\} \vdash_6 A$.

Lemma 6. Let S be a finite set for formulas of $\mathrm{QC}_=^2$.
(a) Let A and B be constant-free formulas of $\mathrm{QC}_=^2$. Then there is a constant-free derivation of $A \supset (B \equiv B)$ from S in $\mathrm{QC}_=^2$.
(b) Let A be an atomic formula of $\mathrm{QC}_=^2$ that is constant-free, and Y be an individual variable of $\mathrm{QC}_=^2$. Then there is a constant-free derivation from S in $\mathrm{QC}_=^2$ of

$$(\forall X)(X = Y) \supset ((\forall X)A \equiv A(Y/X)),$$

$$(\forall X)(X = Y) \supset ((\forall X)A \equiv (\forall X)A(Y/X)),$$

$$(\forall X)(Y = X) \supset ((\forall X)A \equiv A(X/Y)),$$

and

$$(\forall X)(X = X) \supset ((\forall X)A \equiv (\forall X)A(X/Y)).$$

(c) If there is a constant-free derivation of $A \supset (B \equiv C)$ from S in $\mathrm{QC}_=^2$, then there is one of $A \supset (\sim B \equiv \sim C)$.
(d) If there is a constant-free derivation of $A \supset (B \equiv B')$ from S in $\mathrm{QC}_=^2$, and one of $A \supset (C \equiv C')$, then there is one of $A \supset ((B \supset C) \equiv (B' \supset C'))$.
(e) If there is a constant-free derivation of $A \supset (B \equiv C)$ from S in $\mathrm{QC}_=^2$, then there is one of $A \supset ((\forall X)B \equiv (\forall X)C)$, so long as X does not occur free in A.
(f) A being a formula of $\mathrm{QC}_=^2$, B being one of the kind $A(Y/X)$, where exactly one of X and Y is an individual constant of $\mathrm{QC}_=^2$, and Z being an individual variable of $\mathrm{QC}_=^2$ that does not occur in A and is distinct from Y, let A' and B' be the results of replacing by an occurrence of Z any occurrence in A and B, respectively, of any individual constant of $\mathrm{QC}_=^2$, and let A'' and B'' be the results of replacing by an occurrence of $(\forall Z)C$ any occurrence in A' and B', respectively, of any atomic formula C of $\mathrm{QC}_=^2$ that contains Z. Then there is a constant-free derivation of $(\forall Z)(Z = Y) \supset (A'' \supset B'')$ from S in $\mathrm{QC}_=^2$ if X is an individual constant of $\mathrm{QC}_=^2$, otherwise one of $(\forall Z)(X = Z) \supset (A'' \supset B'')$.
(g) If there is a constant-free derivation of $A \supset (B \equiv C)$ from S in $\mathrm{QC}_=^2$, then there is one of $A \supset (B \supset C)$.

Lemma 7. Let S be a finite set of constant-free formulas of $\mathrm{QC}_=^i$, A be a constant-free formula of $\mathrm{QC}_=^\infty$, and $i = 1$ or 2. If $S \vdash_i A$, then there is a constant-free derivation of A from S in $\mathrm{QC}_=^i$.

Lemma 8. (a) If $\vdash_1 A$, then $\vdash_5 A$.
(b) If $\vdash_2 A$, then $\vdash_6 A$.[15]

Lemma 9. Let every individual constant of $QC\overset{1}{=}$ (hence, $QC\overset{2}{=}$, $QC\overset{5}{=}$, and $QC\overset{6}{=}$) that occurs in one or more members of S occur in A.
(a) If $S \vdash_1 A$, then $S \vdash_5 A$.
(b) If $S \vdash_2 A$, then $S \vdash_6 A$, so long as every member of S is closed or A is open.

Lemma 10. Let S' consist of every closed formula of $QC\overset{1}{=}$ (hence, $QC\overset{5}{=}$ and $QC\overset{6}{=}$) of the kind E!X.[16]
(a) If $S \cup S' \vdash_1 A$, then $S \vdash_0 A$.
(b) If $S \cup S' \vdash_5 A$, then $S \vdash_3 A$.
(c) If $S \cup S' \vdash_6 A$, then $S \vdash_4 A$.

Lemma 11. Let $7 \leq i \leq 10$.
(a) If $S \vdash_i A$, then $S \cup S' \vdash_i A$ for every set S' of formulas of $QC\overset{i}{=}$.
(b) If $S \vdash_i p \ \& \sim p$, then $S \vdash_i A$.

Lemma 12. Let every individual constant of $QC\overset{1}{=}$ (hence, $QC\overset{2}{=}$, $QC\overset{9}{=}$, and $QC\overset{10}{=}$) that occurs in A occur in one or more members of S.
(a) If $S \vdash_1 A$, then $S \vdash_9 A$.
(b) If $S \vdash_2 A$, then $S \vdash_{10} A$.

Lemma 13. Let S' consist of every closed formula of $QC\overset{9}{=}$ (hence, $QC\overset{10}{=}$) of the kind E!X, where X occurs in one or more members of S.
(a) If $S \cup S' \vdash_9 A$, then $S \vdash_7 A$.
(b) If $S \cup S' \vdash_{10} A$, then $S \vdash_8 A$.

Proof of the above lemmas is a routine matter, except possibly for L1(c), L1(h), L1(o), L1(q), L3(c), L3(f), L4(a), L5, L6(f), L7, L8, L9, L11(a), and L12. Since proof of L1(c), L1(h), L3(c), L3(f), and L11(a) can be retrieved from [8], proof of L4(a) can be retrieved from [15], proof of L5(c) is like that of L5(b), proof of L8(b) is like that of L8(a), proof of L9(b) is like that of L9(a), and proof of L12(b) is like that of L12(a), we shall restrict ourselves here to L1(o), L1(q), L5(a)–(b), L6(f), L7, L8(a), L9(a), and L12(a).

For proof of L1(o). Let $S \vdash^\infty (\exists X)A$ and $S \cup \{A(Z/X), E!Z\} \vdash^\infty B$, where Z is as in L1(o). Then in view of L1(a) and L1(c) there is a finite subset S' of S such that $S' \vdash^\infty (\exists X)A$ and $S' \cup \{A(Z/X), E!Z\} \vdash^\infty B$, and hence, in particular, a finite column of formulas of $QC\overset{\infty}{=}$, say, the formulas $C_1, C_2, \ldots, C_p$, that counts as a derivation of B from $S' \cup \{A(Z/X), E!Z\}$ in $QC\overset{\infty}{=}$. Now let Y be the alphabetically earliest individual variable of $QC\overset{\infty}{=}$ that does not occur in any member of $S' \cup \{A(Z/X), E!Z\}$ nor in any one of $C_1, C_2, \ldots, C_p$; and for each i from 1 through p let C'_i be $C_i(Y/Z)$. In view of the restrictions placed upon Z, C'_i ($i = 1, 2, \ldots, p$) is sure to be C_i if C_i belongs to S', C_i again if C_i is B, and $A(Y/X)$ if C_i is $A(Z/X)$. But, if so, then the column made up of $C'_1, C'_2, \ldots, C'_p$ is sure to count as a derivation of B from $S' \cup \{A(Y/X), E!X\}$ in $QC\overset{\infty}{=}$. Hence in view of L1(h) $S' \cup \{A(Y/X)\} \vdash^\infty E!Y \supset B$, and hence

Completeness Theorems for Some Presupposition-free Logics 33

in view of L1(n) and L1(i) $S' \cup \{A(Y/X)\} \vdash^\infty B$. But Y is sure not to occur free in $(\exists X)A$. Hence, since $S' \vdash^\infty (\exists X)A$, then $S' \vdash^\infty B$ in view of L1(l), and hence $S \vdash^\infty B$ in view of L1(c).

For proof of L1(q).[18] Let $S \vdash^\infty (\forall X)A$. Then in view of L1(a) there is a finite subset S' of S such that $S' \vdash^\infty (\forall X)A$. Hence in view of L1(c) $S' \cup \{E!Z, Y = Z\} \vdash^\infty (\forall X)A$, where Y is the alphabetically earliest individual variable of $QC_=^\infty$ that does not occur in any member of $S' \cup \{E!Z\}$ nor in $(\forall X)A$. But in view of L1(b) $S' \cup \{E!Z, Y = Z\} \vdash^\infty (\forall X)A \supset A(Y/X)$. Hence in view of L1(i) $S' \cup \{E!Z, Y = Z\} \vdash^\infty A(Y/X)$. But in view of L1(b) $S' \cup \{E!Z, Y = Z\} \vdash^\infty Y = Z$, and $S' \cup \{E!Z, Y = Z\} \vdash^\infty Y = Z \supset (A(Y/X) \supset A(Z/X))$. Hence in view of L1(i) $S' \cup \{E!Z, Y = Z\} \vdash^\infty A(Z/X)$. But in view of L1(b) and L1(p) $S' \cup \{E!Z\} \vdash^\infty (\exists Y)(Y = Z)$. Hence in view of L1(l) $S' \cup \{E!Z\} \vdash^\infty A(Z/X)$, hence in view of L1(h) $S' \vdash^\infty E!Z \supset A(Z/X)$, and hence in view of L1(c) $S \vdash^\infty E!Z \supset A(Z/X)$.

For proof of L5(a). Let X and i be as in L5(a). The following column of formulas of $QC_=^i$,

1   $\sim A$

2   $1 \supset (\sim\sim(f(X) \vee \sim f(X)) \supset \sim A)$ (Axiom)

3   $\sim\sim(f(X) \vee \sim f(X)) \supset \sim A$ (**R2** or **R4**, 1, 2)

4   $3 \supset (A \supset \sim(f(X) \vee \sim f(X)))$ (Axiom)

5   $A \supset \sim(f(X) \vee \sim f(X))$ (**R2** or **R4**, 3, 4)

6   $(\forall X)5$ (**R7**, 5)

7   $6 \supset ((\forall X)A \supset (\forall X)\sim(f(X) \vee \sim f(X)))$ (Axiom)

7   $(\forall X)A \supset (\forall X)\sim(f(X) \vee \sim f(X))$ (**R2** or **R4**, 6, 7),

counts as a derivation of $(\forall X)A \supset (\forall X)\sim(F(X) \vee \sim f(X))$ from $\{(\exists x)(f(x) \vee \sim f(x)), \sim A\}$ in $QC_=^i$. Hence in view of L3(k) $\{(\exists x)(f(x) \vee \sim f(x)), \sim A\} \vdash_i (\exists X)(f(X) \vee \sim f(X)) \supset \sim(\forall X)A$. But in view of L3(b) and L3(q) $\{(\exists x)(f(x) \vee \sim f(x)), \sim A\} \vdash_i (\exists X)(f(X) \vee \sim f(X))$. Hence in view of L3(g) $\{(\exists x)(f(x) \vee \sim f(x)), \sim A\} \vdash_i \sim(\forall X)A$, hence in view of L3(f) $\{(\exists x)(f(x) \vee \sim f(x))\} \vdash_i \sim A \supset \sim(\forall X)A$, hence in view of L3(j) $\{(\exists x)(f(x) \vee \sim f(x))\} \vdash_i (\forall X)A \supset A$, and hence in view of L3(f) $\vdash_i (\exists x)(f(x) \vee \sim f(x)) \supset ((\forall X)A \supset A)$.

For proof of L5(b). Let $S \vdash_1 A$. Then in view of L3(a) and L3(c) there is a finite subset S' of S such that $S' \cup \{(\exists x)(f(x) \vee \sim f(x))\} \vdash_1 A$, and hence there is a finite column of formulas of $QC_=^1$, say, the formulas $B_1, B_2, \ldots, B_p$ ($p > 0$), that counts as a derivation of A from $S' \cup \{(\exists x)(f(x))\}$ in $QC_=^1$. But, if so, then $S' \cup \{(\exists x)(f(x) \vee \sim f(x))\} \vdash_2 B_j$—$S'' \vdash_2 B_j$, for short—for each j from 1 through p, as can be shown by mathematical induction on j. For suppose that B_j belongs to S'' or is an axiom of $QC_=^1$ that counts as an axiom of $QC_=^2$. Then in view of L3(b) $S'' \vdash_2 B_j$. Or suppose that B_j is an axiom of $QC_=^1$ that does not count as an axiom of $QC_=^2$. In view of L5(a) and L3(c) $S'' \vdash_2 (\exists x)(f(x) \vee \sim f(x)) \supset B_j$. Hence in view of L3(b) and L3(g) $S'' \vdash_2 B_j$. Or suppose that B_j follows from two previous entries, say, B_g and $B_g \supset B_j$ ($= B_h$), by means of rule **R1**; suppose $S'' \vdash_2 B_g$ and $S'' \vdash_2 B_h$; and suppose that B_g is closed or B_j is open. Then in view of L3(g) $S'' \vdash_2 B_j$. Suppose then that B_g is open and B_j is closed, and suppose that X is the alphabetically earliest individual variable of QC $\stackrel{2}{=}$ not to occur in any member of S'' nor in B_j. Since $S'' \vdash_2 B_h$, then in view of L3(h) $S'' \vdash_2 (f(X) \lor \sim f(X)) \supset B_h$, and hence in view of L3(i) $S'' \vdash_2 ((f(X) \lor \sim f(X)) \supset B_g) \supset ((f(X) \lor \sim f(X)) \supset B_j)$. But since $S'' \vdash_2 B_g$, then in view of L3(h) $S'' \vdash_2 (f(X) \lor \sim f(X)) \supset B_g$. Hence in view of L3(g) $S'' \vdash_2 (f(X) \lor \sim f(X)) \supset B_j$, hence in view of L3(k) $S'' \vdash_2 \sim B_j \supset \sim(f(X) \lor \sim f(X))$, hence in view of L3(m) $S'' \vdash_2 (\forall X)(\sim B \supset \sim(f(X) \lor \sim f(X)))$, hence in view of L3(p) $S'' \vdash_2 (\forall X)\sim B \supset (\forall X)\sim(f(X) \lor \sim f(X))$, and hence in view of L3(k) $S'' \vdash_2 (\forall X)(f(X) \lor \sim f(X)) \supset (\exists X)B_j$. But in view of L3(a) and L3(q) $S'' \vdash_2 (\exists X)(f(X) \lor \sim f(X))$. Hence in view of L3(g) $S'' \vdash_2 (\exists X)B_j$, and hence in view of L3(n) $S'' \vdash_2 B_j$. Or suppose that B_j follows from a previous entry, say, B_h, by means of rule **R7**, and suppose $S'' \vdash_2 B_h$. Then in view of L3(m) $S'' \vdash_2 B_j$, which completes the induction. But, if $S'' \vdash_2 B_j$ for each j from 1 to p, then $S'' \vdash_2 B_p (= A)$. Hence in view of L3(a) $S \cup \{(\exists x)(f(x) \lor \sim f(x))\} \vdash_2 A$.

For proof of L6(f). Let S be as in L6; and let $A, B, X, Y, Z, A', B', A'',$ and B'' be as in L6(f).

Case 1: X is an individual constant of QC $\stackrel{2}{=}$.

Subcase 1.1: Y does not occur free in B, and hence B'' is the same as A''. Then in view of L6(a) there is a constant-free derivation of $(\forall Z)(Z = Y) \supset (A'' \equiv B'')$ from S in QC $\stackrel{2}{=}$.

Subcase 1.2: Y occurs free in B. In view of L6(b)–(e) it readily follows by mathematical induction on the number of occurrences of '$\sim$', '$\supset$', and '$\forall$' in A that there is a constant-free derivation of $(\forall Z)(Z = Y) \supset (A'' \equiv B'')$ from S in QC $\stackrel{2}{=}$. For suppose in particular that A is of the kind $(\forall X_1)A_1$, and hence B of the kind $(\forall X_1)A_1(Y/X_1)$; suppose A_1' and B_1' respectively stand to A_1 and B_1 as A' and B' respectively stand to A and B; and suppose that A_1'' and B_1'' respectively stand to A_1' and A_1' as A'' and B'' respectively stand to A' and B'. Since Y is presumed to occur free in B and hence in $(\forall X_1)B_1''$, then X_1 is sure to be distinct from Y. Hence, if there is a constant-free derivation of $(\forall Z)(Z = Y) \supset (A_1'' \equiv B_1'')$ from S in QC $\stackrel{2}{=}$, then in view of L6(e) there is one of $(\forall Z)(Z = Y) \supset ((\forall X_1)A_1'' \equiv (\forall X_1)B_1'')$.

Case 2: Y is an individual constant of QC $\stackrel{2}{=}$. Proof like that of Case 1.

For proof of L7. Let $S \vdash_i A$, where S, A, and i are as in L7. Then there is a finite column of formulas of QC $\stackrel{i}{=}$, say, the formulas $B_1, B_2, \ldots, B_p$, that counts as a derivation of A from S in QC $\stackrel{i}{=}$. Let X be the alphabetically earliest individual variable of QC $\stackrel{i}{=}$ that does not occur in any one of $B_1, B_2, \ldots, B_p$, and for each j from 1 through p let B'_j be the result of replacing by an occurrence of X any occurrence in B_j of any individual constant of QC $\stackrel{i}{=}$.

Case 1: $i = 1$. Then the column made up of $B_1', B_2', \ldots, B_p'$ counts as a constant-free derivation of $B_p' (= A)$ from S in QC $\stackrel{i}{=}$.

Case 2: $i = 2$. For each j from 1 to p, let B_j'' be the result of replacing by an occurrence of $(\forall Y)C$ any occurrence in B_j' of any atomic formula C of QC $\stackrel{i}{=}$ that contains X. It is easily shown by mathematical induction on j that for each j

Completeness Theorems for Some Presupposition-free Logics   35

from 1 through p there is a constant-free derivation of B_j'' from S in QC$\stackrel{i}{=}$. For suppose that B_j belongs to S or is an axiom of QC$\stackrel{i}{=}$, and suppose in the latter case that B_j'' is an axiom of QC$\stackrel{i}{=}$. Then B_j'' counts as a constant-free derivation of B_j'' from S in QC$\stackrel{i}{=}$. Or suppose that B_j is of the kind $Y = Y$, where Y is an individual constant of QC$\stackrel{i}{=}$. Then the column made up of $X = X$ and $(\forall X)(X = X)$ counts as a constant-free derivation of B_j'' from S in QC$\stackrel{i}{=}$. Or suppose that B_j is of the kind $Y = Z \supset (C' \supset C'(Z/Y))$, where exactly one of Y and Z is an individual constant of QC$\stackrel{i}{=}$. Then in view of L6(f)–(g) there is a constant-free derivation of B_j'' from S in QC$\stackrel{i}{=}$.[19] Or suppose that B_j follows from two previous entries, say, B_g and $B_g \supset B_j$ ($= B_h$), by means of rule **R2**, and suppose that there is a constant-free derivation of B_g'' and one of B_h'' from S in QC$\stackrel{i}{=}$. Since B_h'' is $B_g'' \supset B_j''$ and B_g'' is closed or B_j'' is open, then the column made up of the derivation of B_g'' (from S in QC$\stackrel{i}{=}$), that of $B_g'' \supset B_j''$ and B_j'' counts as a constant-free derivation of B_j'' from S in QC$\stackrel{i}{=}$. Or suppose that B_j follows from a previous entry, say, B_h, by means of rule **R7**, and suppose that there is a constant-free derivation of B_h'' from S in QC$\stackrel{i}{=}$. Then the column made up of the derivation of B_h'' (from S in QC$\stackrel{i}{=}$) and B_j'' counts as a constant-free derivation of B_j'' from S in QC$\stackrel{i}{=}$, which completes the induction. But, if so, then there is a constant-free derivation of B_p'' ($= A$) from S in QC$\stackrel{i}{=}$.

For proof of L8(a). Let $\vdash_1 A$.

Case 1: No individual constant of QC$\stackrel{1}{=}$ occurs in A. Then in view of L7 there is a constant-free derivation of A from $\emptyset$ in QC$\stackrel{1}{=}$, and hence there is a derivation of A and $\emptyset$ in QC$\stackrel{5}{=}$.

Case 2: At least one individual constant of QC$\stackrel{1}{=}$ occurs in A. Since $\vdash_1 A$, there is a finite column of formulas of QC$\stackrel{1}{=}$, say, the formulas $B_1, B_2, \ldots, B_p$, that counts as a derivation of A from $\emptyset$ in QC$\stackrel{1}{=}$. Let $X_1, X_2, \ldots, X_n$ be in alphabetical order all the individual constants of QC$\stackrel{1}{=}$ that occur in A; for each j from 1 through p let B_j' be the result of replacing by an occurrence of X_1 any occurrence in B_j of any individual constant of QC$\stackrel{1}{=}$ that does occur in A; and for each j from 1 through p, let B_p'' be

$$((\ldots(X_1 = X_1 \& X_2 = X_2) \& \ldots) \& X_n = X_n) \supset B_j'.$$

It is easily shown by mathematical induction on j that $\vdash_5 B_j''$ for each j from 1 through p. For suppose that B_j counts as an axiom of QC$\stackrel{1}{=}$ and hence as an axiom of QC$\stackrel{5}{=}$. Then B_j' counts as an axiom of QC$\stackrel{5}{=}$, and hence in view of L3(h) $\vdash_5 B_j''$. Or suppose that B_j follows from two previous entries, say, B_g and $B_g \supset B_j$ ($= B_h$), by means of rule **R1**, and suppose that $\vdash_5 B_g''$ and $\vdash_5 B_h''$. Then in view of L3(i) $\vdash_5 B_g'' \supset B_j''$, and hence in view of L3(g) $\vdash_5 B_j''$. Or suppose that B_j follows from a previous entry, say, B_h, by means of rule **R7**, and suppose that $\vdash_5 B_h''$. Then in view of L3(o) $\vdash_5 B_j''$, which completes the induction. Hence $\vdash_5 B_p''$. But in view L3(b) and L3(l)

$$\vdash_5 (\ldots(X_1 = X_1 \& X_2 = X_2) \& \ldots) \& X_n = X_n.$$

Hence in view of L3(g) $\vdash_5 B_p' (= A)$.

For proof of L9(a). Let $S \vdash_1 A$, where S and A are as in L9. Then in view of

L3(a) there is a finite subset of S, say, $\{B_1, B_2, \ldots, B_n\}$ ($n \geq 0$), such that $\{B_1, B_2, \ldots, B_n\} \vdash_1 A$, hence in view of L3(f) $\vdash_1 B_1 \supset (B_2 \supset (\ldots(B_n \supset A)\ldots))$, hence in view of L8(a) $\vdash_5 B_1 \supset (B_2 \supset (\ldots(B_n \supset A)\ldots))$, and hence in view of L3(c) $\{B_1, B_2, \ldots, B_n\} \vdash_5 B_1 \supset (B_2 \supset (\ldots(B_n \supset A)\ldots))$. But in view of L3(b) $\{B_1, B_2, \ldots, B_n\} \vdash_5 B_j$ for each j from 1 through n. Hence in view of L3(g) $\{B_1, B_2, \ldots, B_n\} \vdash_5 A$, and hence in view of L3(c) $S \vdash_5 A$.

For proof of L12(a). Let $S \vdash_1 A$, where S and A are as in L12. Then there is a finite subset S' of S such that $S' \vdash_1 A$.

Case 1: Every member of $S' \cup \{A\}$ is constant-free. Then in view of L7 there is a constant-free derivation of A from S' in QC$\frac{1}{=}$, and hence a derivation of A and S' in QC$\frac{9}{=}$. Hence in view of L11(a) $S \vdash_5 A$.

Case 2: At least one member of $S' \cup \{A\}$ (and hence of S) is not constant-free. Since $S' \vdash_1 A$, there is a finite column of formulas of QC$\frac{1}{=}$, say, the formulas $B_1, B_2, \ldots, B_p$, that counts as a derivation of A from S' in QC$\frac{1}{=}$. Let $X_1, X_2, \ldots, X_n$ ($n > 0$) be all the individual constants of QC$\frac{1}{=}$ that occur in one or more of $B_1, B_2, \ldots, B_p$, but not in any member of S (nor, as a result, in A); let Y be the alphabetically earliest individual constant of QC$\frac{1}{=}$ to occur in a member of S; and for each j from 1 through p let B'_j be the result of replacing by an occurrence of Y every occurrence in B_j of every one of $X_1, X_2, \ldots, X_n$. Then the column made up of $B'_1, B'_2, \ldots, B'_p$ counts as a derivation of A from $S' \cup \{C\}$ in QC$\frac{9}{=}$, where C is the alphabetically earliest member of S that contains an occurrence of Y. Hence in view of L11(a) $S \vdash_9 A$.

3. Semantics. We next attend to the semantics of QC$\frac{i}{=}$ ($0 \leq i \leq 10$) and QC$\frac{\infty}{=}$. Of the two domains D and D' mentioned in D13 and later definitions, D is the inner domain of Section 1, D' the outer one. Note in connection with clause (ii) of D13 that when an individual constant X of QC$\frac{i}{=}$ [QC$\frac{\infty}{=}$] is assigned a member of $D \cup D'$ that belongs to D, then X designates a value of 'x', 'y', 'z', etc.; when X is assigned a member of $D \cup D'$ that belongs to D', then X designates something not a value of 'x', 'y', 'z', etc.; and when X is not assigned any member of $D \cup D'$ (which is bound to be the case if $D \cup D'$ is empty, but may also happen when $D \cup D'$ has members), then X fails to designate at all.

Definition 13. *Let D and D' be disjoint domains, and $Int_{<D,D'>}$ be any result of assigning:*
(i) *exactly one of the two truth-values **T** and **F** to each sentence variable P of QC$\frac{i}{=}$ the truth-value in question to be known as the value of P under $Int_{<D,D'>}$;*
(ii) *if D is not empty, exactly one member of D to each individual variable X of QC$\frac{i}{=}$ the member in question to be known as the value of X under $Int_{<D,D'>}$;*
(iii) *if $D \cup D'$ is not empty, at most one member of $D \cup D'$ to each indi-*

vidual constant X of $QC\stackrel{i}{=}$, the member in question to be known as the value of X under $Int_{<D,D'>}$; and
(iv) exactly one subset of $(D \cup D')^m$ to each m-adic ($m = 1, 2, \ldots$) predicate variable F of $QC\stackrel{i}{=}$, the subset in question to be known as the value of F under $Int_{<D,D'>}$.
Then $Int_{<D,D'>}$ counts as a $<D, D'>$-interpretation of the variables and constants of $QC\stackrel{i}{=}$ or, for short, as a $<D, D'>$-interpretation of VC^i.

Definition 13$^\infty$. Like D13, but with '$QC\stackrel{\infty}{=}$' in place of '$QC\stackrel{i}{=}$', and 'VC^∞' in place of 'VC^i'.
Remark. Except D19–D21, every further definition in this section will be understood to carry along its analogue for $QC\stackrel{\infty}{=}$.

Definition 14. Let D, D', and $Int_{<D,D'>}$ be as in D13. If every individual constant of $QC\stackrel{i}{=}$ has a value under $Int_{<D,D'>}$, then $Int_{<D,D'>}$ is said to be C-exhaustive.

Definition 15. Let D be a non-empty domain; let D' be a domain disjoint from D; let $Int_{<D,D'>}$ and $Int'_{<D,D'>}$ be $<D, D'>$-interpretations of VC^i; and let X be an individual variable of $QC\stackrel{i}{=}$. If $Int'_{<D,D'>}$ is like $Int_{<D,D'>}$ except possibly for assigning to X a different member of D than $Int_{<D,D'>}$ does, then $Int'_{<D,D'>}$ counts as an X-variant of $Int_{<D,D'>}$.

We next define three notions of satisfaction: satisfaction$_T$, satisfaction$_F$, and (plain) satisfaction. The first is intended for $QC\stackrel{3}{=} - QC\stackrel{6}{=}$, which—the reader will recall—automatically pronounce true any formula that contains a non-designating constant; the second is intended for $QC\stackrel{7}{=} - QC\stackrel{10}{=}$, which automatically pronounce false any such formula; and the third is intended for $QC\stackrel{1}{=}$, $QC\stackrel{2}{=}$, and $QC\stackrel{\infty}{=}$, which under our official account of things require every individual constant to designate something, either a value of a variable or something not a value of a variable. D16–D18 run along anticipated lines when D is not empty, and hence the variables 'x', 'y', 'z', etc., have values under $Int_{<D,D'>}$. When, on the other hand, D is $\emptyset$, then an open formula or a closed one of the kind $(\forall X)A$ is automatically held, e.g., satisfied$_T$ by $Int_{<D,D'>}$, this is the second case because $(\forall X)A$ is held tantamount to $\sim(\exists X)\sim A$, in the first because the formula is held tantamount to its universal closure.

Definition 16. Let A be a formula of $QC\stackrel{i}{=}$, D and D' be disjoint domains; and $Int_{<D,D'>}$ be a $<D, D'>$-interpretation of VC^i.
Case 1: At least one individual constant of $QC\stackrel{i}{=}$ occurring in A has no value under $Int_{<D,D'>}$. Then $Int_{<D,D'>}$ is said to satisfy$_T$ A.
Case 2: Every individual constant of $QC\stackrel{i}{=}$ occurring in A has a value under $Int_{<D,D'>}$.
Case 2.1: D is not empty.

38   Part 1: Existence

(a)   If A is a sentence variable of $QC^i_=$ and the value of A under $Int_{<D,D'>}$ is T, then $Int_{<D,D'>}$ is said to satisfy$_T$ A;
(b)   If A is of the kind $F(X_1, X_2, \ldots, X_m)$ and the m-tuple made up of the values of $X_1, X_2, \ldots,$ and X_m (in that order) under $Int_{<D,D'>}$ belongs to the value of F under $Int_{<D,D'>}$, then $Int_{<D,D'>}$ is said to satisfy$_T$ A;
(c)   If A is of the kind $X = Y$ and the value of X under $Int_{<D,D'>}$ is the same as that of Y, then $Int_{<D,D'>}$ is said to satisfy$_T$ A;
(d)   If A is of the kind $\sim B$ and $Int_{<D,D'>}$ does not satisfy$_T$ B, then $Int_{<D,D'>}$ is said to satisfy$_T$ A;
(e)   If A is of the kind $B \supset C$ and $Int_{<D,D'>}$ does not satisfy$_T$ B or satisfies$_T$ C, then $Int_{<D,D'>}$ is said to satisfy$_T$ A;
(f)   If A is of the kind $(\forall X)B$ and every X-variant of $Int_{<D,D'>}$ satisfies$_T$ B, then $Int_{<D,D'>}$ is said to satisfy$_T$ A;
(g) $Int_{<D,D'>}$ is said to satisfy$_T$ A pursuant only to one or another of (a)–(f).
Case 2.2: D is empty.
Case 2.2.1: A is open. Then $Int_{<D,D'>}$ is said to satisfy$_T$ A.
Case 2.2.2: A is closed.
(a)–(e)   Like (a)–(e) under Case 2.1;
(f)   If A is of the kind $(\forall X)B$, then $Int_{<D,D'>}$ is said to satisfy$_T$ A;
(g)   Like (g) under Case 2.1.

Definition 17.   Let A, D, D', and $Int_{<D,D'>}$ be as in D16.
Case 1: At least one individual constant of $QC^i_=$ occurring in A has no value under $Int_{<D,D'>}$. Then $Int_{<D,D'>}$ is said not to satisfy$_F$ A.
Case 2: Every individual constant of $QC^i_=$ occurring in A has a value under $Int_{<D,D'>}$. Then $Int_{<D,D'>}$ is said to satisfy$_F$ A if $Int_{<D,D'>}$ satisfies$_T$ A.

Definition 18.   Let A, D, and D' be as in D16; and let $Int_{<D,D'>}$ be a C-exhaustive $<D, D'>$-interpretation of VC^i. Then $Int_{<D,D'>}$ is said to satisfy A if $Int_{<D,D'>}$ satisfies$_T$ A.
Remarks. It follows from D16–D18 that, where $Int_{<D,D'>}$ is a C-exhaustive $<D, D'>$-interpretation of VC^i [VC^∞], a formula of $QC^i_=$ [$QC^\infty_=$] is satisfied by $Int_{<D,D'>}$ if and only if satisfied$_T$, and hence satisfied$_F$, by $Int_{<D,D'>}$. It likewise follows from D16–D18 that a closed formula of $QC^i_=$ [$QC^\infty_=$] of the kind E!X satisfied by $Int_{<D,D'>}$ (and hence both satisfied$_T$ and satisfied$_F$ by $Int_{<D,D'>}$ is if and only if the value of X under $Int_{<D,D'>}$ belongs to D.

Definition 19.   Let S be a set of formulas of $QC^i_=$; and D and D' be as in D16.
(a)   Let $Int_{<D,D'>}$ be a $<D, D'>$-interpretation of VC^i. Then $Int_{<D,D'>}$ is said to simultaneously satisfy$_T$ [simultaneously satisfy$_F$] S if $Int_{<D,D'>}$ satisfies$_T$ [satisfies$_F$] each and every member of S.
(b)   Let $Int_{<D,D'>}$ be a C-exhaustive $<D, D'>$-interpretation of VC^i. Then

Completeness Theorems for Some Presupposition-free Logics   39

$Int_{<D,D'>}$ is said to simultaneously satisfy S if $Int_{<D,D'>}$ simultaneously satisfies$_T$ S.

We then turn to the notion of implication and the attendant one of validity. Eleven different cases are in order.

Definition 20. *Let S be a set of formulas of* $QC^i_=$, *and A be a formula of* $QC^i_=$.
(a) *S is said to imply A in* $QC^0_=$ *if, for every non-empty domain D, every C-exhaustive* $<D, \emptyset>$*-interpretation of* VC^0 *that simultaneously satisfies S also satisfies A.*
(b) *S is said to imply A in* $QC^1_=$ *if, for every non-empty domain D and every domain D' disjoint from D, every C-exhaustive* $<D, D'>$*-interpretation of* VC^1 *that simultaneously satisfies S also satisfies A.*
(c) *S is said to imply A in* $QC^2_=$ *if, for every domain D and every domain D' disjoint from D, every C-exhaustive* $<D, D'>$*-interpretation of* VC^2 *that simultaneously satisfies S also satisfies A.*
(d) *S is said to imply A in* $QC^3_=$ *if, for every non-empty domain D, every* $<D, \emptyset>$*-interpretation of* VC^3 *that simultaneously satisfies$_T$ S also satisfies$_T$ A.*
(e) *S is said to imply A in* $QC^4_=$ *if, for every domain D, every* $<D, \emptyset>$*-interpretation of* VC^4 *that simultaneously satisfies$_T$ S also satisfies$_T$ A.*
(f) *S is said to imply A in* $QC^5_=$ *if, for every non-empty domain D and every domain D' disjoint from D, every* $<D, D'>$*-interpretation of* VC^5 *that simultaneously satisfies$_T$ S also satisfies$_T$ A.*
(g) *S is said to imply A in* $QC^6_=$ *if, for every domain D and every domain D' disjoint from D_0 every* $<D, D'>$*-interpretation of* VC^6 *that simultaneously satisfies$_T$ S also satisfies$_T$ A.*
(h) *S is said to imply A in* $QC^7_=$ *if, for every non-empty domain D, every* $<D, \emptyset>$*-interpretation of* VC^7 *that simultaneously satisfies$_F$ S also satisfies$_F$ A.*
(i) *S is said to imply A in* $QC^8_=$ *if, for every domain D, every* $<D, \emptyset>$*-interpretation of* VC^8 *that simultaneously satisfies$_F$ S also satisfies$_F$ A.*
(j) *S is said to imply A in* $QC^9_=$ *if, for every non-empty domain D and every domain D' disjoint from D, every* $<D, D'>$*-interpretation of* VC^9 *that simultaneously satisfies$_F$ S also satisfies$_F$ A.*
(k) *S is said to imply A in* $QC^{10}_=$ *if, for every domain D and every domain D' disjoint from D, every* $<D, D'>$*-interpretation of* VC^{10} *that simultaneously satisfies$_F$ S also satisfies$_F$ A.*
Remark. No $<\emptyset, \emptyset>$-interpretation of VC^2 can be C-exhaustive; hence S implies A in $QC^2_=$ if and only if, for every domain D and every domain D' that is disjoint from D and non-empty if D is empty, every C-exhaustive $<D, D'>$-interpretation of VC^2 that simultaneously satisfies S also satisfies A.

The various restrictions placed in D20(a)–(k) upon D, D', and $Int_{<D,D'>}$, and the kind of satisfaction that is in order in each case, may be tabulated as follows:

TABLE II

	D	D'	Int	Kind of satisfaction
0	non-empty	empty	C-exhaustive	satisfaction
1	non-empty	disjoint from D	C-exhaustive	satisfaction
2	arbitrary	disjoint from D	C-exhaustive	satisfaction
3	non-empty	empty	arbitrary	satisfaction$_T$
4	arbitrary	empty	arbitrary	satisfaction$_T$
5	non-empty	disjoint from D	arbitrary	satisfaction$_T$
6	arbitrary	disjoint from D	arbitrary	satisfaction$_T$
7	non-empty	empty	arbitrary	satisfaction$_F$
8	arbitrary	empty	arbitrary	satisfaction$_F$
9	non-empty	disjoint from D	arbitrary	satisfaction$_F$
10	arbitrary	disjoint from D	arbitrary	satisfaction$_F$

Definition 11. *A formula A of* $QC_=^i$ *is said to be valid in* $QC_=^i$ *if* $\emptyset$ *implies A in* $QC_=^i$.

Remarks. It follows from D20–D21 that a formula A of $QC_=^i$ is not valid in $QC_=^i$ for any i from 7 to 10 unless A is constant-free. To abridge matters, we shall write, e.g., 'A is implied$_1$ by S' for 'A is implied by S in $QC_=^1$', and 'A is valid$_1$' for 'A is valid in $QC_=^1$'.

The following consequences of D13–D21 merit separate recording as lemmas.

Lemma 14. *Let* $(\forall X)A$ *be a formula of* $QC_=^\infty$, *D be a non-empty domain, D' be a domain disjoint from D, and* $Int_{<D,D'>}$ *be a C-exhaustive* $<D, D'>$-*interpretation of* VC^∞.
(a) *Let each member of D be the value under* $Int_{<D,D'>}$ *of some individual constant or other of* $QC_=^\infty$. *If* $Int_{<D,D'>}$ *satisfies* $A(Y/X)$ *for every individual constant Y of* $QC_=^\infty$ *whose value under* $Int_{<D,D'>}$ *belongs to D, then* $Int_{<D,D'>}$ *satisfies* $(\forall X)A$.
(b) *If* $Int_{<D,D'>}$ *does not satisfy* $A(Y/X)$ *for at least one individual constant Y of* $QC_=^\infty$ *whose value under* $Int_{<D,D'>}$ *belongs to D, then* $Int_{<D,D'>}$ *does not satisfy* $(\forall X)A$.

Lemma 15. *Let A be a closed formula of* $QC_=^2$, *A' be the* $\emptyset$-*associate of A, D' be a non-empty domain, and* $Int_{<\emptyset,D'>}$ *be a* $<\emptyset, D'>$-*interpretation of* VC^2. *Then* $Int_{<\emptyset,D'>}$ *satisfies A if and only if* $Int_{<\emptyset,D'>}$ *satisfies A'.*

Lemma 16. *Let A be a closed formula of* $QC_=^i$, *S' consist of the closed members of S, and* $i = 2$ *or* 6. *If S implies$_i$ A, then it is not the case that there is a non-empty domain D' and a C-exhaustive* $<\emptyset, D'>$-*interpretation* $Int_{<\emptyset,D'>}$ *of* VC^i *such that* $Int_{<\emptyset,D'>}$ *simultaneously satisfies* $S' \cup \{\sim A\}$.

Lemma 17. (a) If S implies$_2$ A, then S implies$_1$ A.
(b) If S implies$_5$ A, then S implies$_1$ A.
(c) If S implies$_6$ A, then S implies$_5$ A.
(d) If S implies$_9$ A, then S implies$_1$ A.
(e) If S implies$_{10}$ A, then S implies$_2$ A.

Lemma 18. Let S' consist of every member of S in which there occurs an individual constant of $QC\underline{\underline{i}}$ not occurring in A, S'' be $S - S'$, and $i = 5$ or 6. If S implies$_i$ A, then S'' implies$_i$ A.

Lemma 19. Let S' consist of every closed formula of $QC\underline{\underline{1}}$ (hence, $QC\underline{\underline{5}}$ and $QC\underline{\underline{6}}$) of the kind $E!X$.
(a) If S implies$_0$ A, then $S \cup S'$ implies$_1$ A.
(b) If S implies$_3$ A, then $S \cup S'$ implies$_5$ A.
(c) If S implies$_4$ A, then $S \cup S'$ implies$_6$ A.

Lemma 20. Let at least one individual constant of $QC\underline{\underline{i}}$ that occurs in A fail to occur in any member of S, and $6 \leq i \leq 10$. If S implies$_i$ A, then S implies$_i$ 'p & $\sim p$'.

Lemma 21. Let S' consist of every closed formula of $QC\underline{\underline{9}}$ (hence, $QC\underline{\underline{10}}$) of the kind $E!X$, where X occurs in one or more members of S.
(a) If S implies$_7$ A, then $S \cup S'$ implies$_9$ A.
(b) If S implies$_8$ A, then $S \cup S'$ implies$_{10}$ A.

Proof of L14 can be retrieved from [8],[20] proof of L15, L16, and L17 is obvious; proof of L19(c) is like that of L19(b); and proof of L21(b) is like that of L21(a). We shall therefore restrict ourselves here to L18, L19(a), L19(b), L20, and L21(a).

For proof of L18. Let S', S'', and i be as in L18, and let S imply$_i$ A.
Case 1: $i = 5$. Let D be a non-empty domain, D' be a domain disjoint from D, $Int_{<D,D'>}$ be a $<D, D'>$-interpretation of VC^i that simultaneously satisfies $_T S''$, and $Int_{<D,D'>}$ be like $Int_{<D,D'>}$ except for not assigning any member of $D \cup D'$ to the individual constants of $QC\underline{\underline{i}}$ that do not occur in A. Since $Int_{<D,D'>}$ simultaneously satisfies $_T S'$, then clearly $Int_{<D,D'>}$ simultaneously satisfies $_T S' \cup S''$ ($= S$) as well. Hence, since S implies$_i$ A, then $Int_{<D,D'>}$ satisfies $_T A$. Hence, clearly, so does $Int_{<D,D'>}$. Hence S'' implies$_i$ A.
Case 2: $i = 6$. Proof like that of Case 1, but with D allowed to be empty.

For proof of L19(a). Let S' be as in L19, and suppose that $S \cup S'$ does not imply$_1$ A. Then there is a non-empty domain D, a domain D' disjoint from D, and a C-exhaustive $<D, D'>$-interpretation $Int_{<D,D'>}$ of VC^1 that simultaneously satisfies $S \cup S'$ (and, hence, assigns a member of D to every individual constant of $QC\underline{\underline{1}}$), but does not satisfy A. Now let $Int_{<D,\varnothing>}$ be like $Int_{<D,D'>}$ except for assigning to each m-adic predicate variable F of $QC\underline{\underline{1}}$ the subset of D^m consisting of every member of D^m that belongs to the value of F under $Int_{<D,D'>}$. Clearly, $Int_{<D,\varnothing>}$ simultaneously satisfies $S \cup S'$ if and only if $Int_{<D,D'>}$ does, and fails to satisfy A if and only if $Int_{<D,D'>}$ does. Hence S does not imply$_0$ A. Hence, if S implies$_0$ A, then $S \cup S'$ implies$_1$ A.

For proof of L19(b). Let S' be as in L19, and suppose that $S \cup S'$ does not imply$_5$ A. Then there is a non-empty domain D, a domain D' disjoint from D, and a $<D, D'>$-interpretation $Int_{<D,D'>}$ of VC^5 that simultaneously satisfies $_T$ $S \cup S'$ (and hence, does not assign a member of D' to any individual constant of $QC\underline{\underline{5}}$), but does not satisfy$_T$ A. Now let $Int_{<D,\varnothing>}$ be like $Int_{<D,D'>}$ except for assigning to each m-adic predicate variable F of $QC\underline{\underline{5}}$ the subset of D^m consisting of every member of D^m that belongs to the value of F under $Int_{<D,D'>}$. Clearly, $Int_{<D,\varnothing>}$ simultaneously satisfies$_T$ $S \cup S'$ if and only if $Int_{<D,D'>}$ does, and fails to satisfy$_T$ A if and only if $Int_{<D,D'>}$ does. Hence S does not imply$_3$ A. Hence, if S implies$_3$ A, then $S \cup S'$ implies$_5$ A.

For proof of L20. Let S and A be as in L20.

Case 1: $i = 7$. Suppose that there is a non-empty domain D and a $<D, \varnothing>$-interpretation $Int_{<D,\varnothing>}$ of VC^i such that $Int_{<D,\varnothing>}$ simultaneously satisfies$_F$ S; and let $Int'_{<D,\varnothing>}$ be like $Int_{<D,\varnothing>}$ except for not assigning any member of D to the individual constants of $QC\underline{\underline{i}}$ that occur in A but do not occur in any member of S. Since $Int_{<D,\varnothing>}$ simultaneously satisfies$_F$ S, then clearly so does $Int'_{<D,\varnothing>}$. But $Int'_{<D,\varnothing>}$ does not satisfy$_F$ A. Hence S does not imply$_i$ A. Hence, if S implies$_i$ A, then it is not the case that there is a non-empty domain D and a $_{<D,\varnothing>}$-interpretation $Int_{<D,\varnothing>}$ of VC^i such that $Int_{<D,\varnothing>}$ simultaneously satisfies$_F$ S. Hence, if S implies$_i$ A, then S implies$_i$ 'p & $\sim p$'.

Case 2: $8 \leq i \leq 10$. Proof like that of Case 1.

For proof of L21(a). Let S' be as in L21, and suppose $S \cup S'$ does not imply$_9$ A. Then there is a non-empty domain D, a domain D' disjoint from D, and a $<D, D'>$-interpretation $Int_{<D,D'>}$ of VC^9 that simultaneously satisfies$_F$ $S \cup S'$ (and hence assigns a member of D to every individual constant of $QC\underline{\underline{9}}$ that occurs in one or more members of S), but does not satisfy$_F$ A. Now let $Int_{<D,\varnothing>}$ be the result of assigning to each sentence variable of $QC\underline{\underline{9}}$ the same truth-value as in $Int_{<D,D'>}$, to each individual variable of $QC\underline{\underline{9}}$ the same member of D as in $Int_{<D,D'>}$, to each individual constant of $QC\underline{\underline{9}}$ that occurs in one or more members of S the same member of D as in $Int_{<D,D'>}$, and to each m-adic predicate variable F of $QC\underline{\underline{9}}$ the subset of D^m consisting of every member of D^m that belongs to the value of **F** under $Int_{<D,D'>}$. Clearly, $Int_{<D,\varnothing>}$ simultaneously satisfies$_F$ S if and only if $Int_{<D,D'>}$ does, and fails to satisfy$_F$ A if $Int_{<D,D'>}$ does. Note, in the latter case, that if any individual constant of $QC\underline{\underline{9}}$ that occurs in A has no value under $Int_{<D,\varnothing>}$, then $Int_{<D,\varnothing>}$ fails to satisfy$_F$ A, whereas if every individual constant of $QC\underline{\underline{9}}$ that occurs in A has a value under $Int_{<D,\varnothing>}$, then $Int_{<D,\varnothing>}$ fails to satisfy$_F$ A if and only if $Int_{<D,D'>}$ does. Hence S does not apply$_7$ A. Hence, if S implies$_7$ A, then $S \cup S'$ implies$_9$ A.

4. Completeness Theorems.

In this section we first establish that $QC\underline{\underline{1}}$ is complete both in Henkin's sense and in Gödel's, and then proceed to obtain

Completeness Theorems for Some Presupposition-free Logics   43

similar results for the rest of our calculi. The proofs of the auxiliary theorems T1, T2, and T4 owe much, as the reader will gather, to [3].

Theorem 1. *Let S_0 be a set of formulas of $QC\overset{1}{=}$ that is consistent in $QC\overset{1}{=}$; for each j from 1 on let S_j be $S_{j-1} \cup \{(\exists X_j)A_j \supset A_j(Y/X_j), E!Y\}$, where (i) $(\exists X_j)A_j$ is in alphabetical order the j-th formula of $QC\overset{\infty}{=}$ of the kind $(\exists X)A$, and (ii) Y is the alphabetically earliest individual constant of $QC\overset{\infty}{=}$ not to occur in any member of S_{j-1} nor in $(\exists X_j)A_j$ and let S_∞ be the union of S_0, S_1, $S_2, \ldots$, Then:*
(a)   *For each j from 0 on S_j is consistent in $QC\overset{\infty}{=}$, and*
(b)   *S_∞ is consistent in $QC\overset{\infty}{=}$.*
Proof:
   (a) Suppose that S_j ($j \geq 1$) is inconsistent in $QC\overset{\infty}{=}$. Then in view of L1(o) and L1(r) so is S_{j-1}. But in view of L1(d) S_0 is consistent in $QC\overset{\infty}{=}$. Hence (a) by mathematical induction on j.
   (b) Suppose that S_∞ is inconsistent in $QC\overset{\infty}{=}$. Then in view of L1(e) some finite subset of S_∞ is inconsistent in $QC\overset{\infty}{=}$. But every finite subset of S_∞ is a subset of S_j for some j from 0 on. Hence in view of L1(e) not all of S_0, S_1, $S_2, \ldots$, are consistent in $QC\overset{\infty}{=}$, as against (a). Hence (b).

Theorem 2. *Let S_∞^0 be the set S_∞ of T1; A_k being in alphabetical order the k-th formula of $QC\overset{\infty}{=}$, let S_∞^k be for each k from 1 on $S_\infty^{k-1} \cup \{A_k\}$ or S_∞^{k-1} according as $S_\infty^{k-1} \cup \{A_k\}$ is consistent₁ in $QC\overset{\infty}{=}$ or not; and let S_∞^∞ be the union of S_∞^0, $S_\infty^1, S_\infty^2, \ldots$. Then:*
(a)   *For each k from 0 on S_∞^k is consistent in $QC\overset{\infty}{=}$;*
(b)   *S_∞^∞ is consistent in $QC\overset{\infty}{=}$;*
(c)   *If $S_\infty^\infty \cup \{A\}$ is consistent in $QC\overset{\infty}{=}$, then A belongs to S_∞^∞;*
(d)   *$S_\infty^\infty \vdash_1^\infty A$ if and only if it is not the case that $S_\infty^\infty \vdash_1^\infty \sim A$; and*
(e)   *$(\exists X)A_j$ being in alphabetical order the j-th formula of $QC\overset{\infty}{=}$ of the kind $(\exists X)A$, then for each j from 1 on there is an individual constant Y of $QC\overset{\infty}{=}$ such that $S_\infty^\infty \vdash_1^\infty (\exists X_j)A_j \supset A_j(Y/X_j)$ and $S_\infty^\infty \vdash_1^\infty E!Y$.*
Proof:
   (a) Suppose that S_∞^k ($k \geq 1$) is $S_\infty^{k-1} \cup \{A_k\}$; then S_∞^k is consistent in $QC\overset{\infty}{=}$, and hence is consistent in $QC\overset{\infty}{=}$ if S_∞^{k-1} is. Suppose, on the other hand, that S_∞^k is S_∞^{k-1}; then S_∞^k is consistent in $QC\overset{\infty}{=}$ if S_∞^{k-1} is. But in view of T1(b) S_∞^0 is consistent in $QC\overset{\infty}{=}$. Hence (a) by mathematical induction on k.
   (b) Proof like that of T1(b).
   (c) Suppose that $S_\infty^\infty \cup \{A\}$ is consistent in $QC\overset{\infty}{=}$ and that A is in alphabetical order the k-th formula of $QC\overset{\infty}{=}$. If S_∞^{k-1} were inconsistent in $QC\overset{\infty}{=}$, then in view of L1(c) $S_\infty^\infty \cup \{A\}$ would be inconsistent in $QC\overset{\infty}{=}$, contrary to the assumption. Hence $S_\infty^{k-1} \cup \{A\}$ is consistent in $QC\overset{\infty}{=}$, hence A belongs to S_∞^k, and hence A belongs to S_∞^∞.
   (d) Suppose $S_\infty^\infty \vdash_1^\infty A$ and $S_\infty^\infty \vdash_1^\infty \sim A$. Then in view of L1(f) S_∞^∞ is inconsistent in $QC\overset{\infty}{=}$, as against (b). Suppose, on the other hand, that it is not the case

that $S^\infty_\infty \vdash^\infty_1 A$. Then in view of L1(b) A does not belong to S^∞_∞. Hence in view of (c) $S^\infty_\infty \cup \{A\}$ is consistent in QC$^\infty_=$. Hence in view of L1(g) $S^\infty_\infty \vdash^\infty_1 \sim A$.
(e) Proof by T1 and L1(b).

Theorem 3. *Let S be a set of formulas of* QC$^1_=$ *that is consistent in* QC$^1_=$. *Then there is a set S' of formulas of* QC$^\infty_=$ *such that:*
(a) S *is a subset of* S';
(b) $S' \vdash^\infty_1 A$ *if and only if it is not the case that* $S' \vdash^\infty_1 \sim A$; *and*
(c) $(\exists X_j)A$ *being as in T2(e), for each j from 1 on there is an individual constant Y of* QC$^\infty_=$ *such that* $S' \vdash^\infty_1 (\exists X_j)A_j \supset A_j (Y/X_j)$ *and* $S' \vdash^\infty_1 E!Y$.
Proof by T1–T2.

Theorem 4. *Let S be a set of formulas of* QC$^1_=$. *If S is consistent in* QC$^1_=$, *then there is a non-empty domain D, a domain D' disjoint from D, and a C-exhaustive $<D, D'>$-interpretation* $Int_{<D,D'>}$ *of* VC^1 *such that* $Int_{<D,D'>}$ *simultaneously satisfies S.*

Proof: Let S be consistent in QC$^1_=$. Then in view of T3 there is a set S of formulas of QC$^\infty_=$ of which (a)–(c) in T3 hold true.

Part One. Let T^∞ consist of all the individual signs of QC$^\infty_=$ and R be a dyadic relation on T^∞ such that, for any members X and Y of T^∞, $R(X, Y)$ if and only if $S' \vdash^\infty_1 Y = Y$. In view of L1 (s)–(u) R is an equivalence relation on T^∞, and hence partitions T^∞ into one or more sets, say $T^\infty_1, T^\infty_2, \ldots$, which by definition are pairwise disjoint and exhaustive of T^∞. Now, for each k from 1 on, let U_k be the alphabetically earliest individual variable of QC$^\infty_=$ to belong to T^∞_k if any individual variable of QC$^\infty_=$ belongs to T^∞_k, otherwise the alphabetically earliest individual constant of QC$^\infty_=$ to belong to T^∞_k; and for each individual term X of QC$^\infty_=$ let $\gamma(X)$ be U_k, where T^∞_k is the one subset of T^∞ to which X belongs.[21] It is easily verified that:

(1.1) *For each individual sign X of* QC$^\infty_=$, $S' \vdash^\infty_1 E!X$ *if and only if* $S' \vdash^\infty_1 E!\gamma(X)$;

(1.2) *For each individual variable X of* QC$^\infty_=$, $S' \vdash^\infty_1 E!\gamma(X)$;

(1.3) *There is at least one k such that* $S' \vdash^\infty_1 E!U_k$;

(1.4) $S' \vdash^\infty_1 F(X_1, X_2, \ldots, X_m)$ *if and only if* $S' \vdash^\infty_1 F(\gamma(X_1), \gamma(X_2), \ldots, \gamma(X_m))$; *and*

(1.5) $S' \vdash^\infty_1 X = Y$ *if and only if* $S' \vdash^\infty_1 \gamma(X) = \gamma(Y)$.

Note for proof of (1.1), (1.4), and (1.5) that $S' \vdash^\infty_1 X = \gamma(X)$ by the very definition of $\gamma(X)$. Hence (1.1), (1.4), and (1.5) by repeated uses of L1(v). Note for proof of (1.2) that in view of L1(n) $S' \vdash^\infty_1 E!X$ for each individual variable X of QC$^\infty_=$. Hence (1.2) by (1.1). And hence (1.3).

Part Two. Let $D \cup D'$ be $\{U_1, U_2, \ldots\}$; for each k from 1 on let U_k belong to D if $S' \vdash^\infty_1 E!U_k$, otherwise to D'; and let $Int'_{<D,D'>}$ be the result of assigning:

(i) to each sentence variable P of QC$^\infty_=$ the truth-value **T** if $S' \vdash^\infty_1 P$, otherwise the truth-value **F**;

(ii) to each individual sign X of QC$^\infty_=$ the uniquely determined member $\gamma(X)$ of $D \cup D'$; and

(iii) to each m-adic ($m \geq 1$) predicate variable F of QC$_=^\infty$ the one subset of $(D \cup D')^m$ to which $<U_{i_1}, U_{i_2}, \ldots, U_{i_m}>$ belongs if and only if $S' \vdash_1^\infty F(U_{i_1}, U_{i_2}, \ldots, U_{i_m})$.

It is easily verified that:

(2.1) D is not empty and D' is disjoint from D;

(2.2) $Int'_{<D,D'>}$ assigns a member of D to each individual variable of QC$_=^\infty$, and a member of $D \cup D'$ to each individual constant of QC$_=^\infty$;

(2.3) $Int'_{<D,D'>}$ counts as a C-exhaustive $<D, D'>$-interpretation of VC$^\infty$;

(2.4) $S' \vdash_1^\infty$ E!X, where X is an individual constant of QC$_=^\infty$, if and only if the value of X under $Int'_{<D,D'>}$ belongs to D; and

(2.5) Each member of D is the value under $Int'_{<D,D'>}$ of some individual constant or other of QC$_=^\infty$.

Of these, (2.1) follows from (1.3); (2.2) from (1.2) and (ii); and (2.3) from (2.1)–(2.2) and (i)–(iii). As for (2.4), note that in view of (2.1)$S' \vdash_1^\infty$ E!X if and only if $S' \vdash_1^\infty$ E!$\gamma(X)$; hence (2.4) by (ii) and the definition of D. As for (2.5), if U_k belongs to D, then $S' \vdash_1^\infty$ E!U_k, and hence in view of L1(p) $S' \vdash_1^\infty$ ($\exists X$)($X = U_k$), where X is the alphabetically earliest individual variable of QC$_=^\infty$ to differ from U_k. Hence in view of T3(c) and L1(i) $S' \vdash_1^\infty Y = U_k$ for some individual constant Y of QC$_=^\infty$. Hence Y belongs to T_k^∞. Hence U_k is the value of Y under $Int'_{<D,D'>}$.

Part Three. Let A be a formula of QC$_=^\infty$. It is easily shown by mathematical induction on the number of occurrences of '$\sim$', '$\supset$', and '$\forall$' in A that $Int_{<D,D'>}$ satisfies A if and only if $S' \vdash_1^\infty A$.

Base Step. By (1.4)–(1.5) and (i)–(iii).

Inductive Step. Suppose that A is of the kind $\sim B$. Then in view of T3(b) $S' \vdash_1^\infty A$ if and only if it is not the case that $S' \vdash_1^\infty B$, hence in view of the hypothesis of the induction if and only if $Int'_{<D,D'>}$ does not satisfy B, and hence if and only if $Int'_{<D,D'>}$ satisfies A. Or suppose that A is of the kind $B \supset C$. Then view of T3(b) and L1(j) $S' \vdash_1^\infty A$ if and only if $S' \vdash_1^\infty C$ or it is not the case that $S' \vdash_1^\infty B$, hence in view of the hypothesis of the induction if and only if $Int'_{<D,D'>}$ does not satisfy B or $Int'_{<D,D'>}$ satisfies C, and hence if and only if $Int'_{<D,D'>}$ satisfies A. Or suppose that A is of the kind ($\forall X$)B and $S' \vdash_1^\infty A$. Then in view of L1(q) $S' \vdash_1^\infty$ E!$Y \supset B(Y/X)$ for every individual constant Y of QC$_=^\infty$; hence in view of (2.4) and L1(i) $S' \vdash_1^\infty B(Y/X)$ for every individual constant Y of QC$_=^\infty$ whose value under $Int'_{<D,D'>}$ belongs to D; and hence in view of (2.5) and L14(a) Int' satisfies A. Or suppose that A is of the kind ($\forall X$)B and it is not the case that $S' \vdash_1^\infty A$. Then in view of T3(b) $S' \vdash_1^\infty \sim(\forall X)B$; hence in view of L1(m) $S' \vdash_1^\infty (\exists X)\sim B$; hence in view of T3(c) and L1(i) $S' \vdash_1^\infty \sim B(Y/X)$ and $S' \vdash_1^\infty$ E!Y for at least one individual constant Y of QC$_=^\infty$; hence in view of T3(b) and (2.4) it is not the case that $S' \vdash_1^\infty B(Y/X)$ for at least one individual constant Y of QC$_=^\infty$ whose value under $Int'_{<D,D'>}$ belongs to D; hence in view of the hypothesis of the induction $Int'_{<D,D'>}$ does not satisfy $B(Y/X)$ for at least one individual constant Y of QC$_=^\infty$ whose value under $Int'_{<D,D'>}$ belongs to D; and hence in view of L14(b) $Int'_{<D,D'>}$ does not satisfy A.

Part Four. Let A be a member of S, and $Int_{<D,D'>}$ be the result of assigning to each sentence variable of QC$_=$ the same truth-value as in $Int'_{<D,D'>}$, to each individual sign of QC$_=$ the same member of $D \cup D'$ as in $Int'_{<D,D'>}$, and to each m-adic predicate variable of QC$_=$ the same subset of $(D \cup D')^m$ as in $Int'_{<D,D'>}$. Since in view of T3(a) A belongs to S', then in view of L1(b) $S' \vdash_1^\infty A$, hence in view of Part Three $Int'_{<D,D'>}$ satisfies A, and hence so does $Int_{<D,D'>}$. Hence T4 in view of (2.1) and (2.3).

Theorem 5. *Let S be a set of formulas of* QC $\frac{1}{=}$, *and A be a formula of* QC $\frac{1}{=}$.
(a) *If S implies$_1$ A, then $S \vdash_1 A$.*
(b) *If A is valid$_1$, then $\vdash_1 A$.*
Proof:
(a) Let S imply$_1$ A. Then it is not the case that there is a non-empty domain D, a domain D' disjoint from D, and a C-exhaustive $<D, D'>$-interpretation $Int_{<D,D'>}$ of VC^1 such that $Int_{<D,D'>}$ simultaneously satisfies $S \cup \{\sim A\}$. Hence in view of T4 $S \cup \{\sim A\}$ is inconsistent in QC $\frac{1}{=}$. Hence in view of L3(d) $S \vdash_1 A$.
(b) Let A be valid$_1$. Then $\emptyset$ implies$_1$ A. Hence $\vdash_1 A$ in view of (a).

In view of T5(a) QC $\frac{1}{=}$ may be said to be *complete in Henkin's sense*, and in view of T5(b) to be *complete in Gödel's*.
We next establish that QC $\frac{2}{=}$ is likewise complete in both senses.

Theorem 6. *Let S be a set of closed formulas of* QC $\frac{2}{=}$, *and let $S \cup \{\sim(\exists x)(f(x) \lor \sim f(x))\}$ be consistent in* QC $\frac{2}{=}$. *Then there is a non-empty domain D' and a C-exhaustive $<\emptyset, D'>$-interpretation $Int_{<D,D'>}$ of VC^2 such that $Int_{<\emptyset,D'>}$ simultaneously satisfies S.*
Proof:
Part One. Let S'_0 consist of the $\emptyset$-associates of the members of S; A_j being in alphabetical order the j-th closed and quantifier-free formula of QC $\frac{2}{=}$, let S'_j be for each j from 1 on $S'_{j-1} \cup \{A_j\}$ or S'_{j-1} according as $S'_{j-1} \cup \{A_j\}$ is consistent in QC $\frac{2}{=}$ or not; and let S'_∞ be the union of $S'_0, S'_1, \ldots$. In view of L4(a) S'_0 is consistent in QC $\frac{2}{=}$. Hence by the same reasoning as in the proof of T2(a)–(d), but with L3(b), L2(a), L3(c), L2(b), and L2(c) respectively doing duty for L1(b), L1(e), L1(c), L1(f), and L1(g):
(1) $S'_\infty \vdash_2 A$ *if and only if it is not the case that* $S'_\infty \vdash_2 \sim A$.
Part Two. Let C^2 consist of all the individual constants of QC $\frac{2}{=}$, and let R be a dyadic relation on C^2 such that, for any members X and Y of C^2, $R(X, Y)$ if and only if $S'_\infty \vdash_2 X = Y$. In view of L2(e)–(g) R is an equivalence relation on C^2, and hence partitions C^2 into one or more sets, say, $C^2_1, C^2_2, \ldots$, which by definition are pairwise disjoint and exhaustive of C^2. Now, for each k from 1 on, let U_k be the alphabetically earliest individual constant of QC $\frac{2}{=}$ to belong to C^2_k; and for each individual constant X of QC $\frac{2}{=}$, let $\gamma(X)$ be U_k, where C^2_k is the one subset of C^2 to which X belongs. It is easily verified with the aid of L2(h) that:
(2) $S'_\infty \vdash_2 F(X_1, X_2, \ldots, X_m)$, *where* $X_1, X_2, \ldots,$ *and* X_m *are indi-*

vidual constants of QC $\underline{\underline{2}}$, if and only if $S'_\infty \vdash_2 F(\gamma(X_1), \gamma(X_2), \ldots, \gamma(X_m))$, and

(3) $S'_\infty \vdash_2 X = Y$, where X and Y are individual constants of QC $\underline{\underline{2}}$, if and only if $S'_\infty \vdash_2 \gamma(X) = \gamma(Y)$.

Part Three. Let D' be $\{U_1, U_2, \ldots\}$, and let $Int_{<\varnothing,D'>}$ be the result of assigning:

(i) to each sentence variable P of QC $\underline{\underline{2}}$ the truth-value **T** if $S'_\infty \vdash_2 P$, otherwise the truth-value **F**;

(ii) to each individual constant X of QC $\underline{\underline{2}}$ the uniquely determined member $\gamma(X)$ of D'; and

(iii) to each m-adic predicate variable F of QC $\underline{\underline{2}}$ the one subset of D'^m to which $<U_{i_1}, U_{i_2}, \ldots, U_{i_m}>$ belongs if and only if $S'_\infty \vdash_2 F(U_{i_1}, U_{i_2}, \ldots, U_{i_m})$.

It is easily verified that:

(4) D' is not empty and $Int_{<\varnothing,D'>}$ counts as a C-exhaustive $<\varnothing, D'>$-interpretation of VC^2.

Part Four. By the same reasoning as in Part Three of the proof of T4, but with the induction carried on the number of occurrences of '$\sim$' and '$\supset$' (rather than '$\sim$', '$\supset$', and '$\forall$') in A, and with (1)–(3) above and L2(d) doing duty for T3(b), (1.4), (1.5), and L1(j), it is easily shown that, where A is a closed and quantifier-free formula of QC $\underline{\underline{2}}$, $Int_{<\varnothing,D'>}$ satisfies A if and only if $S'_\infty \vdash_2 A$. Hence $Int_{<\varnothing,D'>}$ simultaneously satisfies S'_∞, hence S'_0 (S'_0 being a subset of S'_∞), and hence in view of L15 S itself. Hence T6 in view of (4).

Theorem 7. *Let S be a set of formulas of* QC $\underline{\underline{2}}$, *and A be a formula of* QC $\underline{\underline{2}}$.
(a) *If S implies$_2$ A, then $S \vdash_2 A$.*
(b) *If A is valid$_2$, then $\vdash_2 A$.*
Proof:
(a) Let S imply$_2$ A. Then in view of L17(a) S implies$_1$ A, and hence in view of T5(a) $S \vdash_1 A$.
Case 1: A is open. Then in view of L5(b) $S \cup \{(\exists x)(f(x) \vee \sim f(x))\} \vdash_2 A$. But in view of L4(b) and L3(c) $S \cup \{\sim(\exists x)(f(x) \vee \sim f(x))\} \vdash_2 A$. Hence $S \vdash_2 A$ in view of L3(e).
Case 2: A is closed. Let S' consist of all the closed members of S. Since S implies$_2$ A, in view of L16 it is not the case that there is a non-empty domain D' and a C-exhaustive $<\varnothing, D'>$-interpretation $Int_{<\varnothing,D'>}$ of VC^2 such that $Int_{<\varnothing,D'>}$ simultaneously satisfies $S' \cup \{\sim A\}$. Hence in view of T6 $S' \cup \{\sim(\exists x)(f(x) \vee \sim f(x)), \sim A\}$ is inconsistent in QC $\underline{\underline{2}}$, hence in view of L3(d) $S' \cup \{\sim(\exists x)(f(x) \vee \sim f(x))\} \vdash_2 A$, and hence in view of L3(c), $S \cup \{\sim(\exists x)(f(x) \vee \sim f(x))\} \vdash_2 A$. On the other hand, since $S \vdash_1 A$, in view of L5(b) $S \cup \{(\exists x)(f(x) \vee \sim f(x))\} \vdash_2 A$. Hence $S \vdash_2 A$ in view of L3(e).
(b) Proof like that of T5(b).

Banking on T5 and T7, we next establish that QC $\underline{\underline{5}}$ and QC $\underline{\underline{6}}$ are complete in Henkin's sense and in Gödel's.

Theorem 8. Let S be a set of formulas of $QC\stackrel{5}{=}$, and A be a formula of $QC\stackrel{5}{=}$.
(a) If S implies$_5$ A, then $S \vdash_5 A$.
(b) If A is valid$_5$, then $\vdash_5 A$.
Proof:
 (a) Let S imply$_5$ A, and S'' be as in L18. Then in view of L18 S'' implies$_5$ A, hence in view of L17(b) S'' implies$_1$ A, hence in view of T5(a) $S'' \vdash_1 A$, hence in view of L9(a) $S'' \vdash_5 A$, and hence in view of L3(c) $S \vdash_5 A$.
 (b) Proof like that of T5(b).

Theorem 9. Let S be a set of formulas of $QC\stackrel{6}{=}$, and A be a formula of $QC\stackrel{6}{=}$.
(a) If S implies$_6$ A, then $S \vdash_6 A$.
(b) If A is valid$_6$, then $\vdash_6 A$.
Proof:
 (a) Let S imply$_6$ A. Then in view of L17(c) S implies$_5$ A, and hence in view of T8(a) $S \vdash_5 A$.
Case 1: A is open. Then $S \vdash_6 A$ by the same reasoning as in the proof of T7(a), Case 1, but with L5(c) doing duty for L5(b).
Case 2: A is closed. Let S'' be as in L18, and let S''' consist of all the closed members of S''. Since S implies$_6$ A, then in view of L18 S'' implies$_6$ A, and hence in view of L16 it is not the case that there is a non-empty domain D' and a C-exhaustive $<\varnothing, D'>$-interpretation $Int_{<\varnothing,D'>}$ of VC^6 such that $Int_{<\varnothing,D'>}$ simultaneously satisfies $S''' \cup \{\sim A\}$. Hence in view of T6 $S''' \cup \{\sim(\exists x)(f(x) \lor \sim f(x)), \sim A\}$ is inconsistent in $QC\stackrel{2}{=}$, hence in view of L3(d) $S''' \cup \{\sim(\exists x)(f(x) \lor \sim f(x))\} \vdash_2 A$, hence in view of L9(b) $S''' \cup \{\sim(\exists x)(f(x) \lor \sim f(x))\} \vdash_6 A$, and hence in view of L3(c) $S \cup \{\sim(\exists x)(f(x) \lor \sim f(x))\} \vdash_6 A$. On the other hand, since $S \vdash_5 A$, in view of L5(c) $S \cup \{(\exists x)(f(x) \lor \sim(fx))\} \vdash_6 A$. Hence $S \vdash_6 A$ in view of L3(e).
 (b) Proof like that of T5(b).

Banking on T5 and T8 – T9, we next establish that $QC\stackrel{0}{=}$, $QC\stackrel{3}{=}$, and $QC\stackrel{4}{=}$ are complete in Henkin's sense and in Gödel's.

Theorem 10. Let S be a set of formulas of $QC\stackrel{i}{=}$, A be a formula of $QC\stackrel{i}{=}$, and $i = 0, 3,$ or 4.
(a) If S implies$_i$ A, then $S \vdash_i A$.
(b) If A is valid$_i$, then $\vdash_i A$.
Proof:
 (a) Let S' consist of every closed formula of $QC\stackrel{i}{=}$ of the kind $E!X$.
Case 1: $i = 0$. If S implies$_i$ A, then in view of L9(a) $S \cup S'$ implies$_1$ A, hence in view of T5(a) $S \cup S' \vdash_1 A$, and hence in view of L10(a) $S \vdash_i A$.
Case 2: $i = 3$ or 4. Proof like that of Case 1, but with L19(b)–(c) doing duty for L19(a), T8(a)–T9(a) for T5(a), and L10(b)–(c) for L10(a).
 (b) Proof like that of T5(b).

Finally, banking on T5 and T7, we establish that $QC_=^7$, $QC_=^8$, $QC_=^9$, and $QC_=^{10}$ are complete in Henkin's sense and in Gödel's.

Theorem 11. *Let S and A be as in T10, and $7 \leq i \leq 10$.*
(a) *If S implies$_i$ A, then $S \vdash_i A$.*
(b) *If A is valid$_i$, then $\vdash_i A$.*
Proof:
    (a) *Case 1: $i = 9$. Subcase 1.1:* Every individual constant of $QC_=$ that occurs in A occurs in one or more members of S. If S implies$_i$ A, then in view of L17(c) S implies$_1$ A, hence in view of T5(a) $S \vdash_1 A$, and hence in view of L12(a) $S \vdash_i A$.
Subcase 1.2: At least one individual constant of $QC_=^i$ that occurs in A does not occur in any member of S. If S implies$_i$ A, then in view of L20 S implies$_i$ 'p & $\sim p$', hence in view of Subcase 1.1 $S \vdash_i p$ & $\sim p$, and hence in view of L11(b) $S \vdash_i A$.
Case 2: $i = 10$. Proof like that of Case 1, but with L17(d) doing duty for L17(c), T7(b) for T5(b), and L12(b) for L12(a).
Case 3: $i = 7$. Subcase 3.1: Every individual constant of $QC_=^i$ that occurs in A occurs in one or more members of S. Let S' be as in L21. If S implies$_i$ A, then in view of L21(a) $S \cup S'$ implies$_9$ A, hence in view of Case 1 $S \cup S' \vdash_9 A$, and hence in view of L13(a) $S \vdash_7 A$.
Subcase 3.2: At least one individual constant of $QC_=^i$ that occurs in A does not occur in any member of S. If S implies$_i$ A, then in view of L20 S implies$_i$ 'p & $\sim p$', hence in view of Subcase 3.1 $S \vdash_i p$ & $\sim p$, and hence in view of L11(b) $S \vdash_i A$.
Case 4: $i = 8$. Proof like that of Case 3, but with L21(b) doing duty for L21(a), and L13(b) for L13(a).
    (b) Proof like that of T5(b).

The converse of each one of our completeness theorems also holds true, as the reader may verify:

Theorem 12. *Let S and A be as in T10, and $0 \leq i \leq 10$.*
(a) *If $S \vdash_i A$, then S implies$_i$ A.*
(b) *If $\vdash_i A$, then A is valid$_i$.*

In view of T12(a) $QC_=^0 - QC_=^{10}$ may be said to be sound in Henkin's sense; and in view of T12(b) to be sound in Gödel's sense.

5. Closing Remarks. With T5 and T7−T12 at hand, the claims made in the introduction for $QC_=^1 - QC_=^{10}$ are easily defended. (i) The inner domains that figure in clauses (c), (e), (g), (i), and (k) of D20 need not have members. (ii) The $<D, D'>$-interpretations that figure in the last eight clauses of the

50 Part 1: Existence

definition need not be C-exhaustive. (iii) And those that figure in clauses (b), (c), (f), (g), (j), and (k), when C-exhaustive, may assign a member of D' rather than D to any individual constant of $QC_=$. Hence, in view of T7–T12 and (i), $QC_=^2$, $QC_=^4$, $QC_=^6$, $QC_=^8$, and $QC_=^{10}$ *do* lift the restriction usually placed on the individual variables of $QC_=$, namely, that they have values. Hence, in view of T5, T7–T12, and (ii)–(iii), $QC_=^1$, $QC_=^2$, $QC_=^5$, $QC_=^6$, $QC_=^9$, and $QC_=^{10}$ allow the individual constants of $QC_=$ to designate something not a value of a variable; $QC_=^2 - QC_=^{10}$ allow them not to designate at all; and, hence all ten of $QC_=^1 - QC_=^{10}$ *do* lift the restriction usually placed on the individual constants of $QC_=$, namely, that they each designate a value of a variable.

Appendix 1. We abide in the main text by Hailperin's suggestion in [2] that a formula A of $QC_=^i$ of the kind $(\forall X)B$ be held satisfied by any $<\emptyset, D'>$-interpretation $Int_{<\emptyset,D'>}$ of the variables and constants of $QC_=^i$. Another course is open, and was adopted by Mostowski in [13]: letting A be satisfied $Int_{<\emptyset,D'>}$ so long as X occurs free in B, otherwise requiring that B be satisfied by $Int_{<\emptyset,D'>}$ if A is to be satisfied by $Int_{<\emptyset,D'>}$. The changes that must be brought to Sections $2-3$ when Mostowski's policy towards $(\forall X)B$ is enforced, are as follows:

(1) Amend (d) in D6, Case 2, to read: If A is of the kind $(\forall X)B$, where X occurs free in B, then '$p \supset p$' counts as the $\emptyset$-associate of A; if A is of the kind $(\forall X)B$, where X does not occur free in B, and B' is the $\emptyset$-associate of B, then B' counts as the $\emptyset$-associate of A.

(2) Amend (c) in D7 to read: A formula of $QC_=^i$ counts as an axiom of $QC_=^2$, $QC_=^6$, and $QC_=^{10}$ if it is of one of the eight kinds listed under (a), but with Y understood to be an individual variable of $QC_=^i$ when the formula is of the kind $(\forall X)A \supset A(Y/X)$, and X understood to occur free in B when the formula is of the kind $(\forall X)(A \supset B) \supset ((\forall X)A \supset (\forall X)B)$.

(3) Amend (d) in D7 to read: A formula of $QC_=^i$ counts as an axiom of $QC_=^4$ and $QC_=^8$ if it is of one of the eight kinds listed under (a), but with X understood to occur free in B when the formula is of the kind $(\forall X)(A \supset B) \supset ((\forall X) A \supset (\forall X)B)$.

(4) In L3(p) require X to occur free in B when $i = 2, 4$, or 6.

(5) Retrieve proof L4(a) from [13] (rather than [15], which follows Hailperin).

(6) Amend (a) in L5 to read: Let X be an individual variable of $QC_=^i$ that does not occur in B, and $i = 2$ or 6. Then $\vdash_i (\exists x)(f(x) \vee \sim f(x)) \supset ((\forall X)(A \supset B)) \supset ((\forall X)A \supset (\forall X)B)$. Proof of the lemma is as follows.
Part One. The following column of formulas of $QC_=^i$,

1 $(\forall X)(A \supset B)$

2 $1 \supset (A \supset B)$ \hfill (Axiom)

3 $A \supset B$ (**R2** or **R4**, 1, 2)

4 $3 \supset ((f(X) \vee \sim f(X)) \supset (A \supset B))$ (Axiom)

5 $(f(X) \vee \sim f(X)) \supset (A \supset B)$ (**R2** or **R4**, 3, 4)

6 $5 \supset (((f(X) \vee \sim f(X)) \supset A) \supset ((f(X) \vee \sim f(X)) \supset B))$ (Axiom)

7 $((f(X) \vee \sim f(X)) \supset A) \supset ((F(X) \vee \sim f(X)) \supset B)$ (**R2** or **R4**, 5, 6)

8 A

9 $8 \supset ((f(X) \vee \sim f(X)) \supset A)$ (Axiom)

10 $(f(X) \vee \sim f(X)) \supset A$ (**R2** or **R4**, 8, 9)

11 $(f(X) \vee \sim f(X)) \supset B$ (**R2** or **R4**, 7, 10)

12 $11 \supset (\sim B \supset \sim (f(X) \vee \sim f(X)))$ (Axiom)

13 $\sim B \supset \sim (f(X) \sim f(X))$ (**R2** or **R4**, 11, 12)

counts as a derivation of $\sim B \supset \sim (f(X) \vee \sim f(X))$ from $\{(\forall X)(A \supset B), A\}$ in QC$\stackrel{i}{=}$. Hence in view of L3(f)

$$\{(\forall X)(A \supset B)\} \vdash_i A \supset (\sim B \supset \sim (f(X) \vee \sim f(X))),$$

hence in view of L3(m)

$$\{(\forall X)(A \supset B)\} \vdash_i (\forall X)(A \supset (\sim B \supset \sim (f(X) \vee \sim f(X)))),$$

hence in view of L3(p)

$$\{(\forall X)(A \supset B)\} \vdash_i (\forall X)A \supset (\forall X)(\sim B \supset \sim (f(X) \vee \sim f(X))),$$

and hence in view of L3(c)

$$\{(\exists x)(f(x) \vee \sim f(x)), (\forall X)(A \supset B)\} \vdash_i (\forall X)A \supset (\forall X)(\sim B \supset \sim (f(X) \vee \sim f(X))).$$

Part Two. In view of L3(b) and L3(p)

$$\{(\forall X)(\sim B \supset \sim (f(X) \vee \sim f(X)))\} \vdash_i (\forall X) \sim B \supset (\forall X) \sim (f(X) \vee \sim f(X)),$$

hence in view of L3(k)

$$\{(\forall X) \sim B \supset \sim (f(X) \vee \sim f(X)))\} \vdash_i (\exists X)(f(X) \vee \sim f(X)) \supset (\exists X)B,$$

and hence in view of L3(c)

$$\{(\exists x)(f(x) \vee \sim f(x)), (\forall X)(\sim B \supset \sim (f(X) \vee \sim f(X)))\} \vdash (\exists X)(f(X) \vee \sim f(X)) \supset (\exists X)B.$$

But in view of L3(b) and L3(q)

$$\{(\exists x)(f(x) \vee \sim f(x)), (\forall X) \sim B \supset \sim (f(X) \vee \sim f(X)))\} \vdash_i (\exists X)(f(X) \vee \sim f(X)).$$

Hence in view of L3(g)

$$\{(\exists x)(f(x) \lor \sim f(x)), (\forall X)(\sim B \supset \sim (f(X) \lor \sim f(X)))\} \vdash_i (\exists X)B,$$

hence in view of L3(n)

$$\{(\exists x)(f(x) \lor \sim f(x)), (\forall X)(\sim B \supset \sim (f(X) \lor \sim f(X)))\} \vdash_i B,$$

hence in view of L3(m)

$$\{(\exists x)(f(x) \lor \sim f(x)), (\forall X)(\sim B \supset \sim (f(X) \lor \sim f(X)))\} \vdash_i (\forall X)B,$$

hence in view of L3(f)

$$\{(\exists x)(f(x) \lor \sim f(x))\} \vdash_i (\forall X)(\sim B \supset \sim (f(X) \lor \sim f(X))) \supset (\forall X)B,$$

hence in view of L3(h)

$$\{(\exists x)(f(x) \lor \sim f(x))\} \vdash_i (\forall X)A \supset ((AC)(\forall X)(\sim B \supset \sim (f(X) \lor \sim f(X))) \supset (\forall X)B,$$

hence in view of L3(i)

$$\{(\exists x)(f(x) \lor \sim f(x))\} \vdash_i ((\forall X)A \supset (\forall X)(\sim B \supset \sim (f(X) \lor \sim f(X)))) \supset ((\forall X)A \supset (\forall X)B),$$

and hence in view of L3(c)

$$\{(\exists x)(f(x) \lor \sim f(x)), (\forall X)(A \supset B)\} \vdash_i ((\forall X)A \supset (\forall X)(\sim B \supset \sim (f(X) \lor \sim f(X)))) \supset ((\forall X)A \supset (\forall X)B).$$

Part Three. In view of Parts One–Two and L3(g)

$$\{(\exists x)(f(x) \lor \sim f(x)), (\forall X)(A \supset B)\} \vdash_i (\forall X)A \supset (\forall X)B.$$

Hence in view of L3(f)

$$\vdash_i (\exists x)(f(x) \lor \sim f(x)) \supset ((\forall X)(A \supset B) \supset ((\forall X)A \supset (\forall X)B)(AC).$$

(7) In L6(e) require X to occur free in both B and C or in neither (as well as not to occur free in A). The restriction does not affect the proof of L6(f) on p. 34.

(8) Amend (f) in D16, Case 2.2.2, to read: If A is of the kind $(\forall X)B$, where X occurs free in B, then $Int_{<D,D'>}$ is said to satisfy$_T$ A; if A is of the kind $(\forall X)B$, where X does not occur free in B, and $Int_{<D,D'>}$ satisfies$_T$ B, then $Int_{<D,D'>}$ is said to satisfy$_T$ A.

Since all of theorems T1–T12 hold true as before, and by the same proofs as before, we end up with five extra variants of QC$_=$ that lift one or both of the restrictions normally placed on the individual terms of QC$_=$.

Appendix 2. The alternative accounts of QC$_=^1$ and QC$_=^2$ that we mentioned in Section 1 call for the following definitions:

Completeness Theorems for Some Presupposition-free Logics 53

Definition 21. Let D and D' be disjoint domains, $i = 1$ or 2, and $Int_{<D,D'>}$ be any result of assigning:
(i) exactly one of the two truth-values **T** and **F** to each sentence variable P of $QC^i_=$, the truth-value in question to be known as the value of P under $Int_{<D,D'>}$;
(ii) if D is not empty, exactly one member of D to each individual variable X of $QC^i_=$, the member in question to be known as the value of X under $Int_{<D,D'>}$;
(iii) if $D \cup D'$ is not empty, at most one member of $D \cup D'$ to each individual constant X of $QC^i_=$, the member in question to be known as the value of X under $Int_{<D,D'>}$;
(iv) exactly one subset of $(D \cap D')^m$ to each m-adic ($m = 1, 2, \ldots$) predicate variable F of $QC^i_=$, the subset in question to be known as the value of F under $Int_{<D,D'>}$; and
(v) if one or more individual constants of $QC^i_=$ have no value under $Int_{<D,D'>}$, exactly one of the two truth-values **T** and **F** to each atomic formula A of $QC^i_=$ that contains such a constant, the truth-value in question to be known as the value of A under $Int_{<D,D'>}$.

If (a) for every individual constant X of $QC^1_=$ such that X has no value under $Int_{<D,D'>}$, $X = X$ has the value **T** under $Int_{<D,D'>}$, (b) for every two individual constants X and Y of $QC^i_=$ such that exactly one of X and Y has a value under $Int_{<D,D'>}$, $X = Y$ has the value **F** under $Int_{<D,D'>}$, and (c) for every two individual constants X and Y of $QC^i_=$ such that each of X and Y has a value under $Int_{<D,D'>}$ or neither does, and for every atomic formula A of $QC^i_=$ that contains an individual constant of $QC^i_=$ without a value under $Int_{<D,D'>}$, A and $A(Y/X)$ have the same value under $Int_{<D,D'>}$ in case X and Y have the same value under $Int_{<D,D'>}$ or $X = Y$ has the value **T** under $Int_{<D,D'>}$, then $Int_{<D,D'>}$ counts as a $<D, D'>$-interpretation of the variables, constants, and atomic formulas of $QC^i_=$.[22]

Definitions 22–23. Like D14–D15, but with $Int_{<D,D'>}$ in the first case, each one of $Int_{<D,D'>}$ and $Int'_{<D,D'>}$ in the other, understood to be a $<D, D'>$-interpretation of the variables, constants and atomic formulas of $QC^i_=$.

Definition 24. Let A be a formula of $QC^i_=$, D and D' be disjoint domains; $Int_{<D,D'>}$ be a $<D, D'>$-interpretation of the variables, constants, and atomic formulas of $QC^i_=$, and $i = 1$ or 2.
Case 1: D is not empty.
(a) If A is a sentence variable of $QC^i_=$ and has the value **T** under $Int_{<D,D'>}$, then $Int_{<D,D'>}$ is said to satisfy A;
(b1) If A is of the kind $F(X_1, X_2, \ldots, X_m)$, each one of $X_1, X_2, \ldots,$ and X_m has a value under $Int_{<D,D'>}$, and the m-tuple made up of the values of $X_1, X_2, \ldots,$ and X_m (in that order) under $Int_{<D,D'>}$ belongs to the value of F under $Int_{<D,D'>}$, then $Int_{<D,D'>}$ is said to satisfy A;

54   Part 1: Existence

(b2) If A is of the kind $F(X_1, X_2, \ldots, X_m)$, at least one of $X_1, X_2, \ldots,$ and X_m has no value under $Int_{<D,D'>}$, and the value of A under $Int_{<D,D'>}$ is T, then $Int_{<D,D'>}$ is said to satisfy A;
(c1) If A is of the kind $X = Y$, each one of X and Y has a value under $Int_{<D,D'>}$, and the value of X under $Int_{<D,D'>}$ is the same as that of Y, then $Int_{<D,D'>}$ is said to satisfy A;
(c2) If A is of the kind $X = Y$, at least one of X and Y has no value under $Int_{<D,D'>}$, and the value of A under $Int_{<D,D'>}$ is T, then $Int_{<D,D'>}$ is said to satisfy A;
(d) If A is of the kind $\sim B$ and $Int_{<D,D'>}$ does not satisfy B, then $Int_{<D,D'>}$ is said to satisfy A;
(e) If A is of the kind $B \supset C$ and $Int_{<D,D'>}$ does not satisfy B or satisfies C, then $Int_{<D,D'>}$ is said to satisfy A;
(f) If A is of the kind $(\forall X)B$ and every X-variant of $Int_{<D,D'>}$ satisfies B, then $Int_{<D,D'>}$ is said to satisfy A;
(g) $Int_{<D,D'>}$ is said to satisfy A pursuant only to one or another of (a)–(f).
Case 2: D is empty.
Case 2.1: A is open. Then $Int_{<D,D'>}$ is said to satisfy A.
Case 2.2: A is closed.
(a)–(e)   Like (a)–(e) under Case 1;
(f) If A is of the kind $(\forall X)B$, then $Int_{<D,D'>}$ is said to satisfy A;
(g) Like (g) under Case 1.

Definition 25.   Let S be a set of formulas of $QC\overset{i}{=}$, D, D' and $Int_{<D,D'>}$ be as in D24 and $i = 1$ or 2. If $Int_{<D,D'>}$ satisfies each and every member of S, then $Int_{<D,D'>}$ is said to simultaneously satisfy S.

Definition 26.   Let S be a set of formulas of $QC\overset{i}{=}$, A be a formula of $QC\overset{i}{=}$, where $i = 1$ or 2.
(a) S is said to imply$_1$ A if, for every non-empty domain D and every domain D' disjoint from D, every $<D, D'>$-interpretation of the variables, constants, and atomic formulas of $QC\overset{i}{=}$ that simultaneously satisfies S also satisfies A.
(b) S is said to imply$_2$ A if, for all disjoint domains D and D', every $<D, D'>$-interpretation of the variables, constants, and atomic formulas of $QC\overset{2}{=}$ that simultaneously satisfies S also satisfies A.

Definition 27.   Let S, A, and i be as in D26.
(a) S is said to imply$_1'$ A if, for every non-empty domain D, every $<D, \emptyset>$-interpretation of the variables, constants, and atomic formulas of $QC\overset{1}{=}$, that simultaneously satisfies S also satisfies A.
(b) S is said to imply$_2'$ A if, for every domain D, every $<D, \emptyset>$-interpretation of the variables, constants, and atomic formulas of $QC\overset{2}{=}$ that simultaneously satisfies S also satisfies A.

It is readily verified (details are left to the reader) that if $S \vdash_1 A$, then S

Completeness Theorems for Some Presupposition-free Logics 55

implies$'_1$ A. But, if S implies$'_1$ A, then S implies$_1$ A (in the sense of D20(b)),[23] and hence in view of T5(a) $S \vdash_1 A$. Hence S implies$'_1$ A if and only if $S \vdash_1 A$, and by the same reasoning (but with T7(a) doing duty for T5(a)) S implies$'_2$ A if and only if $S \vdash_2 A$. Hence QC$\stackrel{1}{=}$ and QC$\stackrel{2}{=}$, which are sound and complete under Account Two, are also sound and complete under Account One, which allows their individual constants to designate a value of a variable, or designate something not a value of a variable, or not designate at all.

It is readily verified also that if $S \vdash_1 A$, then S implies$''_1$ A. But, if S implies$''_1$ A, then S implies$_1$ A,[24] and hence $S \vdash_1 A$. Hence S implies$''_1$ A if and only if $S \vdash_1 A$, and by the same reasoning S implies$''_2$ A if and only if $S \vdash_2 A$. Hence QC$\stackrel{1}{=}$ and QC$\stackrel{2}{=}$, which are sound and complete under either one of Accounts One and Two, are also sound and complete under Account Three, which requires their individual constants to designate a value of a variable or not designate at all.

Three accounts of QC$\stackrel{1}{=}$ and QC$\stackrel{2}{=}$ are thus available. We personally prefer Account One, but for reasons already stated employ Account Two as our official one in the paper.[25]

Notes

1. See in particular [10], [5], and [7]. Leblanc and Hailperin only intended in [10] to eschew presupposition (b). It was Hintikka's intent in [5] to eschew presupposition (a) as well, but he seemingly failed in this. Modifications of QC—the first-order quantificational calculus without identity—that merely eschew presupposition (a) will be found in [2], [6], [13], and [14], and a like-minded one of QC$_=$ will be found in [15]. Note that with one exception references in the text and the notes do not go past 1968. A more comprehensive history of presupposition-free logic will of course be found in the Introduction.

2. One semantical account of the calculus in [5], said calculus so modified as to eschew both of presuppositions (a) and (b), can be retrieved from [16], another from [17]. To our knowledge the semantical interpretation below of the calculus of [10] is the first to reach print.

3. We take a calculus C to be *(semantically) complete in Gödel's sense* if every valid formula of C is derivable from $\emptyset$ in C, and to be *(semantically) complete in Henkin's sense* if every formula of C that is implied by (or, in Tarski's terminology, is a semantical consequence of) a set of formulas of C is derivable from that set in C. Completeness in Henkin's sense was called in [4] *strong completeness*, a label pretty generally accepted by now, and as a result completeness in Gödel's sense is often called *weak completeness*.

4. The notion of an outer domain was mentioned to Leblanc by Joseph S. Ullian in the spring of 1962.

5. We take a calculus C to be *(semantically) sound in Gödel's sense* if every formula of C that is derivable from $\emptyset$ in C is valid, and to be *(semantically) sound in Henkin's sense* if every formula of C that is derivable in C from a set of formulas of C is implied by that set. Soundness in the first sense is often known as *weak soundness*, and soundness in the second as *strong soundness*.

6. An individual constant 'a' of QC$\stackrel{1}{=}$ or QC$\stackrel{2}{=}$ that does not designate at all can always be made to designate something not a value of a variable: adding to D' (the outer domain) some *ad hoc* thing d' not in D (the inner domain), assigning d' to 'a', and adding suitable m-tuples ($m = 1, 2, \ldots$) to the subsets of $(D \cup D')^m$ already assigned to the predicate variables of QC$\stackrel{1}{=}$ or QC$\stackrel{2}{=}$, will do it. And one that designates something not a value of a variable can always be made not to designate at all: assigning suitable truth-values to the atomic formulas of QC$\stackrel{1}{=}$ or QC$\stackrel{2}{=}$ that contain 'a' and editing the subsets of $(D \cup D')^m$ already assigned to the predicate variables of

56   *Part 1: Existence*

$QC_=^1$ or $QC_=^2$, is all that is needed. Hence Accounts Two and Three are sure to fit $QC_=^1$ and $QC_=^2$ if Account One does.

7. [14] borrows heavily from [2], and so to a lesser extent does [15].

8. As the original version of this paper was written, van Fraassen obtained a proof of Theorem 7(a) for the case where S is a set of closed formulas of $QC_=^2$ that contain no sentence variable and A is a closed formula of $QC_=^2$ that contains no sentence variable either. The proof has since appeared in [18].

9. Proof of the completeness in Gödel's sense of $QC_=^0$ goes back of course to Gödel in [1]. Proof of its completeness in Henkin's sense can be retrieved from [3], once the definition of a formal deduction from assumptions is amended to read as in [8], for example. This last matter is further touched on in Note 13.

10. In [13] Mostowski took a vacuous quantification such as '$(\forall x)p$' to amount to 'p' when 'x' has no values, and hence to be true—so to speak— only if 'p' is true. Soon afterwards Hailperin urged in [2] that '$(\forall x)p$' be invariably held true when 'x' has no values. We abide in the main text by Hailperin's recommendation, but list in Appendix 1 the various changes that Mostowski's handling of vacuous quantifications calls for in Sections 2–3. Case 2 of D6 will be one of the items affected.

11. We borrow **R2** from [15]. Mostowski's rule in [13]: "If every individual variable [of $QC_=^1$] that occurs free in A occurs free in B, then B follows from A $A \supset B$," could do duty for **R2**; it would, however, occasionally make for slightly longer proofs.

12. D10–D11 stem from [8]. On derivations (and the problem which— as shown in [12]—the traditional account of derivations posed), see [9].

13. Seemingly missing from our roster of calculi is a modification of $QC_=^0$, call it $QC_=^{0\prime}$, that would stand to $QC_=^0$ as $QC_=^4$ stands to $QC_=^3$ (and $QC_=^8$ to $QC_=^7$), and in which (i) X should occur free in A if $(\forall X)A \supset A(Y/X)$ is to count as an axiom and (ii) A should be closed or B open if B is to follow from A and $A \supset B$. When $QC_=^0$ and $QC_=^0$ have no individual constants (as in the case in [15]), $QC_=^0$ and $QC_=^{0\prime}$ do differ; under the present circumstances, though, they amount to the same. By the same reasoning as in the proof of L5(b) below, A is derivable from $S \cup \{(\exists x)(f(x) \vee \sim f(x))\}$ in $QC_=^{0\prime}$ if A is derivable from S in $QC_=^0$. But, since '$f(a)$ & $\sim f(a)$', where 'a' is an individual constant of $QC_=^{0\prime}$, follows from '$(\forall x)(f(x)$ & $\sim f(x))$' and '$(\exists x)(f(x)$ & $\sim f(x))$' $\supset (f(a)$ & $\sim f(a))$' by means of rule **R2**, '$(\exists x)(f(x) \vee \sim f(x))$' is derivable from $\varnothing$ in $QC_=^{0\prime}$. Hence A is derivable from S in $QC_=^{0\prime}$ if it is derivable from S in $QC_=^0$.

14. Proof is easily had that, where S is finite, A is derivable from S in $QC_=^1$ if and only if A is derivable from S in [10]; and proof can be had that A is derivable from $\varnothing$ in $QC_=^2$ if and only if A is provable in a suitable variant of [5] ruling out $\varnothing$ as a domain. The matter must be left to the reader.

15. Note also that if $\vdash_0 A$, then $\vdash_3 A$. Hence, so far as derivability from $\varnothing$ (though not from arbitrary S) goes, $QC_=^0$ and $QC_=^3$ coincide, as do $QC_=^1$ and $QC_=^5$, as well as $QC_=^2$ and $QC_=^6$, which leaves us with only three variants of $QC_=$: $QC_=^1$, $QC_=^3$, and $QC_=^4$.

16. I.e., let S' consist of every formula of $QC_=^1$ of the kind E!X, where X is an individual constant of $QC_=^1$.

17. [8] uses in place of **R7** a rule that reads: "$(\forall Y)A(Y/X)$ follows from A," and a slightly different notion of derivation (in $QC_=^0$). Nonetheless, the proof of MT2.4.7 on pp. 132–33 readily converts into one of L1(c), L3(c), and L11(a), and the proof of MT2.4.9 on pp. 133–35 into one of L1(h) and L3(f).

18. Proof of L1(q), for the case where S is a finite set of formulas of $QC_=^1$, first appeared in [10]. Proof of the kindred result: "If $\vdash_2 (\forall X)A$, then $\vdash_2$ E!$Z \supset A(Z/X)$," appeared simultaneously in [5]. In the eyes of some these two results marked the advent of presupposition-free logic.

19. Note that when B_j is of the kind $Y = Z \supset (C' \supset C'(Z//Y))$, where both Y and Z are individual constants of $QC_=^{i\,j}$, then B_j'' counts as an axiom of $QC_=^i$ and hence as a constant-free derivation of B_j'' from S in $QC_=^i$.

20. See the proof of MT2.5.35 on p. 158.

21. For each k from 1 on U_k can be thought of as the representative of the various individual signs of $QC_=^\infty$ that belong to $(\mathbf{T}_k^\infty$; and hence, for each individual sign X of $QC_=^\infty$, $\gamma(X)$ can be thought of as the

representative of the various individual signs of $QC\overset{\infty}{=}$ that belong to the same subset of $\mathbf{T}^\infty$ as X does.
22. The phrasing of D21 in the original version of this paper was incorrect.
23. Concerning this point, see the first half of Note 6.
24. Concerning this point, see the second half of Note 6.
25. Thanks are due to Hintikka and Henry Hiż, who commented at the 1966 Meeting of the American Philosophical Association on an early draft of this paper (see [11]); and to van Fraassen, whose results in [16]–[17] considerably influenced our thinking on non-designating constants.

References

[1] Gödel, K. 1930. "Die Vollständigkeit der Axiome des logischen Funktionenkalküls." *Monatshefte für Mathematik und Physik* 37: 349–60.
[2] Hailperin, T. 1953. "Quantification Theory and Empty Individual Domains." *The Journal of Symbolic Logic* (hereafter *JSL*) 18: 197–200.
[3] Henkin, L. 1949. "The Completeness of the First-Order Functional Calculus." *JSL* 14: 159–66.
[4] ———. 1963. "An Extension of the Craig-Lyndon Interpolation Theorem." *JSL* 28: 201–16.
[5] Hintikka, J. 1959. "Existential Presuppositions and Existential Commitments." *The Journal of Philosophy* (hereafter *JP*) 56: 125–37.
[6] Jaśkowski, S. 1934. "On the Rules of Supposition in Formal Logic." *Studia Logica* 1: 5–32.
[7] Lambert, K. 1963. "Existential Import Revisited." *Notre Dame Journal of Formal Logic* (hereafter *NDJFL*) 4: 288–92.
[8] Leblanc, H. 1966. *Techniques of Deductive Inference.* Englewood Cliffs: Prentice-Hall.
[9] ———. 1979. "Generalization in First-Order Logic." *NDJFL* 20: 835–57 (#35 in this volume).
[10] Leblanc, H., and Hailperin, T. 1959. "Nondesignating Singular Terms." *The Philosophical Review* 68: 239–43 (#1 in this volume).
[11] Leblanc, H., and Thomason, R. H. 1966. "Completeness Theorems for Some Presupposition-Free Logics." *JP* 63: 699–700 (#2 in this volume).
[12] Montague, R., and Henkin, L. 1956. "On the Definition of 'Formal Deduction'." *JSL* 21: 129–36.
[13] Mostowski, A. 1951. "On the Rules of Proof in the Pure Functional Calculus of First Order." *JSL* 16: 107–11.
[14] Quine, W. V. 1954. "Quantification and the Empty Domain." *JSL* 19: 177–79.
[15] Schneider, H. H. 1961. "A Syntactical Characterization of the Predicate Calculus with Identity and the Validity in all Individual Domains." *Portugaliae Mathematica* 20: 105–17.
[16] Van Fraassen, B. C. 1966. "The Completeness of Free Logic." *Zeitschrift für mathematische Logik und Grundlagen der Mathematik* (hereafter *ZMLGM*) 12: 219–34.
[17] ———. 1966. "Singular Terms, Truth-Value Gaps, and Free Logic." *JP* 67: 481–95.
[18] ———. 1968. "A Topological Proof of the Löwenheim-Skolem, Compactness, and Strong Completeness Theorems for Free Logic." *ZMLGM* 14: 245–54.

3

On Prefacing (∀X) A ⊃ A(Y/X) with (∀Y): A Free Quantification Theory Without Identity

R. K. Meyer, coauthor

1. Introduction. When writing [20], Russell regretted (in a footnote) that logic presupposes something to be, as it indeed does by holding valid such a well-formed formula (wff, for short) as '(∃x)(f(x) ∨ ~f(x))'. And Leonard has since deplored in [15] that, by holding valid the wff 'f(y) ⊃ (∃x)f(x)' and hence holding every substitution instance of 'f(y) ⊃ (∃x)f(x)' true no matter what, logic further presupposes all singular terms to designate something.

Russell's complaint has been met in a number of "inclusive" quantification theories—Mostowski's, Quine's, Leblanc and Meyer's, to name just three—which, owning the null set ∅ as a domain, do not require the individual variables that occur bound in a wff to have values.[1] Quine's permits proof of closed wffs only. The other two permit proof of open wffs as well, Mostowski (who as a result has to place a restriction on Modus Ponens) certifying an open wff automatically valid in ∅, Leblanc and Meyer (who don't) certifying it valid in ∅ if—upon replacement of every universal quantification in the wff by 'p ⊃ p', and of every existential one by '~(p ⊃ p)'—it proves to be a tautology.[2]

Leonard's complaint has been met in the "free" logics of Hintikka's, Leblanc and Hailperin's, Lambert's, Meyer and Lambert, Schock's, van Fraassen's, Cocchiarella's, Leblanc and Thomason's, and so on. These do not require the individual variables that occur free in a wff to have a value each, and hence sanction the inference from a premise of the form 'f(y)' to a conclusion of the form '(∃x)f(x)' only if the singular term substituted for 'y' is reported in a further premise to designate something. Leblanc and Hailperin's still requires that the individual variables occurring bound in a wff have values; the others don't, and hence meet Russell's complaint as well.[3]

All but one of the above free logics have a predicate that does not figure in standard quantification theory: the identity predicate '=' in most cases, the existence predicate 'E!' in the rest. The lone exception is an intriguing logic of Lambert's in [9], called hereafter QC*, whose primitive signs are just those of standard quantification theory, and whose axiom schemata and rules of infer-

On Prefacing (∀X)A ⊃ A(Y/X) with (∀Y)   59

ence are standard ones except for *Specification*, which now reads (∀Y)((∀X)A ⊃ A(Y/X)). (As Lambert places no restriction on Modus Ponens, his open wffs must be certified valid in ∅ after the manner of [13] rather than [17].)[4]

We shall establish here that QC* is both sound and complete, and that its theorems are those of Quine's inclusive quantification theory in [19], plus all "parametric" instances of Quine's theorems. The first result should be welcome to those who share Russell's and Leonard's discomfort over the existential presuppositions written into standard quantification theory. The second throws interesting light on the behavior of free individual variables in a free logic without identity.

To facilitate the exposition, we shall use two different runs of letters as individual variables: one run—for which the appellation 'individual variables' is saved—ocurring only bound in the wffs of QC*, the other—called *individual parameters*–occurring only free in them. And for consistency's sake what the literature would call sentence or predicate variables will turn up here as sentences or predicate parameters.

2. The Syntax of QC*. The (primitive) *signs* of QC* are to be $\aleph_0$ sentence parameters (among them 'p'), for each $m \geq 1$ $\aleph_0$ m-place predicate parameters (among them the one-place 'f' and the two-place 'g'),[5] $\aleph_0$ individual variables (among them 'x' and 'y'), $\aleph_0$ individual parameters (among them 'a'), the connectives '∼' and '⊃', the quantifier letter '∀', the comma ',', and the parentheses '(' and ')'. We shall understand by a *formula* of QC* any finite sequence of signs of QC*, and shall presume that the formulas of QC* (hence, in particular, the individual variables of QC*, the individual parameters of QC*, and the formulas of QC* soon to be acknowledged as well-formed) have been arranged in a definite order, to be known as the *alphabetic order* of the formulas of QC*. We shall say that a sign of QC* is *foreign to a formula* of QC* if it does not occur in the formula, and is *foreign to a set of formulas* of QC* if it is foreign to every member of the set. We shall refer to the predicate parameters of QC* by means of the letter 'F'; to its individual variables by means of the letters 'X', 'Y', and 'Z'; to its individual parameters by means of the letters 'P' and 'Q'; to its individual signs (i.e., individual variables and individual parameters) by means of the letter 'I'; and to its formulas (eventually to its well-formed formulas and quasi-well-formed formulas only) by means of the letters 'A', 'B', and 'C'. And we shall refer by means of '$(A)(I_1/I_1)$' to the result of replacing I_1 everywhere in A by I'_1; by means of '$(A)(I'_1, I'_2/I_1, I_2)$' to the result of simultaneously replacing I_1 everywhere in A by I'_1, and I_2 by I'_2; and so on.

By a *well-formed formula* (wff, again, for short) of QC* we shall understand (i) any sentence parameter of QC*, plus any formula of QC* of one of the following four sorts: (ii) $F(P_1, P_2, \ldots, P_m)$, where F is for some $m \geq 1$ an m-place predicate parameter of QC* and $P_1, P_2, \ldots, P_m$ are individual parameters of QC*, (iii) ∼A, where A is a wff of QC*, (iv) $(A \supset B)$, where A

and B are wffs of QC*, and (v) $(\forall X)(A)(X/P)$, where A is a wff of QC*, X is an individual variable of QC* that is foreign to A, and P is an individual parameter of QC* (that may, but need not, occur in A).[6] By a *quasi-wff* (qwff) of QC* we shall understand any wff of QC*, plus any formula of QC* of the sort $(A)(X/P)$, where A is a qwff of QC* and X is an individual variable of QC* that is foreign to A. By an *atomic qwff* of QC* we shall understand any qwff of QC* in which none of '$\sim$', '$\supset$', and '$\forall$' occurs; and by a *Q-wff* of QC* understand any wff of QC* in which no individual parameter of QC* occurs.

From now on we shall use the letters 'A', 'B', and 'C' to refer exclusively to qwffs of QC*, and use the letter 'S' to refer to sets of wffs of QC*. To abridge matters, we shall refer to '$\sim(p \supset p)$' by means of 'f', and to qwffs of QC* of the sorts $(\sim A \supset B)$, $\sim(A \supset \sim B)$, and $\sim(\forall X)\sim A$ by means of '$(A \lor B)$', '$(A \& B)$', and '$(\exists X)A$', respectively; and, when no ambiguity threatens, we shall drop sundry parentheses.

By an *axiom* of QC* we shall understand any wff of QC* of one of the seven sorts:

A1. $A \supset (B \supset A)$

A2. $(A \supset (B \supset C)) \supset ((A \supset B) \supset (A \supset C))$

A3. $(\sim A \supset \sim B) \supset (B \supset A)$

A4. $A \supset (\forall X)A$

A5. $(\forall X)(A \supset B) \supset ((\forall X)A \supset (\forall X)B)$

A6. $(\forall Y)((\forall X)A \supset A(Y/X))$

A7. $(\forall X)(\forall Y)A \supset (\forall Y)(\forall X)A$,

or of the sort $(\forall X)A(X/P)$, where A is an axiom of QC*.[7] Where A and B are wffs of QC*, we shall refer to B as the *ponential* of A and $A \supset B$. By a *derivation* in QC* of a wff A of QC* from a set S of wffs of QC* (for short, when S is the empty set $\emptyset$, a *proof* of A in QC*) we shall understand any finite column of wffs of QC* the last one of whose entries is A and every one of whose entries belongs to S, is an axiom of QC*, or is the ponential of two previous entries in the column. Lastly, we shall say that: (i) a wff A of QC* is *derivable* in QC* from a set S of wffs of QC* (for short, when S is $\emptyset$, that A is *provable* in QC* or is a *theorem* of QC*) if there is a derivation in QC* of A from S, (ii) a set S of wffs of QC* is *inconsistent* in QC* if 'f' is derivable in QC* from S, and (iii) a set S of wffs of QC* is *consistent* in QC* if S is not inconsistent in QC*.

To abridge matters, we shall write '$S \vdash A$' for 'A is derivable from S in QC*', and '$\vdash A$' for 'A is provable in QC*'.

3. The Semantics of QC*. Admitting $\emptyset$ as a *bona fide* domain, and hence

On Prefacing (∀X)A ⊃ A(Y/X) with (∀Y)   61

allowing the individual variables of QC* to go without values, presents little problem.[8] By *a valuation of* QC* *over* ∅ we shall understand any result of assigning a truth-value to each atomic qwff of QC*. And, where V is a valuation of QC* over ∅ and A is a qwff of QC*, we shall take A to be *true under V* if A is of the sort (∀X)B; otherwise, (i) when A is atomic, we shall take A to be true under V if and only if V(A) = **T**, (ii) when A is a negation ~B, take A to be true under V if and only if B is not true under V, and (iii) when A is a conditional B ⊃ C, take A to be true under V if and only if B is not true under V or C is true under V.

Allowing any individual parameter of QC* to go without a value when the individual variables of QC* have values, is a bit more work and calls for more caution.

In the standard account of things, members of a non-empty domain D would be assigned to the individual variables of QC* and *all* the individual parameters of QC*, truth-values would be assigned to the sentence parameters of QC*, and subsets of D^m would be assigned to the m-place predicate parameters of QC*, the result being known as a *valuation of* QC* *over D*. A valuation V' (of QC* over D) would next be declared an *X-variant of a valuation* V (of QC* over D) if V' agrees with V on all the parameters of QC* and on all the variables of QC* except possibly X.[9] And the conditions which must be met if a qwff A of QC* is to be *true under a valuation* V (of QC* over D) would then be spelled out, one of them to the effect that when A is of the sort (∀X)B, A is true under V if and only if B is true under every X-variant of V.

Here, understanding α to be a (possibly empty) set of individual parameters of QC* and talking of an α-valuation V of QC* over D, we shall first attend to the sentence parameters, predicate parameters, and individual variables of QC* in the usual manner, next assign members of D to all and only those individual parameters of QC* that belong to α, and then assign truth-values to the atomic qwffs of QC* that contain an individual parameter not in α (and hence contain an individual parameter that as regards V has no value). However, to insure that *any two wffs of* QC* (say, '(∀x)g(x,a)' and '(∀y)g(y,a)') *that are equivalent under V when all their individual parameters are in α, stay so when some of their individual parameters chance not to be in α*,[10] we shall require that, for any atomic qwff A of QC* with a truth-value in V and any two individual signs I and I' of QC* such that V(I) = V(I'), A and the result A(I'/I) of replacing I everywhere in A by I' be assigned the same truth-value in V (**Restriction 1**).

As for the X-variants of an α-valuation V (of QC* over D), we shall of course expect them to agree with V on all the individual variables of QC* other than X, on all the individual parameters of QC* in α, and on all the atomic qwffs of QC* with a truth-value in V, so long as the qwffs in question do not contain X. We shall also expect every X-variant V' of V to agree with V on the rest of the atomic qwffs of QC* with a truth-value in V if the member of D that is assigned in V' to X is not assigned in V itself to any individual sign of QC*. However, to preserve the italicized principle of the last paragraph, we shall require in the contrary case[11] that, for any atomic qwff A of QC* that has a truth-value in V and contains X, and for any individual sign I of QC* such that $V'(X) = V(I)$, A have in V' the truth-value assigned in V to $A(I/X)$ (rather than the one assigned in V to A itself) (**Restriction 2**).

As a sample mishap that **Restrictions 1** and **2** prevent, suppose D to consist of the two integers 1 and 2, α to consist of all the individual parameters of QC* except 'a', integer 1 to be assigned in an α-valuation V (of QC* over D) to 'x' and 'y', integer 2 to be assigned in V to the rest of the individual variables of QC*, and truth-value **T** to be assigned in V to all the qwffs of QC* of the sort $g(X, a)$ other than '$g(y,a)$'. Then '$g(x,a)$' will come out true under all the x-variants of V, and hence '$(\forall x)g(x, a)$' will come out true under V. On the other hand, if—in violation of **Restriction 1**—'$g(y, a)$' were assigned truth-value **F** in V, then '$(\forall y)g(y, a)$' would come out false under V.

Or suppose D to consist again of the two integers 1 and 2, α to consist again of all the individual parameters of QC* except 'a', integer 1 to be assigned in V to 'x', integer 2 to be assigned in V to the rest of the individual variables of QC*, truth-value **T** to be assigned in V to '$g(x, a)$', and truth-value **F** to '$g(y, a)$'. If—in violation of **Restriction 2**—any α-valuation (of QC* over D) that agrees with V on everything other than variable 'x' counted as an x-variant of V, then '$(\forall x)g(x, a)$' would come out true and '$(\forall y)g(y, a)$' come out false under V.

Full details are as follows.

First, where D is a non-empty domain and α is a (possibly empty) set of individual parameters of QC*, we shall understand by an α-*valuation* of QC* *over* D any result V of assigning a member of D to each individual variable of QC* and to each member of α, a truth-value to each sentence parameter of QC*, a subset of D^m to each m-place predicate parameter of QC* (this for each $m \geq 1$), and a truth-value to each atomic qwff of QC* that contains an individual parameter of QC* not in α, this subject to the restriction that, where A is such a qwff and I and I' are individual signs of QC* such that $V(I) = V(I')$, then $V(A) = V(A(I'/I))$.

Next, where D is a non-empty domain, α is a set of individual parameters of QC*, V and V' are α-valuations of QC* over D, and X is an individual variable of QC*, V' will count as an *X-variant of* V if and only if:

(1) V' is the same as V,

(2) in the case that V' and V disagree on X, but $V'(X)$ is not assigned in V to any individual sign of QC*, then V' and V agree on everything but X,

(3) in the case that V' and V disagree on X, and $V'(X)$ is assigned in V to some individual sign of QC*, then (3.1) V' and V agree on all the individual signs of QC* other than X, all the sentence parameters of QC*, all the predicate parameters of QC*, and all the atomic qwffs of QC* that do not contain X, and (3.2) $V'(A) = V(A(I/X))$ for every atomic qwff A of QC* that has a truth-value in V' and contains X, and for every individual sign I of QC* such that $V'(X) = V(I)$.

Next, where D is a non-empty domain, α is a set of individual parameters of QC*, V is an α-valuation of QC* over D, and A is a qwff of QC*, we shall take A to be *true under V* if and only if: (i) in the case that A is atomic and has a truth-value in V, $V(A) = \mathbf{T}$, (ii) in the case that A is of the sort $F(I_1, I_2, \ldots, I_m)$ and has no truth-value in V, $<V(I_1), V(I_2), \ldots, V(I_m)>$ belongs to $V(F)$, (iii) in the case that A is a negation $\sim B$, B is not true under V, (iv) in the case that A is a conditional $B \supset C$, B is not true under V or C is true under V, and (v) in the case that A is a universal quantification $(\forall X)B$, F is true under V if X is foreign to B, otherwise under every X-variant of V.[12]

Lastly, we shall take a qwff A of QC* to be *valid*[13] if and only if: (i) for every valuation V of QC* over $\varnothing$, A is true under V, and (ii) for every non-empty domain D, every set α of individual parameters of QC*, and every α-valuation V of QC* over D, A is true under V; and we shall take a set S of wffs of QC* to be *verifiable* (or to *have a model*) if and only if there is a valuation V of QC* over $\varnothing$ or—for some non-empty domain D and some set α of individual parameters of QC*—an α-valuation V of QC* over D such that every member of S is true under V.

Our main task will of course be to show that a wff of QC* is valid if and only if provable in QC*.

4. Soundness and Completeness Theorems for QC*.
Our first lemma will be appealed to both in the proof of Lemma 2 and that of Lemma 4.

Lemma 1. *Let A be a qwff of* QC*; *let X be an individual variable and I an individual sign of* QC* *such that no qwff of* QC* *of the sort* $(\forall X)B$ *or the sort* $(\forall I)B$ *occurs in A; let D be a non-empty domain and* α *be a set of individual parameters of* QC*; *let V be an* α-*valuation of* QC* *over D; and let V' be the X-variant of V such that* $V'(X) = V(I)$. *Then A is true under V' if and only if* $A(I/X)$ *is true under V.*

Proof by mathematical induction on the number of occurrences of '$\sim$', '$\supset$', and '$\forall$' in A.

Base Case: Suppose A is atomic, V' is the same as V, and hence $V'(X) = V(I)$. If every individual parameter of QC* that occurs in A belongs to α, then by standard considerations A is true under V' if and only if $A(I/X)$ is true under V. If at least one individual parameter of QC* that occurs in A falls outside α, and hence A and $A(I/X)$ have truth-values in V, then $V'(A) = V(A(I/X))$ by **Restriction 1** on p. 61, and hence A is true under V' if and only if $A(I/X)$ is true under V. Or suppose A is atomic, and V' is distinct from V. If every individual parameter of QC* that occurs in A belongs to α, then by standard considerations again A is true under V' if and only if $A(I/X)$ is true under V. If at least one individual parameter of QC* that occurs in A falls outside α, and hence A is assigned a truth-value in V' and $A(I/X)$ one in V, then $V'(A) = V(A(I/X))$ by **Restriction 2** on pp. 61–62, and hence A is true under V' if and only if $A(I/X)$ is true under V.

64 Part 1: Existence

Inductive Case: Suppose A is a non-vacuous quantification $(\forall Y)B$, Y being an individual variable of QC* which by hypothesis is sure to be distinct from X and I. If $((\forall Y)B)(I/X)$ (i.e., $(\forall Y)B(I/X)$) is not true under V, then $B(I/X)$ is not true under some Y-variant V'' of V, and hence by the hypothesis of the induction B is not true under the X-variant V''' of V'' such that $V'''(X) = V''(I)$. But V''' is a Y-variant of V'. Hence B is not true under some Y-variant of V'. Hence $(\forall Y)B$ is not true under V'. But, by a similar reasoning, if $(\forall Y)B$ is not true under V', then $((\forall Y)B)(I/X)$ is not true under V. Hence $(\forall Y)B$ is true under V' if and only if $((\forall Y)B)(I/X)$ is true under V.

Proof that every theorem of QC* is valid will be had after two more lemmas.

Lemma 2. *Every qwff of QC* of any one of the seven sorts A1–A7 is valid.*
Proof for the case where the qwff is of the sort $(\forall Y)((\forall X)A \supset A(Y/X))$ (= **A6**). (1) Let D, α, and V be as in Lemma 1. If $(\forall X)A$ is not true under V, then $(\forall X)A \supset A(Y/X)$ is true under V. If, on the other hand, $(\forall X)A$ is true under V, then A is true under every X-variant of V, hence A is true under the X-variant V' of V such that $V'(X) = V(Y)$, hence by Lemma 1 $A(Y/X)$ is true under V, and hence again $(\forall X)A \supset A(Y/X)$ is true under V. (2) $(\forall Y)((\forall X)A \supset A(Y/X))$ is sure to be true under every valuation of QC* over $\emptyset$. Hence, if $(\forall Y)((\forall X)A \supset A(Y/X))$ failed to be valid, then there would be a non-empty domain, a set α of individual parameters of QC*, and an α-valuation V of QC* over D such that $(\forall Y)((\forall X)A \supset A(Y/X))$, and hence $(\forall X)A \supset A(Y/X)$, would fail to be true under V, as against (1). Hence $(\forall Y)((\forall X)A \supset A(Y/X))$ is valid.

Lemma 3. *Every axiom of QC* is valid.*
Proof: Every axiom of QC* is of the sort

$$(\forall X_1)(\forall X_2) \ldots (\forall X_n)A(X_1, X_2, \ldots, X_n/P_1, P_2, \ldots, P_n),$$

where $n \geq 0$ and $A(X_1, X_2, \ldots, X_n/P_1, P_2, \ldots, P_n)$ is a qwff of QC* of one of the seven sorts **A1–A7**. Hence Lemma 3 by Lemma 2.

Hence Theorem 1, in which A is presumed to be a *wff* of QC*:

Theorem 1. *If $\vdash A$, then A is valid.*
Proof: The ponential of any two valid wffs of QC* is sure to be valid. Hence Theorem 1 by Lemma 3.

Proof that every valid wff of QC* is a theorem of QC* will be had after four lemmas.

Lemma 4. *Let $(\forall X)A$ be a wff of QC*, D be a non-empty domain, α be a set of individual parameters of QC*, and V be an α-valuation of QC* over D such that every member of D is assigned in V to some member or other of α. Then*

On Prefacing (∀X)A ⊃ A(Y/X) with (∀Y) 65

(∀X)A is true under V if and only if A(P/X) is true under V for every member P of α.

Proof: For every X-variant V' of V there is by hypothesis a member P of α, and for every member P of α an X-variant V' of V, such that V'(X) = V(P), and hence by Lemma 1 such that A is true under V' if and only if A(P/X) is true under V. Hence Lemma 4.

In the next three lemmas A is again presumed to be a wff of QC*.

Lemma 5. *If* $\{A, (\exists x)(f(x) \lor \sim f(x))\}$ *is consistent in* QC*, *then* $\{A\}$ *is verifiable.*

Proof:[14]
Part One: Let S_0 be $\{A, (\exists x)(f(x) \lor \sim f(x))\}$ and be consistent in QC*; let S_1 consist of the two members of S_0, plus all wffs of QC* of the sort (∀X)B ⊃ B(P/X), where P is an individual parameter of QC* foreign to A, plus $(\exists Y_1)C_1$ ⊃ $C_1(Q_1/Y_1)$, where $(\exists Y_1)C_1$ is the alphabetically first wff of QC* of the sort (∃Y)C and Q_1 is the alphabetically first individual parameter of QC* foreign to A and $(\exists Y_1)C_1$; for each $i \geq 2$ let S_i be $S_{i-1} \cup \{(\exists Y_i)C_i \supset C_i(Q_i/Y_i)\}$, where $(\exists Y_i)C_i$ is the alphabetically i-th wff of QC* of the sort (∃Y)C and Q_i is the alphabetically first individual parameter of QC* foreign to A, $(\exists Y_1)C_1$ ⊃ $C_1(Q_1/Y_1)$, $(\exists Y_2)C_2 \supset C_2(Q_2/Y_2)$, ..., $(\exists Y_{i-1})C_{i-1} \supset C_{i-1}(Q_{i-1}/Y_{i-1})$, and $(\exists Y_i)C_i$; and let S_∞ be the union of $S_0, S_1, S_2, \ldots$. Then:
(1) For each $i \geq 0$ S_i is consistent in QC*,
(2) S_∞ is consistent in QC*,
(3) For every wff of QC* of the sort (∀X)B, $S_\infty \vdash (\forall X)B \supset B(P/X)$ for every individual parameter P of QC* foreign to A, and
(4) For every wff of QC* of the sort (∃Y)C, $S_\infty \vdash (\exists Y)C \supset C(P/Y)$ for at least one individual parameter P of QC* foreign to A.

For proof of (1) suppose that S_i ($i > 0$), and hence some finite subset of S_i, is inconsistent in QC*. Then there is sure to be an n ($n \geq 1$) such that

$((\forall X_1)B_1 \supset B_1(P_1/X_1)$ & $(\forall X_2)B_2 \supset B_2(P_2/X_2)$ & $\ldots$ & $(\forall X_n)B_n \supset B_n(P_n/X_n)) \supset (((\exists Y_1)C_1 \supset C_1(Q_1/Y_1)$ & $(\exists Y_2)C_2 \supset C_2(Q_2/Y_2)$ & $\ldots$ & $(\exists Y_i)C_i \supset C_i(Q_i/Y_i)) \supset f)$[15]

is derivable from S_0 in QC*, where $P_1, P_2, \ldots, P_n$ are (not necessarily distinct) individual parameters of QC* foreign to A. Now, for each $j = 1, \ldots, n$ in one case, $j = 1, \ldots, i$ in the other, let B'_j and C'_j respectively be $B_j(Z_1, Z_2, \ldots, Z_{n+i}/P_1, P_2, \ldots, P_n, Q_1, Q_2, \ldots, Q_i)$ and $C_j(Z_1, Z_2, \ldots, Z_{n+i}/P_1, P_2, \ldots, P_n, Q_1, Q_2, \ldots, Q_i)$, where $Z_1, Z_2, \ldots, Z_{n+i}$ are the alphabetically earliest $n + i$ individual variables of QC* foreign to A and the above displayed conditional. Then

$(\forall Z_1)(\forall Z_2) \ldots (\forall Z_{n+i})((\forall X_1)B'_1 \supset B'_1(Z_1/X_1)$ & $(\forall X_2)B'_2 \supset B'_2(Z_2/X_2)$ & $\ldots$ & $(\forall X_n)B'_2 \supset B'_n(Z_n/X_n)) \supset (\forall Z_1)(\forall Z_2) \ldots (\forall Z_{n+i})(((\exists Y_1)C'_1 \supset C'_1(Z_{n+1}/Y_1)$ & $(\exists Y_2)C'_2 \supset C'_2(Z_{n+2}/Y_2)$ & $\ldots$ & $(\exists Y_i)C'_i \supset C'_i(Z_{n+i}/Y_i)) \supset f)$

is derivable from S_0 in QC*.[16] But for each $j = 1, \ldots, n$

$$(\forall Z_1)(\forall Z_2) \ldots (\forall Z_{j-1}) \ldots (\forall Z_{n-1})(\forall Z_j)((\forall X_j)B'_j \supset B'_j(Z_j/X_j))$$

is an axiom of QC*. Hence

$$(\forall Z_1)(\forall Z_2) \ldots (\forall Z_{n+i})(((\exists Y_1)C'_1 \supset C'_1(Z_{n+1}/Y_1) \ \& \ (\exists Y_2)C'_2 \supset C'_2(Z_{n+2}/Y_2)$$
$$\& \ldots \& \ (\exists Y_i)C'_i \supset C'_i(Z_{n+i}/Y_i)) \supset f)$$

is derivable from S_0 in QC*, and hence so is

$$(\forall Z_1)(\forall Z_2) \ldots (\forall Z_n)(Z_{n+1})(\exists Z_{n+2}) \ldots (\exists Z_{n+i})((\exists Y_1)C'_1 \supset C'_1(Z_{n+1}/Y_1)$$
$$\& \ (\exists Y_2)C'_2 \supset C'_2(Z_{n+2}/Y_2) \ \& \ldots \& \ (\exists Y_i)C'_i \supset C'_i(Z_{n+i}/Y_i)) \supset$$
$$(\forall Z_1)(\forall Z_2) \ldots (\forall Z_n)(\exists Z_{n+1})(\exists Z_{n+2}) \ldots (\exists Z_{n+i})f.$$

But, for each $j = 1, \ldots, i$, Z_{n+j} is foreign to $(\exists Y_1)C'_1 \supset C'_1(Z_{n+1}/Y_1)$, $(\exists Y_2)C'_2 \supset C'_2(Z_{n+2}/Y_2), \ldots, (\exists Y_{j-1})C'_{j-1} \supset C'_{j-1}(Z_{n+j-1}/Y_{j-1})$; and hence

$$(\forall Z_1)(\forall Z_2) \ldots (\forall Z_j)(\exists Z_{n+j})((\exists Y_j)C'_j \supset C'_j(Z_{n+j}/Y_j))$$

is derivable from $\{(\exists x)(f(x) \lor \sim f(x))\}$ in QC*. Hence

$$(\forall Z_1)(\forall Z_2) \ldots (\forall Z_n)(\exists Z_{n+1})(\exists Z_{n+2}) \ldots (\exists Z_{n+i})f$$

is derivable from S_0 in QC*. But

$$(\forall Z_1)(\forall Z_2) \ldots (\forall Z_n)(\exists Z_{n+1})(\exists Z_{n+2}) \ldots (\exists Z_{n+i})f \supset f$$

is derivable from $\{(\exists x)(f(x) \lor \sim f(x))\}$ in QC*. Hence S_0 is inconsistent in QC* if S_i is. Hence (1), and hence (2), which readily follows from (1).

Part Two: Let S_∞^0 be S_∞; B_i being the alphabetically i-th wff of QC*, let S_∞^i be $S_\infty^{i-1} \cup \{B_i\}$ or $S_\infty^{i-1} \cup \{\sim B_i\}$ according as $S_\infty^{i-1} \cup \{B_i\}$ is consistent or not in QC*; and let S_∞^∞ be the union of $S_\infty^0, S_\infty^1, S_\infty^2, \ldots$. Then, clearly:

(5) S_∞^∞ is consistent in QC* and

(6) If a wff B of QC* does not belong to S_∞^∞, then $S_\infty^\infty \cup \{B\}$ is inconsistent in QC*.

Hence, given (3)–(4) above:

(7) For every negation $\sim B$ of QC*, $S_\infty^\infty \vdash \sim B$ if and only if it is not the case that $S_\infty^\infty \vdash B$,

(8) For every conditional $B \supset C$ of QC*, $S_\infty^\infty \vdash B \supset C$ if and only if it is not the case that $S_\infty^\infty \vdash B$ or (it is the case that) $S_\infty^\infty \vdash C$, and

(9) For every universal quantification $(\forall X)B$ of QC*, $S_\infty^\infty \vdash (\forall X)B$ if and only if $S_\infty^\infty \vdash B(P/X)$ for every individual parameter P of QC* foreign to A.

Part Three: Let D consist of all the individual parameters of QC* foreign to A; let α be D; and let V be the result of assigning:

(i) to each individual variable of QC* an arbitrary member of D,

(ii) to each member P of α the parameter P itself,

(iii) to each sentence parameter B of QC* the truth-value **T** if $S_\infty^\infty \vdash B$, otherwise the truth-value **F**,

(iv) to each m-place ($m \geq 1$) predicate parameter F of QC* the subset of D^m

that $<P_1, P_2, \ldots, P_m>$ belongs to if and only if $S_\infty^\infty \vdash F(P_1, P_2, \ldots, P_m)$, and

(v) to each atomic qwff B of QC* that contains an individual parameter of QC* not in α, the truth-value **T** if $S_\infty^\infty \vdash A(V(X_1), V(X_2), \ldots, V(X_n)/X_1, X_2, \ldots, X_n)$ otherwise the truth-value **F**, $X_1, X_2, \ldots, X_n$ being in alphabetical order all the individual variables of QC* that occur in A.

It is easily verified that $V(B) = V(B(I'/I))$ for every atomic qwff B of QC* that contains an individual parameter of QC* not in α, and for every two individual signs I and I' of QC* such that $V(I) = V(I')$; and hence that V constitutes an α-valuation of QC* over D. It can further be shown by mathematical induction on the number of occurrences '$\sim$', '$\supset$', and '$\forall$' in an arbitrary wff B of QC* that B is true under V if and only if $S_\infty^\infty \vdash B$, (iii) – (iv) seeing the base case through, (7)–(9) and Lemma 4 seeing the inductive one through. But $S_\infty^\infty \vdash A$. Hence A is true under V. Hence $\{A\}$ is verifiable. Hence Lemma 5.

Lemma 6. *If* $\{A, \sim(\exists x)(f(x) \lor \sim f(x))\}$ *is consistent in* QC*, *then* $\{A\}$ *is verifiable.*

Proof:
Part One: Let S_0 be $\{A, \sim(\exists x)(f(x) \lor \sim f(x))\}$ and be consistent in QC*; B_i being the alphabetically i-th wff of QC*, let S_i be $S_{i-1} \cup \{B_i\}$ or $S_{i-1} \cup \{\sim B_i\}$ according to $S_{i-1} \cup \{B_i\}$ is consistent or not in QC*; and let S_∞ be the union of $S_0, S_1, S_2, \ldots$. Then:

(1) S_∞ is consistent in QC*,

(2) If a wff B of QC* does not belong to S_∞, then $S_\infty \cup \{B\}$ is inconsistent in QC*,

(3) For every wff of QC* of the sort $(\forall X)B$, $S_\infty \vdash (\forall X)B$.

For proof of (3) note that $\sim(f(a) \lor \sim f(a)) \supset B$ is provable in QC*, hence so is $(\forall X)(\sim(f(X) \lor \sim f(X)) \supset B)$, hence so is $(\forall X)\sim(f(X) \lor \sim f(X)) \supset (\forall X)B$, hence so is $\sim(\exists X)(f(X) \lor \sim f(X)) \supset (\forall X)B$, and hence so is $\sim(\exists x)(f(x) \lor \sim f(x)) \supset (\forall X)B$.

Part Two: Let V be the result of assigning to each atomic wff B of QC* the truth-value **T** if $S_\infty \vdash B$, otherwise the truth-value **F**. It is easily verified, given (1)–(3) above, that a wff B of QC* is true under V if and only if $S_\infty \vdash B$. But $S_\infty \vdash A$. Hence A is true under V. Hence $\{A\}$ is verifiable. Hence Lemma 6.

Hence:

Lemma 7. *If* $\{A\}$ *is consistent in* QC*, *then* $\{A\}$ *is verifiable.*

Hence Theorem 2, in which A is presumed again to be a *wff*:

Theorem 2. *If A is valid, then* $\vdash A$.

5. The Substitution Theorem.
Proof that the theorems of QC* are those of

Quine's inclusive quantification theory, plus all "parametric" instances of Quine's theorems, calls for some auxiliary notions, some new, some adapted from Church's [1], and some adapted from Quine's [18]–[19].

With N^1 understood to be the set of the natural numbers, and N^{m+1} to be $N^m \times N^1$, arrange the members of N^m in some *alphabetic order*, this for each $m \geq 1$; and take the *index* of the alphabetically *i*-th member of N^m to be i, this for each $i \geq 1$ and each $m \geq 1$. Take the index of each individual variable of QC* to be 0; and that of the alphabetically *i*-th individual parameter of QC* to be *i*, this for each $i \geq 1$. For each $m \geq 1$ take the *m*-place predicate parameter of QC* to be:

$$f_1^m, f_2^m, f_3^m, \ldots$$

For each $m \geq 1$ and each $j \geq 1$ draft as *auxiliary predicate parameters* of QC* the $\aleph_0$

$$f_{j_1}^m, f_{j_2}^m, f_{j_3}^m, \ldots$$

And, for each $m \geq 1$, each $j \geq 1$ and each $k \geq 1$, take '$f_{j_k}^m$' to be *h-place*, where h is the number of zero entries in the alphabetically *k*-th member of N^m.

This done, take the *first-stage transform of a qwff* of QC* of the sort $F(I_1, I_2, \ldots, I_m)$, where at least one of $I_1, I_2, \ldots, I_m$ is an individual parameter of QC*, to be as in the following table, where for every individual parameter P of QC* $i(P)$ is the index of P:

$F^1(P) \mapsto F_{j_k}^1$, where k is the index of $<i(P)>$,

$F_j^2(X, P) \mapsto F_{j_k}^2(X)$, where k is the index of $<0, i(P)>$,

$F_j^2(P, X) \mapsto F_{j_k}^2(X)$, where k is the index of $<i(P), 0>$,

$F_j^2(P, Q) \mapsto F_{j_k}^2$, where k is the index of $<i(P), i(Q)>$,

$F_j^3(X, Y, P) \mapsto F_{j_k}^3(X, Y)$, where k is the index of $<0, 0, i(P)>$,

and so on. Take the *first-stage transform of a wff A* of QC* to be the result of replacing everywhere in A every qwff of QC* of the sort $F(I_1, I_2, \ldots, I_m)$, where at least one of $I_1, I_2, \ldots, I_m$ is an individual parameter of QC*, by its first-stage transform. And, where M is some one-to-one mapping of the sentence parameters, predicate parameters, and auxiliary predicate parameters of QC* into the sentence and predicate parameters of QC*, said mapping such that the M-image of a sentence parameter or 0-place auxiliary predicate parameter of QC* is a sentence parameter of QC*, and the M-image of an *m*-place ($m \geq 1$) predicate or auxiliary predicate parameter of QC* is an *m*-place predicate of QC*, take the *second-stage transform* of a wff A of QC* to be the result of replacing everywhere in A every sentence parameter, predicate parameter, and auxiliary predicate parameter of QC* by its M-image.

It is easily verified that, where the column made up of the wffs $B_1, B_2, \ldots, B_p$ ($p \geq 1$) of QC* constitutes a proof in QC* of a wff A of QC*,

On Prefacing (∀X)A ⊃ A(Y/X) with (∀Y)   69

then the column made up of the second-stage transforms of $B_1, B_2, \ldots, B_p$ constitutes a proof in QC* of the second-stage transform of A. Hence:

Lemma 8. *If A is provable in* QC*, *then the second-stage transform of A is provable in* QC*.

In view of Lemma 8, which incidentally would fail if *Specification* (= **A6**) read $(\forall X)A \supset A(P/X)$, the individual variables of QC* that *"occur free"*–as the usual terminology has it—*in any theorem of* QC* do not *"essentially"* occur in the theorem, and hence are exactly what we termed them, *parameters*.[17]

Next for the notion of a parametric instance. Let (1) A and B be wffs of QC*, (2) F be for some $m \geq 1$ an m-place predicate parameter of QC*, (3) $P_1, P_2, \ldots, P_m$ be distinct individual parameters of QC*, and (4) $F(I_{1_1}, I_{1_2}, \ldots, I_{1_m})$, $F(I_{2_1}, I_{2_2}, \ldots, I_{2_m}), \ldots, F(I_{k_1}, I_{k_2}, \ldots, I_{k_m})$, where $k \geq 0$, be all the components of A of the sort $F(I_1, I_2, \ldots, I_m)$. If A has a component of the sort $(\forall X)A'$, and B one of the sort $(\forall X)B'$ (X the same individual variable is both cases), $(A)(B/F(P_1,P_2, \ldots, P_m))$ will be A. Otherwise, $(A)(B/F(P_1,P_2, \ldots, P_m))$ will be the result of putting $B(I_{i_1}, I_{i_2}, \ldots, I_{i_m}/P_1, P_2, \ldots, P_m)$ everywhere in A for $F(I_{i_1}, I_{i_2}, \ldots, I_{i_m})$, this for each $i \geq k$.[18] Where A is a wff of QC* that contains at least one individual parameter of QC*, and B is a wff of QC*, we shall count A as an *immediate parametric instance* of B if A is $B(C/F(P_1,P_2, \ldots, P_m))$ for some wff C of QC*, some m-place ($m \geq 1$) predicate parameter F of QC*, and some distinct individual parameters $P_1, P_2, \ldots, P_m$ of QC*. And, where A and B are as before, we shall count A as a *parametric instance* of B if there are n wffs $A_1, A_2, \ldots, A_n$ of QC* such that A_1 is A_n is B, and A_{i+1} is for each $i = 1, \ldots, n - 1$ an immediate parametric instance of A_i.

It is easily verified that:

Lemma 9. *A is provable in* QC*, *then every parametric instance of A is provable in* QC*.[19]

Finally for Quine's account of a theorem in [18].[20] In the case that a qwff A of QC* is atomic, take all the individual variables of QC* that occur in A to *occur free* in A; in the case that A is a negation $\sim B$, take all those that occur free in B to occur free in A; in the case that A is a conditional $B \supset C$ take all those that occur free in B or occur free in C to occur free in A; and in the case that A is a universal quantification $(\forall X)B$, take all those other than X that occur free in B to occur free in A. Where A is a qwff of QC* and $X_1, X_2, \ldots, X_n$ ($n \geq 0$) are in *alphabetic order* all the individual variables of QC* that occur free in A, take $(\forall X_1)(\forall X_2) \ldots (\forall X_n)A$ (()A, for short) to be the *closure* of A. By a *Q-axiom* of QC* ('*Q*' for 'Quine') understand any Q-wff of QC* of anyone of the following sorts:

QA1. $()(A \supset (B \supset A))$,

QA2. $()((A \supset (B \supset C)) \supset ((A \supset B) \supset (A \supset C)))$,

QA3. $()((\sim A \supset \sim B) \supset (B \supset A))$,

QA4. $()(A \supset (\forall X)A)$, where X does not occur free in A,

QA5. $()((\forall X)(A \supset B) \supset ((\forall X)A \supset (\forall X)B))$,

QA6. $()((\forall X)A \supset A(Y/X))$, where X occurs free in A,

QA7. $()((\forall X)(\forall Y)A \supset (\forall Y)(\forall X)A)$

By a *Q-proof* in QC* of a Q-wff A of QC* understand any finite column of wffs of QC* of the last one of whose entries is A and every one of whose entries is a Q-axiom of QC* or the potential of two previous entries in the column. And take a Q-wff A of QC* to be *Q-provable* in QC* or be a *Q-theorem* of QC* if there is a Q-proof of A in QC*.

It is easily verified that:

Lemma 10. *If A is a Q-wff of* QC*, *then A is provable in* QC* *if and only if A is Q-provable in* QC*.

Incidentally, Quine's result in [18] that a Q-wff of QC* is Q-provable in QC* if and only if valid, immediately follows from Theorems 1 and 2 and Lemma 10.

The result we announced in Section 1 is now at hand.

Theorem 3. *A is a theorem of* QC* *if and only if A is a Q-theorem of* QC* *or a parametric instance of a Q-theorem of* QC*.

Proof:

(a) Suppose A is a theorem of QC*. In the case that A is a Q-wff, then A is sure in view of Lemma 10 to be a Q-theorem of QC*. In the contrary case the second-stage transform of A is sure in view of Lemma 8 to be a theorem of QC*, and hence—being a Q-wff—sure in view of Lemma 10 to be a Q-theorem of QC*. But A counts as a parametric instance of its second-stage transform. Hence A is a parametric instance of a Q-theorem of QC*.

(b) Suppose A is a Q-theorem of QC*. Then A is sure in view of Lemma 10 to be a theorem of QC*. Or suppose A is a parametric instance of a Q-theorem of QC*, and hence in view of Lemma 10 a parametric instance of a theorem of QC*. Then A is sure in view of Lemma 9 to be a theorem of QC*.

6. An Alternate Interpretation of QC*. In [14] designating singular terms are free to designate something not a value of a variable as well of course as (something) a value of one. This is accomplished by introducing—besides the *inner* domain D that served as the range of values of the variables—an *outer* domain D' disjoint from D, and assigning to singular terms members of the union $D \cup D'$ of the two domains. Outer domains can likewise be introduced here, and the individual parameters of QC* construed as always having a value each, the value in question hailing from some outer domain D' when not from D.

Details are as follows.

Where D is a possibly empty domain and D' a non-empty one disjoint from D, understand by a *valuation of* QC* *over D and D'* any result of assigning a member of D to each individual variable of QC* (this of course when D is not empty), a member of $D \cup D'$ to each individual parameter of QC*, a truth-value to each sentence parameter of QC*, a subset of $(D \cup D')^m$ to each m-place predicate parameter of QC*, this for each $m \geq 1$, and—when D is empty—a truth-value to each atomic qwff of QC*. Next, where D and D' are non-empty and disjoint domains, V and V' are valuations of QC*, and X is an individual variable of QC*, count V' as an *X-variant* of V if V' and V agree on everything except possibly X. Then, where D is a possibly empty domain, D' is a non-empty one disjoint from D, V is a valuation of QC* over D and D', and A is a qwff of QC*, (i) in the case that A is atomic and has a truth-value in V, take A to be *true under V* if and only if $V(A) = \mathbf{T}$, (ii) in the case that A is of the sort $F(I_1, I_2, \ldots, I_m)$ and has no truth-value in V, take A to be true under V if and only if $<V(I_1), V(I_2), \ldots, V(I_m)>$ belongs to $V(F)$, (iii) in the case that A is a negation $\sim B$, take A to be true under V if and only if B is not true under V, (iv) in the case that A is a conditional $B \supset C$, take A to be true under V if and only if B is not true under V or C is true under V, (v) in the case that A is a universal quantification $(\forall X)B$ and D is empty, take A to be true under V no matter what, and (vi) in the case that A is a universal quantification $(\forall X)B$ and D is not empty, take A to be true under V if and only if B is true under every X-variant of V. Lastly, take a wff A of QC* to be *valid in the sense of* [14] if and only if, for every domain D, every non-empty domain D' disjoint from D, and every valuation V of QC* over D and D', A is true under V.

That every theorem of QC* is valid in the sense of [14] is clear. Towards showing conversely that every wff of QC* valid in the sense of [14] is a theorem of QC*, let S_∞^∞ be as in the proof of Lemma 5; let D consist of all the individual parameters of QC* foreign to A; let D' consist of all those occurring in A; and let V be the result of assigning to each individual variable of QC* an arbitrary member of D, to each individual parameter P of QC* the parameter P itself, to each sentence parameter B of QC* the truth-value $\mathbf{T}$ if $S_\infty^\infty \vdash B$, otherwise the truth-value $\mathbf{F}$, and to each m-place predicate parameter F of QC* the subset of $(D \cup D')^m$ that $<P_1, P_2, \ldots, P_m>$ belongs to if and only if $S_\infty^\infty \vdash F(P_1, P_2, \ldots, P_m)$. It is easily verified that a wff B of QC* is true under V (a valuation of QC* over D and D') if and only if $S_\infty^\infty \vdash B$, and hence that A is true under V if $\{'A, (\exists x)(f(x) \vee \sim f(x))\}$ is consistent in QC*.

That QC* is sound under both accounts of its individual parameters, the one in Section 3 and the present one, was noted by Church in [2]. So long indeed as values not values of variables count, the individual parameters of QC* can be construed as always having a value each (as well as possibly having no

72 Part 1: Existence

values).[21] However, we would hardly conclude with Church (italics ours): "The existence of (the alternate interpretation) shows . . . that Lambert *does not go far enough* to characterize in a distinctive way a logic that allows true assertions having denotationless names as their subjects." For, ironically enough, *the individual parameters of standard quantification theory (QC, for short) can be construed as possibly having no values* (as well of course as having a value each). Where D is a non-empty domain and α is a (possibly empty) set of individual parameters of QC, understand by an α-valuation of QC over D any result of assigning a member of D to each individual variable of QC and to each member of α, a truth-value to each sentence parameter of QC, and a subset of D^m to each m-place predicate parameter of QC. And, where D and α are as above, V is an α-valuation of QC over D, and A is a wff of QC, (i) in the case that each parameter occurring in A belongs to α, take A to be true under V if and only if Church would, and (ii) in the contrary case, follow Mostowski's example in [17] and take A to be automatically true under V. A will be valid in the accepted sense (Church's) if and only if, for every non-empty domain D, every set α of individual parameters of QC, and every α-valuation of QC over D, A is true under V. But, if so, the individual parameters of QC, like those of QC*, can be accounted for in two widely different ways. Are we then to reproach Church for not having gone far enough in [1] to characterize in a distinctive way a logic that bars true assertions having denotationless names as their subjects?[22]

Appendix. As reported on p. 74 note 12, Shipley has found that, given the semantics of the *original* version of this paper,

(1) some wffs of QC* of the sort **A4** are *not* valid.

He has also found that, given the semantics in question,

(2) the notion of an X-variant is *not* symmetrical, i.e., one α-valuation V of QC* may count as an X-variant of another α-valuation V' without V' counting as an X-variant of V, and

(3) the so-called *Coincidence Theorem*, according to which two valuations V and V' of QC* are sure to agree on a qwff A of QC* if V and V' agree on the parameters of QC* that occur in A and the individual variables of QC* that occur free in A, is *not* provable.

The present version of clause (v) on p. 63 does dispose of (1): all wffs of QC* of the sort **A4** are now valid. However, (2) and (3) still hold true here, a possibly unfortunate turn of events. Since Shipley's own semantics for QC* in [21] is free of all three defects, we outline it here. The sketch may prove handy, [21] being available only in microfilm form.

(a) By a $\emptyset$-*valuation* of QC* understand what we called on p. 61 a valuation of QC* over $\emptyset$, and take a qwff A of QC* to be *true under a $\emptyset$-valuation* of QC* if the conditions in paragraph 1 of that page are met.

(b) Where D is a non-empty domain and α is a (possibly empty) set of indi-

On Prefacing (∀X)A ⊃ A(Y/X) with (∀Y)   73

vidual parameters of QC*, understand by a $<D, \alpha>$-*valuation* of QC* what we called on p. 61 an α-valuation of QC* over D.

(c) Where D and α are as in (b) and Σ is a set of $<D, \alpha>$-valuations of QC* that agree on all the parameters (individual, sentence, and predicate parameters of QC), call Σ *coherent* if—for any atomic qwff A of QC* that contains an individual parameter not in α, and for any two members V and V' of Σ—$V(A) = V'(A)$.

(d) Where D and α are as in (b) and Σ is as in (c), call Σ *complete* if—for any mapping M of the individual variables of QC* into D—there is a member of Σ that agrees with M on the said variables.

(e) Where D and α are as in (b), Σ is as in (c), V is a member of Σ, and X is an individual variable of QC*, understand by an *X-variant* of V any member of Σ that agrees with V on all the individual variables of QC* except possibly X.

(f) Let A be a qwff of QC*, D be a non-empty domain, α be a (possibly empty) set of individual parameters of QC*, Σ be a coherent and complete set of $<D, \alpha>$-valuations of QC*, and V be a member of Σ. Then A is said to be *true under V* if the conditions in paragraph 1 of p. 63 are met, but with (v) amended to read: (v) in the case that A is a universal quantification $(\forall X)B$, B is true under every member of Σ that counts as an X-variant of V.

(g) A qwff A of QC* is said to be *valid* if (a) A is true under every ∅-valuation of QC* and (b) no matter the non-empty domain D, the (possibly empty) set α of individual parameters of QC*, the set Σ of $<D, \alpha>$-valuations of QC* that is coherent and complete, and the member V of Σ, A is true under V.

Given (a)–(g), the Coincidence Theorem (which fails for both the original and the present version of this paper), the Soundness Theorem (which failed for the original version of this paper), and the Completeness Theorem are all forthcoming for QC*, as persusal of [21] will show.

Notes

1. The earliest inclusive quanitfication theory is possibly that of Jaśkowski's in [8], which from Shock's account of it in [22] resembles Quine's in [19] and permits proof of closed wffs only. [19] is an outgrowth of [5].

2. Mostowski's inclusive quantification theory in [17] and Quine's in [18] differ in a further respect which is played up in [5] and [19], namely: Mostowski takes a vacuous quantification $(\forall X)A$ (in the context of this paper a quantification $(\forall X)A$ such that X is foreign to A) to be true in ∅, so to speak, if and only if A is, whereas Quine (following Hailperin's precedent in [5]) takes it to be automatically true in ∅. However, Mostowski's (Quine's) axioms are easily amended to suit Quine's (Mostowski's) handling of vacuous quantifications. Leblanc and Meyer in [13] cover both possibilities.

3. With many I doubt that in Hintikka's free logic ∅ can serve as a domain. However, it definitely can in Leblanc and Thomason's, Lambert's, etc.

4. For convenience's sake we shall handle vacuous quantifications the Hailperin-Quine way.

5. In Section 5 we shall presume the predicate parameters of QC* to be 'f_1^m', 'f_2^m', 'f_3^m', etc., this for each m from 1 on.

74   Part 1: Existence

6. By requiring X to be foreign to A, we forego wffs in which identical quantifiers overlap, but skirt some of the technicalities that usually attend the substitution of variables for variables. When P does not occur in A, $(\forall X)(A)(X/P)$ is of course the same as $(\forall X)A$; and, as X does not occur in A, the quantification is what we called in earlier notes a vacuous one. Clause (v) could equivalently read: (v') $(\forall X)A$, where for some individual parameter P of QC* $A(P/X)$ is a wff of QC*.

7. So far as we know the trick of counting $(\forall X)A(X/P)$ as an axiom if A is one, and thereby dispensing with Generalization as a rule of inference, stems from [4]. See [11] on this matter. Axiom schema **A6** was discovered independently by Leblanc, but later found to be in [9]. Axiom schema **A7** did not appear in the original version of this paper, Meyer and I presuming it to be forthcoming as a theorem. But Trew reported in [23] that he was unable to prove it, and we now suspect it to be independent of our other axiom schemata.

8. As mentioned in Section 1, we follow here the precedent of [13].

9. We take two valuations (later two α-valuations) to agree on a variable if both have the same value for that variable; and to agree on a parameter or an atomic qwff if both have the same value for that parameter or qwff, or neither one has a value for it.

10. We take two wffs to be equivalent under an α-valuation if both come out true or both come out false under the valuation.

11. I.e., when the member of D assigned in V' to X is already assigned in V to some individual sign of QC*.

12. In the original version of this paper, A—when of the sort $(\forall X)B$—was taken to be true under V if and only if B is true under every X-variant of V. Unfortunately, Shipley showed in [21] that axioms of the sort **A4** are not all valid under this account of things. We trust that the present version of (v) does the trick. Shipley has a different way of mending things, which we sketch out in the Appendix.

13. Though our main concern is with the valid *wffs* of QC*, we shall have occasion to talk (more generally) of the valid *qwffs* of QC*.

14. Our proof of Lemma 5 is an adaptation of a familiar proof of Henkin's in [6].

15. The antecedent of the conditional, and the antecedent of its consequent, are to be understood of course as conjunctions of conditionals.

16. This by repeated applications of the derived rule of inference: "If $S \vdash A(P/X)$, then $S \vdash (\forall X)A$, so long as P is foreign to S and $(\forall X)A$."

17. A like transformation of the wffs of QC* into what we called up on p. 60 Q-wffs has been used by van Fraassen to show (in effect) that a wff of QC* is valid if and only if its second-stage transform is valid. Van Fraassen communicated the result to us just as we were proving Theorem 3 below.

18. Our $A(B/F(P_1, P_2, \ldots, P_m))$ matches in effect Church's $\check{S}_B^{f(X_1, X_2, \ldots, X_m)} A|$ on pp. 192–93 of [1].

19. It can likewise be verified that any wff of QC* that contains an individual parameter is a parametric instance of its second-stage transform.

20. Note that the reference is to the original rather than the revised version of *Mathematical Logic*.

21. Yet another interpretation of things will be found in [10]. It uses truth-value assignments instead of valuations, and—in the case that the individual variables of QC* have values—allows all but an arbitrary one of the individual parameters of QC* to go without a value.

22. We wish to thank Bas C. van Fraassen for his numerous suggestions and the inspiration that [24] has been to us. The main results of this paper were announced by the senior author at a Philosophy Forum on Aspects of Non-Standard Logics held at Temple University on 28 March 1968, and the paper itself was read by him at the university of Calgary in July of 1969.

References

[1] Church, A. 1956. *Introduce to Mathematical Logic, Volume I*. Princeton: Princeton University Press.

[2] ———. 1965. Review of [9]. *The Journal of Symbolic Logic* (hereafter *JSL*) 30: 103–104.

[3] Cocchiarella, N. 1966. "A Logic of Possible and Actual Objects." *JSL*: 688–89.
[4] Fitch, F. B. 1948. "Intuitionistic Modal Logic with Quantifiers." *Portugaliae Mathematica* 7: 113–18.
[5] Hailperin, T. 1953. "Quantification Theory and Empty Individual Domains." *JSL* 18: 197–200.
[6] Henkin, L. 1949. "The Completeness of the First-Order Functional Calculus." *JSL* 14: 159–66.
[7] Hintikka, J. 1959. "Existential Presuppositions and Existential Commitments." *The Journal of Philosophy* 56: 125–37.
[8] Jaśkowski, S. 1934. "On the Rules of Supposition in Formal Logic." *Studia Logica* 1: 5–32.
[9] Lambert, K. 1963. "Existential Import Revisited." *Notre Dame Journal of Formal Logic* (hereafter *NDJFL*) 4: 288–92.
[10] Leblanc, H. 1971. "Truth-Value Semantics for a Logic of Existence." *NDJFL* 12: 153–68 (#4 in this volume).
[11] ———. 1979. "Generalization in First-Order Logic." *NDJFL* 20:835–57 (#35 in this volume).
[12] Leblanc, H., and Hailperin, T. 1959. "Nondesignating Singular Terms." *The Philosophical Review* 68: 129–36 (#1 in this volume).
[13] Leblanc, H., and Meyer, R. K. 1969. "Open Formulas and the Empty Domain." *Archiv für mathematische Logik und Grundlagenforschung* 12: 78–84 (#5 in this volume).
[14] Leblanc, H., and Thomason, R. H. 1968. "Completeness Theorems for Some Presupposition-Free Logics." *Fundamenta Mathematicae* 62: 125–64 (#2 in this volume).
[15] Leonard, H. 1956. "The Logic of Existence." *Philosophical Studies* 7: 49–64.
[16] Meyer, R. K., and Lambert, K. 1968. "Universally Free Logic and Standard Quantification Theory." *JSL* 33: 8–26.
[17] Mostowski, A. 1951. "On the Rules of Proof in the Pure Functional Calculus of the First Order." *JSL* 16: 107–11.
[18] Quine, W. V. 1940. *Mathematical Logic*. New York: Norton.
[19] ———. 1954. "Quantification and the Empty Domain." *JSL* 19: 177–79.
[20] Russell, B. 1919. *Introduction to Mathematical Philosophy*. London: Allen and Unwin.
[21] Shipley, C. T. 1972. "A Semantical Theory and Several Deductive Systems for Universally Free Logic." Ph.D. dissertation, University of Nebraska.
[22] Schock, R. 1968. *Logics without Existence Assumptions*. Stockholm: Almqvist & Wiksell.
[23] Trew, A. 1970. "Non-Standard Theories of Quantification and Identity." *JSL* 35: 267–94.
[24] van Fraassen, B. 1966. "The Completeness of Free Logic." *Zeitschrift für mathematische Logik und Grundlagen der Mathematik* 12: 219–34.

4

*Truth-Value Semantics
for a Logic of Existence*

1. **Introduction.** Recall the opening moves in the interpretation of a first-order language L: (i) items, thought of as forming a domain D, are made the values of the (bound) individual variables of L, (ii) a member of D is assigned to each individual constant of L, (iii) a (possibly empty) set of members of D is assigned to each one-place predicate constant of L, (iv) a (possibly empty) set of pairs of members of D is assigned to each two-place predicate constant of L, and so on. Löwenheim's theorem of 1915 tells us that, as regards logical truth (i.e., truth under any interpretation whatever), logical falsehood (falsehood under any interpretation whatever), and the like, all but $\aleph_0$ members of any infinite domain D may be discounted.[1] A 1959 theorem of Beth's (implicit in results of Henkin, Hasenjaeger, and others) goes one better, and tells us that, as regards logical truth, logical falsehood, and the like, all but such members of any domain D as have been assigned to the individual constants of L may be discounted, *provided L has $\aleph_0$ individual constants*.[2] The latter result supplies the rationale for the "substitution" interpretation of the quantifiers, according to which a universal quantification $(\forall X)A$ of L is true if every replacement of X everywhere in A by an individual constant of L is true, and an existential one $(\exists X)A$ true if some replacement of X everywhere in A by an individual constant of L is true.[3]

Like considerations apply to the first-order quantificational calculus QC. Suppose that, as in many recent presentations of QC, two different runs of letters ($\aleph_0$ letters per run) serve as individual variables: one run—for which the appellation 'individual variables' is often saved—occurring only bound in the well-formed formulas (wffs) of QC, and one run—called *individual parameters*—occurring only free in them. Löwenheim's Theorem tells us that, as regards validity, contravalidity, and the like, any domain whose members are made the values of the individual variables of QC may be presumed of size $\aleph_0$; Beth's that all but such members as have been assigned to the individual parameters of QC may be discounted.

Beth's Theorem issues into a fresh characterization of the valid wffs of QC—

Truth-Value Semantics for a Logic of Existence 77

as a matter of fact, into a truth-value semantics for QC that runs largely like the ordinary semantics for the sentential calculus SC. Given an assignment α of truth-values to the atomic wffs of QC, calculate the truth-value under α of a negation, conjunction, disjunction, and so on of QC as you would that of a negation, conjunction, disjunction, and so on of SC under an assignment of truth-values to the letters 'p', 'q', 'r', and so on; and certify a universal quantification ($\forall X$)A (an existential quantification ($\exists X$)A) of QC true under α if every (some) replacement of X everywhere in A by an individual parameter of QC is true under α, otherwise certify the quantification false under α. This done, declare a wff of QC valid (contravalid) if it comes out true (false) under every assignment of truth-values to the atomic wffs of QC. It is readily shown that a wff of QC is valid (contravalid) in this truth-value sense of the word if and only if valid (contravalid) in the model-theoretic one of old.[4]

My main concern here will be to outfit Lambert's free logic FQ, rechristened for the occasion QC!, with a truth-value semantics.[5] Earlier free logics were, in general, first-order languages with an identity predicate in which the requirement that individual constants designate something—plus in some cases the requirement that (bound) individual variables have values—was lifted. Lambert's QC!, by a slight but interesting contrast, is a first-order quantificational calculus (with an existence but without an identity predicate) whose individual variables and parameters are free to have no values. Like so many of us, Lambert treats individual parameters (i.e., free individual variables) as place-holders for individual constants or singular terms, and hence has an excellent reason for allowing them to go without a value: not all singular terms designate something. He adduces the same reasons that Russell and others have for allowing individual variables to go without values. Beth's Theorem suggests yet another one. Think indeed of Lambert's individual variables as ranging over just the values of his individual parameters. The former will have values so long as one or more of the latter do; otherwise, they won't.

The truth conditions above for ($\forall X$)A and ($\exists X$)A fail of course for QC!. Think of the individual parameter 'a' in the wff '$f(a)$' as standing for a singular term that does not designate, hence in effect think of 'a' as having no value, and think of 'f' as standing for 'does not exist'. Under this interpretation of 'a' and 'f', the existential quantification '($\exists x$)$f(x)$' is clearly false even though replacement of 'x' everywhere in '$f(x)$' by 'a' is true. Our truth conditions are easily put to rights, however, as the predicate 'E!' from *Principia Mathematica,* *14, figures among the (primitive) signs of QC!. The wff 'E!a', which is assigned a truth-value α(E!a) in any assignment of truth-values to the atomic wffs of QC!, is intended of course to be read: 'a exists', and for that reason I labelled Lambert's free logic *a logic of existence*. But 'a exists' is tantamount here to "'a' has a value', or—to be more exact—'α(E!a) = **T**' is tantamount to "'a' has a value under α', the very qualification that is called for in the foregoing truth conditions for ($\forall X$)A and ($\exists X$)A. Take then an existential quantification ($\exists X$)A (a universal quantification ($\forall X$)A) of QC! to be true under a truth-value assignment α if, *for some (every) individual parameter P of* QC!

such that $\alpha(E!P) = \mathbf{T}$, replacement of X everywhere in A by P is true under α, and the above difficulty is met.

Note incidentally that, with the individual variables of QC! taken to range over *just* the values of the individual parameters of QC!, at least one of the latter will be sure to have a value when the former have values. QC! can be outfitted with a model-theoretical semantics under which no individual parameter of QC! need ever have a value. The semantics in question may be more faithful to Lambert's intent, and it does make for a neater picture. I must save it, though, for another occasion.

After detailing in Section 2 the key syntactical features of QC! and some of the semantics that I intend here for Lambert's calculus, I establish in Section 3 that every wff of QC! that is provable in QC! is valid in my sense, and vice-versa. Meyer and Lambert have already shown in [17] that QC! is complete, but their characterization of the valid wffs of QC! is of a model-theoretic (and rather complicated) sort, and the reasoning by which they arrive at their result is (to me, at any rate) somewhat roundabout. In Section 4 I attend to the problem of implication in truth-value semantics, and show that QC! is both strongly sound and strongly complete. Lastly, I study three further concepts of validity (one tantamount to provability in the sense of [15], another to provability in the sense of [14]).

2. The Syntax and Semantics of QC!. QC! is to have as its (primitive) signs $\aleph_0$ sentence variables (among them 'p'); for each $m \geqslant 1$, $\aleph_0$ m-place predicate variables (among them the one-place 'f' and the two-place 'g'); $\aleph_0$ individual variables (among them 'x' and 'y'); $\aleph_0$ parameters; the one-place predicate constant 'E!'; the two connectives '∼' and '⊃'; the one quantifier letter '∀'; the comma ','; and the two parentheses '(' and ')'. I shall understand by a *formula* of QC! any finite sequence of primitive signs of QC!, and shall presume that the formulas of QC! (hence, in particular, the individual variables of QC!, the individual parameters of QC!, and the formulas of QC! to be soon acknowledged as well-formed) have been arranged in a definite order, to be known as the *alphabetical order* of the formulas of QC!. I shall say that a sign of QC! is *foreign to a formula* of QC! if it does not occur in the formula, and is *foreign to a set of formulas* of QC! if it is foreign to every member of the set. I shall refer to the predicate variables of QC! by means of the letter 'F'; to its individual variables by means of the letters 'X', 'Y', and 'Z'; to its individual parameters by means of the letters 'P', 'Q', and 'R'; to its individual signs (i.e., individual variables and individual parameters) by means of the letter 'I'; and to its formulas by means of the letters 'A', 'B', and 'C'. And I shall refer by means of '$(A)(I_1'/I_1)$' to the result of replacing I_1 everywhere in A by I_1'; by means of '$(A)(I_1',I_2'/I_1,I_2)$' to the result of replacing I_1 everywhere in A by I_1', and I_2 by I_2'; and so on.

By a *well-formed formula* (wff) of QC! I shall understand any sentence variable of QC!, plus any formula of QC! of one of the following five sorts:

Truth-Value Semantics for a Logic of Existence 79

(i) $F(P_1, P_2, \ldots, P_m)$, where F is for some $m \geq 1$ an m-place predicate variable of QC! and $P_1, P_2, \ldots, P_m$ are individual parameters of QC!, (ii) E!P, where P is an individual parameter of QC!, (iii) $\sim A$, where A is a wff of QC!, (iv) $(A \supset B)$, where A and B are wffs of QC!, and (v) $(\forall X)A(X/P)$, where A is a wff of QC!, X is an individual variable of QC! that is foreign to A, and P is an individual parameter of QC!.[6] By an *atomic* wff of QC! I shall understand any wff of QC! that contains no occurrence of any one of '$\sim$', '$\supset$', and '$\forall$'; by an E!-*less* wff of QC! any wff of QC! that contains no occurrence of 'E!' (i.e., any wff of QC!); and by an *infinitely extendible* set of wffs of QC! any set of wffs of QC! to which $\aleph_0$ individual parameters of QC! are foreign.[7] From now on I shall use the letters 'A', 'B', and 'C' to refer exclusively to wffs of QC! and to well-formed results of replacing individual parameters of QC! in a wff of QC! by individual variables of QC! foreign to the wff; and I shall use the letter 'S' to refer to sets of wff of QC!. To abridge matters, I shall refer to '$\sim(p \supset p)$' by means of 'f', and to wffs of QC! of the sorts $(\sim A \supset B)$, $\sim(A \supset \sim B)$, $\sim((A \supset B) \supset \sim(B \supset A))$, and $\sim(\forall X)\sim A$ by means of '$(A \lor B)$', '$(A \& B)$', '$(A \equiv B)$', and '$(\exists X)A$', respectively; and, when no ambiguity arises, I shall write '$A \supset B$', '$A \lor B$', '$A \equiv B$', '$A_1 \& A_2 \& \ldots \& A_n$', '$A(I'_1/I_1)$', '$A(I'_1,I'_2/I_1,I_2)$', and so on, for '$(A \supset B)$', '$(A \lor B)$', '$(A \equiv B)$', '$(\ldots(A_1 \& A_2) \& \ldots) \& A_n$', '$(A)(I'_1/I_1)$', and '$(A)(I'_1,I'_2/I_1,I_2)$', respectively.

A wff of QC! will count as an *axiom* of QC! if (i) it is of one of the seven sorts

A1. $A \supset (B \supset A)$,

A2. $(A \supset (B \supset C)) \supset ((A \supset B) \supset (A \supset C))$,

A3. $(\sim A \supset \sim B) \supset (B \supset A)$,

A4. $A \supset (\forall X)A$,

A5. $(\forall X)(A \supset B) \supset ((\forall X)A \supset (\forall X)B)$,

A6. $(\forall X)A \supset (E! P \supset A(P/X))$,

A7. $(\forall X)E!X$,

or (ii) it is of the sort $(\forall X)A(X/P)$, where A is an axiom of QC!.[8] B will be said to *follow from A and $A \supset B$* by Modus Ponens. By a *derivation* in QC! of A from S (for short, when S is the empty set $\varnothing$, a *proof* of A in QC!) I shall understand any finite column of wffs of QC! that closes with A and every one of whose entries belongs to S, is an axiom of QC!, or follows from two previous entries in the column by Modus Ponens. Lastly, I shall say that: (i) A is *derivable* from S in QC! (for short, $S \vdash A$) if there is a derivation in QC! of A from S, (ii) A is *provable* in QC! (for short, $\vdash A$) if $\varnothing \vdash A$, (iii) S is *inconsistent* in QC! if $S \vdash f$, and (iv) S is *consistent* in QC! if S is not inconsistent in QC!.

By a *truth-value assignment* for QC! I shall understand any function from the set of the atomic wffs of QC! to {**T**,**F**}, where **T** is the truth-value "true" and **F** the truth-value "false". I shall say that A is *true* under a truth-value assignment α for QC! if (i) in the case that A is atomic, $\alpha(A) = $ **T**, (ii) in the case that A is (a negation) $\sim B$, B is not true under α, (iii) in the case that A is (a conditional) $B \supset C$, B is not true under α or C is, and (iv) in the case that A is (a quantification) $(\forall X)B$, $B(P/X)$ is true under α for every individual parameter P of QC! such that $\alpha(E!P) = $ **T**. I shall say that S is *tv-verifiable* (i.e., *truth-value verifiable*) if there is a truth-value assignment for QC! under which every member of S is true. And I shall say that A is *valid* if $\{\sim A\}$ is not tv-verifiable, hence if A is true under every truth-value assignment for QC!

Note that if any existential quantification $(\exists X)A$ of QC! is true under any truth-value assignment α for QC!, then—in view of clauses (ii) and (iv) above—$\alpha(E!P)$ is sure to be **T** for at least one individual parameter P of QC!. Hence, in effect, if the individual variables of QC! have values under any truth-value assignment for QC!, at least one individual parameter of QC! is sure to have a value under α.

Attention will be paid in Section 5 to truth-value assignments for QC! of two special sorts: (i) those, to be called *null* assignments, under which E!P is false for every individual parameter P of QC!, and (ii) those, to be called *standard assignments*, under which E!P is true for every individual parameter P of QC!.

3. Soundness and Completeness Theorems for QC!. That a wff of QC! is not provable in QC! unless valid, nor valid unless provable in QC!, is established after four lemmas.

Lemma 1. *If A is an axiom of* QC!, *then A is valid.*
Proof: Let α be an arbitrary truth-value assignment for QC!. (1) Let A be an axiom of QC! of one of the seven sorts **A1–A7**. It is easily ascertained that A is true under α. For suppose in particular that A is of the sort $B \supset (\forall X)B$. Since X is sure to be foreign to B, $B(P/X)$ is the same as B. Hence, if B is true under α, so is $B(P/X)$ for every individual parameter P of QC! such that $\alpha(E!P) = $ **T**, and hence so is $(\forall X)B$. (2) Let A be as in (1), and P and Q be arbitrary individual parameters of QC!. It is easily ascertained that $A(Q/P)$ is of one of the seven sorts **A1–A7**, and hence in view of (1) is true under α. For suppose in particular that A is of the sort $(\sim B \supset \sim C) \supset (C \supset B)$, and hence that $A(Q/P)$ is of the sort $((\sim B \supset \sim C) \supset (C \supset B))(Q/P)$. Since $((\sim B \supset \sim C) \supset (C \supset B))(Q/P)$ is the same as $(\sim B \supset \sim C)(Q/P) \supset (C \supset B)(Q/P)$, $(\sim B \supset \sim C)(Q/P)$ the same as $(\sim B)(Q/P) \supset (\sim C)(Q/P)$, $(\sim B)(Q/P)$ the same as $\sim B(Q/P)$, and so on, $A(Q/P)$ is the same as $(\sim B(Q/P) \supset \sim C(Q/P)) \supset (C(Q/P) \supset B(Q/P))$, and hence $A(Q/P)$ is of the sort **A3**. Or suppose that A is of the sort $(\forall X)B \supset (E!R \supset B(R/X))$, and that R is the same as P. Since $((\forall X)B \supset (E!P \supset B(P/X)))(Q/P)$ is the same as $((\forall X)B)(Q/P) \supset (E!P \supset B(P/X))(Q/P)$, $((\forall X)B)(Q/P)$ the same as $(\forall X)(B(Q/X))$, and so on, $A(Q/P)$ is the same as

Truth-Value Semantics for a Logic of Existence 81

$(\forall X)(B(Q/P)) \supset (E!Q \supset (B(P/X))(Q/P))$. But $(B(P/X))(Q/P)$ is the same as $(B(Q/P))(Q/X)$. Hence $A(Q/P)$ is of the sort **A6**. (3) Let A be an axiom of QC! of the sort $(\forall X)B(X/P)$, where B is of one of the seven sorts **A1**–**A7**. In view of (2) $B(Q/P)$ is true under α for every individual parameter Q of QC!. But $(B(X/P))(Q/X)$ is the same as $B(Q/P)$. Hence $(B(X/P))(Q/X)$ is true under α for every individual parameter Q of QC! such that $\alpha(E!Q) = \mathsf{T}$. Hence A is true under α. (4) Let A be an axiom of QC! of the sort $(\forall X_1)(\forall X_2) \ldots (\forall X_n)(B(X_1,X_2,\ldots,X_n/P_1,P_2,\ldots,P_n))$, where $n > 1$ and B is of one of the seven sorts **A1**–**A7**. Then by the same reasoning as in (3), but using (3) where (3) uses (2), A is true under α. (5) Let A be an axiom of QC!. Since A is sure to be as in (1), (3), or (4), A is sure to be true under α.

Lemma 2. *If S is inconsistent in QC!, then S is not tv-verifiable.*
Proof: Suppose S is inconsistent in QC!, and the column made up of A_1, $A_2, \ldots, A_p$ constitutes a derivation in QC! of 'f' from S. It is easily established by mathematical induction on i that $S \cup \{\sim A\}$ is not tv-verifiable for any i from 1 through p. Suppose A_i is an axiom of QC!. Since in view of Lemma 1 A_i is true under every truth-value assignment for QC!, $S \cup \{\sim A_i\}$ is not tv-verifiable. Or suppose A_i follows from A_g and $A_g \supset A_i (= A_h)$ by Modus Ponens, and neither one of $S \cup \{\sim A_g\}$ and $S \cup \{\sim A_h\}$ is tv-verifiable. Then $S \cup \{\sim A_i\}$ is not either. Hence $S \cup \{\sim f\}$ is not tv-verifiable. But '$\sim f$' is true under every truth-value assignment for QC!. Hence S is not tv-verifiable.

Lemma 3. (a) *If A belongs to S or is an axiom of* QC!, *then $S \vdash A$.*
(b) *If $S \vdash A$, then there is a finite subset S' of S such that $S \vdash A$.*
(c) *If $S \vdash A$, then $S \cup S' \vdash A$.*
(d) $\vdash A \supset A$.
(e) *If $S \vdash A$ and $S \vdash A \supset B$, then $S \vdash B$.*
(f) *If $S \cup \{A\} \vdash B$, then $S \vdash A \supset B$.*
(g) *If $S \cup \{\sim A\}$ is inconsistent in* QC!, *then $S \vdash A$.*
(h) *If $S \vdash A$ and $S \vdash \sim A$ for any A, then S is inconsistent in* QC!.
(i) *If $S \vdash A$, then $S \cup \{\sim A\}$ is inconsistent in* QC!.
(j) *If $S \vdash (\forall X)A$ and $S \vdash (\forall X)(A \supset B)$, then $S \vdash (\forall X)B$.*
(k) *If $S \vdash A$, then $S \vdash (\forall X)A(X/P)$, so long as P is foreign to S.*
Proof: (a)−(c), (e), and (j) are immediate, and proof of (d) familiar from the literature.[9]

For proof of (f), suppose that the column made up of $C_1, C_2, \ldots, C_p$ constitutes a derivation in QC! of $B(= C_p)$ from $S \cup \{A\}$. It is readily shown by mathematical induction on i that $S \vdash A \supset C_i$ for each i from 1 through p, and hence that $S \vdash A \supset C_p(= A \supset B)$. For suppose C_i belongs to $S \cup \{A\}$, but is other than A, or is an axiom of QC!. Then in view of (a) $S \vdash C_i$. But $C_i \supset (A \supset C_i)$ is an axiom of QC!. Hence in view of (a) and (e) $S \vdash A \supset C_i$. Or suppose C_i is A. Then in view of (d) and (c) $S \vdash A \supset C_i$. Or suppose C_i follows from C_g and $C_g \supset C_i(= C_h)$ by Modus Ponens, and suppose $S \vdash A \supset C_g$ and $S \vdash A \supset C_h$. Since $(A \supset C_h) \supset ((A \supset C_g) \supset (A \supset C_i))$ is an axiom of QC!, in view of (a) and (e) $S \vdash (A \supset C_g) \supset (A \supset C_i)$, and hence in view again of (e) $S \vdash A \supset C_i$.

For proof of (g), suppose $S \cup \{\sim A\} \vdash f$, and hence in view of (f) $S \vdash \sim A \supset f$. Since $(\sim A \supset f) \supset ((p \supset p) \supset A)$ is an axiom of QC!, in view of (a) and (e) $S \vdash (p \supset p) \supset A$. But in view of (d) and (c) $S \vdash p \supset p$. Hence in view of (e) $S \vdash A$.

For proof of (h), suppose $S \vdash \sim A$. Since $\sim A \supset (\sim f \supset \sim A)$ is an axiom of QC!, in view of (a) and (e) $S \vdash \sim f \supset \sim A$. But $(\sim f \supset \sim A) \supset (A \supset f)$ is an axiom of QC!. Hence in view again of (a) and (e) $S \vdash A \supset f$. Hence, if $S \vdash A$, then in view of (e) S is inconsistent in QC!.

For proof of (i), suppose $S \vdash A$. Then in view of (c) $S \cup \{\sim A\} \vdash A$. But in view of (a) $S \cup \{\sim A\} \vdash \sim A$. Hence in view of (h) $S \cup \{\sim A\}$ is inconsistent in QC!.

For proof of (k), suppose the column made up of $B_1, B_2, \ldots, B_p$ constitutes a derivation in QC! of $A (= B_p)$ from S; and let Y be X if X is foreign to $\{B_1, B_2, \ldots, B_{p-1}\}$ (with $(\forall X)A(X/P)$ presumed to be a wff of QC!, X is sure to be foreign to B_p), otherwise let Y be the alphabetically earliest individual variable of QC! that is foreign to $\{B_1, B_2, \ldots, B_p\}$. It can be shown by mathematical induction on i that $S \vdash (\forall Y)B_i(Y/P)$ for each i from 1 through p. Suppose B_i belongs to S. Since P is presumed to be foreign to S, then $B_i(Y/P)$ is the same as B_i. Hence in view of (a) $S \vdash B_i(Y/P)$. But $B_i(Y/P) \supset (\forall Y)B_i(Y/P)$ ($= B_i \supset (\forall Y)B_i$) is an axiom of QC!. Hence in view of (a) and (e) $S \vdash (\forall Y)B_i(Y/P)$. Or suppose B_i is an axiom of QC!. Then so is $(\forall Y)B_i(Y/P)$, and hence in view of (a) $S \vdash (\forall Y)B_i(Y/P)$. Or suppose B_i follows from B_g and $B_g \supset B_i$ ($= B_h$) by Modus Ponens, and suppose $S \vdash (\forall Y)B_g(Y/P)$ and $S \vdash (\forall Y)B_h(Y/P)$. Since $(\forall Y)B_h(Y/P)$ is the same as $(\forall Y)(B_g(Y/P) \supset B_i(Y/P))$, in view of (j) $S \vdash (\forall Y)B_i(Y/P)$. Hence $S \vdash (\forall Y)A(Y/P)$, and hence $S \vdash (\forall X)A(X/P)$ if Y is X. Otherwise, since Y is foreign to A, $(A(Y/P))(P/Y)$ is the same as A, hence $(\forall Y)A(Y/P) \supset (E!P \supset A)$ is an axiom of QC!, and hence so is $(\forall X)((\forall Y)A(Y/P) \supset (E!X \supset A(X/P)))$. Hence in view of (a) $S \vdash (\forall X)((\forall Y)A(Y/P) \supset (E!X \supset A(X/P)))$. But $(\forall Y)A(Y/P) \supset (\forall X)(\forall Y)A(Y/P)$ is an axiom of QC!. Hence in view of (a) and (e) $S \vdash (\forall X)(\forall Y)A(Y/P)$. Hence in view of (j) $S \vdash (\forall X)(E!X \supset A(X/P))$. But $(\forall X)E!X$ is an axiom of QC!. Hence in view of (a) and (e) $S \vdash (\forall X)E!X$. Hence in view of (j) $S \vdash (\forall X)A(X/P)$.

Lemma 4. *Let S be an infinitely extendible set of wffs of* QC!. *If S is consistent in* QC!, *then S is tv-verifiable.*
Proof: Let S be consistent in QC!.[10]
Part One: Take S_0 to be S; A_i being the alphabetically i-th wff of QC!, define S_i as follows for each i from 1 on:
  (i) if $S_{i-1} \cup \{A_i\}$ is inconsistent in QC!, let S_i be $S_{i-1} \cup \{\sim A_i\}$,[11]
  (ii) if $S_{i-1} \cup \{A_i\}$ is consistent in QC! and A_i is not of the sort $\sim(\forall X)A$, let S_i be $S_{i-1} \cup \{A_i\}$, and
  (iii) if $S_{i-1} \cup \{A_i\}$ is consistent in QC! and A_i is a negated quantification

Truth-Value Semantics for a Logic of Existence 83

$\sim(\forall X)A$, let S_i be $S_{i-1} \cup \{\sim(\forall X)A, E!P, \sim A(P/X)\}$, where P is the alphabetically earliest individual parameter of QC! that is foreign to $S_{i-1} \cup \{\sim(\forall X)A\}$; and let S_∞ be the union of $S_0, S_1, S_2, \ldots$. It is easily ascertained that:
(1) For each $i \geq 0$, S_i is consistent in QC!,
(2) S_∞ is consistent in QC!,
(3) For every wff A of QC!, if A does not belong to S_∞, then $S_\infty \vdash \sim A$, and
(4) For every negated quantification $\sim(\forall X)A$ of QC!, if $S_\infty \vdash \sim(\forall X)A$, then there is an individual parameter P of QC! such that $S_\infty \vdash E!P$ and $S_\infty \vdash \sim A(P/X)$.

For proof of (1), suppose S_i is as in (i), hence $S_{i-1} \cup \{A_i\}$ is inconsistent in QC!, and hence in view of Lemma 3(f) $S_{i-1} \vdash A_i \supset f$. If S_i is inconsistent in QC!, then in view of Lemma 3(g) $S_{i-1} \vdash A_i$, and hence in view of Lemma 3(e) S_{i-1} is inconsistent in QC!. Hence S_i is consistent in QC! if S_{i-1} is. Next, suppose S_i is as in (ii). Then S_i is consistent in QC!, and hence is consistent in QC! if S_{i-1} is. Lastly, suppose S_i is as in (iii) and is inconsistent in QC!. Then in view of Lemmas 3(g) and 3(f) $S_{i-1} \cup \{\sim(\forall X)A\} \vdash E!P \supset A(P/X)$. But P is presumed to be foreign to $S_{i-1} \cup \{\sim(\forall X)A\}$. Hence in view of Lemma 3(k) $S_{i-1} \cup \{\sim(\forall X)A\} \vdash (\forall X)(E!X \supset (A(P/X))(X/P))$. But, with P presumed to be foreign to $\sim(\forall X)A$ and hence to A, A is the same as $(A(P/X))(X/P)$. Hence $S_{i-1} \cup \{\sim(\forall X)A\} \vdash (\forall X)(E!X \supset A)$. But $(\forall X)E!X$ is an axiom of QC!. Hence in view of Lemma 3(a) $S_{i-1} \cup \{\sim(\forall X)A\} \vdash (\forall X)E!X$. Hence in view of Lemma 3 (j) $S_{i-1} \cup \{\sim(\forall X)A\} \vdash (\forall X)A$, and hence in view of Lemma 3(i) $S_{i-1} \cup \{\sim(\forall X)A\}$ ($= S_{i-1} \cup \{A_i\}$) is inconsistent in QC!, as against the hypothesis in (iii). Hence S_i is consistent in QC!, and hence is consistent in QC! if S_{i-1} is. But S_0 is presumed to be consistent in QC!. Hence (1) by mathematical induction on i.

For proof of (2), suppose S_∞ is inconsistent in QC!. Then in view of Lemma 3(b) some finite subset of S_∞ is also inconsistent in QC!. But every finite subset of S_∞ is a subset of at least one of $S_0, S_1, S_2, \ldots$. Hence in view of Lemma 3(c) at least one of $S_0, S_1, S_2, \ldots$ is inconsistent in QC!, as against (1). Hence (2).

For proof of (3), suppose A does not belong to S_∞ and is the alphabetically i-th wff of QC!. Then S_i is $S_{i-1} \cup \{\sim A\}$, and hence in view of Lemma 3(a) $S_\infty \vdash \sim A$.

For proof of (4), suppose $S_\infty \vdash \sim(\forall X)A$ and $\sim(\forall X)A$ is the alphabetically i-th wff of QC!. Then $S_{i-1} \cup \{\sim(\forall X)A\}$ is consistent in QC!, for otherwise in view of Lemmas 3(f) and 3(c) $S_\infty \vdash (\forall X)A$, and hence in view of Lemma 3(h) S_∞ is inconsistent in QC!, as against (2). But, if $S_{i-1} \cup \{\sim(\forall X)A\}$ is consistent in QC!, then S_i is $S_{i-1} \cup \{\sim(\forall X)A, E!P, \sim A(P/X)\}$, where P is as in (iii). Hence in view of Lemma 3(a) there is an individual parameter P of QC! such that $S_\infty \vdash E!P$ and $S_\infty \vdash \sim A(P/X)$.

Part Two: Let S' be the set S_∞ of *Part One*. It is easily ascertained with the aid of (2)–(4) in *Part One* that:

(5) For every negation $\sim A$ of QC!, $S' \vdash \sim A$ if and only if it is not the case that $S' \vdash A$,

(6) For every conditional $A \supset B$ of QC!, $S' \vdash A \supset B$ if and only if it is not the case that $S' \vdash A$ or it is the case that $S' \vdash B$.

(7) For every quantification $(\forall X)A$ of QC!, $S' \vdash (\forall X)A$ if and only if $S' \vdash A(P/X)$ for every individual parameter P of QC! such that $S' \vdash E!P$.

For proof of (5), suppose $S' \vdash \sim A$ and $S' \vdash A$. Then in view of Lemma 3(h) S' is inconsistent in QC!, as against (2). Suppose, on the other hand, it is not the case that $S' \vdash A$. Then in view of Lemma 3(a) A does not belong to S', and hence in view of (3) $S' \vdash \sim A$.

For proof of (6), suppose that $S' \vdash A \supset B$ and $S' \vdash A$. Then in view of Lemma 3(e) $S' \vdash B$. Next, suppose it is not the case that $S' \vdash A$. Then in view of (5) $S' \vdash \sim A$. But $\sim A \supset (\sim B \supset \sim A)$ is an axiom of QC!. Hence in view of Lemmas 3(a) and 3(e) $S' \vdash \sim B \supset \sim A$. But $(\sim B \supset \sim A) \supset (A \supset B)$ is an axiom of QC!. Hence in view of the same two lemmas $S' \vdash A \supset B$. Lastly, suppose that $S' \vdash B$. Since $B \supset (A \supset B)$ is an axiom of QC!, then in view of Lemmas 3(a) and 3(e) $S' \vdash A \supset B$.

For proof of (7), suppose $S' \vdash (\forall X)A$. Since $(\forall X)A \supset (E!P \supset A(P/X))$ is an axiom of QC!, in view of Lemmas 3(a) and 3(e) $S' \vdash E!P \supset A(P/X)$, and hence in view again of Lemma 3(e) $S' \vdash A(P/X)$ for every individual parameter P of QC! such that $S' \vdash E!P$. Suppose, on the other hand, it is not the case that $S' \vdash (\forall X)A$. Then in view of (5) $S' \vdash \sim(\forall X)A$, hence in view of (4) there is an individual parameter P of QC! such that $S' \vdash E!P$ and $S' \vdash \sim A(P/X)$, and hence in view of (5) there is an individual parameter P of QC! such that $S' \vdash E!P$ and it is not the case that $S' \vdash A(P/X)$.

Part Three: Let α be the truth-value assignment for QC! such that, for every atomic wff A of QC!, $\alpha(A) = \mathbf{T}$ if and only if $S' \vdash A$. Given (5)–(7) in *Part Two*, it is easily shown by mathematical induction on the number of occurrences of '$\sim$', '$\supset$', and '$\forall$' in an arbitrary wff A of QC!, that A is true under α if and only if $S' \vdash A$. For suppose in particular that A is a quantification $(\forall X)B$. By the hypothesis of the induction $B(P/X)$ is true under α if and only if $S' \vdash B(P/X)$, and this for every individual parameter P of QC!. Hence $B(P/X)$ is true under α for every individual parameter P of QC! such that $\alpha(E!P) = \mathbf{T}$ if and only if $S' \vdash B(P/X)$ for every individual parameter P of QC! such that $\alpha(E!P) = \mathbf{T}$. But $E!P$ being atomic, $\alpha(E!P) = \mathbf{T}$ if and only if $S' \vdash E!P$. Hence in view of (7) $(\forall X)B$ is true under α if and only if $S' \vdash (\forall X)B$. Consider then an arbitrary member A of S. Since A belongs to S', in view of Lemma 3(a) $S' \vdash A$. Hence A is true under α. Hence every member of S is true under α.

Our soundness and completeness theorems for QC! are now at hand.

Theorem 1. *If $\vdash A$, then A is valid.*

Proof: Suppose $\vdash A$. Then in view of Lemma 3(i) $\{\sim A\}$ is inconsistent in QC!, hence in view of Lemma 2 $\{\sim A\}$ is not tv-verifiable and hence A is valid.

Theorem 2. *If A is valid, then* ⊢ *A*.
Proof: Suppose A is valid, and hence $\{\sim A\}$ is not tv-verifiable. Since $\{\sim A\}$ is infinitely extendible, in view of Lemma 4 $\{\sim A\}$ is inconsistent in QC!, and hence in view of Lemma 3(g) ⊢ A.

4. That Matter of Implication.

In 1919 Löwenheim's Theorem was generalized by Skolem, who showed that, as regards the satisfiability of infinite sets of wffs (a set S of wffs of QC being satisfiable when S has a model), the implication of wffs by infinite sets of wffs (a wff A of QC being implied by a set S of wffs of QC when every model of S is one of $\{A\}$), and the like, domains of size greater than $\aleph_0$ may be ignored.[12] Unfortunately, Beth's Theorem does not likewise generalize, as Dunn and Belnap, Thomason, and others have noticed.[13] The set $\{f(a_1), f(a_2), f(a_3), \ldots, \sim(\forall x)f(x)\}$, where '$a_1$', '$a_2$', '$a_3$', ... are presumed to be all the individual parameters of QC, is satisfiable in the model-theoretic sense, since '$f(a_1)$', '$f(a_2)$', '$f(a_3)$', ..., '$\sim(\forall x)f(x)$' all come out true when 'a_1', 'a_2', 'a_3', ... are all assigned the same member of any domain D of size 2 and 'f' is assigned either one of the two subsets of D other than $\varnothing$ and D. Yet there is no assignment of truth-values to the atomic wffs of QC under which all the members of $\{f(a_1), f(a_2), f(a_3), \ldots, \sim(\forall x)f(x)\}$ are true. The same difficulty arises with the set $\{f(a_1), f(a_2), f(a_3), \ldots, E!a_1, E!a_2, E!a_3, \ldots, \sim(\forall x)f(x)\}$, one member of which is bound to be false under any assignment of truth-values to the atomic wffs of QC!.

With nameability by $\aleph_0$ individual parameters falling short of denumerability at this juncture, we cannot pronounce a wff A of QC! implied by a set S of wffs of QC! if A is true under any assignment of truth-values to the atomic wffs of QC! under which the members of S are all true. One way of meeting the difficulty is to pronounce A implied by a finite set of wffs of QC!, say $\{B_1, B_2, \ldots, B_n\}$, if $B_1 \supset (B_2 \supset (\ldots \supset (B_n \supset A) \ldots))$ is valid, and pronounce it implied by an infinite set of wffs of QC! if it is implied by some finite subset of the set. It is rather *ad hoc*. Another, favored by Belnap and Dunn in the case of QC, is to pronounce A implied by a set S of wffs of QC! if, for every parametric extension of QC! (i.e., every plying of QC! with fresh individual parameters) and every assignment of truth-values to the atomic wffs of the extension, A is true under the assignment if every member of S is. I resort to a third, which—as I mentioned in [10]—I owe in part to Hintikka.[14]

Where S is a set of wffs of QC!, Σ_S is the set of all the individual parameters of QC! occurring in members of S, and M is a one-to-one mapping of Σ_S into the set of all the individual parameters of QC!, (1) I shall take the *M-image* $M(A)$ of a member of S to be A itself when no individual parameter of QC! occurs in A, otherwise to be $A(M(P_1), M(P_2), \ldots, M(P_m)/P_1, P_2, \ldots, P_m)$, where the $P_1, P_2, \ldots, P_m$ are in alphabetical order all the individual parameters of QC! that occur in A, and (2) I shall take the *M-image*

86   Part 1: Existence

$M(S)$ of S to be S itself when S is empty, otherwise to be the set of the M-images of the various members of S. Where S and S' are sets of wffs of QC!, and Σ_S is as above, I shall say that S' is *isomorphic* to S if S' is $M(S)$ for some one-to-one mapping of Σ_S into the set of all the individual parameters of QC!. And, where S is a set of wffs of QC! and A is a wff of QC!, I shall say that S *implies* A (or, to use Tarski's terminology, A is a semantic consequence of S) if no set of wffs of QC! that is isomorphic to $S \cup \{\sim A\}$ is tv-verifiable.

Proof that $S \vdash A$ if and only if S implies A in my sense of the word (and, hence, that QC! is both strongly sound and strongly complete) calls for a few extra lemmas.[15]

Lemma 5. *If S is inconsistent in* QC!, *then so is every set of wffs of* QC! *that is isomorphic to S.*
Proof: Let Σ_S consist of all the individual parameters of QC! occurring in members of S; let M be an arbitrary one-to-one mapping of Σ_S into the set of all the individual parameters of QC!; and let the column made up of $A_1, A_2, \ldots, A_p$ constitute a derivation in QC! of 'f'($= A_p$) from S. It is easily verified that the column made up of $M(A_1), M(A_2), \ldots, M(A_p)$ constitutes a derivation in QC! of 'f'($= M(A_p)$) from $M(S)$. For suppose A_i belongs to S. Then $M(A_i)$ belongs to $M(S)$. Or suppose A_i is an axiom of QC!. Then so is $M(A_i)$. Or suppose A_i follows from A_g and $A_g \supset A_i$ ($= A_h$) by Modus Ponens. Since $M(A_h)$ is the same as $M(A_g) \supset M(A_i)$, $M(A_i)$ follows from $M(A_g)$ and $M(A_h)$ by Modus Ponens. Hence $M(S)$ is inconsistent in QC! if S is.

Lemma 6. *If S is inconsistent in* QC!, *then no set of wffs of* QC! *that is isomorphic to S is tv-verifiable.*
Proof by Lemma 2 and Lemma 5.

Lemma 7. *Let S be a set of wffs of* QC!; *let Σ_S be the set of all the individual parameters of* QC! *occurring in members of S; and let M be the one-to-one mapping of Σ_S into the set of all the individual parameters of* QC! *such that, where P is the alphabetically i-th individual parameter of* QC!, $M(P)$ *is the alphabetically $2i$-th individual parameter of* QC!. *If S is consistent in* QC!, *then so is $M(S)$.*
Proof: Let the column made up of $A_1, A_2, \ldots, A_p$ constitute a derivation in QC! of 'f'($= A_p$) from $M(S)$. It is easily verified that the column made up of $M'(A_1), M'(A_2), \ldots, M'(A_p)$, where M' is the inverse of M, constitutes a derivation of QC! of 'f' ($= M'(A_p)$) from $M'(M(S))$. But $M'(M(S))$ is S. Hence $M(S)$ is consistent in QC! if S is.

Lemma 8. *If S is consistent in* QC!, *then at least one set of wffs of* QC! *that is isomorphic to S is tv-verifiable.*
Proof: Suppose S is infinitely extendible. Since S is isomorphic to itself, Lemma 8 by Lemma 4. Suppose on the other hand, S is not infinitely extendible,

and let M be as in Lemma 7. $M(S)$ is infinitely extendible, and in view of Lemma 7 is consistent in QC! if S is. Hence Lemma 8 by Lemma 4.

Theorem 3. $S \vdash A$ *if and only if S implies A.*[16]
Proof like that of Theorems 1–2, but using Lemmas 6 and 8 in place of Lemmas 2 and 6.

Hence Corollary 1, in view of which validity is tantamount—as expected—to implication by the null set:

Corollary 1. *A is valid if and only if $\varnothing$ implies A.*
Proof by Theorems 1–3.

5. Further Concepts of Validity. Recalling the various kinds of truth-value assignments for QC! described at the close of Section 2, pronounce a wff of QC! $valid_1$ if true under every null and every standard truth-value assignment for QC!, $valid_2$ if true under every non-null truth-value assignment for QC!, and $valid_3$ if true under every standard truth-value assignment for QC!. With regards to $validity_1$ every individual parameter of QC! has to have a value (and, hence, the individual variables of QC! have to have values) if anyone does, the option considered in [15]. With regards to $validity_2$ the individual variables of QC! have to have values (hence, under the present understanding of things, at least one individual parameter of QC! has to have a value), the stand taken in [14]. And with regards to $validity_3$ every individual parameter of QC! has to have a value (and, hence, the individual variables of QC! have to have values), the norm outside free logic.
Addition of

A8$_1$. $(\exists x)\text{E}!x \supset \text{E}!P$

to the axiom schemata **A1–A7** of Section 2 will permit proof in QC! of all the wffs of QC! that are $valid_1$; addition of the antecedent

A8$_2$. $(\exists x)\text{E}!x$

of **A8$_1$** permit proof in QC! of all those that are $valid_2$; and addition of the consequent

A8$_3$. E!P

of **A8$_1$** permit proof in QC! of all those that are $valid_3$.[17] Consider indeed the set S' and the truth-value assignment α in the proof of Lemma 4. If wffs of QC! of the sort **A8$_1$** count as extra axioms of QC!, then in view of Lemma 3(a) $S' \vdash (\exists x)\text{E}!x \supset \text{E}!P$ for every individual parameter P of QC!, hence $(\exists x)\text{E}!x \supset \text{E}!P$ is true under α for every individual parameter P of QC! and hence $\alpha(\text{E}!P) = \mathbf{F}$ for every individual parameter P of QC! or $\alpha(\text{E}!P) = \mathbf{T}$ for every individual parameter P of QC!. If **A8$_2$** counts as an extra axiom of QC!, then in view of

88   Part 1: Existence

Lemma 3(a) $S' \vdash (\exists x)\mathrm{E}!x$, hence '$(\exists x)\mathrm{E}!x$' is true under α, and hence $\alpha(\mathrm{E}!P)$ = **T** for at least one individual parameter P of QC!. And if wffs of QC! of the sort **A8**$_3$ count as extra axioms of QC!, then in view of Lemma 3(a) $S' \vdash \mathrm{E}!P$ for every individual parameter P of QC!, and hence $\alpha(\mathrm{E}!P)$ = **T** for every individual parameter P of QC!.

The E!-less wffs of QC! (i.e., the wffs of QC) that are valid$_1$ are axiomatizable, as shown in [15]. So are the valid$_2$ ones, as I recently discovered. And of course so are the valid$_3$ ones: they are the wffs of QC valid in the standard sense. Assume throughout that $(\forall X)A(X/P)$ is an axiom* if A is. Then **A1–A5** and

A9$^*_1$. $(\forall X)A \supset ((\exists x)(f(x) \lor \sim f(x)) \supset A(P/X))$

permit proof* of every valid$_1$ E!-less wff of QC!; **A1–A5, A6$^*_1$–A6$^*_2$**, and

A9$^*_2$. $(\forall X)A \supset A$

permit proof* of every valid$_2$ E!-less wff of QC!; and, of course, **A1–A5 and**

A9$^*_3$. $(\forall X)A \supset A(P/X)$

permit proof* of every valid$_3$ E!-less wff of QC!. Note as regards the second case that since '$(\forall y)((\forall x)\sim(f(x) \lor \sim f(x)) \supset \sim(f(y) \lor \sim f(y)))$' counts as an axiom*, '$(\forall y)((f(y) \lor \sim f(y)) \supset (\exists x)(f(x) \lor \sim f(x)))$' is sure to be provable*, hence so is '$(\forall y)(f(y) \lor \sim f(y)) \supset (\forall y)(\exists x)(f(x) \lor \sim f(x))$', and hence so is '$(\forall y)(\exists x)(f(x) \lor \sim f(x))$'. Hence, if '$(\forall y)(\exists x)(f(x) \lor \sim f(x)) \supset (\exists x)(f(x) \lor \sim f(x))$' also counts as an axiom*, then '$(\exists x)(f(x) \lor \sim f(x))$'—a common rendering of "Something exists"—is provable*.[18]

Notes

1. See [17] Skolem's generalization of Löwenheim's theorem is discussed in Section 4.
2. See [1], Section 89. What I call here Beth's Theorem should not be confused with his more celebrated theorem on definability.
3. The interpretation, which goes back to Wittgenstein, has recently been championed by Ruth Barcan Marcus and others. As announced on p. 13, it is the chief topic of Part 2 of this volume.
4. For further details, see [1], [2], [10], [12], [20], etc. Hintikka's model-set semantics in [6] and later papers is but another brand of what I call here *truth-value semantics*.
5. See [9], [11], and [18]. The version of QC! that I employ here comes from [18], and is credited by Lambert to Meyer. The one in [9], which uses '∃' rather than '∀' as primitive quantifier letter, has very attractive axioms, but proves less handy to work with.
6. By requiring in (v) that X be foreign to A, I forego wffs in which identical quantifiers overlap, but avoid difficulties that would otherwise beset the substitution of parameters- for variables. Essentially the same point is made in [19], p. 15, Note 1.
7. I owe the phrase 'infinitely extendible' to R. K. Meyer.
8. As reported in the preceding paper, the trick of counting $(\forall X)A(X/P)$ as an axiom when A is one, and thereby dispensing with Generalization as a rule of inference, stems from [3]. It clears up all the difficulties that in some formulations of QC have beset, in others have blocked, proof of Lemma 3(c) in Section 3 (see [13] on this whole matter). Note as regards **A4** that, with $A \supset (\forall X)A$ presumed to be a wff of QC!, X is sure to be foreign to A.

9. When Generalization serves as a rule of inference, proof of (c)—as noted in note 8—can be tricky, and proof of (f) has an extra case (which can be tricky too).
10. The following proof borrows from [4], [5], [12], [16], and [22]. The simplification brought in [22], p. 96, to the argument of [5] is credited by Smullyan to Henkin.
11. Or, equivalently, let S_{j-1}. The course adopted in the text makes for a shorter proof of (3) below, the one reported here for a shorter proof of (1).
12. See [21].
13. See [2] and [10].
14. For further details on this whole matter, see [10] and [12].
15. In what follows I borrow in part from [12].
16. One half of the standard Compactness Theorem clearly holds for QC!, namely: If a set S of wffs is tv-verifiable, so is every finite subset of S. The other half fails, since every finite subset of $\{f(a_1), f(a_2), f(a_3), \ldots, E!a_1, E!a_2, E!a_3, \ldots, \sim(\forall x)f(x)\}$ is tv-verifiable, but the set itself is not. The following weakening of that half holds, however: If every finite subset of S is tv-verifiable, then so is some set of wffs of QC! that is isomorphic to S. Suppose indeed that no set of wffs of QC! that is isomorphic to S is tv-verifiable. Then in view of Lemma 8 S is inconsistent in QC!, hence in view of Lemma 3(b) some finite subset of S is inconsistent in QC!, and hence in view of Lemma 2 some finite subset of S is not tv-verifiable. The following also holds in view of Theorem 3 and Lemmas 3(b) and 3(c): S implies a wff A of QC! if and only if some finite subset of S implies A.
17. With $A8_3$ at hand (and $(\forall X)A(X/P)$ counting as an axiom when A does), $A7$ is of course redundant.
18. My thanks go to Lambert, Meyer, van Fraassen, and John T. Kearns, who read an early version of this paper. The results proved here were announced at a symposium on The Logic of Existence held at Indiana University in the spring of 1969.

References

[1] Beth, E. W. 1959. *The Foundations of Mathematics*. Amsterdam: North-Holland.
[2] Dunn, M., and Belnap, Jr., N. D. 1968. "The Substitution Interpretation of the Quantifiers." *Noûs* 2: 177–85.
[3] Fitch, F. B. 1948. "Intuitionistic Modal Logic with Quantifiers." *Portugaliae Mathematica* 7: 113–18.
[4] Hasenjaeger, G. 1953. "Eine Bemerkung zu Henkin's Beweis für die Vollständigkeit des Prädikatenkalkuls der ersten Stufe." *The Journal of Symbolic Logic* (hereafter *JSL*) 18: 42–48.
[5] Henkin, L. 1949. "The Completeness of the First-Order Functional Calculus." *JSL* 14: 159–66.
[6] Hintikka, J. 1955. "Two Papers on Symbolic Logic." *Acta Philosophica Fennica*.
[7] ———. 1959. "Existential Presuppositions and Existential Commitments." *The Journal of Philosophy* 56: 125–37.
[8] Lambert, K. 1963. "Existential Import Revisited." *Notre Dame Journal of Formal Logic* (hereafter *NDJFL*) 4: 288–92.
[9] ———. 1967. "Free Logic and the Concept of Existence." *NDJFL* 8: 133–44.
[10] Leblanc, H. 1968. "A Simplified Account of Validity and Implication for Quantificational Logic." *JSL* 33: 231–35 (#8 in this volume).
[11] ———. 1968. "On Meyer and Lambert's Quantificational Calculus FQ." *JSL* 33: 275–80.
[12] ———. 1969. "A Simplified Strong Completeness Proof for QC$_=$." *Akten des XIV. Internationalen Kongresses für Philosophie* 3: 83–95 Vienna: Verlag Herder (#9 in this volume).
[13] ———. 1979. "Generalization in First-Order Logic." *NDJFL* 20: 835–57 (#35 in this volume).
[14] Leblanc, H., and Hailperin, T. 1959. "Nondesignating Singular Terms." *The Philosophical Review* 68: 129–36 (#1 in this volume).

[15] Leblanc, H., and Meyer, R. K. 1969. "Open Formulas and the Empty Domain." *Archiv für mathematische Logik und Grundlagenforschung* 12: 78–84 (#5 in this volume).
[16] Leblanc, H., and Thomason, R. H. 1968. "Completeness Theorems for some Presupposition-Free Logics." *Fundamenta Mathematicae* 62: 125–64 (#2 in this volume).
[17] Löwenheim, L. 1915. "Über Moglichkeiten im Relativkalkül." *Mathematische Annalen* 76: 447–70.
[18] Meyer, R. K., and Lambert, K. 1968. "Universally Free Logic and Standard Quantification Theory." *JSL* 33: 8–26.
[19] Prawitz, D. 1965. *Natural Deduction: A Proof-Theoretical Study.* Stockholm: Almqvist and Wiksell.
[20] Schütte, K. 1962. *Lecture Notes in Mathematical Logic, Volume I.* The Pennsylvania State University.
[21] Skolem, T. 1920. "Logisch-kombinatorische Untersuchungen über die Erfüllbarkeit oder Beweisbarkeit matehmatischer Sätze nebst einem Theoreme über dichte Mengen." *Skrifter utgit av Videnskappsselskapet i Kristiana, I, Mathematisk-naturvidenskabelig klasse* 1919 3: 1–36.
[22] Smullyan, R. M. 1968. *First-Order Logic.* New York: Springer-Verlag.

5
Open Formulas and the Empty Domain
R. K. Meyer, coauthor

Following Church's lead in [1] and Hailperin's in [2], Quine remarks on p. 177 of [12]: "An easy . . . test enables us . . . to decide whether a formula (of the first-order quantificational calculus without identity) holds for the empty domain. We have only to mark the universal quantifications as true and the existential ones as false, and apply truth-table considerations." Quine implicitly presupposes here that the formula under scrutiny is closed, and in [13], pp. 96–97, where he proposes the same test, he explicitly addresses himself to closed formulas only.

What, however, if the formula is open?

We then have two major options: (i) submit the formula to the very same test, thus taking it to hold for the empty domain if and only if—its universal quantifications once marked true and its existential ones false—it proves to be a tautology, or (ii) take it to automatically hold for the empty domain, this on the grounds that its universal closure does and that for the empty as for any other domain a formula should hold true if its universal closure does.[1] As regards validity the issue is not idle: under (ii) the familiar formula '$(\forall x)f(x) \supset f(y)$' is valid for $\emptyset$ (as well as for every non-empty domain), whereas under (i) it is not. Nor is the issue idle as regards implication. Under (i) no assignment of a truth-value to '$f(y)$' satisfies both '$f(y)$' and '$f(y) \supset (\exists x)f(x)$'; hence none that satisfies both '$f(y)$' and '$f(y) \supset (\exists x)f(x)$' fails to satisfy '$(\exists x)f(x)$'; hence, according to a common reading of the verb 'to imply', '$f(y)$' and '$f(y) \supset (\exists x)f(x)$' imply '$(\exists x)f(x)$'. Under (ii), on the other hand, both '$f(y)$' and '$f(y) \supset (\exists x)f(x)$' hold for $\emptyset$, whereas '$(\exists x)f(x)$' does not; hence '$f(y)$' and '$f(y) \supset (\exists x)f(x)$' do not imply '$(\exists x)f(x)$'. Most writers who have busied themselves with this (Mostowski, Kalish and Montague, Leblanc and Thomason, Schneider, etc.) opt for (ii). (i), however, may well be the most astute option for Modus Ponens, which fails under (ii), holds under (i), and a brand of "inclusive" quantification theory that has Modus Ponens may have a future as well.[2]

92 Part 1: Existence

1. Derivability and Implication in "Exclusive" Quantification Theory. Let a formula of QC, the first-order quantificational calculus without identity,[3] count as an axiom if it is of one of the following six sorts:

A1. $A \supset (B \supset A)$,

A2. $(A \supset (B \supset C)) \supset ((A \supset B) \supset (A \supset C))$,

A3. $(\sim A \supset \sim B) \supset (B \supset A)$,

A4. $A \supset (\forall X)A$, where X does not occur free in A,

A5. $(\forall X)(A \supset B) \supset ((\forall X)A \supset (\forall X)B)$,

and

A6. $(\forall X)A \supset A(Y/X)$, where $A(Y/X)$ is like A except for displaying free Y wherever A displays free X.

Where A and B are formulas of QC, let B be said to follow from A and $A \supset B$ by application of **R1** (Modus Ponens); and, where $(\forall X)A$ is a formula of QC and Y is an individual variable of QC that does not occur free in $(\forall X)A$, let $(\forall X)A$ be said to follow from $A(Y/X)$ by application of **R2** (Generalization). Where K is a finite column of formulas of QC, $(\forall X)A$ is an entry in K that follows from a previous entry by application of **R2** and $A(Y/X)$ is the earliest entry in K from which $(\forall X)A$ follows by application of **R2**, let Y be said to be generalized upon in K if Y is identical with X, otherwise let Y be said to be quasi-generalized upon in K. Where S is a finite set of formulas of QC and A is a formula of QC, let a finite column K of formulas of QC count as a derivation of A from S if: (a) K has A as its last entry, (b) every entry in K belongs to S, or is an axiom, or follows from previous entries in K by application of **R1** or **R2**, and (c) no individual variable of QC that is generalized or quasi-generalized upon in K occurs free in any member of S. Lastly, where S is again a finite set of formulas of QC, let a formula A of QC be said to be derivable from S ($S \vdash A$, for short) if there is a derivation of A from S; and, where S is an infinite set of formulas of QC, let A be said to be derivable from S ($S \vdash A$, again, for short) if there is a finite subset S' of S such that $S' \vdash A$.[4]

With a formula A of QC said to be implied by a set S of formulas of QC if, for every non-empty domain D, every D-interpretation of the variables of QC fails to satisfy a member of S or satisfies A,[5] and A said to be valid if implied by the null set of formulas of QC, we can show following [3] that $S \vdash A$ if S implies A, and hence that $\emptyset \vdash A$ if A is valid:

Lemma 1. *If S implies A, then $S \vdash A$.*[6]

It is easily verified, on the other hand, that S implies A if $S \vdash A$, and hence that A is valid if $\emptyset \vdash A$. The present account of "exclusive" quantification theory is thus complete and sound as regards both implication and validity.[7]

Open Formulas and the Empty Domain 93

2. Derivability and Implication in "Inclusive" Quantification Theory.

Suppose A^* to count as the $\emptyset$-associate of a formula A of QC if: (a) when A is atomic, A^* is A, (b) when A is of the sort $\sim B$, A^* is $\sim B^*$, where B^* is the $\emptyset$-associate of B, (c) when A is of the sort $B \supset C$, A^* is $B^* \supset C^*$, where B^* is the $\emptyset$-associate of B and C^* that of C, and (d) when A is of the sort $(\forall X)B$, A^* is '$p \supset p$'.[8] Next, suppose that, A being a formula and S a set of formulas of QC, A is said to be implied by S in the inclusive sense (for short, A is said to be I-implied by S) if A is implied by S as in Section 1 and—following option (i)—*every assignment of truth-values to the atomic formulas of* QC *fails to satisfy the $\emptyset$-associate of a member of S or satisfies the $\emptyset$-satisfies the $\emptyset$-associate of A*; and A is said to be valid in the inclusive sense (for short, A is I-valid) if A is I-implied by the null set of formulas of QC. Then, suppose that a column K of the sort described on p. 92 counts as a derivation of A from S in the inclusive sense (for short, as an I-derivation of A from S) if every entry in K that does not belong to S nor follows from previous entries in K by application of **R1** or **R2**, is of one of the five sorts **A1–A5** on p. 92 or of the sixth sort:

A6'. $(\exists x)(f(x) \vee \sim f(x)) \supset ((\forall X)A \supset A(Y/X))$, where $A(Y/X)$ is as in **A6**.[9]

Lastly, suppose that A is said to be derivable from S in the inclusive sense ($S \vdash_I A$, for short) if: (a) when S is finite, there is an I-derivation of A from S, and (b) when S is infinite, there is a finite subset S' of S such that $S' \vdash_I A$.

It is readily seen that S I-implies A if $S \vdash_I A$, hence that A is I-valid if $\emptyset \vdash_I A$, and hence that our brand of "inclusive" quantification theory is sound as regards implication and validity. It is readily proved, on the other hand, that $S \vdash_I A$ if S I-implies A, hence that $\emptyset \vdash_I A$ if A is I-valid, and hence that our brand of "inclusive" quantification theory is complete as regards implication and validity.

Four extra lemmas will suffice for showing that $S \vdash_I A$ if S I-implies A.

Lemma 2. *If* $S \vdash A$, *then* $S \cup \{(\exists x)(f(x) \vee \sim f(x))\} \vdash_I A$.
Proof: Suppose the column made up of $A_1, A_2, \ldots, A_p$ counts as a derivation of A from S', where S' is S when S is finite, otherwise a finite subset of S; and for each i from 1 through p let B_i be $(\exists x)(f(x) \vee \sim f(x)) \supset A_i$. Then in view of **A1**, **A2**, and **R1** the column made up of $B_1, B_2, \ldots, B_p$ can be so added onto that it will count as an I-derivation of B_p from S'. Hence $S' \cup \{(\exists x)(f(x) \vee \sim f(x))\} \vdash_I A$ in view of **R1**. Hence $S \cup \{(\exists x)(f(x) \vee \sim f(x))\} \vdash_I A$.

Lemma 3. *Suppose '$\forall$' does not occur in any member of* $S \cup \{A\}$. *If every assignment of truth-values to the atomic formulas of* QC *fails to satisfy a member of S or satisfies A, then $S \vdash_I A$.*
Proof like that of MT1.5.23 on p. 75 of [6].

Lemma 4. $\{\sim(\exists x)(f(x) \vee \sim f(x))\} \vee \sim f(x))\} \vdash_I A \equiv A^*$, *where A^* is the $\emptyset$-associate of A.*

Proof by mathematical induction on the number of times '~', '⊃', and '∀' occur in A. Inductive step when A is of the sort $(\forall X)B$. By a few obvious moves $\vdash_I \sim(f(X) \lor \sim f(X)) \supset B$, hence in view of **R2**, **A5**, and **R1** $\vdash_I (\forall X)$ $\sim f(X) \lor \sim f(X)) \supset (\forall X)B$, and by a few obvious moves $\{\sim(\exists x)(f(x) \lor \sim f(x))\} \vdash_I (\forall X)B \equiv (p \supset p)$.

Lemma 5. *Let S^* consist of the $\varnothing$-associates of the members of S and A^* be the $\varnothing$-associate of A. If $S^* \vdash_I A^*$, then $S \cup \{\sim(\exists x)(f(x) \lor \sim f(x))\} \vdash_I A$.*
Proof by Lemma 4 and a number of routine moves.

Theorem 1. *If S I-implies A, then $S \vdash_I A$.*
Proof: Let S^* and A^* be as in Lemma 5, and S I-imply A. Then (a) S implies A as in Section 1, in which case $S \vdash A$ by Lemma 1, and hence $S \cup \{(\exists x)(f(x) \lor \sim f(x))\} \vdash_I A$ by Lemma 2 and (b) every assignment of truth-values to the atomic formulas of QC fails to satisfy a member of S^* or satisfies A^*, in which case $S^* \vdash_I A^*$ by Lemma 3, and hence $S \cup \{\sim(\exists x)(f(x) \lor \sim f(x))\} \vdash_I A$ by Lemma 5. Hence Theorem 1 by a few obvious moves.[10]

3. Natural Deduction in "Inclusive" Quantification Theory.

Rules **R**, **HE**, **HI**, **NE**, and **NI** in Section 1.2 of [6], plus the two rules **∀E** and **∀I** below for '∀', are readily shown to permit deduction by Fitch's subordinate proof method of a formula A of QC from a finite set S of formulas of QC whenever $S \vdash_I A$ (and, hence, whenever S I-implies A).[11]

∀E	1	A_1		∀I	1	A_1	
	2	A_2			2	A_2	
	.	.			.	.	
	n	A_n			n	A_n	
	.	.			.	.	
	p	$(\exists x)(f(x) \lor \sim f(x))$			p	$(\exists x)(f(x) \lor \sim f(x))$	
	.	.			.	.	
	q	$(\forall X)B$			q	$B(Y/X)$	
	.	.					
	r	$B(Y/X)$	$(\forall E, p, q)$		$q+1$	$(\forall X)B$	$(\forall I, p, q)$

Restriction: In ∀I the individual variables Y is not to occur free in any one of $A_1, A_2, \ldots, A_n$, and $(\forall X)B$.

Deductions (from the null set of formulas of QC) of formulas of QC of the sorts **A4**, **A5**, and **A6'** are as follows:

1	A	
2	$(\exists x)(f(x) \vee \sim f(x))$	
3	A	(**R**, 1)
4	$(\forall X)A$	($\forall$**I**, 2, 3)
5	$A \supset (\forall X)A$	(**HI**, 1, 4)

1	$(\exists x)(f(x) \vee \sim f(x))$	
2	$(\forall X)A$	
3	$(\exists x)(f(x) \vee \sim f(x))$	(**R**, 1)
4	$(\forall X)A$	(**R**, 2)
5	$A(Y/X)$	($\forall$**E**, 3, 4)
6	$(\forall X)A \supset A(Y/X)$	(**HI**, 2, 5)
7	$(\exists x)(f(x) \vee \sim f(x)) \supset ((\forall X)A \supset A(Y/X))$	(**HI**, 1, 6)

1	$(\forall X)(A \supset B)$	
2	$(\forall X)A$	
3	$(\exists x)(f(x) \vee \sim f(x))$	
4	$(\exists x)(f(x) \vee \sim f(x))$	(**R**, 3)
5	$(\forall X)(A \supset B)$	(**R**, 1)
6	$A \supset B$	($\forall$**E**, 4, 5)
7	$(\forall X)A$	(**R**, 2)
8	A	($\forall$**E**, 4, 7)
9	B	(**HE**, 6, 8)
10	$(\forall X)B$	($\forall$**I**, 3, 9)
11	$(\forall X)A \supset (\forall X)B$	(**HI**, 2, 10)
12	$(\forall X)(A \supset B) \supset ((\forall X)A \supset (\forall X)B)$	(**HI**, 1, 11).

4. Closing Remarks. In [11] the $\varnothing$-associate of a formula of QC of the sort $(\forall X)B$ is taken to be B^*, the $\varnothing$-associate of B, when X does not occur free in B

(otherwise, to be '$p \supset p$' as in Section 2).[12] A brand of "inclusive" quantification theory that suits this account of $A*$ (and still abides by option (i)) can be had by turning in axiom schema **A5** of Section 1 for

A5'. $(\forall X)(A \supset B) \supset ((\forall X)A \supset (\forall X)B)$, where X occurs free in B,[13]

and turning in axiom schema **A6** for two axiom schemata: **A6'** and

A6''. $(\forall X)A \supset A$, where X does not occur free in A.

Note indeed that under Mostowski's account of $A*$ the formula '$(\forall x)(f(x) \supset p) \supset ((\forall x)f(x) \supset p)$', whose $\emptyset$-associate runs '$(p \supset p) \supset ((p \supset p) \supset p)$', does not hold for the empty domain, whereas formulas of QC of the sort **A6''**, having $A \supset A$ as their $\emptyset$-associate, hold for it.

Option (ii) calls, as expected, for a definition of implication of its own, A in this case being said to be I-implied by S if: (a) when A *is open*, S implies A as in Section 1, and (b) when A is closed, S implies A as in Section 1 and every assignment of truth-values to the atomic formulas of QC fails to satisfy the $\emptyset$-associate of a *closed* member of S or satisfies the $\emptyset$-associate of A.[14] A brand of "inclusive" quantification theory that abides by option (ii) and suits the account of $A*$ in Section 2 can be had by turning in axiom schema **A6** for

A6'''. $(\forall X)A \supset A(Y/X)$, where X occurs free in A:[15]

and turning in **R1** (Modus Ponens) for either one of the following two rules, due to Mostowski and Schneider, respectively:

R1'. B follows from A and $A \supset B$, so long as every individual variable of QC that occurs free in A also occurs free in B,

and

R1''. B follows from A and $A \supset B$, so long as A is closed or B is open.

One that abides by option (ii) and suits Mostowski's account of $A*$ can be had by turning in axiom schema **A5** for **A5'** above, and again turning in **R1** for either one of rules **R1'** and **R1''**. To those who may have winced at presupposing that "There's something", but would never dream of surrendering Modus Ponens for the likes of **R1'** and **R1''**, we dedicate this modest essay.

Notes

1. Options other than (i)–(ii) (among them, taking an open formula to automatically fail for the empty domain) present little interest.

2. Following [12], p. 177, we call *inclusive* (i.e., inclusive of $\emptyset$) a quantification theory that acknowledges $\emptyset$ as a domain, *exclusive* one that does not. So far as we know, option (i) was first advanced in [9], whose "inclusive" quantification theory abides like ours by (i), but unlike ours permits free individual variables to go without a value when the domain is not empty. For further details on the matter, see note 10.

3. We take '~', '$\supset$', and '$\forall$' to be the only primitive operators of QC; further operators like '$\lor$', '&', '≡', and '∃' are understood to be defined in the customary manner.

Open Formulas and the Empty Domain 97

4. The above account of derivability draws from [5] and [6]. For further details see the last paper in this volume.
5. For a fuller account of things, see [6], pp. 143–48.
6. For a detailed proof of Lemma 1, see [6], pp. 174–79.
7. When the more familiar rule: "$(\forall X)A$ follows from A," does duty for **R2**, the above account of derivability must be made to read as in [10], pp. 131–132, if "exclusive" quantification theory is to prove complete as regards implication. Again see the last paper in this volume.
8. Informally speaking, A^* is the result of replacing every component of A of the sort $(\forall X)B$ by a formula, '$p \supset p$', which Quine would mark true.
9. The more general axiom schema:

A6$'_1$. $(\exists Z)B \supset ((\forall X)A \supset A(Y/X))$, where $A(Y/X)$ is as in **A6**,

would of course do in place of **A6'**; so would:

A6$'_2$. $\sim(\forall Z)B \supset ((\forall X)A \supset A(Y/X))$, where $A(Y/X)$ is as in **A6**.

10. An "inclusive" quantification theory with identity that abides by option (i) can be had by drafting as extra axioms all formulas of either one of the two sorts:

A7. $X = X$

and

A8. $X = Y \supset (A \supset A(Y//X))$, where A is atomic and $A(Y//X)$ is like A except for displaying Y at zero or where A displays X.

Or again by drafting as axioms all formulas that count as axioms in [7], *plus* all formulas of the sort $(\exists x)(f(x) \vee \sim f(x)) \supset (\exists Y)(Y = X)$, where X and Y are distinct from each other, or of the sort $(\exists Z)(Z = X) \supset (\exists Z)(Z = Y)$, where X, Y, and Z are all distinct from one another. The axiom schema $(\exists x)(f(x) \vee \sim f(x)) \supset (\exists Y)(Y = X)$, where X and Y are distinct from each other, obviously guarantees that if the domain is not empty, free individual variables all go with a value.

11. In **∀E** any formula of QC of the sort $(\exists Z)C$ (or the sort $\sim(\forall Z)C$) could do for '$(\exists x)(f(x) \vee \sim f(x))$'. In **∀I** any *valid* formula of QC of the sort $(\exists Z)C$ (or the sort $\sim(\forall Z)C$) could do for '$(\exists x)(f(x) \vee \sim f(x))$'.
12. To suit Mostowski's account of A^*, Quine's test must be amended to read: "When ascertaining whether a formula A of QC holds for the empty domain, replace every component of A of the sort $(\forall X)B$ by B if X does not occur free in B, mark true the remaining components of A of the sort $(\forall X)B$, and apply truth-table considerations."
13. Or for any one of

$$(\exists x)(f(x) \vee \sim f(x)) \supset ((\forall X)(A \supset B) \supset ((\forall X)A \supset (\forall X)B),$$

$$(\exists Y)C \supset ((\forall X)(A \supset B) \supset ((\forall X)A \supset (\forall X)B)), \text{ where } Y \text{ occurs free in } C,$$

and

$$\sim(\forall Y)C \supset ((\forall X)(A \supset B) \supset ((\forall X)A \supset (\forall X)B)), \text{ where } Y \text{ occurs free in } C.$$

Lemma 4 calls for a fresh proof when **A5** is turned in for one of these three axiom schemata; Lemma 2 does when **A5** is turned in for **A5'**.

14. Note as regards (a) that under option (ii) A, when open, automatically holds for the empty domain, and as regards (b) that the open members of S are ignored because taken to automatically hold for the empty domain.
15. Note that '$(p \supset p) \supset p$', the $\emptyset$-associate of '$(\forall x)p \supset p$', is not a tautology. Hence the restriction "where X occurs free in A."

References

[1] Church, A. 1951. "A Formulation of the Logic of Sense and Denotation." *Structure, Method, and Meaning*, eds. P. Henle *et al*, pp. 3–24. New York: Liberal Arts Press.

[2] Hailperin, T. 1953. "Quantification Theory and Empty Individual Domains." *The Journal of Symbolic Logic* (hereafter *JSL*) 18: 197–200.

[3] Henkin, L. 1949. "The Completeness of the First-Order Functional Calculus." *JSL* 14: 159–66.

[4] Kalish, D., and Montague, R. 1965. "On Tarski's Formalization of Predicate Logic with Identity." *Archiv für mathematische Logik und Grundlagenforschung* 7: 81–101.

[5] Leblanc, H. 1966. "Two Shortcomings of Natural Deduction." *The Journal of Philosophy* 63: 29–37 (#25 in this volume).

[6] ———. 1966. *Techniques of Deductive Inference*. Englewood Cliffs: Prentice-Hall.

[7] ———. 1968. "On Meyer and Lambert's Quantificational Calculus FQ." *JSL* 33: 275–80.

[8] Leblanc, H., and Thomason, R. H. 1968. "Completeness Theorems for Some Presupposition-Free Logics." *Fundamenta Mathematicae* 62: 125–64 (#2 in this volume).

[9] Meyer, R. K., and Lambert, K. 1967. "Universally Free Logic and Standard Quantification Theory." *JSL* 33: 8–26.

[10] Montague, R., and Henkin, L. 1956. "On the Definition of 'Formal Deduction'." *JSL* 21: 129–36.

[11] Mostowski, A. 1951. "On the Rules of Proof in the Pure Functional Calculus of the First Order." *JSL* 16: 107–11.

[12] Quine, W. V. 1954. "Quantification and the Empty Domain." *JSL* 19: 177–79.

[13] ———. 1959. *Methods of Logic*, revised edition. New York: Henry Holt.

[14] Schneider, H. H. 1961. "A Syntactical Characterization of the Predicate Calculus with Identity and the Validity in all Individual Domains." *Portugaliae Mathematica* 20: 105–17.

6
A Liberated Version of S5
K. Lambert and R. K. Meyer, coauthors

Efforts to rid classical logic of undesirable existence assumptions have resulted in what Lambert calls *free logic*. Our present aim is to extend slightly the domain in which the writ of liberty runs. Specifically, we propose to extend slightly the well-known Kripke explication of the doctrine that necessary truth is truth in all possible worlds, and allow the possibility that there are no possible worlds. We shall supply and prove complete a version of S5 that conforms to this broader notion of necessary truth.[1]

Our modified S5, henceforth S5*, shall have wffs (A, B, C, etc.) built up as usual from a denumerable stock of sentence variables ('p', 'q', 'r', etc.), '$\sim$', '$\supset$', the necessity sign '$\Box$', and the two parentheses '(' and ')'. Other truth-functional connectives and modal operators are presumed defined in customary ways; in particular, $\Diamond A$ (possibly A) is presumed to be short for $\sim \Box \sim A$.

Now consider the following modification of the truth-value semantics for S5 that Kripke developed in [2] and subsequent papers in his.[2] Let an *assignment* be a function defined on the sentence variables of S5* and with values in {**T**, **F**}. Where f is an assignment, let an *assignment-class for* f be a class G of assignments such that (a) f belongs to G or else (b) G is empty. (The twist, of course, lies in condition (b)).[3] Where f is an assignment and G an assignment-class for f, let an *interpretation* be a function f_G recursively defined on the wffs of S5*, with values in {**T**, **F**} and subject to the following four conditions:
 (i) If A is a sentence variable of S5*, then $f_G(A) = f(A)$,
 (ii) $f_G(\sim A) = $ **T** if and only if $f_G(A) = $ **F**,
 (iii) $f_G(A \supset B) = $ **T** if and only if $f_G(A) = $ **F** or $f_G(B) = $ **T**, and
 (iv) $f_G(\Box A) = $ **T** if and only if, for every member h of G, $h_G(A) = $ **T**.
 (Hence, in particular, $f_G(\Box A) = $ **T** for every empty G.)
Finally, let a wff A of S5* be *valid** if and only if A has the value **T** on all possible interpretations.[1]

To pause for a second on the semantics of S5*, take a sentence to be *logically true* if it arises by substitution from a valid* wff of S5*. It follows from the above that no wff of S5* of the sort $\Diamond A$ is valid*, hence that no sentence

99

of the sort $\Diamond A$ is logically true. From the standpoint of S5*, logic does not presuppose that there are possible worlds; accordingly, there are no purely logical grounds for saying of any sentence A that A is true in some possible world. On the other hand, we do not deny logical truth wholesale to sentences of the sort $\Box A$, nor for that matter to sentences without modal operators. Were there no possible world, some sentences would still, we hold, be true by logic alone, among them: '$\Box$(Socrates skipped town or he didn't)' and 'If Socrates had a wife, then he did'.[5]

We next propose an axiom set for S5*, which we shall prove both sound and complete with respect to the above semantics. It is an adaptation of an axiom set supplied in [3] for a non-modal quantificational calculus whose theorems are valid in all domains including the empty one; as a result, S5* bears the same relationship to the monadic fragment of the quantificational calculus of [3] that S5 bears to the standard monadic quantificational calculus.[6] The axioms of S5* are given by the following five schemata:

A1. $\Box(A \supset B) \supset (\Box A \supset \Box B)$,

A2. $A \supset \Box A$, provided every sentence variable occurring in A occurs in a well-formed part of A of the sort $\Box B$,

A3. $\Diamond A \supset (\Box B \supset B)$,

A4. A, where A is truth-functionally valid, and

A5. $\Box A$, where A is an axiom.

The sole rule of inference of S5* is Modus Ponens—from A and $A \supset B$ infer B. Soundness relative to the above semantics is trivial; as is usual in such cases, one need only observe that the axioms of S5* are valid*, and that validity* is preserved under Modus Ponens.

Completeness relative to the above semantics calls for one definition and four lemmas. Where A is a wff of S5*, let the *null-associate* A_0 of A be the result of replacing every well-formed part of A of the sort $\Box B$ by '$p \supset p$'. We first show:

Lemma 1. *If a wff A of S5* is valid*, then A_0 is provable in S5*.*
Proof: Suppose A is valid*. Then A has the value **T** on all interpretations f_G for which G is empty. But on these interpretations a wff of S5* of the sort $\Box B$ has the same values as '$p \supset p$'. Hence A_0 has the value **T** on all interpretations f_G for which G is empty. Hence A_0 is truth-functionally valid. Hence A_0 is an instance of **A4**.

We next show:

Lemma 2. *Let A be a wff of S5*; $\Box B_1$, $\Box B_2$, . . . , $\Box B_n$ ($n \geq 0$) being in some arbitrary order all the well-formed parts of A of the sort $\Box C$, let B be (. . .(B_1 & B_2) & . . .) & B_n if $n > 0$, otherwise be '$p \supset p$'; and let D be an arbitrary well-formed part of A. Then*

$$\Box B \supset (D_0 \equiv D) \tag{1}$$

is provable in S5*.
Proof by mathematical induction on the number k of occurrences of '$\sim$', '$\supset$', and '$\Box$' in D.
Base Case: $k = 0$. Then (1) counts as an instance of **A4**.
Inductive Case: Suppose first that $n = 0$. Then (1) counts again as an instance of **A4**. Next, suppose that $n > 0$ and D is of the sort $\sim E$ or the sort $E \supset F$. Then—given the hypothesis of the induction—(1) is provable in S5* by a few obvious moves. Finally, suppose that $n > 0$ and D is of the sort $\Box E$. Then D is one of $\Box B_1, \Box B_2, \ldots, \Box B_n$. Hence $B \supset E$ is an instance of **A4**, and hence $\Box(B \supset E)$ one of **A5** but $\Box(B \supset E) \supset (\Box B \supset \Box E)$ is an instance of **A1**. Hence $\Box B \supset \Box E$ is provable in S5* by application of Modus Ponens. Hence (1) is provable in S5* by a few obvious moves.

Lemma 3. *If a wff A of* S5* *is valid*, then $\Box B \supset A$ is provable in* S5* *for some wff B of* S5*.
Proof by Lemma 1, Lemma 2, and a few obvious moves.

It is readily verified that all the theorems of S5 can be obtained by Modus Ponens from **A1–A2, A4–A5**, and the following strengthened version of **A3**:

A3'. $\Box B \supset B$.

We avail ourselves of the fact when showing:

Lemma 4. *Let a wff A of* S5* *be provable in* S5. *Then, for every wff B of* S5*, $\Diamond \sim B \supset A$ is provable in* S5*.
Proof: Let the column made up of $C_1, C_2, \ldots, C_p$ (in that order) constitute a proof of A in S5. It is readily shown by mathematical induction on p that for each i from l through p the wff $\Diamond \sim B \supset C_i$ is provable in S5*. For suppose C_i is an instance of **A3'**. Then $\Diamond \sim B \supset C_i$ is one of **A3**. Or suppose C_i is an instance of **A1, A2, A4**, or **A5**. Since $C_i \supset (\Diamond \sim B \supset C_i)$ is an instance of **A4**, then $\Diamond \sim B \supset C_i$ is provable in S5* by application of Modus Ponens. Or suppose C_i follows from two previous entries C_g and $C_g \supset C_i (= C_h)$ by application of Modus Ponens, and suppose $\Diamond \sim B \supset C_g$ and $\Diamond \sim B \supset C_h$ are both provable in S5*. Since $(\Diamond \sim B \supset C_h) \supset ((\Diamond \sim B \supset C_g) \supset (\Diamond \sim B \supset C_i))$ is an instance of **A4**, $\Diamond \sim B \supset C_i$ is provable in S5* by two applications of Modus Ponens.

Completeness is now at hand:

Theorem 1. *If a wff A of* S5* *is valid*, then A is provable in* S5*.
Proof: Suppose A is valid*. Then A is valid in Kripke's sense and hence provable in S5. Hence, by Lemma 4, $\Diamond \sim B \supset A$ is provable in S5* for every wff B of S5*; and hence, by a few obvious moves, so is $\sim \Box B \supset A$. But, by Lemma 3, $\Box B \supset A$ is provable in S5* for some wff B of S5*. Hence both $\sim \Box B \supset A$

and $\Box B \supset A$ are provable in S5* for some wff B of S5*. But $(\sim\Box B \supset A) \supset ((\Box B \supset A) \supset A)$ is an instance of **A4**. Hence A is provable in S5* by two applications of Modus Ponens.

In conclusion, we wish to note that other modal logics besides S5* (M*, S4*, etc.) can be gotten by analogous adaptations of Kripke's semantics;[7] so, for that matter, can be various subsystems of S5*, in which **A3'** is further weakened.[8] Free modal quantificational logic also beckons. But let this suffice as a first foray into the wonderland of what must, and might, be.

Notes

1. An approach to modal logic with certain affinities to the present one was discussed by Milton Fisk in his contribution to a colloquium on free logic at East Lansing, Michigan, in June of 1967.
2. See also Massey [5].
3. I.e., dropping (b) yields the Kripke semantics for S5.
4. Note that if A has the value **T** on all interpretations f_G for which G is empty, then A is truth-functionally valid, and vice-versa. We shall avail ourselves of the fact below.
5. Łukasiewicz argues in [4] against any wff of the sort $\Box A$ being valid. This too has its point (though not for S5*), but—in our opinion, at any rate—wffs of the sort $\Diamond A$ rather than the sort $\Box A$ involve definite (though minimal) ontological assumptions which logic should eschew.
6. Specifically, let QC_1^* be the monadic fragment of the system of [3], A transformation T that takes theorems of S5* into theorems of QC_1^* (and non-theorems into non-theorems) is as follows: Let 'p', 'q', 'r', 'p'', 'q'', . . . , be (in alphabetic order) the sentence variables of S5*, and 'F', 'G', 'H', 'F'', 'G'', . . . , be (again in alphabetic order) the monadic predicate variables of QC_1^*; where 'x' is the alphabetically first individual variable of QC_1^*, let $T('p') = $ '$F(x)$', $T('q') = $ '$G(x)$', . . . ; and let $T(\sim A) = \sim T(A)$, $T(A \supset B) = T(A) \supset T(B)$, and $T(\Box A) = (\forall x)T(A)$. Then A is provable in S5* if and only if $T(A)$ is provable in QC_1^*, as is easily shown using [3] and Theorem 1 below. T, we note, is a one-to-one mapping of the set of the wffs of S5* onto the set of (what Quine calls in [8]) the *uniform* monadic wffs of QC_1^*, and hence S5* is isomorphic to this fragment of QC_1^*. That A is provable in S5 if and only if $T(A)$ is provable in the standard monadic quantificational calculus is well known; see [1], Chapter 2, Section 1.
7. See among others [7] (where M is referred to as T.)
8. For example, consider the system S5** whose theorems are as follows: A is provable in S5** if and only if $T(A)$ is provable in Lambert's free quantificational calculus in [6], where T is the transformation defined in note 6. Not only are **A3** and hence **A3'** unprovable in S5**; so are all but the weakest analogues of **A3** and **A3'**.

References

[1] Feys, R. 1965. *Modal Logics*, ed. J. Dopp. Louvain: Nauwelaerts.
[2] Kripke, S. 1959. "A Completeness Theorem in Modal Logic." *The Journal of Symbolic Logic* (hereafter *JSL*) 24: 1–14.
[3] Leblanc, H., and Meyer, R. K. 1969. "Open Formulas and the Empty Domain." *Archiv für mathematische Logik und Grundlagenforschung* 12: 78–84 (#5 in this volume).
[4] Łukasiewicz, J. 1951. *Aristotle's Syllogistic*. Oxford: The Clarendon Press.
[5] Massey, G. J. 1966. "The Theory of Truth Tabular Connectives, Both Truth Functional and Modal." *JSL* 31: 593–608.
[6] Meyer, R. K., and Lambert, K. 1968. "Universally Free Logic and Standard Quantification Theory." *JSL* 33: 8–26.
[7] Morgan, C. G. 1970. "Weak Liberated Versions of **T** and S4." *JSL* 40: 25–36.
[8] Quine, W. V. 1959. *Methods of Logic*, revised edition. New York: Holt.

7

On Dispensing with Things and Worlds

Some like their logic mixed with a lot of ontology. To them first-order logic, for example, adjudicates on basic matters of existence, and any semantic account of it should come with things, sets of things, and relations between things. They likewise think of modal logic as adjudicating on basic questions of possibility, and to them any semantic account of it should be complete with possible worlds, possible individuals, and so on.

Others prefer their logic straight. They view it as a handbook (of a highly sophisticated kind, to be sure) for drawing inferences. Of course, there are things, and if one is to discourse about them, he must—sooner or later—think of them as belonging to sets, bearing relations to one another, and so on. But first-order logic *can be, and hence is perhaps best*, explicated without recourse to "models": *What is dispensable simply is not of the essence*. And those who so wish may of course ponder over possible worlds, possible individuals, ways in which the latter preserve their identity from one possible world to another, and so on. But modal logic *can be, and hence is perhaps best*, explicated without recourse to (Leibniz's and) Kripke's musings.[1]

The present paper is a report on recent successes at ridding logic of much expendable ontology, and in particular at making of modal logic a sheer manual of inference.

From a model-theoretic viewpoint, the formula

(1) $\quad (\exists x)(f(x) \lor \sim f(x))$

demands that "bound" variables have values (or, as the matter has been put, that there exist things); and the formula

(2) $\quad (\exists x)(f(x) \lor \sim f(x)) \supset (g(y) \supset (\exists x)g(x))$

demands that "free" variables have values (hence, that free variables stand for designating terms) when bound variables have values. Borrowing in part from Lambert, I shall study in Section 1 a variant of QC (the first-order quantificational calculus) which bars proof of formulas (1) and (2).[2]

The returns, however, are still modest ones. So, moving on, I shall present in Section 2 a new semantics for QC which does without models at all. Quantifications will be understood *substitutionally*, and validity explicated by means of truth-value assignments to the atomic well-formed formulas of QC. The semantics in question, known as *truth-value semantics*,[3] makes for innocuous readings of formulas (1) and (2). To meet all preferences, though, I shall include a variant of it suiting Lambert's QC.

Lastly, I shall treat in Section 3 of eight modal logics with quantifiers, and supply a truth-value interpretation of each. (In the first four of these logics *both* the "Barcan formula"

$$(\forall x)\Box f(x) \supset \Box(\forall x)f(x)$$

and its converse will be provable, whereas in the last four neither one will be.) Besides truth-value assignments I shall employ there sets of truth-value assignments and a relation R (like that of Kripke) on these sets. A recent paper by Dunn would suggest that R is dispensable.[4] But possible worlds and possible individuals will be gone, at any rate, and with them a good deal of needless ontology.

1. Most presentations of QC use just one run of individual variables, to wit: 'x', 'y', 'z', and so on,[5] and then declare some of their occurrences—in well-formed formulas of QC—*bound*, the rest *free*. The first two occurrences of 'x' in

$$(\forall x)f(x) \supset f(x),$$

for example, would be declared bound, the third one free; both occurrences of 'x' in

$$(\forall x)f(x) \supset f(y)$$

would similarly be declared bound, the one occurrence of 'y' free; and so on.

I implicitly adhered to that practice on p. 103, but henceforth I shall use two runs of individual symbols: (1) 'x', 'y', 'z', and so on, for which I save the appellation 'individual variables', and (2) 'a', 'b', 'c', and so on, to be known as *individual parameters*. In well-formed formulas of QC, 'x', 'y', 'z', and so on, will always "occur bound," whereas 'a', 'b', 'c', and so on, will always "occur free." So I shall write, say,

$$(\forall x)f(x) \supset f(a)$$

where others would '$(\forall x)f(x) \supset f(x)$', or '$(\forall x)f(x) \supset f(y)$', or '$(\forall x)f(x) \supset f(z)$'. However, in this part of the paper, formulas like '$(\forall x)f(x) \supset f(x)$', '$(\forall x)f(x) \supset f(y)$', and so on, though not acknowledged as well-formed, will nonetheless play some role, and I shall refer to them as *quasi*-well-formed formulas. So, 'x', 'y', 'z', and so on, though never occurring free in well-formed formulas, will occasionally do so in quasi-well-formed ones.

For uniformity's sake I shall likewise call the letters 'p', 'q', 'r', and so on,

On Dispensing with Things and Worlds   105

sentence parameters; and the letters '*f*', '*g*', '*h*', and so on, *predicate parameters*. These, of course, are not quantified in QC.

The primitive symbols of QC will thus be the two connectives '∼' and '⊃', the one quantifier symbol '∀',[6] the two parentheses '(' and ')', the comma ',', $\aleph_0$ individual variables (referred to by means of '*X*' and '*Y*'), $\aleph_0$ individual parameters (referred to by means of '*P*'), $\aleph_0$ sentence parameters, and—for each *k* from 1 on—$\aleph_0$ *k*-adic predicate parameters (referred to by means of 'F^k').[7] The formulas of QC will be, as usual, all finite (but non-empty) sequences of primitive symbols of QC. And, where *A* is a formula of QC, and *I* and *I'* are two individual symbols of QC, $(A)(I'/I)$ should be understood as the result of putting *I'* everywhere in *A* for *I*.

The well-formed formulas (wffs, for short) of QC will be all sentence parameters of QC, plus all formulas of QC of one of the following four kinds: (1) $F^k(P_1,P_2, \ldots ,P_k)$, where F^k is a *k*-adic predicate parameter, and P_1, $P_2, \ldots, P_k$ are (not necessarily distinct) individual parameters, (2) ∼*A*, where *A* is a wff, (3) $(A \supset B)$, where *A* and *B* are (not necessarily distinct) wffs, and (4) (∀*X*)*A*, where—for any individual parameter *P*—$(A)(P/X)$ is a wff. The quasi-well-formed formulas (qwffs, for short) of QC will be all formulas of QC of the kind $(A)(X/P)$, where *A* is a wff or qwff, *X* is an individual variable that does not occur in *A*, and *P* is an individual parameter that does. Finally, the atomic wffs of QC will be all wffs—and the atomic qwffs of QC will be all qwffs—of QC that contain no connective or quantifier symbol.

Clause (4) in my account of a wff insures that, where (∀*X*)*A* is well-formed, any result of putting an individual parameter of QC for *X* in *A* is likewise well-formed. So parameters can be substituted for variables without any ado.[8]

The interpretation normally placed upon QC runs as follows. First, you acknowledge as a *domain* (alternatively, as a range of values for the individual symbols of QC) *any non-empty set*.[9] Second, *D* being a domain, you acknowledge as a *D-valuation* any result of assigning a truth-value to each sentence parameter of QC, a member of *D* to each *individual symbol of* QC, and a subset of the Cartesian product

$$\underbrace{D \times D \times \ldots \times D}_{k \text{ times}} (= D^k)$$

to each *k*-adic predicate parameter of QC, this for each *k* from 1 on.[10] Third, *D* being a domain, V_D and V'_D being *D*-valuations, and *X* being an individual variable of QC, you count V'_D an *X-variant* of V_D if V'_D agrees with V_D on all the parameters of QC and on all the individual variables of QC other than *X*.[11] Fourth, *A* being a wff or qwff of QC, *D* being a domain, and V_D being a *D*-valuation, you take *A* to be true on V_D if:

(1) in case *A* is a sentence parameter, $V_D(A) = \mathbf{T}$,
(2) in case *A* is of the kind $F^k(I_1,I_2, \ldots ,I_k)$, $<V_D(I_1), V_D(I_2)$, $\ldots, V_D(I_k)>$—the *k*-tuple consisting of the members of *D* respectively assigned in V_D to the individual symbols $I_1, I_2, \ldots, I_k$—belongs to $V_D(F^k)$,

106   Part 1: Existence

(3) in case A is a negation $\sim B$, B is not true on V_D,
(4) in case A is a conditional $(B \supset C)$, B is not true on V_D or C is, and
(5) in case A is a quantification $(\forall X), B$, B is true on every X-variant of V_D.

And, fifth, you declare a wff A of QC *valid*, (that is, *valid in the standard or model-theoretic sense*), if, no matter the domain D nor the D-valuation V_D, A is true on V_D.

(More model-theoretic sounding definitions can be had by taking A *to be true in a model* $<D, V_D>$—D a domain and V_D a D-valuation— when A is true on V_D, and to be *valid* when A is true in every model. A wff of QC valid on either account will of course be valid on the other.)

Now count as your axioms all wffs of QC of the following kinds:[12]

A1. $A \supset (B \supset A)$

A2. $(A \supset (B \supset C)) \supset ((A \supset B) \supset (A \supset C))$

A3. $(\sim A \supset \sim B) \supset (B \supset A)$

A4. $(\forall X)(A \supset B) \supset ((\forall X)A \supset (\forall X)B)$

A5. $A \supset (\forall X)A$[13]

A6. $(\forall X)A \supset A(P/X)$, this for any individual parameter P of QC

and

A7. $(\forall x)A$, where—for any individual parameter P of QC foreign to $(\forall X)A$—$A(P/X)$ is an axiom;

and let Modus Ponens be your (sole) rule of inference.[14]

It can be shown, as in [5] or [6], that all and only those wffs of QC valid in the foregoing sense are provable. But, as was stressed on p. 105, domains must be non-empty, and—in D-valuations—members of these domains must be assigned to all of 'x', 'y', 'z', and so on, and all of 'a', 'b', 'c', and so on. So, *from a model-theoretic standpoint*, the axioms above do demand that the individual symbols of QC have values.

Lifting the requirement that 'x', 'y', 'z', and so on, have values is easy. First, weaken **A6** to read:

A6'. $(\exists x)(f(x) \vee \sim f(x)) \supset ((\forall X)A \supset A(P/X))$

Then, acknowledge $\emptyset$ as a domain; understand by a $\emptyset$-*valuation* any result of assigning a truth-value to each atomic wff or qwff of QC; take an atomic wff or qwff A of QC to be true on a $\emptyset$-valuation $V_\emptyset$ if $V_\emptyset(A) = \mathbf{T}$; take a negation $\sim A$ of QC to be true on $V_\emptyset$ if A is not; take a conditional $A \supset B$ to be true on $V_\emptyset$ if A is not true on $V_\emptyset$ or B is; mindful that $(\forall X)A$ is equivalent to $\sim(\exists X)\sim A$, take a quantification $(\forall X)A$ of QC to be automatically true on $V_\emptyset$; and declare a wff A of QC *valid'* if—for any domain D, empty or not, and any D-valuation V_D—A is true on V_D. As simple additions to Gödel's argument or Henkin's will show, all and only those wffs of QC that are valid' are provable

On Dispensing with Things and Worlds   107

by means of **A1** through **A5**, **A6′ A7** and Modus Ponens,[15] and hence
'$(\exists x)(f(x) \vee \sim f(x))$'—a wff false on any $\varnothing$-valuation—is no longer forthcoming as a theorem.

Note, however, that for any non-empty domain D each individual parameter of QC is still assigned, in any D-valuation V_D, a member of D. So our revised axioms still demand that 'a', 'b', 'c', and so on, have values when 'x', 'y', 'z', and so on do.[16]

Lifting that requirement too calls for more drastic measures. **A6**—again the culprit—is readily weakened to suit the occasion. Run it as Lambert did in [12]:

A6$_1$. $(\forall Y)((\forall X)A \supset A(Y/X))$,

and adopt an extra axiom schema, to wit:

A6$_2$. $(\forall X)(\forall Y)A \supset (\forall Y)(\forall X)A$.[17]

But the notion of a D-valuation for non-empty D, and that of an X-variant of a D-valuation, must be thoroughly revamped.

Talking now of a D-valuation *relative to a set Σ of individual parameters of QC* (said set Σ possibly empty), *one allocates members of D only to those individual parameters of QC that belong to Σ, and then assigns a truth-value to each atomic wff or qwff of QC that contains an individual parameter of QC not in Σ*. However, to preserve the equivalence of wffs like '$(\forall x)f(x, a)$' and '$(\forall y)f(y, a)$', we must require that—for any two individual symbols I and I' of QC—A and $A(I'/I)$ be assigned the same truth-value when I and I' are assigned the same member of D.

Turning to the other task, let D be a non-empty domain, Σ be a set of individual parameters of QC, $V_{D,\Sigma}$ and $V'_{D,\Sigma}$ be D-valuations relative to Σ, and X be an individual variable of QC. If $V'_{D,\Sigma}$ is to count as an X-variant of $V_{D,\Sigma}$, $V'_{D,\Sigma}$ must of course agree with $V_{D,\Sigma}$ on all the parameters of QC, all the individual variables of QC other than X, and all the atomic wffs or qwffs of QC that are assigned a truth-value in $V_{D,\Sigma}$ and do not contain X. Furthermore, when $V'_{D,\Sigma}(X)$ is not assigned in $V_{D,\Sigma}$ to any individual symbol of QC, $V'_{D,\Sigma}$ should also agree with $V_{D,\Sigma}$ on any atomic qwff A of QC that is assigned a truth-value in $V_{D,\Sigma}$ and contains X. Suppose, however, that $V'_{D,\Sigma}(X)$ is already assigned in $V_{D,\Sigma}$ to one or more individual symbols of QC. To preserve again the equivalence of wffs like '$(\forall x)f(x, a)$' and '$(\forall y)f(y, a)$', we must require that, for any individual symbol I of QC such that $V'_{D,\Sigma}(X) = V_{D,\Sigma}(I)$, A be assigned in $V'_{D,\Sigma}$ the truth-value assigned in $V_{D,\Sigma}$ to $A(I/X)$ (rather than the one assigned to A).

This done, take a quantification $(\forall x)A$ of QC to be true—for a non-empty domain D and a set Σ of individual parameters of QC—on a D-valuation $V_{D,\Sigma}$ relative to Σ if A is true on $V_{D,\Sigma}$ in case X is foreign to A, otherwise if A is true on every X-variant of $V_{D,\Sigma}$;[18] and take a wff A of QC to be *valid''* if (1) for every $\varnothing$-valuation $V_\varnothing$, A is true on $V_\varnothing$ and (2) for every non-empty domain D, every set Σ of individual parameters of QC, and every D-valuation $V_{D,\Sigma}$ relative to Σ, A is true on $V_{D,\Sigma}$.

108 *Part 1: Existence*

As a long (and somewhat complicated) argument will show, all and only those wffs of QC that are valid'' are provable in QC,[19] and hence '$(\exists x)(f(x) \lor \sim f(x)) \supset (g(a) \supset (\exists x)g(x))$'—a wff false for non-empty D on any D-valuation relative to $\varnothing$ that assigns **T** to '$g(a)$' and $\varnothing$ to 'g'—is no longer forthcoming as a theorem.

So, touched up as in [12], QC no longer requires (model-theoretically speaking) that 'x', 'y', 'z', and so on, have values; nor—when they do—that 'a', 'b', 'c', and so on, also have values. But, as promised earlier, more substantial savings are in store.

2. When axiomated as on p. 106,[20] QC can be shown to be complete by extending $\{\sim A\}$, A here any wff of QC not provable in QC, into a set S of wffs of QC which is maximally consistent and ω-complete.[21] A model $<D, V_D>$ is then constructed in which every member of S—hence, in particular, $\sim A$—is sure to be true. So, if as presumed A is not provable in QC, then there is a model in which $\sim A$ is true and, by rebound, A is not. So, if a wff of QC is true in every model (that is, valid), then the wff is provable in QC.

The model $<D, V_D>$ used in the foregoing proof has an important feature: each member of D is assigned in V_D to an individual symbol of QC. This peculiarity, when fully exploited, yields a whole new semantics for QC: it bridges the gap between *models* and (what I call) *truth-value assignments*, and thereby permits proof that all and only the wffs of QC true on all true-value assignments are theorems of QC.

To go more fully into the matter, understand by a *truth-value assignment* (for QC) any result of assigning one of the two truth-values **T** and **F** to each atomic wff of QC. Where A is a wff of QC and α a truth-value assignment, take A to be true on α if:

(1) in case A is atomic, $\alpha(A) = $ **T**,
(2) in case A is a negation $\sim B$, B is not true on α,
(3) in case A is a conditional $B \supset C$, B is not true on α or C is,

and

(4) in case A is a quantification $(\forall X)B$, every result of putting an individual parameter for X in B (that is, every substitution instance $(\forall X)B$) is true on α.

Call a model $<D, V_D>$ a *Henkin model* if for every member d of D there is an individual parameter P of QC such that $V_D(P) = d$. And by the *truth-value counterpart of a Henkin model* $<D, V_D>$ understand the result of assigning **T** to all atomic wffs of QC true on V_D, and **F** to the rest.

It is readily shown that a wff A of QC is true in a Henkin model $<D, V_D>$ if and only if A is true on the truth-value counterpart α of $<D, V_D>$. The proof is by mathematical induction on the number k of occurrences of '$\sim$', '$\supset$', and '$\forall$' in A. Suppose first that $k = 0$. Then A is atomic, and by the very construction of α is true on V_D if and only if true on α. Suppose next that the result to be proved holds true for any wff of QC with fewer than k occurrences of '$\sim$', '$\supset$', and '$\forall$'. When A is a negation $\sim B$ or a conditional $B \supset C$, the inductive hypothesis immediately yields that A is true on V_D if and only if true on α. So only one case remains to be covered: that where A is a quantification $(\forall X)B$.

By definition $(\forall X)B$ is true on V_D if and only if B is true on every X-variant of V_D, whereas $(\forall X)B$ is true on α if and only if $B(P/X)$ is true on α for every individual parameter P of QC. However, it can be shown that—with $<D, V_D>$ presumed to be a Henkin model—B is true on every X-variant of V_D if and only if $B(P/X)$ is true on V_D for every individual parameter P of QC. (For example, let V_D' be the X-variant of V_D such that $V_D'(X)$ is, say, $V_D(a)$. Then B will be true on V_D' if and only if $B(a/X)$ is true on V_D.) So the inductive hypothesis will again yield that A is true on V_D if and only if true on α.

The induction can thus be completed, and the members of the set S on p. 108 are now sure to be true on the truth-value counterpart of $<D, V_D>$ as well as on V_D. Hence any wff of QC true on all truth-value assignments is provable in QC. But, as the reader may wish to verify, any wff of QC provable in QC is true on all truth-value assignments. So, take a wff of QC to be *valid in the truth-value sense* if it is true on all truth-value assignments, and exactly the same wffs of QC as were valid in the standard sense will be valid in the truth-value sense.[22]

Discarded here is the whole paraphernalia of models in favor of just these:

(1) the two truth-values **T** and **F**

and

(2) assignments of the truth-values in (1) to the atomic wffs of QC—more formally, functions from the atomic wffs of QC to the truth-values in (1).

So first-order validity *can* be explicated without recourse to things, sets of things, and relations between things, indeed without appeal to any but the twin notions of truth and falsehood. The result should be welcome news to anyone with a stake in "pure" logic.

Under the present account of things, an existential quantification $(\exists X)A$ of QC is certified true on any truth-value assignment on which one of $A(a/X)$, $A(b/X)$, $A(c/X)$, and so on is true. So wffs which from a model-theoretic viewpoint demanded that variables have values, or that parameters have values when variables do, are now innocuously valid. For example,

$$(\exists x)(f(x) \vee \sim f(x))$$

turns out to be valid because, say, '$f(a) \vee \sim f(a)$' is true on any truth-value assignment; and

$$(\exists x)(f(x) \vee \sim f(x)) \supset (g(a) \supset (\exists x)g(x))$$

turns out to be valid because '$(\exists x)g(x)$' is true on any truth-value assignment that assigns **T** to '$g(a)$'.

However, theorems like these might still jolt some who—however first-order validity be explicated—would count a sentence

110 Part 1: Existence

$$(\exists x)(x \text{ is thus and so})$$

true only if putting a *designating* term for 'x' in

$$x \text{ is thus and so}$$

gave a truth. Readers of this persuasion could, of course, think of 'a', 'b', 'c', and so on, as standing for designating terms only.[23] Or they could adjust the foregoing semantics to suit their understanding of '$\exists$' and their choice of theorems for QC.

Indeed, A being a wff of QC, α a truth-value assignment, and Σ a (possibly empty) set of individual parameters of QC, take A to be *true on* α_Σ, that is, take A to be *true on α as relativized to Σ*, if:

(1') in case A is atomic, $\alpha(A) = \mathbf{T}$,
(2') in case A is a negation $\sim B$, B is not true on α_Σ,
(3') in case A is a conditional $B \supset C$, B is not true on α_Σ or C is,

and

(4') in case A is a quantification $(\forall X)B$, $B(P/X)$ is true on α_Σ for every member P of Σ,[24]

and take A to be valid'' *in the truth-value sense* if, no matter the truth-value assignment α nor the set Σ of individual parameters of QC, A is true on α_Σ. The argument in [14] is easily adapted to show that all and only the wffs of QC valid'' in the truth-value sense are provable by means of **A1** through **A5**, **A6$_1$**, **A6$_2$**, **A7**, and Modus Ponens. So '$(\exists x)(f(x) \vee \sim f(x))$' (which is false on any truth-value assignment relativized to $\emptyset$) and '$(\exists x)(f(x) \vee \sim f(x)) \supset (g(a) \supset (\exists x)g(x))$' (which is false on any truth-value assignment relativized to $\{b\}$ that assigns $\mathbf{T}$ to '$g(a)$' and $\mathbf{F}$ to '$g(b)$') are no longer forthcoming as theorems; and 'a', 'b', 'c', and so on, can now stand for *all* terms, that is, for *all* expressions which function as subjects or objects in sentences.

So far, I have exclusively talked of validity. Other semantic concepts can be explicated in terms of truth-value assignments. A key one is, of course, that of *simultaneous satisfiability* or—as some would rather say—*semantic consistency*. In standard semantics you take a set S of wffs of QC to be semantically consistent if there is a model in which every member of S is true, and you readily have proof that the set is semantically consistent if and only if no contradiction is derivable from it. In truth-value semantics you may likewise take S, *when S is finite*, to be semantically consistent if there is a truth-value assignment on which all the members of S are true (or, should **A6$_1$**–**A6$_2$** substitute for **A6**, if there is a truth-value assignment α and a set Σ of individual parameters of QC such that all the members of S are true on α_Σ). However, a problem arises in connection with some infinite sets of wffs.

Consider the set

$$\{f(a), f(b), f(c), \ldots, \sim(\forall x)f(x)\}$$

It is semantically consistent in the standard sense. Indeed, let D consist of, say, the two integers 1 and 2, and let V_D be any D-valuation that assigns 1 to all the individual symbols of QC and the subset $\{1\}$ of D to 'f'. The members of the set will all be true on V_D, and hence be true in the model $<D, V_D>$. Yet there is no truth-value assignment on which all of '$f(a)$', '$f(b)$', '$f(c)$', ..., and '$\sim(\forall x)f(x)$' are true: one of '$f(a)$', '$f(b)$', '$f(c)$', and so on, must be false on any truth-value assignment on which '$\sim(\forall x)f(x)$' is true, and '$\sim(\forall x)f(x)$' must be false on any truth-value assignment on which all of '$f(a)$', '$f(b)$', '$f(c)$', and so on, are true. (Nor—in case $A6_1$–$A6_2$ substitute for **A6**—is there, for any truth-value assignment α, a set Σ of individual parameters of QC such that all of '$f(a)$', '$f(b)$', '$f(c)$', ..., and '$\sim(\forall x)f(x)$' are true on α_Σ.)

The difficulty can be met in a number of ways. The simplest is to certify S, *when S is infinite*, semantically consistent in the truth-value sense if at least one finite subset of S is semantically consistent in that sense. Since '$f(a)$' and '$\sim(\forall x)f(x)$' are true on any truth-value assignment (on any truth-value assignment relativized to $\{b\}$) that assigns **T** to '$f(a)$' and **F** to '$f(b)$', set $\{f(a), \sim(\forall x)f(x)\}$ is semantically consistent in the truth-value sense, and hence so will be $\{f(a), f(b), f(c), \ldots, \sim(\forall x)f(x)\}$. More sophisticated handlings of the matter will be found in [13] and [14].

Higher-order quantificational calculi (both ramified and unramified) admit, as does QC, of a truth-value interpretation, and hence can be semantically explicated at bargain rates. The subject is covered in [16] and other papers in Part 2.

3. Modal logics with quantifiers have multiplied almost beyond reckoning since the publication of [1] and [3]. I shall study eight of them here, respectively labelled QC_M, QC_B ('B' for 'Brouwersche'), QC_4 ('4' for 'S4'), QC_5 ('5' for 'S5'), QC_M'', QC_B'', QC_4'', and QC_5''.[25] In all eight cases add '$\square$' to the list of primitive symbols on p. 105, count $\square A$ well-formed when A is, and use '$\Diamond A$' as short for '$\sim\square\sim A$'. The axiom schemata of my eight calculi are to be as in the following table, with **A8** through **A14** respectively reading:

A8. $\square(A \supset B) \supset (\square A \supset \square B)$

A9. $\square A \supset A$

A10. $\square A$, where A is an axiom

A11. $A \supset \square \Diamond A$

A12. $\square A \supset \square\square \Diamond A$

A13. $\Diamond A \supset \square \Diamond A$

and

A14. $(\forall X)\Box A \supset \Box(\forall X)A$

And Modus Ponens is again to be the sole rule of inference.

Table of Axiom Schemata

A1–A5	All eight calculi
A6	QC_M, QC_B, QC_4, and QC_5
$A6_1$–$A6_2$	QC_M'', QC_B'', QC_4'', and QC_5''
A7	All eight calculi
A8–A10	All eight calculi
A11	QC_B and QC_B''
A12	QC_4 and QC_4''
A13	QC_5 and QC_5''
A14	QC_M and QC_4

As the reader doubtless knows, wffs of the sort $(\forall X)\Box A \supset \Box(\forall X)A$ are provable by means of the axioms on p. 107, **A8–A10**, *plus* either one of **A11** and **A13**. And wffs of the sort $\Box(\forall X)A \supset (\forall X)\Box A$ are provable by means of the axioms on p. 107 and **A8–A10** alone. So both the Barcan formula and its converse turn up as theorems in the first four of my calculi. Neither formula, though, is provable in the last four.[26]

Kripke's semantics is best studied in separate installments.[27] So limit yourself initially to S5; K being a non-empty set (to Kripke a non-empty set of "possible worlds") and G being a member of K (to Kripke a "world" in K), understand by a *K-valuation function* any function that pairs with each member G of K a truth-value assignment (to the sentence parameters of S5); K being as before, Φ being a valuation for K, and G being a member of K, take a wff A of S5 to be *true on the triple* $<K, \Phi, G>$ if:

(1) in case A is a sentence parameter, A is assigned **T** in $\Phi(G)$,
(2) in case A is of the sort $\sim B$, B is not true on $<K, \Phi, G>$,
(3) in case A is of the sort $B \supset C$, B is not true on $<K, \Phi, G>$ or C is,

and

(4) in case A is of the sort $\Box B$, B is true on $<K, \Phi, H>$ for every member H of K;

and take a wff A of S5 to be *valid* if A is true on every triple $<K, \Phi, G>$ of the kind just described (that is, A is true on $<K, \Phi, G>$ no matter the non-empty set K, given any K no matter the valuation function Φ for K, and given any K and any Φ no matter the member G of K).

Proof can be retrieved from [9] that all and only those wffs of S5 valid in the

On Dispensing with Things and Worlds 113

foregoing sense are provable in S5 (that is, are provable by means of **A1** through **A3, A9** through **A11**, and Modus Ponens).

When turning in [10] to M, B, and S4, Kripke intercalates a relation R on K. To use M as a sample, he takes a wff A to M to be *true on a quadruple* $<K, \Phi, R, G>$, where R is an arbitrary *reflexive* relation on K, if:

(1) in case A is a sentence parameter, A is assigned **T** in $\Phi(G)$,
(2) in case A is of the sort $\sim B$, B is not true on $<K, \Phi, R, G>$,
(3) in case A is of the sort $B \supset C$, B is not true on $<K, \Phi, R, G>$ or C is,

and

(4) in case A is of the sort $\Box B$, B is true on $<K, \Phi, R, H>$ for every member H of K such that $R(G, H)$.

(It follows from these clauses that if $R(G, H)$ and A are true on $<K, \Phi, R, H>$, then $\Diamond A$ is true on $<K, \Phi, R, G>$, hence—informally—that any wff "true in a world H" is "possible in any world" that bears R to H.)

This done, Kripke takes a wff A of M to be *valid* if A is true on every quadruple of the sort $<K, \Phi, R, G>$, and goes on to show that all and only those wffs of M valid in this sense are probable in M.

Like results hold for B when R is required to be reflexive *and* symmetrical for S4 when R is required to be reflexive *and* transitive, and—expectedly enough—for S5 when R is required to be reflexive, symmetrical, and transitive.

Now for Kripke's handling of quantifications. I limit myself initially to QC_5'', where R is dispensable.[28]

(1) K being a non-empty set (of "possible worlds"), understand by a K-*domain function* any function that pairs with each ("world") G in K a non-empty set (said by Kripke to comprise "the individuals existing in world G");[29]

(2) K being a non-empty set, ψ being a domain function for K, and D being $\bigcup_{G \in K} \psi(G)$, understand by a $<K, \psi>$-*valuation of the parameters of* QC_5'' any result of assigning a truth-value to each sentence parameter of QC_5'', a member of D to each individual parameter of QC_5'', and a subset of D^k to each k-adic predicate parameter of QC_5'', this for each k from 1 on;

(3) K and ψ being as in (2), understand by a $<K, \psi>$-*valuation function for the parameters of* QC_5'' any function that pairs with each G in K a $<K, \psi>$-valuation of the parameters of QC_5'';

(4) K and Ψ being as in (2) and G being a member of K, understand by a $<K, \psi, G>$-*valuation of the variables of* QC_5'' any result of assigning a member of $\psi(G)$ to each individual variable of QC_5'';[30]

(5) K and ψ being as in (2), understand by a $<K, \psi>$-*valuation function for the variables of* QC_5'' any function that pairs with each G in K a $<K, \Phi, G>$-valuation of the variables of QC_5'';

(6) K, ψ, and G being as in (2), V being a $<K, \psi>$-valuation function for

the variables of QC_5'', and X being an individual variable of QC_5'', understand by an *X-variant of* $V(G)$ any $<K, \Phi, G>$-valuation of the variables of QC_5'' that is like $V(G)$ except for possibly assigning to X another member of $\Phi(G)$ than $V(G)$ does;

(7) K, ψ, and G being as in (2), P being a $<K,\psi>$-valuation function for the parameters of QC_5'', and V being one for the variables of QC_5'', take a wff or qwff A of QC_5'' to be true on the quintuple $<K,\psi,G,P(G),V(G)>$ if:

   (i) in case A is a sentence parameter, A is assigned **T** in $P(G)$,

   (ii) in case A is of the sort $F^k(I_1, \ldots, I_k)$, $<d_1, d_2, \ldots, d_k>$—the k-tuple consisting of the members of $\underset{G \epsilon K}{\cup} \psi(G)$ respectively assigned in $P(G)$ and/or $V(G)$ to $I_1, I_2, \ldots, I_k$—belongs to the subset of $\underset{G \epsilon K}{\cup} \psi(G)$ assigned in $P(G)$ to F^k,

   (iii) in case A is of the sort $\sim B$, B is not true on $<K, \psi, G, P(G), V(G)>$,

   (iv) in case A is of the sort $B \supset C$, B is not true on $<K, \psi, G, P(G), V(G)>$ or C is,

   (v) in case A is of the sort $\square B$, B is true on $<K, \psi, H, P(H), V(H)>$ for every member H of K, and

   (vi) in case A is of the sort $(\forall X)B$, B is true on $<K, \psi, G, P(G), V(G)'>$ for every X-variant $V(G)'$ of $V(G)$.

(8) By a *valuation of the atomic wffs of* QC_5'' understand any result of assigning a truth-value to each atomic wff of QC_5'';

(9) K being a non-empty set, understand by a *K-valuation function for the atomic wffs of* QC_5'' any function that pairs with each G in K a valuation of the atomic wffs of QC_5'';

(10) K being as in (9), G being a member of K, W being a K-valuation function for the atomic wffs of QC_5'', and A being a wff of QC_5'', take A to be automatically *true on the triple* $<K, G, W(G)>$ when A is of the sort $(\forall X)B$; otherwise, take A to be *true on* $<K, G, W(G)>$ if:

   (i) in case A is atomic, A is assigned **T** in $W(G)$,

   (ii) in case A is of the sort $\sim B$, B is not true on $<K, G, W(G)>$,

   (iii) in case A is of the sort $B \supset C$, B is not true on $<K, G, W(G)>$ or C is, and

   (iv) in case A is of the sort $\square B$, B is true on $<K, H, W(H)>$ for every member H of K.

This done, certify a wff A of QC_5'' *valid* if A is true on every quintuple of the sort $<K, \Phi, G, P(G), V(G)>$ and on every triple of the sort $<K, G, W(G)>$. Adaptation of Kripke's argument in [9] will show that all and only those wffs of QC_5'' valid in this sense are provable in QC_5'' (that is, provable by means of **A1** through **A5**, **A7** through **A11**, **A14**, and Modus Ponens).

Treatment in [11] of QC_M'', QC_B'', and QC_4'' calls again for a (binary) relation R on K, which in the case of QC_M'', you require to be reflexive, in that of QC_B'' to be reflexive and symmetrical, and in the case of QC_4'' to be reflexive and transitive. Sextuples of the sort $<K, \psi, R, G, P(G), V(G)>$ will then do duty for the quintuples $<K,\psi,G,P(G),V(G)>$ above, quadruples of the sort

$<K,R,G,W(G)>$ will do duty for the triples $<K,G,W(G)>$ above, and QC_5'' can again be accommodated within this broader framework by requiring R to be an equivalence relation.[31]

As Kripke notes, wffs of the sort $(\forall X(\Box A \supset \Box(\forall X)A$ will turn out to be valid if, for any two members G and G' of K such that $R(G,G')$, $\Psi(G')$ is required to be a subset of $\Psi(G)$, and wffs of the sort $\Box(\forall X)A \supset (\forall X)\Box A$ will if, for any two such members of K, $\Psi(G)$ is required to be a subset of $\Psi(G')$.

Kripke does not attend to calculi such as QC_M, QC_B, QC_4, and QC_5. To provide for these within his own semantics, drop the domain function ψ in favor of an arbitrary domain D common to *all* the worlds in the set K, (thus talking of a sextuple $<K,D,R,G,P(G),V(G)>$ where I just talked of $<K,\psi,R,G,P(G),V(G)>$), disregard (8)–(10) on p. 114, and take a wff A of, say, QC_M to be valid if A is true on every sextuple of the sort $<K,D,R,G,P(G),V(G)>$ for reflexive R. A will then be valid if and only if provable in QC_M (i.e., provable by means of the axioms on p. 107, **A8–A10, A14**, and Modus Ponens).[32]

Kripke's 1959 and 1963 papers were major breakthroughs, ranking with Gödel's and Henkin's completeness papers. They teem, though, with references to "possible worlds," "possible individuals," and the like, and you cannot delete these without robbing the account of its intuitive appeal. So to readers with more frugal tastes an alternative treatment of things may be welcome.

Using QC_M'' as a sample, understand by a *truth-value assignment* (for QC_M'') any result of assigning a truth-value to every atomic wff of QC_M''; K being a non-empty set of truth-value assignments, each relativized to a set of individual parameters of QC_M'', R being a reflexive relation on K, and α_Σ being a member of K, take a wff A of QC_M'' to be *true on the triple* $<K,R,\alpha_\Sigma>$ if:

(1) in case A is atomic, $\alpha_\Sigma (A) = $ **T**
(2) in case A is of the sort $\sim B$, B is not true on $<K,R,\alpha_\Sigma>$,
(3) in case A is of the sort $B \supset C$, B is not true on $<K,R,\alpha_\Sigma>$ or C is,
(4) in case A is of the sort $\Box B$, B is true on $<K,R,\alpha'_{\Sigma'}>$ for every member $\alpha'_{\Sigma'}$ of K such that $R(\alpha_\Sigma,\alpha'_{\Sigma'})$,

and

(5) in case A is of the sort $(\forall X)B$, $B(P/X)$ is true on $<K,R,\alpha_\Sigma>$ for every individual parameter P of QC_M'' in Σ;

and take a wff A of QC_M'' to be *valid in the truth-value sense* if A is true on every triple of the sort $<K,R,\alpha_\Sigma>$.

Note, by the way, that the individual parameters 'a', 'b', 'c', and so on, may be treated here as they were on p. 107. Kripke must think of them as drawing their values from possibly different worlds; we may think of them as simply standing for non-designating as well as designating terms. The savings are considerable.

116 *Part 1: Existence*

The wanted definitions for QC_B'', QC_4'', and QC_5'' can be had the usual way: Require in the case of QC_B'' that R be reflexive and symmetrical, in the case of QC_4'' that R be reflexive and transitive, and in the case of QC_5'' that R be reflexive, symmetrical, and transitive (or, in this last case, dispense with R altogether, use pairs of the sort $<K, \alpha_\Sigma>$ instead of triples, and take $\Box B$ to be true on $<K, \alpha_\Sigma>$ if B is true on $<K, \alpha'_\Sigma>$ for every member α'_Σ of K).

Finally, when it comes to QC_M, QC_B, QC_4, and QC_5, just think of K as a set of *unrelativized* truth-value assignments, use triples of the sort $<K, R, \alpha>$ rather than the sort $<K, R, \alpha_\Sigma>$, and certify $(\forall X)B$ true on $<K, R, \alpha>$ if $B(P/X)$ is true on $<K, R, \alpha>$ for every individual parameter P of your calculus.

Proof that any wff of, say, QC_M which is valid in my sense is provable in QC_M can be retrieved from [22] and [25]. So can proof that any wff of, say, QC_M'' which is valid in that sense is provable in QC_M''. In this case, though, some delicate maneuvers are needed to make up for the missing axiom schema **A14**.[33] The two proofs are then adjusted to cover the remaining six of my calculi. Details, which are too lengthy for inclusion here, can be found in [17] or retrieved from [2].

Another account of QC_M'', QC_B'', QC_4'', and QC_5'' which does without "possible worlds" and "possible individuals" can of course be found in Hintikka. It uses model sets in lieu of truth-value assignments, and sets of model sets (called *model systems*) in lieu of sets of truth-value assignments.[34]

So, the reader for whom the "real world" is already enough of a concern need not despair. The behavior of '$\Box$', like that of '$\forall$', can be explicated with a minimum of ontology, and inferences that employ '$\Box$' can be performed by all: those who deal in "other worlds" and the heathens who do not.[35]

Notes

1. In some passages Kripke describes the K in his triple $<G, K, R>$ as an arbitrary (non-empty) set, G as an arbitrary member of K, and R as an arbitrary reflexive relation on K (see, for example, [11], p. 84, lines 7 and 8). In other passages, though, he talks of K as the set of all "possible worlds," of G as the "real world," and of R as a relation of "relative possibility between worlds"; and deleting the latter passages robs Kripke's account of its intuitive appeal (see p. 115).

2. See [12], [15], and [19]. In previous writings I have understood the formula '$f(y) \supset (\exists x)f(x)$' as requiring that free variables have values (or stand for designating terms). However, '$(\exists x)(f(x) \lor \sim f(x)) \supset (g(y) \supset (\exists x)g(x))$', which under the account of p. 106 always evaluates to **T** when the domain is empty, but sometimes evaluates to **F** when it is not, suits my purpose better. (Whether any formula of QC requires that free variables have values when bound ones do not is a moot question which I would rather avoid here.)

3. The appellation was suggested to me by Quine. For a short history of truth-value semantics, see pp. 123–135; see also [16] and [17].

4. See [4].

5. That is, 'x', 'y', 'z', and their $\aleph_0$ accented variants 'x'', 'y'', 'z'', 'x''', 'y''', 'z''', and so on.

6. I presume the extra operators '&', '$\lor$', '$\equiv$', and '$\exists$' to be defined in the usual manner. So '$(\exists x)(f(x) \lor \sim f(x))$', for example, is short for '$\sim(\forall x)\sim(\sim f(x) \supset \sim f(x))$'.

7. Throughout 'f' and 'g' will serve as monadic predicate parameters.

8. Because of clause (4) formulas like '$(\forall x)(f(x) \supset (\forall x)g(x))$' in which identical quantifiers

overlap do not count as well-formed. But all of '$(\forall x)(f(x) \supset (\forall y)g(y))$', '$(\forall x)(f(x) \supset (\forall z)g(z))$', and so on, do and these well make up for the missing '$(\forall x)(f(x) \supset (\forall x)g(x))$'.

9. Note the italicized *"any."* It is a common misapprehension that only an "individual" should serve as a value of, say, 'x'. *Any*thing can.

10. Each monadic predicate parameter of QC is thereby assigned a set of members of D, each dyadic one a set of pairs of members of D (that is, a dyadic relation), each triadic one a set of triples of members of D (that is, a triadic relation), and so on.

11. And possibly X as well. Any D-valuation thus counts as one of its X-variants.

12. To abridge matters I drop from now on a number of easily restored parentheses.

13. With $A \supset (\forall X)A$ presumed here to be well-formed, $(\forall X)A$ is sure to be a "vacuous quantification."

14. **A7** is a congener of (ii) on p. 79, and because of it no rule of Generalization is needed here. See the closing paper in this volume for fuller details on the matter.

15. For proof of the result see [18], where **A6'** made its first appearance.

16. Note indeed that (2) on p. 103 is still forthcoming as a theorem.

17. Axiom schema **A6$_2$** did not appear in the original version of this paper, for I believed it then to be forthcoming as a theorem. But, as remarked on p. 74, note 7, there are grounds for suspecting it independent of **A1–A5**, **A6$_1''$**, and **A7**.

18. For fuller details on the matter, see pp. 61–63.

19. For proof of the result, see [19]. Different, but equivalent, accounts of things will be found in [23] and [26].

20. I.e., with **A6** (rather than **A6'** or **A6$_1$**) serving as *Specification Axiom*, and without **A6$_2$**, which under the circumstances is redundant.

21. This way of showing QC complete goes back to [6]. A set S of wffs of QC is said to be maximally consistent if S is *syntactically* consistent (that is, no contradiction is derivable from S) and would become syntactically inconsistent upon addition to S of any other wff of QC; and S is said to be ω-complete if a quantification $(\forall X)A$ is not derivable from S unless all the substitution instances of $(\forall X)A$ are also derivable from S.

22. For a detailed proof of the result, see [17]; see also [14].

23. Readers of [21] are asked to do just that. The text uses truth-value semantics as its official semantics.

24. In case A is an existential quantification $(\exists X)B$, A proves to be true on α_Σ if only if $B(P/X)$ is true on α_Σ for at least one member P of Σ; the parameter in Σ can thus be thought of as standing for designating terms only. Note that when Σ is $\emptyset$, $(\forall X)B$ is automatically true, and $(\exists X)B$ automatically false, on α_Σ.

25. I save the customary appellations 'M', 'B', 'S4', and 'S5' for modal logics without quantifiers (that is, for modal logics with just sentence parameters, '~', '$\supset$', '□', '(', and ')' as their primitive symbols).

26. On this matter see [8], pp. 181–82, and [17], pp. 228–29 and 240–41. Proofs of the Barcan formula and its converse make essential use of **A6**.

27. [9] deals exclusively with QC$_5$ (and hence S5); [10] extends the semantics [9] to M, B, and S4; and [11] extends the semantics of [10] to QC$_M''$, QC$_B''$, QC$_4''$, and QC$_5''$. Throughout I adapt Kripke's terminology and symbolism.

28. I depart in what follows from the original version of this paper, which—as R. J. Cosgrove noticed—was defective at one point.

29. Those individuals would of course be "real" ones when G is the "real" world, "merely possible" ones when G is not. How to determine individual d_G in world G and individual d_H in world H are the same has been widely discussed.

30. Note that in view of (2) and (5) the entire set D serves as the range of values of 'a', 'b', 'c', etc., whereas just its subset $\psi(G)$ serves as the range of values of 'x', 'y', 'z', etc. In effect, what Kripke has here are two domains: an *inner* ($\psi(G)$) and an *outer* one (D minus $\psi(G)$). See [20], where versions of QC$_=$ with $(\exists X)(X = P) \supset ((\forall X)A \supset A(P/X))$ as their *Specification Axiom* are accounted for in terms of inner and outer domains.

31. Kripke acknowledges only closed wffs as theorems of QC''_M, QC''_B, QC''_4, and QC''_5; but the restriction is inessential and—in my opinion—best lifted.

32. With one domain D common to all worlds in K, P and V may give way to a single valuation function, and hence sextuples give way to quintuples. Details are left to the reader.

33. See [17], Chapter 9 for full details.

34. See in particular [7]. For an extended variant of Hintikka's semantics, see [24].

35. Early drafts of this paper were read at SUNY at Buffalo and at a seminar on ontology run by the New York University Institute of Philosophy in 1970–71.

References

[1] Barcan, R. 1946. "A Functional Calculus of First-Order Based on Strict Implication." *The Journal of Symbolic Logic* (hereafter *JSL*) 11: 1–16.

[2] Barnes, R. P., and Gumb, R. D. 1979. "The Completeness of Presupposition-Free Tense Logic." *Zeitschrift für mathematische Logik und Grundlagen der Mathematik* (hereafter *ZMLGM*) 25:193–208.

[3] Carnap, R. 1946. "Modalities and Quantification." *JSL* 11: 33–64.

[4] Dunn, J. M. 1973. "A Truth-Value Semantics for Modal Logic." *Truth, Syntax and Modality*, pp. 87–100. Amsterdam: North-Holland.

[5] Gödel, K. 1930. "Die Vollständigkeit der Axiome des logischen Funktionenkalküls." *Monatshefte für Mathematik und Physik* 37: 349–60.

[6] Henkin, L. 1949. "The Completeness of the First-Order Functional Calculus." *JSL* 14: 159–66.

[7] Hintikka, J. 1969. *Models for Modalities*. Holland: Dordrecht.

[8] Hughes, G. E., and Cresswell, M. J. 1968. *An Introduction to Modal Logic*. London: Methuen.

[9] Kripke, S. 1959. "A Completeness Theorem in Modal Logic." *JSL* 24: 1–15.

[10] _____. 1963. "Semantical Analysis of Modal Logic I." *ZMLGM* 9: 67–96.

[11] _____. 1963. "Semantical Considerations on Modal Logic." *Modal and Many-Valued Logics*. Helsinki: Societas Philosophica 16: 83–94.

[12] Lambert, K. 1963. "Existential Import Revisited." *Notre Dame Journal of Formal Logic* (hereafter *NDJFL*) 4: 288–92.

[13] Leblanc, H. 1968. "A Simplified Account of Validity and Implication for Quantificational Logic." *JSL* 33: 231–35 (#8 in this volume).

[14] _____. 1969. "A Simplified Strong Completeness Proof for $QC_=$." *Akten des XIV. Internationalen Kongresses für Philosophie* 3: 83–95. Vienna: Verlag Herder (#9 in this volume).

[15] _____. 1971. "Truth-Value Semantics for a Logic of Existence." *NDJFL* 12: 153–68 (#4 in this volume).

[16] _____. 1973. "Semantic Deviations." *Truth, Syntax and Modality*. Amsterdam: North-Holland, 1–16 (#20 in this volume).

[17] _____. 1976. *Truth-Value Semantics*. Amsterdam: North-Holland.

[18] Leblanc, H., and Meyer, R. K. 1969. "Open Formulas and the Empty Domain." *Archiv für mathematische Logik und Grundlagenforschung*. 12: 78–84 (#5 in this volume).

[19] _____. 1970. "On Prefacing $(\forall X)A \supset A(Y/X)$ with $(\forall Y)$: A Free Quantification Theory without Identity." *ZMLGM* 16: 447–62 (#3 in this volume).

[20] Leblanc, H., and Thomason, R. H. 1968. "Completeness Theorems for some Presupposition-Free Logics." *Fundamenta Mathematicae* 62: 125–64 (#2 in this volume).

[21] Leblanc H., and Wisdom, W. A. 1976. *Deductive Logic*, 2d edition. Boston: Allyn and Bacon.

[22] Makinson, D. C. 1966. "On some Completeness Theorems in Modal Logic." *ZMLGM* 12: 379–84.

[23] Shipley, C. T. 1972. "A Semantical Theory and Several Deductive Systems for Universally Free Logic." Ph.D. dissertation, University of Nebraska.

[24] Snyder, D. P. 1971. *Modal Logic and its Applications*. New York: van Nostrand.
[25] Thomason, R. H. 1970. "Some Completeness Results for Modal Predicate Calculi." *Philosophical Problems in Logic: Some Recent Developments*. Holland: Dordrecht, 56−76.
[26] Van Fraassen, B. C. 1966. "The Completeness of Free Logic." *ZMLGM* 12: 219–34.

Part 2: Truth

Introduction

The reader doubtless knows of the two major interpretations of the quantifiers: the *standard*—or, as Quine would put it, *objectual*—interpretation and the *substitution(al)* one.[1] According to the first, a universal quantification

$$(\forall x)(x \text{ is thus-and-so}) \qquad (1)$$

is true relative to some domain (or, as the older phrase goes, universe of discourse) D if, no matter the member of D that the individual variable 'x' may take as a value,

$$x \text{ is thus-and-so} \qquad (2)$$

is true. According to the second, (1) is true relative to D if every substitution instance of (1), i.e., every result of substituting an individual term for 'x' in (2), is true. The two interpretations amount to the same when the terms substituted for 'x' in (2)

(i) designate *only* members of D, a condition normally met however '$(\forall x)$' be interpreted,

and

(ii) designate *all* the members of D, a condition which can of course be met only when one's language boasts as many individual terms as D has members.

The substitution interpretation of the quantifiers is commonly attributed to Wittgenstein. Though nowhere spelled out in the *Tractatus*, it underlies much of that classic, in particular Wittgenstein's contention that all "propositions" are truth-functions of their elementary components, his contention that all truths of logic (i.e., all theorems of *Principia Mathematica*) are tautologies, etc. Though it is frequently associated with his name, and justly so, Wittgenstein came (ironically enough) to abjure the interpretation. To quote from Moore's *Philosophical Papers*, "he [Wittgenstein] said that there was a temptation, to which he had yielded in the *Tractatus*, to say that $(x) \cdot fx$ is identical with the logical product '$fa \cdot fb \cdot fc \ldots$', ($\exists x$) · fx identical with the logical sum '$fa \lor fb \lor fc \lor \ldots$'; but that this was in both cases a mistake."[2]

In papers dated 1915 and 1926,[3] F. P. Ramsey reported on the interpretation as Wittgenstein's, defended it against an objection of Hilbert's,[4] and stated that, with the quantifiers interpreted Wittgeinstein's way, all axioms of *Principia Mathematica* other than the Axiom *of Reducibility* hold true. The claim, unfortunately, is hard to assess: whether the semantics Ramsey envisaged for *Principia Mathematica* was of the standard (= model-theoretic) sort with 'All' and 'Some' substitutionally understood, or whether it was a truth-value one like that in, say, #15, is unclear.[5]

To my knowledge little was heard (in any event, little was made) of the substitution interpretation of the quantifiers for the next fifteen years. Quine, incidentally, reports in *Ontological Relativity and Other Essays*, p. 63, that Leśniewski favored that interpretation, but adds: "I cannot locate an adequate statement of Stanislaw Leśniewski's philosophy of quantification in his writings; I have it from his conversations." The interpretation then turned up in a succession of books and papers by Carnap, beginning with *Introduction to Semantics* (1942) and culminating in *Logical Foundations of Probability* (1950). The latter book is quite instructive: the account of truth you find there is a model-theoretic one, but the account of logical truth, logical implication, logical equivalence, etc., is not.

Given a domain D, understand by (a) a *D-interpretation* of a first-order language L any result of assigning a member of D to each individual term and a (possibly empty) set of m-tuples of members of D to each m-place predicate of L, this for each m from 1 on, and by (b) a Henkin D-interpretation of L any D-interpretation of L in which each member of D is assigned to at least one individual term of L. Presuming given, for each language L in his *Logical Foundations of Probability*, some domain D of size $\aleph_0$ or less and—relative to that D—some Henkin D-interpretation I_D of L, Carnap lists on p. 69 the conditions that a sentence A of L must meet to be true on I_D. These add up to conditions (2)–(4) on pp. 105–106 (with 'I_D' in place of 'V_D') *plus* the following, which makes for a first use in the book of the substitution interpretation:

(5) in case A is a quantification $(\forall X)B$, $B(T/X)$ is true on I_D for every individual term T of L.

One would then expect Carnap to certify A logically true if—no matter the domain D or the D-interpretation I_D—A is true on I_D. Instead, Carnap takes a cue from the *Tractatus*, and on p. 84 pronounces A *logically true* if A holds in all state-descriptions in L.

To expand briefly on this, a *state-description* in a language L is a set S of sentences of L such that (i) for each atomic sentence A of L, exactly one of A and $\sim A$ belongs to S and (ii) no other sentence of L belongs to S. And a sentence A of L is said to *hold* in a state-description S in L if

(a) when A is atomic, A belongs to S,

(b) when A is a negation $\sim B$, B does not hold in S,
(c) when A is a conditional $B \supset C$, B does not hold in S or C does, and
(d) when A is a quantification $(\forall X)B$, $B(T/X)$ holds in S for every individual term T of L.

Clause (d), incidentally, makes for a second use in Carnap's book of the substitution interpretation.

Carnap goes on to show that any sentence of L that would count as an axiom of quantification in Quine's *Mathematical Logic*, first edition, is logically true (i.e., holds in all state-descriptions in L), and that the ponential of any two sentences of L that are logically true is logically true. He concludes therefrom that every sentence of L provable in Chapter Two of *Mathematical Logic* is logically true, a soundness theorem of sorts.

There are thus two different accounts of things in Carnap's book. The first is standard except for understanding quantifiers substitutionally. It was to recur in Robinson's *On the Metamathematics of Algebra* (1951), Shoenfield's *Mathematical Logic* (1967), and various recent texts, some of which mention no other interpretation of the quantifiers. The second, which is of greater interest here, dispenses with models and hence *presages* what—following Quine's suggestion—I have called *truth-value semantics*. I remarked that Carnap limits himself to models with countable domains, i.e., with finite domains or with infinite ones of size $\aleph_0$. Robinson and Shoenfield rather presume that the first-order languages they deal with have as many individual terms as the occasion may call for, a rather bold (and controversial) move which guarantees that condition (ii) on p. 123 can always be met.

My choice and italicizing of the verb 'presages' above was deliberate. Carnap's characterization of logical truths as sentences true in all state-descriptions is strictly syntactic. So you cannot hail it the beginnings of a new semantics. But, as it readily converts into a semantic characterization of logical truth, it is an intimation—if you will—of things to come. And so is the characterization in Hintikka's *Two Papers on Symbolic Logic* (1955) of validity in QC in terms of model sets.

Talking again of *individual parameters* where much of the literature would talk of free individual variables, understand by a *model set* any non-empty set S of wffs of QC such that

(1) at least one individual parameter of QC occurs in (a member of) S,
(2) if $\sim A$ belongs to S, where A is atomic, then A does not belong to S, and
(3) (a) if $\sim\sim A$ belongs to S, then so does A,
  (b) if $A \supset B$ belongs to S, then at least one of $\sim A$ and B does,
  (c) if $\sim(A \supset B)$ belongs to S, then so do both A and $\sim B$,
  (d) if $(\forall X)A$ belongs to S, then so does $A(P/X)$ for every individual parameter P occurring in (any member of) S, and
  (e) if $\sim(\forall X)A$ belongs to S, then so does $\sim A(P/X)$ for at least one individual parameter P.

It can be shown, following instructions of Hintikka's, that a wff A of QC is valid in the standard sense if and only if its negation $\sim A$ does not belong to any model set, and—so long again as QC is outfitted with a sufficient number of individual parameters—that a set S of wffs of QC has a model if and only if S is a subset of some model set or other. Turn these results into definitions of validity and semantic consistency (or, if you wish, simultaneous satisfiability), and you will have dispensed with models at two critical points in your accounting of QC.

Four years after the appearance of Hintikka's monograph came what I consider the *first* contribution to truth-value semantics, Beth's proof in *The Foundations of Mathematics*, Section 89, that

(A) if a closed wff A of QC evaluates to **T** on all *truth-value assignments* (Beth calls them *regular functions*) for QC, then A is provable in QC, and, more generally,

(B) if a set S of *closed* wffs of QC is (syntactically) consistent, then there is a truth-value assignment for QC on which all members of S evaluate to **T**.

(A)–(B) presuppose two definitions easily retrieved from #7, but which I rehearse for the record.[6] A *truth-value assignment* for QC is a function from the *atomic* wffs of QC to {**T**, **F**}; and a wff A of QC is said to *evaluate to* **T**—or, more simply, *be true*—on a truth-value assignment α for QC if:

(a) in case A is atomic, $\alpha(A) = $ **T**,

(b) in case A is a negation $\sim B$, B is not true on α,

(c) in case A is a conditional $B \supset C$, B is not true on α or C is, and

(d) in case A is a quantification $(\forall X)B$, $B(P/X)$ is true on α for every individual parameter P of QC.

The first definition matches that of a state-description in Carnap; and (a)–(d) in the second match the circumstances under which A would hold in a state-description.

To arrive at (A), Beth uses (among other things) a function s on the positive integers which, he writes, was independently discovered by Henkin, Hasenjaeger, and himself, and, to pass from (A) to (B), he appeals to a Compactness Theorem for SC (= the sentential calculus). A different proof of (B) will be found in #7, #9, #11, *Truth-Value Semantics*, etc.[7] Staying closer to the completeness proof in Henkin's 1949 paper, it better suggests the seminal role (on which I elaborate briefly) that this paper played in the semantics of Beth, Schütte, and others.

There are essentially two steps to Henkin's proof. You extend a set S of closed wffs of QC, said set S presumed for the occasion to be consistent, into a maximally consistent and ω-complete set S_∞ (hence, in particular, into a set to which a quantification belongs if and only if all of its instances do).[8] Then, with the set of all the individual parameters of QC serving as your D, you show all members of S_∞ (and hence of S) to be true on a certain D-interpretation I_D of the predicate parameters and the individual parameters of QC. The D-interpretation in question meets condition (ii) on p. 123 and hence is what I called a *Henkin interpretation*. So you can exploit the fact that a quantification is true on a Henkin interpretation if and only if all of its instances are, and con-

Introduction 127

clude that the quantification belongs to S_∞ if and only if all of its instances are true on I_D.

I report in #10 and fully document in *Truth-Value Semantics*, Section 4.2, that Henkin models translate into truth-value assignments.[9] The model $<D, I_D>$ of the preceding paragraph is no exception. So what I do in #7, #9, #11, etc., once I have extended set S into set S_∞, is to call on the truth-value counterpart α of $<D, I_D>$, and instead of showing the members of S to be true on I_D show them to be true on α. Given clauses (b)–(d) three paragraphs back, the required argument is of the simplest,[10] and it guarantees that S—when numbering only closed wffs as members and consistent—is what I call *truth-value verifiable* (for short, *tv-verifiable*).

Henkin's completeness proof can thus be edited into a proof of (B). It can also be edited into a proof of (A), and—as already noted—a Compactness Theorem for SC will lead from (A) to (B). Beth saw this, and the insight marked the beginning of truth-value semantics.

Beth did not concern himself with open wffs of QC. The earliest writers to do so may have been Schütte in 1962 and Leblanc in 1968. Nor did Beth investigate wffs from calculi other than QC. The first writer to do so may have been Schütte, who offered in a paper published in 1960 a truth-value semantics for STT, the simple theory of types.[11]

I shall return below to Leblanc's 1968 paper (#8 in this volume). As for Schütte's 1960 paper, "Syntactical and Semantical Properties of Simple Type Theory," the author introduced there the concept of a *total valuation* and that of a *partial valuation* for the wffs (non-atomic as well as atomic) of STT. Total valuations assign—subject to expected restrictions—one of the two truth-values **T** and **F** to each wff of STT. They behave, as Schütte points out, like the general models in Henkin's 1950 completeness paper, and hence like the general truth-value functions in #11;[12] they also behave like generalizations to STT of the truth sets in note 8. Partial valuations, on the other hand, assign *at most one—but not necessarily at least one—*of the two truth-values **T** and **F** to each wff of STT. They behave, as Schütte again points out, like generalizations to STT of Hintikka's model sets.

To match this semantic distinction Schütte acknowledged two kinds of provability in SST: *strict provability*, which amounts to provability without Cut in Takeuti's 1953 paper, and *provability*, which amounts to provability with Cut in that paper.[13] And he went on to show that:

(C) a wff A of STT is strictly provable in STT if and only if A does not evaluate to **F** on any partial valuation for STT, and

(D) a wff A of STT is provable in STT if and only if A evaluates to **T** on every total valuation for STT.

Schütte's 1960 paper was a major contribution to the new semantics. Where Beth had shown how to treat the quantificational calculus of order one, Schütte showed (in effect) how to treat the quantificational calculus of order ω, and hence how to explicate validity no matter the type-theoretic order of one's formula. Counterparts of (C) and (D), incidentally, are easily had for RTT, the ramified theory of types, and the whole of *Principia Mathematica* supplied in the process with the kind of semantics that Wittgenstein and Ramsey may have envisioned.[14]

Schütte returned to truth-value semantics in his 1962 *Lecture Notes in Mathematical Logic, Volume I*. He attended there to each of SC, QC, and STT separately. His treatment of STT is like that in the 1960 paper, but more detailed. His treatment of QC is as in #7, but attention is paid only to wffs (rather than to both wffs and sets of wffs). Proof that a wff of QC is provable if and only if valid in the truth-value sense is given. It uses the machinery of positive and negative parts dear to Schütte.

The next two contributions to truth-value semantics, Dunn and Belnap's "The Substitution Interpretation of the Quantifiers" and Leblanc's "A Simplified Account of Validity and Implication for Quantificational Logic" (#8 in this volume), appeared almost simultaneously: one in May 1968 and the other in June of that year.[15] They both attend to sets of wffs, and in particular to sets which—though semantically consistent—are not tv-verifiable.[16]

Dunn and Belnap study, not QC itself, but an arbitrary first-order language L outfitted with $\aleph_0$ individual terms and the so-called *term extensions* of L, i.e., the first-order languages exactly like L except for possibly having extra individual terms besides those of L. They assign truth-values to the atomic sentences of each extension L^+ of L; L^+ being an arbitrary extension of L and α a truth-value assignment for L^+, they mark a sentence A of L^+ true on α if A meets conditions (a)–(d) on p. 126 (with 'T' substituting for 'P' in (d), and 'L^+' for 'QC'); they declare a sentence A of L logically true if A is true on all truth-value assignments for L; and they take a sentence A of L to be logically implied (or *entailed*, as we frequently put it) by a set S of sentences of L if, no matter the extension L^+ of L nor the truth-value assignment α for L^+, A is true on α if all members of S are.

Dunn and Belnap remark that standard weak completeness proofs for QC (such as those of Beth, Schütte, Hintikka, or Kanger) can be edited into proof of:

(E) if a sentence A of L is logically true, then A is provable in L,

and that Henkin's (strong) completeness proof for QC in his 1949 paper can be edited into proof of:

(F) if a sentence A of L is logically implied by a set S of sentences of L, then A is provable from S in L.

They then proceed to "defend the substitution interpretation against a number of potential misapprehensions."[17]

Leblanc's 1968 paper deals with QC, $QC_=$, and (in its original version) presupposition-free brands of the two calculi.[18] *Normal* truth-value assignments, renamed in the present version *identity-normal*, are used in connection with $QC_=$; these are functions from the atomic wffs of $QC_=$ to $\{T, F\}$ which ensure that the usual axioms for $QC_=$ are valid. Two definitions of logical implication are supplied, respectively due to Hintikka and Leblanc. They differ from, but of course have the same force as, the Dunn-Belnap definition sketched above.

The problem, as the reader of #4 and #7 will recall, is to keep such a set as $\{f(p_1), f(p_2), f(p_3), \ldots\}$, where '$p_1$', '$p_2$', '$p_3$', etc., are all the individual parameters of (say) QC, from logically implying '$(\forall x)f(x)$', or—to switch from logical implication to semantic consistency—to ensure that such a set as $\{f(p_1), f(p_2), f(p_3), \ldots, \sim(\forall x)f(x)\}$, though not tv-verifiable, is nonetheless semantically consistent. Dunn and Belnap circumvent the difficulty by declaring a set S of sentences of their language L semantically consistent if, for some term-extension L^+ of L, there is a truth-value assignment for L^+ on which all members of S are true; Hintikka declares a set S of wffs of QC semantically consistent if either S itself or, say, the result of replacing in S 'p_1' by 'p_2', 'p_2' by 'p_4', 'p_3' by 'p_6', etc., is tv-verifiable;[19] and Leblanc, turning the Compactness Theorem into a definition, declares S semantically consistent if every finite subset of S is tv-verifiable. I used to favor Hintikka's account, as touched up in my 1968 paper and later publications, over its two rivals. #20, which recapitulates much of the material in Part 2, attests to this, as does my *Truth-Value Semantics*. Recently, however, I have come to find the Dunn-Belnap account very serviceable.

Like #1 and #2, my earliest papers in truth-value semantics (to wit, #8, #9, and #11) used just one run of individual variables. This made for unnecessary complications, many of them untold as soundness proofs were given only in outline form. Beth's *Foundations of Mathematics*, as reported in Note 6, labored under the same curse. Schütte's writings, by contrast, have two runs of individual variables, and the Dunn-Belnap paper has the equivalent thereof. After the publication of #11, I followed suit and generally employed either (i) two runs of individual variables, one run behaving like the *bound* 'x', 'y', 'z', etc., of #8 and for which the appellation 'variable' is saved, the other run behaving like the *free* 'x', 'y', 'z', etc., of #8 and dubbed *parameters*, or (ii) one run of individual variables, occurring only bound in the wffs of my calculi, and one run of individual terms (or, if you want, individual constants).

#8 provides only definitions. For proofs you have to await "A Simplified Strong Completeness Theorem for $QC_=$," #9 in this volume, where $QC_=$ is shown by cases to be strongly (and hence weakly) complete in the truth-value sense. I first presume that infinitely many individual variables do not occur free in my set S and by an adaptation of the proof on pp. 82–84 show it to be tv-verifiable if consistent; tackling next the contrary case, I construct a set S' isomorphic to S, show that S' is consistent if S is, and—as infinitely many individual variables do not occur free in S'—conclude by virtue of the first case that S' is tv-verifiable if S is consistent. In the first three sections of the paper truth-values are assigned to *all* the atomic wffs of $QC_=$. In the closing one, though, questions of "relevance" are raised, and proof is sketched that

(G) a wff A of $QC_=$ is valid if and only if A is true on all identity-normal truth-value assignments *to its atomic subformulas*.

I shall return below to (G) and its counterparts in other logics.

I was unaware, when writing #8, of Beth's 1959 results, and so were Dunn and Belnap (see footnote 1 of their paper). It is van Fraassen who brought Section 89 of Beth's book to my attention and theirs. I was also unfamiliar with Schütte's 1960 paper and 1962 monograph. So, done with QC and $QC_=$, I turned in 1969 to QC^2, the quantificational calculus of order two; introduced in "Three Generalizations of a Theorem of Beth's" (#11) what I came to call the *truth-value functions of Class 1* and of *Class 3* for QC^2;[20] and, using Henkin's distinction between *provability** and *provability*** in QC^2,[21] offered proof that

(H) a wff A of QC^2 is provable* in QC^2 if and only if A evaluates to **T** on all truth-value functions of Class 1 for QC^2, and

(I) a wff A of QC^2 is provable** in QC^2 if and only if A evaluates to **T** on all truth-value functions of Class 3 for QC^2,

a result that can be retrieved from Schütte's 1960 paper. The strategy used owes much to Henkin's 1949 paper.

An intermediary class of truth-value functions (call it *Class 2*) for QC^2 can of course be had by requiring B on line 32 of p. 173 to be a wff of QC rather than one of QC^2. The functions in question, it so happens, are those suiting $QC^{2!}$, the *predicative* quantificational calculus of order two. And proof will be forthcoming that

(J) a wff A of $QC^{2!}$ is provable in $QC^{2!}$ if and only if A evaluates to **T** on all truth-value functions of Class 2 for QC^2.[22]

The theory of types now beckoned, and with the aid of Robert K. Meyer I turned to it. In the paper embodying our results, "Truth-Value Semantics for the Theory of Types" (#12), we introduced truth-value functions of Class 3 (or general truth-value functions) for STT and proved STT to be both strongly sound and strongly complete in the truth-value sense. As hinted at earlier, our functions were total valuations (in the sense of Schütte) that satisfied the *Axiom of Extensionality*. Calling on the so-called *parametric extensions* of STT and on especially designed truth-value functions for these extensions, we then supplied a truth-value account of standard validity for STT (and, hence, for the quantificational calculus of order ω).[23] Finally, we looked into questions of "truth-functionality," and showed in effect that our interpretation of STT—though *truth-functional*—was not *strictly truth-functional*.[24] The result, largely due to Meyer, was a startling one, to be discussed later on.

Further logics were eventually equipped with a truth-value semantics: QC!, $QC^{2/\infty}$, QC_3, various tense logics, various modal logics, etc. QC!, treated in #4, is a presupposition-free quantificational calculus of order one with an existence predicate (the *Principia* 'E!') as an extra primitive. Due to Lambert and Meyer, it was shown—the reader may recall—strongly sound and complete under an interpretation using truth-value assignments relativized to sets of individual parameters. $QC^{2/\infty}$, the ramified quantificational calculus of order two, is a fragment of RTT, the ramified theory of types. Weaver and I treat it in #15. The answers we supply there to questions of truth-functionality and our proof that upon addition of Russell's *Axiom of Reducibility* $QC^{2/\infty}$ reduces to QC^2, readily generalize to RTT as a whole. QC_3 is a quantificational calculus

Introduction 131

of order one with three (rather than two) truth-values. Treated in #18, it issues from Łukasiewicz's three-valued sentential calculus (= SC_3) that George Weaver, Harold Goldberg, and I had shown strongly complete in #17. Thanks are due in connection with #18 to Atwell R. Turquette, who supplied some of the more difficult proofs and whose *Many-Valued Logics*—written in collaboration with J. B. Rosser and published in 1952—has a strong truth-value flavor. The book, which antedates Beth's *Foundations of Mathematics* by seven years and Schütte's "Syntactical and Semantical Properties of Simple Type Theory" by eight, could in point of fact be hailed a first, though somewhat reticent, contribution to truth-value semantics. Tense logic comes up in #19, a paper written in collaboration with R. P. McArthur and which borrows some from McArthur's dissertation of 1972. The calculi treated there (QK_t and various extensions thereof) have an unrestricted *Axiom of Specification* and hence are of the ordinary rather than the truth-value sort. As a result tense analogues

$$(\forall X)\mathbf{G}A \supset \mathbf{G}(\forall X)A$$

and

$$(\forall X)\mathbf{H}A \supset \mathbf{H}(\forall X)A\,{}^{25}$$

of the Barcan Formula

$$(\forall X)\Box A \supset \Box(\forall X)A$$

are provable in QK_t. Presupposition-free brands of the calculus and extensions thereof are shown strongly sound and complete under a truth-value interpretation in Robert F. Barnes and Raymond D. Gumb's "The Completeness of Presupposition-Free Tense Logic." Modal logic comes in #7, the reader may recall, but fuller treatment of it (and of most topics mentioned in this Introduction) will be found in *Truth-Value Semantics*. Ordinary brands of the main modal quantificational calculi (i.e., QK, QM, QB, QS4, and QS5) are shown to be strongly sound and complete in the latter text, as are presupposition-free brands of three of them. However, presupposition-free brands of QB and QS5, for which the Kripke relation R has to be symmetrical, proved to be somewhat refractory. Strong soundness and completeness proofs for the two calculi can now be retrieved (with minimum effort) from the Barnes-Gumb paper.

Still further logics have recently been equipped with a truth-value semantics of the sort espoused here (among them relevant quantificational logics due to Anderson and Belnap and investigated by Meyer, Dunn, and Leblanc); and some first-order logics have been equipped by Richard Routley with a truth-value semantics of a different sort. But space prevents survey of these contributions here.

Papers #8 through #20 and the other sources mentioned in this Introduction establish beyond a doubt that as regards various calculi (hence, various *language forms*) validity, satisfiability, entailment, etc., can be explicated—and unimpeachably explicated—without resort to models. Truth-value assignments, truth-value functions, and the like will do the trick. Further, various notions relating to models can be so redefined as to suit truth-value assignments, truth-value functions, etc. Cardinality is a case in point. As one may talk of the cardinality (finite or infinite, and—when infinite—denumerable or not) of a model, so one may talk of the cardinality of a truth-value assignment and prove counterparts of such celebrated results as Löwenheim's Theorem, Skolem's Theorem, etc. Paper #10 here, Section §3.3 of *Truth-value Semantics*, and recent findings of mine bear this out. Isomorphy, and by rebound categoricity, is another notion among many that can be accommodated within truth-value semantics.

However, talk of models is indispensable or well-nigh indispensable where *languages* rather than language forms are concerned. Truth-value semantics does provide a perfectly adequate account of logical truth. Indeed, a sentence from, say, a first-order language is logically true in the model-theoretic sense of the appelation if and only if logically true in its truth-value sense. But truth in a model and truth on a truth-value assignment do not always match for denumerable languages, i.e., for languages with no more than $\aleph_0$ individual terms, and understandably so. Truth-value assignments match all and only Henkin models, and many a model is not a Henkin one. Some, as reported earlier, get around the difficulty by plying their languages with as many individual terms as the occasion calls for, but the solution smacks of trickery. Others remind the reader, as I do in #14 and #20, that if a first-order sentence is true in any model at all, then it is sure to be true in a Henkin one, and hence sure to be true on a truth-value assignment. But this corollary of Löwenheim's Theorem may be of little solace to those with a stake in the original model.

I hope at a later time to review these matters and the fate in truth-value semantics of Tarski's Convention T, the subject of much dispute at the moment.[26] I shall only insist here that, however the new semantics' handling of truth be assessed, its handling of logical truth is above reproach and of a luminous simplicity that model-theoretic semantics cannot begin to match.

Popper, Leblanc, Harper, Field, and others, incidentally, have over the last twenty years devised yet another semantics that does without models: *probabilistic semantics*. Probability functions of the so-called *Popper sort* play there the role assigned here to truth-value assignments, truth-value functions, etc. Space, unfortunately, prevented inclusion of the relevant papers in the present volume.[27]

Now for #13 through #16.

A calculus $\mathfrak{C}$ is said to have a *truth-functional interpretation* if there is a set Σ of functions from the wffs (non-atomic as well as atomic) of $\mathfrak{C}$ to $\{T, F\}$ such that:

(a) the theorems of $\mathfrak{C}$ and the wffs of $\mathfrak{C}$ evaluating to T on all members of Σ coincide and

(b) the truth-values that the non-atomic wffs of $\mathfrak{C}$ assume on members of Σ hinge exclusively on the truth-values of their components or—in the case of quantifications—those of their instances.

And 𝕮 is said to have a *strictly truth-functional interpretation* if the set Σ in question also obeys the following condition:
(c) members of Σ that agree on the atomic wffs of 𝕮 agree on the non-atomic ones as well.

SC, the sentential calculus, has a truth-functional interpretation, and a strictly truth-functional one at that. For let Σ' consist of every function α from the wffs of SC to {T, F} such that (i) α(~A) = T if and only if α(A) = F and (ii) α(A ⊃ B) = T if and only if α(A) = F or α(B) = T. It is easily verified that Σ' meets all three of conditions (a)–(c), a result which was known to Wittgenstein (and to many of his predecessors) and because of which he talked of the wffs of SC as truth-functions of their elementary (= atomic) components.

As expected, QC has a strictly truth-functional interpretation. Let Σ' consist of every function α from the wffs of QC to {T, F} that meets (i)–(ii) and the extra condition:
(iii) α((∀X)A) = T if and only if α(A(P/X)) = T for every individual parameter *P* of QC,
and the trick is done. The result is implicit in Wittgenstein's *Tractatus*. Since, however, the instances of a non-vacuous quantification (∀X)A do figure among the components of (∀X)A, it is best to talk here of *subformulas*, a notion possibly introduced and in any event extensively used by Gentzen, and declare the wffs of QC truth-functions of their elementary (= atomic) subformulas.[28]
And, among the extensions of QC, QC₌ for instance has a strictly truth-functional interpretation. Let Σ' consist this time of every *identity-normal* function from the wffs of QC₌ that meets (i)–(iii), and the trick is done.

Truth-functionality remains the rule when you move to second-order logic, but strict truth-functionality becomes the exception.

I talked earlier of three different classes of truth-value functions for second-order logic. They correspond to three different notions of provability in a single calculus or—equivalently—to three different calculi, each with a *Specification Axiom* (and hence each with a provability notion) of its own. The calculi in question are occasionally referred to as QC²*, QC²! (= the predicative quantificational calculus of order two), and QC² (= the ordinary quantificational calculus of order two).[29] In the first of these

$$(\forall F^d)A \supset A(F^d/F^d),$$

F^d a predicate variable of degree d, F^d a predicate parameter of the same degree, and $A(F^d/F^d)$ the result of replacing F^d everywhere in A by F^d, serves as Specification Axiom; in the second

$$(\forall F^d)A \supset A(B/F^d(X_1, X_2, \ldots, X_d)),$$

F^d as before, *B a first-order wff*, $X_1, X_2, \ldots, X_d$ distinct individual parameters, and $A(B/F^d(X_1, X_2, \ldots, X_d))$ understood as on pp. 172–173, serves in that capacity; and in the third the same conditional, *but with B free to be any second-order wff*, does.

In all three calculi a quantification of the sort $(\forall X)A$ has the same instances as before, namely: all results of replacing X in A by an individual parameter. A quantification of the sort $(\forall F^d)A$, on the other hand, has three different classes of instances. Wffs of the sort $A(F^d/F^d)$ constitute its instances of Class 1, while wffs of the sort $A(B/F^d(X_1, X_2, \ldots, X_d))$ constitute its instances of Class 2 when B is a first-order wff, otherwise its instances of Class 3.

With these distinctions on hand, characterization of our three classes of functions is straightforward, a truth-value function of Class i (i = 1, 2, and 3) being any function from second-order wffs to $\{T, F\}$ which meets the usual conditions as regards negations, conditionals, and quantifications of the sort $(\forall X)A$, and on which a quantification of the sort $(\forall F^d)A$ evaluates to T if and only if all its instances of Class i do.

It can be shown (largely by dint of (H)–(J) on p. 130) that of the truth-value functions just defined those of Class 1 constitute a truth-functional interpretation for QC^{2*}, those of Class 2 constitute one for $QC^{2!}$, and those of Class 3 constitute one for QC^2. It can further be shown (by a routine argument in one case, but a rather sophisticated one in the other) that the first two interpretations are strictly truth-functional at that. The third interpretation, on the other hand, is not, as the reader will perhaps have gathered from an earlier remark. Meyer and I constructed in 1969 a pair of truth-value functions of Class 3 that agree on the atomic wffs of QC^2 and yet disagree on the wff '$(\exists f)(\exists x)(\exists y)(f(x) \ \& \ \sim f(y))$'.

Similar results hold for the ramified quantificational calculus of order two, which is the absence of Russell's *Axiom of Reducibility* has a strictly truth-functional interpretation, but in the presence of the axiom reduces to and hence fares like QC^2. Similar results also hold for the ramified quantificational calculus of order ω, i.e., for Whitehead and Russell's *Principia Mathematica*, which triggered Wittgenstein's concerns with truth-functionality.

The foregoing matters are covered in #12, #13, #15, and—more extensively—in Section 7.3 of *Truth-Value Semantics*.

#16 answers in the affirmative a question of some historical interest: "Does QC^2 have a so-called "predicative" interpretation?" By implication it affirmatively answers another question: "Does QC^2 have any interpretation at all that is strictly truth-functional?" Ignoring here the first question, let Σ' consist of all truth-value functions of Class 1 on which the *Axiom of Comprehension*, i.e., on which wffs of the sort

$$(\exists F^d)(\forall X_1)(\forall X_2) \ldots (\forall X_d)(F^d(X_1, X_2, \ldots, X_d) \equiv A)$$

(F^d foreign to A, and $X_1, X_2, \ldots, X_d$ distinct individual variables), evaluate to T. It is easily verified that a wff of QC^2 is provable in QC^2 if and only if it evaluates to T on all members of Σ'. But Σ' does clearly meet conditions (b)–(c) on pp. 132–133. Hence QC^2 has a strictly truth-functional interpretation, to wit: Σ'. The interpretation is somewhat ad hoc, and it widens the gap between model-theoretic and truth-value semantics.[30] Indeed, there are general models

Introduction   135

that translate into truth-value functions of Class 3, but do not translate into truth-value functions of Class 1. But it rates mention in any treatment of QC².
#14 studies a matter close to strict truth-functionality: *relevance*. Where A is a wff of SC, its truth-value *depends* upon the truth-values of *just* the atomic components of A; and, when A is a wff of QC (or of QC$_=$), its truth-value *depends* upon the truth-values of *just* the atomic subformulas of A. The story becomes more complex as one turns to second-order logic and, interestingly enough, to first-order modal logic. For instance, when A is a wff of QC²*, its truth-value *depends* upon the truth-values of *just* the atomic subformulas of A. However, when A is a wff of QC²!, its truth-value may depend upon the truth-values of other atomic wffs as well; and, when A is a wff of QC², its truth-value may depend upon the truth-values of non-atomic wffs as well. For a more detailed and comprehensive coverage than that supplied in #14, the reader may wish to consult Sections 7.3, 9.2, and 9.3 of *Truth-Value Semantics*.

Notes

1. For Quine's more recent views on these two interpretations of the quantifiers, see *Ontological Relativity and Other Essays*. In the remarks that follow I limit myself to universal quantifiers; "dual" remarks apply of course to existential ones. Some of the material in this Introduction is adapted from the Appendix to my *Truth-Value Semantics*.
2. See p. 297. The remark was made by Wittgenstein in the course of a lecture in 1932.
3. The papers are respectively entitled "The Foundations of Mathematics" and "Mathematical Logic," and are reproduced in *The Foundations of Mathematics and Other Logical Essays*.
4. Hilbert objected, not unexpectedly, to the *infinite* product '*fa* & *fb* & *fc* & . . .' and the infinite sum '*fa* ∨ *fb* ∨ *fc* ∨ . . .' as being meaningless. Infinite wffs have since gained some measure of respectability. It seems best, though, to skirt the whole issue, and—rather than treating, say, '(∀x)f(x)' as shorthand for '*f(a)* & *f(b)* & *f(c)* & . . .'—to certify '(∀x)f(x)' true if each one of '*f(a)*', '*f(b)*', '*f(c)*', etc., is true. This is what the substitution interpretation of '(∀x)f(x)' has come to mean, and that is what I take it to mean in the papers that follow and in *Truth-Value Semantics*.
5. And yet crucial. It is one thing to retain the whole machinery of models (i.e., domains and interpretations) and talk of a wff from a calculus 𝔈 being true in a model M, but with the wff—when of the sort (∀X)A—adjudged true in M if all its instances are true in M; it is quite another to discard models in favor, say, of truth-value assignments and talk of a wff from 𝔈 being true on a truth-value assignment α if conditions such as (a)–(d) on p. 126 are met. In the first case one is still doing model-theoretic semantics, though to be sure interpreting (∀X)A substitutionally; in the second one does what I call *truth-value semantics*. The point should be borne in mind when I discuss Carnap's *Logical Foundations of Probability* below.
6. In the definitions I again presume QC to have two infinite runs of individual runs, i.e., one infinite run of individual variables and one infinite run of individual parameters. The latter, as the reader knows, may be thought of either as *free* individual variables or as individual terms. Beth himself used only one run of individual signs. His characterization of an instance of (∀X)A was therefore a good deal more complicated than the one here (where B(P/X), the result of replacing individual variable X everywhere in B by individual parameter P, does the trick). See p. 129 for further details on the matter.
7. The relevant section in *Truth-Value Semantics* is §2.3.
8. As the reader may recall from note 21, p. 117, a set S of wffs of QC is said to be *maximally consistent* if (i) S is consistent (i.e., there is no wff A of QC such that A and ~A are provable from S) and (ii) for any wff A of QC not in S, S ∪ {A} is inconsistent; and S is said to be ω-*complete* if,

for any quantification $(\forall X)A$ of QC, $(\forall X)A$ is provable from S if every instance of $(\forall X)A$ is provable from S. A maximally consistent and ω-complete set S (of wffs of QC) is what is known as a *truth set*, i.e., a set S such that:

(b') for any negation $\sim B$, $\sim B$ belongs to S if and only if B does not,
(c') for any conditional $B \supset C$, $B \supset C$ belongs to S if and only if B does not or C does, and
(d') for any quantification $(\forall X)B$, B belongs to S if and only if $B(P/X)$ belongs to S for every individual parameter P of QC.

That S_∞ is a truth set is critical to Henkin's argument and to the one in #7, #9, #11, etc. For a detailed study of truth sets and model sets, see *Truth-Value Semantics*, Sections 3.1 and 3.2, respectively.

9. The translation is quite straightforward: where M is a Henkin model and A is an atomic wff of QC, assign **T** to A if A is true in M, otherwise **F**.

10. The analogy between (b)–(d) and the three conditions (b')–(d') of note 8 hardly needs stressing.

11. Or, equivalently, for QC$^\infty$, the quantificational calculus of order ω.

12. In *Truth-Value Semantics*, Section 6.1, I refer to general truth-value functions as truth-value functions *of Class 3*. I limit myself there and in #11 below to QC^2, the quantificational calculus of order two, but definitions and theorems easily extend in both texts to QC$^\infty$.

13. The rule Cut is studied in several of the papers in Part Three.

14. For clues on how to turn the semantics in Schütte's 1960 paper or that in #12 into a truth-value semantics for RTT, see *Truth-Value Semantics*, Section 7.3.

15. Both papers, incidentally, were presented at the very same conference (the East Lansing Colloquium on Free Logic, June 1967) and at the same session of that conference.

16. An example of a set of wffs of QC that is semantically consistent and yet not tv-verifiable was supplied in two papers from Part One and will be reproduced a few paragraphs hence.

17. Belnap tells me that he would now disown the term extensions and simply declare first-order languages strongly incomplete when interpreted the truth-value way.

18. The passage relating to the presupposition-free brands of QC and QC$_=$ contained an error. I consequently deleted it when editing #8 for inclusion in this volume. The matter is set to rights in Section 5.3 of *Truth-Value Semantics* (with p. 147 there corrected along the lines of #35. pp. 439–44).

19. Or, to phrase matters more abstractly and more broadly, if some set of wffs of QC to which S is *isomorphic* is tv-verifiable. In papers assembled here and in *Truth-Value Semantics* I define semantic consistency in this second manner.

20. Truth-value functions, as understood here, are assignments of truth-values to *all* the wffs of a calculus, hence (more formally) functions from the wffs (both atomic and non-atomic) of a calculus to $\{\mathbf{T}, \mathbf{F}\}$.

21. See Henkin's "Banishing the Rule of Substitution for Functional Variables." His terminology differs from mine (he has two calculi rather than two notions of provability for a single one), but immaterially so.

22. More will be said about QC$^{2!}$ below, and a detailed coverage of all present matters will be found in Chapters 6 and 7 of *Truth-Value Semantics*.

23. A wff of STT is said to be *standardly* valid (in *Truth-Value Semantics*, *normally* valid) if it is true in all *standard (normal)* models. It is the standardly valid wffs of STT that Gödel showed in his 1931 paper to be, so to speak, unaxiomatizable. By contrast, the *generally* valid wffs of STT (i.e., the wffs of STT true in all *general* models) are axiomatizable, as (I) in the text intimates and as Henkin showed in his 1950 completeness paper.

24. In *Truth-Value Semantics* I talk of *strong* rather than *strict* truth-functionality, but it seemed preferable to abide here by the terminology of #12, #13, etc.

25. In these wffs '**G**' is short for 'It will always be the case that', and '**H**' short for 'It has always been the case that'.

26. As regards this dispute the reader may wish to consult Kripke's "Is There a Problem with Substitutional Quantification?"

Introduction 137

27. The reader may wish to consult on this matter Leblanc's "Probabilistic Semantics: An Overview" and its bibliography.
28. As regards subformulas, note that A is a subformula of itself; when A is of the sort $\sim B$, B is a subformula of A; when A is of the sort $B \supset C$, B and C are subformulas of A; when A is of the sort $(\forall X)B$, $B(P/X)$ is—for each individual parameter P—a subformula of A; and any subformula of a subformula of A is a subformula of A.
29. In Henkin's 1953 paper QC^{2*} appears as F*, and QC^2 as F**.
30. This despite the fact that in model-theoretic semantics general validity is often defined in terms of models in which the Axiom of Comprehension is true. For details on this see Church's *Introduction to Mathematical Logic*, pp. 308–09 (Church, by the way, talks of *secondary* validity where along with Henkin I talk of general validity), and Henkin's 1953 paper.

References

[1] Barnes, R. F. and Gumb, R. D. 1979. "The Completeness of Presupposition-Free Tense Logics," *Zeitschrift für mathematische Logik und Grundlagen der Mathematik* 25: 193–208.
[2] Beth, E. W. 1959. *The Foundations of Mathematics*. Amsterdam: North-Holland.
[3] Carnap, R. 1942. *Introduction to Semantics*. Cambridge, Mass.: Harvard University Press.
[4] ———. 1950. *Logical Foundations of Probability*. Chicago: Chicago University Press.
[5] Church, A. 1956. *Introduction to Mathematical Logic, Volume I*. Princeton: Princeton University Press.
[6] Dunn, J. M., and Belnap, N. D., Jr. 1968. "The Substitution Interpretation of the Quantifiers." *Noûs* 2: 177–85.
[7] Gödel, K. 1931. "Über formal unentscheidbare Sätze der Principia Mathematica und verwandter Systeme. I." *Monatshefte für Mathematik und Physik* 38: 173 – 98.
[8] Hasenjaeger, G. 1953. "Eine Bemerkung zu Henkin's Beweis für die Vollständigkeit des Prädikatenkalkuls der ersten Stufe." *The Journal of Symbolic Logic* (hereafter *JSL*) 18: 42–48.
[9] Henkin, L. A. 1949. "The Completeness of the First-Order Functional Calculus." *JSL* 14: 159 – 66.
[10] ———. 1950. "Completeness in the Theory of Types." *JSL* 15: 81–91.
[11] ———. 1953. "Banishing the Rule of Substitution for Functional Variables." *JSL* 18: 201–208.
[12] Hintikka, J. 1955. *Two Papers on Symbolic Logic. Acta Philosophica Fennica*, vol. 8.
[13] Kanger, S. 1957. *Provability in Logic*. Stockholm: Almqvist and Wiksell.
[14] Kripke,S. 1976. "Is There a Problem with Substitutional Quantification?" *Truth and Meaning*, pp. 325–419. Oxford: Clarendon Press.
[15] Leblanc, H. 1976. *Truth-Value Semantics*. Amsterdam: North-Holland.
[16] ———. 1980. "Probabilistic Semantics: An Overview." *Philosophia* 9: 231–49.
[17] Łukasiewicz, J. 1920. "O logice trojwarttosciowej." *Ruch filosoficzny* 5: 169–71.
[18] McArthur, R. P. 1972. "Truth-Value Semantics for Tense Logic," Ph.D. dissertation, Temple University.
[19] Meyer, R. K., Dunn, J. M., and Leblanc, H. 1974. "Completeness of Relevant Quantification Theories." *Notre Dame Journal of Formal Logic* 15: 16–24.
[20] Moore, G. E. 1959. *Philosophical Papers*. London: Allen and Unwin.
[21] Quine, W. V. 1940. *Mathematical Logic*. New York: Norton.
[22] ———. 1969. *Ontological Relativity and Other Essays*. New York: Columbia University Press.
[23] Ramsey, F. P. 1931. *The Foundations of Mathematics and Other Logical Essays*, R. B. Braithwaite, ed. London: Kegan Paul.
[24] Robinson, A. 1951. *On the Metamathematics of Algebra*. Amsterdam: North-Holland.
[25] Rosser, J. B., and Turquette, A. R. 1952. *Many-Valued Logics*. Amsterdam: North-Holland.

[26] Routley, R. 1971. "Domainless Semantics for Free, Quantification, and Significance Logics." *Logique et Analyse* 14: 603–26.
[27] Schütte, K. 1960. "Syntactical and Semantical of Simple Type Theory." *JSL* 25: 305–26.
[28] ———. 1962. *Lecture Notes in Mathematical Logic, Volume I*. Department of Mathematics, The Pennsylvania State University.
[29] Shoenfield, J. R. 1967. *Mathematical Logic*. Reading Mass.: Addison-Wesley.
[30] Whitehead, A. N., and Russell, B. 1910–13. *Principia Mathematica*. Cambridge: Cambridge University Press.
[31] Wittgenstein, L. 1922. *Tractatus Logico-Philosophicus*. London: Routledge and Kegal Paul.

8
A Simplified Account of Validity and Implication for Quantificational Logic

As those of us who instruct him are well aware, customary accounts of validity and implication for quantificational logic often bewilder the novice. For his benefit, I present here an account of validity, due (in effect) to the late E. W. Beth, and two accounts of implication, one my own, the other Jaakko Hintikka's, which add up to what the better textbooks say, but, *making no mention whatever of domains*, say it far more simply.[1]

1. Presuming known what counts as a formula of SC (the sentential calculus) or of QC (the first-order quantificational calculus without identity),[2] an atomic formula of SC or of QC, a component of a formula of SC or of QC, a free (bound) occurrence in a formula of QC of an individual variable of QC, an individual variable of QC that occurs free (bound) in a formula of QC, and an open (closed) formula of QC, I attend in (i)–(ii) to notational matters and in (iii) to a key notion: that of a subformula of a formula of QC. (i) Where A is a formula of QC, X an individual variable of QC, and Y an individual variable of QC not necessarily distinct from X, I shall take $A(Y/X)$ to be A if X occurs free in at least one component of A of the sort $(\forall Y)B$; otherwise, $A(Y/X)$ will be the result of replacing every free occurrence of X in A by an occurrence of Y. (ii) With A, X, and Y as in (i), I shall take $A[Y/X]$ to be, when X occurs free in at least one component of A of the sort $(\forall Y)B$, the result of replacing: *first*, every bound occurrence of Y in A by an occurrence of the alphabetically earliest individual variable of QC that is foreign to A,[3] and *then* every free occurrence of X (in the resulting formula) by an occurrence of Y; otherwise, $A[Y/X]$ will be $A(Y/X)$. (iii) Where A is a formula of QC and B a formula of QC not necessarily distinct from A, A will count as a subformula of B if (and only if): (a) B is the same as A; (b) B being of the sort $\sim C$, A is a subformula of C; (c) B being of the sort $C \supset D$, A is a subformula of C or of D; and (d) B being of the sort $(\forall X)C$, A is a subformula of $C[Y/X]$ for some individual variable Y of QC. It follows from (iii), and the customary definition of a component of a formula of

QC, that when a formula A of QC has no component of the sort $(\forall X)B$, then the atomic subformulas of A, being just the atomic components of A, are finite in number; on the other hand, when A has a component of the sort $(\forall X)B$, its atomic subformulas are $\aleph_0$ in number.

2. A formula A of SC is declared valid when A is satisfied by every assignment of truth-values to the sentence variables of SC that occur in A; hence, when A is satisfied by every assignment of truth-values to the atomic components of A. Interestingly enough for our purpose, a like definition, with truth-values assigned to the atomic subformulas rather than the atomic components of A, will do *when A is a formula of* QC. Where S_{AF} is a set of atomic formulas of QC to which belongs every atomic subformula of A, and *Asst* is any result of assigning one of the two truth-values **T** and **F** to each member of S_{AF}, let A be said to be satisfied by *Asst* if (and only if): (a) when A is atomic, A is assigned **T** in *Asst*; (b) when A is of the sort $\sim B$, B is not satisfied by *Asst*; (c) when A is of the sort $B \supset C$, B is not satisfied by *Asst* or C is; and (d) when A is of the sort $(\forall X)B$, $B[Y/X]$ is satisfied by *Asst* for every individual variable Y of QC. Beth showed in [1] that *A is valid in the standard (= model-theoretic) sense of the word if and only if satisfied by every assignment of truth-values to the atomic formulas of* QC.[4] But the atomic formulas of QC that do not figure among the atomic subformulas of A are clearly idle here. So, sharpening Beth's result, we may conclude that *A is valid in the standard sense if and only if satisfied by every assignment of truth-values to its atomic subformulas*.

3. Now for implication. A set S of formulas of SC is often said to imply a formula A of SC (or, for those who favor Tarski's terminology, A is said to be a semantic consequence of S) when every assignment of truth-values to the sentence variables of SC that occur in the various members of $S \cup \{A\}$ fails to satisfy a member of S or else satisfies A; hence, when every assignment of truth-values to the atomic components of the various members of $S \cup \{A\}$ fails to satisfy a member of S or else satisfies A. A like definition, with truth-values assigned to the atomic subformulas rather than the atomic components of the various members of $S \cup \{A\}$, will do when S is a finite set of formulas of QC, and A a formula of QC. Note for proof that, where $A_1, A_2, \ldots, A_n$ $(n \geqslant 0)$, and A are formulas of QC, $\{A_1, A_2, \ldots, A_n\}$ implies A in the standard sense of the word 'implies' if and only if the formula $A_1 \supset (A_2 \supset (\ldots (A_n \supset A) \ldots))$ is valid in the standard sense of the word 'valid'; hence if and only if every assignment of truth-values to the atomic subformulas of the various members of $\{A_1, A_2, \ldots, A_n, A\}$ fails to satisfy a member of $\{A_1, A_2, \ldots, A_n\}$ or else satisfies A.

4. When S is infinite, and every member of S is closed, S is likewise sure to imply a formula A of QC, in the standard sense of the word 'imply', if every

A Simplified Account of Validity and Implication for Quantificational Logic 141

assignment of truth-values to the atomic subformulas of the various members of $S \cup \{A\}$ fails to satisfy a member of S or else satisfies A (proof of the fact may be found in [1].) Not so, however, when at least one member of S is open. Suppose indeed S consists of '$f(x)$', '$f(y)$', '$f(z)$', etc., and A is '$(\forall x)f(x)$' (a formula that has '$f(x)$', '$f(y)$', '$f(z)$', etc., as its atomic subformulas). Every assignment of truth-values to '$f(x)$', '$f(y)$', '$f(z)$', etc., will satisfy '$(\forall x)f(x)$' if it satisfies each and every one of '$f(x)$', '$f(y)$', '$f(z)$', etc. Yet the set consisting of '$f(x)$', '$f(y)$', '$f(z)$', etc., does not imply '$(\forall x)f(x)$' in the standard sense of the word 'imply'.[5] A theorem comes to our rescue, fortunately, the Compactness Theorem, according to which an infinite set S of formulas of QC implies a formula A of QC, as the word 'implies' is customarily used, if and only if some finite subset of S implies A, again as the word 'implies' is customarily used; hence, if and only if every assignment of truth-values to the atomic subformulas of the various members of $S' \cup \{A\}$ for some finite subset S' of S fails to satisfy a member of S' or else satisfies A. But, if so, then *a set S of formulas of QC may be said to imply a formula A of QC if: (a) when S is finite, every assignment of truth-values to the atomic subformulas of the various members of $S \cup \{A\}$ fails to satisfy a member of S or else satisfies A, and (b) when S is infinite, some finite subset of S implies A (in the sense of (a)).*

5. Professor Hintikka has shown me another way of defining implication that makes no mention of domains. It calls for three ancillary notions, but, unlike mine, covers finite and infinite sets of formulas of QC at a stroke. (1) Σ and Σ' being sets of individual variables of QC, M being a one-to-one mapping of Σ onto Σ', A being a formula of QC, and X_1, X_2, . . . , X_n ($n \geq 0$) being in alphabetical order all the members of Σ that occur free in A, let A_0 be A, and for each i from 1 to n let A_i be $A_{i-1}[X'_i/X_i]$, where X'_i is $M(X_i)$.[6] Then A_n is to count as the $M(\Sigma, \Sigma')$-correlate of A. (2) Where S and S' are sets of formulas of QC, S' is to be isomorphic with S if S' consists—for some sets Σ and Σ' of individual variables of QC and some one-to-one mapping M of Σ onto S'—of the $M(\Sigma, \Sigma')$-correlates of the various members of S. (3) A set S of formulas of QC is to be simultaneously satisfiable (in Beth's sense) if there is an assignment of truth-values to the atomic subformulas of the various members of S that satisfies each and every member of S. With (1)–(3) on hand, it is readily shown that *a set S of formulas of* QC—*be the set finite or infinite*—*implies a formula A of* QC, *as the word 'implies' is customarily used, if and only if no set of formulas of* QC *that is isomorphic with* $S \cup \{\sim A\}$ *is simultaneously satisfiable (in Beth's sense).*

6. Beth's account of validity, and either of the above accounts of implication, are easily made to suit $QC_=$, the first order quantificational calculus with identity. Where A is an atomic formula of $QC_=$, and X and Y are individual variables of $QC_=$, understand by $A(Y//X)$ any result of replacing zero or more occurrences of X in A by occurrences of Y. Next, declare an assignment *Asst* of truth-values to the atomic formulas of $QC_=$ *identity-normal* if: (i) for every individual variable X of $QC_=$, $X = X$ is assigned **T** in *Asst* and (ii) for every two individual variables X and Y of $QC_=$ and every atomic formula A of $QC_=$ A and $A(Y//X)$ are assigned the same truth-value in *Asst* if $X = Y$ is assigned **T** in *Asst*. Next, declare an assignment *Asst* of truth-values to the members of a set S_{AF} of atomic formulas of $QC_=$ *identity-normal* if *Asst* is the restriction to S_{AF} of an identity-normal assignment of truth-values to the atomic formulas of $QC_=$.[7] Then, take a formula A of $QC_=$ to be valid if A is satisfied (in the sense of Section 2) by every identity-normal assignment of truth-values to the atomic subformulas of A; and, to restrict ourselves to one account of implication, take A to be implied by a set S of formulas of $QC_=$ if: (a) in the case that S is finite, every identity-normal assignment of truth-values to the atomic subformulas of the various members of $S \cup \{A\}$ fails to satisfy a member of S or else satisfies A, (b) in the case that S is infinite, A is implied (in the sense of (a)) by some finite subset of S.

7. A good deal of interest has recently been accorded to $\emptyset$ as a domain. Indeed some prefer to call a formula A of $QC_=$ (QC, for that matter) valid only if A is valid in every nonempty domain *and in* $\emptyset$. Their preference is easily met. A serving as A_0, and the result of replacing the left-most component of A_{i-1} of the sort $(\forall X)B$ by '$p \supset p$' serving for each i from 1 on as A_i, appoint as the $\emptyset$-associate of a closed formula A of $QC_=$ the first one of A_0, A_1, A_2, ..., that has no component of the sort $(\forall X)B$.[8] Then, (a) take A, when open, to be valid if A is valid in the sense of Section 6; (b) take A, when closed, to be valid if A is valid in the sense of Section 6, and —A^* being the $\emptyset$-associate of A—A^* is satisfied by every assignment of truth-values to the atomic components of A^*; (c) take A, when open, to be implied by a set S of formulas of $QC_=$ if A is implied by S in the sense of Section 6; and (d) take A, when closed, to be implied by S if A is implied by S in the sense of Section 6, and—S^* consisting of the $\emptyset$-associates of the closed members of S and A^* being the $\emptyset$-associate of A—every assignment of truth-values to the atomic components of the various members of $S^* \cup \{A^*\}$ fails to satisfy a member of S^* or else satisfies A^*.[9]

Notes

1. Further grounds for dispensing with domains and, more generally, models are offered on pp. 102–118.

2. I take '$\sim$' and '$\supset$' to serve as the only primitive connectives of QC (and hence of SC), and '$\forall$' to serve as the only primitive quantifiers letter of QC. The formulas of this paper would normally be called *well-formed formulas* (*wffs*, for short).

3. For the sake of definiteness the individual variables of QC may be understood to run in the following alphabetic order: 'x', 'y', 'z', 'x'', 'y'', 'z'', etc.

4. I owe the reference to B. C. van Fraassen. The reader may wish to verify that in clause (d) of our definition of satisfaction $B(Y/X)$ cannot do duty for $B[Y/X]$.

A Simplified Account of Validity and Implication for Quantificational Logic 143

5. This because every individual variable of QC may, for example, be assigned the same member d of a given domain D of cardinality greater than 2 and 'f' be assigned some superset of $\{d\}$ short of D, in which case each one of '$f(x)$', '$f(y)$', '$f(z)$', etc. comes out true in D, but '$(\forall x)f(x)$' does not. I owe the example to R. H. Thomason.

6. I.e., where X'_i is the member of Σ' correlated under M with X_i. That $A_{i-1}(X'_i/X_i)$ cannot do duty here for $A_{i-1}[X'_i/X_i]$, was brought to my attention by van Fraassen.

7. In the original version of this paper *Asst* was said to be *identity-normal* if (i) for every individual variable X of QC$_=$, $X = X$ is assigned **T** in *Asst* if $X = X$ belongs to S_{AF} and (ii) for every two individual variables X and Y of QC$_=$, every atomic formula A of QC$_=$ that belongs to S_{AF}, and every (atomic) formula B of QC$_=$ of the sort $A(Y//X)$ that belongs to S_{AF}, A and B are assigned the same truth-value in *Asst* if $X = Y$ belongs to S_{AF} and is assigned **T** in *Asst*. Under this definition the assignment of **T** to '$f(x)$', '$x = y$', and '$y = z$', and of **F** to '$f(z)$', though failing to satisfy the valid formula '$f(x) \supset (x = y \supset (y = z \supset f(z)))$', counted as identity-normal. I noted the error while writing [3] and reported it on p. 298 of the book.

8. I follow here Hailperin's handling of vacuous quantifications in [2].

9. The original version of this paper had a closing paragraph on individual constants which called for correction and as a result is deleted. When the individual constants which either of QC and QC$_=$ may come with each have to designate a so-called *value* of 'x', 'y', 'z', etc., treat them the way free individual variables are treated here; when they have leave to designate nothing or to designate something not a value of 'x', 'y', 'z', etc., treat them as in [4]. The results in this paper were first announced at a colloquium on free logic at East Lansing, Michigan, in June of 1967.

References

[1] Beth, E. W. 1959. *The Foundations of Mathematics*. Amsterdam: North-Holland.
[2] Hailperin, T. 1953. "Quantification Theory and Empty Individual Domains." *The Journal of Symbolic Logic* 18: 197–200.
[3] Leblanc, H. 1976. *Truth-Value Semantics*. Amsterdam: North-Holland.
[4] Leblanc, H., and Thomason, R. H. 1969. "Completeness Theorems for some Presupposition-Free Logics." *Fundamenta Mathematicae* 62: 125–64 (#2 in this volume).

9
A Simplified Strong Completeness
Proof for QC$_=$

That QC, the first-order quantificational calculus without identity, permits proof of all its valid formulas, and hence is *complete*, was first established by Gödel in 1930. Some nineteen years later Henkin obtained the same result as a corollary of the following lemma: "*Any consistent set of closed formulas of* QC *is simultaneously satisfiable in a domain of size* $\aleph_0$." As Henkin knew at the time and others have shown since, the lemma does hold of every consistent set of formulas of QC, and—thus generalized—has the following corollary, because of which QC is often said to be *strongly complete*: "*If S implies A (i.e., if S* ∪ {~A} *is not simultaneously satisfiable in any non-empty domain), then* QC *permits derivation of A from S.*" Both Gödel and Henkin went on to show that QC$_=$, the first-order quantificational calculus with identity, is complete, and others have shown since that it is strongly complete as well.

Using a novel account of implication, due in good part to Hintikka, I submit here yet another proof that QC$_=$, and by rebound QC, is strongly complete. Half of the proof, the half found in Section 3 of the paper, is new, to my knowledge at any rate. The other half, found in Section 2, borrows from Henkin's proof of his 1949 Lemma. It is, however, considerably simpler, as I dispense with all the individual constants that Henkin resorted to, need but two (syntactical) lemmas (L1(k) and L1(l) below, respectively) to show that the sets S_1, S_2, S_3, etc. of Lemma 2 are consistent and dispense with semantical lemmas of any sort, the definitions of satisfaction and of implication in Section 1 seeing the argument through wholly on their own. My handling of identity, lastly, of the simplest, the notion of an identity-normal assignment of truth-values bearing most of the burden.

The definition of implication that I employ has a brief, but possibly interesting, history. In the fall of 1966 I noticed that a formula of QC is valid if and only if satisfied (in a sense to be defined shortly) by every assignment of truth-values to the atomic formulas of QC.[1] I wondered at the time whether—more generally—a set S of formulas of QC implies a formula A of QC if and only if every assignment of truth-values to the atomic formulas of QC that satisfies S

satisfies A. Thomason reminded me, unfortunately, that—though every assignment of truth-values to the atomic formulas of QC that satisfies the set $\{f(x),f(y),f(z), \ldots\}$ satisfies the formula '$(\forall x)f(x)$'—$\{f(x),f(y),f(z), \ldots\}$ does not imply '$(\forall x)f(x)$'.[2] A substitute definition of implication then occurred to me: When S is finite, take S to imply A if $S \cup \{\sim A\}$ is not satisfied by any assignment of truth-values to the atomic formulas of QC; in the contrary case, take S to imply A if, as the Compactness Theorem assures us, some finite subset of S implies A. And in January in 1967 Hintikka wrote of yet another definition, under which S implies A if no set of formulas of QC that is isomorphic (in a sense to be defined shortly) with $S \cup \{\sim A\}$ is satisfied by any assignment of truth-values to the atomic formulas of QC. It is Hintikka's definition of implication, suitably amended to suit $QC_=$, that I use here.

Shortly after hearing from Thomason, incidentally, I learned through van Fraassen of the following result of Beth's in [1], a book published in 1959, "*A set of closed formulas of* QC *is consistent if and only if satisfied by at least one assignment of truth-values to the atomic formulas of* QC." The result, which I generalize and prove afresh below, readily yields that: (a) a formula A of QC, be A closed or not, is valid if and only if A is satisfied by every assignment of truth-values to the atomic formulas of QC, and (b) a set S of closed formulas of QC implies a formula A of QC, whether A be closed or not, if and only if $S \cup \{\sim A\}$ is not satisfied by any assignment of truth-values to the atomic formulas of QC. Beth had thus anticipated the criterion of quantificational validity that I devised in the fall of 1955,[3] and shown my ill-fated criterion of quantificational implication to hold good whenever S exclusively consists of closed formulas. His line of reasoning on pp. 263–67 of [1], like mine in Section 2, is a simplification of Henkin's in [7].[4]

1. Syntactical and Semantical Preliminaries. To abridge matters, I shall presume known what counts as a formula of $QC_=$,[5] an atomic formula of $QC_=$, a quantifier-free formula of $QC_=$, a component of a formula of $QC_=$, a free (bound) occurrence in a formula of $QC_=$ of an individual variable of $QC_=$, an individual variable of $QC_=$ occurring free (bound) in a formula of $QC_=$, and an open (closed) formula of $QC_=$; and I shall call a set S of formulas of QC = a *formula set of Type I* if infinitely many individual variables of $QC_=$ do not occur free in any member of S,[6] otherwise a *formula set of Type II*. I shall also presume that the individual variables of $QC_=$ and the formulas of $QC_=$ are arranged in some fixed alphabetical order, and shall refer to the alphabetically second individual variable of $QC_=$, its alphabetically fourth one, its alphabetically sixth one, etc., as the *evenly indexed individual variables of* $QC_=$. A being a formula of $QC_=$, and X and Y being not necessarily distinct individual variables of $QC_=$, I shall take $A(Y/X)$ to be A if X occurs free in a component of A of the sort $(\forall Y)B$; otherwise, $A(Y/X)$ will be the result of replacing every free occurrence of X in A by an occurrence of Y. A being again a formula of $QC_=$, and $X_1, X_2, \ldots, X_n, X'_1, X'_2, \ldots, X'_n$ ($n \geq 1$)

being not necessarily distinct individual variables of $QC_=$, I shall take $(A)[X'_1/X_1]$ $(A'[X'_1/X_1]$, for short, whenever the occasion permits) to be the result of replacing, *first*, every bound occurrence of X'_1 in A by an occurrence of the alphabetically earliest individual variable of $QC_=$ that is foreign to A, and *then* every free occurrence of X_1 in the resulting formula by an occurrence of X'_1, and take $(A)[X'_1, X'_2, \ldots, X'_n/X_1, X_2, \ldots, X_n]$ $(A[X'_1, X'_2, \ldots, X'_n/X_1, X_2, \ldots, X_n]$, for short, whenever the occasion permits) to be $(A[X'_2, X'_3, \ldots, X'_n/X_2, X_3, \ldots, X_n])[X'_1/X_1]$. M being a one-to-one mapping of the set of the individual variables of $QC_=$ into itself, A being a formula of $QC_=$, and X_1, $X_2, \ldots, X_n$ ($n \geq 0$) being in alphabetical order all the individual variables of $QC_=$ that occur free in A, I shall take *the M-image* of A to be A when n equals 0, otherwise to be $A[M(X_1), M(X_2), \ldots, M(X_n)/X_1, X_2, \ldots, X_n]$. And, S and S' being not necessarily distinct sets of formulas of $QC_=$, I shall take S to be *isomorphic to* S if: (i) in the case that S is empty, S' is empty as well, and (ii) in the contrary case, S' consists—for some one-to-one mapping M of the set of the individual variables of $QC_=$ into itself—of the M-images of the various members of S.

Following recent practice, I shall count as an *axiom* any formula of $QC_=$ that:

(i) is of one of the eight sorts

A1. $A \supset (B \supset A)$,

A2. $(A \supset (B \supset C)) \supset ((A \supset B) \supset (A \supset C))$,

A3. $(\sim A \supset \sim B) \supset (B \supset A)$,

A4. $A \supset (\forall X)A$, where X does not occur free in A,

A5. $(\forall X)A \supset A(Y/X)$,

A6. $(\forall X)(A \supset B) \supset ((\forall X)A \supset (\forall X)B)$,

A7. $X = X$,

and

A8. $X = X' \supset (A \supset A')$, where X and X' are two distinct individual variables of $QC_=$, A is an atomic formula of $QC_=$, and A' is any result of replacing X by X' at one or more places in A,

or (ii) is of the sort $(\forall X)A$, where A is an axiom.[7]

A and B being formulas of $QC_=$, I shall take B to follow from A and $A \supset B$ by application of Modus Ponens. S being a set of formulas of $QC_=$ and A a formula of $QC_=$, I shall count as a *derivation of A from S* any finite column of formulas of $QC_=$ whose last entry is A and every one of whose entries belongs to S, is an axiom, or follows from two previous entries by application of Modus Ponens; and take A to be *derivable* from $S(S \vdash A$, for short) if there is a derivation of A from S. Lastly, I shall take a set S of formulas of QC$_=$ to be *inconsistent* if $S \vdash p \mathrel{\&} {\sim}p$, otherwise to be *consistent*.

Turning then to semantical matters, I shall declare an assignment *Asst* of truth-values to the atomic formulas of QC$_=$ *identity-normal* if: (i) for every individual variable X of QC$_=$ *Asst* assigns the truth-value **T** to $X = X$, and (ii) for every two distinct individual variables X and X' of QC$_=$, every atomic formula A of QC$_=$, and every result A' of replacing X by X' at one or more places in A, *Asst* assigns the same truth-value to both A and A' if it assigns **T** to $X = X'$. *Asst* being an assignment of truth-values to the atomic formulas of QC$_=$ and A a formula of QC$_=$, I shall say that *Asst* satisfies A if: (a) when A is atomic, *Asst* assigns **T** to A, (b) when A is of the sort ${\sim}B$, *Asst* does not satisfy B, (c) when A is of the sort $B \supset C$, *Asst* does not satisfy B or *Asst* satisfies C, and (d) when A is of the sort $(\forall X)B$, *Asst* satisfies $B[Y/X]$ for every individual variable Y of QC$_=$.[8] *Asst* being again an assignment of truth-values to the atomic formulas of QC$_=$ and S a set of formulas of QC$_=$, I shall say that *Asst satisfies S* if *Asst* satisfies every member of S. Lastly, S being a set of formulas of QC$_=$ and A a formula of QC$_=$, I shall say that *S implies A* (or, in Tarski's terminology, A is a semantic consequence of S) if no set of formulas of QC$_=$ that is isomorphic to $S \cup \{{\sim}A\}$ is satisfied by any identity-normal assignment of truth-values to the atomic formulas of QC$_=$; and I shall say that a formula A of QC$_=$ is *valid* if $\varnothing$ implies A.

When proving that $S \vdash A$ if S implies A, I first consider the case where S is a formula set of Type I (i.e., a set such that infinitely many individual variables of QC$_=$ do not occur free in any member of S); I then pass on to the case where S is a formula set of Type II (i.e., a set such that at most finitely many individual variables of QC$_=$ do not occur free in any member of S). The reader will note that among the formula sets of Type I turn up all sets of closed formulas of QC$_=$, all finite sets of formulas of QC$_=$, etc.

2. A Strong Completeness Proof for QC$_=$: Case I. The following five lemmas pave the way for Case I of my strong completeness proof for QC$_=$. In the first of them the set S may be of either one of Types I and II; in the remaining four it is explicitly required to be of Type I. Proof of the various clauses of Lemma 1 is routine.

Lemma 1. (a) *If $S \vdash A$, then $S' \vdash A$ for some finite subset S' of S.*
(b) *If A belongs to S, then $S \vdash A$.*
(c) *If $S \vdash A$, then $S \cup S' \vdash A$ for any set S' of formulas of QC$_=$.*
(d) *If $S \vdash A$ and $S \vdash {\sim}A$, then $S \vdash p \mathrel{\&} {\sim}p$.*
(e) *If $S \cup \{A\} \vdash p \mathrel{\&} {\sim}p$, then $S \vdash {\sim}A$.*
(f) *If $S \cup \{{\sim}A\} \vdash p \mathrel{\&} {\sim}p$, then $S \vdash A$.*
(g) *If $S \vdash A$ and $S \vdash A \supset B$, then $S \vdash B$.*
(h) *If $S \vdash {\sim}A$ or $S \vdash B$, then $S \vdash A \supset B$.*

148   Part 2: Truth

(i)   If $S \vdash A \supset B$ and $S \vdash {\sim}B$, then $S \vdash {\sim}A$.
(j)   If $S \vdash (\forall X)A$, then $S \vdash A[Y/X]$ for any individual variable Y of $QC_=$.
(k) $\vdash (\exists X)(A \supset (\forall X)A)$.
(l)   If $\vdash (\exists X)A$ and $S \cup \{A[Y/X]\} \vdash B$, then $S \vdash B$, so long as Y does not occur free in any member S, nor in $(\exists X)A$, nor in B.
(m) $S \vdash X = X$.
(n)   If $S \vdash X = X'$, then $S \vdash A$ iff $S \vdash A'$, where X and X' are distinct individual variables of $QC_=$, A is an atomic formula of $QC_=$, and A' is any result of replacing X by X' at one or more places in A.

Lemma 2.   Let S_0 be a consistent formula set of Type I; for each i from 1 on let S_i be $S_{i-1} \cup \{A_i[Y/X_i] \supset (\forall X_i)A_i\}$, where (i) $(\forall X_i)A_i$ is the alphabetically i-th formula of $QC_=$ of the sort $(\forall X)A$, and (ii) Y is the alphabetically earliest individual variable of $QC_=$ that does not occur free in any member of S_{i-1} nor in $(\forall X_i)A_i$ and let S_∞ be the union of S_0, S_1, S_2, etc. Then:
(a)   For each i from $\emptyset$ on S_i is consistent;
(b)   For each finite subset S' of S_∞ there is an i($i \geq 0$) such that S' is a subset of S_i, S_{i+1}, S_{i+2}, etc.;
(c) S_∞ is consistent; and
(d)   For each formula of $QC_=$ of the sort $(\forall X)A$ there is an individual variable Y of $QC_=$ such that $A[Y/X] \supset (\forall X)A$ belongs to S_∞.
Proof:
   (a) Suppose S_i($i \geq 1$) were consistent. Then in view of L1(k)–(l) so would S_{i-1} be. But S_0 is presumed to be consistent. Hence (a) by mathematical induction on i.
   (b) For each member A of S' there is an i($i \geq 0$) such that A belongs to each one of S_i, S_{i+1}, S_{i+2}, etc. Hence, S' being finite, there is an i($i \geq 0$) such that each member of S' belongs to S_i, S_{i+1}, S_{i+2}, etc.
   (c) Suppose S_∞ were inconsistent. Then in view of L1(a) some finite subset of S_∞ would be inconsistent, and hence in view of (b) and L1(c) there would be an i($i \geq 0$) such that each one of S_i, S_{i+1}, S_{i+2}, etc., is inconsistent. Hence (c) in view of (a).

Lemma 3.   Let S_∞^0 of Lemma 2; A_j being the alphabetically j-th formula of $QC_=$, let S_∞^j be for each j from 1 on $S_\infty^{j-1} \cup \{A_j\}$ or S_∞^{j-1} according as $S_\infty^{j-1} \cup \{A_j\}$ is consistent or not; and let S_∞^∞ be the union of $S_\infty^0, S_\infty^1, S_\infty^2$, etc. Then:
(a)   For each i from 0 on S_∞^i is consistent;
(b)   For each finite subset S' of S_∞^∞ there is an i such that S' is a subset of S_∞^i, $S_\infty^{i+2}, S_\infty^{i+2}$, etc.;
(c) S_∞^∞ is consistent;
(d)   If A does not belong to S_∞^∞, then $S_\infty^\infty \cup \{A\}$ is inconsistent; and
(e)   For each formula of $QC_=$ of the sort $(\forall X)A$ there is an individual variable Y of $QC_=$ such that $A[Y/X] \supset (\forall X)A$ belongs to S_∞^∞.
Proof:
   (a) Suppose S_∞^j ($j \geq 1$) is $S_\infty^{j-1} \cup \{A_j\}$; then S_∞^j is consistent, and hence is

A Simplified Strong Completeness Proof for $QC_=$ 149

consistent if S_∞^{j-1} is. Suppose, on the other hand, S_∞^j is S^{j-1}, then S_∞^j is consistent if S_∞^{j-1} is. But in view of L2(c) S_∞^0 is consistent. Hence (a) by mathematical induction on j.

(b)–(c) Proofs like those of L2(b)–(c).

(d) Suppose A is the alphabetically j-th formula of $QC_=$. If $S_\infty^\infty \cup \{A\}$ is consistent, then in view of L1(c) so is $S_\infty^{j-1} \cup \{A_j\}$ ($= S_\infty^j$), hence A belongs to S_∞^j, and hence A belongs to S_∞^∞.

Lemma 4. *For every consistent formula set S of Type I there exists a set S' of formulas of $QC_=$, the set S_∞^∞ of Lemma 3, such that:*
(a) S is a subset of S';
(b) $S' \vdash \sim A$ iff it is not the case that $S' \vdash A$;
(c) $S' \vdash A \supset B$ iff $S' \vdash B$ if $S' \vdash A$; and
(d) $S' \vdash (\forall X)A$ iff $S' \vdash A[Y/X]$ for each individual variable Y of $QC_=$.

Proof:
(a) By Lemmas 2–3.

(b) Suppose $S' \vdash A$. If $\sim A$ were also derivable from S', then in view of L1(d) S' would be inconsistent, as against L3(c). Suppose, on the other hand, it is not the case that $S' \vdash A$. Then in view of L1(b) A does not belong to S', hence in view of L3(d) $S' \cup \{A\}$ is inconsistent, and hence in view of L1(e) $S' \vdash \sim A$. Hence (b).

(c) If $S' \vdash A \supset B$ and $S' \vdash A$, then in view of L1(g) $S' \vdash B$. Conversely, if it is not the case that $S' \vdash A$, then in view of (b) and L1(h) $S' \vdash A \supset B$; and, if $S' \vdash B$, then in view of L1(h) $S' \vdash A \supset B$. Hence (c).

(d) If $S' \vdash (\forall X)A$, then in view of L1(j) $S' \vdash A[Y/X]$ for each individual variable Y of $QC_=$. Suppose, on the other hand, it is not the case that $S' \vdash (\forall X)A$. Then in view of (b) $S' \vdash \sim(\forall X)A$. But in view of L3(e) and L1(b) $S' \vdash A[Y/X] \supset (\forall X)A$ for some individual variable Y of $QC_=$. Hence in view of L1(i) and (a) it is not the case that $S' \vdash A[Y/X]$ for at least one individual variable Y of $QC_=$. Hence (d).

Lemma 5. *For every consistent formula set S of Type I there exists an identity-normal assignment of truth-values to the atomic formulas of $QC_=$ that satisfies S.*
Proof: Since S is consistent, then in view of Lemma 4 there exists a formula set S' such that (a)–(d) as in Lemma 4. Suppose then *Asst* is the result of assigning **T** or **F** to each atomic formula A of $QC_=$ according as $S' \vdash A$ or not. (i) In view of L4(b)−(d) it is readily shown by mathematical induction on the number of occurrences of '$\sim$', '$\supset$', and '$\forall$' in a formula A of $QC_=$ that *Asst* satisfies A if and $S' \vdash A$. For suppose, in particular, that A is of the sort $\sim B$. Then in view of L4(b) $S' \vdash \sim B$ only if it is not the case that $S' \vdash B$, hence by the hypothesis of the induction $S' \vdash \sim B$ only if *Asst* does not satisfy B, and hence $S' \vdash \sim B$ only if *Asst* satisfies $\sim B$. And so on. (ii) Suppose A belongs to S, and hence in view of L4(a) to S'. Then in view of L1(b) $S' \vdash A$, and hence in view of (i) *Asst* satisfies A. Hence *Asst* satisfies S. (iii) In view of L1(m) S'

150   *Part 2: Truth*

⊢ $X = X$, and hence in view of (i) *Asst* assigns **T** to $X = X$ for each individual variable X of QC$_=$. Suppose, on the other hand, that *Asst* assigns **T** to $X = X'$, where X and X' are distinct individual variables of QC$_=$, suppose that A is an atomic formula of QC$_=$, and suppose that A' is any result of replacing X by X' at one or more places in A. Then in view of (i) $S' ⊢ X = X'$, hence in view of L1(n) $S' ⊢ A$ if and only if $S' ⊢ A'$, and hence in view of (i) *Asst* assigns the same truth-value to A and A'. Hence *Asst* is identity-normal. Hence Lemma 5.

Case I of our strong completeness theorem is now readily proved.

Theorem 1.   *Let S be a formula of Type I. If S implies A, then $S ⊢ A$.*
Proof: Suppose S implies A. Since S is isomorphic to itself, no identity-normal assignment of truth-values to the atomic formulas of QC$_=$ *satisfies* $S ∪ \{\sim A\}$. But $S ∪ \{\sim A\}$ is a formula set of Type I if S is. Hence in view of Lemma 5 $S ∪ \{\sim A\}$ is inconsistent. Hence in view of L1(f) $S ⊢ A$.

Theorem 1 has some interesting corollaries, which we record as T3(a)–(d). Proof of the auxiliary Theorem 2 is left to the reader.

Theorem 2.   (a)   *If $S ⊢ A$, then S implies A.*
(b)   *If $S ⊢ A$, then no identity-normal assignment of truth-values to the atomic formulas of* QC$_=$ *satisfies $S ∪ \{\sim A\}$.*

Theorem 3.   *Let S in (a)–(b) be a formula set of Type I, and hence in particular a set of closed formulas of* QC$_=$ *or a finite set of formulas of* QC$_=$.
(a)   *S implies A if and only if no identity-normal assignment of truth-values to the atomic formulas of* QC$_=$ *satisfies $S ∪ \{\sim A\}$.*
(b)   *S is consistent if and only if some identity-normal assignment of truth-values to the atomic formulas of* QC$_=$ *satisfies S.*
(c)   *A is valid if and only if every identity-normal assignment of truth-values to the atomic formulas of QC$_=$ satisfies A.*
Proof:
(a)   Suppose no identity-normal assignment of truth-values to the atomic formulas of QC$_=$ satisfies $S ∪ \{\sim A\}$. Since $S ∪ \{\sim A\}$ is a formula set of Type I if S is, in view of Theorem 1 and L1(f) $S ⊢ A$, and hence in view of T2(a) S implies A. Conversely, if S implies A, then in view of Theorem 1 and T2(b) no identity-normal assignment of truth-values to the atomic formulas of QC$_=$ satisfies $S ∪ \{\sim A\}$. Hence (a).

(b)   In view of (a) S is consistent if and only if some identity-normal assignment of truth values to the atomic formulas of QC$_=$ satisfies $S ∪ \{\sim(p \ \& \sim p)\}$. But every assignment of truth-values to the atomic formulas of QC$_=$ satisfies '$\sim(p \ \& \sim p)$'. Hence (b).

(c)   By (a).

As noted above, proof of T3(b) for the special case where S is a set of closed formulas of QC was first offered by Beth. Sharper versions of T3(a)–(c) will be found in Section 4.

3. A Strong Completeness Proof for $QC_=$: Case II. The following three lemmas pave the way for Case II of my strong completeness proof for $QC_=$. Proof of the last four clauses of Lemma 6 is routine.

Lemma 6. (a) $\varnothing$ *is consistent.*
(b) *If* $\{A_1, A_2, \ldots, A_n\} \vdash B$ ($n \geq 1$), *then* $\vdash ((\ldots(A_1 \& A_2) \& \ldots) \& A_n) \supset B$.
(c) *If* $S \vdash A$ *and* $S \vdash B$, *then* $S \vdash A \& B$.
(d) *If* $S \vdash A$, *then* $S \vdash A[Y/X]$ *for any two individual variables X and Y of* $QC_=$.
(e) *Let* A' *be the result of replacing every bound occurrence of X in A by an occurrence of* X'. *If* $S \vdash A$, *then* $S \vdash A'$, *so long as* X' *is foreign to A.*
Proof:
  (a) Every assignment of truth-values to the atomic formulas of $QC_=$ satisfies '$\sim(p \& \sim p)$'. Hence (a) by T_2(b).

Lemma 7. *Let S be a formula set of Type II; let Σ consist of all the individual variables of $QC_=$ And Σ' of all the evenly indexed individual variables of $QC_=$; let M be the one-to-one mapping of Σ onto Σ' such that, where X is the alphabetically i-th individual variable of $QC_=$, M(X) is the alphabetically $(2 \times i)$-th individual variable of $QC_=$; and let S' be S if S is $\varnothing$, otherwise consist of the M-images of the various members of S. Then:*
(a) S' *is isomorphic to S,*
(b) S' *is of Type I, and*
(c) S' *is consistent if S is.*
Proof:
  (c) Suppose S' is inconsistent. Then in view of L1(a) and L6(a) there is a subset $\{A'_1, A'_2, \ldots, A'_n\}$ ($n \geq 1$) of S' such that

$$\{A'_1, A'_2, \ldots, A'_n\} \vdash p \& \sim p,$$

hence in view of L6(b) such that

$$\vdash ((\ldots(A'_1 \& A'_2) \& \ldots) \& A'_n) \supset (p \& \sim p),$$

and hence in view of L6(d) such that $\{A_1, A_2, \ldots, A_n\} \vdash ((\ldots(A'_1 \& A'_2) \& \ldots) A'_n)[X_1, X_2, \ldots, X_k/X'_1, X'_2, \ldots, X'_k] \supset (p \& \sim p)$, where (i) for each i from 1 through n A_i is the formula of $QC_=$ of which A'_i is the M-image, (ii) $X'_1, X'_2, \ldots, X'_k$ are in alphabetical order all the members of Σ' that occur free in $(\ldots(A'_1 \& A'_2) \& \ldots) \& A'_n$, and (iii) for each i from 1 through k X_i is the member of Σ such that $M(X'_i)$ is X_i. Now, Y_1 being the alphabetically first individual variable of $QC_=$ that is foreign to $(\ldots(A'_1 \& A'_2) \& \ldots) \& A'_n$, Y_2 the first one that is foreign to $((\ldots (A'_1 \& A'_2) \& \ldots) \& A'_n)[X_1/X'_2], \ldots,$

152   Part 2: Truth

and Y_k the first one that is foreign to $((\ldots(A_1' \& A_2') \& \ldots) A_n')[X_1, X_2, \ldots, X_{k-1}/X_1', X_2', \ldots, X_{k-1}']$, let B_i be the result of replacing all the free occurrences of $X_1', X_2', \ldots, X_k'$ in A_i by occurrences of $Y_1, Y_2, \ldots, Y_k$, respectively. Then in view of L1(b) and L6(e)

$$\{A_1, A_2, \ldots, A_n\} \vdash B_i$$

for each i from 1 through n, and hence in view of L6(c)

$$\{A_1, A_2, \ldots, A_n\} \vdash (\ldots(B_1 \& B_2) \& \ldots) \& B_n.$$

But $(\ldots(B_1 \& B_2) \& \ldots) \& B_n$ is the same as $((\ldots(A_1' \& A_2') \& \ldots) \& A_n')[X_1, X_2, \ldots, X_k/X_1', X_2', \ldots, X_k']$. Hence in view of L1(g)

$$\{A_1, A_2, \ldots, A_n\} \vdash p \& \sim p.$$

Hence in view of L1(c) S is inconsistent. Hence Lemma 7.[9]

Lemma 8.   *For every consistent formula set S of Type II there exists an identity-normal assignment of truth-values of the atomic formulas of* $QC_=$ *that satisfies some formula set isomorphic to S.*
Proof by Lemmas 5 and 7.

Case II of our strong completeness theorem is now readily proved:

Theorem 4.   *Let S be a formula set of Type II. If S implies A, then $S \vdash A$.*
Proof: Suppose S implies A. Then in view of Lemma 8 $S \cup \{\sim A\}$ is inconsistent. Hence in view of L1(f) $S \vdash A$.

Hence, to throw together Theorems 1 and 4:

Theorem 5.   (a)   *If S implies A, then $S \vdash A$.*
(b)   *If A is valid, then $\vdash A$.*
Proof:
   (a)   By T1 and T4.
   (b)   By (a).

Note, incidentally, that if the column made up of the formulas $B_1, B_2, \ldots, B_p$ of $QC_=$ constitutes a derivation of a formula A of QC from a set S of formulas of QC, then the column in question can be converted into a derivation of A from S all of whose entries are formulas of QC. Suppose indeed that $X_1, X_2, \ldots, X_m$ ($m \geq 0$) are all the individual variables of QC, and $F_1, F_2, \ldots, F_n$ ($n \geq 0$) all the predicate variables of QC, that occur in anyone of $B_1, B_2, \ldots,$ and B_p. Next, in the case that $n > 0$, take $C_j(Y, Z)$ to be for each j from 1 through n and for any two individual variables Y and Z of QC
   (I)   when F_j is 1-place, the biconditional

$$F_j(X) \equiv F_j(Y),$$

A Simplified Strong Completeness Proof for QC₌   153

(II) when F_j is 2-place, the conjunction

$$(\forall X')(F_j(X',X) \equiv F_j(X',Y)) \ \& \ (\forall X')(F_j(X,X') \equiv F_j(Y,X')),$$

where X' is the alphabetically earliest individual variable of QC distinct from X and Y, and so on. Lastly, for each i from 1 to p, let B'_i be the result of replacing $X = Y$ everywhere in B_i by $f(X,Y) \supset f(X,Y)$ ('f' an arbitrary 2-place predicate variable of QC) when $n = 0$, otherwise by $C_1(X,Y) \ \& \ C_2(X,Y) \ \& \ldots \ \& \ C_n(X,Y)$. Then the column made up of $B'_1, B'_2, \ldots, B'_p$ either constitutes a proof of A from S all of whose entries are formulas of QC or can be mechanically converted into one.[10]

Note also that if there is a derivation of a formula A of SC, the ordinary sentential calculus, from a set S of formulas of SC, then the result of replacing in each entry: (i) each component of the sort $(\forall X)B$ by B, (ii) each component of the sort $X = X$ by '$p \supset p$', (iii) each component of the sort $X = Y$, where X and Y are distinct individual variables of QC₌, by '$\sim(p \supset p)$', and (iv) every other atomic component that is not a sentence variable of QC₌ by 'p'[11] is readily converted into a derivation of A from S all of whose entries are formulas of SC.

That QC and SC are strongly complete is thus an immediate corollary of our Theorem 5.

4. Subformula Matters. Let a formula A of QC₌ count as a subformula of a formula B of QC₌ if: (i) B is the same as A, (ii) B being of the sort $\sim C$, A is a subformula of C, (iii) B being of the sort $C \supset D$, A is a subformula of C or one of D, and (iv) B being of the sort $(\forall X)C$, A is a subformula of $C[Y/X]$ for some individual variable Y of QC₌. It can be shown by a simple enough induction that if a formula A of QC₌ is satisfied by an identity-normal assignment *Asst* of truth-values to the atomic formulas of QC₌, then A is satisfied by the restriction of *Asst* to the atomic subformulas of A, and vice-versa. And it is seen at a glance that the atomic subformulas of a quantifier-free formula A are the same as the atomic components of A. This being so, let an assignment *Asst* of truth-values to the members of a set S_{AF} of atomic formulas of QC₌ be said to be identity-normal if *Asst* is the restriction to the members of S_{AF} of an identity-normal assignment of truth-values to the atomic formulas of GC₌.[12] Let a formula A of QC₌ be said to be satisfied by an assignment of truth-values to the members of S_{AF}, where S_{AF} *is a set of atomic formulas of QC₌* to which belongs every atomic subformula of A, if conditions (a)–(d) on p. 147, paragraph 2, are met. Let a quantifier-free formula A of QC₌ be said to be satisfied by an assignment of truth-values to the various members of S_{AF}, where S_{AF} is a set of atomic formulas of QC₌ to which belongs every atomic component of A, if the first three of those conditions are met. Let a set S of formulas of QC₌ be said to be satisfied by an assignment of truth-values to the members of S_{AF}, where S_{AF} is a set of atomic formulas of QC₌ to which belongs every subformula of every member of S, if the assignment satisfies every member of S. And

154   Part 2: Truth

let a set S of quantifier-free formulas of $QC_=$ be said to be satisfied by a given assignment of truth-values to the various members of S_{AF}, where S_{AF} is a set of atomic formulas of $QC_=$ to which belongs every atomic component of every member of S, if the assignment satisfies every member of S. The following are then forthcoming as theorems:

Theorem 6. *S implies A if and only if no formula set $S' \cup \{\sim A'\}$ that is isomorphic to $S \cup \{\sim A\}$ is satisfied by any identity-normal assignment of truth-values to the atomic subformulas of the members of $S' \cup \{\sim A\}$.*

Theorem 7. *Let S in (a)–(b) be a formula set of Type I, and hence in particular a set of closed formulas of $QC_=$ or a finite set of formulas of $QC_=$.*
(a)   *S implies A if and only if no identity-normal assignment of truth-values to the atomic subformulas of the members of $S \cup \{\sim A\}$ satisfies $S \cup \{\sim A\}$.*
(b)   *S is consistent if and only if some identity-normal assignment of truth-values to the atomic subformulas of the members of S satisfies S.*
(c)   *A is valid if and only if every identity-normal assignment of truth-values to the atomic subformulas of A satisfies A.*

Theorem 8. *Let S be a set of quantifier-free formulas of $QC_=$, and A be a quantifier-free formula of $QC_=$.*
(a)   *S implies A if and only if no identity-normal assignment of truth-values to the atomic components of the members of $S \cup \{\sim A\}$ satisfies $S \cup \{\sim A\}$.*
(b)   *S is consistent if and only if some identity-normal assignment of truth-values to the atomic components of the members of S satisfies S.*
(c)   *A is valid if and only if every assignment of truth-values to the atomic components of A satisfies A.*
(d)   *$(\forall X_1)(\forall X_2) \ldots (\forall X_n) A$ ($n \geq 0$) is valid if and only if every assignment of truth-values to the atomic components of A satisfies A.*

The first of these theorems figures in [8] as a definition of implication for the case where S is infinite, clause (a) of the second as a definition of implication for the case where S is finite, and clause (c) of the same theorem as a definition of implication for the case where S is finite, and clause (c) of the same theorem as a definition of validity. Clause (d) of the third theorem is familiar from the literature, and—incidentally—prompted my search for new criteria of quantificational validity and implication.[13]

Notes

1. The result was reported in [8]. Dunn and Belnap, who had independently arrived at the same result, reported it in [3], a paper published the same year as [8].
2. Dunn and Belnap report in [3] that the same counterexample occurred to them a few years before they wrote the paper.
3. The criterion had also been anticipated, I later found out, by Schütte in [10].

A Simplified Strong Completeness Proof for $QC_=$ 155

4. Beth mentions in this connection [6], a paper of Hasenjaeger's in which some simplifications had already been brought to Henkin's argument.

5. '$\sim$', '$\supset$', and '$\forall$' are understood here to serve as the primitive operators of $QC_=$, and '$\lor$', '&', '$\equiv$', and '$\exists$' to be defined in the customary manner. The formulas of this paper would normally be called *wffs*.

6. In later papers of mine formula sets of Type I are called *infinitely extendible*, a term I owe to R. K. Meyer.

7. So far as I know, the above way of specifying the axioms of $QC_=$—and thereby dispensing with Generalization as a rule of inference—goes back to [4]. For further details on the matter, see the closing paper in this volume.

8. Consider the result *Asst* of assigning **T** to all the atomic formulas of $QC_=$ but '$f(y,y)$'. If $B(Y/X)$ did duty in (d) for $B[Y/X]$, then '$(\forall x)(\forall y)f(x,y)$' would be satisfied by *Asst* even though '$f(y,y)$' is not. In papers written from 1970 on I use two runs of individual variables and thereby avoid the difficulties besetting substitutions here. See p. 129 on this matter.

9. The above proof would not go through if on p. 146 the M-image of A were taken to be $A(M(X_1), M(X_2), \ldots, M(X_k)/X_1, X_2, \ldots, X_k)$ rather than $A[M(X_1), M(X_2), \ldots, M(X_k)/X_1, X_2, \ldots, X_k]$ when $k > 0$. Suppose indeed that S had '$(\forall y)f(x,y)$ & $g(y)$' and '$\sim g(x)$' among its members, that 'x' counted as the alphabetically first individual variable of $QC_=$, and that 'y' counted as the second. Since 'x' occurs free in a component of '$(\forall y)f(x,y)$ & $g(y)$' in which 'y' occurs bound, the M-image of '$(\forall y)f(x,y)$ & $g(y)$' would be '$(\forall y)f(x,y)$ & $g(y)$' itself, and hence S would have '$(\forall y)f(x,y)$ & $g(y)$)' and '$\sim g(y)$' as two of its members, and hence S' would not be consistent even if S were. I owe the example to van Fraassen.

10. This paragraph owes some to R. K. Meyer.

11. I borrow (iv) from [2], footnote 182, where it is credited to J. G. Kemeny.

12. In the original version of this paper identity-normal assignments were defined as on p. 143, note 7. The error was first reported in [9].

13. The results of this paper were announced at the Fourteenth International Congress for Philosophie, Vienna, 2–9, September 1968. Thanks are due to J. Hintikka, R. K. Meyer, R. H. Thomason, and B. C. van Fraassen for their kind advice and encouragement.

References

[1] Beth, E. W. 1959. *The Foundations of Mathematics*. Amsterdam: North-Holland.
[2] Church, A. 1956. *Introduction to Mathematical Logic, Volume 1*. Princeton: Princeton University Press.
[3] Dunn, M., and Belnap, N. D., Jr. 1968. "The Substitution Interpretation of the Quantifiers." *Noûs* 2: 177–85.
[4] Fitch, F. B. 1948. "Intuitionistic Modal Logic with Quantifiers." *Portugaliae Mathematica* 7: 113–18.
[5] Gödel, K. 1930. "Die Vollständigkeit der Axiome des logischen Functionenkalküls." *Monatshefte für Mathematik und Physik* 37: 349–60.
[6] Hasenjaeger, G. 1953. "Eine Bemerkung zu Henkin's Beweis für die Vollständigkeit des Prädikatenkalkuls der ersten Stufe." *The Journal of Symbolic Logic* (hereafter *JSL*) 18: 42–48.
[7] Henkin, L. 1949. "The Completeness of the First-Order Functional Calculus." *JSL* 14: 159–66.
[8] Leblanc, H. 1968. "A Simplified Account of Validity and Implication for Quantificational Logic." *JSL* 33: 231–35 (#8 in this volume).
[9] ———. 1976. *Truth-Value Semantics*. Amsterdam: North-Holland.
[10] Schütte, K. 1962. *Lecture Notes in Mathematical Logic, Volume 1*. The Pennsylvania State University.

10
Truth-Value Assignments
and Their Cardinality

Readers of Beth, Schütte, and their followers know of course how the notions of satisfiability and validity for QC are defined in truth-value semantics. As a summary for the uninitiated, suppose that QC has two runs of individual letters: (i) 'a', 'b', 'c', 'a'', 'b'', 'c'', etc., to function as *free* individual variables do in the literature and be called here *individual parameters*, and (ii) 'x', 'y', 'z', 'x'', 'y'', 'z'', etc., to function as *bound* individual variables ordinarily do and be called here *individual variables*.[1] Understand by a *truth-value assignment to a set S of one or more atomic wffs of* QC any function from S to $\{\mathbf{T},\mathbf{F}\}$, atomic wffs of QC being wffs of the sort $F^m(P_1,P_2,\ldots,P_m)$, where F^m is a sentence parameter[2] in case $m = 0$, otherwise F^m is an m-place predicate parameter[3] and $P_1, P_2, \ldots, P_m$ are (not necessarily distinct) individual parameters.[4] And, given a wff A of QC and a set S of atomic wffs of QC, among them all the atomic subformulas of A,[5] take A to be *true on a truth-value assignment* α *to S* if

 (a) in case A is atomic, $\alpha(A) = \mathbf{T}$,
 (b) in case A is of the sort $\sim B$, B is not true on α,
 (c) in case A is of the sort $B \supset C$, B is not true on α or C is, and
 (d) in case A is of the sort $(\forall X)B$, the result $B(P/X)$ of putting P everywhere in B for X is true on α for every individual parameter P of QC.[6]

This done, you certify A *satisfiable in the truth-value sense*—*tv-satisfiable*, for short—if A is true on at least one truth-value assignment to the atomic subformulas of A;[7] and you certify A *valid in the truth-value sense*—*tv-valid*, for short—if A is true on every truth-value assignment to the atomic subformulas of A.

It is easily shown that A is tv-satisfiable if and only if A has a model,[8] and that A is tv-valid if and only if $\sim A$ has none. For proof, call a model $\langle D, I_D \rangle$ a *Henkin model* if, no matter the member d of D, there is at least one individual parameter P of QC such that $I_D(P) = d$. To each truth-value assignment α there corresponds a *(Henkin) model* $\langle D, I_D \rangle$ known as the model-theoretic *counterpart of* α and such that a *wff of* QC *is true on* α *if and only if true in*

Truth-Value Assignments and Their Cardinality 157

$<D,I_D>$ (= **Theorem 1**),[9] and *to each Henkin model $<D,I_D>$ there corresponds a truth-value assignment α known as the truth-value counterpart of $<D,I_D>$ and such that a wff of QC is true in $<D,I_D>$ if and only if true on α* (= **Theorem 2**). But, as review of Henkin's completeness proof for QC will disclose, any wff of QC that has a model is sure to have a Henkin one.[10] So a wff A of QC is tv-satisfiable if and only if A has a model, and hence A is tv-valid if and only if ~A has none. Since in the standard literature a wff of QC is counted satisfiable if it has a model, and valid if its negation has none, it further follows that *A is tv-satisfiable if and only if satisfiable in the ordinary sense, and tv-valid if and only if valid in that sense* (= **Theorem 3**).[11]

Now for the cardinality of models, and—my main topic in this paper—the cardinality of truth-value assignments.

A model $<D,I>$ is said to be of *cardinality* $\mathfrak{C}$ ($\mathfrak{C}$ a finite or an infinite cardinal) when the domain D in $<D,I_D>$ is of cardinality $\mathfrak{C}$, to be *finite* when D is finite, and to be *infinite* when D is infinite. Scores of theorems about the cardinality of models will be found in the literature. One assures us that *if a wff A of QC has a model of cardinality $\mathfrak{C}$ ($\mathfrak{C}$ again finite or infinite), then A will have one of cardinality $\mathfrak{C}$ for any cardinal $\mathfrak{C}$ larger than $\mathfrak{C}$* (= **Theorem 4**). Another, due to Löwenheim, assures us that *if A has any model at all, .then A will have one of cardinality $\aleph_0$* (= **Theorem 5**), and hence by Theorem 4 *will have one of cardinality $\mathfrak{C}$ for each cardinal $\mathfrak{C}$ from $\aleph_0$ on*. So the only cardinalities that truly matter are the infinite one $\aleph_0$ and, to a lesser extent, the finite ones 1, 2, 3, etc.[12]

The cardinality $\mathfrak{C}$ of a truth-value assignment may be defined in two different (and, in case $\mathfrak{C}$ is finite, demonstrably equivalent) ways. Let α be a function from one or more atomic wffs of QC to $\{\mathbf{T},\mathbf{F}\}$. I shall say that α *is of cardinality $\mathfrak{C}$ in the sense of* (1) if

(1) there is a set Σ of $\mathfrak{C}$ individual parameters of QC such that, no matter the quantification $(\forall X)A$ of QC, $(\forall X)A$ is true on α if $A(P/X)$ is true on α for every member P of Σ.

I shall say that α *is of cardinality $\mathfrak{C}$ in the sense of* (2) if

(2) there is a set Σ of $\mathfrak{C}$ individual parameters of QC and a function R from the complement of Σ to Σ such that, for every atomic wff A of QC, $\alpha(A) = \alpha(R(A))$, where $R(A)$ is the result of replacing in A every member P of the complement of Σ by $R(P)$.

I shall say that α is of (in)finite cardinality if, for some (in)finite cardinal $\mathfrak{C}$, α is of cardinality $\mathfrak{C}$ in the sense of (1). And I shall say that a wff A of QC is *(in)finitely tv-satisfiable* if A is true on a truth-value assignment of (in)finite cardinality.

Proof that *if α is of (finite) cardinality p (p > 0) in the sense of* (1), *then α is sure to be of cardinality p in the sense of* (2), was obtained some years ago by David Kaplan. It runs as follows.

Let Σ be a set of p individual parameters of QC such that, no matter the quantification $(\forall X)B$ of QC, $(\forall X)B$ is true on α if $B(P/X)$ is true on α for every member P of Σ; let $P_1, P_2, \ldots, P_p$ be the members of Σ; and suppose for *reductio* that there is no function R from the complement of Σ to Σ such that, for every atomic wff A of QC, $\alpha(A) = \alpha(R(A))$. Then there is sure to be a member Q of the complement of Σ such that, no matter the integer i from 1 through p, there is an atomic wff A_i of QC such that $\alpha(A_i) \neq \alpha(A_i(P_i/Q))$. Now let A'_i ($i = 1, 2, \ldots, p$) be $\sim A_i$ if $\alpha(A_i) = \mathbf{T}$, otherwise let A'_i be A_i.

(i) Because of its construction A'_i is not true on α for any i from 1 through p, and hence

$$(\ldots(A'_1 \vee A'_2) \vee \ldots) \vee A'_p \qquad (a)$$

is not true on α.

(ii) By the same token $A'_i(P_i/Q)$ is true on α for each i from 1 through p. Hence

$$(\ldots(A'_1(P_i/Q) \vee A'_2(P_i/Q)) \vee \ldots) \vee A'_p(P_i/Q) \qquad (b)$$

is true on α for each i from 1 through p. But, for any individual variable X of QC,

$$(((\ldots(A'_1 \vee A'_2) \vee \ldots) \vee A'_p)(X/Q))(P_i/X) \qquad (c)$$

is the same as (b). Hence (c) is true on α for each i from 1 through p, hence by the hypothesis on Σ the quantification

$$(\forall X)((\ldots(A'_1 \vee A'_2) \vee \ldots) \vee A'_p)(X/Q)$$

is true on α, and hence so is

$$(((\ldots(A'_1 \vee A'_2) \vee \ldots) \vee A'_p)(X/Q))(Q/X). \qquad (d).$$

But (a) is the same as (d). Hence (a) is true on α, as against (i). Hence α, *when of cardinality p ($p > 0$) in the sense of* (1), *is sure to be of cardinality p in the sense of* (2) (= ***Theorem 6***).

The converse of Theorem 6 also holds true, as I discovered a few years ago: α, *when of cardinality p ($p > 0$) in the sense of* (2), *is sure to be of cardinality p in the sense of* (1). My proof uses various notions and theorems from model-theoretic semantics. One calling exclusively on the resources of truth-value semantics would of course be preferable, and—I hope—will soon be found.

Among the model-theoretic prerequisites of my proof is the model $<D, I_D>$ mentioned in Theorem 1, pp. 156–157. Assuming for simplicity's sake that α has a value for every atomic wff of QC, you fashion its *model-theoretic counterpart* as follows: use as your D the set of all the individual parameters of QC, and select as your I_D the function that pairs with each individual parameter P of QC that very parameter, with each sentence parameter F^0 of QC the truth-value $\alpha(F^0)$, and with each predicate parameter F^m of QC of degree m ($m = 1, 2, 3, \ldots$) the set of m-tuples of individual parameters of QC to which $<P_1, P_2, \ldots, P_m>$ belongs if and only if $\alpha(F^m(P_1, P_2, \ldots, P_m)) = \mathbf{T}$. (As noted on pp. 156–157 and proved at length in [2], pp. 93–94, a wff A of QC is true on α if and only if A is true in $<D, I_D>$.)

This first matter disposed of, consider a truth-value assignment α with a value for every atomic wff of QC; suppose that for two non-empty, mutually exclusive, and jointly exhaustive sets Σ and Σ' of individual parameters of QC there is a function R from Σ' to Σ such that, for every atomic wff B of QC, $\alpha(B) = \alpha(R(B))$; let $<D, I_D>$ be the model-theoretic counterpart of α; let D' be Σ; and let $I_{D'}$ be the function that pairs with each member P of Σ that very parameter, with each member Q of Σ' the parameter $R(Q)$, with each sentence parameter F^0 of QC the truth-value $I_D(F^0)$, and with each predicate parameter F^m of QC of degree m ($m = 1, 2, 3, \ldots$) the set of m-tuples of members of Σ to which $<P_1, P_2, \ldots, P_m>$ belongs if and only if $\alpha(R(F^m(P_1, P_2, \ldots, P_m))) = \mathsf{T}$. It can be shown by mathematical induction on the length of a wff A of QC that A *is true in* $<D, I_D>$ *if and only if* A *is true in* $<D', I_{D'}>$ (= **Theorem 7**). The proof, a fairly easy one in any event, can be found in [2], pp. 100–11.

This second matter disposed of, consider a Henkin model $<D, I_D>$, and let Σ be any set of individual parameters of QC such that—no matter the member d of D—$I_D(P) = d$ for some member or other P of Σ. It can be shown that *a quantification* $(\forall X)A$ *of* QC *is true in* $<D, I_D>$ *if and only if* $A(P/X)$ *is true in* $<D, I_D>$ *for every member* P *of* Σ (= **Theorem 8**). The point is an obvious one, but—as consulting [2], pp. 90–91, will attest—full-fledged proof of it can be singularly arduous.

Done with these preliminaries, suppose there is a set Σ of p ($p > 0$) individual parameters of QC and a function R from the complement of Σ to Σ such that, for every atomic wff B of QC, $\alpha(B) = \alpha(R(B))$; and let $(\forall X)A$ be an arbitrary quantification of QC such that, for every member P of Σ, $A(P/X)$ is true on α. Then, for every member P of Σ, $A(P/X)$ is sure by Theorem 1 to be true in the model-theoretic counterpart—call it $<D, I_D>$—of α, and hence sure by Theorem 7 to be true in the model $<D', I_{D'}>$ fashioned in the preamble to that theorem. But $<D', I_{D'}>$ is a Henkin model, and—no matter the member d' of D'—$I_{D'}(P) = d'$ for some member P or other of Σ. Hence $(\forall X)A$ is sure by Theorem 8 to be true in $<D', I_{D'}>$, hence sure by Theorem 7 again to be true in the model-theoretic counterpart $<D, I_D>$ of α, and hence sure by Theorem 1 to be true on α itself. Hence α, *when of cardinality p* ($p > 0$) *in the sense of* (2), *is sure to be of cardinality p in the sense of* (1) (= **Theorem 9**).

So much for the equivalence of (1) and (2) when $\mathfrak{E}$ is finite. Wanted next is proof that *a wff A of* QC *is true in a model* $<D, I_D>$ *of finite cardinality p* ($p > 0$) *if and only if A is true on a truth-value assignment* α *of that cardinality*. In both Step One and Step Two of the proof we take the cardinality of α to be explicated as in (1) on p. 157.

Step One: Suppose there is a truth-value assignment α of cardinality p on which A is true; let Σ be a set of p individual parameters of QC such that—no matter the quantification $(\forall X)B$ of QC—$(\forall X)B$ is true on α if $B(P/X)$ is for every member P of Σ; let R be a function from the complement of Σ to Σ such that, for every atomic wff C of QC, $\alpha(C) = \alpha(R(C))$; let D be Σ: and let I_D be the function that pairs with each member P of Σ that very parameter, with each member Q of the complement of Σ the parameter $R(Q)$, with each sentence parameter F^0 of QC the truth-value $\alpha(F^0)$, and with each predicate parameter F^m of QC of degree m ($m = 1,2,3, \ldots$) the set of m-tuples of members of Σ to which $<P_1,P_2, \ldots, P_m>$ belongs if and only if $\alpha(F^m(P_1,P_2, \ldots, P_m)) =$ **T**. It is easily shown by mathematical induction on the length of A that A is true in $<D,I_D>$ if and only if A is true on α, and hence that *A is true in a model of cardinality p if true on a truth-value assignment of that cardinality.*

(Two cases in the induction call for special attention: that in which A is of the sort $F^m(P_1,P_2, \ldots, P_m)$ for some non-zero m and that in which A is of the sort $(\forall X)B$. *Case 1:* Let $Q_1, Q_2, \ldots$, and Q_k be all the individual parameters among $P_1, P_2, \ldots$, and P_m that do not belong to Σ, and suppose first that $k = 0$. By the construction of I_D, A *is true in* $<D,I_D>$ if and only if $<P_1,P_2, \ldots, P_m>$ belongs to $I_D(F^m)$, and hence if and only if A is true on α (Case 1.1.). Suppose then that $k > 0$. Since $I_D(Q_i) = I_D(R(Q_i))$ for each i from 1 through k, A is true in $<D,I_D>$ if and only if $R(A)$ ($= A(R(Q_1),R(Q_2), \ldots, R(Q_k)/Q_1,Q_2, \ldots, Q_k)$) is true in $<D,I_D>$.[13] But by Case 1.1 $R(A)$ is true in $<D,I_D>$ if and only if $R(A)$ is true on α. Hence A is true in $<D,I_D>$ if and only if $R(A)$ is true on α. But $\alpha(A) = \alpha(R(A))$. Hence A is true in $<D,I_D>$ if and only if A is true on α (Case 1.2). *Case 2:* $<D,I_D>$ is a Henkin model, and for each member d of $D(= \Sigma)$ there is an individual parameter P in Σ such that $I_D(P) = d$. Hence by Theorem 8 $(\forall X)B$ is true in $<D, I_D>$ if and only if $B(P/X)$ is true in $<D,I_D>$ for every member P of Σ. Hence by the hypothesis of the induction $(\forall X)B$ is true in $<D,I_D>$ if and only if $B(P/X)$ is true on α for every member P of Σ. Hence, by the hypothesis on Σ, $(\forall X)B$ ($= A$) is true in $<D,I_D>$ if and only if $(\forall X)B$ is true on α.)

Step Two: Suppose there is a model $<D,I_D>$ of cardinality p in which A is true. (i) Let $d_1, d_2, \ldots, d_k$ ($k \leq p$) be the members of D paired by I_D with the individual parameters of QC, and in case $k < p$ let $d_{k+1}, d_{k+2}, \ldots, d_p$ be the remaining members of D; let P_i ($1 \leq i \leq k$) be the alphabetically earliest individual parameter of QC such that $I_D(P_i) = d_i$; let P_{k+i} ($1 \leq i \leq p - k$) be the alphabetically earliest individual parameter of QC foreign to A and distinct from $P_1, P_2, \ldots, P_k$;[14] when $k = p$, let I_D^p be I_D; otherwise, let I_D^k be I_D and let I_D^{k+1} be the P_{k+1}-variant of I_D^{k+i} such that $I_D^{k+1}(P_{k+1}) = d_{k+1}$. It is easily verified that, with $P_{k+1}, P_{k+2}, \ldots, P_p$ foreign to A, A is true in $<D,I_D>$. But $<D,I_D^p>$ is a Henkin model. Hence by Theorem 2 A is sure to be true on the truth-value counterpart α of $<D,I_D>$, a truth-value assignment obtained by pairing **T** with each atomic wff of QC true in $<D,I_D>$ and **F** with every other one. (ii) Let Σ be $\{P_1, P_2, \ldots, P_p\}$, where P_i ($1 \leq i \leq p$) is the alphabetically earliest individual parameter of QC such that $I_D^p(P_i) = d_i$; let $(\forall X)B$ be an arbitrary quantification of QC; and suppose $B(P_i/X)$ is true on α for every i from 1 through p. Then by Theorem 2 $B(P_i/X)$ is true in $<D, I_D^p>$ for every i from 1 through p, hence by Theorem 8 $(\forall X)B$ is true in $<D, I_D^p>$, and hence by Theorem 2 again $(\forall X)B$ is true on α. Hence α is sure to be of cardinality p. (iii) By (i)–(ii) *A is true on a truth-value assignment of cardinality p if true in a model of that cardinality.*

Truth-Value Assignments and Their Cardinality 161

Hence *a wff of* QC *is true in a model of cardinality* p ($p > 0$) *if and only if true on a truth-value assignment of that cardinality* (= ***Theorem 10***); and hence *a wff of* QC *has a finite model if and only if it is finitely tv-verifiable* (= ***Theorem 11***).

Turning now to infinite cardinalities, I have proof of course that *every truth-value assignment is of cardinality* $\aleph_0$ *in the sense of* (1) (= ***Theorem 12***), and hence that *every tv-satisfiable wff of* QC *is true on a truth-value assignment of cardinality* $\aleph_0$ *in the sense of* (1) (= ***Theorem 13***). Let Σ in (1) be $\{$'a', 'b', 'c', 'a''', 'b''', 'c''', ...$\}$, and the trick is done. I have no proof, though, that a truth-value assignment is of cardinality $\aleph_0$ in the sense of (1) if and only if of cardinality $\aleph_0$ in the sense of (2), and hence I have no proof that every tv-satisfiable wff of QC is true on a truth-value assignment of cardinality $\aleph_0$ in the sense of (2).

Theorem 13 is the truth-value counterpart of Löwenheim's Theorem. It guarantees with an assist from Theorem 2 that *any wff of* QC *with a model of cardinality* $\aleph_0$ *is true on a truth-value assignment of that cardinality* (= ***Theorem 14***). As for the converse of this, note that the model-theoretic counterpart of a truth-value assignment is (by construction) of cardinality $\aleph_0$. So by Theorem 1 *any wff of* QC *that is true on a truth-value assignment— hence, by the way, any one that is infinitely tv-satisfiable—has a model of cardinality* $\aleph_0$ (= ***Theorem 15***). Hence *a wff of* QC *is true in a model of cardinality* $\aleph_0$ *if and only if true on a truth-value assignment of that cardinality* (= ***Theorem 16***).

Theorems 15 and 16 guarantee in turn that *a wff of* QC *has an infinite model if and only if it is infinitely tv-satisfiable* (= ***Theorem 17***). Note indeed that if our wff has an infinite model, then by Löwenheim's Theorem it has one of cardinality $\aleph_0$, and hence by Theorem 16 it is infinitely tv-satisfiable. Hence Theorem 17 by Theorem 15.

Since the individual parameters of QC are $\aleph_0$ in number, accounts (1) and (2) of the cardinality $\mathfrak{C}$ of a truth-value assignment α will not suit $\mathfrak{C}$'s larger than $\aleph_0$. I can think of two ways of "patching up" things.

(a) Following Hintikka's practice in [1], p. 52, take the individual parameters of QC to be $\mathfrak{C}$ in number, where $\mathfrak{C}$ is any cardinal you wish. Accounts (1) and (2) would now suit any cardinal from 1 through $\mathfrak{C}$, but none larger. So (a) strikes me as little more than a makeshift.

(b) Discarding (1) and (2), take α to be of cardinality $\mathfrak{C}$ if α is equivalent to a model of cardinality $\mathfrak{C}$ (a truth-value assignment being equivalent to a model if the wffs of QC true on the assignment are all and only those true in the model). The account would suit any cardinal there is, but—*as it mentions models*—it is hardly welcome in truth-value semantics.

Fuller discussion of the problem must be saved for another occasion.

Returning at long last to Theorem 4, I prove two special, but critical, cases of its truth-value counterpart.[15] Suppose there is a set Σ of p ($p > 0$) individual parameters of QC such that, no matter the quantification $(\forall X)A$ of QC, $(\forall X)A$ is true on a truth-value assignment α if $A(P/X)$ is true on α for every member P

of Σ; let Σ' be a superset of Σ of cardinality p', where p' is larger than p, or of cardinality $\aleph_0$; let $(\forall Y)B$ be an arbitrary quantification of QC; and suppose $B(P'/Y)$ is true on α for every member P' of Σ'. Then $B(P/X)$ is sure to be true on α for every member P' of Σ'. Then $B(P/X)$ is sure to be true on α for every member P of Σ; and hence, by the hypothesis on Σ, $(\forall Y)B$ is sure to be true on α. So:

A *wff of* QC *true on a truth-value assignment of cardinality p ($p > 0$) is sure, for some p' larger than p, to be true on one of cardinality p'* (= ***Theorem 18***),
and

A *wff of* QC *true on a truth-value assignment of cardinality p ($p > 0$) is sure to be true on one of cardinality* $\aleph_0$ (= ***Theorem 19***).

The material on p. 156 must be *adjusted* at several points when we pass to $QC_=$, the first-order quantificational calculus with identity.[16] Needed first and foremost are what I call *identity-normal* truth-value assignments. In case α is defined for *all* the atomic wffs of $QC_=$, rate α identity-normal if

(a) for any atomic wff A of $QC_=$ of the sort $P = P$, $\alpha(A) = \textbf{T}$
and

(b) for any other atomic wff A of $QC_=$ and any two individual parameters P and Q of $QC_=$ such that $\alpha(P = Q) = \textbf{T}$, $\alpha(A) = \alpha(A(Q/P))$;
and in case α is defined for *only some* atomic wffs of QC, rate α identity-normal if α is the restriction to these wffs of an identity-normal truth-value assignment to all the atomic wffs of $QC_=$.[17] This done, you certify a wff A of $QC_=$ *tv-satisfiable* if A is true on at least one identity-normal truth-value assignment to the atomic subformulas of A; and you certify A *tv-valid* if A is true on every identity-normal truth-value assignment to those subformulas.

It is easily shown that *a wff of* $QC_=$ *is tv-satisfiable if and only if satisfiable in the ordinary sense, and tv-valid if and only if valid in that sense* (= ***Theorem 20***).[18]

However, my treatment on p. 157 of the cardinality of a truth-value assignment α must be *totally revamped*. With '$QC_=$' substituted throughout for 'QC', account (1) on p. 157 of the cardinality of α would still permit proof of (a) Theorems 18 and 19 above and (b) Theorem 13 on p. 161. Yet, as the reader well knows, Theorems 4 and 5 fail for $QC_=$: the wff '$(\exists x)(\forall y)(y = x)$', for example, which has models of cardinality 1, has none of cardinality larger than 1, and hence in particular none of cardinality $\aleph_0$. So the truth-value counterparts of Theorems 4 and 5 should also fail for $QC_=$.

An account that better suits the occasion occurred to me some years back. I again distinguish between truth-value assignments defined for *all* the atomic wffs of $QC_=$ and truth-value assignments defined for *only some* of those wffs; and, to abridge things, I refer to the former as assignments of *Type I* and to the latter as assignments of *Type II*.

Let α be an identity-normal truth-value assignment, and in case α is of Type II let A_1, A_2, A_3, etc. be all the atomic wffs of $QC_=$ for which α is defined.

(a) α is said to be *of (finite) cardinality p* $(p > 0)$ if
  (a1) in case α is of Type I, $(\exists X_1)(\exists X_2) \ldots (\exists X_p)((X_1 \neq X_2 \;\&\; X_1 \neq X_3 \;\&\; \ldots \;\&\; X_1 \neq X_p \;\&\; X_2 \neq X_3 \;\&\; X_2 \neq X_4 \;\&\; \ldots \;\&\; X_2 \neq X_p \;\&\; \ldots \;\&\; X_{p-1} \neq X_p) \;\&\; (\forall Y)(Y = X_1 \vee Y = X_2 \vee \ldots \vee Y = X_p))$ is true on α, and
  (a2) in case α is of Type II, α is the restriction to A_1, A_2, A_3, etc. of an assignment of Type I of cardinality p.

(b) α is said to be *of cardinality* $\aleph_0$ if
  (b1) in case α is of Type I, α is not of cardinality p for any p from 1 on, and
  (b2) in case α is of Type II, α is the restriction to A_1, A_2, A_3, etc. of an assignment of Type I of cardinality $\aleph_0$.[19]

Proof that *any wff of* QC$_=$ *true on a truth-value assignment of cardinality p* $(p > 0)$ *has a model of that cardinality* is essentially as on pp. 159–160, and proof that *any wff of* QC$_=$ *with a model of cardinality p* $(p > 0)$ *is true on a truth-value assignment of that cardinality* runs as on p. 160 but for (ii) amended to read: (ii) For each i from 1 through p let P_i be the alphabetically earliest individual parameter of QC such that $I_D^p(P_i) = d_i$. It is easily verified that $(P_1 \neq P_2 \;\&\; P_1 \neq P_3 \;\&\; \ldots \;\&\; P_1 \neq P_p \;\&\; P_2 \neq P_3 \;\&\; P_2 \neq P_4 \;\&\; \ldots \;\&\; P_2 \neq P_p \;\&\; \ldots \;\&\; P_{p-1} \neq P_p) \;\&\; (\forall y)(y = P_1 \vee y = P_2 \vee \ldots \vee y = P_p)$ is true in the model $<D, I_D^p>$, and hence by Theorem 2 is true on the truth-value theoretic counterpart α of $<D, I_D^p>$. Hence α is sure to be of cardinality p.

Hence *a wff of* QC$_=$ *is true in a model of (finite) cardinality p* $(p > 0)$ *if and only if true on a truth-value assignment of that cardinality* (= **Theorem 21**); and hence *a wff of* QC$_=$ *has a finite model if and only if it is finitely tv-satisfiable* (= **Theorem 22**).

Proof that *a wff of* QC$_=$ *is true in a model of cardinality* $\aleph_0$ *if and only if true on a truth-value assignment of that cardinality* is probably easy enough. I have not looked into the matter yet.

I remarked earlier that Löwenheim's Theorem does not hold for QC$_=$. A weaker version of it does, however, according to which *any wff of* QC$_=$ *that has any model at all has a finite model or one of cardinality* $\aleph_0$ (= **Theorem 23**); and, with truth-value assignments of cardinality $\aleph_0$ accounted for as above, the truth-value counterpart of this weaker version, to wit: *any tv-satisfiable wff of* QC$_=$ *is true on a truth-value assignment of finite cardinality or one of cardinality* $\aleph_0$ (= **Theorem 24**), holds by definition.

Mindful that a wff of QC$_=$ has a model of cardinality $\aleph_0$ if it has an infinite one, I limited myself in (a)–(b) to those cardinalities that truly matter here (the finite ones 1, 2, 3, etc., and the infinite one $\aleph_0$),[20] and accordingly got Theorem 24 on the cheap. A fuller and more sophisticated treatment is wanted, though, which would own cardinalities larger than $\aleph_0$ and in which Theorem 24 would accordingly call for a fresh (and more difficult) proof.

One might of course borrow from p. 161 and declare α of (infinite) cardinality $\mathfrak{E}$ if α is equivalent to a model of cardinality $\mathfrak{E}$ (= (b$'$)). (b$'$) would permit proof that—no matter the infinite cardinal $\mathfrak{E}$—a wff of QC$_=$ is true on a truth-value assignment of cardinality $\mathfrak{E}$ if and only if true on one of cardinality $\aleph_0$,

164   Part 2: Truth

thus excusing our use of (b). And clauses (a) and (b') would permit proof of Theorem 24. However, (b') makes mention of models, and what we deemed an embarrassment four pages back cannot but be one here.

So there are open problems in this chapter of truth-value semantics, open problems which—I hope—some will want to tackle. But much work has already been done, and *the new semantics* (as truth-value semantics has been called) should shortly measure up to its rival.[21]

Notes

1. With two runs of individual letters at hand, matters of substitution are far easier to handle as clause (d) below and clause (iv) in each one of notes 4 and 5 attest.
2. For uniformity's sake I talk of sentence parameters where the literature would talk of *free sentence variables*.
3. For uniformity's sake I talk of predicate parameters where the literature would talk of *free predicate variables*.
4. The wffs of QC will consist of (i) all the atomic wffs of QC, (ii) all formulas of the sort $\sim A$, where A is a wff of QC, (iii) all formulas of QC of the sort $(A \supset B)$, where A and B are wffs of QC, and (iv) all formulas of the sort $(\forall X)A$, where—for any individual parameter P of QC—the result $B(P/X)$ of putting P everywhere in B for the individual variable X is a wff of QC. The three operators '&', '∨', and '∃' will be presumed to be defined in the customary manner.
5. For those unfamiliar with the notion of a subformula, (i) any wff of QC is a subformula of itself, (ii) A is a subformula of $\sim A$, (iii) A and B are subformulas of $A \supset B$, (iv) for any individual parameter P of QC, $A(P/X)$ is a subformula of $(\forall X)A$, and (v) any subformula of a subformula of a wff of QC is a subformula of the wff. The atomic subformulas of a wff are of course those subformulas of the wff that are atomic.
6. The results $B(a/X)$, $B(b/X)$, $B(c/X)$, etc. of successively putting 'a', 'b', 'c', etc. everywhere in B for X are of course the substitution-instances of $(\forall X)B$. Our interpretation of '$\forall$' is thus of the substitution kind.
7. In other writings I use 'tv-verifiable' in lieu of 'tv-satisfiable', but the latter epithet better suits the comparison drawn here between truth-value and standard semantics.
8. Or, as the matter is also put, if and only if A is true in a model. A few definitions may be in order here. Where D is a non-empty set, called for the occasion a domain, and Σ is a non-empty set of parameters of QC, understand by a D-interpretation of Σ any function pairing with each individual parameter in Σ a member of D, with each sentence parameter in Σ a truth-value, and with each m-place ($m > 0$) predicate parameter in Σ a set of m-tuples of members of D. Where D and Σ are as just specified, I_D is a D-interpretation of Σ, and P is an individual parameter in Σ, understand by a P-variant of I_D any D-interpretation of Σ that agrees with I_D except possibly on P. Where D, Σ, I_D, and P are as just specified, and I'_D is a P-variant of I_D, call the pair $<D, I_D>$ a model, and the pair $<D, I'_D>$ a P-variant of $<D, I_D>$. Finally, where A is a wff of QC, D is a domain, Σ is a set of parameters of QC to which belongs every parameter in A plus some arbitrary individual parameter P foreign to A, and I_D is a D-interpretation of Σ, take A to be true in the model $<D, I_D>$ if
   (i) in case A is a sentence parameter, $I_D(A) = \mathbf{T}$,
   (ii) in case A is of the sort $F^m(P_1, P_2, \ldots, P_m)$ ($m > 0$), the m-tuple $<I_D(P_1), I_D(P_2), \ldots, I_D(P_m)>$ belongs to $I_D(F^m)$,
   (iii) in case A is of the sort $\sim B$, B is not true in $<D, I_D>$,
   (iv) in case A is of the sort $B \supset C$, B is not true in $<D, I_D>$ or C is, and
   (v) in case A is of the sort $(\forall X)B$, $B(P/X)$ is true in $<D, I'_D>$ for every P-variant $<D, I'_D>$ of $<D, I_D>$.
(The letter 'Σ', used here to refer to sets of parameters *in general*, will *exclusively* refer in the main text to sets of *individual* parameters.)

9. Note that a wff of QC is said to be true *on* an assignment, but to be true *in* a model. A single preposition would be preferable, but I conform here to current practice.

10. For a presentation of Henkin's proof in which this feature is made quite perspicuous, see [3], pp. 285–92.

11. Proofs of these various results will be found in [2], §4.1–§4.2.

12. The foregoing material on the cardinality of models is doubtless familiar to most. I include it with an eye to later results which rest on it. I use the letter '$\mathfrak{C}$' to refer to cardinals in general (whether finite or infinite), *When only finite cardinals are intended, I shall use the letter 'p'*.

13. $A(R(Q_1), R(Q_2), \ldots, R(Q_k)/Q_1, Q_2, \ldots, Q_k))$ is of course the result of simultaneously putting $R(Q_1), R(Q_2), \ldots,$ and $R(Q_k)$ everywhere in A for $Q_1, Q_2, \ldots,$ and Q_k, respectively.

14. By the alphabetic order of our individual parameters we understand the order in which they are listed on p. 156.

15. Proof of the general case must await definition of 'α is of cardinality $\mathfrak{C}$' for $\mathfrak{C}$'s larger than $\aleph_0$.

16. When passing to QC$_=$, count all formulas of the sort $(P = Q)$, where P and Q are individual parameters of QC$_=$, as atomic wffs, and take these to be true in a model $<D, I_D>$ if $I_D(P) = I_D(Q)$.

17. Let α and α' be truth-value assignments, the latter to a set S' of atomic wffs of QC$_=$ and the former to a subset S of S'. α will of course count as the restriction of α' to S if, for every member A of S, $\alpha(A) = \alpha'(A)$.

18. Proofs of these results will be found in [2], §5.1.

19. Concerning (b) see p. 163, lines 36–39, and Note 20. To abridge matters I presume hereafter all truth-value assignments to be identity-normal.

20. Hence my declaring α in (b) *not of infinite cardinality*, as the reader possibly anticipated, but *of cardinality* $\aleph_0$.

21. The results in this paper were announced at the Detroit meeting of the Society for Exact Philosophy, Spring 1976, and the paper itself was delivered at the 22d Conference on the History of Logic, held in Cracow, Summer 1976.

References

[1] Hintikka, J. 1955. "Two Papers on Symbolic Logic." *Acta Philosophica Fennica*.
[2] Leblanc, H. 1976. *Truth-Value Semantics*. Amsterdam, North-Holland.
[3] Leblanc, H., and Wisdom, W. A. 1976. *Deductive Logic*, second edition. Boston: Allyn and Bacon.

11

Three Generalizations of a Theorem of Beth's

Exploiting an argument of Henkin's in [4], Beth established in Section 89 of [1], that a set S of *closed* wffs of QC^1 is consistent in QC^1 if and only if (every member of) S is satisfied by at least one assignment of truth-values to the atomic wffs of QC^1.[1] The result has two interesting corollaries: one to the effect that a wff A of QC^1 (A possibly open) is provable in QC^1 if and only if A is satisfied by every assignment of truth-values to the atomic wffs of QC^1, the other one to the effect that a wff A of QC^1 is derivable in QC^1 from a set S of closed wffs of QC^1 if and only if A is satisfied by every assignment of truth-values to the atomic wffs of QC^1 that satisfies S.

In Section 1 of this paper I shall obtain a first generalization of Beth's Theorem,[2] and show that a set S of wffs of QC^1 (said wffs possibly *open*) is consistent in QC^1 if and only if at least one set of wffs of QC^1 that is isomorphic to S (in a sense to be explicated below) is satisfied by at least one assignment of truth-values to the atomic wffs of QC^1. It will readily follow from the result that a wff A of QC^1 is derivable in QC^1 from a set S of wffs of QC^1 if and only if no set of wffs of QC^1 that is isomorphic to $S \cup \{\sim A\}$ is satisfied by any assignment of truth-values to the atomic wffs of QC^1. Since A is implied by S in the standard sense of the word 'implies' if and only if A is derivable from S in QC^1, it will further follow from my first result that A is implied by S if and only if no set of wffs of QC^1 that is isomorphic to $S \cup \{\sim A\}$ is satisfied by any assignment of truth-values to the atomic wffs of QC^1. As announced in [7], the notion of first-order implication (and by rebound that of first-order validity) can thus be explicated without recourse to models.[3]

Passing on to QC^2, the second-order quantificational calculus, and taking a set of wffs of QC^2 to be consistent* in QC^2 if—*roughly*—'p & $\sim p$' is not derivable from S in Henkin's fragment F^* of QC^2 in [6],[4] I shall establish in Section 2 that S is consistent* in QC^2 if and only if at least one set of wffs of QC^2 that is isomorphic to S is satisfied by at least one assignment of truth-values to the atomic wffs of QC^2, or—to use a fresh terminology explicated below—if and only if at least one set of wffs of QC^2 that is isomorphic to S is satisfied by at least one truth-value function for QC^2. And, taking a set S of wffs of QC^2 to be consistent** in QC^2 if—*roughly again*—'p & $\sim p$' is not derivable from S in Henkin's version F^{**} of QC^2,[5] I shall establish in Section 3 that S is consistent** in QC^2 if and only if at least one set of wffs of QC^2 that is isomorphic to S is satisfied by at least one *general* truth-value function for QC^2. It will follow from these two extra generalizations of Beth's Theorem that notions of second-order implication* and second-order implication** (roughly equivalent, the first to derivability in Henkin's F^*, the second to derivability in Henkin's F^{**}) can be explicated without mention of models, and hence—in particular—that Henkin's notion of general validity, which is tantamount to second-order implication** by $\emptyset$, can be explicated without mention of general models of the Henkin sort. The last result may be welcome news to those who find the notion of general validity somewhat *ad hoc*.

Robert K. Meyer and I have an account of order ω validity** (a notion tantamount to provability in the quantificational calculus of order ω), and one of order ω validity, which likewise make no mention of models. They can be found in [12].

1. When establishing that *if a set S of wffs of QC^1 is consistent in QC^1, at least one set of wffs of QC^1 that is isomorphic to S is satisfied by at least one assignment of truth-values to the atomic wffs of QC^1*, I consider first the case where infinitely many individual variables of QC^1 do not occur in any member of S, then turn to the contrary case. To abridge matters, I call a set of the first sort a *wff set of Type I*, and one of the second sort a *wff set of Type II*. I also use the following substitution convention. A being a wff of QC^1, X_1, X_2, ..., X_n ($n \geq 1$) being distinct individual variables of QC^1, and for each i from 1 through n Y_i being an individual variable of QC^1 not necessarily distinct from X_i. I shall take $(A)[Y_1/X_1]$ to be the result of replacing every free occurrence of X_1 in A by an occurrence of Y_1 if X_1 does not occur free in any component of A of the sort $(\forall Y_1)B$; otherwise, I shall take $(A)[Y_1/X_1]$ to be the result of *first* replacing every bound occurrence of Y_1 in A by an occurrence of the alphabetically earliest individual variable of QC^1 that is foreign to A, and *then* replacing every free occurrence of X_1 in the resulting formula by an occurrence of Y_1; and I shall take $(A)[Y_1, Y_2, \ldots, Y_n/X_1, X_2, \ldots, X_n]$ to be $((A)[Y_1, Y_2, \ldots, Y_{n-1}/X_1, X_2, \ldots, X_{n-1}])[Y_n/X_n]$.

Proof of Case 1 is as follows. (1) S being a wff set of Type 1, let S_0 be S; for each i from 1 on let S_i be $S_{i-1} \cup \{A_i[Y/X_i] \supset (\forall X_i)A_i\}$, where $(\forall X_i)A_i$ is in some predetermined order the i-th wff of QC^1 of the sort $(\forall X)A$ and Y is the alphabetically first individual variable of QC^1 that does not occur in any member of $S_{i-1} \cup (\forall X_i)A_i$; and let S_∞ be the union of S_0, S_1, S_2, ... It is easily verified that S_∞ is consistent in QC^1 if S is, and that for each i from 1 on there is an individual variable Y of QC^1 such that $A_i[Y/X_i] \supset (\forall X_i)A_i$ belongs to S_∞. (2) S_∞^0 being the set S_∞ of (1), let S_∞^i be for each i from 1 on $S_\infty^{i-1} \cup \{A_i\}$, where A_i is in some predetermined order the i-th wff of QC^1, if $S_\infty^{i-1} \cup \{A_i\}$ is consistent in QC^1, otherwise let S_∞^i be S_∞^{i-1}; and let S_∞^∞ be the union of S_∞^0, S_∞^1,

S^2_∞, ... It is easily verified that S^∞_∞ is consistent in QC^1 if S_∞ is; and that, if S^∞_∞ is consistent in QC^1, then: (i) $\sim A$ belongs to S^∞_∞ if and only if A does not, (ii) $A \supset B$ belongs to S^∞_∞ if and only if A does not or B does, and (iii) $(\forall X)A$ belongs to S^∞_∞ if and only if $A[Y/X]$ does for every individual variable Y of QC^1.[6] (3) Let a wff A of QC^1 be said to be satisfied by an assignment $Asst$ of truth values to the atomic wffs of QC^1 if: (i) in the case that A is atomic, A is assigned the truth-value **T** in $Asst$, (ii) in the case that A is of the sort $\sim B$, B is not satisfied by $Asst$, (iii) in the case that A is of the sort $B \supset C$, B is not satisfied by $Asst$ or C is, and (iv) in the case that A is of the sort $(\forall X)B$, $B[Y/X]$ is satisfied by $Asst$ for every individual variable Y of QC^1. Next, let $Asst$ be the result of assigning the truth-value **T** to every atomic wff of QC^1 that belongs to the set S^∞_∞ of (2), the truth-value **F** to every other one. It is easily verified that, if S^∞_∞ is consistent in QC^1, then in view of (i)–(iii) in (2) a wff A of QC^1 belongs to S^∞_∞ if and only if A is satisfied by $Asst$.[7] Hence, if S is consistent in QC^1, there is an assignment of truth-values to the atomic wffs of QC^1 that satisfies S. (4) M being a one-to-one mapping of the set of the individual variables of QC^1 into itself, A being a wff of QC^1, and $X_1, X_2, \ldots,$ and X_n being in alphabetical order all the individual variables of QC^1 that occur free in A, let the M-image of A be A itself when $n = 0$, otherwise let it be $A[M(X_1), M(X_2), \ldots, M(X_n)/X_1, X_2, \ldots, X_n]$. And, S and S' being not necessarily distinct sets of wffs of QC^1, let S' be said to be isomorphic to S if: (i) in the case that S is empty, S' is empty as well, and (ii) in the contrary case, S' consists—for some one-to-one mapping M of the set of the individual variables of QC^1 into itself—of the M-images of the various members of S. It immediately follows from (3) that, if S is consistent in QC^1, there is an assignment of truth-values to the atomic wffs of QC^1 that satisfies at least one set of wffs of QC^1 isomorphic to S, the set in question being S itself.

Proof of Case 2 is as follows. S being a wff set of Type II, and M the one-to-one mapping of the set of the individual variables of QC^1 into itself such that, where X is the alphabetically i-th individual variable of QC^1, $M(X)$ is the alphabetically $(2 \times i)$-th individual variable of QC^1, let S' be $\emptyset$ if S is $\emptyset$, otherwise let S' consist of the M-images of the various members of S. It is easily verified that S' is a wff set of Type I, is isomorphic to S, and is consistent in QC^1 if S is. Hence, in view of Case 1, if S is consistent in QC^1, there is an assignment of truth-values to the atomic wffs of QC^1 that satisfies at least one set of wffs of QC^1 isomorphic to S, said set being S'.[8]

S being a wff set of Type I or of Type II, suppose next that S is not consistent in QC^1. Then, as the reader may verify on his own, no set of wffs of QC^1 that is isomorphic to S is consistent in QC^1 either. But, as the reader may again verify on his own, a set of wffs of QC^1 is not satisfied by an assignment of truth-values to the atomic wffs of QC^1 unless it is consistent in QC^1. Hence no set of wffs of QC^1 that is isomorphic to S is satisfied by any assignment of truth-values to the atomic wffs of QC^1.

Hence, my first generalization of Beth's Theorem: *A set S of wffs of QC^1 is consistent in QC^1 if and only if at least one set of wffs of QC^1 that is isomor-*

phic to S is satisfied by at least one assignment of truth-values to the atomic wffs of QC^1. Hence, as a corollary: *A set S of wffs of QC^1 implies a wff A of QC^1* (this in the standard sense of the word 'implies') *if and only if no set of wffs of QC^1 that is isomorphic to $S \cup \{\sim A\}$ is satisfied by any assignment of truth-values to the atomic wffs of QC^1*. Hence, as a further corollary: *A wff of QC^1 is valid* (this in the standard sense of the word 'valid') *if and only if A is satisfied by every assignment of truth-values to the atomic wffs of QC^1*.

A word may be in order, before I pass to QC^2, concerning the notion of derivability in QC^1 (and, hence, consistency in QC^1, a set S of wffs of QC^1 being said here to be consistent in QC^1 if 'p & $\sim p$' is not derivable from S in QC^1). Following in this the example of Fitch in [3], I count a wff A of QC^1 as an axiom of QC^1 if:

(i) A is of one of the six sorts

A1. $B \supset (C \supset B)$

A2. $(B \supset (C \supset D)) \supset ((B \supset C) \supset (B \supset D))$

A3. $(\sim B \supset \sim C) \supset (C \supset B)$

A4. $(\forall X)(B \supset C) \supset ((\forall X)B \supset (\forall X)C)$

A5. $B \supset (\forall X)B$, where X does not occur free in B

A6. $(\forall X)B \supset B'$, where B' is like B except for containing free occurrences of some individual variable X' of QC^1 wherever B contains free occurrences of X, or

(ii) A is of the sort $(\forall X)B$, where B is an axiom of QC^1.

I count a finite column of wffs of QC^1 as a derivation in QC^1 of a wff A of QC^1 from a set S of wffs of QC^1 if: (i) the column closes with A and (ii) every entry in the column belongs to S, is an axiom of QC^1, or follows from two previous entries in the column by application of Modus Ponens. And I take a wff A of QC^1 to be derivable in QC^1 from a set S of wffs of QC^1 if there is a derivation in QC^1 of A from S, to be provable in QC^1 if A is derivable from $\emptyset$ in QC^1. It immediately follows from this account of things that, if a wff of QC^1 is derivable in QC^1 from a set S of wffs of QC^1, then A is derivable in QC^1 from any set of wffs of QC^1 that has S as a subset. As Montague and Henkin have shown in [13], the result—in the absence of which QC^1 fails to be strongly complete[9]—is blocked when derivability in QC^1 is accounted for as in [2].[10]

2. My second generalization of Beth's Theorem calls for the following syntactical and semantical preliminaries.

First, where A is a wff of QC^2, and F and G are (not necessarily distinct) predicate variables of QC^2 of the same degree, I shall take $(A)[G/F]$ to be the result of replacing every free occurrence of F in A by an occurrence of G if F does not occur free in any component of A of the sort $(\forall G)B$; otherwise, I shall

170 Part 2: Truth

take $(A)[G/F]$ to be the result of *first* replacing every bound occurrence of G in A by an occurrence of the alphabetically earliest predicate variable of QC^2 that is of the same degree as G and is foreign to A, and *then* replacing every free occurrence of F in the resulting formula by an occurrence of G.

Next, where A is a wff of QC^2, $V_1, V_2, \ldots, V_n$ ($n \geq 1$) are distinct variables of QC^2, and for each i from 1 through n V'_i is an individual variable of QC^2 when V_i is one, otherwise a predicate variable of QC^2 of the same degree of V_i, I shall take $(A)[V'_1, V'_2, \ldots, V'_n/V_1, V_2, \ldots, V_n]$ to be $((A)[V'_1, V'_2, \ldots, V'_{n-1}/V_1, V_2, \ldots, V_{n-1}])[V'_n/V_n]$.

Next, where (a) M is a one-to-one mapping of the set of the variables of QC^2 into itself such that, for every individual variable X of QC^2, MX) is an individual variable of QC^2, and, for every m from 1 on and every predicate variable F of QC^2 of degree m, MF) is a predicate variable of QC^2 of degree m, (b) A is a wff of QC^2, and (c) $V_1, V_2, \ldots, V_n$ are in alphabetical order all the variables of QC^2 that occur free in A, I shall take the M-image of A to be A itself when $n = 0$, otherwise to be $A[MV_1), M(V_2), \ldots, M(V_n)/V_1, V_2, \ldots, V_n]$. And, S and S' being (not necessarily distinct) sets of wffs of QC^2, I shall take S' to be isomorphic to S if: (i) in the case that S is empty, S' is empty as well, and (ii) in the contrary case, S' consists—for some one-to-one mapping M of the aforedescribed sort—of the M-images of the various members of S.

Then, I shall count a wff A of QC^2 as an axiom* of QC^2 if:

(i) A is of one of the aforementioned sorts **A1 – A6**,

(ii) A is of one of the three extra sorts

A7. $(\forall F)(B \supset C) \supset ((\forall F)B \supset (\forall F)C)$

A8. $B \supset (\forall F)B$, where F does not occur free in B

A9. $(\forall F)B \supset B'$, where B' is like B except for containing free occurrences of some predicate variable F' of QC^2 of the same degree as F wherever B contains free occurrences of F, or

(iii) A is of one of the two sorts $(\forall X)B$ and $(\forall F)B$, where B is an axiom* of QC^2.

I shall count a finite column of wffs of QC^2 as a derivation* of a wff A of QC^2 from a set S of wffs of QC^2 if: (i) the column closes with A and (ii) every entry in the column belongs to S, is an axiom* of QC^2, or follows from two previous entries in the column by application of Modus Ponens. I shall take a wff A of QC^2 to be derivable* in QC^2 from a set S of wffs of QC^2 if there is a derivation* of A from S in QC^2, to be provable* in QC^2 if A is derivable* from $\varnothing$ in QC^2. And I shall take a set S of wffs of QC^2 to be consistent* in QC^2 if 'p & $\sim p$' is not derivable* from S in QC^2.

Finally, where A is a wff of QC^2 and *Asst an assignment of truth-values to the atomic wffs of QC^2*, I shall say that A is satisfied by *Asst* if: (i) in the case that A is atomic, A is assigned the truth-value **T** in *Asst*, (ii) in the case that A is of the sort $\sim B$, B is not satisfied by *Asst*, (iii) in the case that A is of the sort $B \supset C$, B is not satisfied by *Asst* or C is, (iv) in the case that A is of the sort

Three Generalizations of a Theorem of Beth's 171

$(\forall X)B$, $B[Y/X]$ is satisfied by $Asst$ for every individual variable Y of QC^2, and (v) is the case that A is of the sort $(\forall F)B$, $B[G/F]$ is satisfied by $Asst$ for every predicate variable G of QC^2 that is of the same degree as F.

Proof that *if a set S of wffs of* QC^2 *is consistent* in* QC^2, *at least one set of wffs of* QC^2 *that is isomorphic to S is satisfied by at least one assignment of truth-values to the atomic wffs of* QC^2, can be had by essentially the same argument as in Section 1. First, count a set S of wffs of QC^2 as a *wff set of Type I* if infinitely many individual variables of QC^2 and—for each m from 1 on—infinitely many predicate variables of QC^2 of degree m do not occur in any member of S, otherwise count S as a *wff set of Type II*. Second, where S is a wff set of Type I, let S_0 be S; for each i from 1 on let S_i be $S_{i-1} \cup \{A_i(Y/X_i) \supset (\forall X_i)A_i\}$ where $(\forall X_i)A_i$ is in some predetermined order the i-th of QC^2 of the sort $(\forall X)A$ and Y is the alphabetically earliest individual variable of QC^2 that does not occur in any member of S_{i-1} nor in $(\forall X_i)A_i$; let S_{∞_0} be the union of $S_0, S_1, S_2, \ldots$; for each i from 1 on let S_{∞_i} be $S_{\infty_{i-1}} \cup \{A_i[\bar{G}/F_i] \supset (\forall F_i)A_i\}$, where $(\forall F_i)A_i$ is in some predetermined order the i-th wff of QC^2 of the sort $(\forall F)A$ and G is the alphabetically earliest predicate variable of QC^2 that is of the same degree as F_i and does not occur in any member of $S_{\infty_{i-1}}$ nor in $(\forall F_i)A_i$; let $S_{\infty_\infty}^0$ be the union of $S_{\infty_0}, S_{\infty_1}, S_{\infty_2}, \ldots$; for each i from 1 on let $S_{\infty_\infty}^i$ be $S_{\infty_\infty}^{i-1} \cup \{A_i\}$, where A_i is in some predetermined order the i-th wff of QC^2, if $S_{\infty_\infty}^{i-1} \cup \{A_i\}$ is consistent* in QC^2; otherwise let $S_{\infty_\infty}^i$ be $S_{\infty_\infty}^{i-1}$; and let $S_{\infty_\infty}^\infty$ be the union of $S_{\infty_\infty}^0, S_{\infty_\infty}^1, S_{\infty_\infty}^2, \ldots$. It is easily verified that $S_{\infty_\infty}^\infty$ is consistent* in QC^2 if S is, and—in particular—that if $S_{\infty_\infty}^\infty$ is consistent* in QC^2, then an arbitrary wff of QC^2 of the sort $(\forall F)A$ belongs to $S_{\infty_\infty}^\infty$ if and only if $A[G/F]$ does for every predicate variable G of QC^2 of the same degree as F. Third, let $Asst$ be the result of assigning **T** to every atomic wff of QC^2 that belongs to $S_{\infty_\infty}^\infty$, **F** to every other one. It is easily verified that, if $S_{\infty_\infty}^\infty$ is consistent* in QC^2, then a wff A of QC^2 belongs to $S_{\infty_\infty}^\infty$ if and only if A is satisfied by $Asst$.[11] Hence, if S is consistent* in QC^2, there is an assignment of truth-values to the atomic wffs of QC^2 that satisfies S, and hence that satisfies at least one set of wffs of QC^2 isomorphic to S.

Proof of the same result for the case where S is a wff set of Type II, and proof of the converse result when S is a wff set either of Type I or of Type II, proceeds as in Section 1.

Hence, my second generalization of Beth's Theorem: *A set S of wffs of* QC^2 *is consistent* in* QC^2 *if and only if at least one set of wffs of* QC^2 *that is isomorphic to S is satisfied by at least one assignment of truth-values to the atomic wffs of* QC^2. Hence, as a corollary: *A wff A of* QC^2 *is derivable* in* QC^2 *from a set S of wffs of* QC^2 *if and only if no set of wffs of* QC^2 *that is isomorphic to S* $\cup \{\sim A\}$ *is satisfied by any assignment of truth-values to the atomic wffs of* QC^2. Hence, as a further corollary: *A wff A of* QC^2 *is provable* in* QC^2 *if and only if A is satisfied by every assignment of truth-values to the atomic wffs of* QC^2. Because of the parallelism between these corollaries and the ones on p. 169. I suggest that a set S of wffs of QC^2 be said to imply* a wff A of QC^2 if no set of wffs of QC^2 that is isomorphic to $S \cup \{\sim A\}$ is satisfied by any assignment of truth-values to the atomic wffs of QC^2, and that a wff A of QC^2 be said to be valid* if A *is satisfied by every assignment of truth-values to the atomic wffs of* QC^2. The reader will note that under this understanding of things a wff A of QC^2 is valid* if and only if A is completely valid with respect to every model of the sort described by Henkin on p. 206 of [6].

The present generalization of Beth's Theorem can be phrased in another— but, of course, equivalent—manner. TV being a function from the set of the wffs of QC^2 to $\{T, F\}$, count TV as a truth-value function for QC^2 if: (i) $TV(\sim A) = T$ if and only if $TV(A) = F$, (ii) $TV(A \supset B) = T$ if and only if $TV(A) = F$ or $TV(B) = T$, (iii) $TV((\forall X)A) = T$ if and only if $TV(A[Y/X]) = T$ for every individual variable Y of QC^2, and (iv) $TV((\forall F)A) = T$ if and only if $TV(A[G/F]) = T$ for every predicate variable G of QC^2 of the same degree as F. And, A being a wff of QC^2 and TV a truth-value function for QC^2, take A to be satisfied by TV if $TV(A) = T$.

Return now to the extension $S_{\infty\infty}^{\infty}$ of S that we constructed four paragraphs back, and let TV be the function from the set of the wffs of QC^2 to $\{T, F\}$ such that, for every wff A of QC^2, $TV(A) = T$ if and only if A belongs to $S_{\infty\infty}^{\infty}$. TV readily proves to be a truth-value function for QC^2 (if $S_{\infty\infty}^{\infty}$ is consistent* in QC^2), and one that satisfies every member of S. Hence, if S is consistent* in QC^2, then at least one set of wffs of QC^2 that is isomorphic to S is satisfied by at least one truth-value function for QC^2. But, as the reader may verify on his own, no set of wffs of QC^2 is satisfied by a truth-value function for QC^2 unless consistent* in QC^2. Hence, *a set S of wffs of* QC^2 *is consistent* in* QC^2 *if and only if at least one set of wffs of* QC^2 *that is isomorphic to S is satisfied by at least one truth-value function for* QC^2. But, if so, then a set S of wffs of QC^2 may be said to imply* a wff A of QC^2 if and only if no set of wffs of QC^2 that is isomorphic to $S \cup \{\sim A\}$ is satisfied by any truth-value function for QC^2, and a wff A of QC^2 may be termed valid* if A is satisfied by every truth-value function for QC^2.

3. My last generalization of Beth's Theorem calls for an extra substitution convention.

Let A and B be (not necessarily distinct) wffs of QC^2; let F be for some m from 1 on a predicate variable of QC^2 of degree m; and let $X_1, X_2, \ldots, X_m$ be distinct individual variables of QC^2.

Case 1: F does not occur free in any component of A of the sort $(\forall V)C$, where V is an individual variable of QC^2 other than $X_1, X_2, \ldots, X_m$ that occurs free in B, or V is a predicate variable of QC^2 that occurs free in B. Then $A[B/F(X_1, X_2, \ldots, X_m)]$ is to be the result of substituting $B[Y_1, Y_2, \ldots, Y_m/X_1, X_2, \ldots, X_m]$ for every component of A of the sort $F(Y_1, Y_2, \ldots, Y_m)$ that contains one of the free occurrences of F in A.

Case 2: F occurs free in at least one component of A of the sort $(\forall V)C$, where V is an individual variable of QC^2 other than $X_1, X_2, \ldots, X_m$ that occurs free in B, or V is a predicate variable of QC^2 that occurs free in B. Let $(\forall V_1)C_1$,

Three Generalizations of a Theorem of Beth's   173

$(\forall V_2)C_2, \ldots,$ and $(\forall V_n)C_n$ be in order of decreasing length all the components of A of the sort $(\forall V)C,$[12] where V is as just described; let A_0 be A; and, V'_i being the alphabetically earliest individual variable of QC^2 that is foreign to C_i when V_i is an individual variable of QC^2, otherwise the alphabetically earliest predicate variable of QC^2 of the same degree as V_i that is foreign to C_i, let A_i be for each i from 1 through n the result of substituting $(\forall V'_i)C_i[V'_i/V_i]$ for every occurrence of $(\forall V_i)C_i$ in A that contains one of the free occurrences of F in A_{i-1}. Then $A[B/F(X_1,X_2, \ldots ,X_m)]$ is to be $A_n[B/F(X_1,X_2, \ldots ,X_m)]$.[13]

Next, count as an axiom** of QC^2 any wff A of QC^2 that
(i) is of one of the aforementioned sorts **A1–A9**, or
(ii) is of the sort

A10. $(\exists F)(\forall X_1)(\forall X_2) \ldots (\forall X_m)(F(X_1,X_2, \ldots ,X_m) \equiv B)$, where for some m from 1 on F is a predicate variable of QC^2 of degree m that does not occur free in B, and $X_1, X_2, \ldots , X_m$ are distinct individual variables of QC^2, or

(iii) is of one of the two sorts $(\forall X)B$ and $(\forall F)B$, where B is an axiom** of QC^2.

Count as a derivation** in QC^2 of a wff A of QC^2 from a set S of wffs of QC^2 any column of wffs of QC^2 that closes with A and everyone of whose entries belongs to S, is an axiom** of QC^2, or follows from two previous entries in the column by application of Modus Ponens. Take a wff A of QC^2 to be derivable* in QC^2 from a set S of wffs of QC^2 if there is a derivation** of A from S in QC^2, to be provable** in QC^2 if A is derivable** from $\emptyset$ in QC^2. And take a set S of wffs of QC^2 to be consistent** in QC^2 if 'p & $\sim p$' is not derivable** from S in QC^2.

Finally, TV being a function from the set of the wffs of QC^2 to $\{\mathbf{T},\mathbf{F}\}$, count TV as a general truth-value function for QC^2 if: (i) $TV(\sim A) = \mathbf{T}$ if and only if $TV(A) = \mathbf{F}$, (ii) $TV(A \supset B) = \mathbf{T}$ if and only if $TV(A) = \mathbf{F}$ or $TV(B) = \mathbf{T}$, (iii) $TV((\forall X)A) = \mathbf{T}$ if and only if $TV(A[Y/X]) = \mathbf{T}$ for every individual variable Y of QC^2, and (iv) $TV((\forall F)A) = \mathbf{T}$, where for some m from 1 on F is a predicate variable of QC^2 of degree m, if and only if $TV(A[B/F(X_1, X_2, \ldots , X_m)]) = \mathbf{T}$ for every wff B of QC^2 and every m individual variables $X_1, X_2, \ldots , X_m$ of QC^2 that are distinct from one another. And, A being a wff of QC^2 and TV a general truth-value function for QC^2, take A to be satisfied by TV if $TV(A) = \mathbf{T}$.

It is easily verified that, for every wff A of QC^2, every predicate variable F of QC^2 of, say, degree m, every predicate variable G of QC^2 of degree m that is foreign to A, and every m individual variables $X_1, X_2, \ldots , X_m$ of QC^2 that are distinct from another, $A[G/F]$ and $A[G(X_1, X_2, \ldots , X_m)/F(X_1, X_2, \ldots , X_m)]$ are the same. Consider then the set $S^0_{\infty\infty}$ on p. 171. Since for each i from 1 on there is a predicate variable G of QC^2 of the same degree, say, m, as F_i such that $A_i[G/F_i] \supset (\forall F_i)A_i$ belongs to $S^0_{\infty\infty}$, then for each i from 1 on there are distinct individual variables $X_1, X_2, \ldots , X_m$ of QC^2 (the alphabetically first m individual variables of QC^2 will do), and a wff B of QC^2 (to wit: $G(X_1,$

$X_2, \ldots, X_m$)) such that $A_i[B/F_i(X_1,X_2, \ldots, X_m)] \supset (\forall F_i)A_i$ belongs to $S^0_{\infty\infty}$. Now for each i from 1 on let $S^i_{\infty\infty}$ be $S^{i-1}_{\infty\infty} \cup \{A_i\}$, where A_i is in some predetermined order the i-th wff of QC^2, if $S^{i-1}_{\infty\infty} \cup \{A_i\}$ is consistent** in QC^2; otherwise let $S^i_{\infty\infty}$ be $S^{i-1}_{\infty\infty}$; and let $S^\infty_{\infty\infty}$ be the union of $S^0_{\infty\infty}, S^1_{\infty\infty}, S^2_{\infty\infty}, \ldots$. It is easily verified (i) that $S^\infty_{\infty\infty}$ is consistent** in QC^2 if S is, and (ii) since $(\forall F)A \supset A[B/F(X_1, X_2, \ldots, X_m)]$ is provable** in QC^2 for any predicate variable F of QC^2, any two wffs A and B of QC^2, and any m (m the degree of F) individual variables $X_1, X_2, \ldots, X_m$ of QC^2 that are distinct from one another,[14] that, if $S^\infty_{\infty\infty}$ is consistent** in QC^2, then an arbitrary wff of QC^2 of the sort $(\forall F)A$ belongs to $S^\infty_{\infty\infty}$ if and only if $A[B/F(X_1,X_2, \ldots ,X_m)]$ does for every wff B of QC^2 and every m individual variables $X_1, X_2, \ldots, X_m$ of QC^2 that are distinct from one another. Let then TV be the function from the set of the wffs of QC^2 to $\{T, F\}$ such that, for every wff A of QC^2, $TV(A) = T$ if and only if A belongs to $S^\infty_{\infty\infty}$. TV readily proves to be a general truth-value function for QC^2, (if $S^\infty_{\infty\infty}$ is consistent** in QC^2), and one that satisfies every member of S.

Hence, my third generalization of Beth's Theorem: *A set S of wffs of QC^2 is consistent** in QC^2 if and only if at least one set of wffs of QC^2 that is isomorphic to S is satisfied by at least one general truth-function for QC^2*. Hence, as a corollary: *A wff A of QC^2 is derivable** from a set S of wffs of QC^2 if and only if no set of wffs of QC^2 that is isomorphic to $S \cup \{\sim A\}$ is satisfied by any general truth-value function for QC^2*. Hence, as a further corollary, *A wff A of QC^2 is provable** in QC^2 if and only if A is satisfied by every general truth-value function for QC^2*.[15] Because of the parallelism between these corollaries and the ones on p. 169, I suggest that a set S of wffs of QC^2 be said to imply** a wff A of QC^2 if no set of wffs of QC^2 that is isomorphic to $S \cup \{\sim A\}$ is satisfied by any general truth-value function for QC^2, and that a wff A of QC^2 be said to be valid** if A is satisfied by every general truth-value function for QC^2. The reader will note that under this understanding of things a wff A of QC^2 is valid** if and only if A is valid with respect to every general model of the sort described by Henkin on p. 84 of [5].[16]

Notes

1. As in the literature I take a set S of wffs of QC^1 to be consistent in QC^1 if 'p & $\sim p$', say, is not derivable from S in QC^1; and throughout I take S to be *satisfied by a truth-value assignment* (eventually, *by a truth-value function*) if every member of S is.

2. What I call here *Beth's Theorem* should not be confused with another (and better known) result of Beth's on definability.

3. I was considerably helped, when devising this new account of first-order implication, by Hintikka, R. H. Thomason, and van Fraassen. For further details on this, see [7].

4. *Roughly* because Henkin handles Generalization as in [2], and hence by virtue of [13] his account of provability in F^* from an arbitrary set is weaker than my account of derivability* in QC^2. See Note 10 and the closing paper in this volume.

5. *Roughly again* because Henkin handles Generalization as in [2], and hence by virtue of [13] his account of provability in F^{**} from an arbitrary set is weaker than my account of derivability** in QC^2. See Note 10 and the closing paper in this volume.

6. My construction of the two sets S_∞ and S_∞^∞ is obviously reminiscent of a construction in [4].
7. The proof is by mathematical induction on the number of occurrences of '$\sim$', '$\supset$', and '$\forall$' in A. For fuller details, see [8]; see also [10], Section 2.3. The signs '$\vee$', '&', '$\equiv$', and '$\exists$', incidentally, are presumed to be defined in the customary manner.
8. For more detailed proofs of both cases, see [8]; see also [10], Section 2.3.
9. QC^1 is said to be *strongly complete* if any wff of QC^1 that is implied by a set of wffs of QC^1 is derivable in QC^1 from that set.
10. So Church's account in [2] of provability in F^{1p} from an arbitrary set is weaker than my account of derivability in QC^1. Here as in Church's account of provability in F^{2p} (and hence Henkin's account of provability in F^* and F^{**}) from an arbitrary set, it is Generalization that is at fault. As noted in the closing paper of this volume, the matter is set to rights in later writings of Church's, in [13], etc. But Fitch's way with Generalization still seems to me the best, and I consequently adopt it throughout.
11. The proof is by mathematical induction on the number of occurrences of '$\sim$', '$\supset$', and '$\forall$' in A. For fuller details see [10], Section 6.2.
12. Where A and B are two components of a wff C of QC^2, let A precede B in order of decreasing length if A has fewer symbols than B does or, in case A and B have the same number of symbols, if A alphabetically precedes B.
13. $A[B/F(X_1, X_2, \ldots, X_m)]$ is a generalization of what Church understands by $\check{S}_B^{F(X_1, X_2, \ldots, X_m)} A |$ on pp. 192–93 of [2]. Predicate substitution is far easier to handle when *two* runs of individual signs (*individual variables* acting as *bound* individual variables and *individual parameters* acting as *free* individual variables) are used in lieu of *one*. See p. 129 on the matter.
14. Proof of the result can be found in effect in [6].
15. For fuller details, see [10], Section 6.2. Only after writing this paper and coauthoring the next (with R. K. Meyer) did I discover that a generalization of the corollary to the quantificational calculus of order ω (i.e., the simple theory of types) had already been proved in [14]. See pp. 127–28 on the matter.
16. Analogues of the results in this section can be had for the predicative quantificational calculus of order two, and—as suggested in note 15—generalizations of these results can be had for the theory of types (both the simple theory of types and the ramified one). See [10], Chapters 6–7 in the first case; see the next paper and [10] in the second. Thanks are due to Meyer, who read the original draft of this paper and whose comments and encouragement have proved invaluable. The results in this paper were announced at a meeting of the Association for Symbolic Logic, held at the University of California, Los Angeles, on March 22, 1968.

References

[1] Beth, E. W. 1959. *The Foundations of Mathematics*. Amsterdam: North-Holland.
[2] Church, A. 1956. *Introduction to Mathematical Logic. Volume I*. Princeton: Princeton University Press.
[3] Fitch, F. B. 1948. "Intuitionistic Modal Logic with Quantifiers." *Portugaliae Mathematica* 7: 113–18.
[4] Henkin, L. 1949 "The Completeness of the First-Order Functional Calculus." *The Journal of Symbolic Logic* (hereafter *JSL*) 14: 159–66.
[5] ———. 1950. "Completeness in the Theory of Types." *JSL* 15: 81–91.
[6] ———. 1953. "Banishing the Rule of Substitution for Functional Variables." *JSL* 18: 201–08.
[7] Leblanc, H. 1968. "A Simplified Account of Validity and Implication." *JSL* 33: 231–35 (#8 in this volume).
[8] ———. 1969. "A Simplified Strong Completeness Proof for $QC_=$." *Akten des XIV. Internationalen Kongresses für Philosophie* 3:83–95. Vienna: Verlag Herder (#9 in this volume).
[9] ———. 1972. "Matters of Relevance." *The Journal of Philosophical Logic* 1: 269–86 (#14 in this volume).
[10] ———. 1976. *Truth-Value Semantics*. Amsterdam: North-Holland.

[11] ———. 1979. "Generalization in First-Order Logic." *Notre Dame Journal of Formal Logic* 20: 835–57 (#35 in this volume).
[12] Leblanc, H., and Meyer, R. K. 1970. "Truth-Value Semantics for the Theory of Types." *Philosophical Problems in Logic: Some Recent Developments.* pp. 77–101. Dordrecht: Reidel (#12 in this volume).
[13] Montague, R., and Henkin, L. 1956. "On the Definition of 'Formal Deduction'." *JSL* 21: 129–36.
[14] Schütte, K. 1960. "Syntactical and Semantical of Simple Type Theory." *JSL* 25: 305–26.

12
Truth-Value Semantics for the Theory of Types
R.K. Meyer, coauthor

1. Gödel showed in 1931 that the valid wffs of T, the simple theory of types, outrun the theorems of T, and in fact cannot but outrun them.[1] It was to be almost two decades before Henkin supplied a semantic characterization of these theorems, when he showed in [5] that a wff A of T is provable in T if and only if A is what he called *valid in the general sense* or what we shall call *generally valid*. Further semantic characterizations of provability in T then came in rapid succession, among them Hintikka [7] and Schütte [13]. Both of these dispense with Henkin's *general models*, the former using *general model sets*, the latter *total valuations*.

Pursuing earlier investigations of Leblanc into first-order and second-order implication, we submit a semantic characterization of derivability (and hence provability) in T, and show that a wff A of T is derivable in T from a set $\mathcal{G}$ of wffs if and only if A is what we call *generally implied by* $\mathcal{G}$. Our account of general implication is an extension of Schütte's account of general validity, our *general truth-value functions* coinciding in effect with his *total valuations*; accordingly, our account also dispenses with general models, though we shall show how the account presented here is foreshadowed in the Henkin techniques. We then go on to offer an account of implication (and hence validity) in T, in which what we call *truth-value functions* do duty for models of the ordinary sort. Our results, easily extended to the whole functional calculus of order ω, may be of interest to readers of a nominalist persuasion. Thanks are due to Hintikka, who helped to devise the account of first-order implication in [8] and, by extension, the present account of general implication in T.

2. We shall take *the primitive signs* of T to be the two connectives '$\sim$' and '$\supset$', the quantifier letter '$\forall$', the membership predicate 'ϵ', the colon ':', the two parentheses '(' and ')', and the two braces '{' and '}', and for each natural number t from 0 on $\aleph_0$ variables and $\aleph_0$ parameters of type t.[2] We shall under-

177

178   Part 2: Truth

stand by a *formula* of T any finite sequence of primitive signs of T, and we shall presume that the formulas of T (in particular, the ones we care about, soon to receive the honorific 'well-formed') have been arranged in sequence, and hence have an *alphabetical order*. We shall refer to the variables of T by means of 'X', 'Y', and 'Z'; to the parameters of T by means of 'P', 'Q', and 'R'; to the formulas of T by means of 'S'. These letters (and others adopted later for similar purposes) will occasionally sport primes or numerical subscripts. We shall take an occurrence of X in S to be *bound* if it is in a part of S of the sort $(\forall X)S'$ or $\{X{:}S'\}$ and otherwise to be *free*. We shall say that X *occurs bound (free) in* S if at least one occurrence of X in S is bound (free). Finally, we shall take $S(S'/X)$ to be the result of substituting S' for every *free* occurrence of X in S; $S(S'/P)$, to be the result of substituting S' for every occurrence of P in S.

The *well-formed formulas* of T shall be its *terms* and *sentences*, to be immediately defined. We shall refer to the terms of T by 'K', 'L', and 'M', and to the sentences by 'A', 'B', and 'C'. Letting t be any type from 0 on, we proceed to the appropriate recursive definitions.

(i) Let X be a variable and P be a parameter of the same type t. Then $\{X{:}A(X/P)\}$ is an *abstract* of type $t + 1$.

(ii) If S is a parameter or abstract (of type t), S is a term (of type t).

(iii) If K is of type t and L is of type $t + 1$, $K\epsilon L$ is a sentence.

(iv) $\sim A$ and $(A \supset B)$ are sentences.

(v) Let X and P be as in (i). Then $(\forall X)A(X/P)$ is a sentence.

A formula S shall be well formed only if (possibly iterated) application of (i)–(v) establishes that it is a term or a sentence. (In view of what seems to have become current practice, however, we shall restrict our application of the abbreviation 'wff' to those well-formed formulas which are sentences.) Although the reader will have noted that officially formulas with free variables are not well formed, we slacken our conventions to the extent of occasionally referring to *sentences* by means of '$(\forall X)A$' and '$A(K/X)$', and to *terms* by means of '$\{X{:}A\}$', etc., when A is $B(X/P)$ for some sentence B. And note finally that if $(\forall X)S$ is a wff, where X is free in S, $S(K/X)$ is a wff only if K and X are of the same type.

We name now certain sets of well-formed formulas. Π shall be the set of all parameters of T; λ, the set of all terms of T; for a given type t, Π_t and λ_t shall be respectively the sets of all parameters and of all terms of that type. In view of the parenthetical remark of the last paragraph, W shall be the set of sentences of T. Finally, '$\mathfrak{G}$', subscripted, primed, or otherwise defaced, shall refer to an arbitrary subset of W.

Our last terminological preliminaries will set the stage for the Hintikka-Leblanc ploy exploited in [8]. Since moralistically inclined readers may, when they discover what is going on, accuse us of undue gimmickry, we advise them to skip this paragraph, continuing for the benefit of the more devious among you. As readers of [4] will recall, in proving that every consistent set $\mathfrak{G}$ of first-order formulas has a model, Henkin was obliged to send out in mid-

Truth-Value Semantics for the Theory of Types 179

proof for a fresh supply of constants foreign to $\mathfrak{G}$. The reason, essentially, is that a constant (or parameter) which occurs in $\mathfrak{G}$ is subject therein to special assumptions, while Henkin required for his purposes constants about which no special assumptions were made. Since in the extreme case every constant of a given language might occur in a given set of consistent sentences, it would seem that for the purpose of proving completeness we cannot make do, in general, with the linguistic resources already at hand.

In fact this is false; indeed, Henkin himself avoids the problem in [5] by making use of a choice operator, as he notes. Even without such an operator, however, the problem may be skirted by systematically *rewriting* the formulas of a given $\mathfrak{G}$ in such a way that, when the rewriting is complete, infinitely many parameters do not occur in the set $\mathfrak{G}'$ of rewritten formulas. This is essentially the method of [8], and it serves to motivate the definitions immediately following; the point is that we do not need to exceed the vocabulary of T, so far as our formal language is concerned, in deriving our most interesting results about T.

As we proceed, the key notion at which we are aiming is that of the isomorphism of two sets $\mathfrak{G}$ and $\mathfrak{G}'$ of wffs. First, let us call any function f partially defined on the set λ of terms of T with values in λ *type-preserving* provided that, for each type t and each term K of λ_t on which f is defined, $f(K)$ is also in λ_t. Let f be a type-preserving function defined for each parameter P of a given wff A; by the *f-image* of A we mean the result of simultaneously replacing P with $f(P)$ throughout A, for every P in A.[3] Then we say that two sets $\mathfrak{G}$ and $\mathfrak{G}'$ of wffs are *isomorphic* provided that, where $\Pi(\mathfrak{G})$ is the set of all parameters occurring in wffs of $\mathfrak{G}$, there is a one-one type-preserving mapping $f:\Pi(\mathfrak{G}) \to \Pi$ such that $\mathfrak{G}'$ consists of exactly the f-images of members of $\mathfrak{G}$.[4] In terms of our motivating remarks, two sets are isomorphic if and only if each can be obtained from the other by a systematic rewriting of parameters.

We say now that a sign of T is *foreign* to A if it does not occur in A, and *foreign* to $\mathfrak{G}$ if it is foreign to every member of $\mathfrak{G}$. We call $\mathfrak{G}$ *infinitely extendible* if, for each t from 0 on, $\aleph_0$ parameters of Π_t are foreign to $\mathfrak{G}$. We pause for a trivial lemma.

Lemma 1. *Every set $\mathfrak{G}$ of sentences of T is isomorphic to an infinitely extendible set.*

Proof: Let P_i^t be the i-th parameter in alphabetical order of Π_t and define $f:\Pi \to \Pi$ by $F(P_i^t) = P_{2i}^t$, for all i and t. Clearly an f-image exists for each $A \in W$, where W is the set of *all* sentences of T, but infinitely many parameters of every type (specifically, all parameters P_{2i+1}^t, $0 \le i, t$) fail to occur among the f-images. Accordingly, for any $\mathfrak{G} \subseteq W$ the set $\mathfrak{G}'$ of f-images of members of $\mathfrak{G}$ is inifinitely extendible, while it follows readily from definitions that $\mathfrak{G}$ and $\mathfrak{G}'$ are isomorphic.

3. Our last immediate syntactical concern will be provability in T. We shall count as an *axiom* of T any wff of T of any of the following ten sorts:[5]

180   Part 2: Truth

A1. $A \supset (B \supset A)$

A2. $(A \supset (B \supset C)) \supset ((A \supset B) \supset (A \supset C))$

A3. $(\sim A \supset \sim B) \supset (B \supset A)$

A4. $(\forall X)(A \supset B) \supset ((\forall X)A \supset (\forall X)B)$

A5. $A \supset (\forall X)A$

A6. $(\forall X)A \supset A(P/X)$

A7. $(\forall X)A \supset A(\{Y:B\}/X)$[6]

A8. $K\epsilon\{X:A\} \equiv A(K/X)$[7]

A9. $(\forall X)(X\epsilon K \equiv X\epsilon L) \supset (K\epsilon M \supset L\epsilon M)$[8]

A10. $(\forall X)A(X/P)$, where A is an axiom and P is foreign to any part of A of the sort $(\forall X)B$ or $\{X:B\}$.[9]

We shall count as a *derivation* of A from Ⓖ in T (a *proof* of A in T when Ⓖ is $\emptyset$, for short) any column of wffs of T that closes with A and every one of whose entries belongs to Ⓖ, is an axiom of T, or follows from two previous entries in the column by Modus Ponens. And we say that (i) A is *derivable* from Ⓖ in T (Ⓖ ⊢ A, for short) if there is a derivation of A from Ⓖ in T, and (ii) A is *provable* in T (⊢ A, for short) if there is a proof of A in T. Finally, (iii) Ⓖ is *consistent* in T if it is not the case that Ⓖ ⊢ $\sim(A \supset A)$, for any A.

A few remarks concerning the above axiom system for T may be in order.

(a) In **A8** 'P' could replace 'K', and in **A9** 'P', 'Q', and 'R' could replace 'K', 'L', and 'M', respectively. However, the axioms of T are more easily shown to be generally valid when **A8** and **A9** are written out as above.

(b) Readers who prefer to dispense with set abstracts and the accompanying notation (defining $P\epsilon\{X:A\}$ and $\{X:A\}\epsilon K$ as we did in note 6) may dispense with **A8** above and with condition (v) in the definition of a general truth-value function for T in Section 4 below. **A8** corresponds to one of Quine's definitions of $P\epsilon\{X:A\}$ in [12]. While axiom-chopping, we discovered the following proof in T of the biconditional corresponding to Quine's definition of $\{X:A\}\epsilon K$.[10]

(1) $\{X:A\}\epsilon K \supset ((\forall Z)(Z\epsilon\{X:A\} \equiv Z\epsilon\{X:A\}) \,\&\, \{X:A\}\epsilon K)$ by routine truth-functional moves. Hence in view of **A8**

(2) $\{X:A\}\epsilon K \supset ((\forall Z)(Z\epsilon\{X:A\} \equiv A(Z/X)) \,\&\, \{X:A\}\epsilon K)$. Hence in view **A7**

(3) $(\exists Y)(\{X:A\}\epsilon K \supset ((\forall Z)(Z\epsilon Y \equiv A(Z/X)) \,\&\, Y\epsilon K)$. Hence by routine quantificational moves

(4) $\{X:A\}\epsilon K \supset (\exists Y)((\forall Z)(Z\epsilon Y \equiv A(Z/X)) \,\&\, Y\epsilon K)$, proving half of Quine's biconditional.

On the other hand,

(5) $(\forall Z)(Z\epsilon P \equiv Z\epsilon\{X:A\}) \supset (P\epsilon K \supset \{X:A\}\epsilon K)$ holds by **A9**. Hence, with P presumed foreign to $\{X:A\}$ and to K,

(6) $(\forall Z)(Z\epsilon P \equiv A(Z/X)) \supset (P\epsilon K \supset \{X:A\}\epsilon K)$ by **A8**. Hence by truth-functional and quantificational moves

(7) $(\exists Y)((\forall Z)(Z \epsilon Y \equiv A(Z/X))$ & $Y \epsilon K) \supset \{X:A\} \epsilon K$, the converse of (4).

(c) The familiar *axiom of Comprehension* is of course provable in T, as follows:[11]

(1) $(\forall Y)(Y \epsilon \{Y:A\} \equiv A)$ by **A8** and **A10**. Hence by the dual of **A7** and Modus Ponens

(2) $(\exists X)(\forall Y)(Y \epsilon X \equiv A)$, where X is not free in A.

4. Here is installment one of our semantics for T. Let **2** = {**T**,**F**}, where **T** is the truth-value true and **F** the truth-value false.[12] A function $\alpha: W \to \mathbf{2}$ will count as a *general truth-value function* for T provided that the following conditions are fulfilled for all wffs:[13]

(i) $\alpha(\sim A) \neq \alpha(A)$;
(ii) $\alpha(A \supset B) = \mathbf{T}$ if and only if $\alpha(A) = \mathbf{F}$ or $\alpha(B) = \mathbf{T}$;
(iii) $\alpha((\forall X)A) = \mathbf{T}$ if and only if $\alpha(A(K/X)) = \mathbf{T}$ for all terms K of the same type as X;
(iv) $\alpha(K \epsilon \{X:A\}) = \alpha(A(K/X))$
(v) if $\alpha(K \epsilon L) = \alpha(K \epsilon L')$ for all terms K in λ_t, $0 \leq t$,
   $\alpha(L \epsilon M) = \alpha(L' \epsilon M)$ for each M in λ_{t+2}.

A wff A is *true on a general truth-value function α for* T if $\alpha(A) = \mathbf{T}$. $\mathfrak{G}$ is *generally verifiable* in T if there is a general truth-value function on which every member of $\mathfrak{G}$ is true. If some $\mathfrak{G}'$ isomorphic to $\mathfrak{G}$ is generally verifiable in T, $\mathfrak{G}$ is *weakly generally verifiable*. $\mathfrak{G}$ *generally implies* A (in Tarski's terminology, A is a general consequence of $\mathfrak{G}$) if $\mathfrak{G} \cup \{\sim A\}$ is not weakly generally verifiable. Finally, A is *generally valid* if $\varnothing$ generally implies A, or, what comes to the same thing, if A is true on all general truth-value functions for T.[14]

The following lemma will prove useful.

Lemma 2. *Suppose A is generally valid. Then all wffs $A(K/P)$ are generally valid, where K is a term of the same type as P.*

Proof: Let K and P be of the same type t. Let B be an arbitrary wff and α a general truth-function. We show first that there is a general truth-value function β such that $\alpha(B(K/P)) = \beta(B)$.

Assume first that P does not occur in K (and hence not in $B(K/P)$). Let $P_1, P_2, \ldots, P_{i-1}$ be in alphabetical order all the parameters of type t which occur in $B(K/P)$, let P_i be P, and let $P_{i+1}, P_{i+2}, \ldots$ be the other parameters of type t, again in alphabetical order. Define a function $f: \Pi \to \Pi - \{P\}$ by setting $f(P_j) = P_{j+1}$ for any parameter P_j of type t such that $i \leq j$, and $f(Q) = Q$ for any other parameter Q. Note (i) f is an isomorphism in the sense of Section 2, (ii) the set of f-images of wffs of T is the set of wffs to which P is foreign (temporarily baptized $W - P$), and (iii) the f-image of $B(K/P)$ is $B(K/P)$. Let $\beta: W \to \mathbf{2}$ now be defined by cases as follows: (1) if $C \epsilon W - P$, and is hence the f-image of a wff D, set $\beta(C) = \alpha(D)$; (2) if P occurs in C, set $\beta(C) = \beta(C(K/P))$, noting that the latter is already defined by (1) since on assumption P is foreign to K.

182   Part 2: Truth

Note too that α, being a general truth-value function, β is sure to be one also, since any suspected violation of one of (i)–(v) above by β can be transformed into a violation by α by replacing P by K throughout the suspect context and passing to images under the converse of f. And by definition $\beta(B) = \beta(B(K/P)) = \alpha(B(K/P))$, which was to be proved.

Suppose now that P occurs in K. Let Q be a parameter foreign to B and K and of type t. By what has been shown above, there is at any rate a general truth-value function γ such that $\alpha(B(Q/P)(K/Q)) = \gamma(B(Q/P))$, since Q is foreign to K. But $B(Q/P)(K/Q)$ is just $B(K/P)$, so $\alpha(B(K/P)) = \gamma(B(Q/P))$. Define $f:\Pi \to \Pi$ by setting $f(P) = Q, f(Q) = P$, and, for any other parameter $R, f(R) = R$, and then define $\beta(C) = \mathbf{T}$ if and only if the f-image of C is true on γ. Clearly β is a general truth-value function such that $\beta(B) = \gamma(B(Q/P)) = \alpha(B(K/P))$, completing the demonstration that for any α we can find a β such that $\alpha(B(K/P)) = \beta(B)$.

We complete the proof of Lemma 2 by assuming A generally valid. Suppose for *reductio* that $A(K/P)$ is not generally valid. Then there is a general truth-value function α such that $\alpha(A(K/P)) = \mathbf{F}$, by our alternate definition of general validity. But by what has been just demonstrated there is then another general truth-value function β such that $\beta(A) = \mathbf{F}$, contradicting the assumed general validity of A and ending the proof.

5.   We now establish the soundness of our axioms for T, given the semantics of the previous section.

Lemma 3.   *Suppose* ⊢ *A. Then A is generally valid.*
Proof: We assume that A is a theorem of T and show it true on all general truth-value functions α. Proof is by induction. There are two cases, according as A is an axiom or a consequence of predecessors by Modus Ponens. We employ a secondary induction on the number of prefaced universal quantifiers if A is an axiom.
Case 1: A is an axiom.
  1.1 A is not of the form $(\forall X)B$. Then it is of one of the sorts **A1–A9**. It is readily verified that A is true on arbitrary α. For suppose in particular that A is $(\forall X)(B \supset C) \supset ((\forall X)B \supset (\forall X)C)$, and that $(\forall X)(B \supset C)$ and $(\forall X)B$ are both true on α. Then $(B \supset C)(K/X)$ and $B(K/X)$ are both true on α for every term K of T of the same type as X. But $B(K/X) \supset C(K/X)$ is the same as $(B \supset C)(K/X)$. Hence $C(K/X)$ is true on α for K of the same type as X; hence $(\forall X)C$ is true on α. Or suppose that A is $B \supset (\forall X)B$. Since X cannot occur free in B, $B(K/X)$ is the same as B for every term K; hence if B is true on α, so is $(\forall X)B$. Finally, note that if A is an extensionality axiom of the sort **A9**, it is true on α by (v) of Section 4.
  1.2 A is of the form $(\forall X)B$. We may assume by the hypothesis of the secondary induction that $B(P/X)$ is generally valid, for some P of the same type as X and foreign to B. But then by Lemma 2, $B(P/X)(K/P)$ is generally valid for

every term K of the type of X; since P is foreign to B, $B(P/X)(K/P)$ is $B(K/X)$ for every such K, and hence $(\forall X)B$ is generally valid by (iii) of Section 4.
Case 2: A is the consequence of predecessors B and $B \supset A$. Trivial, given the hypothesis of the primary induction, ending the proof of Lemma 3.

Lemma 4. *Suppose $\mathfrak{G}$ is weakly generally verifiable. Then $\mathfrak{G}$ is consistent in* T.
Proof: We prove the lemma first for the case in which $\mathfrak{G}$ is itself generally verifiable. Then there is a general truth-value function α on which all members of $\mathfrak{G}$ are true. Using Lemma 3, one establishes by a straightforward induction on length of derivation that every wff B derivable from $\mathfrak{G}$ is true on α. Since $\vdash A \supset A$ for every A in T, however, by Lemma 3 no wff $\sim(A \supset A)$ is true on α. Hence neither is any such wff derivable from $\mathfrak{G}$, establishing the consistency of generally verifiable $\mathfrak{G}$.

Suppose now that $\mathfrak{G}$ is weakly generally verifiable; then $\mathfrak{G}$ is isomorphic to a generally verifiable $\mathfrak{G}'$; $\mathfrak{G}'$ is consistent by what has been just shown. Assume that $\mathfrak{G}$ is nevertheless inconsistent, for *reductio*. We finish the proof by showing how a derivation of $\sim(A \supset A)$ from $\mathfrak{G}$ can, for some B, be turned into a derivation of $\sim(B \supset B)$ from $\mathfrak{G}'$, a contradiction.

Indeed, by the definition of 'isomorphic' there is a type-preserving one-one mapping f from the parameters of $\mathfrak{G}$ onto the parameters of $\mathfrak{G}'$. For each $C \epsilon W$, let C' be its f-image in the sense of p. 179. Then where $A_1, A_2, \ldots, A_n$ is the assumed derivation of $\sim(A \supset A)$ from $\mathfrak{G}$, $A'_1, A'_2, \ldots, A'_n$ is a derivation of $\sim(A' \supset A')$ from $\mathfrak{G}'$; this is the promised contradiction, completing the proof of the consistency of weakly generally verifiable $\mathfrak{G}$.

Corollary. *Suppose A is derivable from $\mathfrak{G}$ in* T. *Then $\mathfrak{G}$ generally implies A.*
Proof: Clearly, if $\mathfrak{G} \vdash A$, $\mathfrak{G} \cup \{\sim A\}$ is inconsistent. By the lemma, $\mathfrak{G} \cup \{\sim A\}$ is not weakly generally verifiable, which was to be proved.

6. We turn now to completeness, proving the converses of the lemmas of the previous section. (Proofs in the present section are in large part an adaptation of results in Henkin's [4] and in Section 89 of Beth's [1].)

Lemma 5. *Let $\mathfrak{G}$ be infinitely extendible. If $\mathfrak{G}$ is consistent in* T, *then $\mathfrak{G}$ is generally verifiable.*
Proof: Suppose $\mathfrak{G}$ is consistent and infinitely extendible. For every i from 1 on, let $(\forall X_i)A_i$ be the alphabetically i-th wff of T of the sort $(\forall X)A$; and letting $\mathfrak{G}_0$ be $\mathfrak{G}$, let $\mathfrak{G}_i$ be $\mathfrak{G}_{i-1} \cup \{A_i(P/X_i) \supset (\forall X_i)A_i\}$, where P is the alphabetically earliest parameter of T that is of the same type as X_i and is foreign to $\mathfrak{G}_{i-1}$ and A_i. Let $\mathfrak{G}_\omega$ be the union of $\mathfrak{G}_0, \mathfrak{G}_1, \mathfrak{G}_2 \ldots$. It is easily verified that $\mathfrak{G}_\omega$ is consistent in T if $\mathfrak{G}$ is, and that, for every wff of T of the sort $(\forall X)A$, there is a parameter (and hence a term) K of T of the same type as X such that $\mathfrak{G}_\omega \vdash A(K/X) \supset (\forall X)A$.

184   Part 2: Truth

Next, let $\mathfrak{G}_\omega^0$ be $\mathfrak{G}_\omega$; where B_i is the alphabetically i-th wff of T, let $\mathfrak{G}_\omega^i$ be $\mathfrak{G}_\omega^{i-1} \cup \{B_i\}$ or $\mathfrak{G}_\omega^{i-1}$ according as $\mathfrak{G}_\omega^{i-1} \cup \{B_i\}$ is consistent or not in T. Let $\mathfrak{G}_\omega^\omega$ be the union of $\mathfrak{G}_\omega^0$, $\mathfrak{G}_\omega^1$, $\mathfrak{G}_\omega^2$, ... It is easily verified that: (a) $\mathfrak{G}_\omega^\omega$ is consistent in T if $\mathfrak{G}_\omega$ (and hence if $\mathfrak{G}$) is; (b) if $\mathfrak{G}_\omega^\omega$ is consistent in T, then (i) $\mathfrak{G}_\omega^\omega \vdash {\sim}A$ if and only if it is not the case that $\mathfrak{G}_\omega^\omega \vdash A$, (ii) $\mathfrak{G}_\omega^\omega \vdash A \supset B$ if and only if it is not the case that $\mathfrak{G}_\omega^\omega \vdash A$ or (it is the case that) $\mathfrak{G}_\omega^\omega \vdash B$, (iii) where X is a variable of T of type t, $0 \leq t$, $\mathfrak{G}_\omega^\omega \vdash (\forall X)A$ if and only if $\mathfrak{G}_\omega^\omega \vdash A(K/X)$ for every term K of type t.

Let α be the function from the set of wffs of T to $\{\mathbf{T}, \mathbf{F}\}$ such that, for every A, $\alpha(A) = \mathbf{T}$ if and only if $\mathfrak{G}_\omega^\omega \vdash A$. Since $K\epsilon\{X{:}A\} \equiv A(K/X)$ is an axiom of T, $\mathfrak{G}_\omega^\omega \vdash K\epsilon\{X{:}A\} \equiv A(K/X)$; hence $\alpha(K\epsilon\{X{:}A\} \equiv A(K/X)) = \mathbf{T}$, and hence $\alpha(K\epsilon\{X{:}A\}) = \alpha(A(K/X))$. Applying similar considerations to axioms of the sort **A9**, we see that if $\alpha(K\epsilon L) = \alpha(K\epsilon L')$ for all terms K in λ_t, $\alpha(L\epsilon M) = \alpha(L'\epsilon M)$ for each M in λ_{t+2}. Hence α meets the conditions (i)–(v) defining a general truth-value function in Section 4. But since $\mathfrak{G}$ is a subset of $\mathfrak{G}_\omega^\omega$, $\mathfrak{G}_\omega^\omega \vdash A$ for every member A of $\mathfrak{G}$. Hence every member of $\mathfrak{G}$ is true on α. Hence every consistent and infinitely extendible set $\mathfrak{G}$ is generally verifiable.

Lemma 6. *For every set $\mathfrak{G}$ of wffs of T, if $\mathfrak{G}$ is consistent in T then $\mathfrak{G}$ is weakly generally verifiable.*
Proof: Let $\mathfrak{G}$ be a consistent set of wffs of T. By Lemma 1, $\mathfrak{G}$ is isomorphic to an infinitely extendible set of wffs $\mathfrak{G}'$. By the argument which concludes the proof of Lemma 4, $\mathfrak{G}'$ is consistent. By Lemma 5, $\mathfrak{G}'$ is generally verifiable; hence $\mathfrak{G}$ is isomorphic to a generally verifiable set of wffs, which was to be proved.

Corollary. *If $\mathfrak{G}$ generally implies A, $\mathfrak{G} \vdash A$. If A is generally valid, $\vdash A$.*
Proof: We note that the second statement is the specialization of the first to the case $\mathfrak{G} = \varnothing$. Assume then that it is not the case that $\mathfrak{G} \vdash A$. It follows readily that $\mathfrak{G} \cup \{{\sim}A\}$ is consistent and hence, by the lemma, weakly generally verifiable. So if $\mathfrak{G} \cup \{{\sim}A\}$ is not weakly generally verifiable, A is derivable from $\mathfrak{G}$ in T, which was to be proved.

We sum up the considerations of this and the preceding section in the following two theorems, which can be thought of as combined soundness and completeness theorems for T:

Theorem 1. $\mathfrak{G} \vdash A$ *if and only if $\mathfrak{G}$ generally implies A.*

Theorem 2. $\vdash A$ *if and only if A is generally valid.*

7. We turn now to comparison and contrast between the semantics presented for T in Section 4, which we shall henceforth call the *general truth-value semantics* for T, and a Henkin-style semantics for T, which we shall call the

general model-theoretic semantics for T.[15] The equivalence of the two semantical approaches yields the following philosophically interesting conclusion: T is consistent with the assumption that the only things which need to be admitted to the range of variables of quantification are those which are nameable in the vocabulary of T.[16] We pause to introduce the requisite model-theoretic notions, beginning with those of the *standard model-theoretic semantics* for T.[17]

8. Let S be a non-empty set.[18] By $\Gamma(S)$, we mean the power set of S—i.e., $\Gamma(S) = \{S': S' \subseteq S\}$. For each non-negative integer t, we define Γ^t recursively as follows: (i) $\Gamma^0(S) = S$; (ii) $\Gamma^{t+1}(S) = \Gamma(\Gamma^t(S))$. $U(S)$ shall be $\cup_{t<\omega}\Gamma^t(S)$.[19] Furthermore,

(a) by the *standard system $D(S)$ of domains* for T over S, understand the sequence $<\Gamma^0(S), \Gamma^1(S), \Gamma^2(S), \ldots>$;

(b) by a $D(S)$-*interpretation of the parameters* of T, understand any function $I: \Pi \rightarrow U(S)$ such that, for each parameter P of type t, $I(P) \in \Gamma^t(S)$;

(c) where I and I' are $D(S)$-interpretations of the parameters of T, and P is a parameter of T, count I' as a P-*variant* of I if, for every parameter Q of T other than $P, I'(Q) = I(Q)$ (we shall refer to the P-variants of I by 'I'');

(d) where I is a $D(S)$-interpretation of the parameters of T, let a *complete interpretation CI (agreeing with I)* be a function defined on the set λ of terms of T with values in $U(S)$ and on the set W of sentences of T with values in **2** ($= \{\mathbf{T}, \mathbf{F}\}$), subject to the following conditions:

(i) $CI(P) = I(P)$;
(ii) $CI(K\epsilon L) = \mathbf{T}$ if and only if $CI(K) \epsilon CI(L)$;
(iii) $CI(\sim A) \neq CI(A)$;
(iv) $CI(A \supset B) = \mathbf{T}$ if and only if $CI(A) = \mathbf{F}$ or $CI(B) = \mathbf{T}$;
(v) where P is the alphabetically earliest parameter of **T** of the same type as X that is foreign to A, $CI((\forall X)A) = \mathbf{T}$ if and only if $CI^P(A(P/X)) = \mathbf{T}$ for every complete interpretation CI^P agreeing with a P-variant I^P of I;
(vi) where P is as in (v), $CI(\{X:A\}) = \{I^P(P): CI^P(A(P/X)) = \mathbf{T}\}$;

(e) by a *standard model* for T, understand any pair $<D(S), CI>$, where $D(S)$ is the standard system of domains for T over some non-empty set S, and CI is a complete interpretation of T agreeing with some $D(S)$-interpretation I of the parameters of T;

(f) take a set $\mathfrak{G}$ of wffs of T to be *model-theoretically verifiable* if there is a standard model $<D(S), CI>$ for T such that every member of $\mathfrak{G}$ is true on CI (i.e., $CI(A) = \mathbf{T}$ for all $A \in \mathfrak{G}$); take $\mathfrak{G}$ to *model-theoretically imply* A if $\mathfrak{G} \cup \{\sim A\}$ is not model-theoretically verifiable, and A to be *valid* if $\emptyset$ model-theoretically implies A.

Despite the crispness which we have attempted to inject into our characterization of the standard model-theoretic semantics for T by stipulations (a)–(f), the reader, who has already been warned in note 17, will note that the crispness is illusory without specification of the set theory which we are using along with the one, namely T, which we are mentioning. Leaving this choice to the reader (and thus subjecting the choice of what shall eventually count as a standard model for T to the reader's set-theoretical standards), we pass on to an analogous account of Henkin's *general model-theoretic semantics*, adapted here to T.

9. We assume the preliminaries of Section 8. Then

(a) by a *Henkin system* $\mathfrak{H}(S)$ *of domains for* T *over* S, understand any sequence $<S_0, S_1, S_2, \ldots>$, where S_0 is S and where for every t from 0 on, $S_{t+1} \subseteq \Gamma(S_t)$;

(b) by an $\mathfrak{H}(S)$-*interpretation of the parameters* of T, understand any function $I : \Pi \to U(S)$ such that, for each parameter P of type $t, I(P) \in S_t$;

(c) where I is an $\mathfrak{H}(S)$-interpretation of the parameters of T, take I^P to be a *P-variant* of I, defined, *mutatis mutandis*, as in (c) of the preceding section;

(d) where I is an $\mathfrak{H}(S)$-interpretation of the parameters of T, let *a complete* $\mathfrak{H}(S)$-*interpretation CI (agreeing with I)* be any function defined on the set λ of terms of T with values in $U(S)$ and on the set W of sentences of T with values in **2** which meets conditions (i)–(vi) in (d) of the preceding section;

(e) call *CI*, when a complete $\mathfrak{H}(S)$ interpretation of T, an *admissible* interpretation provided that, for every t from 0 on and for every term K of type $t, CI(K) \in S_t$; and call $\mathfrak{H}(S)$ *a general system of domains* provided that every complete $\mathfrak{H}(S)$-interpretation is admissible;

(f) by a *general model* for T, understand any pair $<\mathfrak{H}(S), CI>$, where $\mathfrak{H}(S)$ is a general system of domains for T and *CI* is a complete (and hence admissible) $\mathfrak{H}(S)$-interpretation; take a set $\mathfrak{G}$ of wffs of T to be *model-theoretically generally verifiable* if there is a general model $<\mathfrak{H}(S), CI>$ such that every member of $\mathfrak{G}$ is true on *CI*; define corresponding notions of model-theoretic general implication and of model-theoretic general validity in exact analogy with the definition in (f) of the last section.

10. We now relate the general model-theoretic semantics of Section 9 to the general truth-value semantics of Section 4. Interestingly, model-theoretic general verifiability relates, on the truth-value side, not to general verifiability but to weak general verifiability. (There are indeed sets of wffs which are generally verifiable in the model-theoretic but not in the truth-value sense; cf. [8].) We proceed to the appropriate theorems.[20]

Lemma 7. *Suppose* $\mathfrak{G}$ *is model-theoretically generally verifiable; then* $\mathfrak{G}$ *is consistent.*
Proof as in Lemmas 3 and 4.

We prove the converse of Lemma 7 by showing first that every general truth-value function determines a general model. We shall abbreviate the proof,

Truth-Value Semantics for the Theory of Types   187

which is largely an adaptation of a similar result in [5]. By a *canonical system of domains* for T, we mean a Henkin system of domains $\mathfrak{H}(v_0)$, where $v_0 \subseteq \Pi_0$. By a *canonical general model*, we mean a general model $<\mathfrak{H}(v_0), CI>$.

Let α be a general truth-value function. It is readily verified that the relation $\leftrightarrow$ defined on Γ_0 by

(i) $P \leftrightarrow Q$ if and only if $\alpha((X)(P \epsilon X \equiv Q \epsilon X)) = \mathbf{T}$

is an equivalence relation. Let v_0 be any exhaustive set of representatives of the equivalence classes into which Π_0 is partitioned by $\to$.[21] By the *canonization of α relative to v_0*, understand the pair $Z\alpha = <\mathfrak{H}(v_0), CI>$, which is defined in accordance with the following specifications:
(ii) for all wffs A of T, $CI(A) = \alpha(A)$;
(iii) if $P \epsilon v_0$, $CI(P) = P$;
(iv) if $P, Q \epsilon \Gamma_0$, $CI(P) = CI(Q)$ if and only if $P \leftrightarrow Q$;
(v) for $t > 0$, if $L \epsilon \lambda_t$ then $CI(L) = \{CI(K) : \alpha(K \epsilon L) = \mathbf{T}\}$;
finally, define $\mathfrak{H}(v_0) = <S_0, S_1, S_2, \ldots>$ by defining each S_t from 0 on as the set of values of CI for arguments in λ_t.

Lemma 8. *Let α and $Z\alpha = <\mathfrak{H}(v_0), CI>$ be as above. Then $Z\alpha$ is a canonical general model for T.*
Proof: It suffices to show CI a complete $\mathfrak{H}(v_0)$ interpretation of T and to show $\mathfrak{H}(v_0)$ a general system of domains. Proof of the former may be had by checking that each of conditions (i)–(vi) in (d) of Section 9 is met, proceeding by an induction on the length of a well-formed formula. To finish the proof, show $\mathfrak{H}(v_0)$ a general system of domains by proving that any $\mathfrak{H}(v_0)$-interpretation of the parameters of T can be extended to a complete $\mathfrak{H}(v_0)$-interpretation CI'. This is clear if P is a parameter, since $I'(P)$ must be $CI(K)$ for some K. Show then for any wff A and for any term L that, where $P_1, \ldots, P_n$ are the parameters in A or L respectively, $I'(P_1) = CI(K_1)$, $I'(P_2) = CI(K_2), \ldots$, $I'(P_n) = CI(K_n)$, if A^* is the result of replacing K_1 with P_1, K_2 with $P_2, \ldots, K_n$ with P_n simultaneously throughout A and that if L^* is the result of making similar replacements in L, then $CI(A^*) = CI'(A)$ and $CI(K^*) = CI'(K)$, which completes the proof of the lemma and establishes that $Z\alpha$ is a general model.

Lemma 9. *If $\mathfrak{G}$ is consistent, $\mathfrak{G}$ has a general model and hence $\mathfrak{G}$ is model-theoretically generally verifiable. (Henkin completeness theorem for T)*
Proof: If $\mathfrak{G}$ is consistent, there is a general truth-value function α on which all members of a set $\mathfrak{G}'$ isomorphic to $\mathfrak{G}$ are true, by Lemma 6. By Lemma 8, all members of $\mathfrak{G}'$ are true on CI, where $Z\alpha = <\mathfrak{H}(v_0), CI>$ is a canonical general model. Let $f: \Pi \to \Pi$ be the type-preserving mapping of p. 179 from the parameters of $\mathfrak{G}$ onto those of $\mathfrak{G}'$ (extended if necessary to all of Π by setting $f(P) = P$ if P is foreign to $\mathfrak{G}$). Let $I'(P)$ be defined, for each parameter of T, as $f(I(P))$. It is readily verified that $<\mathfrak{H}(v_0), CI'>$ is a general model for T and that all members of $\mathfrak{G}$ are true on CI', ending the proof of the lemma.

188 Part 2: Truth

Theorem 3. ⑤ *model-theoretically generally implies A if and only if* ⑤ *generally implies A.*

Theorem 4. *A is model-theoretically generally valid if and only if A is generally valid.*
Proof by Theorems 1 and 2, Lemmas 7 and 9, and definitions.

11. We now address ourselves to the problem of constructing *a standard truth-value semantics for* T. We warn the reader, however, that although in our opinion the general truth-value semantics of Section 4 offers ontological and perhaps conceptual economies over against the general model-theoretic semantics of Section 9, no similar economies are to be sought in this part. But if one's model-theoretic view of truth-value semantics is that the range of the quantifiers has been restricted to those entities actually *named* (on a given interpretation) by terms of our type-theoretic language, a view implicit in the treatment of the universal quantifiers in (iii) of Section 4, then it would seem that one could simulate any standard model for T by making provision in one's truth-value semantics for the addition of an appropriately large supply of names. One must, of course, also lay down conditions which insure that all entities of the model do, in effect, receive names. As noted, this is not an economical procedure; it is the work of Sections 2–6, not that of this part, that we commend to those of thrifty philosophic inclination. On the other hand, it is of interest to think from a more freewheeling point of view about what it takes to build a truth-value semantics equivalent to the (standard) model-theoretic account of Section 8. Although we make no claim that the particular stipulations which we have chosen are the most economical or interesting, they are reasonably direct. Given a modicum of indulgence toward our propensity to presume that a set (e.g., of parameters) is well ordered, we shall prove them sufficient.

12. Syntactical preliminaries are as in Section 2. A *parametric extension* of T is like T except for containing zero or more additional parameters. We shall refer to parametric extensions of T by 'T^*'; to the sets of sentences, parameters, terms, parameters of type t, and terms of type t respectively for a given T^* by means of 'W^*', 'λ^*', 'Π_t^*', and 'λ_t^*', extending in a natural way the conventions of Section 2. Similarly, define a *general truth-value function for* T^*, *mutatis mutandis*, as in Section 4.

13. Installment two of our truth-value semantics for T follows. Let T^* be a parametric extension of T and let α be a general truth-value function for T^*. α will be called a *truth-value function* for T^* provided that, in addition to (i)–(v) of Section 4, the following three conditions are fulfilled.

(vi) There exists a sequence $v = \langle v_0, v_1, v_2, \ldots \rangle$, where
  (a) for every type t, $v_t \subseteq \Pi_t^*$;
  (b) for every type t, if v_t has exactly n members (where n may be finite or infinite), v_{t+1} has 2^n members;
  (c) v_0 is non-empty.

(vii) The sequence v (of sets of parameters of T^*) being as in (vi), there exists for each t from 1 on a one-one mapping f_t from v_t onto $\Gamma(v_{t-1})$, such that for any parameter Q of v_{t-1} and R of v_t, $\alpha(Q \in R) = \mathbf{T}$ if and only if $Q \in F_t(R)$.

(viii) There exists, for each t from 0 on, a function g_t from λ_t^* to v_t, where v_t is as in (vi), such that
  (a) if $K \in v_t$, $g_t(K) = K$;
  (b) if K and L are of consecutively ascending types t and $t + 1$ respectively, then $\alpha(K \in L) = \alpha(g_t(K) \in g_{t+1}(L))$.

If T^* is a parametric extension of T and α is a truth-value function for T^*, we say that a wff A of T^* is *true on* α if $\alpha(A) = \mathbf{T}$. If $\mathfrak{G}$ is a set of wffs of T and A is a wff of T, we shall say that (1) $\mathfrak{G}$ is *verifiable* if, for some parametric extension T^* of T and some truth-value function α for T^*, every member of $\mathfrak{G}$ is true in α; (2) $\mathfrak{G}$ *implies* A if $\mathfrak{G} \cup \{\sim A\}$ is not verifiable; and (3) A is *valid* if $\{\sim A\}$ is not verifiable (alternatively, and equivalently, if A is true on all truth-value functions α).

14. It may be obvious that the model-theoretic notions of Section 8 coincide with their analogues in Section 13, in the sense that a set $\mathfrak{G}$ of wffs of T is verifiable if and only if model-theoretically verifiable, etc. As suggested in our initial motivating remarks, conditions (vi)–(viii) have been incorporated into the characterization of a truth-value function to have just this effect. For conditions (vi) and (vii) assure that each member of v_0 may be viewed as a (non-redundant) name of a particular member of a given non-empty set S; similarly, for $0 < t$ the members of v_t are names of sets—specifically, each names, again non-redundantly, a member of $\Gamma^t(S)$, while conversely each member of $\Gamma^t(S)$ is named by one and only one parameter in v_t. Accordingly the sequence v of (vi) simulates the *standard* system of domains $D(S)$ over S.

On the other hand, condition (viii) of the last section assures that each term of T^* *not* in the v_t of its type will be redundant; for by (b) under (viii), the systematic replacement of any such term K by $g_t(K)$ will not affect truth-values; hence K may be viewed as a synonym of $G_t(K)$, naming the same item in an associated standard model. So, though our quantifier (and, by the way, our abstraction operator) continues to look at names and not at things, all the things which one takes to exist in a model-theoretic standard interpretation of type theory may be *viewed* as named on some truth-value function. We turn now to proofs.

15. Let T^* be a parametric extension of T. Extending the definitions of Section 8 *mutatis mutandis* to T^*, let $\langle D(S), CI^* \rangle = M$ be called a standard model for T^*. M will be called *full* provided that the restriction of CI^* to a given Π_t^* is *onto* $\Gamma^t(S)$, for all types t. (In terms of our motivating remarks, a model is full if each type-theoretic entity of the model has a name among the parameters of T^*.) And call two models T-*equivalent* if they make the same wffs of T true. The following lemmas are trivial.

Lemma 10. *Let* $M = <D(S), CI>$ *be a standard model for* T. *Then for some parametric extension* T^* *of* T, *there is a* T-*equivalent full model* M^*. (For proof, add a new parameter P of type t for each item in $\Gamma^t(S)$ and for every type t, and extend CI in obvious fashion.)

Lemma 11. *Let* $M^* = <D(S), CI^*>$ *be a standard model for* T^*, *and* CI *be the restriction of* CI^* *to terms and wffs of* T. $M = <D(S), CI>$ *is a standard model for* T *and is* T-*equivalent to* M^*. (Proof obvious.)

Let T^* be a parametric extension of T, and let ν_0 be a (non-empty) subset of Π_0^*. $M_c = <D(\nu_0), CI>$ will be called a *normal canonical model for* T^* provided that the following conditions are fulfilled:
(1) M_c is a standard model for T^*;
(2) M_c is full;
(3) for $P\epsilon\nu_0$, $CI(P) = P$.
Let M and M' be full standard models for T^*, where M is $<D(S), CI>$ and M' is $<D(S'), CI'>$. For every type t, let h_t be a bijection from $\Gamma^t(S)$ onto $\Gamma^t(S')$; for each term K in λ_t^*, let $CI'(K)$ be $h_t(CI(K))$; and for every wff A, let $CI(A) = CI'(A)$. If all of these conditions can be fulfilled, we call M and M' *isomorphic*.

Lemma 12. *Every full standard model* M *for* T^* *is isomorphic to a normal canonical model* M_c *for* T^*.
Proof: Let $M = <D(S), CI>$ be a full standard model for T^*; we give a recipe for constructing an isomorphic normal canonical model. The relation of having the same value under CI partitions the members of Π_0^* into equivalence classes; let P be a member of ν_0 if and only if it is an alphabetically first member of its equivalence class. Set $h_0(P) = CI(P)$, for each $P\epsilon\nu_0$. h_t having been defined on all members of $\Gamma^t(\nu_0)$, if $r\epsilon\Gamma^{t+1}(\nu_0)$, let $h_{t+1}(r) = \{h_t(q):q\epsilon r\}$. Clearly each of the h_t's is a one-one correspondence from $\Gamma^t(\nu_0)$ to $\Gamma^t(S)$.
For each parameter P of Π_t^*, let $I'(P) = h_t^{\circ}(CI(P))$, where h° is the inverse of h. It is then readily verified that $<D(\nu_0), CI'>$ is a normal canonical model isomorphic to M. In particular, (2) holds of it since M is full; (3), by the definition of ν_0 and of h_0.

Corollary. *A set* $\mathfrak{G}$ *of wffs of* T *is model-theoretically verifiable if and only if there is a normal canonical model* $M_c = <D(\nu_0), CI>$ *for some parametric extension* T^* *of* T *such that* $CI(A) = \mathbf{T}$ *for every* A *in* $\mathfrak{G}$.
Proof: If $\mathfrak{G}$ has a model, by Lemmas 10 and 12 $\mathfrak{G}$ has a normal canonical

model M_c for some T^*; conversely, by Lemma 11 a normal canonical model for T^* is T-equivalent to some standard model for T, completing the proof of the corollary.

We now show that normal canonical models determine truth-value functions.

Lemma 13. *Let* $M = \langle D(v_0), CI \rangle$ *be a normal canonical model for a parametric extension* T^* *of* T. *Then the restriction of CI to sentences is a truth-value function.*

Proof: We must show that conditions (i)–(v) of Section 4 and (vi)–(viii) of Section 13 are fulfilled by CI for T^*. That CI meets (i) and (ii) is obvious, given the definition of a complete interpretation in (d) of Section 8. To prove (iii), it suffices to recall that M is full. Hence $A(K/X)$ is true for every term K of the same type as X if and only if $A(P/X)$ is true for all parameters P of that type on CI, since there is sure to be a parameter P such that $CI(K) = CI(P)$ for each term K. But $A(P/X)$ is true for every parameter P of the same type as X if and only if $(X)A$ is true on CI, since among the $CI(P)$ are *all* items of the appropriate level. (iv) and (v) hold respectively by items (ii) and (vi) under (d) of Section 8 and by the principle of extensionality for sets.

To prove (vi), choose v_0 itself as the first member of the sequence v; for $t > 0$, let a parameter P of type t be a member of v_t if and only if for every alphabetic predecessor Q of type t of P, $CI(P) \neq CI(Q)$; clearly each v_t is in one-one correspondence with $\Gamma^t(v_0)$. To find the mappings f_t required by (vii), let I_t be the restriction of CI to members of v_t and let I_t^{-1} be the inverse image of I_t: i.e., the function $h: \Gamma^{t+1}(v_0) \to \Gamma(v_t)$ such that $Q \epsilon H(s)$ if and only if $I^t(Q) \epsilon s$. Then for each t from 0 on, define $f_{t+1}: v_{t+1} \to \Gamma(v_t)$ by setting $f_{t+1}(P) = I_t^{-1}(I_{t+1}(P))$. It is then clear that CI meets condition (vii), since the following equivalences follow from definitions for every $Q \epsilon v_t$ and $R \epsilon v_{t+1}$:

$$CI(Q \epsilon R) = T \Leftrightarrow CI(Q) \epsilon CI(R) \Leftrightarrow I_t(Q) \epsilon I_{t+1}(R) \Leftrightarrow Q \epsilon I_t^{-1}(I_{t+1}(R)) \Leftrightarrow Q \epsilon f_{t+1}(R);$$

furthermore, since each I_t is a one-one correspondence, so is each f_{t+1}. Finally, for each term K in λ_t^*, let $g_t(K)$ be the unique parameter P of type t in v_t such that $CI(K) = CI(P)$; because M is full there must be such a P. Accordingly condition (viii) holds. This completes the proof of Lemma 13.

We have just seen that normal canonical models straightforwardly determine truth-value functions. We now prove the converse. Where α is a truth-value function for T^*, we shall define its *normal canonization* $Z_v \alpha$ by building on the work of Sections 7–10.

Suppose then that α is a truth-value function. Let the sequence $v = \langle v_0, v_1, v_2, \ldots \rangle$, the functions f_t, and the functions g_t be those whose existence is guaranteed by (vi)–(viii) of Section 13. By the *normal canonization* $Z_v \alpha$ of α (relative to v), we mean the pair $\langle D(v_0), CI \rangle$, where $D(v_0)$ is the standard

192 Part 2: Truth

system of domains over the initial set v_0 in the sequence v, and CI agrees with α on sentences of T^* and is defined as follows on terms:
(1) if $P\epsilon v_0$, $CI(P) = P$;
(2) if $P\epsilon v_{t+1}$, $CI(P) = \{CI(Q):Q\epsilon f_{t+1}(P)\}$;
(3) if K is a term of T^* of type t, $CI(K) = CI(g_t(K))$.
It is readily verified that (1)–(3) serve to define inductively CI for each term of T^*. Here is the converse of Lemma 13 (and the analogue of Lemma 8 for the standard type-theoretic semantics).

Lemma 14. Let α be a truth-value function for a parametric extension T^* of T, and let $Z_v\alpha = <D(v_0),CI>$ be the normal canonization of α just defined. Then $Z_v\alpha$ is a normal canonical model for T^*.

Proof: To show that $Z_v\alpha$ is a normal canonical model, it clearly suffices to show that it is a full standard model. We first show $Z_v\alpha$ full, assuming on inductive hypothesis for $t < i$ that every member of $\Gamma^t(v_0)$ is the image under CI of some parameter P in v_t (and hence of some parameter in Π_t^*) and showing that this statement remains true when $t = i$. We note that this is clear if $i = 0$, since $CI(P) = P$ for every P in v_0 by (1) above.

Suppose now that $0 < i$. Let s be an arbitrary member of $\Gamma^i(v_0)$. On inductive hypothesis, each member s_j of s is the image under CI of some parameter Q_j in v_{i-1}. But there is by (vii) of Section 13 some parameter P in v_i such that $f_i(P) = \{Q_j:CI(Q_j)\epsilon s\}$. But then by (2) above $CI(P) = s$. This completes the inductive argument and shows $Z_v\alpha$ full.

We must now show $Z_v\alpha$ a standard model. For this it will suffice to show CI a complete interpretation in the sense of (d) of Section 8, since by definition $D(v_0)$ is a standard system of domains. Since the strategy is essentially that lately employed in proving Lemma 8, we can safely leave most of this task to the reader. Inasmuch as we have carried the abstraction notation into this part (via the syntactical preliminaries) while ignoring it in pratice, we at least owe it to the reader to make it plausible that (3) above correctly defines CI on abstracts. We do this by showing that every sentence of T^* of the form

(4) $(\forall X)(X\epsilon\{Y:A\} \equiv X\epsilon P)$, where P is $g_t(\{Y:A\})$,

is true on α.

In fact if (4) is not true on α, there is by definition of a truth-value function some term K of type $t - 1$ such that $\alpha(K\epsilon\{Y:A\}) \neq \alpha(K\epsilon P)$. But by (b) under (viii) of Section 13, $\alpha(K\epsilon\{Y:A\}) = \alpha(g_{t-1}(K)\epsilon g_t\{Y:A\})$ and $\alpha(K\epsilon P) = \alpha(g_{t-1}(K)\epsilon g_t(P))$. But on assumption and by (a) under (viii) of Section 13, $g_t\{Y:A\} = g_t(P) = P$, which shows that there is no term K which refutes (4); hence (4) is true on α. Entrusting other details to the reader, we pronounce $Z_v\alpha$ a standard, and hence by what has already been shown a normal canonical, model for T^*.

We have proved enough lemmas.

Theorem 5. *Let $\mathfrak{G}$ be a set of wffs of T. Then $\mathfrak{G}$ is verifiable if and only if $\mathfrak{G}$ is model-theoretically verifiable.*
Proof: Suppose $\mathfrak{G}$ is verifiable. Then there is a truth-value function α on which every member of $\mathfrak{G}$ is true, for some parametric extension T^* of T. By Lemma 14 there is a normal canonical model $<D(v_0), CI>$ such that CI agrees with α on sentences of T^*; by the Corollary to Lemma 12, $\mathfrak{G}$ is model-theoretically verifiable.

Suppose on the other hand that $\mathfrak{G}$ is model-theoretically verifiable. Again by the Corollary to Lemma 12, there is a normal canonical model $<D(v_0), CI>$ for a parametric extension T^* of T such that every member of $\mathfrak{G}$ is true on CI. But by Lemma 13, the restriction of CI to sentences of T^* is a truth-value function. Hence $\mathfrak{G}$ is verifiable, completing the proof of the theorem.

Theorem 6. *Let $\mathfrak{G}$ be a set of sentences of T and A be a sentence of T.*
(a) *$\mathfrak{G}$ model-theoretically implies A if and only if $\mathfrak{G}$ implies A;*
(b) *A is model-theoretically valid if and only if A is valid.*
Proof by Theorem 5 and definitions.

This completes the proof of our principal theorems.

16. In conclusion, we should like to remark that both the standard and the general versions of our truth-value semantics are easily adapted to variations on the syntactic or the semantic side. In particular, type-theoretic versions of the axioms of infinity and choice are easily accommodated (the latter perhaps particularly appropriate in view of our relaxed attitude toward the use of that axiom in the last part), while on the other hand one may drop the axioms of extensionality if one wishes; one might even drop the axioms of specification (**A6** and **A7**) to get a *free* type theory.

Of perhaps greater interest is the question whether one can modify the account of a general truth-value function in Section 4 in such a way that the truth-value of a given sentence would be fixed when (a) the truth-values of all shorter sentences are fixed. (We could recast our account of a truth-value function rather easily to meet condition (a), since on that account the truth-value of a sentence $(\forall X)A$ is in fact fixed when the truth-value of $A(P/X)$ is fixed for every parameter P of appropriate type; but, as we have noted above, abstracts are essentially along for the ride in our standard truth-value semantics, for that story would remain about the same if the abstraction machinery were dropped. On the other hand, abstracts play a crucial role in our general truth-value semantics, as we shall immediately demonstrate.)

Observation ω. *There is a general truth-value function α and a formula $(\forall X)A$ such that (1) all sentences $A(K/X)$ shorter than $(\forall X)A$ are true on α, but (2) $(\forall X)A$ is false on α.*

Proof: Let q be the set whose only member is Quine, and let $D(q)$ be the standard system of domains for T over q.[22] Define an interpretation I of the parameters of T by setting $I(P) =$ Quine for all parameters of type 0; if $0 < t$ and P is of type t, let $I(P) = \Gamma^{t-1}(q)$, for all types t and parameters P. Let $<D(q), CI>$ be the (standard, and hence general) model determined by I.

Let α be the restriction of CI to wffs. Then α is a general truth-value function. To show this, it will suffice to show that—for every t—if $s\epsilon\Gamma^t(q)$, then $s = CI(K)$ for some K in λ_t. (Informally, what we are showing is that on each level in this particular model all sets are named by some term of T; in fact this must hold for any general model such that (i) the level zero set is finite and (ii) all members of the level zero set have names, since under these circumstances the sets of any level must also be finite and in fact have names; we remark moreover that perforce any general model satisfying (i) is a standard model.)

Returning to our immediate task, let us establish by induction on i that—for every s—if $s\epsilon\Gamma^i(q)$, $CI(K) = s$ for some K in λ_i. This is clear if $i = 0$, for all of our $\aleph_0$ parameters of type zero have been temporarily set aside as names of Quine.[23] Supposing our proposition true for arbitrary i, we prove it for $i + 1$. Let s then belong to $\Gamma^{i+1}(q)$; i.e., $s \subseteq \Gamma^i(q)$. $\Gamma^i(q)$, as noted, is finite. Accordingly we may informally specify s as $\{x:x\epsilon\Gamma^i(q)$ & $(x = s_1 \lor x = s_2 \lor \ldots \lor x = s_n)\}$, where $s_1, s_2, \ldots, s_n$ are all the members of s (and substituting $x \neq x$ for the parenthesized condition if s is empty). Where X is a variable of type i, Y is a variable of type $i + 1$, and (employing the inductive hypothesis) let K_s be $\{X:(\forall Y)(X\epsilon Y \equiv K_1\epsilon Y) \lor (\forall Y)(X\epsilon Y \equiv K_2\epsilon Y) \lor \ldots \lor (\forall Y)(X\epsilon Y \equiv K_n\epsilon Y)\}$, where $CI(K_1) = S_1$ and $CI(K_2) = S_2$ and $\ldots$ and $CI(K_n) = s_n$ when $s_1, s_2, \ldots, s_n$ are the members of s; when s is empty, let K_s be $\{X:\sim(A \supset A)\}$, where A is the alphabetically first sentence of T. In view of the extensionality axioms, it is clear that $CI(K_s) = s$, completing the inductive argument.

It is then easy to go on to show, in the spirit of Lemma 13, that α is a general truth-value function. We now confirm observation ω. For let A be $P\epsilon X$, where P and X are respectively of types 0 and 1. $(\forall X)A$ is not true on α, since Quine is not a member of the null set. But $A(K/X)$ is true when K is a parameter, since for every type 1 parameter Q, $CI(Q) = q$. But only when K is a parameter is $A(K/X)$ shorter than $(\forall X)A$. Q.E.D.

The observation has an interesting corollary.[24]

Observation $\omega + 1$. *There are two distinct general truth-value functions α and β which agree on all sentences of T in which no abstracts or quantifiers occur.*
Proof: Let $<D(q), CI>$ be as in the preceding observation, and let α again be the restriction of CI to sentences. Let $r = \{0,1\}$. Let $CI'(P) = 0$ for the alphabetically first parameter of Π_0; otherwise if $Q\epsilon\Pi_0$, $CI'(Q) = 1$. If $0 < t$, let $CI'(R) = \Gamma^{t-1}(r)$ for each parameter R in Π_t. Arguing as above, note that the extension of CI' to a complete $D(r)$-interpretation yields a standard model $<D(r), CI'>$, and that the restriction of CI' to wffs of T is a general truth-

value function β. Clearly all sentences of T in which neither connectives nor quantifiers nor abstracts occur are true both on α and on β, whence α and β agree on sentences free of both quantifiers and abstracts. On the other hand, where X and Y are of type 0 and Z is of type 1, the sentence $(\exists X)(\exists Y)(\exists Z)(X \epsilon Z \& \sim(Y \epsilon Z))$ is true on β but not on α.

Although the observations just made are relatively trivial, that they can be made at all suggests that truth-value semantics may be more than just a recasting of model-theoretic semantics. In Sections 2–6 of this paper, and in the earlier papers of Leblanc cited therein, proof was given that truth-value semantics can be accommodated to those systems of logic for which *bona fide* completeness results may be obtained from the model-theoretic viewpoint. What we should like to see in addition are results which show truth-value semantics to have a life of its own, not necessarily dependent on the model-theoretic insights from which it arose and into which, as we have showed, it can for certain purposes be translated. Noting that one of the abiding purposes of modern logical research has been the reduction of facts about "things" to facts about appropriately constructed formal languages, we welcome the increasing interest of recent years in one or another form of what we have called 'truth-value semantics' and trust that it may herald genuinely deeper insights into, among other things, the theory of types.

Notes

1. 'T' is short here for the 'STT' of the Introduction.

2. Parameters and variables will play here the roles respectively assigned elsewhere to free variables and bound ones. By using two runs of letters per type, we avoid some of the difficulties that would otherwise be involved in giving a correct account of substitution (of terms) for free variables. Neither our parameters nor our variables are to be associated with relations of more than one argument; as in [12], such relations may be simulated using the well-known Wiener-Kuratowski techniques.

3. The notion of simultaneous replacement or substitution may be defined as on pp. 4–5 of [11].

4. The technique of the papers of Leblanc cited earlier has been revised here to make the relation of isomorphism between sets of wffs of T an equivalence relation. Note that if π contains no parameters (in particular, if ᛃ is empty), every set isomorphic to ᛃ is identical with ᛃ by our definitions (since f is here the empty function). We shall, by the way, refer to f itself as an isomorphism if it meets the conditions laid down in the text.

5. We presume '&', '∨', '≡', and '∃' defined in the customary manner. Note that only sentences are axioms.

6. We might dispense with the braces and colon as primitive signs, following rather Quine's example in [12] by defining $P\epsilon\{X:A\}$ as $A(P/X)$ and $\{X:A\}\epsilon K$ as $(\exists Y)((\forall Z)(Z\epsilon Y \equiv A(Z/X))$ & $Y\epsilon K)$. In that case **A7** could be replaced by the *axiom* (scheme) *of Comprehension*, $(\exists X)(\forall Y)(Y\epsilon X \equiv A)$, where X is not free in A. However, because of the crucial role played by abstracts in our account of a general truth-value function for T, we prefer to have $P\epsilon\{X:A\}$ and $\{X:A\}\epsilon K$ count as genuine wffs of T (rather than as mere definitional rewrites).

7. If X is not free in $A, A(K/X)$ is of course just A.

8. This is the familiar *axiom of Extensionality*. It may of course be dropped (as is, e.g., in [13]), turning T into a theory of attributes rather than of classes. If **A9** is dropped, then in the semantical account of Section 4, (v) must also be dropped.

196   Part 2: Truth

9. The trick of counting $(\forall X)A(X/P)$ as an axiom when A is an axiom stems from [3].
10. Analogous moves will show that the biconditional in question can do duty for **A9**.
11. This proof borrows from [6], p. 203.
12. Recall that 'T' is our latel here for the simple theory of types; **T** and **F**, on the other hand, are as usual the truth-values "true" and "false."
13. Note that a general truth-value function is not "recursive" in the sense that the truth-values of longer sentences is invariably determined by the truth-values of shorter ones. See the observation on p. 193.
14. The above account of general implication and validity adapts to T the suggestion of Hintikka to Leblanc acknowledged at the outset. Cf. [8] on the matter.
15. Our account below borrows significantly from [5], [4], and from Section 53 of [2].
16. We are partially indebted to John Corcoran for this way of putting the matter.
17. In view of the Gödel result cited on p. 177, completeness proofs (and hence the possibility of sharp syntactic characterization of semantical concepts which such proofs afford) are out of the question when we turn to the standard model-theoretic semantics for T. Accordingly, although the account below summarizes what we take to be intended by the standard model theory for T, as do corresponding accounts in [5] and (for the second-order calculus) in [2], the standards involved seem to us as little secure as is the gold standard nowadays.
18. We have long since lost interest in ill-formed formulas, which frees the letter 'S' to refer (henceforth) to arbitrary sets; we use 's', and on occasion 'q' and 'r', for the same purpose. '$\mathfrak{G}$' continues to refer to sets of *sentences*.
19. $U(S)$ is thus the type-theoretic (standard) *universe* over S, while each of the $\Gamma^t(S)$ is the collection of all type-theoretic entities of level t. On the intended interpretation, $\Gamma^0(S)$—i.e., S itself—is of course a collection of individuals, which do not themselves have further members. ($U(S)$, naturally, is unmentionable according to the canons of simple type theory itself.)
20. For the remainder of this section, we leave most of the details in carrying out proofs to the reader.
21. I.e., v_0 contains exactly one parameter from each equivalence class. One may, of course, specify a unique v_0 for any α by requiring that each equivalence class be represented by its alphabetically first member.
22. We distinguish q from its illustrious member, despite the reluctance which he has showed in [12] and elsewhere to do so.
23. The reader who things this unduly profligate may, if he wishes, decrease temporarily the number of parameters of T for each given type to finite size; in order to preserve the uniformity of our account of a general truth-value function for T, however, we shall not do so.
24. The question which the corollary answers was put to us by N. D. Belnap, Jr.

References

[1] Beth, E. W. 1959. *The Foundations of Mathematics*. Amsterdam: North-Holland.
[2] Church, A. 1956. *Introduction to Mathematical Logic, Volume I*. Princeton: Princeton University Press.
[3] Fitch, F. B. 1948. "Intuitionistic Modal Logic with Quantifiers." *Portugaliae Mathematica* 7: 113–18.
[4] Henkin, L. 1949. "The Completeness of the First-Order Functional Calculus." *The Journal of Symbolic Logic* (hereafter *JSL*) 14: 159–66.
[5] ———. 1950. "Completeness in the Theory of Types." *JSL* 15: 81–91.
[6] ———. 1953. "Banishing the Rule of Substitution for Functional Variables." *JSL* 18: 201–08.
[7] Hintikka, J. 1955. "Two Papers on Symbolic Logic." *Acta Philosophica Fennica*.
[8] Leblanc, H. 1968. "A Simplified Account of Validity and Implication for Quantificational Logic." *JSL* 33: 231–35 (#8 in this volume).
[9] ———. 1969. "A Simplified Strong Completeness Theorem for QC$_=$." *Akten des XIV*.

Internationalen Kongresses für Philosophie 3: 83–95. Vienna: Verlag Herder (#9 in this volume).

[10] ――――. 1969. "Three Generalizations of a Theorem of Beth's." *Logique et Analyse* 12: 205–20 (#11 in this volume).

[11] ――――. 1976. *Truth-Value Semantics*. Amsterdam: North-Holland.

[12] Quine, W. V. 1963. *Set Theory and its Logic*. Cambridge: Harvard University Press.

[13] Schütte, K. 1960. "Syntactical and Semantical Properties of Simple Type Theory." *JSL* 25: 305–26.

13
Wittgenstein and the Truth-Functionality Thesis

Wittgenstein claimed in the *Tractatus* that any statement is a truth-function of its components, indeed a truth-function of its elementary components. Few today would share either view; too many statements resist the kind of analysis that Wittgenstein envisioned. But the kindred claim that Russell's ramified theory of types (a "model language" to the Wittgenstein of the *Tractatus*) has a *strictly truth-functional interpretation* is sound, and I shall defend it here. I shall go one step farther, and show (in outline form) that—upon adoption of Russell's *Axiom of Reducibility*—the principal interpretation of the theory, though still *truth-functional* in a sense, is no longer strictly truth-functional, a result which perhaps justifies Wittgenstein's own uneasiness over the axiom.[1]

To begin with a straightforward example, consider SC (= the sentential calculus); employ, say, '~' and '⊃' as primitive connectives; suppose SC has the same theorems as, say, Church's P_2 in [1]; and, generalizing the notion of a truth-value assignment, understand by a *truth-value function* for SC any function from the wffs (non-atomic as well as atomic) of SC to {**T**, **F**}.

I shall say that SC has a *truth-functional interpretation* if there is a family Σ of truth-value functions for SC such that:

(1) the theorems of SC and the wffs of SC evaluating to **T** under all members of Σ coincide, and

(2) the truth-values that negations and conditionals assume under members of Σ depend on the truth-values of their components, and on those truth-values only.

And I shall say that SC has a *strictly truth-functional interpretation* if there is a family Σ of truth-value functions for SC meeting conditions (1)–(2) *plus* the following condition:

(3) members of Σ that agree on the atomic wffs of SC agree on the non-atomic ones as well.[2]

Now let Σ' consist of every truth-value function α for SC such that: (a) $\alpha(\sim A) = $ **T** if and only if $\alpha(A) = $ **F**, and (b) $\alpha(A \supset B) = $ **T** if and only if $\alpha(A) = $ **F** or $\alpha(B) = $ **T**. It is easily verified that Σ' meets all three of conditions

Wittgenstein and the Truth-Functionality Thesis 199

(1) – (3), and hence that SC has a strictly truth-functional interpretation, a result which owes much to Wittgenstein. (The result can be considerably strengthened. Require in my account of truth-functionality that all truth-value assignments to the atomic wffs of SC figure among the members of Σ (condition (0)). It can be verified that only one family of truth-value functions for SC meets conditions (0)–(2): the family Σ', and hence that all truth-functional interpretations of SC are strictly truth-functional.)

Things get slightly more complicated when you come to QC^1, the first-order quantificational calculus. The truth-value of a negation $\sim A$ will again hinge on that of its component A, and the truth-value of a conditional $A \supset B$ hinge on those of its components A and B. But what will the truth-value of a quantification $(\forall X)A$ hinge on? Wittgenstein supplied the answer in the *Tractatus*: the truth-values of its *substitution instances*.

To handle matters of substitution in the simplest possible way, suppose that in keeping with recent practice we use *two* runs of individual signs: one run (say, the letters 'x', 'y', 'z', etc.) serving in effect as *bound* individual variables, and called *individual variables*; the other (say, the letters 'a', 'b', 'c', etc.) serving as *free* individual variables, and called *individual parameters*. And suppose that formulas of QC^1 in which identical quantifiers overlap are not counted well-formed. The substitution instances of a quantification $(\forall X)A$ of QC^1 will then be all results of putting an individual parameter of QC^1 for each occurrence of X in A; and, in particular, the substitution instances of '$(\forall x)f(x)$' will be—as they were for Wittgenstein—'$f(a)$', '$f(b)$', '$f(c)$', etc.

These preliminaries once disposed of, read 'QC^1' for 'SC' in my accounts of truth-functionality and strict truth-functionality; in condition (2) require the truth-values that quantifications assume under members of Σ to depend on the truth-values of their substitution instances, and on those truth-values only; and let Σ' consist of every truth-value function α for QC^1 such that:[3] (a) α($\sim A$) = **T** if and only if α(A) = **F**, (b) α($A \supset B$) = **T** if and only if α(A) = **F** or α(B) = **T**, and (c) α($(\forall X)A$) = **T** if and only if α(A^*) = **T** for every substitution instance A^* of $(\forall X)A$. It can be verified that Σ' meets all three of conditions (1) – (3), and hence that QC^1 has a strictly truth-functional interpretation, a result to which Wittgenstein contributed some.[4] (Again the result can be considerably strengthened. Require that all truth-value assignments to the atomic wffs of QC^1 figure among the members of Σ (condition (0)). It can be shown that only one family of truth-value functions for QC^1 meets conditions (0)–(2): the family Σ', and hence that all truth-functional interpretations of QC^1 are strictly truth-functional.)

Now let us turn to QC^2 (= the second-order quantificational calculus), and in particular to $QC^{2/\infty}$ (= the ramified second-order quantificational calculus); and let us employ both predicate variables (= *bound* predicate variables) and predicate parameters (= *free* predicate variables).[5] As the reader knows, formulas of the sort $(\forall F^d)A$, where F^d is a predicate variable of degree d ($d \geq 0$) are acknowledged as well-formed both in QC^2 and in $QC^{2/\infty}$. However, whereas QC^2 has a single run of predicate variables, $QC^{2/\infty}$ has one for each so-called level l ($l = 1, 2, 3, \ldots$); and, whereas QC^2 has a single run of predicate parameters, $QC^{2/\infty}$ has one for each level l. To appreciate Russell's distinction between, say, predicates of level 1 and predicates of level 2, compare 'Napoleon had sangfroid on the battlefield' and 'Napoleon had all the qualities of a great general.'[6] The predicate 'had all the qualities of a great general' could be regarded as summary for such predicates of level 1 as 'had sangfroid on the battlefield', 'knew how to pen a victory bulletin', etc., and hence could be adjudged of level 2.

Needed at this point are a substitution convention for predicate variables and a means of assessing the level of a wff of $QC^{2/\infty}$. I shall relegate the first to Appendix 1, and ask the reader to think of

$$A(B/F^{d/l}(X_1, X_2, \ldots, X_d)),$$

where A is a wff or a qwff,[7] B is a wff, $F^{d/l}$ is a predicate variable of degree d and level l, and $X_1, X_2, \ldots,$ and X_d are distinct individual parameters of $QC^{2/\infty}$, as behaving in effect like Church's

$$\check{S}_B^{F^{d/l}(X_1, X_2, \ldots, X_d)} A |$$

in [1]. As to the second desideratum, B being a wff of $QC^{2/\infty}$, let l_P ('P' for 'parameter') be 0 if no predicate parameter of $QC^{2/\infty}$ occurs in B; let l_P be 1 if at least one predicate parameter of level 1 occurs in B but none of level higher than 1 does; let l_P be 2 if at least one predicate parameter of level 2 occurs in B but none of level higher than 2 does; etc. And define l_V ('V' for 'variable') in the same manner, but with the word 'variable' doing duty for 'parameter'. The *level* of B will then be $\max(l_P, l_{V+1})$. This done, you may take the substitution instances of a quantification $(\forall F^{d/l})A$ of $QC^{2/\infty}$ to be all wffs of $QC^{2/\infty}$ of the sort $A(B/F^{d/l}(X_1, X_2, \ldots, X_d))$, and take its *predicative* substitution instances to be all wffs of $QC^{2/\infty}$ of that sort in which B is of level l or less.

The distinction just drawn between the substitution instances of $(\forall F^{d/l})A$ in general, and its predicative ones in particular, is crucial. Indeed, call a substitution instance A^* of a quantification $(\forall V)A$ *permissible* if

$$(\forall V)A \supset A^*$$

is provable in $QC^{2/\infty}$. Without the *Axiom of Reducibility*, $(\forall F^{2/l})A \supset A^*$—though provable in $QC^{2/\infty}$ for every *predicative* substitution instance A^* of $(\forall F^{d/l})A$—fails for many an impredicative one. On the other hand, Russell's axiom (which guarantees that for any property or relation of level higher than 1 there exists a coextensive one of level 1) permits proof of $(\forall F^{d/l})A \supset A^*$ for *every* substitution instance A^* of $(\forall F^{d/l})A$.[8] So, in one case only some of the substitution instances of $(\forall F^{d/l})A$ turn out permissible, whereas in the other they all do.

Now read '$QC^{2/\infty}$' for 'SC' in my accounts of truth-functionality and strict truth-functionality; in (2) require the truth-values that quantifications assume under members of Σ to depend on the truth-values of their permissible substitution instances, and on those truth-values only; let Σ'_1 consist of every truth-value function α for $QC^{2/\infty}$ such that (a) $\alpha(\sim A) = \mathbf{T}$ if and only if $\alpha(A) = \mathbf{F}$, (b) $\alpha(A \supset B) = \mathbf{T}$ if and only if $\alpha(A) = \mathbf{F}$ or $\alpha(B) = \mathbf{T}$, (c) $\alpha((\forall X)A) = \mathbf{T}$ if and only if $\alpha(A^*) = \mathbf{T}$ for every instance A^* of $(\forall X)A$, and (d) $\alpha((\forall F^{d/l})A) = \mathbf{T}$ if and only if $\alpha(A^*) = \mathbf{T}$ for every predicate substitution instance A^* of $(\forall F^{d/l})A$; and let Σ'_2 be similarly defined, but with (d) now reading: $\alpha((\forall F^{d/l})A). = \mathbf{T}$ if and only if $\alpha(A^*) = \mathbf{T}$ for every substitution instance A^* of $(\forall F^{d/l})A$.

It is easily verified that *in the absence of the Axiom of Reducibility* Σ'_1 meets conditions (1)–(2), and *upon the adoption of the axiom* so does Σ'_2. In either case, therefore, $QC^{2/\infty}$ has a strictly truth-functional interpretation. And, aided by George Weaver, I have verified that Σ'_1 meets condition (3) as well.[9] However, Robert K. Meyer and I have isolated two members of Σ'_2 which agree on all the atomic wffs of $QC^{2/\infty}$ and yet disagree on the wff

$$(\exists f)(\exists x)(\exists y)(f(x) \& \sim f(y)).[10]$$

So *in the absence of the Axiom of Reducibility* the main interpretation of $QC^{2/\infty}$, to wit: Σ'_1, *is* strictly truth-functional;[11] but *upon adoption of the axiom* its main interpretation, now Σ'_2, is *not* strictly truth-functional.[12]

Like results hold for $QC^{\infty/\infty}$, Russell's ramified theory of types, and the full *Axiom of Reducibility*: in the absence of that axiom $QC^{\infty/\infty}$ *has* a strictly truth-functional interpretation, but upon adoption of the axiom its main interpretation is *not* strictly truth-functional.

Wittgenstein had misgivings of his own over Russell's axiom, which I find hard to evaluate. The results in the last paragraph may be more to the point, given Wittgenstein's advocacy of strict truth-functionality.

Appendix 1.[13] **Substitution Convention for Predicate Variables.** (1) Let A be a wff or qwff of $QC^{2/\infty}$; let $X_1, X_2, \ldots, X_d$ ($d \geq 0$) be distinct individual parameters of $QC^{2/\infty}$; and let $I_1, I_2, \ldots, I_d$ be (not necessarily distinct) individual signs of $QC^{2/\infty}$. Then $A(I_1, I_2, \ldots, I_d/X_1, X_2, \ldots, X_d)$ is to be the result of simultaneously putting I_1 everywhere in A for X_1, I_2 for $X_2, \ldots, I_d$ for X_d.

(2) Let A be a wff or qwff of $QC^{2/\infty}$; let $F^{2/l}$ be a predicate variable of $QC^{2/\infty}$ of degree d and level l; in case $d > 0$, let $X_1, X_2, \ldots, X_d$ be distinct individual parameters of $QC^{2/\infty}$; let B be a wff of $QC^{2/\infty}$; and let $F^{d/l}(I_1, I_{2_1}, \ldots, I_{d_1}), F^{d/l}(I_{1_2}, I_{2_2}, \ldots, I_{d_2}) \ldots, F^{d/l}(I_{1_k}, I_{2_k}, \ldots, I_{d_k})$ ($k \geq 0$) be all the (distinct) components of A of the sort $F^{d/l}(I_1, I_2, \ldots, I_d)$.

Case 1: $k = 0$. Then $A(B/F^{d/l}(X_1, X_2, \ldots, X_d))$ is to be A.

Case 2: $k \geq 0$. (a) If $F^{d/l}$ occurs in a component of A of the sort $(\forall V)A'$ and B has a component of the sort $(\forall V)B'$ (V the same variable in both cases), $A(B/F^{d/l}(X_1, X_2, \ldots, X_d))$ is to be the result of putting the alphabetically earliest predicate parameter of $QC^{2/\infty}$ of the same degree and level as $F^{d/l}$ everywhere in A for $F^{d/l}$. (b) Otherwise, $A(B/F^{d/l}(X_1, X_2, \ldots, X_d))$ is to be the result of putting

202   Part 2: Truth

$B(I_{1_i}, I_{2_i}, \ldots, I_{d_i}/X_1, X_2, \ldots, X_d)$ everywhere in A for $F^{d/l}(I_{1_i}, I_{2_i}, \ldots, I_{d_i})$, this for each i from 1 through k.

Appendix 2. Truth-Functionality and Strict Truth-Functionality. Note: In the definitions that follow, C may be SC (in which case (2.5) drops out), QC^1, or $QC^{2/\infty}$ (with or without the Axiom of Reducibility); and a *permissible instantial function* for (the quantifications of) C is to be any function that pairs with each quantification $(\forall V)A$ of C a set of permissible substitution instances of $(\forall V)A$.

A calculus C is said *to have a truth-functional interpretation* if there is a family Σ of truth-value functions for C such that:

(1.0) for any wff A of C, A is provable in C if and only if $\alpha(A) = \mathbf{T}$ for every member α of Σ,

(2.1) for any two members α and α' of Σ and any negation $\sim A$ of C, if $\alpha(A) = \alpha'(A)$, then $\alpha(\sim A) = \alpha'(\sim A)$,

(2.2) for any member α of Σ and any two negations $\sim A$ and $\sim A'$ of C, if $\alpha(A) = \alpha(A')$, then $\alpha(\sim A) = \alpha(\sim A')$,

(2.3) for any two members α and α' of Σ and any conditional $A \supset B$ of C, if $\alpha(A) = \alpha'(A)$ and $\alpha(B) = \alpha'(B)$, then $\alpha(A \supset B) = \alpha'(A \supset B)$,

(2.4) for any member α of Σ and any two conditionals $A \supset B$ and $A' \supset B'$ of C, if $\alpha(A) = \alpha(A')$ and $\alpha(B') = \alpha(B')$, then $\alpha(A \supset B) = \alpha(A' \supset B')$, and

(2.5) there is a permissible instantial function I for C such that:

(2.5.1) for any two members α and α' of Σ and any quantification $(\forall V)A$ of C, if $\alpha(A^*) = \alpha'(A^*)$ for every member A^* of $I((\forall V)A)$, then $\alpha((\forall V)A) = \alpha'((\forall V)A)$,

(2.5.2) for any member α of Σ, any two quantifications $(\forall V)A$ and $(\forall V')A'$ (V and V' both individual variables or both predicate variables) of C such that $I((\forall V)A)$ is at least as large as $I((\forall V')A')$, and any function f from $I((\forall V)A)$ onto $I((\forall V')A')$, if $\alpha(A^*) = \alpha(f(A^*))$ for every member A^* of $I((\forall V)A)$, then $\alpha((\forall V)A) = \alpha((\forall V')A')$, and

(2.5.3) for any member α of Σ, any two quantifications $(\forall V)A$ and $(\forall V')A'$ (V and V' as before) of C such that $I((\forall V)A)$ is smaller than $I((\forall V')A')$, and any function f from $I((\forall V')A')$ onto $I((\forall V)A)$, if $\alpha(A'^*) = \alpha(f(A'^*))$ for every member A'^* of $I((\forall V')A')$, then $\alpha((\forall V)A) = \alpha((\forall V')A')$.

And C is said *to have a strictly truth-functional interpretation* if there is a family Σ of truth-value functions for C that meets (1)–(2.5) *plus* the following condition:

(3) for any two members α and α' of Σ if $\alpha(A) = \alpha'(A)$ for every atomic wff A of C, then $\alpha(A) = \alpha'(A)$ for every non-atomic wff A of C.[14]

Notes

1. As was discovered five years after the publication of this paper, there is an interpretation of the ramified theory of types that is strictly truth-functional. But Wittgenstein (and Russell) would

Wittgenstein and the Truth-Functionality Thesis 203

hardly have favored it over the present one. For further details on the matter see pp. 134–35, [2], and [3].

2. So that the truth-values of non-atomic wffs of SC depend entirely upon those of atomic ones. See Appendix 2 for a more formal account of things.

3. I.e., of every function α from the wffs (non-atomic as well as atomic) of QC^1 to $\{T,F\}$ such that . . . . I assume in what follows that QC^1 has in effect the same theorems as Church's F^1 in [1].

4. Ironically, Wittgenstein came to abjure the *substitution interpretation* of the quantifiers. Moore reports in [6], p. 297: "He said that there was a temptation, to which he had yielded in the *Tractatus*, to say that (x) . fx is identical with the logical product 'fa . fb . fc . . .', and $(\exists x)fx$ identical with the logical sum '$fa \lor fb \lor fc$ . . .'; but that this was in both cases a mistake."

5. Sentence variables (parameters) can be thought of as predicate variables (parameters) of degree 0. So nothing is said about them in the text.

6. The example stems from [7].

7. Roughly, qwffs (= quasi-well-formed formulas) are like wffs except for exhibiting variables at places where wffs would exhibit parameters.

8. The *Axiom of Reducibility*, as tailored to suit $QC^{2/\infty}$, reads:

$$(\exists F^{d/1})(\forall X_1)(\forall X_2) \ldots (\forall X_d)(F^{d/1}(X_1, X_2, \ldots, X_d) \equiv F^{d/l}(X_1, X_2, \ldots, X_d)),$$

where $F^{d/l}$ is a predicate parameter of $QC^{2/\infty}$ of degree d and level l ($d \geq 0$ and $l > 1$), and $X_1, X_2, \ldots, X_d$ are distinct individual variables of $QC^{2/\infty}$.

In the absence of the axiom $QC^{2/\infty}$ is presumed here to have in effect the same theorems as $F^{2/\infty}$ in [1].

9. For full details, see [3] and [5].

10. For full details, see [3] and [4].

11. There is some slippage though: the truth-value of a wff of SC depends exclusively upon the truth-values of its atomic *components*, that of a wff of QC^1 depends upon the truth-values of its atomic *subformulas* (not all of which need be components of the wff), and that of a wff of $QC^{2/\infty}$ generally depends upon the truth-values of *all* the atomic wffs of $QC^{2/\infty}$.

12. Whether in the absence of the *Axiom of Reducibility* $QC^{2/\infty}$ has any truth-functional interpretation which is *not* strictly truth-functional is still an open question, and whether upon adoption of the axiom $QC^{2/\infty}$ has any truth-functional interpretation which—unlike its main one—*is* strictly truth-functional was also an open one at the time this paper was written. The answer, to repeat, is now known to be Yes (see Note 1).

13. In what follows '*I*' ranges over individual variables and parameters. All other syntactical variables have already turned up in the main text.

14. The paper was read at the 1971 Meeting of the American Philosophical Association, Pacific Division. Thanks are due to Paul Benacerraf for his invaluable comments, and George Weaver, who helped to devise the criterion of truth-functionality in Appendix 2 and prove that $QC^{2/\infty}$ has a strictly truth-functional interpretation.

References

[1] Church, A. 1956. *Introduction to Mathematical Logic*, Volume I. Princeton: Princeton University Press.

[2] Leblanc, H. 1975. "That *Principia Mathematica*, First Edition, has a Predicative Interpretation after all." *Journal of Philosophic Logic* 4: 32–35 (#16 in this volume).

[3] ———. 1976. *Truth-Value Semantics*. Amsterdam: North-Holland.

[4] Leblanc, H., and Meyer, R. K. 1970. "Truth-Value Semantics for the Theory of Types." *Philosophical Problems in Logic: Some Recent Developments*, pp. 77–101. Dordrecht: Reidel (#12 in this volume).

[5] Leblanc, H., and Weaver, G. 1973. "Truth-Functionality and the Ramified Theory of Types." *Truth, Syntax and Modality*, pp. 148–67. Amsterdam: North-Holland (#15 in this volume).

[6] Moore, G. E. 1959. *Philosophical Papers*. London: Allen and Unwin.
[7] Russell, B. 1919. *Introduction to Mathematical Philosophy*. London: Allen and Unwin.
[8] Whitehead, A. N., and Russell, B. 1910–13. *Principia Mathematica*. Cambridge: Cambridge University Press.
[9] Wittgenstein, L. 1922. *Tractatus Logico-Philosophicus*. London: Routledge and Kegan Paul.

14
Matters of Relevance

Forswearing venerable doctrine, some now claim that the truth-value of a statement A, and—more generally—that of a theory T, hinges upon (the truth-values of) all other statements from the same language as A or T. I should like to investigate this matter as regards languages of four main sorts: first-order languages without a box (called here L^1), first-order languages with a box (called $L^\square$), predicative second-order languages (called $L^{2!}$), and impredicative second-order languages (called L^2).

Paraphrasing at times familiar results, I shall report that: (a) when the statements in a theory T come from a language L^1, only some of the atomic wffs of L^1—those to be known below as *the atomic subformulas of T*—bear on the truth-value of T, and (b) when the statements in T come from a language $L^{2!}$, only the atomic wffs of $L^{2!}$ bear on that truth-value. However, when the statements in T come from a language L^2, some non-atomic wffs of L^2 may affect the truth-value of T, as an example due to Robert K. Meyer and myself attests. The result in (a) can be sharpened somewhat. Indeed, when the statements in T come from a language L^1, the atomic wffs of L^1 that do not figure among the atomic subformulas of T may go truth-valueless, and the truth-value of T will still compute right.

Languages of the sort $L^\square$ will fall into five subfamilies. Those in the first subfamily (called here $L^\square_1$) will have the axioms of I plus the *Barcan Formula*; those in the second (called $L^\square_2$) will have the axioms of M plus the *Barcan Formula*; those in the third (called $L^\square_3$) will have the axioms of B; those in the fourth (called $L^\square_4$) will have the axioms of S4 plus the *Barcan Formula*; and those in the fifth (called $L^\square_5$) will have the axioms of S5.

Breaking possibly new ground, I shall report that, whatever language $L^\square_i$ ($1 \leq i \leq 5$) the statements in a theory T may come from, only the atomic subformulas of T affect the truth-value of T. I shall also note that, when $i = 5$, the other atomic wffs of the language may again go truth-valueless and the truth-value of T will nonetheless compute right. Not so, however, when $i < 5$. As examples due to Brian Chellas, Robert McArthur, and George Weaver show, a shortage of truth-values may occasionally throw the computation off. To prevent such mishaps, truth-values must be assigned to *all* the atomic wffs of the language *or else* indices must be attached to the truth-value assignments, a trick which allows any assignment to figure more than once in the computation.[1]

Modest though they may be, my results should make for a better documented, and hence more responsible, appraisal of Logical Atomism. The doctrine has its limitations, but—as I show—much of it is fact, not just dogma. They should also throw some fresh light on first-order languages with a box. Some of these, the languages $L_5^\square$, behave in a very normal fashion. The rest raise an issue which, in my opinion, Kripke's use of possible worlds simply blurs.

1. I attend in this section to a number of syntactical preliminaries. The *primitive vocabulary* of a language L^1 will consist of:
(a) $\aleph_0$ individual variables,
(b) $\aleph_0$ individual parameters.
(c) anywhere from 0 to $\aleph_0$ individual constants,
(d) anywhere from 1 to $\aleph_0$ predicate constants, each one of them identified as being of degree 1, or degree 2, etc.,
(e) the three logical operators '~', '⊃', and '∀', and
(f) the three punctuation signs '(', ')', and ','.

The primitive vocabulary of a language $L^\square$ will consist of the signs in (a)–(f) *plus* the logical operator '$\square$'. And that of a language L^2 or $L^{2!}$ will consist of the signs in (a)–(e) *plus*—for each d from 1 on—$\aleph_0$ predicate variables of degree d and $\aleph_0$ predicate parameters of that degree. As usual, the *formulas* of a language L will be all finite (but non-empty) strings of primitive signs of L.

My variables are in effect what the literature understands by *bound* variables, and my parameters what it understands by *free* variables. Incidentally, the predicate parameters of a language L^2 or $L^{2!}$ will be presumed to come for each degree d in some definite order, to be known as the *alphabetic order* of these parameters.

Because I use both variables and parameters, my arsenal of syntactic variables will be rather large: 'X' to refer to individual variables, '$\mathbf{X}$' to individual parameters and constants, 'I' to *individual signs* in general (i.e., individual variables, individual parameters, and individual constants), 'F' ('F^d' when the degree matters) to predicate variables, '$\mathbf{F}$' ('$\mathbf{F}^d$' when the degree matters) to predicate parameters and constants, 'V' to variables in general, and 'A', 'B', and 'C' to formulas.[2]

Three substitution conventions will be needed as we proceed. Under **C1**, the first of these, $A(\mathbf{X}/X)$ will be the result of replacing everywhere in the formula A the individual variable X by the individual parameter or constant $\mathbf{X}$; and— with F and $\mathbf{F}$ understood to be of the same degree—$A(\mathbf{F}/F)$ will be the result of replacing everywhere in A the predicate variable F by the predicate parameter or constant $\mathbf{F}$.

In all my languages formulas of the following four sorts will count as *wffs* (= well-formed formulas):

(a) $F^d(X_1, X_2, \ldots, X_d)$, where F^d is a predicate constant and $X_1, X_2, \ldots,$ X_d are individual parameters or constants,
(b) $\sim A$, where A is a wff,
(c) $(A \supset B)$, regularly abridged $A \supset B$, where A and B are wffs, and
(d) $(\forall X)A$, where—for some individual parameter X—$A(X/X)$ is a wff.

In languages $L^\square$ formulas of one extra sort besides (a)–(d) will also count as wffs, to wit:
(e) $\square A$, where A is a wff.

And in languages L^2 and $L^{2!}$ so will formulas of two extra sorts besides (a)–(d), to wit:
(f) $F^d(X_1, X_2, \ldots, X_d)$, where this time around F^d is a predicate parameter, and
(g) $(\forall F)A$, where—for some predicate parameter F of the same degree as F—$A(F/F)$ is a wff.

A few familiar labels will prove handy in what follows. Wffs of the sort $F^d(X_1, X_2, \ldots, X_d)$ (F^d a predicate constant or—when the occasion permits—a predicate parameter, and $X_1, X_2, \ldots, X_d$ as in (a) above) will be called *atomic*. Wffs of a language L^2 or $L^{2!}$ that do not contain any predicate variable or predicate parameter (and hence qualify as wffs of a language L^1) will be known as *first-order wffs*. Wffs that do not contain any parameter whatever will be known as *statements*, whereas wffs that do will be known as *quasi-statements*. And non-empty sets of statements will be known as *theories*.[3] I shall refer to sets of wffs by means of 'S', and to theories by means of 'T'; and I shall say that a theory T *is (couched) in a language L* if every statement in T comes from L.

Here as in all of the literature, any wff will count as one of its *components*; A will count as a component of $\sim A$, $(\forall X)A$, $\square A$, and $(\forall F)A$; A and B will count as components of $A \supset B$; and any component of a component of a wff will count as a component of that wff. Here as in Gentzen, any wff will count as one of its *subformulas*; A will count as a subformula of $\sim A$ and $\square A$; for any individual parameter or constant X, $A(X/X)$ will count as a subformula of $(\forall X)A$; for any predicate parameter or constant F of the same degree as F, $A(F/F)$ will count as a subformula of $(\forall F)A$; and any subformula of a subformula of a wff will count as a subformula of that wff. Finally, any subformula of a member of a theory will count as a subformula of that theory. The atomic subformulas of a theory will star in many of the theorems below.

Now for my last two substitution conventions.

C2. Let A be a wff or a component of one; let $X_1, X_2, \ldots, X_d$ ($d > 0$) be distinct individual parameters; and let $I_1, I_2, \ldots, I_d$ be (not necessarily distinct) individual signs. By $A(I_1, I_2, \ldots, I_d/X_1, X_2, \ldots, X_d)$ I shall understand the result of simultaneously replacing X_1 in A by I_1, X_2 by $I_2, \ldots,$ and X_d by I_d.

C3. Let A be a wff or a component of one; let F^d be a predicate variable of degree d; let $X_1, X_2, \ldots, X_d$ be distinct individual parameters; let B be a wff; and let $F^d(I_{1_1}, I_{2_1}, \ldots, I_{d_1}), F^d(I_{1_2}, I_{2_2}, \ldots, I_{d_2}) \ldots, F^d(I_{1_k}, I_{2_k}, \ldots, I_{d_k})$

208   Part 2: Truth

($k \geq 0$) be all the atomic components of A that begin with F^d. *Case 1: $k = 0$*. Then $A(B/F^d(\mathbf{X}_1,\mathbf{X}_2, \ldots ,\mathbf{X}_d))$ is to be A. *Case 2: $k > 0$*. If F^d occurs in a component of A of the sort $(\forall V)A'$ and B has a component of the sort $(\forall V)B'$ (V the same variable in both cases), $A(B/F^d(\mathbf{X}_1,\mathbf{X}_2, \ldots ,\mathbf{X}_d))$ is to be $A(\mathbf{F}^d/F^d)$, where $\mathbf{F}^d$ is the alphabetically earliest predicate parameter of degree d of the language that A belongs to. Otherwise, $A(B/F^d(\mathbf{X}_1,\mathbf{X}_2, \ldots ,\mathbf{X}_d))$ is to be the result of replacing $F^d(I_{1_i},I_{2_i}, \ldots ,I_{d_i})$ everywhere in A by $B(I_{1_i},I_{2_i}, \ldots ,I_{d_i}/\mathbf{X}_1,\mathbf{X}_2, \ldots ,\mathbf{X}_d)$, this for each i from 1 through k.

My last assignment in this section is a lengthy one: to specify the circumstances under which a set of wffs of a language L (hence, in particular, a theory in L) is syntactically consistent in L. I discharge it in three steps.

(1) Let **A1–A19** be the following *axiom schemata*:
A1. $A \supset (B \supset A)$,
A2. $(A \supset (B \supset C)) \supset ((A \supset B) \supset (A \supset C))$,
A3. $(\sim A \supset \sim B) \supset (B \supset A)$,
A4. $(\forall X)(A \supset B) \supset ((\forall X)A \supset (\forall X)B)$,
A5. $A \supset (\forall X)A$,
A6. $(\forall X)A \supset A(X/X)$, for any individual parameter or constant $\mathbf{X}$,
A7. $(\forall X)A$, where—for some individual parameter $\mathbf{X}$ foreign to $(\forall X)A$—$A(\mathbf{X}/X)$ is an axiom,
A8. $(\forall F)(A \supset B) \supset ((\forall F)A \supset (\forall F)B)$,
A9. $A \supset (\forall F)A$,
A10. $(\forall F^d)A \supset A(B/F^d(\mathbf{X}_1, \mathbf{X}_2, \ldots , \mathbf{X}_d))$, for any wff B and any distinct individual parameters $\mathbf{X}_1, \mathbf{X}_2, \ldots , \mathbf{X}_d$,
A11. Same as **A10**, but with B restricted to be a first-order wff,
A12. $(\forall F)A$, where—for some predicate parameter $\mathbf{F}$ of the same degree as F, but foreign to $(\forall F)A$—$A(\mathbf{F}/F)$ is an axiom,
A13. $\square(A \supset B) \supset (\square A \supset \square B)$,
A14. $\square A$, where A is an axiom,
A15. $(\forall X)\square A \supset \square(\forall X)A$,
A16. $\square A \supset A$,
A17. $A \supset \square \lozenge A$ ('$\lozenge$' short here and in **A19** for '$\sim\square\sim$'),
A18. $\square A \supset \square\square A$, and
A19. $\lozenge A \supset \square\lozenge A$.

The *axioms* of my various languages will then be as indicated in Table I.

(2) S being a set of wffs of a language L, and A a wff of L, I shall say that A is *provable in L from S* if there is a finite column of wffs of L which closes with A and in which every entry belongs to S, is an axiom of L, or follows from two previous entries by Modus Ponens.

(3) And I shall say that a set S of wffs of a language L is *syntactically consistent in L* if there is no wff A of L such that both A and $\sim A$ are provable in L from S.

Table 1

L^1: A1–A7
L^2: A1–A10 and A12
$L^{2!}$: A1–A9 and A11–A12
$L_1^{\square}$: A1–A7 and A13–A15
$L_2^{\square}$: A1–A7 and A13–A16,
$L_3^{\square}$: A1–A7, A13–A14, and A16–A17
$L_4^{\square}$: A1–A7, A13–A16, and A18
$L_5^{\square}$: A1–A7, A13–A14, A16, and A19

(A11, which distinguishes $L^{2!}$ from L^2, is sometimes known as the *Predicative Specification Law*; A15 is the *Barcan Formula* mentioned earlier; and A16–A19 are the so-called *characteristic formulas* of M, B, S4, and S5, respectively.)

2. When it comes to interpreting my various languages, I use truth-value functions rather than models. The account is appropriate, as Theorems 1, 5, and 7 below attest; and it suits my overall purpose to a T. I limit myself in this section to languages without modalities, saving for the next languages with a box.

Understand by a *truth-value function for a language L^1* any function α from the wffs of L^1 to {1,0} such that, for any wff A of L^1,[4]

(i) in case A is a negation $\sim B$, $\alpha(A) = 1$ if and only if $\alpha(B) = 0$,

(ii) in case A is a conditional $B \supset C$, $\alpha(A) = 1$ if and only if $\alpha(B) = 0$ or $\alpha(C) = 1$, and

(iii) in case A is a quantification $(\forall X)B$, $\alpha(A) = 1$ if and only if $\alpha(B(\mathbf{X}/X)) = 1$ for every individual parameter and constant $\mathbf{X}$ of L^1.

Next, understand by a *truth-value function for a language L^2* any function α from the wffs L^2 to {1,0} such that, for any wff A of L^2,

(i)–(iii) as before, and

(iv) in case A is a quantification $(\forall F^d)B$, $\alpha(A) = 1$ if and only if $\alpha(B(C/F^d(\mathbf{X}_1, \mathbf{X}_2, \ldots, \mathbf{X}_d))) = 1$ for every wff C of L^2 and any distinct individual parameters $\mathbf{X}_1, \mathbf{X}_2, \ldots, \mathbf{X}_d$ of L^2.

Then, understand by a *truth-value function for a language $L^{2!}$* any function α from the wffs of $L^{2!}$ to {1,0} that satisfies conditions (i)–(iv), but with C in (iv) restricted to be a first-order wff. Finally, where α is a truth-value function for a language L^i ($i = 1, 2,$ or $2!$), and T is a theory in L_i, take $\alpha(T)$ to equal 1 if and only if $\alpha(A)$ equals 1 for every sentence A in T.

Adapting Henkin's argument in [1], I have shown elsewhere[5] that:

Theorem 1. *A theory T in a language L^i ($i = 1, 2,$ or $2!$) is syntactically* consistent in L_i if and only if $\alpha(T) = 1$ for at least one truth-value function α for L^i.[6]

It follows from the theorem that:
(a) when $i = 1$, $\alpha(T) = 1$ for some truth-value function α for L_i if and only if T has a model,
(b) when $i = 2$, $\alpha(T) = 1$ for some truth-value function α for L_i if and only if T has what Henkin calls a *general model* satisfying the (unrestricted) Axiom of Specification,[7] and
(c) when $i = 2!$, $\alpha(T) = 1$ for some truth-value function α for L^i if and only if T has a general model satisfying the *Predicative Axiom of Specification*.

My semantic account of the languages L^1, L^2, and $L^{2!}$ thus matches the traditional one.

Turning now to questions of relevance, I shall say that, where α is a truth-value function for a language L^i ($i = 1, 2,$ or $2!$) and α^* is a function from just the atomic wffs of L^i to $\{1,0\}$, α has α^* as its *atomic restriction* if α and α^* agree on all the atomic wffs of L^i. And I shall say that *the truth-value of a theory T in L^i depends upon the truth-values of just the atomic wffs of L^i* if, for any two truth-value functions α and α' for L^i that have the same atomic restriction, $\alpha(T) = \alpha'(T)$.

A routine induction will show that, where α is a truth-value function for a language L^1 and α^* is the atomic restriction of α, $\alpha(A) = \alpha^*(A)$ for any wff A of L^1. The induction is on the length of A. Hence:

Theorem 2. *The truth-value of a theory T in a language L^i depends upon the truth-values of just the atomic wffs of L^i.*

A second induction will similarly show that, where α is a truth-value function for a language $L^{2!}$ and α^* is the atomic restriction of α, $\alpha(A) = \alpha^*(A)$ for any wff A of $L^{2!}$. The induction is on the number of quantifications in A of the sort $(\forall F)B$, with subordinate inductions on the length of A seeing both the basis and the inductive step through. Hence:

Theorem 3. *The truth-value of a theory T in a language $L^{2!}$ depends upon the truth-values of just the atomic wffs of $L^{2!}$.*

The two results are not unexpected ones, and I include them only for the record.

The story changes, though, when the statements in T come from a language L^2. Meyer and I have constructed a pair of truth-value functions for a language L^2 that agree on all the atomic wffs of L^2 and yet disagree on the statement '$(\exists f)(\exists x)(\exists y)(f(x) \,\&\, \sim f(y))$' ('$f$' here some predicate variable of L^2 of degree 1, and 'x' and 'y' two individual variables of L^2). The result is announced in [11], and detailed proof of it can be found in [12] and [9]. So, *the truth-value of a theory T in a language L^2* (unlike that of a theory T in a language L^1 or a language $L^{2!}$) *does not always depend upon the truth-values of just the atomic*

Matters of Relevance 211

wffs of L^2. As in the case of the one-statement theory $\{(\exists f)(\exists x)(\exists y)(f(x)$ & $\sim f(y))\}$, it may also depend upon the truth-values of various non-atomic wffs of L^2.

As promised on p. 205, Theorem 2 can be sharpened some. T being a theory in a language L^i ($i = 1$ or 2!), α *a truth-value function for* L^i, and α^* a function from just the atomic subformulas of T to $\{1,0\}$, I shall say that α has α^* as its *atomic T-restriction* if α and α^* agree on all the atomic subformulas of T. And I shall say that *the truth-value of a theory T in L^i depends upon the truth-values of just the atomic subformulas of T* if, for any two truth-value functions α and α' for L^i that have the same atomic T-restriction, $\alpha(T) = \alpha'(T)$.

A routine induction will show that, where T is a theory in a language L^1, α is a truth-value function for L^1, and α^* is the atomic T-restriction of α, $\alpha(A) = \alpha^*(A)$ for any statement A in T. Hence:

Theorem 4. *The truth-value of a theory T in a language L^1 depends upon the truth-values of just the atomic subformulas of T.*

Theorem 3, however, cannot be so sharpened. Given any language $L^{2!}$, let α be a truth-value function for $L^{2!}$ that assigns the truth-value 1 to all the atomic wffs of $L^{2!}$, and let α' be one that agrees with α on all the atomic wffs of $L^{2!}$ but one, say: the wff '**f**(**x**,**x**)' ('**f**' here some predicate parameter of $L^{2!}$ of degree 2, and '**x**' some individual parameter of $L^{2!}$). It is easily verified that the statement '$(\forall f)(\forall x)(\forall y)(f(x) \supset f(y))$' of $L^{2!}$ ('f' here some predicate variable of $L^{2!}$ of degree 1, and 'x' and 'y' two individual variables of $L^{2!}$) has the truth-value 1 under α, but not under α'. So, *the truth-value of a theory T in a language $L^{2!}$* (unlike that of a theory T in a language L^1) *does not always depend upon the truth-values of just the atomic subformulas of T*. As in the case of the one-statement theory $\{(\forall f)(\forall x)(\forall y)(f(x) \supset f(y))\}$, it may also depend upon the truth-values of other atomic wffs of $L^{2!}$.[8]

As Theorems 2–4 suggest, the semantic account on p. 209 of my languages L^1 and $L^{2!}$ can be improved some.

(1) α being a function from the atomic wffs of a language L^i ($i = 1$ or 2!) to $\{1,0\}$, take a wff A of L^i to be *true under* α if:
 (i) in case A is atomic, $\alpha(A) = 1$,
 (ii) in case A is a negation $\sim B$, B is not true under α,
 (iii) in case A is a conditional $B \supset C$, B is not true under α or C is,
 (iv) in case A is a quantification $(\forall X)B$, $B(\mathbf{X}/X)$ is true under α for every individual parameter and constant $\mathbf{X}$ of L^i, and
 (v) in case A is a quantification $(\forall F^d)B$, $B(C/F^d(\mathbf{X}_1,\mathbf{X}_2,\ldots,\mathbf{X}_d))$ is true under α for every first-order wff C of L^i and any distinct individual parameters $\mathbf{X}_1, \mathbf{X}_2, \ldots, \mathbf{X}_d$ of L^i.
Extant proofs of Theorem 1 can be adapted to show that a theory T in L^i is syntactically consistent in L^i if and only if there is a function from the atomic wffs of L^i to $\{1,0\}$ under which every member of T is true.

(2) A being a wff of a language L^1, and α being a function from the atomic

212   Part 2: Truth

subformulas of A and possibly other atomic wffs of L {1,0}, take A to be *true under* α if the first four of the conditions in (1) are met. Extant proofs of Theorem 1 can be adapted to show that a theory T in L^1 is syntactically consistent in L^1 if and only if there is a function from the atomic subformulas of T to {1,0} under which every member of T is true.

3. Next for languages with a box. I begin with those labelled $L_5^\square$, as their story is simpler.

Extending Kripke's approach in [3], understand by a *truth-value pair for a language* $L_5^\square$ any pair of the sort $<K, \alpha>$, where K is a non-empty set of functions from the wffs of $L_5^\square$ to {1,0} and α is a member of K. Next, take a wff A of $L_5^\square$ to be *true* under a truth-value pair $<K,\alpha>$ for $L_5^\square$ if:

(i) in case A is atomic, $\alpha(A) = 1$,
(ii) in case A is a negation $\sim B$, B is not true under $<K,\alpha>$,
(iii) in case A is a conditional $B \supset C$, B is not true under $<K,\alpha>$ or C is,
(iv) in case A is a quantification $(\forall X)B$, $B(X/X)$ is true under $<K,\alpha>$ for every individual parameter and constant X of $L_5^\square$, and
(v) in case A is a modality $\square B, B$ is true under $<K,\beta>$ for every β in K.

And, then, take a theory T of $L_5^\square$ to be *true under a truth-value pair* $<K,\alpha>$ *for* $L_5^\square$ if every sentence in T is true under $<K,\alpha>$.

Adaptation of Makinson's argument in [13] will show that:

Theorem 5. *A theory T in a language $L_5^\square$ is syntactically consistent in $L_5^\square$ if and only if T is true under at least one truth-value pair for $L_5^\square$.*

It follows from the theorem that T is true under a truth-value pair for $L_5^\square$ if and only if T has a Kripke model of the kind appropriate for $L_5^\square$,[9] and hence that my semantic account of the languages $L_5^\square$ matches Kripke's.

Generalizing the second of our criteria of truth-relevance, let T be a theory in a language $L_5^\square$, let $<K,\alpha>$ be a truth-value pair for $L_5^\square$, let K^* be a non-empty set of functions from the atomic subformulas of the members of T to {1,0}, and let α^* be a member of K^*. I shall say that $<K,\alpha>$ has $<K^*,\alpha^*>$ as *one* of its *atomic T-restrictions* if there is a function f from K^* to K such that:

(a)   for any β^* in K^*, β^* and $f(\beta^*)$ agree on all the atomic subformulas of T, and
(b) $f(\alpha^*)$ is α.[10]

And I shall say that *the truth-value of a theory T of $L_5^\square$ depends upon the truth-values of just the atomic subformulas of T* (and, hence, upon those of just the atomic wffs of $L_5^\square$), if, for any two truth-value pairs $<K,\alpha>$ and $<K',\alpha'>$ for $L_5^\square$ that have the same atomic T-restrictions, T is true under $<K,\alpha>$ if and only if T is true under $<K',\alpha'>$.

A simple enough induction will show that, where T is a theory in a language $L_5^\square$, $<K,\alpha>$ is a truth-value pair for $L_5^\square$, and $<K^*,\alpha^*>$ is any atomic T-

restriction of $<K,\alpha>$, a statement in T is true under $<K,\alpha>$ if and only if true under $<K^*,\alpha^*>$. Hence:

Theorem 6. *The truth-value of a theory T in a language $L_5^\square$ depends upon the truth-values of just the atomic subformulas of T (and, hence, upon those of just the atomic wffs of $L_5^\square$).*

First-order theories with an S5 box thus fare exactly like their boxless brethren.

As readers of Kripke will have guessed, treatment of my other modal languages calls for a relation R on K. I supply two accounts. Details of the first, which is simpler but suits only certain theories, are as follows.

Understand by a *truth-value triple for a language* $L_i^\square$ (i = 1, 2, 3, or 4) any triple of the sort $<K,\alpha,R>$, where K is a non-empty set of functions from the wffs of $L_i^\square$ to $\{1,0\}$, α is a member of K, and R is a dyadic relation on K when i = 1, a reflexive one when i = 2, a reflexive and symmetrical one when i = 3, and a reflexive and transitive one when i = 4. Next, take a wff A of $L_i^\square$ to be *true under a truth-value triple $<K,\alpha,R>$ for $L_i^\square$* if:
 (i) in case A is atomic, $\alpha(A)$ = 1,
 (ii) in case A is a negation $\sim B$, B is not true under $<,\alpha,R>$,
 (iii) in case A is a conditional $B \supset C$, B is not true under $<K,\alpha,R>$ or C is,
 (iv) in case A is a quantification $(\forall X)B$, $B(\mathbf{X}/X)$ is true under $<K,\alpha,R>$ for every individual parameter and constant $\mathbf{X}$ of $L_i^\square$, and
 (v) in case A is a modality $\square B$, B is true under $<K,\beta,R>$ for every β in K such that $R(\alpha,\beta)$.
Then, take a theory T in $L_i^\square$ to be true under a truth-value triple $<K,\alpha,R>$ for $L_i^\square$ if every sentence in T is true under $<K,\alpha,R>$. Finally, call a theory T in $L_i^\square$ *infinitely extendible* (as regards the atomic wffs of $L_i^\square$) if $\aleph_0$ atomic wffs of $L_i^\square$ do not figure among the atomic subformulas of T.

Adaptation of Makinson's argument in [13] will show that:

Theorem 7. *An infinitely extendible theory T in a language $L_i^\square$ (i = 1, 2, 3, or 4) is syntactically consistent in $L_i^\square$ if and only if T is true under at least one truth-value triple for $L_i^\square$.*

The result is a generalization of one I announced in [8].

Now, generalizing further my second criterion of truth-relevance, let T be a theory in a language $L_i^\square$ (i = 1, 2, 3, or 4), let $<K,\alpha,R>$ be a truth-value triple for $L_i^\square$, let K^* be a non-empty set of functions from the atomic subformulas of T to $\{1,0\}$, let α^* be a member of K^*, and let R^* be a relation on K^*. I shall say that $<K,\alpha,R>$ has $<K^*,\alpha^*,R^*>$ as *one* of its *atomic T-restrictions* if there exists a one-to-one function f from K^* to K such that:
 (a) for any β^* in K^*, β^* and $f(\beta^*)$ agree on all the atomic subformulas of T,
 (b) $f(\alpha^*)$ is α, and
 (c) for any two β^* and γ^* in K^*, $R^*(\beta^*,\gamma^*)$ if and only if $R(f(\beta^*),f(\gamma^*))$.

And I shall say that *the truth-value of a theory T of $L_i^\square$ depends upon the truth-values of just the atomic subformulas of T* (and, hence, upon those of just the atomic wffs of $L_i^\square$) if, for any two truth-value triples $<K,\alpha,R>$ and $<K',\alpha',R'>$ for $L_i^\square$ that have the same atomic T-restrictions, T is true under $<K,\alpha,R>$ if and only if T is true under $<K',\alpha',R'>$.

It is readily checked that the relation R^* in any atomic T-restriction $<K^*,\alpha^*,R^*>$ of a truth-value triple $<K,\alpha,R>$ for a language $L_i^\square$ is reflexive when R is, symmetrical when R is, etc. So, as one more induction will show, a statement in T is true under $<K,\alpha,R>$ if and only if true under $<K^*,\alpha^*,R^*>$. Hence:

Theorem 8. *The truth-value of an infinitely extendible theory T in a language $L_i^\square$ ($i = 1, 2, 3$, or 4) depends upon the truth-values of just the atomic subformulas of T (and, hence, upon those of just the atomic wffs of $L_i^\square$).*

Do *all* modal first-order theories, then, behave alike? Puzzlingly enough, the answer is *No*, as relativizing the notion of a truth-value pair and that of a truth-value triple will eventually show.

T being a theory in a language $L_5^\square$, understand by a *truth-value T-pair for $L_5^\square$* any pair of the sort $<K,\alpha>$, where K is a non-empty set of functions from the atomic subformulas of T to $\{1,0\}$, and α is a member of K. Then take a member A of T to be true under such a pair if conditions (i)–(v) on p. 212 are met, and take T to be true under the pair if every member of T is. In view of Theorem 6 one might expect that T is syntactically consistent in $L_5^\square$ if and only if T is true under some truth-value T-pair or other for $L_5^\square$, and inspection of the proof of Theorem 6 bears this out:

Theorem 9. *A theory T in a language $L_5^\square$ is syntactically consistent in $L_5^\square$ if and only if T is true under at least one truth-value T-pair for $L_5^\square$.*

As a result, the semantic account on p. 212 of my language $L_5^\square$ can be improved some. A being a wff of $L_5^\square$, K being a non-empty set of functions from the atomic subformulas of A and possibly other atomic wffs of $L_5^\square$ to $\{1,0\}$, and α being a member of K, take A to be true under $<K,\alpha>$ if conditions (i)–(v) on p. 212 are met. And, T being a theory in $L_5^\square$, K being a non-empty set of functions from the atomic subformulas of T to $\{1,0\}$ and α being a member of K, take T to be true under $<K,\alpha>$ if every member of **T** is true under $<K,\alpha>$. This thriftier account, incidentally, makes for a decision procedure when T has only finitely many atomic subformulas.

Now for truth-value triples. T being this time a theory in a language $L_i^\square$ ($i = 1, 2, 3$, or 4), understand by a *truth-value T-triple for $L_i^\square$* any triple of the sort $<K,\alpha,R>$, where K is a non-empty set of functions from the atomic subformulas of T to $\{1,0\}$, α is a member of K, and R is a dyadic relation on K when $i = 1$, a reflexive one when $i = 2$, etc. Then take a member A of T to be true under such a triple if conditions (i)–(v) on p. 213 are met, and take T to be true under the triple if every member of T is.

Theorem 8 notwithstanding, an infinitely extendible theory T in $L_i^\square$ ($i < 5$) may be syntactically consistent in $L_i^\square$ and yet fail to be true under any truth-value T-triple for $L_i^\square$. Cases in point are as follows.

(a) The theory $\{\lozenge\square f(a), \sim\square\square f(a), \sim\lozenge\lozenge f(a)\}$, though syntactically consistent in $L_1^\square$, is not true under any truth-value T-triple for $L_1^\square$. I owe the example to Chellas.[11]

(b) The theory $\{\square f(a), \sim\square\square f(a)\}$, though syntactically consistent in $L_2^\square$, is not true under any truth-value T-triple for $L_2^\square$, and this for a simple enough reason: any reflexive relation on the sets $\{\alpha_1,\alpha_2\}$, $\{\alpha_1\}$, and $\{\alpha_2\}$—α_1 the result of assigning 1 to 'f(a)' and α_2 that of assigning 0 to 'f(a)'—is transitive as well! So, $\{\square f(a), \sim\square\square f(a)\}$, which pans out false under $<\{\alpha_1,\alpha_2\},\alpha_1,R>$, $<\{\alpha_1,\alpha_2\},\alpha_2,R>$, $<\{\alpha_1\},\alpha_1,R>$, and $<\{\alpha_2\},\alpha_2,R>$ for reflexive and transitive R, is sure to do so for reflexive R. I owe the example to McArthur.

(c) The theory $\{\lozenge f(a), \sim\square\lozenge f(a)\}$, though syntactically consistent in $L_3^\square$, is not true under any truth-value T-triple for $L_3^\square$, and this for the same reason as in (b): any reflexive relation on the sets $\{\alpha_1,\alpha_2\}$, $\{\alpha_1\}$, and $\{\alpha_2\}$ in (b) is transitive as well. So, $\{\lozenge f(a), \sim\square\lozenge f(a)\}$, which pans out false under $<\{\alpha_1,\alpha_2\},\alpha_1,R>$, $<\{\alpha_1,\alpha_2\},\alpha_2,R>$, $<\{\alpha_1\},\alpha_1,R>$, and $<\{\alpha_2\},\alpha_2, R>$ for reflexive, symmetrical, and transitive R, is sure to do so for reflexive and symmetrical R. I again owe the example to McArthur.

(d) The theory $\{f(a), \sim\square f(a), \lozenge\square f(a)\}$, though syntactically consistent in $L_4^\square$, is not true under any truth-value T-triple for $L_4^\square$. I owe the example to Weaver.

In all four cases assigning a truth-value (whichever one we please) to one more atomic wff, say 'f(b)', would save the situation. Limiting ourselves to McArthur's first theory, let α_1 be the result of assigning 1 to both 'f(a)' and 'f(b)', α_2 the result of assigning 0 to 'f(a)' and 1 to 'f(b)', and α_3 the result of assigning 1 to 'f(a)' and 0 to 'f(b)'; let α be α_1; and let R be the reflexive—but non-transitive—relation $\{<\alpha_1,\alpha_1>, <\alpha_2,\alpha_2>, <\alpha_3,\alpha_3>, <\alpha_1,\alpha_3>, <\alpha_3,\alpha_2>\}$. The theory $\{\square f(a), \sim\square\square f(a)\}$ will then be true under $<K,\alpha,R>$, as the reader may wish to verify. In other cases truth-values must be assigned to two more atomic wffs, in yet others to three more, etc.

To sum things up, the truth-value of a theory T in a language $L_i^\square$ ($i < 5$) is invariant under all possible truth-value assignments to the atomic wffs of $L_i^\square$ that do not figure among the atomic subformulas of T. But, as (a)–(d) show, truth-values must nonetheless be assigned to those wffs if the truth-value of T is to compute right in all cases.

I promised on p. 213 a second—and wider ranging—account of the languages $L_1^\square$–$L_5^\square$. It throws a rather interesting light on the problem at hand.

Call a pair of the sort $<\Phi,r>$, where Φ is a function from the atomic wffs of a language $L_i^\square$ ($i = 1, 2, 3$, or 4) to $\{1,0\}$ and r is a real number, an *index function from these wffs to* $\{1,0\}$, and understand by a *Kripke truth-value triple for* $L_i^\square$ any triple of the sort $<K,\alpha,R>$, where K is a non-empty set of indexed functions from the atomic wffs of $L_i^\square$ to $\{1,0\}$, α is a member of K, and R is a relation on K of the expected sort.[12] This done, take a wff A of $L_i^\square$ to be true under such a triple of conditions (i)–(v) on p. 213 are met, and take a theory T in $L_i^\square$ to be true under the triple if every member of T is.

Following Makinson once more, one can show that:

Theorem 10. *A theory T in a language $L_i^\square$ (i = 1, 2, 3, or 4) is syntactically consistent in $L_i^\square$ if and only if T is true under at least one Kripke truth-value triple for $L_i^\square$.*

Note that T here may be *any* theory in $L_i^\square$, whether infinitely extendible or not. So the account significantly outstrips the one offered on pp. 214–15.[13]

With Kripke triples substituting for the triples on pp. 214–15, proof is again forthcoming that:

(1) the truth-value of a theory T in a language $L_i^\square$ (i = 1, 2, 3, or 4) is invariant under all possible assignments of truth-values to the atomic wffs of $L_i^\square$ that do not figure among the atomic subformulas of T,

and proof can *now* be had that:

(2) the truth-value of T will always compute right whether or not truth-values are assigned to the atomic wffs of $L_i^\square$ that do not figure among the atomic subformulas of T.

In particular, let the functions Φ in both $<\Phi,1>$ and $<\Phi,2>$ assign the truth-value 1 to 'f(a)', and let the function Φ' in $<\Phi',1>$ assign it the truth-value 0; let K consist of the three indexed functions $<\Phi,1>$ (= α_1), $<\Phi',1>$ (= α_2), and $<\Phi,2>$ (= α_3); and let α and R be as on p. 215. McArthur's theory $\{\square\mathbf{f(a)}, \sim\square\square\mathbf{f(a)}\}$ will again pan out true under the Kripke triple $<K,\alpha,R>$.

So the problem that vexed us on p. 215 has a solution after all: assign truth-values to just the atomic subformulas of your theory T, but outfit the resulting truth-value assignments with indices, thus allowing them to appear under as many different guises as the occasion may call for. Kripke, in effect, does just that when he allows one and the same model to go with different worlds. To the naive his solution sounds of course more exalted, but unlike him I refuse to make metaphysical virtue out of logical necessity. To me indexing one's functions has but one merit: wffs that are irrelevant to the truth-value of a theory can be left truth-valueless, as indeed they should be.

One feature of the above analysis may have puzzled the reader. Only statements are normally said to be true or to be false. Yet many of the atomic wffs—and, on some occasions,[14] all the atomic wffs—whose bearing on the truth-value of a theory I have just investigated are quasi-statements!

So far as first-order languages go, one could skirt the difficulty by banishing all individual parameters and requiring instead that each language L^1 or $L^\square$ come with $\aleph_0$ individual constants. All wffs would now be statements, and theorems in Sections 2 and 3 concerning first-order theories would hold true of first-order theories to which infinitely many individual constants are foreign.

Second-order languages would call for similar, though more extensive, tinkering: banish all individual and all predicate parameters, and require instead that each language $L^{2!}$ or L^2 come with $\aleph_0$ individual constants and—for each d from 1 on—$\aleph_0$ predicate constants of degree d. All wffs would again be statements, and theorems in Section 2 concerning second-order theories would hold true of second-order theories to which infinitely many individual constants and—for any d from 1 on—infinitely many predicate constants of degree d are foreign.

But there is a better answer to the difficulty. Instead of banishing parameters in favor of constants, think of parameters as just so many extra constants!

To illustrate matters, suppose the statements in your theory T come from a language L^1. If T has any model at all, T is sure by Skolem's Theorem to have one whose domain, call it D, is denumerable.[15] So, think of the $\aleph_0$ individual parameters of L^1 as just so many names of the members of D, and the trick is done. Semantically speaking, the quasi-statements of L^1 and, in particular, those of the sort $F^d(X_1, X_2, \ldots, X_d)$—will now behave exactly like statements, and your assigning them truth-values will be entirely proper.

True, the model that I exploit here, call it M, need not be the *intended* model of T. That model, call it M', might well have a nondenumerable domain D', in which case you will not have names for all the members of D'. But I must urge you to take Skolem's Theorem seriously. Whatever the size of D' in the intended model M', there nonetheless exists at least one model M with a denumerable domain D that suits T as well as M' does, indeed is such that exactly the same statements of L^1 are true in M as are true in M'. So, while others orate in T about M', think M instead, and no one will ever find you out.

Like considerations apply when the statements in T come from a language $L^\square$, a language $L^{2!}$, or a language L^2. Note in the last case that if T has a general model satisfying the (unrestricted) *Specification Law*, T is sure by Henkin's generalization of Skolem's Theorem to have one whose system of domains, call it $<D_0, D_1, D_2, \ldots, >$, consists exclusively of denumerable domains.[16] So, think of the $\aleph_0$ individual parameters of L^2 as just so many names of the members of D_0, of the $\aleph_0$ predicate parameters of L^2 of degree 1 as just so many names of the members of D_1, of the $\aleph_0$ predicate parameters of L^2 of degree 2 as just so many names of the members of D_2, etc., and the trick is done. Semantically speaking, the quasi-statements of L^2 will now behave like statements, and your assigning them truth-values will be above reproach.[17]

Notes

1. Similar results can be had for analogues of my languages $L_1^\square$-$L_5^\square$ in which neither the *Barcan Formula* nor its converse are provable. For details on these languages, see [7] and [10].

2. Note again the systematic use of italic letters to refer to variables and bold ones to refer to predicates and constants.

3. Theories are often presumed to be closed under some provability relation or other. Not so here.

4. Because 'T' already ranges here over theories, I use as truth-values '1' in lieu of the customary '**T**' and '0' in lieu of the customary '**F**'.

5. See in particular [5], [6], and [10].

6. Theorem 1 holds true, as shown in [5], [6], and [10], of any set of wffs of L^i that is infinitely extendible as regards the parameters of L^i, i.e., any set of wffs of L^i to which $\aleph_0$ individual parameters and—for each d from 1 on—$\aleph_0$ predicate parameters of degree d are foreign. It does not hold of other sets of wffs of L^i, as noted in earlier papers in this volume. By definition theories are infinitely extendible in the present sense; they need not, however, be infinitely extendible in the sense of p. 213.

7. See [2]. Note that my concern, when $i = 2$, is with *all* general models satisfying the (unrestricted) *Axiom of Specification*, not just those known as *standard* models. As regards the latter, see [11].

8. As reported on pp. 134–35 and more fully explained in [9] and [10], there is an account of truth-value functions under which Theorem 4 holds of theories in L^{2^i} and L^2 as well as L^1. However, for reasons given there, the account has less attraction than the present one and mere mention of it is consequently deemed sufficient.

9. See [4] on this matter.

10. The definition is a generalization by G. Weaver of one I used in an early draft of this paper.

11. The predicate constant of degree one 'f' and the individual constant 'a' are presumed to come in (a) from a language $L_1^\square$, in (b) from a language $L_2^\square$, etc.

12. I call the triples in question Kripke triples to stress their likeness to the models in [3]. As indices of the present sort first turned up (it seems) in [14], I could also have called them *Montague triples* and indeed did so in [10].

13. Proof that Theorem 7 fails for theories that are not infinitely extendible in the sense of p. 213 can be found in [15].

14. I.e., when your language comes without individual constants.

15. As the reader knows, a model for a language L^1 is a pair $<D, I_D>$, where D is a non-empty domain and I_D is an interpretation relative to D of the parameters of L^1 (i.e., some result of assigning to each individual parameter and constant of L^1 a member of D and to each predicate parameter and constant of L^1 of degree d ($d = 1, 2, 3, \ldots$) a subset of D^d).

16. A general model is a pair of the sort $<<D_0, D_1, D_2, \ldots>, I_{<D_0, D_1, D_2, \ldots>}>$, where D_0 is a non-empty domain, for each d from 1 on D_d is a subset of the power set of D_0^d, and $I_{<D_0, D_1, D_2, \ldots>}$ is the result of assigning to each individual parameter and constant of L^2 a member of D_0 and to each predicate parameter and constant of L^2 of degree d ($d = 1, 2, 3, \ldots$) a subset of D_d. For further details on this whole matter, see [2] and [10].

17. The results in this paper were first announced at the Montreal Symposium on Exact Philosophy, 4–5 November 1971.

My thanks go to Brian Chellas, Robert P. McArthur, and G. Weaver for their comments and advice.

References

[1] Henkin, L. 1949. "The Completeness of the First-Order Functional Calculus." *The Journal of Symbolic Logic* (hereafter *JSL*) 14: 159–166.

[2] _____. 1950. "Completeness in the Theory of Types." *JSL* 15: 81–91.

[3] Kripke, S. A. 1959. "A Completeness Theorem in Modal Logic." *JSL* 24: 1–15.

[4] _____. 1963. "Semantical Considerations in Modal Logic." *Modal and Many-Valued Logics, Acta Philosophica Fennica* 16: 83–94.

[5] Leblanc, H. 1969. "A Simplified Strong Completeness Proof for QC$_=$." *Akten des XIV. Internationalen Kongresses für Philosophic.* Vienna: Verlag Herder 3: 83–95 (#9 in this volume).

[6] _____. 1969. "Three Generalizations of a Theorem of Beth's." *Logique et Analyse* 12: 205–20 (#11 in this volume).

[7] _____. 1972. "On Dispensing with Things and Worlds." *Existence and Possible Worlds*, pp. 241–59. New York: New York University Press (#7 in this volume).

Matters of Relevance 219

[8] ———. 1973. "Semantic Deviations." *Truth, Syntax and Modality*, pp. 1–16. Amsterdam: North-Holland (#20 in this volume).
[9] ———. 1975. "That *Principia Mathematica*, First Edition, has a Predicative Interpretation after all." *Journal of Philosophical Logic* 4: 67 – 70 (#16 in this volume).
[10] ———. 1976. *Truth-Value Semantics*. Amsterdam: North-Holland.
[11] Leblanc, H., and Meyer, R. K. 1970. "Truth-Value Semantics for the Theory of Types." *Philosophical Problems in Logic. Some Recent Developments*, pp. 77–101. Dordrecht: Reidel (#12 in this volume).
[12] Leblanc, H., and Weaver, G. 1973. "Truth-Functionality and the Ramified Theory of Types." *Truth, Syntax and Modality*, pp. 148–67. Amsterdam: North-Holland (#15 in this volume).
[13] Makinson, D. C. 1966. "On Some Completeness Theorems in Modal Logic." *Zeitschrift für mathematische Logik und Grundlagen der Mathematik* 12: 379–84.
[14] Montague, R. 1970. "Pragmatics and Intensional Logic." *Synthèse* 22: 68–94.
[15] Weaver, G. 1973. "Logical Consequences in Modal Logic: Alternative Semantic Systems for Normal Modal Logics." *Truth, Syntax and Modality*, pp. 308–17. Amsterdam: North-Holland.

15

Truth-Functionality and the Ramified Theory of Types

G. Weaver, coauthor

Take a calculus C with, say, '$\sim$', '$\supset$', and '$\forall$' as its only logical operators. We shall say that C has a *truth-functional interpretation* if there is a family Σ of functions from the wffs (non-atomic as well as atomic) of C to $\{\mathbf{T}, \mathbf{F}\}$ such that, informally speaking:

(a) the theorems of C and the wffs of C evaluating to $\mathbf{T}$ under all members of Σ coincide

and

(b) the truth-values that the non-atomic wffs of C assume under members of Σ hinge exclusively on the truth-values of their components or—in the case of quantifications—those of their substitution instances.

And we shall say that C has a *strictly truth-functional interpretation* if the family Σ in question also obeys the following condition:

(c) members of Σ that agree on the atomic wffs of C agree on the non-atomic ones as well.[1]

The sentential calculus (SC, for short) has a strictly truth-functional interpretation; and—as follows from results of Beth, Schütte, and others[2]—so does the first-order quantificational calculus (QC^1). By contrast, the *principal* interpretation of QC^2 (the second-order quantificational calculus), though truth-functional, is *not* strictly truth-functional, a result due to Leblanc and Meyer.[3] Passing to $QC^{2/\infty}$ (the ramified second-order quantificational calculus), we establish that:

(1) without Russell's *Axiom of Reducibility*, $QC^{2/\infty}$ fares like SC and QC^1 (Theorems 1 and 3),

but

(2) upon adoption of that axiom, $QC^{2/\infty}$ fares like QC^2 (Theorems 8 and 11).

Our results automatically extend to $QC^{\infty/\infty}$ (the ramified theory of types):

(1') without Russell's axiom, $QC^{\infty/\infty}$ has a strictly truth-functional interpretation, but

(2′) upon adoption of the axiom, its *principal* interpretation—though still truth-functional—is no longer strictly truth-functional.[4]

1. The *primitive signs* of $QC^{2/\infty}$ are to be the three logical operators '$\sim$' '$\supset$', and '$\forall$', the parentheses '(' and ')', the comma ',', *plus* the following parameters and variables:
 (i) $\aleph_0$ individual parameters (among them 'a'),
 (ii) $\aleph_0$ individual variables (among them 'x' and 'y'),
 (iii) for each d from 0 on and each l from 1 on, $\aleph_0$ predicate parameters of degree d and level l (among them 'f', a predicate parameter of degree and level l); and
 (iv) for each d from 0 on and each l from 1 on, $\aleph_0$ predicate variables of degree d and level l (among them 'f', a predicate variable of degree and level 1).[5]

The parameters in (i) and those in (iii) will be presumed to come in a definite order, known as their *alphabetic order*. The individual parameters and variables of $QC^{2/\infty}$ will be said to be of *type 0*; the predicate parameters and variables of $QC^{2/\infty}$ of degree 0, better known as *sentence* parameters and variables, will be said to be of *type −1* and the remaining predicate parameters and variables of $QC^{2/\infty}$ will be said to be of *type 1*. And, as usual, the *formulas* of $QC^{2/\infty}$ are to be all finite (but non-empty) strings of primitive signs of $QC^{2/\infty}$.

Because we use both parameters and variables, our arsenal of syntactic variables will be rather large: 'P' to refer to parameters in general, 'V' to variables in general, 'X' and 'Y' to individual parameters, 'X' to individual variables, 'I' to *individual signs* (i.e., to individual parameters and variables), '$F^{d/l}$', '$G^{d/l}$', and '$H^{d/l}$' to predicate parameters of degree d and level l, '$F^{d/l}$' and '$G^{d/l}$' to predicate variables of degree d and level l, and 'A', 'B', and 'C' to formulas.

Three substitution conventions will be needed as we go along. The first one runs:

C1. Let A be a formula of $QC^{2/\infty}$, V be a variable of $QC^{2/\infty}$, and P be a parameter of the same type, same level, and (when V is a predicate variable) same degree as V. Then $(A)(P/V)$ will be the result of putting V everywhere in A for P, and $(A)(P/V)$ that of putting P everywhere A for V.

The *atomic well-formed formulas* (*atomic wffs*, for short) of $QC^{2/\infty}$ are to be all formulas of $QC^{2/\infty}$ of the sort $F^{d/l}(X_1, X_2, \ldots, X_d)$ where $d \geq 0$.[6] The *well-formed formulas* (*wffs*, for short) of $QC^{2/\infty}$ will be all atomic wffs of $QC^{2/\infty}$, *plus* all formulas of $QC^{2/\infty}$ of the following three sorts: (i) $\sim A$, where A is a wff of $QC^{2/\infty}$, (ii) $(A \supset B)$, where A and B are wffs of $QC^{2/\infty}$, and (iii) $(\forall V)A$, where—for any parameter P of $QC^{2/\infty}$ of the same type, level, and degree as V—$(A)(P/V)$ is a wff of $QC^{2/\infty}$.[7] And the *quasi-wffs* (*qwffs*, for short) of $QC^{2/\infty}$ will be all formulas of $QC^{2/\infty}$ of the sort $(A)(V/P)$, where A is a wff or qwff of $QC^{2/\infty}$, P a parameter of $QC^{2/\infty}$ which occurs in A, and V a variable of $QC^{2/\infty}$ which is of the same type, level, and degree as P but does not occur in A.

As usual, A counts as the *immediate component* of $\sim A$ and of $(\forall V)A$ (this for any variable V of $QC^{2/\infty}$); and A and B count as the two immediate components of $(A \supset B)$. And the *components* of a wff or qwff of $QC^{2/\infty}$ are the wff or qwff itself, its immediate components, and the components of all its components.

For convenience's sake we assign levels to the wffs (as well as to the predicate parameters and variables) of $QC^{2/\infty}$. A being a wff of $QC^{2/\infty}$, let $l_P(A)$ be 0 if no predicate parameter of $QC^{2/\infty}$ occurs in A; let $l_P(A)$ be 1 if at least one predicate parameter of $QC^{2/\infty}$ of level 1 occurs in A but none of higher level than 1 does; let $l_P(A)$ be 2 if at least one predicate parameter of $QC^{2/\infty}$ of level 2 occurs in A but none of higher level than 2 does; etc. And let $l_V(A)$ be similarly defined, but with the word 'variable' doing duty throughout for 'parameter'. We shall then take the *level* $l(A)$ of A to be $\max(l_P(A), l_V(A) + 1)$.

Now for our remaining two substitution conventions:

C2. Let A be a wff or qwff of $QC^{2/\infty}$; let $X_2, X_2, \ldots,$ and X_d ($d \geq 0$) be distinct individual parameters of $QC^{2/\infty}$; and let $I_1, I_2, \ldots,$ and I_d be (not necessarily distinct) individual signs of $QC^{2/\infty}$. By $(A)(I_1, I_2, \ldots, I_d/X_1, X_2, \ldots, X_d)$ we shall understand the result of simultaneously putting I_1 everywhere in A for X_1, I_2 for X_2, $\ldots,$ and I_d for X_d.[8]

C3. Let A be a wff of qwff of $QC^{2/\infty}$; let $F^{d/l}$ be a predicate variable of $QC^{2/\infty}$ of degree d and level l; in case $d > 0$, let $X_1, X_2, \ldots, X_d$ be distinct individual parameters of $QC^{2/\infty}$; let B be a wff of $QC^{2/\infty}$; and let $F^{d/l}(I_{1_1}, I_{2_1}, \ldots, I_{d_1})$, $F^{d/l}(I_{1_2}, I_{2_2}, \ldots, I_{d_2}), \ldots, F^{d/l}(I_{1_k}, I_{2_k}, \ldots, I_{d_k})$ ($k \geq 0$) be all atomic components of A which contain $F^{d/l}$. *Case 1:* $k = 0$. Then $(A)(B/F^{d/l}(X_1, X_2, \ldots, X_d))$ is to be A. *Case 2:* $k > 0$. (a) If $F^{d/l}$ occurs in a component of A of the sort $(\forall V)A'$ and B has a component of the sort $(\forall V)B'$ (V the same variable in both cases), $(A)(B/F^d(X_1, X_2, \ldots, X_d))$ is to be $(A)(F^{d/l}/F^{d/l})$, where $F^{d/l}$ is in alphabetic order the first predicate parameter of $QC^{2/\infty}$ of degree d and level l. (b) Otherwise, $(A)(B/F^{d/l}(X_1, X_2, \ldots, X_d))$ is to be the result of putting $(B)(I_{1_i}, I_{2_i}, \ldots, I_{d_i}/X_1, X_2, \ldots, X_d)$ everywhere in A for $F^{d/l}(I_{1_i}, I_{2_i}, \ldots, I_{d_i})$, this for each i from 1 through k.[9]

The (substitution) *instances* of the quantifications of $QC^{2/\infty}$ will play a considerable role throughout. With **C1** and **C3** on hand, they can be identified as follows: (i) the instances of a quantification of the sort $(\forall X)A$ will be all wffs of $QC^{2/\infty}$ of the sort $A(X/X)$; (ii) the instances of a quantification of the sort $(\forall F^{d/l})A$ will be all wffs of $QC^{2/\infty}$ of the sort $A(B/F^{d/l}(X_1, X_2, \ldots, X_d))$, where B is any wff of $QC^{2/\infty}$ and—in case $d > 0$—$X_1, X_2, \ldots, X_d$ are distinct individual parameters of $QC^{2/\infty}$; and (iii) the *predicative* instances of $(\forall F^{d/l})A$ will be all wffs of $QC^{2/\infty}$ of the sort $A(B/F^{d/l}(X_1 X_2, \ldots, X_d))$, where B

Truth-Functionality and the Ramified Theory of Types 223

is wff of $QC^{2/\infty}$ of *level 1 or less* (and—in case $d > 0$—$X_1, X_2, \ldots, X_d$ are distinct individual parameters of $QC^{2/\infty}$).

Turning at last to the deductive apparatus of $QC^{2/\infty}$, we take the *axioms* of $QC^{2/\infty}$ to be all wffs of $QC^{2/\infty}$ of any of the following seven sorts:

A1. $A \supset (B \supset A)$,
A2. $(A \supset (B \supset C)) \supset ((A \supset B) \supset (A \supset C))$,
A3. $(\sim A \supset \sim B) \supset (B \supset A)$,
A4. $(\forall V)(A \supset B) \supset ((\forall V)A \supset (\forall V)B)$,
A5. $A \supset (\forall V)A$,
A6. $(\forall X)A \supset A^*$, where A^* is an instance of $(\forall X)A$,
A7. $(\forall F^{d/l})A \supset A^*$, where A^* is a predicative instance of $(\forall F^{d/l})A$,

plus all wffs of $QC^{2/\infty}$ of the sort $(\forall V)A$, where—for any parameter P of $QC^{2/\infty}$ of the same type, level, and degree as V that is foreign to $(\forall V)A$—$A(P/V)$ is an axiom of $QC^{2/\infty}$.[10] We understand by the *ponential* of two wffs A and $A \supset B$ of $QC^{2/\infty}$ the wff B. Where A is a wff and S a set of wffs of $QC^{2/\infty}$, we understand by a *proof in* $QC^{2/\infty}$ *of A from S* any column

$$B_1$$
$$B_2$$
$$\cdot$$
$$\cdot$$
$$\cdot$$
$$B_p$$

of wffs of $QC^{2/\infty}$ such that B_p is A and, for each i from 1 through p, B_i belongs to S, is an axiom of $QC^{2/\infty}$, or is the ponential of two earlier wffs in the column; we say that A *is provable in* $QC^{2/\infty}$ *from S* if there is in $QC^{2/\infty}$ a proof of A from S; we say that S is *syntactically consistent* in $QC^{2/\infty}$ if there is no wff of $QC^{2/\infty}$ such that both it and its negation are provable in $QC^{2/\infty}$ from S; and we say that A is a *theorem* of $QC^{2/\infty}$ ($\vdash A$, for short) if there is in $QC^{2/\infty}$ a proof of A from $\emptyset$.

Russell's *Axiom of Reducibility*, as tailored to suit $QC^{2/\infty}$, runs:

A8. $(\exists F^{d/l})(\forall X_1)(\forall X_2) \ldots (\forall X_d)(F^{d/1}(X_1, X_2, \ldots, X_d) \equiv F^{d/l}(X_1, X_2, \ldots, X_d))$, where $d > 0$ and $X_1, X_2, \ldots, X_d$ are distinct individual variables of $QC^{2/\infty}$.

It will count as an axiom of $QC^{2/\infty}$ in Sections 3 and 4 below, where

$$(\forall F^{d/l})A \supset A^*$$

will thereby become provable in $QC^{2/\infty}$ for *every* instance A^* of $(\forall F^{d/l})A$.[11]

2. Towards sharpening our accounts of truth-functionality and strict truth-functionality on p. 220, understand by a *truth-value function* for $QC^{2/\infty}$ any

224 Part 2: Truth

function from the wffs of $QC^{2/\infty}$ to $\{T, F\}$; understand by an *instantial function* for (the quantifications of) $QC^{2/\infty}$ any function that pairs with each quantification $(\forall V)A$ of $QC^{2/\infty}$ a set of instances of $(\forall V)A$; and by a *permissible* instantial function for $QC^{2/\infty}$ understand any instantial function I for $QC^{2/\infty}$ such that, for any quantification $(\forall V)A$ of $QC^{2/\infty}$ and any member A^* of $I((\forall V)A)$, $\vdash (\forall V)A \supset A^*$.

We shall say that $QC^{2/\infty}$ has a *truth-functional interpretation* if there is a family Σ of truth-value functions for $QC^{2/\infty}$ such that:

(1) for any wff A of $QC^{2/\infty}$, $\vdash A$ if and only if $\alpha(A) = T$ for every member α of Σ,

(2.1) for any member α of Σ and any two negations $\sim A$ and $\sim A'$ of $QC^{2/\infty}$, if $\alpha(A) = \alpha(A')$, then $\alpha(\sim A) = \alpha(\sim A')$,

(2.2) for any negation $\sim A$ of $QC^{2/\infty}$ and any two members α and α' of Σ, if $\alpha(A) = \alpha'(A)$, then $\alpha(\sim A) = \alpha'(\sim A)$,

(3.1) for any member α of Σ and any two conditionals $A \supset B$ and $A' \supset B'$ of $QC^{2/\infty}$, if $\alpha(A) = \alpha(A')$ and $\alpha(B) = \alpha(B')$, then $\alpha(A \supset B) = \alpha(A' \supset B')$,

(3.2) for any conditional $A \supset B$ of $QC^{2/\infty}$ and any two members α and α' of Σ, if $\alpha(A) = \alpha'(A)$ and $\alpha(B) = \alpha'(B)$, then $\alpha(A \supset B) = \alpha'(A \supset B)$, and

(4) there is a permissible instantial function I for $QC^{2/\infty}$ such that:

(4.1) for any member α of Σ, any two quantifications $(\forall V)A$ and $(\forall V')A'$ of $QC^{2/\infty}$ (V and V' here variables of the same type, level, and degree) such that $I((\forall V)A)$ is at least as large as $I((\forall V')A')$, and any function f from $I((\forall V)A)$ onto $I((\forall V')A')$, if $\alpha(A^*) = \alpha(f(A^*))$ for every member A^* of $I((\forall V)A)$, then $\alpha((\forall V)A) = \alpha((\forall V')A')$,

(4.2) for any member α of Σ, any two quantifications $(\forall V)A$ and $(\forall V')A'$ of $QC^{2/\infty}$ (V and V' as in (4.1)) such that $I((\forall V)A)$ is smaller than $I((\forall V')A')$, and any function f from $I((\forall V')A')$ onto $I((\forall V)A)$, if $\alpha(A^{*'}) = \alpha(f(A^{*'}))$ for every member $A^{*'}$ of $I((\forall V')A')$, then $\alpha((\forall V)A) = \alpha((\forall V')A')$, and

(4.3) for any quantification $(\forall V)A$ of $QC^{2/\infty}$ and any two members α and α' of Σ, if $\alpha(A^*) = \alpha'(A^*)$ for every member A^* of $I((\forall V)A))$, then $\alpha((\forall V)A) = \alpha'((\forall V)A)$.[12]

And we shall say that $QC^{2/\infty}$ has a *strictly truth-functional interpretation* if there is a family Σ of truth-value functions for $QC^{2/\infty}$ which satisfies conditions (1)–(4) *plus* the following:

(5) for any two members α and α' of Σ, if $\alpha(A) = \alpha'(A)$ for every atomic wff A of $QC^{2/\infty}$, then $\alpha(A) = \alpha'(A)$ for every wff A of $QC^{2/\infty}$.

Now consider the family Σ_1 consisting of every truth-value function α for $QC^{2/\infty}$ such that:

(i) for any negation $\sim A$ of $QC^{2/\infty}$, $\alpha(\sim A) = T$ if and only if $\alpha(A) = F$. if and only if $\alpha(A)$,

(ii) for any conditional $A \supset B$ of $QC^{2/\infty}$, $\alpha(A \supset B) = T$ if and only if $\alpha(A) = F$ or $\alpha(B) = T$,

(iii) for any quantification of $QC^{2/\infty}$ of the sort $(\forall X)A$, $\alpha((\forall X)A) = T$ if and only if $\alpha(A^*) = T$ for every instance A^* of $(\forall X)A$, and

Truth-Functionality and the Ramified Theory of Types 225

(iv) for any quantification of $QC^{2/\infty}$ of the sort $(\forall F^{d/l})A$, $\alpha((\forall F^{d/l})A) = \mathbf{T}$ if and only if $\alpha(A^*) = \mathbf{T}$ for every predicative instance A^* of $(\forall F^{d/l})A$.

It is clear that Σ_1—the *intended* or *principal* interpretation of $QC^{2/\infty}$—satisfies conditions (2)–(4). Towards showing that Σ_1 satisfies condition (1) as well, let S be any finite set of wffs of $QC^{2/\infty}$ that is syntactically consistent in $QC^{2/\infty}$. Following the instructions in [8],[13] one can extend S into a set S_∞ such that: (i_∞) for any negation $\sim A$ of $QC^{2/\infty}$, $\sim A$ belongs to S_∞ if and only if A does not belong to S_∞, (ii_∞) for any conditional $A \supset B$ of $QC^{2/\infty}$, $A \supset B$ belongs to S_∞ if and only if A does not belong to S_∞ or B does, (iii_∞) for any quantification of $QC^{2/\infty}$ of the sort $(\forall X)A$, if $(\forall X)A$ does not belong to S_∞, then there is an individual parameter X of $QC^{2/\infty}$ such that $A(X/X)$ does not belong to S_∞, and (iv_∞) for any quantification of $QC^{2/\infty}$ of the sort $(\forall F^{d/l})A$, if $(\forall F^{d/l})A$ does not belong to S_∞, then there is a predicate parameter $F^{d/l}$ of $QC^{2/\infty}$ of the same degree and level as $F^{d/l}$ such that $A(F^{d/l}/F^{d/l})$ does not belong to S_∞ either. But, if a quantification $(\forall X)A$ of $QC^{2/\infty}$ belongs to S_∞, then in view of **A6** so does every instance of $(\forall X)A$; and, if a quantification $(\forall F^{d/l})A$ of $QC^{2/\infty}$ belongs to S_∞, then in view of **A7** so does every predicative instance of $(\forall F^{d/l})A$. Hence each member of S_∞— and, by rebound, of S—is sure to evaluate to $\mathbf{T}$ under the member α of Σ_1 that assigns $\mathbf{T}$ to every wff of $QC^{2/\infty}$ in S_∞ and $\mathbf{F}$ to everyone not in S_∞. Hence, in particular, if $\{\sim A\}$ is syntactically consistent in $QC^{2/\infty}$, then $\alpha(A) = \mathbf{F}$, this for any wff A of $QC^{2/\infty}$. Hence any wff of $QC^{2/\infty}$ evaluating to $\mathbf{T}$ under all members of Σ_1 is a theorem of $QC^{2/\infty}$. But any theorem of $QC^{2/\infty}$ can be shown to evaluate to $\mathbf{T}$ under all members of Σ_1. Hence Σ_1 meets all four of conditions (1)–(4). Hence:

Theorem 1. *In the absence of the Axiom of Reducibility, $QC^{2/\infty}$ has a truth-functional interpretation.*

Proof that Σ_1 meets condition (5) as well (and, hence, that in the absence of the *Axiom of Reducibility* $QC^{2/\infty}$ has a strictly truth-functional interpretation) is by four inductions. The principal one is on $r(A)$, the *rank* of a wff A of $QC^{2/\infty}$; of the subsidiary inductions, two are on $\ell(A)$, the *length* of A, and the third is on $h_j(A)$, the *height* of A *relative to j* or —for short—the *j-height* of A.

As usual, $\ell(A) = 1$ when A is atomic; $\ell(\sim A) = \ell(A) + 1$; $\ell(A \supset B) = \ell(A) + \ell(B) + 1$; and $\ell((\forall V)A) = \ell(A(P/V)) + 1$, where P is the alphabetically earliest parameter of $QC^{2/\infty}$ of the same type, level, and degree as V.

Definitions of the rank and *j*-height of A are more elaborate. By a *terminating sequence of natural numbers* understand any infinite sequence of the sort $<n_1, n_2, \ldots, n_g, \ldots>$, where either (1) for each k from 1 on, $n_k = 0$, in which case the *rank of the sequence* will be 0, or (2) there is a j such that $n_j > 0$ and—for each k from $j + 1$ on—$n_k = 0$, in which case its rank will be j. For each j from 1 on, take the *j-height of a terminating sequence* of rank r to be $\sum_{m=j}^{r} n^m$ when $j \leq r$, otherwise to be 0. Take one terminating sequence, say $<n_1, n_2, \ldots, n_g, \ldots>$ to *precede* another terminating sequence, say

$<n'_1, n'_2, \ldots, n'_g, \ldots>$, if there is a k such that $n_m = n'_m$ for any m from $k + 1$ on but $n_k < n'_k$. Take the *associated terminating sequence* of A to be $<n_1, n_2, \ldots, n_g, \ldots>$, where—for each l from 1 on—n_l is the number of times '∀' occurs in A flanked on the right by a predicate variable of level l. And, lastly, take the *rank* $r(A)$ and—for each j from 1 on—the *j-height* $h_j(A)$ of A to be those of the associated terminating sequence of A.[14]

Theorem 2. Let α and α' be members of Σ_1 such that $\alpha(A) = \alpha'(A)$ for each atomic wff A of $QC^{2/\infty}$. Then $\alpha(A) = \alpha'(A)$ for each wff A of $QC^{2/\infty}$.
Proof by mathematical induction on the rank $r(A)$ of an arbitrary wff A of $QC^{2/\infty}$.
Basis: $r(A) = 0$, in which case A contains no predicate variable. Proof that $\alpha(A) = \alpha'(A)$ here is by a first induction on the length $\ell(A)$ of A. (i) Suppose $\ell(A)$ 1, in which case A is atomic. Then $\alpha(A)$ $\alpha(A)$ by the hypothesis on α and α. (ii) Suppose $\ell(A)$ 1, and A is of the sort $\sim B$. Since $\ell(B) < \ell(\sim B)$, $\alpha(B) = \alpha'(B)$ by the hypothesis of the first induction on length. Hence $\alpha(\sim B) = \alpha'(\sim B)$. Or suppose A is of the sort $B \supset C$. Since $\ell(B) < \ell(B \supset C)$ and $\ell(C) < \ell(B \supset C)$, $\alpha(B) = \alpha'(B)$ and $\alpha(C) = \alpha'(C)$ by the hypothesis of the first induction on length. Hence $\alpha(B \supset C) = \alpha'(B \supset C)$. Or suppose A is of the sort $(\forall X)B$, and let X be an arbitrary individual parameter of $QC^{2/\infty}$. Since $\ell(B(X/X)) < \ell((\forall X)B)$, $\alpha(B(X/X)) = \alpha'(B(X/X))$ by the hypothesis of the first induction on length. Hence $\alpha((\forall X)B) = \alpha'((\forall X)B)$.
Inductive Step: $r(A) > 0$. When A is of one of the three sorts $\sim B$, $B \supset C$, and $(\forall X)B$, proof that $\alpha(A) = \alpha'(A)$ is by a second induction (this one without *Basis*) on the length $\ell(A)$ of A; when A is of the sort $(\forall F^{d/l})B$, proof that $\alpha(A) = \alpha'(A)$ is by induction on the l-height $h_l(A)$ of A.
Case 1: A is of the sort $\sim B$. Since $\ell(B) < \ell(\sim B)$, $\alpha(B) = \alpha'(B)$ by the hypothesis of the second induction on length, and hence $\alpha(\sim B) = \alpha'(\sim B)$.
Case 2: A is of the sort $B \supset C$. Since $\ell(B) < \ell(B \supset C)$ and $\ell(C) < \ell(B \supset C)$, $\alpha(B) = \alpha'(B)$ and $\alpha(C) = \alpha'(C)$ by the hypothesis of the second induction on length, and hence $\alpha(B \supset C) = \alpha'(B \supset C)$.
Case 3: A is of the sort $(\forall X)B$. Let X be an arbitrary individual parameter of $QC^{2/\infty}$. Since $\ell(B(X/X)) < \ell((\forall X)B)$, $\alpha(B(X/X)) = \alpha'(B(X/X))$ by the hypothesis of the second induction on length, and hence $\alpha((\forall X)B) = \alpha'((\forall X)B)$.
Case 4: A is of the sort $(\forall F^{d/l})B$. Let C be an arbitrary wff of $QC^{2/\infty}$ of level l or less, and—in case $d > 0$—let $X_1, X_2, \ldots, X_d$ be distinct individual parameters of $QC^{2/\infty}$. *Basis:* $h_l(A) = 1$. Then no predicate variable of level l other than $F^{d/l}$ nor any predicate variable of level higher than l can occur in $(\forall F^{d/l})B$. So, with C presumed to be of level l or less, $r(B(C/F^{d/l}(X_1, X_2, \ldots, X_d))) < r((\forall F^{d/l})B)$, hence $\alpha(B(C/F^{d/l}(X_1, X_2, \ldots, X_d))) = \alpha'(B(C/F^{d/l}(X_1, X_2, \ldots, X_d)))$ be the hypothesis of the induction on rank, and hence $\alpha((\forall F^{d/l})B) = \alpha'((\forall F^{d/l})B)$. *Inductive Step:* $h_l(A) > 1$. With C presumed to be of level l or less, $h_l(B(C/F^{d/l}(X_1, X_2, \ldots, X_d))) < h_l((\forall F^{d/l})B)$, hence $\alpha(B(C/F^{d/l}(X_1, X_2, \ldots, X_d))) = \alpha'(B(C/F^{d/l}(X_1, X_2, \ldots, X_d)))$

by the hypothesis of the induction on l-height, and hence $\alpha((\forall F^{d/l})B) = \alpha'((\forall F^{d/l})B)$.[15]

Hence:

Theorem 3. *In the absence of the Axiom of Reducibility, $QC^{2/\infty}$ has a strictly truth-functional interpretation.*

3. Now count as an *axiom$_r$* of $QC^{2/\infty}$ any wff of $QC^{2/\infty}$ of any of the seven sorts **A1–A7** on p. 223, of the sort **A8** on that page (= *the Axiom of Reducibility*), or of the sort $(\forall V)A$, where—for any parameter P of $QC^{2/\infty}$ of the same type, level, and degree as V that is foreign to $(\forall V)A$—$A(P/V)$ is an axiom$_r$ of $QC^{2/\infty}$. Where A is a wff and S a set of wffs of $QC^{2/\infty}$, we shall understand by a *proof$_r$ in $QC^{2/\infty}$ of A from S* any finite column of wffs of $QC^{2/\infty}$ such that: (1) the last entry in the column is A and (2) every entry in the column belongs to S, is an axiom$_r$ of $QC^{2/\infty}$, or is the ponential of two earlier wffs in the column; we shall say that A is *provable$_r$ in $QC^{2/\infty}$ from S* if there is in $QC^{2/\infty}$ a proof$_r$ of A from S; we shall say that S is *syntactically consistent$_r$* in $QC^{2/\infty}$ if there is no wff of $QC^{2/\infty}$ such that both it and its negation are provable$_r$ in $QC^{2/\infty}$ from S; and we shall say that A is a *theorem$_r$* of $QC^{2/\infty}$ ($\vdash_r A$, for short) if there is in $QC^{2/\infty}$ a proof$_r$ of A from S.

We first obtain a generalization of **A8** with '$F^{d/l}$' in place of '$F^{d/1}$', and '$F^{d/l'}$' in place of '$F^{d/1}$' (Theorem 5); and, given this result, we obtain the counterpart in $QC^{2/\infty}$ of the familiar *Axiom of Comprehension* (Theorem 6). Proof that, for any quantification of $QC^{2/\infty}$ of the sort $(\forall F^{d/l})A$ and *any* instance A^* of $(\forall F^{d/l}) A$,

$$(\forall F^{d/l})A \supset A^*$$

is a theorem$_r$ of $QC^{2/\infty}$ can then be retrieved from [5], a task we leave to the reader.[16] In the course of proving Theorems 5 and 6 we use some thirteen lemmas, listed without proof under the common heading Lemma 4. These, as the reader may verify, do not call for **A8**; so throughout we write '$\vdash$' in place of '$\vdash_r$'.

Lemma 4. (a) *If $\vdash A$ and $\vdash A \supset B$, then $\vdash B$.*
(b) $\vdash A \supset ((B \supset B) \equiv A)$.
(c) $\vdash \sim A \supset (\sim(B \supset B) \equiv A)$.
(d) *If $\vdash A \supset B$ and $\vdash \sim A \supset B$, then $\vdash B$.*
(e) $\vdash (\forall X_1)(\forall X_2) \ldots (\forall X_d)(A \equiv B) \supset ((\forall X_1)(\forall X_2) \ldots (\forall X_d)(A \equiv C) \supset (\forall X_1)(\forall X_2) \ldots (\forall X_d)(C \equiv B))$.
(f) $\vdash (\forall X_1)(\forall X_2) \ldots (\forall X_d)(A \equiv B) \supset ((\forall X_1)(\forall X_2) \ldots (\forall X_d)(B \equiv C) \supset (\forall X_1)(\forall X_2) \ldots (\forall X_d)(A \equiv C))$.
(g) *If $\vdash A(P/V) \supset B(P/V)$, then $\vdash (\exists V)A \supset (\exists V)B$, where P is foreign to $(\exists V)A$ and $(\exists V)B$.*

(h) If ⊢ $A(P/V) \supset B$, then ⊢$(\exists V)A \supset B$, where P is foreign to $(\exists V)A$ and to B.

(i) If ⊢ $A \supset (B(P/V) \supset C(P/V))$, then ⊢ $A \supset ((\exists V)B \supset (\exists V)C)$, where P is foreign to A, $(\exists V)B$, and $(\exists V)C$.

(j) If ⊢ $(\exists V)(A \supset B)$, then ⊢ $(\forall V)A \supset B$.[17]

(k) If ⊢ $(\exists V)(A \supset B)$, then ⊢ $A \supset (\exists V)B$.[18]

(l) If ⊢ $A(B/F^{d/l}(X_1, X_2, \ldots, X_d))$, then ⊢ $(\exists F^{d/l})A$, where B is a wff of $QC^{2/\infty}$ of level l or less, and—in case $d > 0$—$X_1, X_2, \ldots, X_d$ are distinct individual parameters of $QC^{2/\infty}$.

(m) ⊢ $(\forall G^{d/l})(\exists F^{d/l})(\forall X_1)(\forall X_2) \ldots (\forall X_d)(G^{d/l}(X_1, X_2, \ldots, X_d) \equiv F^{d/l}(X_1, X_2, \ldots, X_d))$.

Theorem 5. ⊢$_r$ $(\exists F^{d/l})(\forall X_1)(\forall X_2) \ldots (\forall X_d)(F^{d/l}(X_1, X_2, \ldots, X_d) \equiv F^{d/l'}(X_1, X_2, \ldots, X_d))$, where $d > 0$ and $X_1, X_2, \ldots, X_d$ are distinct individual variables of $QC^{2/\infty}$

Proof: Let $G^{d/1}$ be a predicate parameter of $QC^{2/\infty}$ of degree d and level 1 distinct from $F^{d/l}$; let $H^{d/l}$ be a predicate parameter of $QC^{2/\infty}$ of degree d and level l distinct from $G^{d/l}$ and $F^{d/l'}$; and let $G^{d/1}$ be a predicate variable of $QC^{2/\infty}$ of degree d and level 1 distinct from $F^{d/l}$.

By L4(e)

⊢$_r$ $(\forall X_1)(\forall X_2) \ldots (\forall X_d)(G^{d/l}(X_1, X_2, \ldots, X_d) \equiv F^{d/l'}(X_1, X_2, \ldots, X_d)) \supset$
$((\forall X_1)(\forall X_2) \ldots (\forall X_d)(G^{d/1}(X_1, X_2, \ldots, X_d) \equiv$
$H^{d/l}(X_1, X_2, \ldots, X_d)) \supset (\forall X_1)(\forall X_2) \ldots (\forall X_d)(H^{d/l}(X_1, X_2, \ldots, X_d) \equiv$
$F^{d/l'}(X_1, X_2, \ldots, X_d)))$.

Hence by L4(i) and the hypothesis on $H^{d/l}$

⊢$_r$ $(\forall X_1)(\forall X_2) \ldots (\forall X_d)(G^{d/1}(X_1, X_2, \ldots, X_d) \equiv$
$F^{d/l'}(X_1, X_2, \ldots, X_d)) \supset$
$((\exists F^{d/l})(\forall X_1)(\forall X_2) \ldots (\forall X_d)(G^{d/1}(X_1, X_2, \ldots, X_d) \equiv$
$F^{d/l}(X_1, X_2, \ldots, X_d)) \supset (\exists F^{d/l})(\forall X_1)(\forall X_2) \ldots (\forall X_d)$
$(F^{d/l}(X_1, X_2, \ldots, X_d) \equiv F^{d/l'}(X_1, X_2, \ldots, X_d)))$.

Hence by L4(g) and the hypothesis on $G^{d/1}$

⊢$_r$ $(\exists G^{d/1})(\forall X_1)(\forall X_2) \ldots (\forall X_d)(G^{d/1}(X_1, X_2, \ldots, X_d) \equiv$
$F^{d/l'}(X_1, X_2, \ldots, X_d)) \supset (\exists G^{d/1})((\exists F^{d/l})(\forall X_1)(\forall X_2) \ldots (\forall X_d)$
$(G^{d/1}(X_1, X_2, \ldots, X_d) \equiv F^{d/l}(X_1, X_2, \ldots, X_d)) \supset$
$(\exists F^{d/l})(\forall X_1)(\forall X_2) \ldots (\forall X_d)(F^{d/l}(X_1, X_2, \ldots, X_d) \equiv$
$F^{d/l'}(X_1, X_2, \ldots, X_d)))$.

Hence by the *Axiom of Reducibility* and L4(a)

⊢$_r$ $(\exists G^{d/1})((\exists F^{d/l})(\forall X_1)(\forall X_2) \ldots (\forall X_d)(G^{d/1}(X_1, X_2, \ldots, X_d) \equiv$
$F^{d/l}(X_1, X_2, \ldots, X_d)) \supset (\exists F^{d/l})(\forall X_1)(\forall X_2) \ldots (\forall X_d)$
$(F^{d/l}(X_1, X_2, \ldots, X_d) \equiv F^{d/l'}(X_1, X_2, \ldots, X_d)))$.

Hence by L4(j) and the hypothesis on $G^{d/l}$

$\vdash_r (\forall G^{d/l})(\forall F^{d/l})(\exists X_1)(\forall X_2) \ldots (\forall X_d)(G^{d/l}(X_1, X_2, \ldots, X_d) \equiv F^{d/l}(X_1, X_2, \ldots, X_d)) \supset (\exists F^{d/l})(\forall X_1)(\forall X_2) \ldots (\forall X_d)$
$(F^{d/l}(X_1, X_2, \ldots, X_d) \equiv F^{d/l'}(X_1, X_2, \ldots, X_d)).$

Hence by L4(m) and L4(a)

$\vdash_r (\exists F^{d/l})(\forall X_1)(\forall X_2) \ldots (\forall X_d)(F^{d/l}(X_1, X_2, \ldots, X_d) \equiv F^{d/l'}(X_1, X_2, \ldots, X_d)).$

Theorem 6. $\vdash_r (\exists F^{d/l})(\forall X_1)(\forall X_2) \ldots (\forall X_d)(F^{d/l}(X_1, X_2, \ldots, X_d) \equiv A)$, where $F^{d/l}$ is foreign to A and—in case $d > 0$—$X_1, X_2, \ldots, X_d$ are distinct individual variables of $\mathrm{QC}^{2/\infty}$.

Proof: Let $F^{d/l}$ be a predicate parameter of $\mathrm{QC}^{2/\infty}$ of degree d and level l foreign to A.

Case 1: $d = 0$. By L4(b) and L4(c)

$$\vdash_r A \supset ((F^{d/l} \supset F^{d/l}) \equiv A)$$

and

$$\vdash_r A \supset (\sim(F^{d/l} \supset F^{d/l}) \equiv A).$$

Hence by L 4(l)

$$\vdash_r (\exists F^{d/l})(A \supset (F^{d/l} \equiv A))$$

and

$$\vdash_r (\exists F^{d/l})(\sim A \supset (F^{d/l} \equiv A)).$$

Hence by L4(k) and the hypothesis on $F^{d/l}$

$$\vdash_r A \supset (\exists F^{d/l})(F^{d/l} \equiv A)$$

and

$$\vdash_r \sim A \supset (\exists F^{d/l})(F^{d/l} \equiv A).$$

Hence by L4(d)

$$\vdash_r (\exists F^{d/l})(F^{d/l} \equiv A).$$

Case 2: $d > 0$. l' being the level of A, let $G^{d/l'}$ be a predicate parameter of $\mathrm{QC}^{2/\infty}$ of degree d and level l' foreign to A and distinct from $F^{d/l}$, and let $G^{d/l'}$ be a predicate variable of $\mathrm{QC}^{2/\infty}$ of degree d and level l' foreign to A. By L4(f)

$\vdash_r (\forall X_1)(\forall X_2) \ldots (\forall X_d)(F^{d/l}(X_1, X_2, \ldots, X_d) \equiv G^{d/l'}(X_1, X_2, \ldots, X_d)) \supset ((\forall X_1)(\forall X_2) \ldots (\forall X_d)(G^{d/l'}(X_1, X_2, \ldots, X_d) \equiv A) \supset (\forall X_1)(\forall X_2) \ldots (\forall X_d)(F^{d/l}(X_1, X_2, \ldots, X_d) \equiv A)).$

Hence by L4(g) and the hypotheses on $F^{d/l}$ and $G^{d/l'}$

230   Part 2: Truth

$\vdash_r (\exists F^{d/l})(\forall X_1)(\forall X_2) \ldots (\forall X_d)(F^{d/l}(X_1, X_2, \ldots, X_d) \equiv$
$G^{d/l'}(X_1, X_2, \ldots, X_d)) \supset (\exists F^{d/l})((\forall X_1)(\forall X_2) \ldots$
$(\forall X_d)(G^{d/l'}(X_1, X_2, \ldots, X_d) \equiv A) \supset (\forall X_1)(\forall X_2) \ldots$
$(\forall X_d)(F^{d/l}(X_1, X_2, \ldots, X_d) \equiv A))$.

Hence by T5 and L4(a)

$\vdash_r (\exists F^{d/l})((\forall X_1)(\forall X_2) \ldots (\forall X_d)(G^{d/l'}(X_1, X_2, \ldots, X_d) \equiv A) \supset$
$(\forall X_1)(\forall X_2) \ldots (\forall X_d)(F^{d/l}(X_1, X_2, \ldots, X_d) \equiv A))$.

Hence by L4(k) and the hypothesis on $F^{d/l}$

$\vdash_r (\forall X_1)(\forall X_2) \ldots (\forall X_d)(G^{d/l'}(X_1, X_2, \ldots, X_d) \equiv A) \supset$
$(\exists F^{d/l})(\forall X_1)(\forall X_2) \ldots (\forall X_d)(F^{d/l}(X_1, X_2, \ldots, X_d) \equiv A)$.

Hence by L4(h) and the hypotheses on $G^{d/l'}$ and $G^{d/l'}$

$\vdash_r (\exists G^{d/l'})(\forall X_1)(\forall X_2) \ldots (\forall X_d)(G^{d/l'}(X_1, X_2, \ldots, X_d) \equiv A) \supset$
$(\exists F^{d/l})(\forall X_1)(\forall X_2) \ldots (\forall X_d)(F^{d/l}(X_1, X_2, \ldots, X_d) \equiv A)$.

Hence by L4(l) and L4(a)

$\vdash_r (\exists F^{d/l})(\forall X_1)(\forall X_2) \ldots (\forall X_d)(F^{d/l}(X_1, X_2, \ldots, X_d) \equiv A)$.

Hence, by an adaptation of Henkin's argument in [5]:

Theorem 7. $\vdash_r (\forall F^{d/l})A \supset A^*$, *for any instance* A^* *of* $(\forall F^{d/l})A$.

To show that in the presence of **A8** $QC^{2/\infty}$ still has a truth-functional interpretation, read '$\vdash_r A$' for '$\vdash A$' in condition (1) on p. 224, drop the (now idle) qualifier 'permissible' in condition (4) on that page and define Σ_2 as Σ_1 was defined there, but with (iv) now amended to read:

(iv′) for any quantification of $QC^{2/\infty}$ of the sort $(\forall F^{d/l})A$, $\alpha((\forall F^{d/l})A) = \mathbf{T}$ if and only if $\alpha(A^*) = \mathbf{T}$ for every instance A^* of $(\forall F^{d/l})A$.

Supposing a finite set S of wffs of $QC^{2/\infty}$ to be syntactically consistent in $QC^{2/\infty}$, one can again extend S into a set S_∞ boasting features (i_∞)–(iv_∞) on p. 225. But, if a quantification $(\forall X)A$ of $QC^{2/\infty}$ belongs to S_∞, then in view again of **A6** so does every instance of $(\forall X)A$; and if a quantification $(\forall F^{d/l})A$ of $QC^{2/\infty}$, then in view of Theorem 7 so does every instance of $(\forall F^{d/l})A$. Hence each member of S is sure to evaluate to **T** under the member α of Σ_2 that assigns **T** to every wff of $QC^{2/\infty}$ in S_∞ and **F** to everyone not in S_∞. Hence any wff of $QC^{2/\infty}$ evaluating to **T** under all the members of Σ_2 is a theorem$_r$ of $QC^{2/\infty}$. But any theorem$_r$ of $QC^{2/\infty}$ can be shown to evaluate to **T** under all members of Σ_2. Hence Σ_2 meets all four conditions (1)–(4). Hence:

Theorem 8. *In the presence (as well as in the absence) of the Axiom of Reducibility,* $QC^{2/\infty}$ *has a truth-functional interpretation.*

Truth-Functionality and the Ramified Theory of Types 231

4. Proof that Σ_2—now the *principal* interpretation of $QC^{2/\infty}$—fails to meet condition (5) on p. 224 calls for some model-theoretic notions (one of them adapted to serve the purpose at hand).

Take a *model* to be any non-empty set. Where D is a domain, take a D-*interpretation* of the parameters of $QC^{2/\infty}$ to be any function I_D from the predicate parameters of $QC^{2/\infty}$ of degree 0 to $\{T, F\}$, from the individual parameters of $QC^{2/\infty}$ to D, and from the predicate parameters of $QC^{2/\infty}$ of non-zero degree d to the power set of D^d ($= \underbrace{D \times D \times \ldots \times D}_{d \text{ times}}$).[19]

Where D is a domain, I_D a D-interpretation of the parameters of $QC^{2/\infty}$, and P a parameter of $QC^{2/\infty}$, take a P-*variant* of I_D to be any D-interpretation of the parameters of $QC^{2/\infty}$ that agrees with I_D on all the parameters of $QC^{2/\infty}$ other than P (and possibly on P as well). And, where A is a wff of $QC^{2/\infty}$, D a domain, and I_D a D-interpretation of the parameters of $QC^{2/\infty}$, take A to be *true* on I_D if:

(a) in case A is a predicate parameter of $QC^{2/\infty}$ of degree 0, $I_D(A) = T$,

(b) in case A is of the sort $F^{d/l}(X_1, X_2, \ldots, X_d)$ for some non-zero d, $<I_D(X_1), I_D(X_2), \ldots, I_D(X_d)>$ belongs to $I_D(F^{d/l})$,

(c) in case A is of the sort $\sim B$, B is not true on I_D,

(d) in case A is of the sort $B \supset C$, B is not true on I_D or C is, and

(e) in case A is of the sort $(\forall V)B$, $B(P/V)$ (P here the alphabetically earliest parameter of $QC^{2/\infty}$ of the same type, level, and degree as V that is foreign to $(\forall V)B$) is true on every P-variant of I_D.

Crucial among D-interpretations are those—to be called *Henkin D-interpretations*—where each member of the domain D is assigned to an individual parameter of $QC^{2/\infty}$ (more formally, where for each member d of the domain D there is an individual parameter X of $QC^{2/\infty}$ such that $I_D(X) = d$). Extending a familiar result for QC^1, one can indeed show that:

Theorem 9. *Let D be a domain, and I_D be a Henkin D-interpretation of the parameters $QC^{2/\infty}$. Then a quantification $(\forall X)A$ of $QC^{2/\infty}$ is true on I_D if and only if every instance of $(\forall X)A$ is true on I_D.*[20]

And crucial among Henkin D-interpretations are those where the domain D is finite. Take indeed an arbitrary quantification $(\forall F^{d/l})A$ of $QC^{2/\infty}$; let $F^{d/l}$ be the alphabetically earliest predicate parameter of $QC^{2/\infty}$ of the same level and degree as $F^{d/l}$ that is foreign to $(\forall F^{d/l})A$; in case $d > 0$, let $X_1, X_2, \ldots, X_d$ be in alphabetic order the first d individual parameters of $QC^{2/\infty}$ that are foreign to $(\forall F^{d/l})A$; let D be a finite domain; let I_D be a Henkin D-interpretation of the parameters of $QC^{2/\infty}$; and let I'_D be an $F^{d/l}$-variant of I_D. There exists then a wff B of $QC^{2/\infty}$, to be known as the *wff-associate* of I'_D, such that $A(F^{d/l}/F^{d/l})$ is true on I'_D if and only if $A(B/F^{d/l}(X_1, X_2, \ldots, X_d))$ is true on I_D; and, as a result, $(\forall F^{d/l})A$ proves to be true on I_D if and only if all its instances do.

B is as in the following table, where $d_1, d_2, \ldots, d_n$ ($n > 0$) serve as the

232   Part 2: Truth

various members of D, Y_i is for each i from 1 through n the alphabetically earliest individual parameter of $QC^{2/\infty}$ to which member d_i of D is assigned in I'_D, and $I_1 = I_2$ is short for $(\forall f)(f(I_1) \supset f(I_2))$:

d	$I'_D(F^{d/l})$	B
0	T	$\mathbf{x} = \mathbf{x}$
	F	$\sim(\mathbf{x} = \mathbf{x})$
1	$\varnothing$ $\{d_i\}$ $\{d_i, d_j\}$ etc.	$\sim(X_1 = X_1)$ $X_1 = Y_i$ $X_1 = Y_i \lor X_1 = Y_j$ etc.
2	$\varnothing$ $\{<d_{1_i}, d_{2_i}>\}$ $\{<d_{1_i}, d_{2_i}>, <d_{1_j}, d_{2_j}>\}$ etc.	$\sim(X_1 = X_1)$ $X_1 = Y_{1_i}\ \&\ X_2 = Y_{2_i}$ $(X_1 = Y_{1_i}\ \&\ X_2 = Y_{2_i})$ $\lor\ (X_1 = Y_{1_j}\ \&\ X_2 = Y_{2_j})$ etc.
etc.	etc.	etc.

And proof that $A(F^{d/l}/F^{d/l})$ is true on I'_D if and only if $A(B/F^{d/l}(X_1, X_2, \ldots, X_d))$ is true on I_D is by mathematical induction on the length of A.[21]

Now suppose that $(\forall F^{d/l})A$ is true on I_D. Then $A(B/F^{d/l}(X_1, X_2, \ldots, X_d))$ is sure to be true on I_D for any wff B of $QC^{2/\infty}$ and—in case $d > 0$—any distinct individual parameters $X_1, X_2, \ldots, X_d$ of $QC^{2/\infty}$. Suppose, on the other hand, that $(\forall F^{d/l})A$ is not true on I_D. Then there is an $F^{d/l}$-variant I'_D of I_D such that $A(F^{d/l}/F^{d/l})$ is not true on I'_D, and hence by the foregoing result there is a wff B of $QC^{2/\infty}$ (to wit: the wff-associate of I'_D), and—in case $d > 0$—there are distinct individual parameters $X_1, X_2, \ldots, X_d$ of $QC^{2/\infty}$, such that $A(B/F^{d/l}(X_1, X_2, \ldots, X_d))$ is not true on I_D itself. Hence:

Theorem 10. *Let D be a finite domain, and I_D be a Henkin D-interpretation of the parameters of $QC^{2/\infty}$. Then a quantification $(\forall F^{d/l})A$ of $QC^{2/\infty}$ is true on I_D if and only if every instance of $(\forall F^{d/l})A$ is true on I_D.*

Proof of our last theorem is within reach. Indeed, let D and D' respectively be $\{1\}$ and $\{1, 2\}$; let I_D assign T to every predicate parameter of $QC^{2/\infty}$ of degree 0, 1 to every individual parameter of $QC^{2/\infty}$, and D^d to every predicate parameter of $QC^{2/\infty}$ of non-zero degree d; let I'_D assign **T** to every predicate parameter of $QC^{2/\infty}$ of degree 0, 1 to 'a', 2 to every other individual parameter of $QC^{2/\infty}$, and D'^d to every predicate parameter of $QC^{2/\infty}$ of non-zero degree d; let α be the truth-value function for $QC^{2/\infty}$ such that, for every wff A of $QC^{2/\infty}$, $\alpha(A) = \mathbf{T}$ if and only if A is true on I_D; and let α' be the one such that, for any such A, $\alpha'(A) = \mathbf{T}$ if and only if A is true on I'_D. It is easily verified with the aid of Theorems 9 and 10 that α and α' both belong to the family Σ_2 of p. 230, that α and α' agree on all atomic wffs of $QC^{2/\infty}$ (indeed, on all wffs of $QC^{2/\infty}$ of rank 1), and yet that α and α' disagree on '$(\exists f)(\exists x)(\exists y)(f(x)\ \&\ \sim f(y))$', which evaluates to **F** on α but to **T** on α'. (For proof that the wff in question evaluates to **F** on α, note that '$(\exists x)(\exists y)(f(x)\ \&\ \sim f(y))$' cannot be true on either of the two f-variants of I_D; for proof that it evaluates to **T** on α', note that '$(\exists x)(\exists y)(f(x)\ \&\ \sim f(y))$' is true on the f-variant of I'_D that assigns $\{1\}$ to 'f'.)[22]

Hence Σ_2 does not meet condition (5) on p. 224. Hence:

Theorem 11. *In the presence of the Axiom of Reducibility, $QC^{2/\infty}$ has a truth-functional interpretation which is not strictly truth-functional.*[23]

5. Church sketches in [2] a semantic account of $QC^{2/\infty}$ with two truth-values per level.[24] The account uses models. To mimic it here, acknowledge with Church two truth-values $\mathbf{T}^l$ and $\mathbf{F}^l$ for each level l. Understand by a *system of truth-value functions* for $QC^{2/\infty}$ any sequence of the sort $<\alpha_1, \alpha_2, \alpha_3, \ldots>$, where—for each l from 1 on—α^l is a function from the wffs of $QC^{2/\infty}$ of level l to $\{\mathbf{T}^l, \mathbf{F}^l\}$ such that:

(i) $\alpha_l(\sim A) = \mathbf{T}^l$ if and only if $\alpha_l(A) = \mathbf{F}^l$,

(ii) $\alpha_l(A \supset B) = \mathbf{T}^l$ if and only if $\alpha_j(A) = \mathbf{F}^j$ or $\alpha_k(B) = \mathbf{T}^k$ (j here the level of A and k that of B),

(iii) $\alpha_l((\forall X)A) = \mathbf{T}^l$ if and only if $\alpha_l(A(X/X)) = \mathbf{T}^l$ for every individual parameter X of $QC^{2/\infty}$, and

(iv) $\alpha_l((\forall F^{d/j})A) = \mathbf{T}^l(j < l)$ if and only if $\alpha_k(A(B/F^{d/l}(X_1, X_2, \ldots, X_d))) = \mathbf{T}^k$ (k here the level of $A(B/F^{d/j}(X_1, X_2, \ldots, X_d))$) for every wff B of $QC^{2/\infty}$ of level j or less, and—in case $d > 0$—any distinct individual parameters $X_1, X_2, \ldots, X_d$ of $QC^{2/\infty}$.

And take a wff A of $QC^{2/\infty}$ of level l to be *true* on a system $<\alpha_1, \alpha_2, \alpha_3, \ldots>$ of truth-value functions for $QC^{2/\infty}$ if $\alpha_l(A) = \mathbf{T}^l$.

It can be verified that:

(1) $\vdash_r A$ if and only if A is true on every system of truth-value functions for $QC^{2/\infty}$, and

(2) two systems of truth-value functions for $QC^{2/\infty}$ that agree on all the atomic wffs of $QC^{2/\infty}$ are sure to agree on all the non-atomic ones.

Indeed, the induction that saw Theorem 2 through will—*mutatis mutandis*—see (2) through.

234   Part 2: Truth

Suppose, however, that B in condition (iv) is allowed to be of any level whatever. It then follows that:

(3) $\vdash_r A$ if and only if A is true on every system of truth-value functions for $QC^{2/\infty}$,

but (2) fails, as a straightforward generalization of the argument in Section 4 will show.

So analogues of Theorems 1, 3, 8, and 11 hold for Church's account.

Notes

1. For a formal account of the matter, see Section 2, where (b) is broken into three separate conditions: one dealing with negations, one with conditionals, and one with quantifications.

2. See [1], pp. 263–67, [13], pp. 5–14, [3], and [6]. $QC^1_=$, the first-order quantificational calculus with identity, also has a strictly truth-functional interpretation; see [7] on the matter.

3. And first reported in [11]. That QC^2 has a truth-functional interpretation follows in effect from results in [12].

4. Two questions remained open when this paper was written: in the absence of Russell's axiom does $QC^{\infty/\infty}$ (and, in particular, $QC^{2/\infty}$) have any truth-functional interpretation which is not strictly truth-functional; and in the presence of that axiom does $QC^{\infty/\infty}$ (and, in particular, $QC^{2/\infty}$) have a truth-functional interpretation which—unlike its principal one—is strictly truth-functional? The answer to the second question is now known to be Yes. See pp. 134–35, [9], and [10] on the matter.

5. Our variables are what the literature calls *bound* variables, and our parameters what it calls *free* variables.

6. When $d = 0$, $F^{d/l}(X_1, X_2, \ldots, X_d)$ is to be understood as just $F^{d/l}$.

7. Under the present account of things formulas in which identical quantifiers overlap do not count as well-formed. '&', '∨', '≡', and '∃', which we come to employ besides '∼', '⊃', and '∀', are presumed to be defined in the usual manner.

8. Simultaneous substitutions can of course be broken into sequences of single ones. See [2], p. 82, on this point.

9. It is easily verified that if $(\forall F^{d/l})A$ and B are wffs of $QC^{2/\infty}$, then $(A)(B/F^{d/l}(X_1, X_2, \ldots, X_d))$ is sure to be a wff of $QC^{2/\infty}$. From this point on we drop a number of inessential parentheses, thus writing '$A \supset B$' in lieu of '$(A \supset B)$', '$A(P/V)$' in lieu of '$(A)(P/V)$', etc.

10. The trick of counting $(\forall V)A$ an axiom if—for suitable P—$A(P/V)$ is an axiom, stems from Fitch. See on the matter the closing paper of this volume, #35. Note in connection with **A5** that with $A \supset (\forall V)A$—and, hence, A—presumed here to be a wff of $QC^{2/\infty}$, V is sure to be foreign to A.

11. In the absence of **A8**, $(\forall F^{d/l})A \supset A^*$ is provable in $QC^{2/\infty}$ for an occasional non-predicative instance A^* of $(\forall F^{d/l})A$. For example, '$(\forall f)f(a) \supset ((f(a) \& (\forall f)f(a)) \vee (f(a) \& \sim(\forall f)f(a)))$' is provable in $QC^{2/\infty}$, even though the wff '$(f(a) \& (\forall f)f(a)) \vee (f(a) \& \sim(\forall f)f(a))$' is one level higher than the predicate variable 'f'. But only upon adoption of **A8** does $(\forall F^{d/l})A \supset A^*$ become provable in $QC^{2/\infty}$ for *every* non-predicative instance A^* of $(\forall F^{d/l})A$.

12. The reader may wish to verify that conditions (2)–(4) are equivalent to the following:

(2') for any member α of Σ and any negation $\sim A$ of $QC^{2/\infty}$, $\alpha(\sim A) = \mathsf{T}$ if and only if $\alpha(A) = \mathsf{F}$,

(3') for any member α of Σ and any conditional $A \supset B$ of $QC^{2/\infty}$, $\alpha(A \supset B) = \mathsf{T}$ if and only if $\alpha(A) = \mathsf{F}$ or $\alpha(B) = \mathsf{T}$, and

(4') for any member α of Σ and any quantification $(\forall V)A$ of $QC^{2/\infty}$, $\alpha((\forall V)A) = \mathsf{T}$ if and only if $\alpha(A^*) = \mathsf{T}$ for every instance A^* of $(\forall V)A$ such that $\vdash (\forall V)A \supset A^*$.

13. The instructions stem largely from [4].

14. The definition of $r(A)$ in the original version of this paper was incorrect, as Ray Gumb noted. The present one is largely due to him.

15. Note as regards Cases 1 − 3 that $r(B) = r(\sim B)$, $r(B) < r(B \supset C)$, $r(C) < r(B \supset C)$, and $r(B(X/X)) = r((\forall X)B)$. So the hypothesis of the induction on rank cannot be appealed to in any of these three cases.
And note as regards the *Inductive Step* of Case 4 that when $h_I((\forall F^{d/l})B) > 1$, at least one predicate variable of level l besides $F^{d/l}$ is sure to occur in $(\forall F^{d/l})B$ or at least one of level higher than l is. So, with C presumed to be of level l or less, $r(B(C/F^{d/l}(X_1, X_2, \ldots, X_d)))$ is sure to equal $r((\forall F^{d/l})B)$. So the hypothesis of the induction on rank cannot be appealed to in this subcase of Case 4.
16. A detailed proof of the result appears in [10], pp. 177–83.
17. With $(\forall V)A \supset B$ presumed here to be a wff of $QC^{2/\infty}$, V is sure to be foreign to B.
18. With $A \supset (\exists V)B$ presumed here to be a wff of $QC^{2/\infty}$, V is sure to be foreign to A.
19. In model-theoretic accounts of $QC^{2/\infty}$, $I_D(F^{d/l})$, where $d > 0$, would be required to be a subset of D^d of *level l*. But the restriction would play no role here, and is intentionally dropped.
20. Proof of Theorem 9 can be retrieved from Sections 7.1 and 4.1 of [10]. The *D*-interpretations under consideration are called *Henkin D-interpretations* because of the role their counterparts for QC^1 play in [4].
21. For further details see [10], pp. 205–07.
22. The example comes from [11].
23. $QC^{2/\infty}$ (and, more generally, $QC^{\infty/\infty}$) admits of course of other interpretations besides its *principal* or *intended* one. That one of them is strictly truth-functional, and this in the presence of Russell's axiom, was mentioned in Note 4 and will be demonstrated in the next paper.
24. See pp. 347–48, Note 577.

References

[1] Beth, E. W. 1959. *The Foundations of Mathematics*. Amsterdam: North-Holland.
[2] Church, A. 1956. *Introduction to Mathematical Logic, Volume I*. Princeton: Princeton University Press.
[3] Dunn, M., and Belnap, N. D. Jr. 1968. "The Substitution Interpretation of the Quantifiers." *Noûs* 2: 113–18.
[4] Henkin, L. 1949. "The Completeness of the First-Order Functional Calculus." *The Journal of Symbolic Logic* (hereafter *JSL*) 14: 159–66.
[5] ———. 1953. "Banishing the Rule of Substitution for Functional Variables." *JSL* 18: 201–08.
[6] Leblanc, H. 1968. "A Simplified Account of Validity and Implication for Quantificational Logic." *JSL* 33: 231–35 (#8 in this volume).
[7] ———. 1969. "A Simplified Strong Completeness Proof for $QC_=$." *Akten des XIV. Internationalen Kongresses für Philosophie* 3: 83–96. Vienna: Verlag Herder (#9 in this volume).
[8] ———. 1969. "Three Generalizations of a Theorem of Beth's." *Logique et Analyse* 12: 205–20 (#11 in this volume).
[9] ———. 1975. "That *Principia Mathematica*, First Edition, has a Predicative Interpretation After All." *The Journal of Philosophical Logic* 4: 67–70 (#16 in this volume).
[10] ———. 1976. *Truth-Value Semantics*. Amsterdam: North-Holland.
[11] Leblanc, H., and Meyer, R. K. 1970. "Truth-Value Semantics for the Theory of Types." *Philosophical Problems in Logic: Some Recent Developments*. Dordrecht: Reidel, pp. 77–101 (#12 in this volume).
[12] Schütte, K. 1960. "Syntactical and Semantical Properties of Simple Type Theory." *JSL* 25: 305–26.
[13] ———. 1962. *Lecture Notes in Mathematical Logic, Volume I*. The Pennsylvania State University.
[14] Whitehead, A. N., and Russell, B. 1910–13. *Principia Mathematica*. Cambridge: Cambridge University Press.

16
That Principia Mathematica, *First Edition*, Has a Predicative Interpretation After All

Call a wff A of QC^2, the quantificational calculus of order two, *predicative* if A has no component of the sort $(\forall F^d)B$;[1] otherwise, call A *impredicative*. In [4], QC^2 numbers among its axioms *all* wffs of the sort

$$(\exists F^d)(\forall X_1)(\forall X_2) \ldots (\forall X_d)(F^d(X_1, X_2, \ldots, X_d) \equiv A) \quad (Comp)$$

(F^d foreign to A, and $X_1, X_2, \ldots, X_d$ distinct from one another), hence *both* those with a predicative A and those with an impredicative one.[2] By contrast, the predicative fragment $QC^{2!}$ of QC^2 numbers among its axioms *only* those wffs of the sort *Comp* that show a predicative A.[3]

$QC^{2!}$, as expected, has a predicative interpretation. In answer to a question raised some years back, I show that the allegedly impredicative QC^2 also does.[4] The result is readily extended to suit QC^∞, the quantificational calculus of order omega. So *Principia Mathematica*, first edition, has a predicative interpretation after all, a point which may not have been noted before.

Understand by *a truth-value function for* QC^2 any function from the wffs of QC^2 to $\{\mathbf{T}, \mathbf{F}\}$. Call a truth-value function α for QC^2 *general* if α meets the following four conditions:

(a) For any negation $\sim A$ of QC^2, $\alpha(\sim A) = \mathbf{T}$ if and only if $\alpha(A) = \mathbf{F}$,

(b) For any conditional $A \supset B$ of QC^2, $\alpha(A \supset B) = \mathbf{T}$ if and only if $\alpha(A) = \mathbf{F}$ or $\alpha(B) = \mathbf{T}$,

(c) For any quantification $(\forall X)A$ of QC^2, $\alpha((\forall X)A) = \mathbf{T}$ if and only if $\alpha(A(X/X)) = \mathbf{T}$ for every individual parameter X of QC^2,[5] and

(d) For any quantification $(\forall F^d)A$ of QC^2, $\alpha((\forall F^d)A) = \mathbf{T}$ if and only if $\alpha(A(B/F^d(X_1, X_2, \ldots, X_d))) = \mathbf{T}$ for *every wff B of* QC^2 and every d-tuple $<X_1, X_2, \ldots, X_d>$ of distinct individual parameters of QC^2.[6]

Call a truth-function α for QC^2 *predicative* if α meets the first three of the foregoing conditions, plus:

(d') For any quantification $(\forall F^d)A$ of QC^2, $\alpha((\forall F^d)A) = \mathbf{T}$ if and only if

236

That *Principia Mathematica Has a Predicative Interpretation After All* 237

$\alpha(A(B/F^d(X_1,X_2, \ldots,X_d))) = \mathbf{T}$ for *every predicative wff B of* QC^2 and every *d*-tuple $<X_1,X_2, \ldots,X_d>$ of distinct individual parameters of QC^2. Take a set Σ of truth-value functions for QC^2 to count as *an interpretation of* QC^2 if the theorems of QC^2 and the wffs of QC^2 that evaluate to $\mathbf{T}$ under all members of Σ coincide; and take the set to count as *a predicative interpretation of* QC^2 if all members of Σ are predicative.[7]

I showed in [5] (and, more fully, in [8]) that the set Σ' of all general truth-value functions for QC^2 counts as an interpretation of QC^2. Proof will now be given that the set Σ'' of all predicative truth-value functions for QC^2 under which *Comp* evaluates to $\mathbf{T}$ also counts as an interpretation of QC^2, and hence that QC^2 has a predicative (as well as a non-predicative) interpretation.

Σ' and Σ'', incidentally, are distinct sets. Meyer and I constructed in [9] two members of Σ' which, though they agree on all predicative wffs of QC^2, disagree on some impredicative ones. On the other hand, proof will be found in [8] that any two members of Σ'' agreeing on all predicative wffs of QC^2 agree on all impredicative ones as well.[8]

Proof of the result in [5] begins thusly. Given a wff A of QC^2 that is not provable in QC^2, you extend the set $\{\sim A\}$ into a set $\{\sim A\}_\infty$ such that

(i) $\{\sim A\}_\infty$ is maximally consistent,

(ii) For any quantification $(\forall X)B$ of QC^2, $(\forall X)B$ belongs to $\{\sim A\}_\infty$ if and only if $B(X/X)$ belongs to $\{\sim A\}_\infty$ for every individual parameter X of QC^2,

(iii) For any quantification $(\forall F^d)B$ of QC^2, if $(\forall F^d)B$ belongs to $\{\sim A\}_\infty$, then so does $B(C/F^d(X_1,X_2, \ldots,X_d))$ for every wff C of QC^2,[9]

and

(iv) For any quantification $(\forall F^d)B$ of QC^2, if $(\forall F^d)B$ does not belong to $\{\sim A\}_\infty$, then there is a predicate parameter F^d of QC^2 such that $B(F^d/F^d)$ does not belong to $\{\sim A\}_\infty$ either.[10]

Now let α be the result of assigning $\mathbf{T}$ to all wffs of QC^2 that belong to $\{\sim A\}_\infty$ and $\mathbf{F}$ to the rest. It is easily verified, given (i)–(ii), that α meets conditions (a)–(c) on p. 236. But, if there is a predicate parameter F^d of QC^2 such that $B(F^d/F^d)$ does not belong to $\{\sim A\}_\infty$ (see (iv)),[11] then there is a wff C of QC^2—to wit: $F^d(X_1,X_2, \ldots,X_d)$—such that $B(C/F^d(X_1,X_2, \ldots,X_d))$ does not belong to $\{\sim A\}_\infty$. So, given (iii)–(iv), α is sure to meet condition (d) on p. 236. So α is a general truth-value function for QC^2. So any wff of QC^2 that evaluates to $\mathbf{T}$ under all members of Σ' is provable in QC^2.

Note, though, that if $B(C/F^d(X_1,X_2, \ldots,X_d))$ belongs to $\{\sim A\}_\infty$ for every wff C of QC^2 (see (iii)), then $B(C/F^d(X_1,X_2, \ldots,X_d))$ belongs to $\{\sim A\}_\infty$ for every *predicative* wff C of QC^2. Note further that $F^d(X_1,X_2, \ldots,X_d)$ is a *predicative* wff of QC^2. So, if $(\forall F^d)B$ does not belong to $\{\sim A\}_\infty$ (see (iv)), then there is a *predicative* wff C of QC^2 such that $B(C/F^d(X_1,X_2, \ldots,X_d))$ does not belong to $\{\sim A\}_\infty$ either. So α meets condition (d') on pp. 236–237 as well as condition (d), and hence α is a predicative as well as a general truth-value function for QC^2.[12] But, as *Comp* is provable from $\{\sim A\}_\infty$ in QC^2 and $\{\sim A\}_\infty$ is maximally consistent (see (i)), *Comp* is sure to belong to $\{\sim A\}_\infty$. So *Comp* is sure to evaluate

238   Part 2: Truth

to **T** under α. So any wff of QC^2 that evaluates to **T** under all members of Σ'' is provable in QC^2. But, as the reader may wish to verify, any wff of QC^2 that is provable in QC^2 evaluates to **T** under all members of Σ''. So Σ'' (as well as Σ') counts as an interpretation of QC^2.

Notes

1. Equivalently, if A counts as a wff of QC^1, the quantificational calculus of order one. My use of the epithet 'predicative' stems from Russell's, who on p. 189 of [11] talks of a predicative function as one not involving reference to any collection of functions. I take QC^2 to have '$\sim$', '$\supset$', and '$\forall$' as its primitive logical operators. I refer to the individual variables (= bound individual variables) of QC^2 by means of 'X', to its individual parameters (= *free* individual variables) by means of 'X', to its predicate variables (= bound predicate variables) by means of 'F^d', and to its predicate parameters (= free predicate variables) by means of 'F^d'.

2. Henkin shows in [4] that his axiomatization of QC^2 is tantamount—in all essential respects—to Church's on pp. 296–97 of [1]. '*Comp*' is short of course for 'Comprehension', a label pinned in axiomatic set theory on an axiom schema very much like *Comp*.

3. As editing Henkin's argument in [4] will bear out, the axiomatization of $QC^{2!}$ I envisage here is tantamount—in all essential respects—to Church's on pp. 348–49 of [1].

4. The question is discussed (in different, but equivalent, terms) in [6] and [10]. (As established in [8], pp. 208–09, any predicative interpretation of QC^2 is strictly truth-functional.) For further details, see pp. 134–35.

5. $A(X/X)$ here is the result of replacing X everywhere in A by X.

6. The notation '$A(B/F^d(X^1,X^2, \ldots, X_d))$' is explicated on pp. 201–202. It plays essentially the same role as Church's '$\check{S}_B^{F^d(X_1,X_2,\ldots,X_d)}A|$' in [1]. My use of the epithet 'general' stems from [3].

7. My account of a predicative interpretation for QC^2 is deliberately couched in the truth-value idiom I have championed these last few years. It is in line, I believe, with its model-theoretic counterpart, at any rate with such intimations as the literature offers of what a predicative model for QC^2 should be like. Writers on the subject are loath, it seems, to spell this out.

8. Proof of the result is sketched in [10]. But some of the definitions there have to be touched up, as my friend R. D. Gumb pointed out to me.

9. This because $(\forall F^d)B \supset B(C/F^d(X_1,X_2, \ldots, X_d))$ is provable in QC^2 for every wff C of QC^2.

10. This because $\{\sim A\}_\infty$ is so constructed as to contain at least one conditional of the sort $B(F^d/F^d) \supset (\forall F^d)B$ $(B(F^d/F^d)$ the result of replacing F_d everywhere in B by F^d) for every quantification $(\forall F^d)B$ of QC^2. The construction is reminiscent of course by one in [2].

11. $B(F^d/F^d)$ is to be understood as in note 10.

12. Hence, incidentally, the set Σ''' of all *predicative* truth-value functions for $QC^{2!}$ constitutes an interpretation for $QC^{2!}$, the result mentioned in paragraph 2 of the paper.

References

[1] Church, A. 1956. *Introduction to Mathematical Logic, Volume I*. Princeton: Princeton University Press.

[2] Henkin, L. 1949. "The Completeness of the First-Order Functional Calculus." *The Journal of Symbolic Logic* (hereafter *JSL*) 14: 159–66.

[3] ―――. 1950. "Completeness in the Theory of Types." *JSL* 15: 81–91.

[4] ―――. 1953. "Banishing the Rule of Substitution for Functional Variables." *JSL* 18: 201–08.

[5] Leblanc, H. 1969. "Three Generalizations of a Theorem of Beth's." *Logique et Analyse* 12: 205–20 (#11 in this volume).

[6] ———— . 1972. "Matters of Relevance." *Journal of Philosophical Logic* 1: 269–86 (#14 in this volume).
[7] ———— . 1972. "Wittgenstein and the Truth-Functionality Thesis." *American Philosophical Quarterly* 9: 271–74 (#13 in this volume).
[8] ———— . 1976. *Truth-Value Semantics*. Amsterdam: North-Holland.
[9] Leblanc, H., and Meyer, R. K. 1970. "Truth-Value Semantics for the Theory of Types." *Philosophical Problems in Logic. Some Recent Developments*, pp. 77–101. Dordrecht: Reidel (#12 in this volume).
[10] Leblanc, H., and Weaver, G. 1973. "Truth-Functionality and the Ramified Theory of Types." *Truth, Syntax and Modality*, pp. 148–73 (#15 in this volume).
[11] Russell, B. 1919. *Introduction to Mathematical Philosophy*. London: Allen and Unwin.

17

A Strong Completeness Theorem
For Three-Valued Logic: Part I

H. Goldberg and G. Weaver, coauthors

We establish here that Wajsberg's axiomatization of SC_3, the three-valued sentential calculus, is *strongly complete* (= Theorem 1), and by rebound *weakly complete* (= Theorem 2). Theorem 2 is a familiar result, obtained by Wajsberg himself in [5], and Theorem 1 can be recovered from results in [3]. But because of its simplicity and directness our proof of Theorem 1 may be worth reporting.[1]

The *primitive signs* of SC_3 are '~', '⊃', '(', ')', and a denumerable infinity of sentence letters, say 'p', 'q', 'r', 'p'', 'q'', 'r'', etc. The *wffs* of SC_3 are those sentence letters, plus all formulas of the sort $\sim A$, where A is a wff, plus all those of the sort $(A \supset B)$, where A and B are wffs. The *length* $l(P)$ of a sentence letter P is 1; the length $l(\sim A)$ of a negation $\sim A$ is $l(A)+1$; and the length $l((A \supset B))$ of a conditional $(A \supset B)$ is $l(A)+l(B) + 1$. We abbreviate the wff '$\sim(p \supset p)$' as 'f', and wffs of the sort $(A \supset \sim A)$ as $-A$. We also omit outer parentheses whenever clarity permits. The *axioms* of SC_3 are all wffs of SC_3 of the following four sorts:

A1. $A \supset (B \supset A)$,

A2. $(A \supset B) \supset ((B \supset C) \supset (A \supset C))$,

A3. $(-A \supset A) \supset A$,

A4. $(\sim A \supset \sim B) \supset (B \supset A)$.

A wff A of SC_3 is *provable from a set S of wffs of* SC_3—$S \vdash A$, for short—if there is a column of wffs of SC_3 (called a proof of A from S) which closes with A and every entry of which is an axiom, a member of S, or the ponential of two earlier entries in the column. A wff A of SC_3 is *provable*—$\vdash A$, for short—if A is provable from $\emptyset$. A set S of wffs of SC_3 is *syntactically (in)consistent* if there is a (there is no) wff A of SC_3 such that both A and $\sim A$ are provable from S. And S is *maximally consistent* if (a) S is syntactically consistent, and (b) $S \vdash A$ for any wff A of SC_3 such that $S \cup \{A\}$ is syntactically consistent.

240

Our *truth-values* are the designated 1 and the undesignated 2 and 3. *Truth-value assignments* are functions from *all* the sentence letters of SC_3 to $\{1,2,3\}$,[2] and the truth-values under these of negations and conditionals are reckoned as the following matrix directs:

Matrix 1

			B		
$A \supset B$		1	2	3	$\sim A$
	1	1	2	3	3
A	2	1	1	2	2
	3	1	1	1	1

A set *S* of wffs of SC_3 is *semantically consistent* if there is a truth-value assignment under which all members of *S* evaluate to 1. *S entails* a wff *A* of SC_3—$S \models A$, for short—if, no matter the truth-value assignment α, *A* evaluates to 1 under α if all members of *S* do. And *A* is *valid*—$\models A$, for short—if, no matter the truth-value assignment α, *A* evaluates to 1 under α.

We collect in Lemma 1 some auxiliary facts about provability and syntactic inconsistency. L1(a)–(d) hold by definition. Instructions for proving L1(e)–(p) can be found in [5].

Lemma 1. (a) *If* $S \vdash A$, *then* $S' \vdash A$ *for every superset* S' *of* S.[3]
(b) *If* $S \vdash A$, *then there is a finite subset* S' *of* S *such that* $S' \vdash A$.
(c) *If A belongs to S, then* $S \vdash A$.
(d) *If* $S \vdash A$ *and* $S \vdash A \supset B$, *then* $S \vdash B$.
(e) $\vdash (A \supset (A \supset (B \supset C))) \supset ((A \supset (A \supset B)) \supset (A \supset (A \supset C)))$.
(f) $\vdash \sim A \supset (A \supset B)$.
(g) $\vdash A \supset A$.
(h) $\vdash (A \supset -A) \supset -A$.
(i) $\vdash - -A \supset A$.
(j) $\vdash \sim\sim A \supset A$.
(k) $\vdash A \supset \sim\sim A$.
(l) $\vdash (A \supset B) \supset (\sim B \supset \sim A)$.
(m) $\vdash \sim(A \supset B) \supset A$.
(n) $\vdash \sim(A \supset B) \supset \sim B$.
(o) $\vdash A \supset (\sim B \supset \sim(A \supset B))$.
(p) $\vdash -A \supset (- \sim B \supset (A \supset B))$.
(q) *If* $S \cup \{A\} \vdash B$, *then* $S \vdash A \supset (A \supset B)$. (The Stutterer's Deduction Theorem)[4]
(r) *If S is syntactically inconsistent, then* $S \vdash A$ *for every wff A of* SC_3.
(s) *S is syntactically inconsistent if and only if* $S \vdash$ f.
(t) *If* $S \cup \{A\}$ *is syntactically inconsistent, then* $S \vdash -A$.
(u) *If* $S \cup \{-A\}$ *is syntactically inconsistent, then* $S \vdash A$.

Proof:

(q) Suppose the column made up of C_1, C_2, . . . , C_p constitutes a proof of

242   Part 2: Truth

B from $S \cup \{A\}$. We establish by mathematical induction on i that $S \vdash A \supset (A \supset C_i)$ for each i from 1 through p, and hence in particular that $S \vdash A \supset (A \supset B)$.

Case 1: C_i is an axiom or a member of S. Then $S \vdash C_i$ by L1(a) or L1(c). But $S \vdash C_i \supset (A \supset C_i)$ by L1(a''). Hence $S \vdash A \supset C_i$ by L1(d). But $S \vdash (A \supset C_i) \supset (A \supset (A \supset C_i))$ by L1(a''). Hence $S \vdash A \supset (A \supset C_i)$ by L1(d).

Case 2: C_i is A. Then $S \vdash A \supset (A \supset C_i)$ by L1(a'').

Case 3: C_i is the ponential of C_h and $C_h \supset C_i$. Then $S \vdash A \supset (A \supset C_h)$ and $S \vdash A \supset (A \supset (C_h \supset C_i))$ by the hypothesis of the induction. Hence $S \vdash A \supset (A \supset C_i)$ by L1(c) and L1(d).

(r) Suppose $S \vdash B$ and $S \vdash {\sim}B$ for some wff B of SC_3. Then by L1(f) and L1(d) $S \vdash A$ for any wff A of SC_3.

(s) $S \vdash p \supset p$ by L1(g). Hence, if $S \vdash f$, then S is syntactically inconsistent. Hence L1(s) by L1(r).

(t) Suppose $S \cup \{A\}$ is syntactically inconsistent. Then $S \cup \{A\} \vdash {\sim}A$ by L1(r), hence $S \vdash A \supset -A$ by L1(q), and hence $S \vdash -A$ by L1(h) and L1(d).

(u) Proof by L1(t), L1(i), and L1(d).

Now for proof that if a set S of wffs of SC_3 is syntactically consistent, then S is semantically consistent as well. We hew at first to two-valued precedent: i.e., we assume S to be syntactically consistent and then extend S into the familiar superset S_∞ of two-valued textbooks.[5] The members of S_∞, and hence those of S, will thereafter be shown to evaluate to 1 under some truth-value assignment of our own devising. Construction of S_∞, the reader will recall, is as follows: (a) take S_0 to be S, (b) assuming the wffs of SC_3 to be alphabetically ordered and A_i to be—for each i from 1 on—the alphabetically i-th wff of SC_3, take S_i to be $S_{i-1} \cup \{A_i\}$ if $S_{i-1} \cup \{A_i\}$ is syntactically consistent, otherwise take S_i to be S_{i-1} itself, and (c) take S_∞ to be $\sum_{i=0} S_i$.

Here as in the two-valued case, it is easily verified that:

(1) S_∞ is syntactically consistent.

and

(2) S_∞ is maximally consistent.

For proof of (1), suppose S_∞ were syntactically inconsistent. Then by L1(s) and L1(b) at least one finite subset S' of S_∞ would be syntactically inconsistent. But S' is sure to be a subset of S_0, or (failing that) one of S_1, or (failing that) one of S_2, etc., and each one of S_0, S_1, S_2, etc. is syntactically consistent. Hence (1). For proof of (2), suppose not $S_\infty \vdash A$, where A is the alphabetically i-th wff of SC_3. Then by L1(c) A does not belong to S_∞, hence A does not belong to S_i, hence $S_{i-1} \cup \{A\}$ is syntactically inconsistent, and hence by L1(s) and L1(a) so is $S_\infty \cup \{A\}$.

Departing now from two-valued precedent, let α be the result of assigning to each sentence letter P of SC_3 the truth-value 1 if $S_\infty \vdash P$ (and hence, by the syntactic consistency of S_∞, not $S_\infty \vdash {\sim}P$), the truth-value 3 if $S_\infty \vdash {\sim}P$ (and hence, by the syntactic consistency of S_∞, not $S_\infty \vdash P$), otherwise the truth-value 2. We proceed to show of any wff A of SC_3 that:

(i) If $S_\infty \vdash A$ (and, hence, not $S_\infty \vdash {\sim}A$), $\alpha(A) = 1$,
(ii) If $S_\infty \vdash {\sim}A$ (and, hence, not $S_\infty \vdash A$), $\alpha(A) = 3$,
(iii) If neither $S_\infty \vdash A$ nor $S_\infty \vdash {\sim}A$, $\alpha(A) = 2$.

The proof is by mathematical induction on the length l of A.
Basis: $l = 1$, in which case A is a sentence letter. Proof by the very construction of α.
Inductive Step: $l > 1$.
Case 1: A is a negation ${\sim}B$.
   (i) Suppose $S_\infty \vdash {\sim}B$. Then not $S_\infty \vdash B$, hence by the hypothesis of the induction $\alpha(B) = 3$, and hence $\alpha({\sim}B) = 1$.
   (ii) Suppose $S_\infty \vdash {\sim}{\sim}B$. Then by L1(j) and L1(d) $S_\infty \vdash B$, hence by the hypothesis of the induction $\alpha(B) = 1$, and hence $\alpha({\sim}B) = 3$.
   (iii) Suppose neither $S_\infty \vdash {\sim}B$ nor $S_\infty \vdash {\sim}{\sim}B$. If B were provable from S_∞, then by L1(k) and L1(d) so would ${\sim}{\sim}B$ be. Hence neither $S_\infty \vdash B$ nor $S_\infty \vdash {\sim}B$, hence by the hypothesis of the induction $\alpha(B) = 2$, and hence $\alpha({\sim}B) = 2$.
Case 2: A is a conditional $B \supset C$.
   (i) Suppose $S_\infty \vdash B \supset C$. If $S_\infty \vdash {\sim}B$, then $\alpha(B) = 3$ by the hypothesis of the induction. If $S_\infty \vdash C$, then $\alpha(C) = 1$ by the hypothesis of the induction. If $S_\infty \vdash B$, then $S_\infty \vdash C$ by L1(d), and hence again $\alpha(C) = 1$. And, if $S_\infty \vdash {\sim}C$, then $S_\infty \vdash {\sim}B$ by L1(l) and L1(d), and hence again $\alpha(B) = 3$. Hence, if any one of B, ${\sim}B$, C, and ${\sim}C$ is provable from S_∞, then $\alpha(B) = 3$ or $\alpha(C) = 1$, and hence $\alpha(B \supset C) = 1$. If, on the other hand, none of B, ${\sim}B$, C, and ${\sim}C$ is provable from S_∞, then $\alpha(B) = \alpha(C) = 2$ by the hypothesis of the induction, and hence $\alpha(B \supset C) = 1$.
   (ii) Suppose $S_\infty \vdash {\sim}(B \supset C)$. Then by L1(m)–(n) and L1(d) both $S_\infty \vdash B$ and $S_\infty \vdash {\sim}C$, hence by the hypothesis of the induction $\alpha(B) = 1$ and $\alpha(C) = 3$, and hence $\alpha(B \supset C) = 3$.
   (iii) Suppose neither $S_\infty \vdash B \supset C$ nor $S_\infty \vdash {\sim}(B \supset C)$. Then $\alpha(B)$ cannot equal 3 nor can $\alpha(C)$ equal 1, for by the hypothesis of the induction ${\sim}B$ or C would then be provable from S_∞, and hence by L1(f), L1(a), and L1(d) so would $B \supset C$ be. Now suppose *first* that $\alpha(B) = 1$. Then $\alpha(C)$ cannot equal 3, for by the hypothesis of the induction ${\sim}C$ would then be provable from S_∞, and hence by L1(o) and L1(d) so would ${\sim}(B \supset C)$ be. Hence $\alpha(C)$ must equal 2, and hence $\alpha(B \supset C) = 2$. Suppose *next* that $\alpha(B) = 2$. Then $\alpha(C)$ cannot equal 2, for by the hypothesis of the induction neither B nor ${\sim}C$ would then be provable from S_∞, hence by the maximal consistency of S_∞ both $S \cup \{B\}$ and $S \cup \{{\sim}C\}$ would be syntactically inconsistent, hence by L1(t) both $-B$ and $-{\sim}B$ would be provable from S_∞, and hence by L1(p) and L1(d) so would $B \supset C$ be. Hence $\alpha(C)$ must equal 3, and hence $\alpha(B \supset C) = 2$.

244   Part 2: Truth

Since every member of S belongs to S_∞ and hence by L1(c) is provable from S_∞, every member of S is thus sure to evaluate to 1 under α. Hence:

Lemma 2.   *If S is syntactically consistent, then S is semantically consistent.*

Our completeness theorems are now at hand. For suppose $S \vdash A$. Then, as the reader may wish to verify, $S \cup \{-A\}$ is semantically inconsistent, hence by L2, $S \cup \{-A\}$ is syntactically inconsistent, and hence by L1(u) $S \vdash A$. Hence:

Theorem 1.   *If $S \models A$, then $S \vdash A$.* (The Strong Completeness Theorem)

Hence, taking S to be $\varnothing$:

Theorem 2.   *If $\models A$, then $\vdash A$.* (The Weak Completeness Theorem)

Since the converse of Lemma 2 is also provable, it follows from L1(b) and L1(s) that if every finite subset of S is semantically consistent, then S is syntactically consistent. Hence, as a further corollary of Lemma 2:

Theorem 3.   *If every finite subset of S is semantically consistent, then S is semantically consistent.* (The Compactness Theorem)

Four closing remarks are in order.

(1) Słupecki noted in [4] that '$\sim$' and '$\supset$' are not "functionally complete," but '$\sim$', '$\supset$', and the connective '**T**' are (**T**A evaluates to 2 no matter the truth-value of A). If with Słupecki we add to **A1–A4** on p. 240 the following two axiom schemata:
   A5. **T**$A \supset \sim$**T**A,
   A6. $\sim A \supset$ **T**A,
the above proof of L2 easily extends to the case where A is of the sort **T**B. Indeed, neither $S_\infty \vdash$ **T**B nor $S_\infty \vdash \sim$**T**B (by L1(a) and L1(d) S_∞ would otherwise be syntactically inconsistent), and $\alpha(\mathbf{T}B) = \alpha(\sim\mathbf{T}B) = 2$. (i)–(iii) on p. 243 are therefore sure to hold true.

(2) Suppose the truth-values of $\sim A$, $A \supset B$, and **T**A are reckoned as the following matrix directs:

Matrix 2

		B				
$A \supset B$		1	1	3	$\sim A$	**T**A
	1	1	3	1	3	3
A	2	1	1	1	1	3
	3	3	2	1	2	3

Suppose also the truth-value assignment α on pp. 242–43 is so redefined as to assign value 1 to P if $S_\infty \vdash P$, value 2 if $S_\infty \vdash \sim P$, and value 3 if neither $S_\infty \vdash P$ nor $S_\infty \vdash \sim P$. Then the argument on pp. 243–44 will show that: (i′) If $S_\infty \vdash A$, $\alpha(A) = 1$, (ii′) if $S_\infty \vdash \sim A$, $\alpha(A) = 2$, and (iii′) if neither $S_\infty \vdash A$ nor $S_\infty \vdash \sim A$, $\alpha(A) = 3$. So L2 holds true again. But, if $S \models A$, then $S \cup \{-A\}$ is again semantically inconsistent. So Theorems 1–2 hold true whether the truth-values of $\sim A$, $A \supset B$, and TA be beckoned the familiar Łukasiewicz way or as Matrix II directs. That SC_3—as axiomatized by Wajsberg and Słupecki—is strongly (and hence weakly) sound and consistent under *two* different readings of '$\sim$', '$\supset$', and '**T**' (and, incidentally, under two only) may not have been reported before.

(3) As noted on p. 241, our truth-value assignments are to *all* the sentence letters of SC_3 rather than just those occurring in (members of) a set S of wffs of SC_3 or just those occurring in a wff A of SC_3. However, the argument on pp. 243–244 is easily sharpened to show that if S is non-empty and syntactically consistent, then there is a truth-value assignment to just the sentence letters in S under which all members of S evaluate to 1. Hence proof can be had that (a) if, no matter the truth-value assignment α to the sentence letters in $S \cup \{A\}$, A evaluates to 1 under α if all members of S do, then $S \vdash A$, and (b) if, no matter the truth-value assignment α to the sentence letters in A, A evaluates to 1 under α, then $\vdash A$.

(4) S is sometimes taken to entail A if, no matter the truth-value assignment α, A does not evaluate under α to less than any member of S does. The account does not suit Wajsberg's axiomatization of SC_3 since 'f' is provable from (the set consisting of) 'p' and '$\sim p$'.

Notes

1. Wajsberg's proof of Theorem 2 in [5] is "effective": it shows how to prove A whenever A is valid. Ours merely guarantees that A is provable.
2. The possibility of assigning truth-values to just the sentence letters occurring in (members of) a set S of wffs of SC_3 or in a wff A of SC_3 is considered on p. 245.
3. Hence, in particular, if $\vdash A$, then $S \vdash A$ for every set S of wffs of SC_3 (a′); hence, in particular, if A is an axiom of SC_3, then $S \vdash A$ for every S (a″). Because of (a′), each one of (e)–(p) holds prefaced with 'S', a fact we shall regularly take for granted.
4. The familiar Deduction Theorem: "*If* $S \cup \{A\} \vdash B$, *then* $S \vdash A \supset B$," does not hold here. Though '$\sim(p \supset \sim p)$' is provable from $\{p\}$, '$p \supset \sim(p \supset \sim p)$' is not valid and hence not provable. The counterexample given in the original of this paper is in error.
5. See, for instance, [2], p. 73. The primary source is, of course, [1].

References

[1] Henkin, L. 1949. "The Completeness of the First-Order Functional Calculus." *The Journal of Symbolic Logic* 14: 159–66.
[2] Leblanc, H. 1966. *Techniques of Deductive Inference*. Englewood Cliffs: Prentice Hall.
[3] Rosser, J. B., and Turquette, A. R. 1952. *Many-Valued Logics*. Amsterdam: North-Holland.

[4] Słupecki, J. 1967. "The Full Three-Valued Propositional Calculus." *Polish Logic*, pp. 335–37. Oxford: Clarendon Press.
[5] Wajsberg, M. 1967. "Axiomiatization of the Three-Valued Sentential Calculus." *Polish Logic*, pp. 264–84. Oxford: Clarendon Press.

18
A Strong Completeness Theorem for Three-Valued Logic: Part II

Proof was given in the previous paper that SC_3, the three-valued sentential calculus, has a strongly complete axiomatization. Pushing our investigation one step further, we obtain here a like result about QC_3, the three-valued quantificational calculus of order one.[1]

1. The primitive signs of QC_3 are

(a) '$\sim$', '$\supset$', '$\forall$', '(', ')', and ',',
(b) a denumerable infinity of individual variables, to be referred to by means of 'X',[2]
(c) a denumerable infinity of individual parameters, to be referred to by means of 'P',[3] and
(d) for each d from 0 on, a denumerable infinity of predicate parameters of degree d, to be referred to by means of 'F^d'.[4]

We presume the variables in (b), the parameters in (c), and the parameters in (d) to be alphabetically ordered; and we take the alphabetically first parameter of degree 0 in (d) to be 'p'.

The atomic wffs in QC_3 are all formulas of the sort $F^d(P_1, P_2, \ldots, P_d)$, where F^d is a predicate parameter of degree d ($d \geq 0$) and $P_1, P_2, \ldots, P_d$ are individual parameters. The wffs of QC_3 (presumed at one point below to be alphabetically ordered) are the atomic wffs just defined, plus all formulas of the sorts (i) $\sim A$, where A is well-formed, (ii) $(A \supset B)$, where A and B are well-formed, and (iii) $(\forall X)A$, where—for some individual parameter P—the result $A(P/X)$ of replacing X everywhere in A by P is well-formed.[5] The length $l(A)$ of an atomic wff is 1; the length $l(\sim A)$ of a negation $\sim A$ is $l(A)+1$; the length $l((A \supset B))$ of a conditional $(A \supset B)$ is $l(A)+l(B)+1$; and the length $l((\forall X)A)$ of a quantification $(\forall X)A$ is $l(A(P/X))+1$, where P is the alphabetically earliest individual parameter of QC_3. We avail ourselves of the following eleven abbreviations:

247

'f' $=_{df}$ '$\sim(p \supset p)$'

$(A \lor B) =_{df} ((A \supset B) \supset B)$

$\sum_{i=1}^{n} A_i =_{df} ((\ldots (A_1 \lor A_2) \lor \ldots) \lor A_n$

$(A \& B) =_{df} \sim(\sim A \lor \sim B)$

$(A \equiv B) =_{df} ((A \supset B) \& (B \supset A))$

$(A \mid B) =_{df} (A \supset (A \supset B))$

$-A =_{df} (A \supset \sim A)$

$J_1(A) =_{df} \sim(A \supset \sim A)$

$J_3(A) =_{df} \sim(\sim A \supset A)$

$J_2(A) =_{df} \sim(J_1(A) \lor J_3(A))$

$(\exists X)A =_{df} \sim(\forall X) \sim A$;

and we omit outer parentheses whenever clarity permits.

Sets of wffs play a major role in the paper. We take an individual parameter to be foreign to a set S of wffs if the parameter does not occur in any member of the set, and we declare S infinitely extendible if $\aleph_0$ individual parameters are foreign to S. Given a mapping M of one set of individual parameters into another, we understand by the M-rewrite of a wff A the result of simultaneously replacing in A all individual parameters from the first set by their respective values under M; and we understand by the M-rewrite of a set S of wffs the set $\emptyset$ when S is empty, otherwise the set consisting of the M-rewrites of the various members of S. Lastly, given two sets S and S' of wffs, we declare S' isomorphic to S if—for some one-to-one mapping M of the individual parameters of QC_3 occurring in S into all the individual parameters of QC_3—S' is the M-rewrite of S.

The axioms of QC_3 are all wffs of the sorts **A1–A4** on p. 240, plus all those of the sorts:

A5. $(\forall X)(A \supset B) \supset ((\forall X)A \supset (\forall X)B)$,

A6. $A \supset (\forall X)A$, 6

A7. $(\forall X)A \supset A(P/X)$,

plus all those of the sort $(\forall X)A$, where—for some individual parameter P foreign to $(\forall X)A$—$A(P/X)$ is an axiom of QC_3. The notions of provability, syntactic (in)consistency, and maximal consistency are then defined as on p. 240, but with 'QC_3' substituting throughout for 'SC_3'.

Our truth-values are (the designated) 1 and (the undesignated) 2 and 3. Truth-value assignments are functions from the atomic wffs of QC_3 to $\{1, 2, 3\}$, and the truth-values under these of negations and conditionals are reckoned as on p. 241.[7] As for quantifications, $(\forall X)A$ evaluates to 1 under a truth-value assignment α if $A(P/X)$ does so for every individual parameter P of QC_3; $(\forall X)A$ evaluates to 3 under α if $A(P/X)$ does so for at least one individual parameter P of QC_3; otherwise, $(\forall X)A$ evaluates to 2 under α.[8] We take a set S of wffs to be truth-value verifiable if there is a truth-value assignment under which all members of S evaluate to 1; we take S to be semantically consistent if either S or some set isomorphic to S is truth-value verifiable;[9] we take S to entail a wff A if $S \cup \{-A\}$ is semantically inconsistent; and we take the wff A to be valid if $\varnothing$ entails A.

2. Our completeness proof, an extension of that on pp. 241–44, uses five fresh results: L3(c) and L4(a)–(d). Proof of the first result can be recovered from [2], pp. 336–37, and so is omitted here; but proofs of the other four results are given in full. Our first lemma is L1, p. 241; our second deals with extra truth-functional matters; and our third with quantificational ones.

Lemma 2. (a) *If* $S \vdash A \supset B$, *then* $S \vdash (B \supset C) \supset (A \supset C)$.
(b) *If* $S \vdash A \supset B$ *and* $S \vdash B \supset C$, *then* $S \vdash A \supset C$.
(c) *If* $S \vdash {\sim}A \supset {\sim}B$, *then* $S \vdash B \supset A$.
(d) *If* $S \vdash A \supset B$ *and* $S \vdash {\sim}B$, *then* $S \vdash {\sim}A$.
(e) *If* $S \cup \{A\} \vdash B$ *and* $S \vdash A' \supset A$, *then* $S \cup \{A'\} \vdash B$.
(f) *If* $S \vdash A \lor B$, *then* $S \vdash B \lor A$.
(g) *If* $S \vdash A \lor B$ *and* $S \vdash A \supset A'$, *then* $S \vdash A' \lor B$.
(h) *If* $S \vdash A \lor B$ *and* $S \vdash A \supset A'$, *then* $S \vdash (A' \& A) \lor B$.
(i) *If* $S \vdash A \lor B$ *and* $S \vdash B \supset B'$, *then* $S \vdash A \lor B'$.
(j) *If* $S \vdash A \lor (B \lor C)$ *and* $S \vdash B \supset B'$, *then* $S \vdash A \lor (B' \lor C)$.
(k) *If* $S \vdash A \lor (B \lor C)$ *and* $S \vdash C \supset C'$, *then* $S \vdash A \lor (B \lor C')$.
(l) *If* $S \vdash A \lor (B \& C)$ *and* $S \vdash C \supset C'$, *then* $S \vdash A \lor (B \& C')$.
(m) *If* $S \cup \{C\} \vdash A \lor B$, *then* $S \cup \{C\} \vdash A \lor (B \& C)$.
(n) *If* $S \cup \{C\} \vdash A \lor (B \lor {\sim}C)$, *then* $S \cup \{C\} \vdash A \lor B$.
(o) *If* $S \vdash A \mid -A$, *then* $S \vdash -A$.
(p) *If* $S \vdash J_1(A) \lor J_2(A)$, *then* $S \vdash {\sim}J_3(A)$.
(q) $S \vdash {\sim}J_3(A) \supset (J_1(A) \lor J_2(A))$.
(r) $S \vdash -J_3(A) \supset {\sim}J_3(A)$.
(s) *If* $S \cup \{J_3(A)\} \vdash B$, *then* $S \vdash J_3(A) \supset B$.
Proof: (a) Since $(A \supset B) \supset ((B \supset C) \supset (A \supset C))$ is an axiom, $S \vdash (A \supset B) \supset ((B \supset C) \supset (A \supset C))$ by L1(a). So (a) by L1(d).
  (b) By (a) and L1(d).
  (c) Proof like that of (a).
  (d) $S \vdash (A \supset B) \supset ({\sim}B \supset {\sim}A)$ by L1(1) and L1(a). So (d) by L1(d).
  (e) Suppose $S \cup \{A\} \vdash B$. Then $S \vdash A \mid B$ by L1(q), and hence $S \cup \{A'\} \vdash A \mid B$ by L1(a). But $(A \mid B) \supset ((A' \supset A) \supset (A' \mid B))$ is valid in the sense of p. 241. So $S \cup \{A'\} \vdash (A \mid B) \supset ((A' \supset A) \supset (A' \mid B))$ by the completeness

theorem on p. 241 and L1(a), and hence $S \cup \{A'\} \vdash (A' \supset A) \supset (A' \mid B)$ by L1(d). So, if $S \vdash A' \supset A$, then $S \cup \{A'\} \vdash A' \supset A$ by L1(a), hence $S \cup \{A'\} \vdash A' \mid B$ by L1(d), and hence $S \cup \{A'\} \vdash B$ by L1(c)–(d).

(f) Since $(A \vee B) \supset (B \vee A)$ is valid in the sense of [1], $S \vdash (A \vee B) \supset (B \vee A)$ by the completeness theorem on p. 244 and L1(a). Hence (f) by L1(d).

(g)–(l) Proofs like that of (f).
(m)–(n) Proofs like that of (e).
(o)–(p) Proofs like that of (f).
(q)–(r) By the completeness theorem on p. 244 and L1(a).
(s) Proof like that of (e).

Lemma 3. (a) If $S \vdash (\forall X)A \supset B)$, then $S \vdash (\forall X)A \supset (\forall X)B$.
(b) $S \vdash (\forall X')A(X'/X) \supset (\forall X)A$.
(c) If $S \vdash A(P/X)$, then $S \vdash (\forall X)A$, so long as P is foreign to S and $(\forall X)A$.
(d) $S \vdash (\forall X)(A \supset B) \supset (A \supset (\forall X)B)$.[10]
(e) $S \vdash (\forall X)(A \vee B) \supset (A \vee (\forall X)B)$.[11]
(f) If $S \vdash (\forall X)(A \vee B)$, then $S \vdash A \vee (\forall X)B$, so long as X is foreign to A.
(g) $S \vdash A(P/X) \supset (\exists X)A$.
(h) If $S \vdash A(P/X) \vee (B(P/X) \vee C(P/X))$, then $S \vdash (\forall X)A \vee ((\exists X)B \vee (\exists X)C)$, so long as P is foreign to S, $(\forall X)A$, $(\exists X)B$, and $(\exists X)C$.
(i) $S \vdash (\forall X)A \supset (\exists X)A$.
(j) $S \vdash ((\exists X)J_k(A) \;\&\; (\forall X) \sum_{i=1}^{k} J_i(A)) \supset J_k((\forall X)A)$, for any k from 1 through 3.
(k) $S \vdash (\forall X){\sim}J_3(A) \supset (\forall X)(J_1(A) \vee J_2(A))$.
(l) $S \vdash (\forall X) - J_3(A) \supset (\forall X){\sim}J_3(A)$.
(m) $S \vdash -(\forall X) - A \mid (\exists X)A$.
(n) If $S \vdash A \supset (\exists X){\sim}B$, then $S \vdash A \supset {\sim}(\forall X)B$.
(o) If $S \vdash (\forall X)({\sim}{\sim}A \supset B) \supset C$, then $S \vdash (\forall X)(A \supset B) \supset C$.
(p) If $S \vdash A \supset (B \supset (\forall X){\sim}C)$, then $S \vdash A \supset (B \supset {\sim}(\exists X)C)$.
(q) $S \vdash B \supset (\exists X)(A \supset B)$.
(r) $S \vdash (\exists X)(A \supset B) \supset ((\forall X)A \supset B)$.
(s) $S \vdash ((\exists X)(A \supset B) \supset B) \equiv (((\forall X)A \supset B) \supset B)$.

Proof:
(a) Since $(\forall X)(A \supset B) \supset ((\forall X)A \supset (\forall X)B)$ is an axiom, $S \vdash (\forall X)(A \supset B) \supset ((\forall X)A \supset (\forall X)B)$ by L1(a). Hence (a) by L1(d).

(b) In case X' and X are the same, (b) by L1(g) and L1(a). So suppose X' and X are distinct, and let P be foreign to $(\forall X)A$. $(\forall X')A(X'/X) \supset A(P/X)$ $(=(\forall X')A(X'/X) \supset (A(X'/X))(P/X'))$ is an axiom. Hence, by the hypothesis on P, so is $(\forall X)((\forall X')A(X'/X) \supset A)$. Hence, by L1(a), $S \vdash (\forall X)((\forall X')A(X'/X) \supset A)$. Hence, by (a), $S \vdash (\forall X)(\forall X')A(X'/X) \supset (\forall X)A$. But $(\forall X')A(X'/X) \supset (\forall X)(\forall X')A(X'/X)$ is an axiom. Hence, by L1(a), $S \vdash (\forall X')A(X'/X) \supset (\forall X)(\forall X')A(X'/X)$. Hence (b) by L2(b).

(c) See proof of (3.7.12) in [2].

(d) Since $A \supset (\forall X)A$ is an axiom, $S \vdash A \supset (\forall X)A$ by L1(a). Hence $S \vdash ((\forall X)A \supset (\forall X)B) \supset (A \supset (\forall X)B)$ by L2(a). But $(\forall X)(A \supset B) \supset ((\forall X)A \supset (\forall X)B)$ is an axiom. So $S \vdash (\forall X)(A \supset B) \supset ((\forall X)A \supset (\forall X)B)$ by L1(a). So (d) by L2(b).

(e) See proof of Lemma 6.7.2 in [3].

(f) Suppose X is foreign to A, in which case $(\forall X)(A \vee B) \supset (A \vee (\forall X)B)$ is well-formed. Then (f) by (e) and L1(d).

(g) See proof of Lemma 6.8.5 in [3].

(h) Suppose $S \vdash A(P/X) \vee (B(P/X) \vee C(P/X))$, suppose P is foreign to S, $(\forall X)A$, $(\exists X)B$, and $(\exists X)C$, and let X' be new. Then $S \vdash A(P/X) \vee ((\exists X)B \vee C(P/X))$ by (g) and L2(j), hence $S \vdash A(P/X) \vee ((\exists X)B \vee (\exists X)C)$ by (g) and L2(k), hence $S \vdash ((\exists X)B \vee (\exists X)C) \vee A(P/X)$ by L2(f), hence $S \vdash (\forall X')(((\exists X)B \vee (\exists X)C) \vee A(X'/X))$ by (c), hence $S \vdash ((\exists X(B \vee (\exists X)C) \vee (\forall X')A(X'/X)$ by (f) and the hypothesis on X', hence $S \vdash ((\exists X)B \vee (\exists X)C) \vee (\forall X)A$ by (b) and L2(k), and hence $S \vdash (\forall X)A \vee ((\exists X)B \vee (\exists X)C)$ by L2(f).

(i) Let P be an arbitrary individual parameter. Since $(\forall X)A \supset A(P/X)$ is an axiom, $S \vdash (\forall X)A \supset A(P/X)$ by L1(a). Hence (i) by (g) and L2(b).

(j) See proof of Lemma 6.8.24 in [3].

(k) Let P be an individual parameter foreign to $(\forall X)(\sim J_3(A) \supset (J_1(A) \vee J_2(A)))$. By L2(q) $\vdash \sim J_3(A(P/X)) \supset (J_1(A(P/X)) \vee J_2(A(P/X)))$. So, by the hypothesis on P, $\vdash (\forall X)(\sim J_3(A) \supset (J_1(A) \vee J_2(A)))$. So, by L1(a), $S \vdash (\forall X)(\sim J_3(A) \supset (J_1(A) \vee J_2(A)))$. So (k) by (a).

(l) Proof like that of (k), but using L2(r) in place of L2(q).

(m) See proof of Lemma 6.8.29 in [3].

(n) Let P be an individual parameter foreign to $(\forall X)(B \supset \sim\sim B)$. By L1(k) $\vdash B(P/X) \supset \sim\sim B(P/X)$; hence, by (c), $\vdash (\forall X)(B \supset \sim\sim B)$; hence, by (a), $\vdash (\forall X)B \supset (\forall X)\sim\sim B$; hence, by L1(l) and L1(d), $\vdash (\exists X)\sim B \supset \sim(\forall X)B$; hence, by L1(a), $S \vdash (\exists X)\sim B \supset \sim(\forall X)B$; and hence (n) by L2(b).

(o)–(p) Proofs like that of (n).

(q) See proof of Lemma 6.8.10 in [3].

(r) See proof of Lemma 6.8.11 in [3].

(s) See proof of Lemma 6.8.8 in [3].

Lemma 4. (a) $S \vdash (\forall X)\neg A \supset \neg(\exists X)A$.
(b) $S \vdash (\exists X')(A(X'/X) \supset (\forall X)A)$.
(c) If $S \vdash (\forall X)A$, then $S \vdash A(P/X)$ for every individual parameter P of QC_3.
(d) If $S \vdash \sim A(P/X)$ for any individual parameter P of QC_3, then $S \vdash \sim(\forall X)A$.

Proof:
(a) Let P be foreign to $(\forall X)A$, $(\exists X)B$, and $(\exists X)C$. $J_1(A(P/X)) \vee (J_2(A(P/X)) \vee J_3(A(P/X)))$ is valid in the sense of p. 241. So by the completeness theorem of p. 244.

$$\vdash J_1(A(P/X)) \vee (J_2(A(P/X)) \vee J_3(A(P/X))),$$

252 Part 2: Truth

so by L3(h) and the hypothesis on P

$$\vdash (\forall X)J_1(A) \lor ((\exists X)J_2(A) \lor (\exists X)J_3(A)),$$

so by L1(a)

$$\{J_3((\forall X)A), (\forall X)\sim J_3(A)\} \vdash (\forall X)J_1(A) \lor ((\exists X)J_2(A) \lor (\exists X)J_3(A)),$$

so by L2(n)

$$\{J_3((\forall X)A), (\forall X)\sim J_3(A)\} \vdash (\forall X)J_1(A) \lor (\exists X)J_2(A),$$

so by L3(i) and L2(h)

$$\{J_3((\forall X)A), (\forall X)\sim J_3(A)\} \vdash ((\exists X)J_1(A) \,\&\, (\forall X)J_1(A)) \lor (\exists X)J_2(A),$$

so by L3(j) and L2(g)

$$\{J_3((\forall X)A), (\forall X)\sim J_3(A)\} \vdash J_1((\forall X)A) \lor (\exists X)J_2(A),$$

so by L2(m)

$$\{J_3((\forall X)A), (\forall X)\sim J_3(A)\} \vdash J_1((\forall X)A) \lor ((\exists X)J_2(A) \,\&\, (\forall X)\sim J_3(A)),\,^{12}$$

so by L3(k) and L2(l)

$$\{J_3((\forall X)A), (\forall X)\sim J_3(A)\} \vdash J_1((\forall X)A) \lor ((\exists X)J_2(A) \,\&\, (\forall X)(J_1(A) \lor J_2(A))),$$

so by L3(j) and L2(i)

$$\{J_3((\forall X)A), (\forall X)\sim J_3(A)\} \vdash J_1((\forall X)A) \lor J_2((\forall X)A),$$

so by L2(p)

$$\{J_3((\forall X)A), (\forall X)\sim J_3(A)\} \vdash \sim J_3((\forall X)A),$$

so by L1(c) and L1(r)

$$\{J_3((\forall X)A), (\forall X)\sim J_3(A)\} \vdash -(\forall X)-J_3(A),$$

so by L3(l) and L2(e)

$$\{J_3((\forall X)A), (\forall X)-J_3(A)\} \vdash -(\forall X)-J_3(A),$$

so by L1(q)

$$\{J_3((\forall X)A)\} \vdash (\forall X)-J_3(A) \mid -(\forall X)-J_3(A),$$

so by L2(o)

$$\{J_3((\forall X)A)\} \vdash -(\forall X)-J_3(A),$$

so by L3(m) and L1(d)

$$\{J_3((\forall X)A)\} \vdash (\exists X)J_3(A),$$

so by L2(s)

$$\vdash J_3((\forall X)A) \supset (\exists X)J_3(A),$$

so by L3(n)
$$\vdash J_3((\forall X)A) \supset \sim(\forall X)(\sim A \supset A),$$
so by L2(c)
$$\vdash (\forall X)(\sim A \supset A) \supset (\sim(\forall X)A \supset (\forall X)A),$$
so in particular
$$\vdash (\forall X)(\sim\sim A \supset \sim A) \supset ((\exists X)A \supset (\forall X)\sim A),$$
so by L3(o)
$$\vdash (\forall X) - A \supset ((\exists X)A \supset (\forall X)\sim A),$$
so by L3(p)
$$\vdash (\forall X)\text{-}A \supset -(\exists X)A,$$
so by L1(a)
$$S \vdash (\forall X)\text{-}A \supset -(\exists X)A.$$

(b) $(A \supset B) \supset ((B \supset C) \supset (((B \supset A) \equiv (C \supset A)) \supset (C \supset B)))$ is valid in the sense of p. 241. So by the completeness theorem of p. 244.

$$\vdash (A \supset B) \supset ((B \supset C) \supset (((B \supset A) \equiv (C \supset A)) \supset (C \supset B))),$$

so in particular

$$\vdash (B \supset (\exists X)A \supset B)) \supset (((\exists X)(A \supset B) \supset ((\forall X)A \supset B)) \supset ((((\exists X)(A \supset B) \supset B) \equiv (((\forall X)A \supset B) \supset B)) \supset (((\forall X)A \supset B) \supset (\exists X)(A \supset B)))).$$

But
$$\vdash B \supset (\exists X)(A \supset B),$$
$$\vdash (\exists X)(A \supset B) \supset ((\forall X)A \supset B),$$

and

$$\vdash ((\exists X)A \supset B) \supset B) \equiv (((\forall X)A \supset B) \supset B)$$

by L3(q), L3(r), and L3(s), respectively. So by L1(d)

$$\vdash ((\forall X)A \supset B) \supset (\exists X)(A \supset B),$$

so in particular

$$\vdash ((\forall X')A(X'/X) \supset (\forall X)A) \supset (\exists X')(A(X'/X) \supset (\forall X)A),$$

so by L3(b) and L1(d)

$$\vdash (\exists X')(A(X'/X) \supset (\forall X)A),$$

so by L1(a)

$$S \vdash (\exists X')(A(X'/X) \supset (\forall X)A).^{13}$$

(c) $(\forall X)A \supset A(P/X)$ is an axiom of QC_3. So $S \vdash (\forall X)A \supset A(P/X)$ by L1(a). So (c) by L1(d).

(d) $S \vdash (\forall X)A \supset A(P/X)$ by the same steps as in (c). So (d) by L2(d).

3. Let S be a set of wffs that is syntactically consistent *and* infinitely extendible. We extend S into another set S^∞, then extend S^∞ into yet another set S_∞, and proceed to show all members of S_∞ (hence, all members of S) true on a certain truth-value assignment α.

Towards defining S^∞, let S^0 be S; and, $(\forall X_n)A_n$ being the alphabetically n-th quantification of QC_3, let S^n be for each n from 1 on $S^{n-1} \cup \{A_n(P_n/X_n) \supset (\forall X_n)A_n\}$, where P_n is the alphabetically earliest individual parameter of QC_3 foreign to S^{n-1} and $(\forall X_n)A_n$. S^∞ will then be the union of $S^0, S^1, S^2, \ldots$.

Towards defining S_∞, let S_0 be S^∞; and, A_n being the alphabetically n-th wff of QC_3, let S_n be for each n from 1 on $S_{n-1} \cup \{A_n\}$ or S_{n-1} according as $S_{n-1} \cup \{A_n\}$ is syntactically consistent or not. S_∞ will then be the union of $S_0, S_1, S_2, \ldots$. It is easily verified that:

(0) S^∞ *is syntactically consistent*,

(1) S_∞ *is syntactically consistent*,

and

(2) S_∞ *is maximally consistent*.

Proof of (1) is as on p. 242 (but using the syntactic consistency of S^∞ rather than that of S); and so is proof of (2). As for (0), suppose S^n to be syntactically inconsistent, and hence by L1(t) $-(A_n(P_n/X_n) \supset (\forall X_n)A_n)$ to be provable from S^{n-1}, and let X'_n be the alphabetically earliest individual variable of QC_3 foreign to $(\forall X_n)A_n$. Then by L3(c) $S^{n-1} \vdash (\forall X'_n) -(A_n(X'_n/X_n) \supset (\forall X_n)A_n)$. But by L4(a)

$$S^{n-1} \vdash (\forall X'_n) -(A_n(X'_n/X_n) \supset (\forall X_n)A_n) \supset -(\exists X'_n)(A_n(X'_n/X_n) \supset (\forall X_n)A_n).$$

So by L1(d)

$$S^{n-1} \vdash -(\exists X'_n)(A_n(X'_n/X_n) \supset (\forall X_n)A_n),$$

i.e.,

$$S^{n-1} \vdash (\exists X'_n)(A_n(X'_n/X_n) \supset (\forall X_n)A_n) \supset \sim(\exists X'_n)(A_n(X'_n/X_n) \supset (\forall X_n)A_n).$$

But by L4(b)

$$S^{n-1} \vdash (\exists X'_n)(A_n(X'_n/X_n) \supset (\forall X_n)A_n).$$

So by L1(d) S^{n-1} is syntactically inconsistent. So S^n is syntactically consistent if S^{n-1} is. But by assumption S^0 is syntactically consistent. So each one of $S^0, S^1, S^2, \ldots$, is syntactically consistent. So, by a familiar argument using L1(a) and L1(b), S^∞ is syntactically consistent.

A Strong Completeness Theorem for Three-Valued Logic: Part II   255

Now let α be the result of assigning to each atomic wff A of QC_3 the truth-value 1 if $S_\infty \vdash A$, the truth-value 3 if $S_\infty \vdash \sim A$, otherwise the truth-value 2. Mathematical induction on the length $l(A)$ of an arbitrary wff A of QC_3 will show that:
  (i) *If* $S_\infty \vdash A$, $\alpha(A) = 1$,
  (ii) *If* $S_\infty \vdash \sim A$, $\alpha(A) = 3$,
and
  (iii) *If neither* $S_\infty \vdash A$ *nor* $S_\infty \vdash \sim A$, $\alpha(A) = 2$.
Basis: $l(A) = 1$. Proof by the construction of α.
Inductive Step: $l(A) > 1$.
Case 1: A is a negation $\sim B$. See Case 1 on p. 243.
Case 2: A is a conditional $B \supset C$. See Case 2 on p. 243.
Case 3: A is a quantification $(\forall X)B$.

  (i) Suppose $S_\infty \vdash (\forall X)B$. Then by L4(c) $S_\infty \vdash B(P/X)$ for every individual parameter P of QC_3, hence by the hypothesis of the induction $\alpha(B(P/X)) = 1$ for every such P, and hence $\alpha((\forall X)B) = 1$.

  (ii) Suppose $S_\infty \vdash \sim(\forall X)B$, and let P be the alphabetically earliest individual parameter of QC_3 such that $B(P/X) \supset (\forall X)B$ belongs to S_∞. Then by L1(c) $S_\infty \vdash B(P/X) \supset (\forall X)B$, hence by L1(1) and L1(d) $S_\infty \vdash \sim(\forall X)B \supset \sim B(P/X)$, hence by L1(d) $S_\infty \vdash \sim B(P/X)$, hence by the hypothesis of the induction $\alpha(B(P/X)) = 3$, and hence $\alpha((\forall X)B) = 3$.

  (iii) Suppose neither $S_\infty \vdash (\forall X)B$ nor $S_\infty \vdash \sim(\forall X)B$. If $\alpha(B(P/X))$ equaled 3 for any individual parameter P of QC_3, then by the hypothesis of the induction $\sim B(P/X)$ would be provable from S_∞ for that P, and hence by L4(d) $\sim(\forall X)B$ would be provable from S_∞, against the hypothesis on $\sim(\forall X)B$. If, on the other hand, $\alpha(B(P/X))$ equaled 1 for every individual parameter P of QC_3, then by the hypothesis of the induction $B(P/X)$ would be provable from S_∞ for every such P. But $B(P/X) \supset (\forall X)B$ is sure to belong to S_∞, and hence by L1(c) to be provable from S_∞, for at least one individual parameter P of QC_3. So, if $\alpha(B(P/X))$ equaled 1 for every individual parameter P of QC_3, then by L1(d) $(\forall X)B$ would be provable from S_∞, against the hypothesis on $(\forall X)B$. So $\alpha((\forall X)B) = 2$.

Since every member of S belongs to S_∞ and hence by L1(c) is provable from S_∞, every member of S is thus sure to evaluate to 1 under α. Hence:

Lemma 5. *If S is syntactically consistent and infinitely extendible, then S is truth-value verifiable and hence semantically consistent.*

Suppose next that S is syntactically consistent but *not* infinitely extendible; P_i being for each i from 1 on the alphabetically i-th individual parameter of QC_3, let M be the mapping on the individual parameters of QC_3 such that $M(P_i) = P_{2i}$; let M' be the restriction of M to the individual parameters of QC_3 occurring in S; and let S' be the M'-rewrite of S. S' is infinitely extendible, and is easily

256   Part 2: Truth

verified to be syntactically consistent if—as presumed here—S is. So by L5 S' is truth-value verifiable. But S' is isomorphic to S. So S is semantically consistent.

So, whether or not S is infinitely extendible,

Lemma 6. *If S is syntactically consistent, then S is semantically consistent.*

So, by the same argument as on p. 244:

Theorem 1. *If S entails A, then $S \vdash A$.* (Strong Completeness Theorem for QC_3)

So, taking S to be $\emptyset$:

Theorem 2. *If A is valid, then $\vdash A$.* (Weak Completeness Theorem for QC_3)[14]

Notes

1. The result is a generalization of a result in [3].
2. Our individual variables are in effect what the literature calls *bound* individual variables.
3. Our individual parameters are in effect what the literature calls *free* individual variables.
4. Our predicate parameters are in effect what the literature calls *free* predicate variable, and our predicate parameters of degree 0 are as a result what it calls *free sentence* variables.
5. Because of (iii), formulas in which identical quantifiers overlap are not well-formed.
6. With $A \supset (\forall X)A$ presumed to be well-formed, X here is sure to be foreign to A.
7. Given the matrices on p. 241 for $\sim A$ and $A \supset B$, those for $-A$, $\mathbf{J}_1(A)$, $\mathbf{J}_2(A)$, and $\mathbf{J}_3(A)$ respectively run:

A	$-A$	$\mathbf{J}_1(A)$	$\mathbf{J}_2(A)$	$\mathbf{J}_3(A)$
1	3	1	3	3
2	1	3	1	3
3	1	3	3	1

8. Our interpretation of $(\forall X)A$—like that in [3]—is thus of the substitutional sort, and our semantics for QC_3 is of the truth-value sort.
9. Here, as in two-valued logic, *some* syntactically consistent sets of wffs are *not* truth-value verifiable: a case in point is $\{f(a_1), f(a_2), f(a_3), \ldots, \sim(\forall x)f(x)\}$, where '$f$' is a predicate parameter of degree 1, 'a_1', 'a_2', 'a_3', etc. are all the individual parameters of QC_3, and 'x' is an individual variable. But, as we shall establish below, *all* syntactically consistent sets of wffs *are* semantically consistent in the sense just defined. For alternative accounts of semantic consistency in truth-value semantics, see [1].
10. L3(c)–(d) guaranteed that any wff of QC_3 provable by the "axiomatic stipulation" on p. 8 of [3] is provable here, and vice-versa. With $(\forall X)(A \supset B) \supset (A \supset (\forall X)B)$ presumed to be well-formed, X here is sure to be foreign to A.
11. With $(\forall X)(A \lor B) \supset (A \lor (\forall X)B)$ presumed to be well-formed, X here is sure to be foreign to A.
12. From this point on the proof of L4(a) is due to Professor A. R. Turquette.
13. The entire proof of L4(b) is due to Professor Turquette.
14. The results of this paper were announced at the 1975 International Symposium on Multiple-

Valued Logic, Indiana University, Bloomington. Thanks are due to Professor Turquette for helping with the proofs of L4(a)–(b), and to George Weaver for his counsel and advice throughout the writing of the paper.

References

[1] Leblanc, H. 1971. "Truth-Value Semantics for a Logic of Existence." *Notre Dame Journal of Formal Logic* 12: 153–68 (#4 in this volume).
[2] Leblanc, H., and Wisdom, W. A. 1976. *Deductive Logic*, second edition. Boston: Allyn and Bacon.
[3] Rosser, J. B., and Turquette, A. R. 1952. *Many-Valued Logics*. Amsterdam: North-Holland.

19

A Completeness Result for Quantificational Tense Logic

R. P. McArthur, coauthor

We establish in this paper the strong completeness of QK_t, a minimal quantificational tense logic. Our result differs from those already in the literature, say [1], in two major respects. First, unlike Cocchiarella's proof, which utilizes semantic tableaux, ours is run in the Henkin fashion (with modifications found in [4]). And, second, the semantics we employ is of the truth-value rather than the usual model-theoretic sort. So truth-value assignments do duty for models, and the quantifiers are interpreted substitutionally.

Study of a presupposition-free variant of QK_t, known as QK_t^*, was begun in [5]. The strong completeness of QK_t^* will be established in a separate paper by R. F. Barnes, Jr., and R. D. Gumb.[1]

Together with the tense operators '**G**' ('it will always be the case that') and '**H**' ('it has always been the case that'), the *primitive signs* of QK_t include '$\sim$', '$\supset$', '$\forall$', '(', ')', and ',', plus a denumerable stock of each of the following:

(a) *individual variables* (among them 'x'),

(b) *individual parameters* (say, 'p_1', 'p_2', 'p_3', etc.), and

(c) for each m from 0 on, *m-place predicate parameters* (among them, the one-place 'f').

Our individual variables are what the literature calls *bound variables*, and our individual parameters are what it calls *free variables*. 'a_1' will count as the *alphabetically first individual parameter* of QK_t, 'a_2' as the *second*, 'a_3' as the *third*, etc. We refer by means of 'X' and 'Y' to the variables in (a), by means of 'I' to the parameters in (b), by means of 'F' ('F^m', where places matter) to the parameters in (c), by means of 'A', 'B', and 'C' to the formulas of QK_t, and by means of 'S' to sets of (what are shortly to be called) wffs of QK_t. We refer by means of '$A(P/X)$' (by means of '$A(Y/X)$') to the result of substituting parameter P (variable Y) for variable X in A. And we abridge '$\sim$**G**$\sim$' as '**F**' ('it will be the case that'), and '$\sim$**H**$\sim$' as '**P**' ('it has been the case that').

The *atomic wffs* of QK_t are to be all formulas of the kind $F^m(P_1, P_2, \ldots, P_m)$, where F^m is an m-place predicate parameter and—in case $m > 0$—all of $P_1, P_2, \ldots, P_m$ are individual parameters. The *wffs* of QK_t—presumed below to be alphabetically ordered—are to be all atomic wffs of QK_t, plus all formulas of the following four kinds:

(i) $\sim A$, where A is a wff,

(ii) $(A \supset B)$, where A and B are wffs (from here on outer parentheses are omitted),

(iii) $(\forall X)A$, where—for some individual parameter P—$A(P/X)$ is a wff,

(iv) GA or HA, where A is a wff.

The *mirror image of a wff* A—$MP(A)$, for short—is to be the result of simultaneously replacing every occurrence of '**G**' in A by one of '**H**', and every occurrence of '**H**' by one of '**G**'.

The *axioms* of QK_t are to be all wffs of the following eleven kinds:

A1. $A \supset (B \supset A)$,

A2. $(A \supset (B \supset C)) \supset ((A \supset B) \supset (A \supset C))$,

A3. $(\sim A \supset \sim B) \supset (B \supset A)$,

A4. $A \supset (\forall X)A$,

A5. $(\forall X)(A \supset B) \supset ((\forall X)A \supset (\forall X)B)$,

A6. $(\forall X)A \supset A(P/X)$,

A7. $(\forall X)A$, where—for some individual parameter P foreign to $(\forall X)A$—$A(P/X)$ is an axiom.

B1. $G(A \supset B) \supset (GA \supset GB)$,

B2. $A \supset HFA$,

B3. GA, where A is an axiom,

B4. $MP(A)$, where A is an axiom.

Wff B will be said to be the *ponential* of wffs A and $A \supset B$. The tense logics QCR, QCL, etc. have further axioms governing '**G**' and '**H**'. See [5] for details.

We shall say that a *wff* A *is derivable in* QK_t *from a set* S *of wffs*—$S \vdash A$, for short—if there is a finite column of wffs such that (i) each wff in the column is a member of S, an axiom, or the ponential of two earlier wffs in the column, and (ii) the last wff in the column is A. And we shall say that A *is provable in* QK_t—$\vdash A$, for short—if $\emptyset \vdash A$.

Turning to matters of semantics, we shall understand by a *truth-value assignment* (for QK_t) any function from the atomic wffs of QK_t to $\{F, T\}$; we shall understand by an *indexed truth-value assignment* (for QK_t) any pair of the kind $<\alpha, r>$, where α is a truth-value assignment and r is a real number, and we shall understand by a *truth-value triple* (for QK_t) any triple of the kind $<\Sigma, <\alpha, r>, R>$, where Σ is a non-empty set of indexed truth-value assignments,[2] $<\alpha, r>$ is a member of Σ, and R is a binary relation on Σ. In the

260   *Part 2: Truth*

tense logics QCR, QCL, etc., restrictions such as transitivity, connectedness, etc., are placed on R. See [5] on this.

We shall take a *wff A to be true on a truth-value triple* $<\Sigma$, $<\alpha,r>$, $R>$ if:
(a) in case A is atomic, $\alpha(A) = \mathbf{T}$,
(b) in case A is of the kind $\sim B$, B is not true on $<\Sigma$, $<\alpha,r>$, $R>$,
(c) in case A is of the kind $B \supset C$, B is not true on $<\Sigma$, $<\alpha,r>$, $R>$ or C is,
(d) in case A is of the kind $(\forall X)B$, $B(P/X)$ is true on $<\Sigma$, $<\alpha,r>$, $R>$ for every individual parameter P,
(e) in case A is of the kind $\mathbf{G}B$, B is true on $<\Sigma$, $<\alpha',r'>$, $R>$ for every member $<\alpha',r'>$ of Σ such that $R(<\alpha,r>$, $<\alpha',r'>)$,
(f) in case A is of the kind $\mathbf{H}B$, B is true on $<\Sigma, <\alpha',r'>$, $R>$ for every member $<\alpha',r'>$ of Σ such that $R(<\alpha',r'>$, $<\alpha,r>)$.

And we shall take *a set S of wffs to be tv-verifiable* ('tv' short here for 'truth-value') if there is a truth-value triple on which every member of S is true.

The reader unfamiliar with these matters may appreciate a more picturesque phrasing of our semantics for QK_t. (i) Recalling that α assigns a truth-value to each wff of QK_t of the sort $F^m(P_1, P_2, \ldots, P_m)$ and presuming for the occasion that $m \geq 1$, think of $<\alpha,r>$ in $<\Sigma, <\alpha,r>$, $R>$ as detailing

in case $m = 1$, which things belong to which sets at a certain date, a date to be known here as $<\alpha,r>$'s *date*,

in case $m = 2$, which pairs of things belong to which binary relations at $<\alpha,r>$'s date,

in case $m = 3$, which triples of things belong to which ternary relations at $<\alpha,r>$'s date,

etc.

(ii) Think of R in $<\Sigma$, $<\alpha,r>$, $R>$ as ordering the members of Σ in terms of *before and after*, so that member $<\alpha,r>$ of Σ will bear R to member $<\alpha',r'>$ of Σ if and only if $<\alpha,r>$'s date *precedes* $<\alpha',r'>$'s date. (iii) Given a truth-value triple $<\Sigma$, $<\alpha,r>$, $R>$ and a wff A of QK_t, truth-conditions (a)–(f) above stamp either A or its negation $\sim A$ true on $<\Sigma$, $<\alpha,r>$, $R>$. In light of (i)–(iii) you may thus think of $<\Sigma,R>$ as a *chronicle* of sorts, think of $<\Sigma$, $<\alpha,r>$, $R>$ as *the portion of the chronicle covering* $<\alpha,r>$'s *date*, and understand A to be true on $<\Sigma$, $<\alpha,r>$, $R>$ if and only if A *occurs* in that portion of the chronicle. (By the same token $\mathbf{G}B$ will be true on $<\Sigma$, $<\alpha,r>$, $R>$ if and only if B occurs in every later portion of the chronicle, and $\mathbf{H}B$ will be true on $<\Sigma$, $<\alpha,r>,R>$ if and only if B occurs in every earlier portion of the chronicle.)

We could dispense with indices, and so write 'α' where we now have '$<\alpha,r>$'. But the account of entailment in (3) below would have to be materially altered, so would step 3 on p. 264, etc. Note that by allowing a truth-value assignment to sport two different indices, as, for example, in $<\alpha,r>$ and $<\alpha,r'>$, we allow things to be the same at different dates, a possibility some might welcome.

Any set of wffs that is tv-verifiable is consistent, but not vice-versa:

$\{f(a_1), f(a_2), f(a_3), \ldots, \sim(\forall x)f(x)\}$, though consistent, is not tv-verifiable. So we go on to define a broader semantic notion, the notion of satisfiability, which will exactly match the syntactic one of consistency. (1) paves the way for (2), which paves the way for (3).

(1) Given a mapping M of one set of individual parameters into another, we shall understand by the M-*rewrite of a wff* A the result of simultaneously replacing in A all individual parameters from the first set by their respective values under M.

(2) Given two sets of wffs S and S', we shall declare S' *isomorphic to* S if—for some one-to-one mapping M of the individual parameters that occur in S into all of 'a_1', 'a_2', 'a_3', etc.—S' consists of the M-rewrites of the members of S.

(3) We shall say that *a set S of wffs is satisfiable* if S itself or some set isomorphic to S is tv-verifiable.

(4) And mimicking customary practice, we shall say that S *entails a wff* A (in Tarski's terminology, A is a semantic consequence of S) if $S \cup \{\sim A\}$ is not satisfiable.

Our completeness proof, being of the Henkin sort, features of course maximally consistent and ω-complete sets. To rehearse familiar definitions, a set S will be called *consistent* if there is no wff A such that both A and $\sim A$ are derivable from S, and *inconsistent* otherwise. S will be called *maximally consistent* if S is consistent and, for any wff A not in S, $S \cup \{A\}$ is inconsistent. And S will be called ω-*complete* if, no matter the quantification $(\forall X)A$, $(\forall X)A$ is derivable from S if $A(P/X)$ is for every individual parameter P.

Proof of the following lemma proceeds as in the classical case:

Lemma 1. *Let S be maximally consistent and ω-complete. Then:*
(a) For any wff A, if $S \vdash A$, then A belongs to S;
(b) For any negation $\sim A$, $\sim A$ belongs to S if and only if A does not;
(c) For any conditional $A \supset B$, $A \supset B$ belongs to S if and only if A does not belong to S or B does; and
(d) For any quantification $(\forall X)A$, $(\forall X)A$ belongs to S if and only if $A(P/X)$ does for every individual parameter P.

We next describe two methods of extending a consistent set of wffs into one which is maximally consistent and ω-complete. We presume in the first case that S is *infinitely extendible*, i.e., that infinitely many individual parameters are foreign to S; and in the second that S is ω-complete.

The first method, yielding what we call *the normal extension S^+ of S*, is as follows:
take S_0 to be S,
A_n being for each n from 1 on the alphabetically n-th wff of QK_t, take S_n to be
 (a) in case $S_{n-1} \cup \{A_n\}$ is inconsistent, the set S_{n-1},
 (b) in case $S_{n-1} \cup \{A_n\}$ is consistent and A_n is not of the sort $\sim(\forall X)B$, the set $S_{n-1} \cup \{A_n\}$,

(c) in case $S_{n-1} \cup \{A_n\}$ is consistent and A_n is a negated quantification $\sim(\forall X)B$, the set $S_{n-1} \cup \{\sim(\forall X)B, \sim B(P/X)\}$, where P is the alphabetically earliest individual parameter foreign to S_{n-1} and $\sim(\forall X)B$,[3] and, this done, take S^+ to be the union of S_0, S_1, S_2, etc.

The second method, yielding what we call *the special extension S^+ of S*, runs like the first, but with P understood in (c) to be the alphabetically earliest parameter such that $B(P/X)$ is not derivable from $S_{n-1} \cup \{\sim(\forall X)B\}$. (We know from a result in [3] that, with S understood to be ω-complete and $S_{n-1} \cup \{\sim(\forall X)B\}$ understood—as is the case in (c)—to be consistent, there is sure to be at least one such P.)[4]

Proof of Lemma 2 is as in the literature.

Lemma 2. (a) *Let S be consistent and infinitely extendible. Then the normal extension S^+ of S is sure to be maximally consistent and ω-complete.*
(b) *Let S be consistent and ω-complete. Then the special extension S^+ of S is sure to be maximally consistent and ω-complete.*

Special extensions turn up in our next two definitions.

(1) Suppose S to be maximally consistent and ω-complete, and to have at least one member of the sort **F**B; let $S_{[\mathbf{G}]A}$ consist of every wff A such that **G**A belongs to S; and let B be any wff such that **F**B belongs to S. Then the special extension of $S_{[\mathbf{G}]A} \cup \{B\}$ will count as a *future attendant of S*.

(2) Suppose S to be maximally consistent and ω-complete, and to have at least one member of the sort **P**B'; let $S_{[\mathbf{H}]A}$ consist of every wff A such that **H**A belongs to S; and let B' be any wff such that **P**B' belongs to S. Then the special extension of $S_{[\mathbf{H}]A} \cup \{B'\}$ will count as a *past attendant of S*.

The foregoing construction is patterned after one in [4]. Note that a set is accorded future (past) attendants *only* when it has at least one member of the sort **F**B (**P**B'). Note also that when a set has no future (past) attendants but has past (future) attendants, these past (future) attendants *have* future (past) attendants.

We go on to show that (a) each of $S_{[\mathbf{G}]A} \cup \{B\}$ and $S_{[\mathbf{H}]A} \cup \{B'\}$ is consistent and (b) each is ω-complete. (We took that for granted when talking of the special extension of $S_{[\mathbf{G}]A} \cup \{B\}$ and that of $S_{[\mathbf{H}]A} \cup \{B'\}$.)

Lemma 3. *Let S be maximally consistent and ω-complete; let $S_{[\mathbf{G}]A}$ and $S_{[\mathbf{H}]A}$ be as just described; and let **F**B and **P**B' be members of S. Then:*
(a) $S_{[\mathbf{G}]A} \cup \{B\}$ and $S_{[\mathbf{H}]A} \cup \{B'\}$ are consistent, and
(b) $S_{[\mathbf{G}]A} \cup \{B\}$ and $S_{[\mathbf{H}]A} \cup \{B'\}$ are ω-complete.
Proof:
(a) Suppose $S_{[\mathbf{G}]A} \cup \{B\}$ is inconsistent. Then $S_{[\mathbf{G}]A} \vdash \sim B$, and hence $S_{\mathbf{G}A} \vdash \mathbf{G}\sim B$, where $S_{\mathbf{G}A}$ is the result of prefacing each member of $S_{[\mathbf{G}]A}$ with a '**G**'. But, by the construction of $S_{[\mathbf{G}]A}$, $S_{\mathbf{G}A}$ is a subset of S. Hence $S \vdash \mathbf{G}\sim B$, and

A Completeness Result for Quantificational Tense Logic   263

hence $S \vdash {\sim}FB$ ($= {\sim}{\sim}G{\sim}B$). But FB belongs to S, and hence $S \vdash FB$. Hence S is inconsistent, a conclusion that would analogously follow from our supposing $S_{[H]A} \cup \{B'\}$ to be inconsistent.

(b) Suppose $S_{[G]A} \vdash C(P/X)$ for every individual parameter P. Hence, $S_{GA} \vdash GC(P/X)$, and hence as above $S \vdash GC(P/X)$, for every individual parameter P. Then, by the ω-completeness of S, $S \vdash (\forall X)GC$. But $\vdash (\forall X)GC \supset G(\forall X)C$.[5] Hence $S \vdash G(\forall X)C$; hence, by the maximal consistency of S and L1(a), $G(\forall X)C$ belongs to S; hence $(\forall X)C$ belongs to $S_{[G]A}$; hence $S_{[G]A} \vdash (\forall X)C$; hence $S_{[G]A}$ is ω-complete; and hence by a result in [3] so is $S_{[G]A} \cup \{B\}$. A like reasoning would show that $S_{[H]A} \cup \{B'\}$ is also ω-complete.

So, by dint of L2(b):

Lemma 4. *Let S be maximally consistent and ω-complete. Then every future and every past attendant of S is maximally consistent and ω-complete.*

These preliminaries attended to, we show how to construct for any *consistent and infinitely extendible* set S a truth-value triple on which all members of S are true.

Step 1. Take Σ_S to consist of (i) the normal extension S^+ of S and (ii) the future and past attendants of every member of Σ_S (i.e. the future and past attendants of S^+, the future and past attendants of these attendants, etc.). As shown in [5], the members of Σ_S can be alphabetically ordered; so we shall refer to S^+ as S_1^+, and to the remaining members of Σ_S as S_2^+, S_3^+, S_4^+, etc. And, in view of Lemma 2(a) and Lemma 4, these various sets are both maximally consistent and ω-complete.

Lemma 5. *Let S_i^+ be any set in Σ_S, then S_i^+ is maximally consistent and ω-complete.*

Step 2. Take R_S to be the binary relation on Σ_S such that, for any S_i^+ and S_j^+ in Σ_S, $R_S(S_i^+, S_j^+)$ if and only if—no matter the wff GA of QK_t—A belongs to S_j^+ if GA belongs to S_i^+. R_S has the following properties, to be exploited in Lemma 7.

Lemma 6. *Let S_i^+ and S_j^+ be arbitrary sets in Σ_S.*
(a) *If S_j^+ is a future attendant of S_i^+ or S_i^+ is a past attendant of S_j^+, then $R_S(S_i^+, S_j^+)$.*
(b) *If $R_S(S_i^+, S_j^+)$, then—for any wff HA—A belongs to S_i^+ if HA belongs to S_j^+.*
Proof:
(a) When S_j^+ is a future attendant of S_i^+, S_i^+ bears R_S to S_j^+ by definition. So suppose S_j^+ is a past attendant of S_i^+, and suppose A does not belong to S_j^+.

Then by L5 and L1(b), $\sim A$ belongs to S_j^+, and hence is derivable from S_j^+. But $\sim A \supset \mathsf{HF}\sim A$ is an axiom of $\mathrm{QK_t}$. Hence $S_j^+ \vdash \mathsf{HF}\sim A$, hence $S_j^+ \vdash \mathsf{H}\sim\mathsf{G}A$ (= $\mathsf{H}\sim\sim\mathsf{F}\sim A$), and hence by L5 and L1(a) $\mathsf{H}\sim\mathsf{G}A$ belongs to S_j^+. But, with S_j^+ presumed to be a past attendant of S_j^+, $\sim\mathsf{G}A$ is sure to belong to S_i^+ if $\mathsf{H}\sim\mathsf{G}A$ belongs to S_j^+. Hence by L5 and L1(b) $\mathsf{G}A$ does not belong to S_i^+. Hence, if $\mathsf{G}A$ belongs to S_i^+ then A belongs to S_j^+. Hence $R_S(S_i^+, S_j^+)$.

(b) Suppose A does not belong to S_i^+. Then by the same reasoning as for (a), but with axiom $\sim A \supset \mathsf{GP}\sim A$ substituting for axiom $\sim A \supset \mathsf{HF}\sim A$, $\mathsf{G}\sim\mathsf{H}A$ belongs to S_i^+. Suppose further that $R_S(S_i^+, S_j^+)$. Then $\sim\mathsf{H}A$ belongs to S_j^+, and hence by L5 and L1(b) $\mathsf{H}A$ does not belong to S_j^+.

Step 3. For each i from 1 on take the *truth-value assignment corresponding to* S_i^+ to be the result α_i of assigning truth-value **T** to all the atomic wffs of $\mathrm{QK_t}$ that belong to S_i^+ and truth-value **F** to the rest, and take the *indexed truth-value assignment corresponding to* S_i^+ to be the pair $<\alpha_i, i>$.

For certain choices of S the same atomic wffs will belong to several members of Σ_S. The assignment α_i in Step 3 may thus correspond to other members of Σ_S besides S_i^+. But the result $<\alpha_i, i>$ of tacking to α_i the index i corresponds to just S_i^+.

Step 4. Take Σ to consist of $<\alpha_1, 1>$, $<\alpha_2, 2>$, $<\alpha_3, 3>$, etc.

Step 5. Let R be the binary relation on Σ such that $<\alpha_i, i>$ bears R to $<\alpha_j, j>$ if and only if S_i^+ bears R_S to S_j^+ (S_i^+ the *one* member of Σ_S to which $<\alpha_i, i>$ corresponds, and S_j^+ the *one* member of Σ_S to which $<\alpha_j, j>$ does).

It is readily shown that, for any i from 1 on and any wff A of $\mathrm{QK_t}$:

Lemma 7. *A belongs to S_j^+ if and only if A is true on $<\Sigma, <\alpha_i, i>, R>$.*
Proof: Our proof is by mathematical induction on the complexity of A, with L5 and L1(b)–(d) seeing the induction through when A is of one of the three sorts $\sim B$, $B \supset C$, and $(\forall X)B$.
Case 4: A is of the sort $\mathsf{G}B$. (i) Suppose A is not true on $<\Sigma, <\alpha_i, i>, R>$. Then $\sim A$ is true on $<\Sigma, <\alpha_i, i>, R>$, and hence so is $\mathsf{F}\sim B$ (= $\sim\mathsf{G}B$). So there is a member $<\alpha_j, j>$ of Σ such that $R(<\alpha_i, i>, <\alpha_j, j>)$, and B is not true on $<\Sigma, <\alpha_j, j>, R>$. So by the definition of R and the hypothesis of the induction there is a member S_j^+ of Σ_S such that $R_S(R_i^+, S_j^+)$ and B does not belong to S_j^+. But, if B does not belong to S_j^+, then by L5 and L1(b) $\sim B$ belongs to S_j^+. Hence $S_j^+ \vdash \sim B$. But $\sim B \supset \mathsf{H}\sim\mathsf{G}\sim\sim B$ is an axiom of $\mathrm{QK_t}$. Hence $S_j^+ \vdash \mathsf{H}\sim\mathsf{G}\sim\sim B$, hence $S_j^+ \vdash \mathsf{H}\sim\mathsf{G}B$, hence by L5 and L1(a) $\mathsf{H}\sim\mathsf{G}B$ belongs to S_j^+, hence by L6(b) $\sim\mathsf{G}B$ belongs to S_i^+, and hence by L5 and L1(b) $\mathsf{G}B$ (= A) does not belong to S_i^+. (ii) Suppose A does not belong to S_i^+. Then by L5 and L1(b) $\sim A$ does belong to S_i^+, hence $S_i^+ \vdash \sim\mathsf{G}B$, hence $S_i^+ \vdash$

F~B (= ~**G**~~B), hence by L5 and L1(a) **F**~B belongs to S_i^+, and hence S_i^+ is sure to have a future attendant that boasts ~B as a member. But every future attendant of S_i^+ belongs to Σ_S. So there is sure to be a member S_j^+ of Σ_S such that ~B belongs to S_j^+, hence by L5 and L1(b) such that B does not belong to S_j^+, and hence by the hypothesis of the induction such that B is not true on $<\Sigma, <\alpha_j, j>, R>$. But, as S_j^+ is a future attendant of S_i^+, $R_S(S_i^+, S_j^+)$ by L6(a), and hence $R(<\alpha_i, i>, <\alpha_j, j>)$ by the definition of R. Hence A is not true on $<\Sigma, <\alpha_i, i>, R>$.

Case 5: A is of the sort **H**B. Proof similar to that of Case 4, but using axiom ~B ⊃ **G**~**H**~~B in place of ~B ⊃ **H**~**G**~~B.

Hence, in particular, every member of S_1^+ ($= S^+$) is true on $<\Sigma, <\alpha_1, 1>, R>$. But S is a subset of (its normal extension) S^+. Hence every member of S is true on $<\Sigma, <\alpha_1, 1>, R>$, the truth-value triple promised on p. 263.[6] Hence:

Theorem 1. Any consistent and infinitely extendible set of wffs of QK_t is tv-verifiable, and hence satisfiable.

Consider then a set S that is consistent and not infinitely extendible, and let S' be the result of doubling the subscript of every individual parameter occurring in S. It is easily verified that S' is consistent if—as presumed here—S is. But S' is infinitely extendible. Hence, by Theorem 1, S' is tv-verifiable. But S' is isomorphic to S. Hence S is satisfiable. Hence by Theorem 1 again:

Theorem 2. Any consistent set of wffs of QK_t is satisfiable.

Hence, by routine moves:

Theorem 3. If S entails A, then S ⊢ A.

QK_t is thus strongly complete under the truth-value semantics of pp. 259–261.

Notes

1. The controverted analogues $(\forall X)\mathbf{G}A \supset \mathbf{G}(\forall X)A$ and $(\forall X)\mathbf{H}A \supset \mathbf{H}(\forall X)A$ of the *Barcan Formula* are provable in QK_t. They will not be provable in QK_t^*, however, and therein lies the interest of QK_t^*.

2. In view of a result on p. 263, Σ could be presumed to be of cardinality $\aleph_0$, and hence the indices that turn up in its members to be among 1, 2, 3, etc.

3. With S presumed to be infinitely extendible, there are sure to be $\aleph_0$ individual parameters foreign to S_{n-1} and ~$(\forall X)B$.

4. Both of these methods for extending sets are due to Henkin. On the first, see [6], p. 96, which is a simplification of [2]. As for the second, it stems from [3].

5. Note the use of $(\forall X)\mathbf{G}C \supset \mathbf{G}(\forall X)C$ (see Note 1).

6. Since Σ_S is of cardinality $\aleph_0$, so is Σ. If an infinitely extendible set is consistent, there is

thus a truth-value triple $<\Sigma, <\alpha,r>, R>$ with denumerable Σ on which all of its members are true. The converse of this also holds true, as the reader may verify. Hence the point in Note 2.

References

[1] Cocchiarella, N. B. 1967. "Tense Logic. A Study in the Topology of Time." Ph.D. Dissertation. University of California at Los Angeles.

[2] Henkin, L. 1949. "The Completeness of the First-Order Functional Calculus." *The Journal of Symbolic Logic* (hereafter *JSL*) 14: 159–66.

[3] _____. 1957. "A Generalization of the Concept of ω-Completeness." *JSL* 22: 1–14.

[4] Makinson, D. 1966. "On Some Completeness Theorems in Modal Logic." *Zeitschrift für mathematische Logik und Grundlagen der Mathematik.* 12: 379–84.

[5] McArthur, R. P. 1972. "Truth-Value Semantics for Tense Logic." Ph.D. Dissertation. Temple University.

[6] Smullyan, R. M. 1963. *First-Order Logic.* New York: Springer-Verlag.

20
Semantic Deviations

By way of opening this conference,[1] I shall treat briefly of the substitution interpretation of 'All' and 'Some'; illustrate at length what I understand by non-denotational semantics and, in particular, by truth-value semantics; and discuss the point—philosophical as well as mathematical—of these deviations from model-theoretic semantics.

In his classic paper of 1936 Tarski showed how to define truth for a first-order language L. Though familiar by now, the lesson may be worth repeating.[2] Given a pair $<D, I_D>$, D a *domain* and I_D an *interpretation over* D of the individual constants (if any) and the predicate constants of L, understand by a *valuation over* D of the individual variables of L any assignment V_D of members of D to these variables. Next, recursively spell out the circumstances under which a sentence (closed or open) of L is to be *true on* V_D ('satisfied by V_D' would be Tarski's phrase). In particular, where F is an m-adic predicate constant and $I_1, I_2, \ldots, I_m$ are individual constants or variables of L, certify $F(I_1, I_2, \ldots, I_m)$ true on V_D if $<d_1, d_2, \ldots, d_m>$—$d_1, d_2, \ldots, d_m$ the members of D respectively assigned in I_D or in V_D to $I_1, I_2, \ldots, I_m$—is one of the m-tuples assigned in I_D to F; certify $\sim A$ true on V_D if A is not true on V_D; certify $A \supset B$ true on V_D if A is not true on V_D or B is; and certify $(\forall X)A$ true on V_D if A is true on every X-variant of V_D, one valuation counting as an X-variant of another if it agrees with that other on all the individual variables of L except possibly X.[3] Then, take a closed sentence of L to be *true* if it is true on all valuations over D of the individual variables of L, otherwise take it to be false.[4] Should you want to define logical truth as well, take a closed sentence of L to be logically true if it is true no matter what the domain D and the interpretation I_D, i.e., no matter what the *model* $<D, I_D>$.

Tarski's account is quite natural, but an even more natural one can be had. Indeed, read 'Everything is an F' as 'Whatever you may choose, it is an F'. The quantification will then ring true if all the following, known as its *substitution instances,* are true: 'The first thing you choose is an F', 'The second thing you choose is an F', 'The third thing you choose is an F', and so on without end. Hence the substitution interpretation of 'All' (and, by rebound, of 'Some'), according to which a universal quantification is a summary of its substitution instances. So, limiting yourself to closed sentences and dispensing with Tarski's valuations of the individual variables of L, take $F(C_1, C_2, \ldots, C_m)$ to be true if $<d_1, d_2, \ldots, d_m>$—$d_1, d_2, \ldots, d_m$ the members of D respectively assigned in I_D to the individual constants $C_1, C_2, \ldots, C_m$—is one of the m-tuples assigned in I_D to F; take $\sim A$ to be true if A is not; take $A \supset B$ to be true if A is not true or B is; take $(\forall X)A$ to be true if all results of putting an individual constant of L for X in A are true; and you have a full-fledged account of truth, to be known here as *Carnap's account*.

The substitution interpretation of 'All' is *at least* fifty years old: you find it, for example, in Wittgenstein's *Tractatus* and in a 1926–27 paper of Ramsey's. Carnap and Abraham Robinson used it (and the substitution account of truth I just credited to Carnap) in the early fifties, and Ruth Marcus championed it in her oft quoted paper of 1963. It does raise a problem, as Quine has repeatedly warned: "What if you have more things to choose from than names for them?" Carnap meets the difficulty by requiring his domains to be of size $\aleph_0$ or less; Robinson (and Shoenfield after him) by outfitting first-order languages with as many individual constants as the occasion may call for.

Carnap's account of truth departs from standard practice, but only some of the way. Individual constants still denote members of a preselected domain D, monadic predicate constants still denote sets of members of D, dyadic predicate constants still denote sets of pairs of members of D, etc. So, much of Carnap's semantics in *Logical Foundations of Probability* (1950), and all of Robinson's in *On the Metamathematics of Algebra* (1951), remain of the *model-theoretic* or—as Belnap phrased it in a recent letter—of the *denotational* sort. The substitution interpretation of 'All', however, can be put to more radical use. Indeed, when fully exploited, it issues into semantic accounts of the quantificational (= functional) calculus of order one, the quantificational calculus of order two, the simple theory of types, the ramified one, and so on, which do *without* domains and interpretations, and hence are truly *non-denotational*. Specimens of these will be found in Hintikka (1955), Beth (1959), and Schütte (1962), and—interestingly enough—one can be retrieved from Carnap's own book on probability.

So, turning to QC, the (pure) quantificational calculus of order one, suppose that two different runs of individual variables are used, one run occurring only bound in wffs of QC and for which the appellation 'individual variables' is saved, the other occurring only free and called *individual parameters*; for the sake of uniformity, talk of sentence parameters and predicate parameters where others would talk of (free) sentence variables and (free) predicate variables; take $(\forall X)A$ to be well-formed if—for any individual parameter P of QC—the result $A(P/X)$ of putting P everywhere in A for X is well-formed,[5] and call a wff of QC open if it contains at least one individual parameter.

The key notions of validity and semantic consistency (=simultaneous satisfiability) would normally be explicated as follows. D being again a domain and V_D being this time a valuation over D of the parameters of QC,[6] declare a sentence parameter of QC true on V_D if it is assigned **T** in V_D; where F is an m-adic

Semantic Deviations 269

predicate parameter of QC and $P_1, P_2, \ldots, P_m$ are individual parameters of QC, declare $F(P_1, P_2, \ldots, P_m)$ true on V_D if $<d_1, d_2, \ldots, d_m>$—$d_1, d_2, \ldots, d_m$ the members of D respectively assigned in V_D to $P_1, P_2, \ldots, P_m$—is one of the m-tuples assigned in V_D to F; declare a wff of QC of the sort $\sim A$ true on V_D if A is not true on V_D; declare one of the sort $A \supset B$ true on V_D if A is not true on V_D or B is; and declare one of the sort $(\forall X) A$ true on V_D if—P being the alphabetically earliest individual parameter of QC foreign to $(\forall X)A$—$A(P/X)$ is true on every P-variant of V_D. This done, declare a set S of wffs of QC *semantically consistent* if, for some domain D and some valuation V_D over D of the parameters of QC, every member of S is true on V_D; and declare a wff A of QC *valid* if $\{\sim A\}$ is not semantically consistent, i.e., if—no matter the domain D or the valuation V_D over D of the parameters of QC—A is true on V_D.

More model-theoretic sounding definitions will be had if, in case every wff in a set S of wffs of QC is true on V_D, you talk of S as having $<D, V_D>$ for a model. Your set could then be declared semantically consistent if it has a model, and a wff A of QC could be declared valid if $\{\sim A\}$ has none.

Now for Hintikka's departure from this standard account of things. Call a *model set* any set S of wffs of QC that has at least one open member[7] and meets the following six conditions:

(i) if $\sim A$ belongs to S, where A is atomic, then A does not belong to S.

(ii) if $\sim\sim A$ belongs to S, so does A,

(iii) if $A \supset B$ belongs to S, so does at least one of $\sim A$ and B,

(iv) if $\sim(A \supset B)$ belongs to S, so do both A and $\sim B$,

(v) if $(\forall X)A$ belongs to S, so does $A(P/X)$ for every individual parameter P of QC in S, and

(vi) if $\sim(\forall X)A$ belongs to S, so does $\sim A(P/X)$ for at least one individual parameter P of QC.

Hintikka showed in 1955 that any model set has a model, indeed has what I call a *Henkin model*, i.e., a model $<D, V_D>$ such that each member of D is assigned in V_D to some individual parameter of QC. Now suppose that infinitely many individual parameters of QC are foreign to a set S of wffs of QC—or, as Meyer and I have put it, suppose S is *infinitely extendible*. Suppose further that S has a model, and hence is syntactically consistent. Adapting Henkin's instructions in his classic paper of 1949, it is easy to extend S to a model set. Hence an infinitely extendible set of wffs of QC is semantically consistent in the model-theoretic sense if and only if it extends to a model set. But, if so, take an infinitely extendible set of wffs of QC to be semantically consistent if it is a subset of a model set, take a wff of QC to be valid if its negation does not belong to any model set, and you have the beginnings of a non-denotational semantics for QC.

Passing on to Beth and Schütte, understand by a *truth-value assignment for* QC any function from the atomic wffs of QC to $\{T, F\}$; take a wff A of QC to be *true on a truth-value assignment* α *for* QC if:

(a) in case A is atomic, $\alpha(A) = T$,

(b) in case A is a negation $\sim B$, B is not true on α,
(c) in case A is a conditional $B \supset C$, B is not true on α or C is, and
(d) in case A is a quantification $(\forall X)B$, $B(P/X)$ is true on α for every individual parameter P of QC;
and call a set S of wffs of QC *tv-verifiable* if there is a truth-value assignment for QC on which every member of S is true. Relying in part on Henkin, Beth showed in 1959 that a set S of closed wffs of QC is syntactically consistent if and only if S is tv-verifiable; and, using a different argument, Schütte showed in 1962 that a wff A of QC is provable if and only if A is true on every truth-value assignment for QC. Beth's result readily generalizes to the case where S is infinitely extendible.[8] So, take a set of that sort to be semantically consistent if it is tv-verifiable, take a wff of QC to be valid if it is true on every truth-value assignment for QC, and you have the beginnings of another non-denotational semantics for QC, one this time of the *truth-value* variety.

Incidentally, Beth's result and Schütte's can be sharpened some. Following Gentzen, take a wff of QC to be a *subformula* of itself; take A to be a subformula of $\sim A$; take both A and B to be subformulas of $A \supset B$; take $A(P/X)$ to be a subformula of $(\forall X)A$, this for any individual parameter P of QC; and, if A is a subformula of B and B one of C, take A to be a subformula of C. Also, given a non-empty set Σ of atomic wffs of QC, understand by a *truth-value assignment to* Σ any function from Σ to $\{\mathbf{T}, \mathbf{F}\}$; and, given a wff A of QC, a set Σ of atomic wffs of QC to which belongs every atomic subformula of A, and a truth-value assignment α to Σ, take A to be true on α if conditions (a)–(d) above are met. Beth's argument, in particular, is readily adapted to show that A is provable if and only if true on every truth-value assignment to its atomic subformulas.[9] So, as a wff of PC (the propositional calculus) is valid if and only if true on every truth-value assignment to its atomic *components*, one of QC is valid if and only if true on every truth-value assignment to its atomic *subformulas*, a rather neat thing.

Some of this will have a familiar ring to readers of Carnap's 1950 book; his state-descriptions behave very much like truth-value assignments, and indeed they were meant to do so. To facilitate the comparison, understand by a *state-description for* QC any (possibly empty) set of atomic wffs of QC; where A is a wff of QC and Σ a state-description for QC, take A to *hold in* Σ if: (a') in case A is atomic, A belongs to Σ, (b') in case A is a negation $\sim B$, B does not hold in Σ, (c') in case A is a conditional $B \supset C$, B does not hold in Σ or C does, and (d') in case A is a quantification $(\forall X)B$, $B(P/X)$ holds in Σ for every individual parameter P of QC; and take a set S of wffs of QC to hold in a state-description for QC if every member of S does. It will immediately follow that S is tv-verifiable if and only if S holds in a state-description for QC, hence that a wff A of QC is valid if and only if A holds in every state-description for QC. This of course is the non-denotational half of Carnap's semantics, as tailored here to suit QC.

All the findings reported so far hinge on the substitution interpretation of 'All'—more precisely, on treating $(\forall X)A$ as summary for all results of putting an individual parameter of QC for X in A. But readers of Quine need have no fear: proofs of Hintikka's, Beth's, and Schütte's results merely presuppose that QC has $\aleph_0$ individual parameters or free individual variables (say, 'a_1', 'a_2', 'a_3', etc.), and substitute proofs are available when the same letters (say, the familiar 'x', 'y', 'z', etc.) serve both as free and as bound individual variables. Exactly what counts as a substitution instance of $(\forall X)A$ has to be spelled out with extra care, but all else goes through as before.[10]

A difficulty *does* arise with sets that are not infinitely extendible. Consider $\{f(a_1), f(a_2), f(a_3), \ldots, \sim(\forall x)f(x)\}$. The set has a model; but, with 'a_1', 'a_2', 'a_3', etc., presumed—as is the case here—to be *all* the individual parameters of QC, $\{f(a_1), f(a_2), f(a_3), \ldots, \sim(\forall x)f(x)\}$ cannot be true on any truth-value assignment for QC, nor as a result can it extend to a model set. Hintikka in his 1955 paper meets the difficulty *à la Robinson*: he assumes QC to have as many individual parameters as any occasion may call for. So, in his version of QC, $\{f(a_1), f(a_2), f(a_3), \ldots, \sim(\forall x)f(x)\}$—and, more generally, any syntactically consistent set of wffs of QC—does extend to a model set. But the move strikes me as wasteful, and so does an analogous one in a paper by Dunn and Belnap.

A more economical solution can be had, as Hintikka and I came to realize.[11] R being a function (to be known as a *relettering* function) on the individual parameters of QC, understand by the R-*image* $R(A)$ of a wff A of QC the result of replacing each individual parameter P of QC in A by $R(P)$, and understand by the R-image $R(S)$ of a set S of wffs of QC the set consisting of the R-images of the various members of S. Then, S and S' being sets of wffs of QC, take S' to be *isomorphic* to S if—for some one-to-one relettering function R on the individual parameters of QC—S' is the R-image $R(S)$ of S. It is easily verified that: (a) if two sets S and S' of wffs of QC are isomorphic, then S is syntactically consistent if and only if S' is, and (b) to any set of wffs of QC there corresponds one which is infinitely extendible. So, take your set to be semantically consistent if it or some other set isomorphic to it is a subset of a model set, or—should you favor truth-value assignments—if it or some other set isomorphic to it is tv-verifiable, and you have an account of semantic consistency that does without models but exactly matches the model-theoretic one.

My own concern, recently, has been to duplicate within truth-value semantics further model-theoretic notions besides validity and semantic consistency. Take, for example, the notion of finiteness, and suppose the members of a set S of wffs of QC are true on a truth-value assignment α for QC. S will have a *finite model* (i.e., a model with a finite domain) if and only if α meets the following condition:

C1: There is a finite (but non-empty) set Σ_P of individual parameters of QC and a relettering function R from the individual parameters of QC not in Σ_P to those in Σ_P such that, for every atomic wff A of QC, $\alpha(A) = \alpha(R(A))$,

or, equivalently,

C2: There is a finite (but non-empty) set Σ_P of individual parameters of QC such that, for every quantification $(\forall X)A$ of QC, $(\forall X)A$ is true on α if $A(P/X)$ is true on α for every member P of Σ_P.[12]

So take a tv-verifiable set S of wffs of QC to be *finitely tv-verifiable* if S is true on some truth-value assignment α for QC that satisfies C1. It can be shown on the strength of this definition that, as a set S of wffs of QC has a model if and only if S itself or some other set isomorphic to S is tv-verifiable, so S has a finite model if and only if S itself or some other set of isomorphic to S is finitely tv-verifiable.

The notion of isomorphism between truth-value assignments also proves of interest. α and α' being truth-value assignments for QC, take α and α' to be *isomorphic* if there is a one-to-one relettering function R on the individual parameters of QC such that, for every atomic wff A of QC, $\alpha'(A) = \alpha(R(A))$. And take the *model counterpart* of a truth-value assignment α for QC to be $<D, I_D>$, where D consists of the individual parameters of QC and I_D has the following values: (i) for each sentence parameter A of QC the value of A on α, (ii) for each individual parameter P of QC the parameter P itself, and (iii) for each m-adic predicate parameter F of QC the subset of D^m that has $<P_1, P_2, \ldots, P_m>$ as a member if and only if $\alpha(F(P_1, P_2, \ldots, P_m)) = \mathbf{T}$. It will follow that two truth-value assignments for QC are isomorphic in my sense if and only if their model counterparts are isomorphic in the model-theoretic sense.

A rather interesting question arises at this point: "How many truth-value assignments for QC are isomorphic to a given one?" The answer—as Weaver and I noted—is threefold:

(1) If all the atomic wffs of QC are assigned $\mathbf{T}$ in α, or all of them assigned $\mathbf{F}$, just one truth-value assignment is isomorphic to α: α itself;

(2) If only finitely many atomic wffs of QC are assigned $\mathbf{T}$ in α, or only finitely many assigned $\mathbf{F}$, $\aleph_0$ truth-value assignments are isomorphic to α; and

(3) If $\aleph_0$ atomic wffs of QC are assigned $\mathbf{T}$ in α, and equally many are assigned $\mathbf{F}$, $2^{\aleph_0}$ truth-value assignments are isomorphic to α.

As it happens, all sets of wffs of QC true on a truth-value assignment from either one of the first two groups are sure to be finitely tv-verifiable or have a finite model. So, if the wffs true on a truth-value assignment α are to have no finite model, $\aleph_0$ atomic wffs of QC must be assigned $\mathbf{T}$ in α, and as many be assigned $\mathbf{F}$.

Note incidentally that any two isomorphic truth-value assignments for QC are *equivalent as to closed wffs*, i.e., any closed wff of QC true on one is sure to be true on the other. However, two truth-value assignments for QC may be equivalent as to closed wffs and yet not be isomorphic.

Matters of completeness also deserve study. Take a closed set S of wffs of QC to be *complete* if for every wff A of QC at least one of A and $\sim A$ is a consequence of S (i.e., at least one of $S \cup \{A\}$ and $S \cup \{\sim A\}$ is not tv-verifiable); take two closed sets of wffs of QC to be *equivalent* if their consequences are the same; and call the set consisting of the closed wffs of QC true on a truth-value assignment α the *associated truth set* of α. It can be shown of a closed and tv-verifiable set S of wffs of QC that S is complete if and only if S is equivalent to the associated truth set of a truth-value assignment to which no other truth-value assignment is isomorphic. However, a set may be incomplete as to *all* the wffs of QC and nonetheless be complete as to *just the closed* wffs of QC. The set may even be *categorical in the truth-value sense* (i.e., such that any two truth-value assignments on which the members of the set are true are isomorphic), in which case the set is what the literature calls $\aleph_0$-categorical.

But so much for QC. QC^2, the quantificational calculus of order two, raises interesting problems, some solved only recently. Dispense for the occasion with sentence letters, but have both predicate parameters and predicate variables on hand; allow the latter to be quantified as individual variables were in QC; and write '$A(B/F^m(P_1,P_2, \ldots ,P_m))$' ($F_m$ from now on an m-adic predicate variable) where Church would '$\check{S}_B^{F^m(P_1,P_2, \ldots ,P_m)} A|$'.[13]

Borrowing in part from a 1960 paper by Schütte, I shall understand by a *truth-value function of Class One for* QC^2 any function α from the wffs (*non-atomic as well as atomic*) of QC^2 to $\{T,F\}$ such that:

(1) $\alpha(\sim A) = T$ if and only if $\alpha(A) = F$,
(2) $\alpha(A \supset B) = T$ if and only if $\alpha(A) = F$ or $\alpha(B) = T$,
(3) $\alpha((\forall X)A) = T$ if and only if $\alpha(A(P/X)) = T$ for every individual parameter P of QC^2, and
(4) $\alpha((\forall F^m)A) = T$ if and only if $\alpha(A(B/F^m(P_1,P_2, \ldots ,P_m))) = T$ for any wff B of QC^2 of the sort $G^m(P_1,P_2, \ldots ,P_m)$ and any distinct individual parameters $P_1, P_2, \ldots , P_m$ of QC^2.

It can be shown, again by an adaptation of Henkin's completeness argument, that a wff A of QC^2 is provable in QC^{2*}, the fragment of QC^2 which in a 1953 paper Henkin labels F^*, if and only if A has value T on every truth-value function of Class One for QC^2.

Now call your function a *truth-value function of Class Two for* QC^2 if B in clause (4) is allowed to be any wff of QC, and call it a *truth-value function of Class Three for* QC^2 if B there can be any wff of QC^2. Exactly the same argument will show that A is provable in $QC^{2!}$, the fragment of QC^2 which Church calls *the predicative functional calculus of order two,* if and only if A has value T on every truth-value function of Class Two for QC^2, and A is provable in QC^2 if and only if A has value T on every truth-value function of Class Three. A truth-value semantics for each one of QC^{2*}, $QC^{2!}$, and QC^2 can thus be had, thanks in good measure to Schütte and Henkin.[14]

The question naturally arises: "Can truth-values be assigned in QC^2 as in QC and PC to *just* the atomic wffs, and the truth-values of non-atomic ones be calculated from these?". The answer is Yes in the first two cases. Where α and α' are truth-value functions of Class One or of Class Two for QC^2, α and α' will agree on the non-atomic wffs of QC^2 if they agree on the atomic ones. So the interpretation placed here upon QC^2 and that placed upon $QC^{2!}$ are what I call a *strictly truth-functional*. In the third case, though, the answer is No. Meyer and I have constructed truth-value functions of Class Three which agree on all the wffs of QC (and, hence, on all the atomic wffs of QC^2), but disagree on '$(\exists f)(\exists x)(\exists y)(f(x)$ & $\sim f(y))$'. So the interpretation placed here upon QC^2 is not strictly truth-functional.[15]

I recently extended this investigation to $QC^{2/\omega}$, *the ramified quantificational calculus of order two*, and arrived at analogous results. In the absence of the *Axiom of Reducibility*, count as a *truth-value function for* $QC^{2/\omega}$ any function α from the wffs of $QC^{2/\omega}$ to $\{T, F\}$ which meets conditions (1)–(3) above and the following fourth condition, where $F^{m/l}$ is an arbitrary m-adic predicate variable of level l:

(4') $\alpha((\forall F^{m/l})A) = T$ if and only if $\alpha(A(B/F^{m/l}(P_1, P_2, \ldots, P_m))) = T$ for any wff B of $QC^{2/\omega}$ which contains no predicate variable of level higher than $l-1$ nor any predicate parameter of level higher than l, and for any distinct individual parameters $P_1, P_2, \ldots, P_m$ of $QC^{2/\omega}$.

I verified that a wff A of $QC^{2/\omega}$ is provable in that calculus if and only if A has value T on every truth-value function for $QC^{2/\omega}$; and—aided by Weaver—proved that truth-value functions for $QC^{2/\omega}$ which agree on all the atomic wffs of $QC^{2/\omega}$ also agree on all the non-atomic ones. So here too truth-values can be assigned to *just* the atomic wffs, and the truth-values of non-atomic ones calculated from these.

However, add the following Axiom of Reducibility, with $X_1, X_2, \ldots, X_m$ presumed to be distinct individual variables:

$$(\forall G^{m/l})(\exists F^{m/1})(\forall X_1)(\forall X_2) \ldots (\forall X_m)(F^{m/1}X_1, X_2, \ldots, X_m) \equiv G^{m/l}(X_1, X_2, \ldots, X_m)),$$

and the interpretation placed here $QC^{2/\omega}$ is not strictly truth-functional. To any wff A of $QC^{2/\omega}$ there will correspond a unique (and readily specified) wff B of QC^2 such that A is provable in $QC^{2/\omega}$ if and only if B has value T on every truth-value function of Class Three for QC^2. And expectedly so: as Ramsey pointed out in 1926, the ramified theory of types in *Principia Mathematica*, first edition, is but a notational variant of the simple theory of types.[16]

Results like the above hold true of the quantificational calculus of order ω and the ramified quantificational calculus of order ω. Some of the details are to be found in Schütte's paper and the Leblanc-Meyer one.

1959 saw a major breakthrough in semantics when Kripke published his completeness proof for QS5, a quantificational extension of Lewis' S5's. Others soon joined in the undertaking, and by 1962 various semantic accounts of QM (a quantificational extension of von Wright's M), QS4 (a quantificational extension of Lewis's S4), and QS5 were on hand. Kripke in his 1963 paper still uses models, but Hintikka in his paper of the same year does not, model sets doing again duty for models.

Borrowing from both accounts, one readily gets a truth-value semantics for all three of QM, QS4, and QS5. Indeed, α being a truth-value assignment for

QM (i.e., a function from the *atomic* wffs of QM to $\{\mathbf{T},\mathbf{F}\}$), Σ being a set of truth-value assignments for QM that contains α, and R being a reflexive relation on Σ, take a wff A of QM to be true on the triple $<\alpha,\Sigma,R>$ if:
(A) in case A is atomic, $\alpha(A) = \mathbf{T}$,
(B) in case A is of the sort $\sim B$, B is not true on $<\alpha,\Sigma,R>$,
(C) in case A is of the sort $B \supset C$, B is not true on $<\alpha,\Sigma,R>$ or C is,
(D) in case A is of the $(\forall X)B$, $B(P/X)$ is true on $<\alpha,\Sigma,R>$ for every individual parameter P of QM, and
(E) in case A is of the sort $\Box B$, B is true on $<\alpha',\Sigma,R>$ for every member α' of Σ such that $R(\alpha,\alpha')$.
It can be shown that a wff A of QM is provable in QM if and only if A is true on every triple $<\alpha,\Sigma,R>$ of the kind just described. And like results obtain for QS4 when R is required to be transitive as well as reflexive, and for QS5 when R is required to be transitive and symmetrical as well as reflexive (or when R is dropped altogether and, as Kripke had it in his 1959 paper, $\Box B$ is held true on $<\alpha,\Sigma>$ if B is true on $<\alpha',\Sigma>$ for every member α' of Σ).[17]

In all three cases, the reader will note, truth-values are assigned to *just* the atomic wffs, and the truth-values of non-atomic ones are calculated from these. So QM, QS4, and QS5 have strictly truth-functional interpretations, and hence are *extensional* after all.

I could parade further logics boasting a truth-value semantics, but the point of all these deviations from standard practice has yet to be discussed. So let me move on.

I repeatedly talked above of semantics that do without models. I am not urging, though, that we do away with models altogether and—to parody Hume—commit to the flames all volumes of model theory. There are facts about models which you can report in the tongue of Beth, Schütte, and others—say, that a set of wffs of QC has a model, that the set has a finite model, that all its models are isomorphic, etc. *But* there are other facts you cannot. Similarly, you may think of truth-value assignments as models of a sort. *But* these are all Henkin ones, and—important though Henkin models may be—other models cannot be wished away. So, admittedly, model theory outruns truth-value semantics, Hintikka's theory of model sets, Carnap's theory of state-descriptions, and the like.

However, model theory and semantics are quite different things, and my concern here is with the latter, more specifically, with semantic accounts of QC, QC^2, the theory of types (both ramified and not), QM, QS4, QS5, etc. Until recently, the wffs held provable, and the sets of wffs held syntactically consistent, in these calculi were exclusively described in model-theoretic terms. I am agreeable of course to the practice but wish to enter a plea for alternate ones, which might well prove equally noteworthy.

I have also assumed that truth-value semantics—though attentive only to matters of truth—is a *bona fide* semantics. Some will doubtless object to this, insisting that matters of denotation be covered as well. In reply I could point to the standard account of a tautology, in which only truth figures. I could also list various notions—synonymy one of them—which are rated semantical by many, and yet do not figure in standard accounts of validity, semantic consistency, and the like. But these would be mere *quid pro quos*. I shall urge instead that whenever validity, semantic consistency, and the like can be explicated in terms of truth alone, as is demonstrably the case with all of the above calculi, talk of denotation—though allowable, to be sure—is dispensable. To be blunt, find a flaw in extant proofs that, say, a set of wffs of QC is syntactically consistent so long as it or some set isomorphic to it is tv-verifiable, or learn to live with truth-value semantics. I shall return to the subject a few pages hence.

Hintikka's model set semantics, *as reported above*, is something else. The notion of a model set is strictly syntactical, and hence so is the characterization of a valid wff of QC as one whose negation belongs to no model set. But that entire account can be so revamped as to be of the truth-value sort. Indeed, partial truth-value functions—reminiscent of those in Schütte's 1960 paper—will readily do duty for Hintikka's model sets, and a valid wff of QC will then be one whose negation does not evaluate to **T** on any such function.

These preliminaries out of the way, let me sketch out what—philosophically as well as mathematically—may entitle the new semantics to consideration.

Take the theorems of QC. They are, of course, the wffs of QC whose negations have no models. But they are also the wffs of QC that prove true no matter what the truth-values of their atomic subformulas. The second characterization is no less enlightening than the first. It also makes for a smooth transition from the logic of connectives to the logic of quantifiers. And within the latter it makes for a sharp divide between mere instances of tautologies and wffs that owe their validity to '$\forall$' (note the difference between '$(\forall x)f(x) \supset (\forall x)f(x)$', which is true on all truth-value assignments to '$(\forall x)f(x)$', and '$(\forall x)f(x) \supset f(a_1)$', which—though false on one truth-value assignment to just '$(\forall x)f(x)$' and '$f(a_1)$'—is true on all truth-value assignments to '$(\forall x)f(x)$', '$f(a_1)$', '$f(a_2)$', '$f(a_3)$', etc.).

Or take the sets of wffs of QC that are rated syntactically consistent. I find it enlightening—even from a model-theoretic point of view—that all the infinitely extendible ones are tv-verifiable, that some of the rest are not (so that Henkin models will not do duty for *all* denumerable models), and that the difficulty can be met by simply reshuffling one's individual parameters. And Henkin's completeness proof becomes pellucid when viewed as systematically extending an infinitely extendible set to a model one.[18]

Or take the matter of strict truth-functionality. There are various ways of phrasing the difference between $QC^{2!}$, the predicate fragment of QC^2, and QC^2 itself. But I find it enlightening that in one case the truth-value of a non-atomic wff depends exclusively upon the truth-values of its atomic subformulas, but not in the other. Like results hold true—as I reported earlier—of RT, the ramified theory of types. Wittgenstein, you will recall, favored a strictly truth-functional logic and rightly sensed that the substitution interpretation of the quantifiers was the key to it. Quite consistently with that stance of his, he balked at the Axiom of Reducibility, but his objections may have missed the target. We know of a better one now: in the absence of Russell's axiom the theory's main interpretation is strictly truth-functional, in the presence of the axiom it is not.[19]

The literature is silent on this, and on many other questions regarding RT. For example, you will find in Henkin's 1950 paper a semantic characterization of the theorems of T, the simple theory of types, but nowhere will you find one of the theorems of RT. These, in truth-value semantics, are simply the wffs of RT true on all truth-value functions for RT.

Attention has been drawn by Quine to the ontological presuppositions of logic and by rebound to those of rival semantics for logic. The semantics of Beth, Schütte, and others fares rather well on this score. Consider again QC. Where model-theoretic semantics must acknowledge truth-values, functions from the sentence parameters of QC to these truth-values, domains (and domains of all conceivable cardinalities at that), functions from the individual parameters of QC to members of these domains, functions from the monadic predicate parameters of QC to sets of members of these domains, functions from the dyadic predicate parameters of QC to sets of pairs of members of these domains, and so on, truth-value semantics makes do with just truth-values, functions from the atomic wffs of QC to these truth-values, and relettering functions on the individual parameters of QC. The contrast is startling.

Or consider QC^2. Where Henkin has to call in truth-values, functions from the sentence parameters of QC^2 to these truth-values, *systems of domains*, and functions from the individual and predicate parameters of QC^2 to the domains in these systems, truth-value semantics uses just truth-values, functions from the wffs of QC^2 to these truth-values, and relettering functions on the paremeters of QC^2. And the restrictions that Henkin must place on his *models* to ensure that the respective axioms of $QC^{2!}$ and QC^2 are valid become in truth-value semantics just different conditions which $(\forall F)A$ must meet to be true on a truth-value function.

Or, to vary the illustrations, consider the first-order arithmetic A_0 of Church,[20] count 'a_0' as an extra individual parameter, and let α be the result of assigning **T** to just the atomic wffs of A_0 of the two sorts $\Sigma(a_i, a_j, a_k)$ and $\Pi(a_i, a_j, a_k)$, where in the first case $i + j = k$ and in the second $i \times j = k$. The closed wffs of A_0 true on α (or any truth-value assignment for A_0 isomorphic to α) are of course the truths of elementary arithmetic, which can thus be explicated without reference to 0, 1, 2, 3, etc. The news should be welcome to nominalists who acknowledge elementary arithmetic, but wince at mention of abstract entities like numbers.

Like results can be had for any first-order theory whose *intended* model is finite or denumerably infinite. Some truth-value assignment, easily specified in each case, can always substitute for the model. When individual constants are around, these must be mapped with some of the individual parameters, but the mapping is usually no problem. Suppose, for example, that the two numerals '0' and '1' did turn up as primitives in A_0. You could take $R(`0')$ to be 'a_0', take $R('1')$ to be 'a_1', and use in lieu of the above α the truth-value assignment α', where—for every atomic A of A_0—$\alpha'(A) = \alpha(R(A))$. The truths of elementary arithmetic would then prove to be all (and only) the closed wffs of A_0 true on α'.

The ontological presuppositions of familiar logics like QC, QC^2, the theory of types, etc., and of familiar first-order theories like elementary arithmetic, thus boil down in the new semantics to just truth-values, assignments of truth-values to wffs, and—should semantic consistency be explicated as well—relettering functions. As a result, the main emphasis is on the wff, not on what goes into its making. This brings us back to an earlier and crucial subject.

From Hobbes down to Quine some have claimed that meaning accrues to a statement through its being true or its being false—hence, that meaning accrues to a statement directly, *not* through the meanings or alleged meanings of its component parts. Hobbes's thesis has made its way into linguistics, students of speech now assuring us that children—far from first speaking words which they then combine into sentences—speak sentences from the very start. It is further alleged that children do not match nouns with things, and verbs with properties of things or relations between things, but rather match whole sentences with these parents' responses (sometimes approbative, sometimes not) to these sentences. I won't argue that the young show us the way here. I shall only insist that its exclusive attention to truth—far from telling against the new semantics—may well speak for it.

These then should commend truth-value semantics to your attention: the fresh light it sheds on validity and semantic consistency in first-order logic, the badly needed light it sheds on theoremhood in higher-order ones, its findings as regards strict truth-functionality in the theory of types and modal logic, the ontological thrift it displays when accounting for all manners of logics and formal theories, and the stress it places on truth, a *large* part—if not, as some claim, the whole—of meaning.

Notes

1. As noted earlier, "Semantic Deviations" was the opening address at the Temple University Conference on Alternative Semantics, 1970. Some of the material had been presented at meetings of the Association for Symbolic Logic and in talks delivered at the University of California at Los Angeles, the University of Alberta, etc.

2. The presentation in the text differs somewhat from Tarski's, but is equivalent to it. For Tarski's own phrasing of the matter, see Note 4.

3. Throughout, '~' and '⊃' will be the only connectives, and '∀' the only quantifier letter, to serve as primitive.

4. Now for Tarski's own phrasing of the matter. Given a model $<D, I_D>$ Tarski talks of a sentence of L being satisfied *by an infinite sequence of members of D* rather than *by a valuation over D of the individual variables of L*. Presuming the individual variables of L to be, say, 'x_1', 'x_2', 'x_3', etc., and S_D to be an infinite sequence of members of D, he declares $F(I_1, I_2, \ldots, I_m)$ satisfied by S_D if $<d_1, d_2, \ldots, d_m>$ belongs to $I_D(F)$, where (i) in case I_i ($1 \leq i \leq m$) is an individual constant of L, d_i is $I_D(I_i)$ and (ii) otherwise, d_i is the first entry in S_D if I_i is 'x_1', the second entry in S_D if I_i is 'x_2', the third entry in S_D if I_i is 'x_3', etc.; and he declares $(\forall X)A$ satisfied by S_D if—X being the n-th individual variable of L—A is satisfied by every sequence of members of

D agreeing with S_D except possibly on entry n. This done, he takes a closed sentence of L to be true if it is satisfied by every infinite sequence of members of D, otherwise to be false.

5. Note that under the present account of things formulas of L in which identical quantifiers overlap do not count as well-formed.

6. I.e., V being a function from the sentence parameters of QC to $\{T, F\}$, from the individual parameters of QC to D, and from the m-adic ($m = 1, 2, 3$, etc.) predicate parameters of QC to the power set of D^m.

7. As Hintikka points out, the restruction can be lifted when $\emptyset$ is acknowledged as a domain.

8. See my paper "Three Generalizations of a Theorem of Beth's" in this volume.

9. See my paper "A Simplified Strong Completeness Proof for $QC_=$" in this volume.

10. See my papers "A Simplified Account of Validity and Implication for Quantificational Logic," "Three Generalizations of a Theorem of Beth's," and "A Simplified Strong Completeness Proof for $QC_=$" in this volume. It became clear as I wrote these that using two runs of individual signs rather than one, two runs of predicate signs rather than one, etc., would immensely simplify matters, and I have done so every since.

11. See my paper "A Simplified Account of Validity and Implication for Quantificational Logic" in this volume.

12. An early proof of mine that C2 implies C1 was in error. A correct one has since been supplied by David Kaplan and will be found on pp. 157–58 and in my *Truth-Value Semantics*, pp. 71–72.

13. See Church's *Introduction to Mathematical Logic, Volume I*, pp. 192–93. With two runs of individual letters and two of predicate letters, $A(B/F(P_1, P_2, \ldots, P_m))$ is readily accounted for. See "Truth-Functionality and the Ramified Theory of Types" in this volume.

14. In view of Gödel's Incompleteness Theorem the wffs of QC^2 provable in QC^2 (i.e., those true on all truth-value functions of Class Three for QC^2) are *but some* of the valid wffs of QC^2. For a truth-value account of the latter, see "Truth-Value Semantics for the Theory of Types" in this volume.

15. For further details, see the three papers "Truth-Value Semantics for the Theory of Types," "Wittgenstein and the Truth-Functionality Thesis," and "That *Principia Mathematica*. First Edition, has a Predicative Interpretation After All" in this volume. As the reader will recall from p. 236, an interpretation of QC^2 that is strictly truth-functional turns up in the third of these papers. It is, however, rather *ad hoc*, in my opinion at any rate.

16. For further details, see "Truth-Functionality and the Ramified Theory of Types" in this volume. As noted in my 1975 paper on *Principia Mathematica*, an interpretation of $QC^{2/\omega}$ (and, more generally, of the ramified theory of types) that is strictly truth-functional can be had. It is, however, rather *ad hoc*, in my opinion at any rate.

17. I assume that the Barcan Formula (provable in QS5) counts as an axiom of QM and QS4. The semantics sketched in the text can be so amended that neither the Barcan formula nor its converse are valid in any of QM, QS4, and QS5. On this point, see my paper "On Dispensing with Things and Worlds" in this volume.

18. Henkin's own instructions extend the set into a special sort of model set known as a *truth set*, i.e., into a set S such that (i) a negation $\sim A$ of QC belongs to S if and only if A does not, (ii) a condition $A \supset B$ of QC belongs to S if and only if A does not belong to S or B does, and (iii) a quantificational $(\forall X)A$ of QC belongs to S if and only if $A(P/X)$ does for every individual parameter P of QC.

19. By the *main* interpretation of RT I understand the interpretation issuing from that of $QC^{2/\omega}$ in "Truth-Functionality and the Ramified Theory of Types" once predicate variables and parameters are enlisted for all types.

20. See Church's *Introduction to Mathematical Logic, Volume I*, pp. 318–19.

References

[1] Beth, E. W. 1959. *The Foundations of Mathematics*. Amsterdam: North-Holland.
[2] Carnap, R. 1950. *Logical Foundations of Probability*. Chicago: University of Chicago Press.

[3] Church, A. 1956. *Introduction to Mathematical Logic, Volume I*. Princeton: Princeton University Press.
[4] Dunn, J. M., and Belnap, N. D., Jr. 1968. "The Substitution Interpretation of the Quantifiers." *Noûs* 2: 177–85.
[5] Gentzen, G. 1934–35. "Untersuchungen über das logische Schliessen." *Mathematische Zeitschrift* 39: 176–210, 405–31.
[6] Henkin, L. 1949. "The Completeness of the First-Order Functional Calculus." *The Journal of Symbolic Logic* (hereafter *JSL*) 14: 159–66.
[7] ———. 1950. "Completeness in the Theory of Types." *JSL* 15: 81–91.
[8] ———. 1953. "Banishing the Rule of Substitution for Functional Variables." *JSL* 18: 201–08.
[9] Hintikka, J. 1955. "Two Papers on Symbolic Logic." *Acta Philosophica Fennica* 8.
[10] ———. 1963. "The Modes of Modality." *Modal and Many-Valued Logics. Acta Philosophica Fennica.* 16: 65–81.
[11] Kripke, S. 1963. "Semantical Considerations on Modal Logic." *Acta Philosophica Fennica.* 16: 83–94.
[12] Leblanc, H. 1976. *Truth-Value Semantics*. Amsterdam: North-Holland.
[13] Marcus, R. B. 1963. "Modal Logics I: Modalities and Intensional Languages." *Boston Studies in Philosophy of Science*, ed. M. W. Wartofsky, pp. 77–96. Dordrecht: Reidel.
[14] Ramsey, F. P. 1926. "The Foundations of Mathematics." *Proceedings of the London Mathematical Society*, Series 2, 25: 338–84.
[15] ———. 1926–27. "Mathematical Logic." *The Mathematical Gazette* 13: 185–94.
[16] Robinson, A. 1951. *On the Metamathematics of Algebra*. Amsterdam: North-Holland.
[17] Schütte, K. 1960. "Syntactical and Semantical Properties of Simple Type Theory." *JSL* 25: 305–26.
[18] ———. 1962. *Lecture Notes in Mathematical Logic*. The Pennsylvania State University, Department of Mathematics.
[19] Shoenfield, J. R. 1967. *Mathematical Logic*. Reading, Mass.: Addison-Wesley.
[20] Tarski, A. 1936. "Der Wahrheitsbegriff in den formalisierten Sprachen." *Studia Philosophica* 1: 261–405.
[21] Wittgenstein, L. 1922. *Tractatus Logico-Philosophicus*. London: Routledge and Kegan Paul.

Part 3: Provability

Introduction

Unlike Parts 1 and 2, which had a single theme each, Part 3 has a variety of them: #21–#26 deal with the twin topics of *natural deduction* and *sequenzen kalküle*, #27–#30 deal with ways of strengthening intuitionist logic into classical logic and study the demarcation line between these two logics, #31–#32 deal with ways of converting axioms and rules of inference for Boolean Algebra into axioms and rules of inference for SC (= the sentential calculus), #33 deals with a novel choice of primitive operators for elementary logic, #34 deals with so-called matters of separation, and lastly #35 deals with the rule of Generalization. In all cases but two a brief review of these themes should suffice. The lone exceptions are natural deduction and sequenzen.

Prior to 1934 one commonly understood by a *deduction* (or *derivation*) any column of wffs that consisted of (i) assumptions (or, to use the more familiar phrase, premises), (ii) axioms, and (iii) wffs gotten from earlier wffs in the column by dint of a rule of inference. Cases in point are the following two columns of wffs, one constituting a deduction of 'p' from the set of premises $\{\sim p \supset q, q \supset \sim r, r\}$ and the other a deduction of '$p \supset p$' from the null set of premises.[1] All wffs concerned are presumed to be from SC, and all wffs of SC of the sorts **A1–A3** on p. 000 are presumed to count as axioms. The one rule of inference appealed to is of course Modus Ponens (**MP**, for short).

1 $\sim p \supset q$		1 $p \supset ((p \supset p) \supset p)$		(**A1**)
2 $q \supset \sim r$		2 $p \supset (p \supset p)$		(**A1**)
3 r		3 $1 \supset (2 \supset (p \supset p))$		(**A2**)
4 $2 \supset (\sim p \supset (q \supset \sim r))$	(**A1**)	4 $2 \supset (p \supset p)$		(**MP**, 1, 3)
5 $\sim p \supset (q \supset \sim r)$	(**MP**, 2, 4)	5 $p \supset p$		(**MP**, 2, 4)
6 $5 \supset (1 \supset (\sim p \supset \sim r))$	(**A2**)			
7 $1 \supset (\sim p \supset \sim r)$	(**MP**, 5, 6)			

283

8 $\sim p \supset \sim r$ (**MP**, 1, 7)
9 $8 \supset (r \supset p)$ (**A3**)
10 $r \supset p$ (**MP**, 8, 9)
11 p (**MP**, 3, 10)

Deductions of this sort will be known here as *axiomatic deductions*. Easy to characterize,[2] they turned up in many papers of Part 1 and Part 2 as our official means of deducing a wff from a set of wffs, be it in first- or in higher-order logic, in standard or in presupposition-free logic, in two- or in three-valued logic, etc. Whenever there are quantifiers about, however, they can be quite difficult to construct, even with the aid of computers.

Fortunately for practitioners of logic, Gentzen and Jaśkowski devised in 1934 a novel sort of deductions, known as *natural deductions*.[3] These are harder to characterize than axiomatic deductions,[4] but they are vastly easier to come by and they better mimic the ways we informally reason. Particularly noteworthy about natural deductions is that they dispense with axioms (but as a result employ more rules of inference than axiomatic deductions do) and permit deductions within deductions. For illustration's sake I supply a natural deduction of 'p' from $\{\sim p \supset q, q \supset \sim r, r\}$ and one of '$p \supset p$' from $\varnothing$.[5] '**R**' is short throughout for 'Reiteration', '**HE**' for 'Horseshoe Elimination', '**HI**' for 'Horseshoe Introduction', '**NE**' for 'Negation Elimination', and '**NI**' for 'Negation Introduction'.

1	$\sim p \supset q$			1		p	
2	$q \supset \sim r$			2		p	(**R**, 1)
3	r			3	$p \supset p$		(**HI**, 1, 2)
4		$\sim p$					
5		$\sim p$	(**R**, 4)				
6		$\sim p \supset q$	(**R**, 1)				
7		q	(**HE**, 5, 6)				
8		$q \supset \sim r$	(**R**, 2)				
9		$\sim r$	(**HE**, 7, 8)				
10		r	(**R**, 3)				
11	$\sim\sim p$		(**NI**, 4–(9, 10))				
12	p		(**NE**, 11)				

The first of these two natural deductions is longer to be sure, but far easier, than its axiomatic counterpart; the second is both shorter and easier.

A variety of rules have been advanced over the years as *natural deduction rules*. Those in the Gentzen-Jaśkowski tradition (to me the only ones deserving consideration) comprise **R**, sometimes labeled a *structural rule*, plus rules for either *intr*oducing or *elim*inating logical operators and known as *intelim rules*.[6] **HI** and **NI** in the foregoing illustrations are introduction rules for '$\supset$' and '$\sim$', respectively, while **HE** and **NE** are elimination rules for these connectives.

Now for #25. Montague and Henkin reported in 1956 that strong completeness cannot be had[7] if variables are generalized upon in Church's 1944 manner.[8] I show in #25 that the corresponding introduction rule for '$\forall$' and elimination rule for '$\exists$' create a like problem, and propose various solutions to it. I then address myself to a *separation* matter.

Let a wff A (a set S of wffs) of QC be said to be *in K, K* a subset of $\{\sim, \supset, \&, \vee, \equiv, \forall, \exists\}$, if every logical operator that occurs in A (in one or more members of S) belongs to K. It can be shown—given results in #23 and #24— that in 76 out of 128 cases a wff A, when entailed by a set S of premises in K, is invariably deducible from S by means of **R** and the intelim rules *for only such logical operators as belong to K*. In the remaining 52 cases, however, recourse to **NI** and **NE** proves ineluctable whenever A is not intuitionistically entailed by S.

In 48 of these 52 cases things can be put to rights, I go on to show, if the elimination rule for '$\supset$' is strengthened along lines suggested by Kanger and the elimination rule for '$\equiv$' strengthened along lines suggested by Leblanc and Bernays. The last four cases call for a rule of Fitch's that introduces two operators at a time, the connective '$\vee$' and the quantifier letter '$\forall$'.[9]

The natural deductions in #25 match Gentzen's N-sequents and hence feature only single wffs. Natural deductions matching Gentzen's L-sequents can also be had in which figure sequences of two or more wffs as well as single wffs. They are studied in the closing pages of #26 and constitute another solution to the second problem reported in #25.

#22 and #23 call for some additional preliminaries. The rules employed in the natural deductions of p. 284 are often formulated as follows:

$$
\begin{array}{r|ll}
1 & A_1 & \\
2 & A_2 & \\
\cdot & \cdot & \\
n & A_n & \\
\cdot & \cdot & \\
p & A_i & (\mathbf{R},\ i)
\end{array}
$$

```
1 | A₁                              1 | A₁
2 | A₂                              2 | A₂
. | .                               . | .
n | Aₙ                              n | Aₙ
. | .                               . | .
p |   | B                           p | B       (or B ⊃ C)
  |   |                             . | .
. | .                               q | B ⊃ C   (or B)
q |   | C                           . | .
q+1 | B ⊃ C    (HI, p–q)            r | C       (HE, p, q)

1 | A₁                              1 | A₁
2 | A₂                              2 | A₂
. | .                               . | .
n | Aₙ                              n | Aₙ
. | .                               . | .
p |   | B                           p | ~~B
. | .                               . | .
q |   | C   (or ~C)                 q | B       (NE, p)
. | .
r |   | ~C  (or C)
r+1 | ~B    (NI, p–(q,r))
```

They have also been formulated as follows:

R: For each i from 1 through n, A_i is deductible from $\{A_1, A_2, \ldots, A_n\}$;

HI: If C is deducible from the superset $\{A_1, A_2, \ldots, A_n, B\}$ of $\{A_1, A_2, \ldots, A_n\}$, then $B \supset C$ is deducible from $\{A_1, A_2, \ldots, A_n\}$;

HE: If both B and $B \supset C$ are deducible from $\{A_1, A_2, \ldots, A_n\}$, then so is C;

NI: If for some wff C both C and $\sim C$ are deducible from the superset $\{A_1, A_2, \ldots, A_n, B\}$ of $\{A_1, A_2, \ldots, A_n\}$, then $\sim B$ is deducible from $\{A_1, A_2, \ldots, A_n\}$;

NE: If $\sim\sim B$ is deducible from $\{A_1, A_2, \ldots, A_n\}$, then so is B;

or, to use the turnstile of p. 6, as follows:

Introduction 287

R: $A_1, A_2, \ldots, A_n \vdash A_i$ for each i from 1 through n;
HI: If $A_1, A_2, \ldots, A_n, B \vdash C$, then $A_1, A_2, \ldots, A_n \vdash B \supset C$;
HE: If $A_1, A_2, \ldots, A_n \vdash B$ and $A_1, A_2, \ldots, A_n \vdash B \supset C$, then $A_1, A_2, \ldots, A_n \vdash C$;
NI: If $A_1, A_2, \ldots, A_n, B \vdash C$ and $A_1, A_2, \ldots, A_n, B \vdash \sim C$, then $A_1, A_2, \ldots, A_n \vdash \sim B$;
NE: If $A_1, A_2, \ldots, A_n \vdash \sim\sim B$, then $A_1, A_2, \ldots, A_n \vdash B$.

(As pointed out on p. 6, formulations such as the last one constitute in effect recursive definitions of '⊢' for SC, **R** serving as the base clause of the definition and the remaining four rules serving as so many inductive clauses. Adoption of intelim rules for '∀' would yield a recursive definition of '⊢' for QC.)

In #22 and #23 I refer to a *metastatement* of the sort

$$A_1, A_2, \ldots, A_n \vdash B$$

as a *turnstile statement* or—for short—as a *T-statement*, and (in effect) declare it *valid* if (i) in case $n = 0$, B is valid and (ii) in case $n > 0$, the conditional $A_1 \supset (A_2 \supset (\ldots(A_n \supset B)\ldots))$ is valid, a move which ensures that $A_1, A_2, \ldots, A_n \vdash B$ is valid if and only if B is entailed by, and hence deducible from, the set $\{A_1, A_2, \ldots, A_n\}$.[10]

#23, restricted to T-statements in which all the A's (the so-called *antecedent formulas*) and B (the so-called *succedent formula*) are wffs of SC, supplies algorithms—or, as the paper puts it, routines—for proving

$$A_1, A_2, \ldots, A_n \vdash B$$

whenever valid.[11] In each and every case the proof that issues employs intelim rules *for only such connectives as occur in the T-statement*; and it readily converts into a natural deduction of B from $\{A_1, A_2, \ldots, A_n\}$ using **R** and intelim rules *for only such connectives as occur in* $A_1, A_2, \ldots, A_n$ or B. So far as I know, #23 was the first paper to mechanize the conducting of natural deductions, and as a result it may deserve a cursory glance.

#26 deals for the most part with N-sequents. But the argument there immediately yields as a corollary that, with 'A_1', 'A_2', $\ldots$ 'A_n', 'B' now ranging over wffs of QC,

$$A_1, A_2, \ldots, A_n \vdash B$$

is sure—when valid—to have a proof using intelim rules *for only such connectives and quantifier letters as occur in the T-statement*. In view of Church's Theorem, algorithms are of course out of the question; but, however arrived at, the proof is sure to convert into a natural deduction of B from $\{A_1, A_2, \ldots, A_n\}$ using **R** and intelim rules *for only such logical operators as occur in* $A_1, A_2, \ldots, A_n$, or B.

The so-called *separation problem* (i.e., given a set $\{A_1, A_2, \ldots, A_n\}$ of wffs and a wff B such that $\{A_1, A_2, \ldots, A_n\}$ entails B, is there a proof of the

T-statement $A_1, A_2, \ldots, A_n \vdash B$ or—equivalently—a deduction of B from $\{A_1, A_2, \ldots, A_n\}$ that exhibits no logical operators other than those in $A_1, A_2, \ldots, A_n$, or B?) is thus solved for both SC and QC.

The table of rules used in #23 to prove valid T-statements contains three "structural" rules. One is a weakened version of the **R** the reader has met with in these pages. It reads:

$$A \vdash A.^{12}$$

Another is the Permutation rule **P**, needed in #23 because the antecedent formulas of a T-statement are thought of as constituting an *ordered sequence* rather than a set. It reads:

If $A_1, A_2, \ldots, A_{i-1}, A_i, A_{i+1}, A_{i+2}, \ldots, A_n \vdash B$, then $A_1, A_2, \ldots,$
$A_{i-1}, A_{i+1}, A_i, A_{i+2}, \ldots, A_n \vdash B.$

The third is the Thinning rule **T**, which runs:

If $A_1, A_2, \ldots, A_n \vdash B$, then $A_1, A_2, \ldots, A_n, C \vdash B$.

The main result of #22 is to the effect that if **R** is left to read:

$$A_1, A_2, \ldots, A_n \vdash A_i,$$

and a T-statement $A_1, A_2, \ldots, A_n \vdash B$ is provable by **R**, **P**, and the four rules **HI**, **HE**, **NI**, and **NE** on p. 287, then $A_1, A_2, \ldots, A_n, C \vdash B$ is sure to be provable by the same rules. At times, therefore, **T** is dispensable.

A proof that features only logical operators occurring in its last line has been called *operator-minded* (in #21 *operator-preserving*); and one that features only subformulas of that last line has been called *subformula-minded* (in #21 *subformula-preserving*). Proofs of the traditional sort were sometimes (though not always) operator-minded: that of '$p \supset p$' on p. 283, for example, exhibits no connective but '$\supset$'.[13] But they generally were not subformula-minded, nor could they hope to be, since (i) the subformulas of a valid wff are generally not valid, but (ii) all steps in a proof of the traditional sort must be valid.

It was Gentzen's ambition in his 1934 paper to devise means of proof both for classical and for intuitionist logic that would yield subformula-minded (and hence operator-minded) proofs. The method of natural deduction, where proofs are deductions from the empty set, made for operator-minded proofs, as Gentzen stated but did not bother to establish.[14] It did not, however, always make for subformula-minded proofs: the first deduction on p. 283, easily extended into a proof of the wff '$(\sim p \supset q) \supset ((q \supset \sim r) \supset (r \supset p))$' from $\emptyset$, is bound to exhibit '$\sim\sim p$'.[15] So Gentzen quickly disposed of natural deductions and turned to his principal concern, to wit: brands of the classical and the intuitionist first-order quantificational calculus respectively known as LK and LJ and which boast subformula-minded proofs.

Gentzen's LK has one more primitive sign than QC, the arrow '$\rightarrow$', which is closely related to our turnstile '$\vdash$' but belongs to LK rather than its metalanguage. LK, as a result, has further formulas besides those of QC, to wit: the formulas

$$A_1, A_2, \ldots, A_n \to B_1, B_2, \ldots, B_m,$$

where $A_1, A_2, \ldots, A_n$ ($n \geq 0$), $B_1, B_2 \ldots, B_m$ ($m \geq 0$) are wffs of QC. These were called by Gentzen *sequenzen* and will be known here as *L-sequents*. When $m = 1$, L-sequents are closely related to our T-statements, but they belong to LK rather than its metalanguage. An L-sequent is classically (as opposed to intuitionistically) valid when and only when—in effect—$\{A_1, A_2, \ldots, A_n, \sim B_1, \sim B_2, \ldots, \sim B_m\}$ is not classically satisfiable.

Gentzen supplied in his paper an axiom schema (to wit: $A \to A$), six structural rules, and a pair of *introduction* rules for each of the operators '$\sim$', '$\supset$', '&', 'V', '∀', and '∃', which make for subformula-minded proofs of all classically valid L-sequents.[16]

LJ is exactly like LK except for one structural rule and one introduction rule, which are special cases of their LK-counterparts. Provable now are only those L-sequents which are intuitionistically valid, but the proofs are still subformula-minded. I shall not supply here, incidentally, nor did I supply in the papers collected below, a definition of intuitionist validity. The first one to reach print, Kripke's, still strikes me as the best, and—having no space to reproduce it here—I must ask the reader to consult the author's 1965 paper, "Semantical Analysis of Intuitionistic Logic I."

We remarked in passing that when $m=1$ L-sequents are near relatives of T-statements. Because of this kinship L-sequents of the sort

$$A_1, A_2, \ldots, A_n \to B$$

are often known as *N-sequents* ('N' as in 'Natural Deduction'). They made their first appearance in a 1936 paper of Gentzen's. Mimicking his earlier paper, one can devise an NK calculus, which has as its theorems all classically valid N-sequents, and an NJ calculus, which has as its theorems all intuitionistically valid ones. Whereas LK and LJ use just introduction rules, NK and NJ use both introduction and elimination rules. These can be adaptations of Gentzen's natural deduction rules and hence of my own rules for proving T-statements. They make for operator-minded proofs of all classically valid N-sequents and subformula-minded proofs of all intuitionistically valid ones. As a consequence Gentzen's natural deduction rules for intuitionist logic do permit subformula-minded deduction of B from $\{A_1, A_2, \ldots, A_n\}$ whenever B is intuitionistically entailed by $\{A_1, A_2, \ldots, A_n\}$.

These various matters are cursorily treated in #21 (a paper that readers unfamiliar with sequents should definitely peruse) and at length in #24 and #26. Some of the results in #24 and #26 were known at the time the papers were published; the balance, though, were new.[17]

#27–#30 study the gap between intuitionist and classical logic and ways of bridging it, especially ways of converting intelim rules for the former into intelim rules suiting the latter. It has long been known, for example, that strengthening the intuitionist elimination rule for '$\sim$' (be it "If $A_1, A_2, \ldots, A_n \vdash D$ and $A_1, A_2, \ldots, A_n \vdash \sim B$, then $A_1, A_2, \ldots, A_n \vdash C$," or the more perspicuous "If $A_1, A_2, \ldots, A_n \vdash \sim B$ and $A_1, A_2, \ldots, A_n \vdash \sim\sim B$, then $A_1, A_2, \ldots, A_n \vdash B$") to read like **NE** on p. 287 would do the trick. In collaboration with Beth in #27 and with Belnap in #28 I showed that

(i) strengthening the intuitionist elimination for '$\supset$' (= **HE**) to read (in effect): "If $A_1, A_2, \ldots, A_n \vdash B \supset C$ and $A_1, A_2, \ldots, A_n \vdash (B \supset D) \supset C$, then $A_1, A_2, \ldots, A_n \vdash C$,"[18]

or

(ii) strengthening the intuitionist elimination rule for '$\equiv$' ("If $A_1, A_2, \ldots, A_n \vdash B$ and either $A_1, A_2, \ldots, A_n \vdash B \equiv C$ or $A_1, A_2, \ldots, A_n \vdash C \equiv B$, then $A_1, A_2, \ldots, A_n \vdash C$") to read (in effect): "If $A_1, A_2, \ldots, A_n \vdash B$ and $A_1, A_2, \ldots, A_n \vdash (D \equiv B) \equiv (D \equiv C)$, then $A_1, A_2, \ldots, A_n \vdash C$,"[19] would also do the trick.

Belnap and I surmised in #28 that any classical rule for either of '&' and '∨' was bound to hold in intuitionist logic (and hence that there were but three ways of converting intelim rules for intuitionist logic into intelim rules suiting classical logic). Vesley challenged us on this point and advanced a rule which belied our conjecture and to him counted as an introduction rule for '∨'. This prompted the writing of #29, a paper in which Belnap, Thomason, and I explicated what is commonly understood by a rule, a structural rule, and an intelim rule for a logical operator. Under this analysis Vesley's rule did not qualify as a rule for '∨', and the conjecture in #28 was shown to hold true.

#30, written in collaboration with Thomason, sorts out the L-sequents, and then the N-sequents, which are sure—if classically valid—to be intuitionistically valid as well, and thus sharpens the demarcation line between the two logics.

#31–#32 solve a problem analogous to that in #27–#29. Students of Boolean Algebra (the alleged Algebra of Logic) frequently assume that it converts into the full sentential calculus once complement, intersection, and union signs are made into tildes, ampersands, and wedges. The truth is otherwise, as C. I. Lewis noted as early as 1918. Indeed, under the foregoing editing standard postulate sets for Boolean Algebra will deliver as theorems only tautologies of the sort $A \equiv B$. Ways of capturing the remaining tautologies are proposed in the two papers, and the gap between Boolean Algebra and the sentential calculus is thereby bridged.

The last three papers in Part 3 return to QC (and occasionally QC$_=$). #33 provides a list of all (*singulary*) quantifiers;[20] shows that a little noted one, 'All or none', permits definition of all others; and, with '$\sim$', '$\supset$', and this quantifier serving as primitive operators, supplies axioms and rules of inference that prove both sound and complete. #34 demonstrates a weak separation theorem for two axiomatizations of QC$_=$, one intuitionistically and the other classically sound and complete. '$\supset$' plays here the role that '$\vdash$' and '$\rightarrow$' did in earlier papers, and as a result figures in the proof of many a theorem that is horseshoeless. As for #35, it studies at length the problem Montague and Henkin noted in 1956 (see p. 431). Various solutions are reviewed, in particular one due to Fitch and which, *initially*, allows variables to be generalized upon only in axioms. Full-fledged rules of Generalization are then obtained, as are the metatheorems whose proofs Church's 1944 handling of Generalization blocked. All results are extended to presupposition-free brands of QC and $QC_=$, with #35 thus ending on an axiomatic treatment of matters from #1.

Notes

1. I.e., a proof of '$p \supset p$'. Deductions from $\varnothing$ are proofs.
2. Difficulties met when axiomatic deductions were initially characterized have since been cleared up. See #35 on this point. The appellation 'axiomatic deduction', incidentally, is of my own coining. I use it for lack of a better one.
3. Gentzen and Jaśkowski arrived at natural deduction independently of each other.
4. Indeed, natural deductions are frequently characterized by means of examples, a practice I followed in *Techniques of Deductive Inference* and (with Wisdom) in *Deductive Logic*.
5. I.e., a proof of '$p \supset p$'. See Note 1.
6. I borrow the appellation 'intelim rules' from Fitch's *Symbolic Logic*.
7. For instance, '$(\forall y)(g(y) \supset g(y))$', though entailed by $\{g(y)\}$, cannot be derived from it.
8. See Church's 1944 *Introduction to Mathematical Logic*, p. 45. The handling of Generalization in his 1956 *Introduction* circumvents the present difficulty.
9. Kanger's rule for '$\supset$' was suggested to me in a letter; my rule for '$\equiv$' first appeared in #28 and Bernays's simplification of it is in a review in the *Journal of Symbolic Logic*; and Fitch's rule for '$\lor$' and '$\forall$' first appeared in his *Symbolic Logic*. For additional information concerning these three rules, see pp. 350–357.
10. On further reflection I would now declare $A_1, A_2, \ldots, A_n \vdash B$ *true* rather than *valid* when condition (i) or condition (ii) is met. The occurrence of the word 'valid' in (i)–(ii) is probably to blame for the mislabeling, which I do not trouble to correct.
11. Proofs of T-statements will be found aplenty in my *Techniques of Deductive Inference*. For illustration's sake I include two, which stem in obvious ways from the natural deductions of p. 284.

Example 1:

1 $\sim p \supset q, q \supset \sim r, r, \sim p \vdash \sim p$		(R)
2 $\sim p \supset q, q \supset \sim r, r, \sim p \vdash \sim p \supset q$		(R)
3 $\sim p \supset q, q \supset \sim r, r, \sim p \vdash q$		(HE, 1, 2)
4 $\sim p \supset q, q \supset \sim r, r, \sim p \vdash q \supset \sim r$		(R)
5 $\sim p \supset q, q \supset \sim r, r, \sim p \vdash \sim r$		(HE, 3, 4)
6 $\sim p \supset q, q \supset \sim r, r, \sim p \vdash r$		(R)
7 $\sim p \supset q, q \supset \sim r, r, \vdash \sim\sim p$		(NI, 5, 6)
8 $\sim p \supset q, q \supset \sim r, r \vdash p$		(NE, 7)

Example 2:

1 $p \vdash p$ (R)

2 $\vdash p \supset p$ (HI, 1)

12. In the papers below $A \vdash A$ is sometimes referred to as **SR** (= Special Reiteration), but in most cases as **R**. $A_1, A_2, \ldots, A_n \vdash A_i$ is usually referred to as **R**, but sometimes as **GR** (= Generalized Reiteration).

13. For further information on this point, see #34. Of the sets of axioms and rules of inference proposed so far the one in #34 comes as close as any to making for operator-minded proofs. Note, however, that as the axioms all exhibit '⊃', any proof of '∼(p & ∼p)' has got to exhibit '⊃' and hence none can be operator-minded.

14. The first proofs of Gentzen's claim may have been in Prawitz's *Natural Deduction* and, by implication, in #24. The point in the text is pursued on pp. 293–300.

15. Proof of the point is too long for inclusion here. It hinges on the fact that '(∼p ⊃ q) ⊃ ((q ⊃ ∼r) ⊃ (r ⊃ p))' is not intuitionistically valid.

16. LK (and, it will turn out, LJ) has no elimination rules. This accounts in large part for the subformula-minded proofs it can boast of.

17. The literature on L- and N-sequents is enormous. A particularly comprehensive survey (one incidentally written by a major contributor to the subject) is Curry's *Foundations of Mathematical Logic*.

18. See Note 9 on the provenance of the rule.

19. See Note 9 on the provenance of the rule.

20. For a definition of singular quantifiers, see Borkowski's 1958 paper (or Leblanc and Wisdom's *Deductive Logic*, pp. 250–53). There are eight of these, as Dubislav may have been the first to notice.

References

[1] Bernays, P. 1962. Review of H. Leblanc's "Etudes sur les règles d'inférence dites règles de Gentzen." *The Journal of Symbolic Logic* (hereafter *JSL*) 27: 248–49.

[2] Borkowski, L. 1958. "On Proper Quantifiers I." *Studia Logica* 8: 65–130.

[3] Church, A. 1944. *Introduction to Muthematical Logic, Part I*. Princeton: Princeton University Press.

[4] ———. 1956. *Introduction to Mathematical Logic, Vol. I*. Princeton: Princeton University Press.

[5] Curry, H. B. 1963. *Foundations of Mathematical Logic*. New York: McGraw-Hill.

[6] Dubislav, W. 1929. "Elementarer Nachweis der Widerspruchslosigkeit des Logik-Kalküls." *Journal für die reine und angewandte Mathematik* 161: 107–12.

[7] Fitch, F. B. 1948. "Intuitionistic Modal Logic with Quantifiers." *Portugaliae Mathematica* 17: 113–18.

[8] Gentzen, G. 1934. "Untersuchungen über das logische Schliessen." *Mathematische Zeitschrift* 39: 176–210 and 406–31.

[9] ———. 1936. "Widerspruchsfreiheit der Zahlentheorie." *Mathematische Annalen* 112: 493–565.

[10] Jaśkowski, S. 1934. "On the Rules of Suppositions in Formal Logic." *Studia Logica* 1: 1–32.

[11] Kripke, S. A. 1965. "Semantical Analysis of Intuitionistic Logic I." *Formal Systems and Recursive Functions*, pp. 92–130. Amsterdam: North-Holland.

[12] Leblanc, H. 1966. *Techniques of Deductive Inference*. Englewood Cliffs: Prentice-Hall.

[13] Leblanc, H., and Wisdom, W. A. 1976. *Deductive Logic*, second edition. Boston: Allyn and Bacon.

[14] Lewis, C. I. 1918. *A Survey of Symbolic Logic*. Berkeley: University of California Press.

[15] Montague R., and Henkin, L. 1956. "On the Definition of 'Formal Deduction'." *JSL* 21: 129–36.

[16] Prawitz, D. 1965. *Natural Deduction, A Proof-Theoretical Study*. Stockholm: Almqvist and Wiksell.

[17] Vesley, R. E. 1963. "On Strengthening Intuitionistic Logic." *Notre Dame Journal of Formal Logic* 4: 80.

21
Marginalia on Gentzen's Sequenzen-Kalküle

1. As many a reader knows, Gentzen fashioned in [3] two novel versions of elementary logic or, to be more precise, of the quantificational calculus of first order (QC). One kalkül, called LK, sports besides the standard primitives of QC a fresh primitive, the symbol '$\to$'; it also sports besides the standard formulas of QC so-called *sequents*, that is, expressions of the kind

$$A_1, A_2, \ldots, A_n \to B_1, B_2, \ldots, B_m,$$

where $A_1, A_2, \ldots, A_n$ ($n \geq 0$), $B_1, B_2, \ldots, B_m$ ($m > 0$ if $n = 0$, otherwise $m \geq 0$) are standard formulas of QC. As for Gentzen's other kalkül, NK, it can be thought of as a fragment of LK, a fragment that also boasts the primitive '$\to$' but only owns sequents of the sort

$$A_1, A_2, \ldots, A_n \to B,$$

where $A_1, A_2, \ldots, A_n$ ($n \geq 0$), and B are again standard formulas of QC.[1]
Since Gentzen meant a sequent of the kind

$$A_1, A_2, \ldots, A_n \to B_1, B_2, \ldots, B_m,$$

where $n \geq 1$ and $m \geq 1$, to be valid when and only when the formula

$$(A_1 \mathbin{\&} A_2 \mathbin{\&} \ldots \mathbin{\&} A_n) \supset (B_1 \lor B_2 \lor \ldots \lor B_m)$$

of QC is valid, the commas which interspace the so-called *antecedent formulas* $A_1, A_2, \ldots, A_n$ in $A_1, A_2, \ldots, A_n \to B_1, B_2, \ldots, B_m$ may be treated as so many conjunction signs, those which interspace the so-called *consequent formulas* $B_1, B_2, \ldots, B_m$ as so many disjunction signs, and the arrow '$\to$' as a conditional sign. Under this understanding of Gentzen's commas and arrows,[2] a sequent of the kind

$$A_1, A_2, \ldots, A_n \to B_1, B_2, \ldots, B_m,$$

where $n \geq 1$ and $m \geq 1$, may be treated as an inference-form with $A_1, A_2, \ldots, A_n$ as premises and the disjunction $B_1 \lor B_2 \lor \ldots \lor B_m$ as conclusion. Sequents without antecedent formulas, on the other hand, are tantamount to

293

sequents with '$p \lor \sim p$' as antecedent formula, and sequents without consequent formulas tantamount to sequents with '$p \mathbin{\&} \sim p$' as consequent formula.

Gentzen supplied in [3] a list, revised in [4], of so-called *introduction* and *elimination rules of inference* for NK; only in [4], however, did he trouble to write out the one axiom schema and the so-called *structural rules of inference* he contemplated for that kalkül. Borrowing from [4] and recent papers of mine, I shall take NK to be fitted here with the following axiom schema:

$$A \to A,$$

occasionally known as the Reiteration Rule, and the following fifteen rules of inference, in which the Greek capitals 'Γ' and 'Δ' range over (possibly empty) arrays of formulas and commas:

TABLE 1

Structural rules of NK:

Permutation: $\quad \dfrac{\Gamma, A, B, \Delta \to C}{\Gamma, B, A, \Delta \to C}$

Thinning: $\quad \dfrac{\Gamma \to A}{B, \Gamma \to A}$

Contraction: $\quad \dfrac{A, A, \Gamma \to B}{A, \Gamma \to B}$

Int(roduction-)elim(ination) rules of NK:

	Introduction rules	Elimination rules
For '⊃':	$\dfrac{\Gamma, A \to B}{\Gamma \to A \supset B}$	$\dfrac{\Gamma \to A \supset B \text{ and } \Gamma \to (A \supset C) \supset A}{\Gamma \to B}$
For '∼':	$\dfrac{\Gamma, A \to B \text{ and } \Gamma, A \to \sim B}{\Gamma \to \sim A}$	$\dfrac{\Gamma \to \sim\sim A}{\Gamma \to A}$
For '&':	$\dfrac{\Gamma \to A \text{ and } \Gamma \to B}{\Gamma \to A \mathbin{\&} B}$	$\dfrac{\Gamma \to A \mathbin{\&} B \text{ and } \Gamma, A, B \to C}{\Gamma \to C}$
For '∨':	$\dfrac{\Gamma \to A \text{ or } \Gamma \to B}{\Gamma \to A \lor B}$	(a) $\Gamma \to A \lor B$, (b) $\Gamma, A \to C$, and (c) $\Gamma, B \to C$ over $\Gamma \to C$
For '∀':	$\dfrac{\Gamma \to A(Y/X)}{\Gamma \to (\forall X)A}$	$\dfrac{\Gamma \to (\forall X)A \text{ and } \Gamma, A(Y/X) \to B}{\Gamma \to B}$
For '∃':	$\dfrac{\Gamma \to A(Y/X)}{\Gamma \to (\exists A)X}$	$\dfrac{\Gamma \to (\exists X)A \text{ and } \Gamma, A(Y/X) \to B}{\Gamma \to B}$

Notes: (a) In the intelim rules for '∀' and '∃' $A(Y/X)$ is to be like A except for exhibiting free occurrences of the individual variable Y wherever A exhibits free occurrences of the individual variable X.
(b) In the introduction rule for '∀' the individual variable Y is presumed not to be free in $\Gamma \to (\forall X)A$.
(c) In the elimination rule for '∃' the individual variable Y is presumed not to be free in $\Gamma \to (\exists X)A$ nor in B.

Gentzen lavished more attention on LK, for which he proposed the axiom schema

$$A \to A$$

and the following sixteen rules of inference, in which the Greek capitals 'Γ', 'Δ', 'Θ', and 'Λ' range over (possibly empty) arrays of formulas and commas:

TABLE 2

Structural rules of LK:

	in the antecedent	in the consequent
Permutation:	$\dfrac{\Gamma, A, B, \Delta \to \Theta}{\Gamma, B, A, \Delta \to \Theta}$	$\dfrac{\Gamma \to \Delta, A, B, \Theta}{\Gamma \to \Delta, B, A, \Theta}$
Thinning:	$\dfrac{\Gamma \to \Delta}{A, \Gamma \to \Delta}$	$\dfrac{\Gamma \to \Delta}{\Gamma \to \Delta, A}$
Contraction:	$\dfrac{A, A, \Gamma \to \Delta}{A, \Gamma \to \Delta}$	$\dfrac{\Gamma \to \Delta, A, A}{\Gamma \to \Delta, A}$
Cut:	$\dfrac{\Gamma \to \Delta, A \text{ and } A, \Theta \to \Lambda}{\Gamma, \Theta \to \Delta, \Lambda}$	

Introduction rules of LK:

For '⊃':	$\dfrac{\Gamma \to \Delta, A \text{ and } B, \Theta \to \Lambda}{A \supset B, \Gamma, \Theta \to \Delta, \Lambda}$	$\dfrac{A, \Gamma \to \Delta, B}{\Gamma \to \Delta, A \supset B}$
For '∼':	$\dfrac{\Gamma \to \Delta, A}{\sim A, \Gamma \to \Delta}$	$\dfrac{A, \Gamma \to \Delta}{\Gamma \to \Delta, \sim A}$
For '&':	$\dfrac{A, \Gamma \to \Delta, \text{ or } B, \Gamma \to \Delta}{A \& B, \Gamma \to \Delta}$	$\dfrac{\Gamma \to \Delta, A \text{ and } \Gamma \to \Delta, B}{\Gamma \to \Delta, A \& B}$
For '∨':	$\dfrac{A, \Gamma \to \Delta \text{ and } B, \Gamma \to \Delta}{A \vee B, \Gamma \to \Delta}$	$\dfrac{\Gamma \to \Delta, A \text{ or } \Gamma \to \Delta, B}{\Gamma \to \Delta, A \vee B}$
For '∀':	$\dfrac{A(Y/X), \Gamma \to \Delta}{(\forall X)A, \Gamma \to \Delta}$	$\dfrac{\Gamma \to \Delta, A(Y/X)}{\Gamma \to \Delta, (\forall X)A}$
For '∃':	$\dfrac{A(Y/X), \Gamma \to \Delta}{(\exists X)A, \Gamma \to \Delta}$	$\dfrac{\Gamma \to \Delta, A(Y/X)}{\Gamma \to \Delta, (\exists X)A}$

Notes: (d) In the introduction rules for '∀' and '∃' this formula $A(Y/X)$ is to be as in Note (a).
(e) In the introduction rule for '∀' in the consequent the individual variable Y is presumed not to be free in $(\forall X)A, \Gamma \to \Delta$, and in the introduction rule for '∃' in the antecedent it is presumed not to be free in $(\exists X)A, \Gamma \to \Delta$.

With the above axiom schema and rules of inference on hand, I shall say: (a) that a finite column of sequents of NK or of LK constitutes in that kalkül a proof of a sequent S of the kalkül if, first, every entry in the said column is an axiom or follows from previous entries in the column by means of a rule of inference of the kalkül, and, second, the closing entry in the column is S; (b) that a sequent S of NK or of LK is *provable* in that kalkül if there exists a proof of S in the kalkül; and (c) that a sequent S of NK or of LK is *provable* in that kalkül by means of m ($m \geq 0$) given rules of inference of the kalkül, say R_1, $R_2, \ldots, R_m$, if there exists a proof of S in the kalkül and every entry in the said proof that follows from previous entries in the proof follows from them by means of $R_1, R_2, \ldots, R_m$.

Passing on to semantical matters, let the formula associate of a sequent

$$A_1, A_2, \ldots, A_n \to B$$

of NK be B or $(A_1 \& A_2 \& \ldots \& A_n) \supset B$ according as $n = 0$ or $n > 0$, that of a sequent

$$A_1, A_2, \ldots, A_n \to B_1, B_2, \ldots, B_m$$

of LK be $B_1 \lor B_2 \lor \ldots \lor B_m$, $\sim(A_1 \& A_2 \& \ldots \& A_n)$ or $(A_1 \& A_2 \& \ldots \& A_n) \supset (B_1 \lor B_2 \lor \ldots \lor B_m)$ according as (i) $n = 0$ and $m > 0$, (ii) $n > 0$ and $m = 0$, or (iii) $n > 0$ and $m > 0$. I shall then say that a sequent S is *classically valid* or, for short, valid if the formula associate of S is classically valid; *intuitionistically* valid, on the other hand, if the formula associate of S is intuitionistically valid.[3] I shall also say that a rule of inference R is *intuitionistically sound* if any sequent that follows by means of R from one or more intuitionistically valid sequents is itself intuitionistically valid.

2. In one respect NK and LK run neck and neck: "*Every valid sequent of either kalkül is provable in that kalkül*", as Gentzen showed of LK and as is easily shown of the present version of NK. Gentzen, nonetheless, preferred LK to NK because—as he saw it—the valid sequents of LK are susceptible in LK of more direct proofs than those of NK are in NK. I should like to assess here the comparative merits of his two kalküle and justify his partiality for LK in the light of some results of his and mine.

Let a formula A be declared (i) a subformula of A, (ii) a subformula of $\sim B$ if A is a subformula of B, (iii) a subformula of $B \supset C$, $B \& C$, and $B \lor C$ if A is a subformula of B or of C, and (iv) a subformula of $(\forall X)B$ if A is a subformula of B or of $B(Y/X)$, where $B(Y/X)$ is like B except for exhibiting free occurrences of Y wherever B exhibits free occurrences of X. Next, let a finite column of sequents, say, the sequents $S_1, S_2, \ldots, S_q$, constitute a *subformula-preserving proof* of S_q if the column constitutes a proof of S_q and any antecedent or consequent formula of any one of $S_1, S_2, \ldots, S_{q-1}$ is a subformula of some antecedent or consequent formula of S_q. Then, let such a column constitute an *operator-preserving proof* of S_q if the column constitutes a proof of S_q and any connective or quantifier letter that occurs in any one of $S_1, S_2, \ldots,$

Marginalia on Gentzen's Sequenzen-Kalküle 297

S_{q-1} also occurs in S_q. Finally, let a sequent S be susceptible of a *subformula-preserving proof* if there exists a subformula-preserving proof of S, susceptible of an *operator-preserving proof* if there exists an operating-preserving proof of S.

The reader need only glance at the various rules of inference of LK to realize that any sequent of LK which is provable in LK by means of the rules of inference of LK minus **Cut** is susceptible in LK of a subformula-preserving proof. But Gentzen effectively proved—the result is known as the "Hauptsatz"—that any sequent of LK which is provable in LK is provable in LK by means of the rules of inference of LK minus **Cut**.[4] Hence:

Theorem 1. *Every valid sequent of* LK *is susceptible in* LK *of a subformula-preserving proof.*

This corollary of Gentzen's "Hauptsatz" has a corollary of its own, which Gentzen did not bother to record, namely:

Theorem 2. *Every valid sequent of* LK *is susceptible in* LK *of an operator-preserving proof.*

Since a subformula-preserving proof never strays—so to speak—from its closing entry[5] and an operator-preserving one strays less than others from that entry, the valid sequents of LK are thus susceptible in LK of direct proofs in two senses (a stronger one and a weaker one) of the word 'direct'.

So much, however, for LK. Consider now those sequents of NK, dubbed for the occasion *propositional* sequents, in which neither one of '∀' and '∃' occurs. Gentzen's intelim rules for '⊃', '~', '&', '∨', '∀', and '∃' in [3] were all intuitionistically sound.[6] To permit proof of sequents which, though classically valid, are not intuitionistically valid, Gentzen accordingly had to appoint a second axiom schema for NK, to wit: → $A \lor \sim A$. In such a version of NK a good many valid propositional sequents of NK were simply not susceptible of operator-preserving, let alone subformula-preserving, proofs, and the race was thrown from the very start. The present version of NK, however, fares much better than Gentzen's. I effectively showed in [6] that every valid propositional sequent S of NK is provable in NK by means of the structural rules of NK and the intelim rules of NK for such and such only of the connectives '⊃', '~', '&', and '∨' as occur in S.[7] It accordingly follows that:

Theorem 3. *Every valid propositional sequent of* NK *is susceptible in* NK *of an operator-preserving proof.*

a result which at least puts NK back in the running.

The instructions supplied in [6] make for proofs which, besides being operator-preserving, are also variable-preserving. They unfortunately do not always make for subformula-preserving proofs, nor can they be so amended as to always make for subformula-preserving proofs, for some valid sequents of NK are simply not susceptible in NK of such proofs. Consider, for instance, the sequent

$$(p \supset q) \supset p \to p.$$

Since the sequent, though classically valid, is not intuitionistically valid, and since—among the structural rules of NK and the intelim rules of NK for '⊃'— only the elimination rule for '⊃', call it **HE**, is not intuitionistically sound, at least one entry in any proof of '$(p \supset q) \supset p \to p$' must, for one thing, follow by **HE** from two previous entries in the proof and, for another, fail to be intuitionistically valid. But among the sequents which qualify as entries in a subformula-preserving proof of '$(p \supset q) \supset p \to p$', each and every one that follows by **HE** from two others in the group is intuitionistically valid as well as classically valid. '$(p \supset q) \supset p \to p$' is therefore not susceptible in NK of a subformula-preserving proof. Hence:

Theorem 4. *Not every valid propositional sequent of* NK *is susceptible in* NK *of a subformula-preserving proof.*

I have not pursued this matter any further, but would conjecture that Theorem 4 holds true whatever rules of inference of the familiar sort NK may be fitted with, and hence that the valid propositional sequents of NK are at best susceptible in NK of operator-and-variable preserving proofs.[8]

An even more disappointing result is in store when it comes to the non-propositional or, if you wish, quantificational sequents of NK. Consider, for instance, the sequent

$$(\forall x)(p \lor f(x)) \to p \lor (\forall x)f(x).$$

Since the sequent, though classically valid, is not intuitionistically valid, and since all the structural rules of NK and all the intelim rules of NK for '∀' and '∨' are intuitionistically sound, no operator-preserving, let alone subformula-preserving, proof of '$(\forall x)(p \lor f(x)) \to p \lor (\forall x)f(x)$' is possible in NK. Hence the two negative results:

Theorem 5. *Not every valid quantificational sequent of* NK *is susceptible in* NK *of an operator-preserving proof.*

Theorem 6. *Not every valid quantificational sequent of* NK *is susceptible in* NK *of a subformula-preserving proof.*

I would conjecture that Theorems 5 and 6 hold true whatever rules of inference of the familiar sort NK may be fitted with. We know, for one thing, that any structural rule and any intelim rule for '∨' NK may be fitted with is intuitionistically sound.[9] I suspect, for another, that any intelim rule for '∀' NK may be fitted with is likewise intuitionistically sound. If this surmise of mine is borne out, then the sequent '$(\forall x)(p \lor f(x)) \to p \lor (\forall x)f(x)$' will not be susceptible in any version of NK of an operator-preserving proof (not, a fortiori, of a subformula-preserving one).

Our box score thus reads:

(i) All valid sequents of LK are susceptible in LK of direct proofs in both our senses of the word 'direct';

(ii) All valid propositional sequents of NK are susceptible in NK of direct proofs in the weaker sense of the word 'direct';

(iii) Not all valid propositional sequents of NK are susceptible in NK of direct proofs in the stronger sense of the word 'direct';

(iv) Not all valid quantificational sequents of NK are susceptible in NK of direct proofs in the weaker (nor, a fortiori, in the stronger) sense of the word 'direct'.

The reader will have noticed that both '$(p \supset q) \supset p \to p$', the sequent I used to obtain Theorem 4, and '$(\forall x)(p \lor f(x)) \to p \lor (\forall x)f(x)$', the one I used to obtain Theorems 5 and 6, fail to be intuitionistically valid. He might, as a result, wonder whether NJ, the intuitionist kin of NK, does not fare better than NK. A somewhat offhand remark of Gentzen's in [3] suggests that it does,[10] and proof of the fact will be found in [7].[11]

LJ, the intuitionist kin of LK, fares as well as LK, a result due to Gentzen himself. This fourth kalkül sports sequents of only two kinds:

$$A_1, A_2, \ldots, A_n \to B,$$

where $n \geq 0$, and

$$A_1, A_2, \ldots, A_n \to ,$$

where $n > 0$, and is fitted, subject to amendments (a)–(c) below, with the same axiom schema and rules of inference as LK:

(a) **Permutation in the consequent** and **Contraction in the consequent** are dropped as inoperative;

(b) 'Δ' is deleted in **Thinning in the consequent, Cut,** the two introduction rules for each one of '$\supset$' and '$\sim$', and the introduction in the consequent rule for each one of '&', '$\lor$', '$\forall$', and '$\exists$';

(c) 'Δ' is understood in **Thinning in the antecedent, Contraction in the antecedent,** and the introduction in the antecedent rule for each one of '&', '$\lor$', '$\forall$', and '$\exists$', to range over a single formula or no formula at all; so is 'Θ' in **Permutation in the antecedent**; so, finally, is 'Λ' in **Cut** and the introduction in the antecedent rule for '$\supset$'.

Since Gentzen's "Hauptsatz" holds true of LJ as well as LK, every intuitionistically valid sequent of LJ is susceptible in LJ of a subformula-preserving proof and hence of an operator-preserving one.

Notes

1. The present account of NK, though departing from that in [3], stems from [4], p. 512, Note 9, and hence meets Gentzen's intentions.

2. See [3], p. 180.
3. For an account of intuitionistic validity, see [5].
4. To simplify matters I assume here with Gentzen that no individual variable is permitted to occur both bound and free in a sequent.
5. To quote Gentzen's own characterization of a subformula-preserving proof, "Er macht keine Umwege." See [3], p. 177.
6. Or, to be more exact, Gentzen's intelim rules for the said operators and the propositional constant 'f', which Gentzen also adopts as a primitive sign of NK (though not of LK).
7. In [6] '⊦' does duty for '→' and is intended as a primitive sign of the metalanguage of PC, the propositional calculus, rather than a primitive sign of PC; all results, nonetheless, carry over. In the paper in question '≡' also figures as a primitive sign, governed by two intelim rules of its own, and the result obtained runs (*mutatis mutandis*): "Every valid propositional sequent S of NK is provable in NK by means of the structural rules of NK and the intelim rules of NK for such and such only of the connectives '⊃', '~', '&', 'V', and '≡' as occur in S."
8. Requirements to be met by a rule if it is to qualify as a structural rule or an intelim rule of such a kalkül as NK are laid down in [1].
9. See [1] and [2].
10. See [3], p. 177.
11. An earlier proof of nearly the same result can be found in [8], a text to which [7] owes some.

References

[1] Belnap, N. D., Jr., Leblanc, H., and Thomason, R. H. 1963 "On *Not* Strengthening Intuitionistic Logic." *Notre Dame Journal of Formal Logic* (hereafter *NDJFL*) 4: 313–20 (#29 in this volume).

[2] Belnap, N. D., Jr., and Thomason, R. H. 1963. "A Rule-Completeness Theorem." *NDJFL* 4: 39–43.

[3] Gentzen, G. 1934. "Untersuchungen über das logische Schliessen." *Mathematische Zeitschrift* 39: 176–210 and 406–31.

[4] ———. 1936. "Widerspruchsfreiheit der Zahlentheorie." *Mathematische Annalen* 112: 493–565.

[5] Kripke, S. A. 1965. "Semantical Analysis of Intuitionistic Logic I." *Formal Systems and Recursive Functions*, pp. 92–130. Amsterdam: North-Holland.

[6] Leblanc, H. 1963. "Proof Routines for the Propositional Calculus." *NDJFL* 4: 81–104 (#23 in this volume).

[7] ———. 1966. "Two Separations Theorems for Natural Deduction." *NDJFL* 7: 159–80 (#24 in this volume).

[8] Prawitz, D. 1965. *Natural Deduction: A Proof-Theoretical Study*. Stockholm: Almqvist and Wiksell.

22
Structural Rules of Inference

On many occasions the following three rules:

R: $A \vdash A$ (**Reflexivity**),

T: If $A_1, A_2, \ldots, A_n \vdash B$, then $A_1, A_2, \ldots, A_n, C \vdash B$ (**Thinning**),

P: If $A_1, A_2, \ldots, A_{i-1}, A_i, A_{i+1}, A_{i+2}, \ldots, A_n, A_{n+1}, A_{n+2} \vdash B$, then $A_1, A_2, \ldots, A_{i-1}, A_{i+1}, A_i A_{i+2}, \ldots, A_n, A_{n+1}, A_{n+2}, \vdash B$, where $i \leq n + 2$ (**Permutation**),

are appointed as structural rules of inference for the propositional calculus;[1] on others, **P** and the following generalization of **R**:

GR: $A_1, A_2, \ldots, A_n \vdash (A_i$, where $i \leq n$ (**Generalized Reflexivity**),

are made to serve in that capacity.[2] I examine here the impact of this switch from **R** and **T** to **GR** upon the proving and deriving of rules of inference for the said calculus.

Let PC be a (pure) propositional calculus with '$\sim$' and '$\supset$' as primitive connectives. Let 'A', 'B', and 'C' range in the metalanguage MPC of PC over the wffs of PC. Let (meta)statements of MPC of the form 'B *is implied in* PC *by* (or *deducible in* PC *from*) $A_1, A_2, \ldots,$ *and* A_n' be abbreviated to read '$A_1, A_2, \ldots, A_n \vdash B$' and called turnstile statements or, for short, T-statements. Let the following four rules serve as intelim rules for '$\sim$' and '$\supset$':

NI: If $A_1, A_2, \ldots, A_n, B \vdash C$ and $A_1, A_2, \ldots, A_n, B \vdash \sim C$, then $A_1, A_2, \ldots, A_n \vdash \sim B$,

NE: If $A_1, A_2, \ldots, A_n \vdash \sim \sim B$, then $A_1, A_2, \ldots, A_n \vdash B$,

HI: If $A_1, A_2, \ldots, A_n, B \vdash C$, then $A_1, A_2, \ldots, A_n \vdash B \supset C$,

HE: If $A_1, A_2, \ldots, A_n \vdash B$ and $A_1, A_2, \ldots, A_n \vdash B \supset C$, then $A_1, A_2, \ldots, A_n \vdash C$.

Let a finite column of T-statements qualify as a *derivation* in MPC from p ($p \geq 0$) T-statements $T_1, T_2, \ldots, T_p$ if every T-statement in the column is one of $T_1, T_2, \ldots, T_p$, or is of the form **GR**, or follows from previous T-statements in the column by application of **P**, **NI**, **NE**, **HI**, or **HE**. Let a T-statement be said to be *derivable* in MPC from p ($p \geq 0$) T-statements $T_1, T_2, \ldots, T_p$ if it comes last in a derivation in MPC from $T_1, T_2, \ldots, T_p$. Let a finite column of T-statements qualify as a *proof* in MPC if it qualifies as a derivation in MPC from zero T-statements. Finally, let a T-statement be said to be *provable* in MPC if it comes last in a proof MPC.

It is easily shown that:

Theorem 1. *If a given T-statement $A_1, A_2, \ldots, A_n \vdash B$ is provable in MPC, so is the corresponding T-statement $A_1, A_2, \ldots, A_n, C \vdash B$, where C is any wff of PC.*

Proof: Let

$$A_{1_1}, A_{1_2}, \ldots, A_{1_{n_1}} \vdash B_1,$$
$$A_{2_1}, A_{2_2}, \ldots, A_{2_{n_2}} \vdash B_2,$$
$$\vdots$$
$$A_{q_1}, A_{q_2}, \ldots, A_{q_{n_q}} \vdash B_q,$$

constitute the proof of $A_1, A_2, \ldots, A_n \vdash B$ in MPC. The result of inserting ', C' to the left of '$\vdash$' in each one of the T-statements in question either qualifies or can be so supplemented as to qualify as a proof of $A_1, A_2, \ldots, A_n, C \vdash B$ in MPC. For suppose that $A_{j_1}, A_{j_2}, \ldots, A_{j_{n_j}} \vdash B_j$ is of the form **GR**; then $A_{j_1}, A_{j_2}, \ldots, A_{j_{n_j}}, C \vdash B_j$ is likewise of the form **GR**. Or suppose that $A_{j_1}, A_{j_2}, \ldots, A_{j_{n_j}} \vdash B_j$ follows from $A_{j_1}, A_{h_2}, \ldots, A_{h_{n_h}} \vdash B_h$, where $h < j$, by application of **P** or **NE**; then $A_{j_1}, A_{j_2}, \ldots, A_{j_{n_j}}, C \vdash B_j$ likewise follows from $A_{h_1}, A_{h_2}, \ldots, A_{h_{n_h}}, C \vdash B_h$ by application of **P** or **NE**. Or suppose that $A_{j_1}, A_{j_2}, \ldots, A_{j_{n_j}} \vdash B_j$ follows from $A_{h_1}, A_{h_2}, \ldots, A_{h_{n_h}} \vdash B_h$ and $A_{i_1}, A_{i_2}, \ldots, A_{i_{n_i}} \vdash B_i$, where $h < j$ and $i < j$, by application of **HE**; then $A_{j_1}, A_{j_2}, \ldots, A_{j_{n_j}}, C \vdash B$ will likewise follow from $A_{h_1}, A_{h_2}, \ldots, A_{h_{n_h}}, C \vdash B_h$ and $A_{i_1}, A_{i_2}, \ldots, A_{i_{n_i}}, C \vdash B_i$ by application of **HE**. Or suppose that $A_{j_1}, A_{j_2}, \ldots, A_{j_{n_j}} \vdash B_j$—$B_j$ being of the form $\sim A_{h_{n_h}}$, and $\sim A_{i_{n_i}}$—follows from $A_{h_1}, A_{h_2}, \ldots, A_{h_{n_h}} \vdash B_h$ and $A_{i_1}, A_{i_2}, \ldots, A_{i_{n_i}} \vdash B_i$, where $h < j$ and $i < j$, by application of **NI**; then $A_{h_1}, A_{h_2}, \ldots, C, A_{h_{n_h}} \vdash B_h$ follows from $A_{h_1}, A_{h_2}, \ldots, A_{h_{n_h}}, C \vdash B_h$ by application of **P**, $A_{i_1}, A_{i_2}, \ldots, C, A_{i_{n_i}} \vdash B_i$ follows from $A_{i_1}, A_{i_2}, \ldots, A_{i_{n_i}}, C \vdash B_i$ by application of **P**, and $A_{j_1}, A_{j_2}, \ldots, A_{j_{n_j}}, C \vdash B_j$ follows from $A_{h_1}, A_{h_2}, \ldots, C, A_{h_{n_h}} \vdash B_h$ and $A_{i_1}, A_{i_2}, \ldots, C, A_{i_{n_i}} \vdash$

B_i by application of **NI**. Or suppose that $A_{j_1}, A_{j_2}, \ldots, A_{j_{n_j}} \vdash B_j$—$B_j$ being of the form $A_{h_{n_h}} \supset B$—follows from $A_{h_1}, A_{h_2}, \ldots, A_{h_{n_h}} \vdash B_h'$, where $h < j$, by application of **HI**; then $A_{h_1}, A_{h_2}, \ldots, C, A_{h_{n_h}} \vdash B_h$ follows from $A_{h_1}, A_{h_2}, \ldots, A_{h_{n_h}}, C \vdash B_h$ by application of **P**, and $A_{j_1}, A_{j_2}, \ldots, A_{j_{n_j}}, C \vdash B_j$ follows from $A_{h_1}, A_{h_2}, \ldots, C, A_{h_{n_h}} \vdash B_h$ by application of **HI**. Hence T1.

It is easily shown also that:

Theorem 2. *If a given T-statement $A_1, A_2, \ldots, A_n, C \vdash B$ is provable in MPC, then it is derivable in MPC from the corresponding T-statement $A_1, A_2, \ldots, A_n \vdash B$.*
Proof: The column of T-statements made up of $A_1, A_2, \ldots, A_n \vdash B$, followed by the proof of $A_1, A_2, \ldots, A_n, C \vdash B$, qualifies by definition as a derivation in MPC from $A_1, A_2, \ldots, A_n \vdash B$. Hence T2.

Theorem 2 is trivial enough. I include it, though, to throw into relief Theorem 3, according to which a given T-statement $A_1, A_2, \ldots, A_n, C \vdash B$ is not derivable in MPC from the corresponding T-statement $A_1, A_2, \ldots, A_n \vdash B$ unless $A_1, A_2, \ldots, A_n, C \vdash B$ is, as required in Theorem 2, provable in MPC.

Theorem 3. *If a given T-Statement $A_1, A_2, \ldots, A_n, C \vdash B$ is not provable in MPC, then it is not derivable in MPC from the corresponding T-statement $A_1, A_2, \ldots, A_n \vdash B$.*
Proof:
Part one: Consider (1) any column, call it C_1, of T-statements which qualifies as a derivation in MPC from p ($p \geq 0$) T-statements $T_1, T_2, \ldots, T_p$, and (2) the column, call it C_2, which results from C_1 when all the T-statements in C_1 exhibiting fewer wffs of PC than the last T-statement in C_1, have been deleted from C_1. C_2 qualifies by definition as a derivation in MPC from those T-statements among $T_1, T_2, \ldots, T_p$, call them $T'_1, T'_2, \ldots, T'_m$, where $m \leq p$, which figure in C_2. For suppose that a given T-statement from C_1 which figures in C_2 happened to be one of $T_1, T_2, \ldots, T_p$; that statement will now be one of $T'_1, T'_2, \ldots, T'_m$. Or suppose that a given T-statement from C_1 which figures in C_2 happened to be of the form **GR**; that statement will still be of the form **GR**. Or suppose that a given T-statement from C_1 which figures in C_2 happened to follow from one or two previous T-statements in C_1 by application of **P, NI, NE, HI,** or **HE**; the one or two T-statements from which that statement followed are bound to figure in C_2[3] and the statement will still follow from them by application of **P, NI, NE, HI,** or **HE**.
Part two: Suppose $A_1, A_2, \ldots, A_n, C \vdash B$ were derivable in MPC from $A_1, A_2, \ldots, A_n \vdash B$. By virtue of part one, the derivation in MPC from $A_1, A_2, \ldots, A_n \vdash B$ that closed with $A_1, A_2, \ldots, A_n, C \vdash B$ could be trimmed into

a proof in MPC closing with $A_1, A_2, \ldots, A_n, C \vdash B$, and hence $A_1, A_2, \ldots, A_n, C \vdash B$ would be provable in MPC. Hence T3.

The fate of **T**, once **GR** is made to do duty for **R** and **E**, should now be clear. **T** will be forthcoming, in the presence of **P**, **NI**, **NE**, **HI**, and **HE**, under the provability form of Theorem 1; it will be forthcoming under the derivability form of Theorems 2 and 3 when and only when $A_1, A_2, \ldots, A_n, C \vdash B$ is already provable in MPC and hence is trivially derivable in MPC from $A_1, A_2, \ldots, A_n \vdash B$. This anomaly is reminiscent of the one recently brought out by Hiz and others in connection with Modus Ponens in axiomatic presentations of PC.[4]

The first theorem, one's main excuse for switching from **R** and **T** to **GR**, would still hold if **NE** and **HE** were modified to read, as often happens:

NE': $A_1, A_2, \ldots, A_n, \sim\sim B \vdash B$,

HE': $A_1, A_2, \ldots, A_n, B, B \supset C \vdash C$.[5]

I suspect, however, that Theorem 1 would no longer hold if **NE** and **HE** were weakened to read, as often happens:

NE'': $\sim\sim A \vdash A$,

HE'': $A, A \supset B \vdash B$,

and **GR**, **P**, and the following rule,

C: If $A_1, A_2, \ldots, A_n, B \vdash C$ and $A_1, A_2, \ldots, A_n \vdash B$, then $A_1, A_2, \ldots, A_n \vdash C$ (**Cut**),

were appointed to serve as structural rules of inference for PC.[6] I also suspect that Theorem 1 would no longer hold if **GR**, **P**, **NI**, **NE**, **HI**, **HE**, and the following two intelim rules for '∀':

∀I: If $A_1, A_2, \ldots, A_n \vdash B$, then $A_1, A_2, \ldots, A_n \vdash (\forall W)B$, where the individual variable W is not free in any one of $A_1, A_2, \ldots, A_n$,

∀E: If $A_1, A_2, \ldots, A_n \vdash (\forall W)B$, then $A_1, A_2, \ldots, A_n \vdash B'$, where B' is like B except for containing free occurrences of an individual variable W' at all the places where B contains free occurrences of W.

were appointed as rules of inference for a (pure) quantificational calculus with '∼' and '⊃' as primitive connectives and '∀' as primitive quantifier letter.[7]

Notes

1. See, for example, [2], pp. 214–15, which sports a further structural rule, (III), easily shown to be redundant in the presence of **R**, **T**, **P**, **HI**, and **HE**. The three rules **R**, **T**, and **P** stem from [3].

2. See, for example, [5] and [7].

3. Note for proof that the one or two T-statements from which a given T-statement exhibiting r

($r \geq 1$) wffs of PC follows by **P, NI, NE, HI,** or **HE** are bound to exhibit r or $r + 1$ wffs of PC and hence to figure in C_2 if the said T-statement does.
4. See [4] and [6].
5. See, for example, [5].
6. See, for example, [1].
7. My thanks go to Nuel D. Belnap, Jr., with whom I discussed the results of this paper. I owe him, among other things, the distinction drawn in the text between the provability and the derivability version of **T**.

References

[1] Beth, E. W., and Leblanc, H. 1960. "A Note on the Intuitionistic and the Classical Propositional Calculus." *Logique et Analyse* 11–12: 174–75 (#27 in this volume).
[2] Church, A. 1956. *Introduction to Mathematical Logic, Volume I*. Princeton: Princeton University Press.
[3] Gentzen, G. 1934. "Untersuchungen über das logische Schliessen." *Mathematische Zeitschrift* 39: 176–210 and 405–31.
[4] Hiz, H. 1959. "Extendible Sentential Calculus." *The Journal of Symbolic Logic* 24: 193–202.
[5] Jaśkowski, S. 1934. "On the Rules of Supposition in Formal Logic." *Studia Logica* 1: 5–32.
[6] Leblanc, H. 1961. "The Algebra of Logic and the Theory of Deduction." *The Journal of Philosophy* 58: 553–58 (#32 in this volume).
[7] Popper, K. R. 1947. "New Foundations for Logic." *Mind* 56: 193–235.

23

Proof Routines for the Propositional Calculus

I prove in the pages that follow a conjecture of mine, to wit:

Any metastatement of the form

$$A_1, A_2, \ldots, A_n \vdash B,$$

where $A_1, A_2, \ldots, A_n$ ($n \geq 0$), *and B are wffs of* PC *and* '$\vdash$' *is the customary yields sign, is provable, when valid, by means of the three structural rules in Table 1 and the intelim rules in Table 1 for such of the connectives* '$\sim$', '$\supset$', '&', '$\vee$', *and* '$\equiv$' *as occur in* $A_1, A_2, \ldots, A_n \vdash B$.

and sketch a routine for proving $A_1, A_2, \ldots, A_n \vdash B$, when valid, for each one of the thirty-two cases covered by the conjecture.[1] I also discuss a related conjecture of mine concerning the intuitionist fragment of PC.

1. Let all five of '$\sim$', '$\supset$', '&', '$\vee$', and '$\equiv$' be elected to serve as the *primitive connectives* of PC; let '*A*', '*B*', '*C*', and '*D*' be elected to range over the well-formed formulas (wffs) of PC; let a metastatement of the form $A_1, A_2, \ldots, A_n \vdash B$, called for short a T-statement, be rated *valid* if, in case $n = 0$, B is satisfied by any assignment of truth-values to the propositional variables occurring in B, or, in case $n > 0$, B is satisfied by any assignment of truth-values to the propositional variables occurring in $A_1, A_2, \ldots, A_n\, B$ which simultaneously satisfies $A_1, A_2, \ldots, A_n$; let a T-statement be rated *provable* if it is the last entry in a finite column of T-statements each one of which is of the form **R** in Table 1 or follows from one or more previous T-statements in the column by application of one of the remaining rules in Table 1; and, finally, let a T-statement be rated *provable by means of the structural rules in Table 1* (to be collectively referred to as **S**) *and zero or more of the intelim rules in Table 1* if it is the last entry in a finite column of T-statements each one of which is of the form **R** or follows from one or more previous T-statements in the column by application of **T**, **P**, or one of the intelim rules in question.

306

TABLE 1

Structural rules:

R: $A \vdash A$;

T: If $A_1, A_2, \ldots, A_n \vdash B$, then $A_1, A_2, \ldots, A_{n+1} \vdash B$;

P: If $A_1, A_2, \ldots, A_{n+2} \vdash B$, then $A_1, A_2, \ldots, A_{i-1}, A_{i+1}, A_i, A_{i+2}, \ldots, A_{n+2} \vdash B$, where $i \leq n + 1$.

Intelim rules for '$\sim$', '$\supset$', '&', '$\vee$', and '$\equiv$':

NI: If (1) $A_1, A_2, \ldots, A_{n+1} \vdash B$ and (2) $A_1, A_2, \ldots, A_{n+1} \vdash \sim B$, then $A_1, A_2, \ldots, A_n \vdash \sim A_{n+1}$;

NE: If $A_1, A_2, \ldots, A_n \vdash \sim\sim B$, then $A_1, A_2, \ldots, A_n \vdash B$;

HI: If $A_1, A_2, \ldots, A_{n+1} \vdash B$, then $A_1, A_2, \ldots, A_n \vdash A_{n+1} \supset B$;

HE: If (1) $A_1, A_2, \ldots, A_n \vdash B \supset C$ and (2) $A_1, A_2, \ldots, A_n \vdash (B \supset D) \supset B$, then $A_1, A_2, \ldots, A_n \vdash C$;

CI: If (1) $A_1, A_2, \ldots, A_n \vdash B$ and (2) $A_1, A_2, \ldots, A_n \vdash C$, then $A_1, A_2, \ldots, A_n \vdash B \& C$;

CE: If (1) $A_1, A_2, \ldots, A_n \vdash B \& C$ and (2) $A_1, 2A_2, \ldots, A_n, B, C \vdash D$, then $A_1, A_2, \ldots, A_n \vdash D$;

DI: If $A_1, A_2, \ldots, A_n \vdash B$, then (1) $A_1, A_2, \ldots, A_n \vdash B \vee C$ and (2) $A_1, A_2, \ldots, A_n \vdash C \vee B$;

DE: If (1) $A_1, A_2, \ldots, A_n \vdash B \vee C$, (2) $A_1, A_2, \ldots, A_n, B \vdash D$, and (3) $A_1, A_2, \ldots, A_n, C \vdash D$, then $A_1, A_2, \ldots, A_n \vdash D$;

BI: If (1) $A_1, A_2, \ldots, A_n, B \vdash C$ and (2) $A_1, A_2, \ldots, A_n, C \vdash B$, then $A_1, A_2, \ldots, A_n \vdash B \equiv C$;

BE: If (1) $A_1, A_2, \ldots, A_n \vdash B$ and (2) either $A_1, A_2, \ldots, A_n \vdash (D \equiv B) \equiv (D \equiv C)$ or $A_1, A_2, \ldots, A_n \vdash (D \equiv C) \equiv (D \equiv B)$, then $A_1, A_2, \ldots, A_n \vdash C$.

It is easily shown that:

Theorem 1. *If $A_1, A_2, \ldots, A_n \vdash B$ is provable, then $A_1, A_2, \ldots, A_n \vdash B$ is valid.*

I shall accordingly leave this matter to the reader and restrict myself to proving—as announced before—the following theorem:

Theorem 2. *If $A_1, A_2, \ldots, A_n \vdash B$ is valid, then $A_1, A_2, \ldots, A_n \vdash B$ is provable by means of* **S** *and the intelim rules for such of the connectives* '$\sim$', '$\supset$', '&', '$\vee$', *and* '$\equiv$' *as occur in $A_1, A_2, \ldots, A_n \vdash B$,* from which the converse of T1, namely:

Theorem 3. *If $A_1, A_2, \ldots, A_n \vdash B$ is valid, then $A_1, A_2, \ldots, A_n \vdash B$ is provable,*

trivially follows.[2]

Of theorems T2 and T3, the second still holds when the elimination rules for '⊃' and '≡' are phrased in the more traditional fashion:

HE′: If (1) $A_1, A_2, \ldots, A_n \vdash B$ and (2) $A_1, A_2, \ldots, A_n \vdash B \supset C$, then $A_1, A_2, \ldots, A_n \vdash C$,

and

BE′: If (1) $A_1, A_2, \ldots, A_n \vdash B$ and (2) either $A_1, A_2, \ldots, A_n \vdash B \equiv C$ or $A_1, A_2, \ldots, A_n \vdash C \equiv B$, then $A_1, A_2, \ldots, A_n \vdash C$.

The first, however, fails, as I shall establish in Section 4.[3]

2. I address myself in this section to the case where $A_1, A_2, \ldots, A_n \vdash B$ exhibits no connective (Case 1) and to the fifteen cases, reduced by various inductions to Case 1, where $A_1, A_2, \ldots, A_n \vdash B$ exhibits any one, any two, any three, or all four of the connectives '⊃', '&', '∨', and '≡'. The conditions under which a wff of PC is said in the proof of Case 6 to be in conjunctive normal form and the routine employed to put a wff of PC in conjunctive normal form need no rehearsing here. As for the conditions under which an occurrence of a connective in a wff of PC is said in the proofs of Cases 2–3 and Cases 7–10 to be either nested or unnested, they read: *Let A be a wff of PC of one of the four forms $B \supset C$, $B \& C$, $B \lor C$, and $B \equiv C$; then (1) every occurrence (if any) of '⊃', '&', '∨', or '≡' in B or in C is a nested occurrence of that connective, and (2) every occurrence (if any) of '⊃', '&', '∨', or '≡' in A that is not nested is unnested.*

Case 1: No connective occurs in $A_1, A_2, \ldots, A_n \vdash B$.
Proof: Suppose $A_1, A_2, \ldots, A_n \vdash B$ is valid. Then there is bound to be an i such that A_i is B,[4] in which case $A_1, A_2, \ldots, A_n \vdash B$ follows from $B \vdash B$ (= **R**) by means of **T** and **P**. Hence T2.

Case 2: The only connective that occurs in $A_1, A_2, \ldots, A_n \vdash B$ is '⊃'.
Proof: (a) By induction on p, the number of occurrences of '⊃' in B, (b) when $p = 0$, by induction on q, the number of nested occurrences of '⊃', in $A_1, A_2, \ldots, A_n$, and (c) when $q = 0$, by induction on the number of unnested occurrences of '⊃' in $A_1, A_2, \ldots, A_n$.
Step 1: $p = 0$.

Proof Routines for the Propositional Calculus 309

Step 1.1: $q = 0$. Suppose $A_1, A_2, \ldots, A_n \vdash B$ is valid. Then (1) there is bound to be an i such that A_i is B, in which case

$$A_1, A_2, \ldots, A_{j-1}, A_{j+1}, \ldots, A_n \vdash B, \tag{2.1}$$

where A_j ($j < i$ or $j > i$) is the left-most one of $A_1, A_2, \ldots, A_n$ to exhibit an occurrence of '⊃', is valid and hence—in view of Case 1 or of the hypothesis of induction—provable by means of **S**, **HI**, and **HE**, or (2) there is bound to be an i and there is bound to be a j ($j < i$ or $j > i$) such that A_i is $A_j \supset A_{i_2}$, in which case

$$A_1, A_2, \ldots, A_{i-1}, A_{i+1}, A_{i+1}, \ldots, A_n \vdash B \tag{2.2}$$

is valid and hence—in view of Case 1 or of the hypothesis of induction—provable by means of **S**, **HI**, and **HE**.[5] But $A_1, A_2, \ldots, A_n \vdash B$ follows from (2.1), in one case, by means of **S** and from (2.2), in the other, by means of **S**, **HI**, and **HE**. Hence T2.

Step 1.2: $q > 0$. Then there is bound to be an i such that A_i is of one of the two forms $(A_{i_1} \supset A_{i_2}) \supset A_{i_3}$ and $A_{i_1} \supset (A_{i_2} \supset A_{i_3})$. Now suppose $A_1, A_2, \ldots, A_n \vdash B$ is valid and A_i is of the form $(A_{i_1} \supset A_{i_2}) \supset A_{i_3}$. Then both

$$A_1, A_2, \ldots, A_{i-1}, A_{i_1}, A_{i_2} \supset A_{i_3}, A_{i+1}, \ldots, A_n \vdash B \tag{2.3}$$

and

$$A_1, A_2, \ldots, A_{i-1}, A_{i_3}, A_{i+1}, \ldots, A_n \vdash B \tag{2.4}$$

are bound to be valid and hence—in view of the hypothesis of induction—provable by means of **S**, **HI**, and **HE**.[6] Or suppose $A_1, A_2, \ldots, A_n \vdash B$ is valid and A_i is of the form $A_{i_1} \supset (A_{i_2} \supset A_{i_3})$. Then both

$$A_1, A_2, \ldots, A_{i-1}, A_{i_1} \supset A_{i_3}, A_{i+1}, \ldots, A_n \vdash B \tag{2.5}$$

and

$$A_1, A_2, \ldots, A_{i-1}, A_{i_2} \supset A_{i_3}, A_{i+1}, \ldots, A_n \vdash B \tag{2.6}$$

are bound to be valid and hence—in view of the hypothesis of induction—provable by means of **S**, **HI**, and **HE**.[7] But $A_1, A_2, \ldots, A_n \vdash B$ follows from (2.3)–(2.4) in one case and from (2.5)–(2.6) in the other by means of the said rules. Hence T2.

Step 2: $p > 0$. Then B is bound to be of the form $B_1 \supset B_2$. Now suppose $A_1, A_2, \ldots, A_n \vdash B$ is valid. Then

$$A_1, A_2, \ldots, A_n, B_1 \vdash B_2 \tag{2.7}$$

is bound to be valid and hence—in view of Case 1 or of the hypothesis of induction-provable by means of **S**, **HI**, and **HE**. But $A_1, A_2, \ldots, A_n \vdash B$ follows from (2.7) by means of the said rules. Hence T2.[8]

Case 3: The only two connectives that occur in $A_1, A_2, \ldots, A_n \vdash B$ are '$\supset$' and '&'.
Proof: (a) By induction on p, the number of occurrences of '$\supset$' and '&' in B, (b) when $p = 0$, by induction on q, the number of nested occurrences of '$\supset$' and '&' in $A_1, A_2, \ldots, A_n$, and (c) when $q = 0$, by induction on the number of unnested occurrences of '&' in $A_1, A_2, \ldots, A_n$.
Step 1: $p = 0$.
Step 1.1: $q = 0$. Then there is bound to be an i such that A_i is of the form A_{i_1} & A_{i_2}. Now suppose $A_1, A_2, \ldots, A_n \vdash B$ is valid. Then

$$A_1, A_2, \ldots, A_{i-1}, A_{i_1}, A_{i_2}, A_{i+1}, \ldots, A_n \vdash B \quad (3.1)$$

is bound to be valid and hence—in view of Case 2 or of the hypothesis of induction—provable by means of **S, HI, HE, CI,** and **CE**. But $A_1, A_2, \ldots, A_n \vdash B$ follows from (3.1) by means of the said rules. Hence T2.
Step 1.2: $q > 0$. Then there is bound to be an i such that A_i is of one of the eight forms $(A_{i_1} \supset A_{i_2}) \supset A_{i_3}$, $A_{i_1} \supset (A_{i_2} \supset A_{i_3})$, $(A_{i_1} \& A_{i_2}) \& A_{i_3}$, $A_{i_1} \& (A_{i_2} \& A_{i_3})$, $(A_{i_1} \supset A_{i_2}) \& A_{i_3}$, $A_{i_1} \& (A_{i_2} \supset A_{i_3})$, $(A_{i_1} \& A_{i_2}) \supset A_{i_3}$, and $A_{i_1} \supset (A_{i_2} \& A_{i_3})$, where in the last case A_{i_1} is a propositional variable.[9]
Step 1.2.1: A_i is of one of the first two forms listed. Proof similar to the proof of Case 2, Step 1.2, but with **S, HI, HE, CI,** and **CE** doing duty for **S, HI,** and **HE**.
Step 1.2.2: A_i is of one of the next four forms listed. Proof similar to the proof of Step 1.1.
Step 1.2.3: A_i is of the form $(A_{i_1} \& A_{i_2}) \supset A_{i_3}$. Suppose $A_1, A_2, \ldots, A_n \vdash B$ is valid. Then both

$$A_1, A_2, \ldots, A_{i-1}, A_{i_1} \supset A_{i_3}, A_{i+1}, \ldots, A_n \vdash B \quad (3.2)$$

and

$$A_1, A_2, \ldots, A_{i-1}, A_{i_2}, A_{i_2} \supset A_{i_3}, A_{i+1}, \ldots, A_n \vdash B \quad (3.3)$$

are bound to be valid and hence—in view of Case 2 or of the hypothesis of induction—provable by means of **S, HI, HE, CI,** and **CE**.[10] But $A_1, A_2, \ldots, A_n \vdash B$ follows from (3.2)–(3.3) by means of the said rules. Hence T2.
Step 1.2.4: A_i is of the form $A_{i_1} \supset (A_{i_2} \& A_{i_3})$, where A_{i_1} is a propositional variable. Suppose $A_1, A_2, \ldots, A_n \vdash B$ is valid. Then

$$A_1, A_2, \ldots, A_{i-1}, A_{i_1} \supset A_{i_2}, A_{i_1} \supset A_3, A_{i+1}, \ldots, A_n \vdash B \quad (3.4)$$

is bound to be valid and hence—in view of Case 2 or of the hypothesis of induction—provable by means of **S, HI, HE, CI,** and **CE**.[11] But $A_1, A_2, \ldots, A_n \vdash B$ follows from (3.4) by means of the said rules. Hence T2.
Step 2: $p > 0$. Then B is bound to be of one of the two forms $B_1 \supset B_2$ and $B_1 \& B_2$.
Step 2.1: B is of the form $B_1 \supset B_2$. Proof similar to the proof of Case 2, Step

Proof Routines for the Propositional Calculus 311

2, but minus the reference to Case 1 and with **S, HI, HE, CI,** and **CE** doing duty for **S, HI,** and **HE**.
Step 2.2: B is of the form $B_1 \mathbin{\&} B_2$. Suppose $A_1, A_2, \ldots, A_n \vdash B$ is valid. Then both

$$A_1, A_2, \ldots, A_n \vdash B_1 \qquad (3.5)$$

and

$$A_1, A_2, \ldots, A_n \vdash B_2 \qquad (3.6)$$

are bound to be valid and hence—in view of Case 2 or of the hypothesis of induction—provable by means of **S, HI, HE, CI,** and **CE**. But $A_1, A_2, \ldots, A_n \vdash B$ follows from (3.5)–(3.6) by means of **CI**. Hence T2.

Case 4: The only connective that occurs in $A_1, A_2, \ldots, A_n \vdash B$ is '&'.
Proof by induction on the number of occurrences of '&' in $A_1, A_2, \ldots, A_n$, and B.
Step 1: There is an i such that A_i is of the form $A_{i_1} \mathbin{\&} A_{i_2}$. Proof similar to the proof of Case 3, Step 1.1, but with Case 1 doing duty for Case 2 and with **S, CI,** and **CE** doing duty for **S, HI, HE, CI,** and **CE**.[12]
Step 2: B is of the form $B_1 \mathbin{\&} B_2$. Proof similar to the proof of Case 3, Step 2.2, but with Case 1 doing duty for Case 2 and with **S, CI,** and **CE** doing duty for **S, HI, HE, CI,** and **CE**.

Case 5: The only connective that occurs in $A_1, A_2, \ldots, A_n \vdash B$ is '$\vee$'.
Proof by induction on p, the number of occurrences of '$\vee$' in $A_1, A_2, \ldots, A_n$, and, when $p = 0$, by induction on the number of occurrences of '$\vee$' in B.
Step 1: $p = 0$. Then B is bound to be of the form $B_1 \vee B_2$. Now suppose $A_1, A_2, \ldots, A_n \vdash B$ is valid. Then (1) there is bound to be an i such that A_i is or occurs in B_1, in which case

$$A_1, A_2, \ldots, A_n \vdash B_1 \qquad (5.1)$$

is valid and hence—in view of Case 1 or of the hypothesis of induction—provable by means of **S, DI,** and **DE**, or (2) there is bound to be an i such that A_i is or occurs in B_2, in which case

$$A_1, A_2, \ldots, A_n \vdash B_2 \qquad (5.2)$$

is valid and hence—in view of Case 1 or of the hypothesis of induction—provable by means of **S, DI,** and **DE**.[13] But $A_1, A_2, \ldots, A_n \vdash B$ follows from (5.1) in one case and from (5.2) in the other by means of **DI**. Hence T2.
Step 2: $p > 0$. Then there is bound to be an i such that A_i is of the form $A_{i_1} \vee A_{i_2}$. Now suppose $A_1, A_2, \ldots, A_n \vdash B$ is valid. Then both

$$A_1, A_2, \ldots, A_{i-1}, A_{i_1}, A_{i+1}, \ldots, A_n \vdash B \qquad (5.3)$$

and

$$A_1, A_2, \ldots, A_{i-1}, A_{i_2}, A_{i+1}, \ldots, A_n \vdash B \qquad (5.4)$$

312   Part 3: Provability

are bound to be valid and hence—in view of Case 1 or of the hypothesis of induction—provable by means of **S**, **DI**, and **DE**. But $A_1, A_2, \ldots, A_n \vdash B$ follows from (5.3)–(5.4) by means of the said rules. Hence T2.[14]

Case 6: The only two connectives that occur in $A_1, A_2, \ldots, A_n \vdash B$ are '∨' and '&'.
Proof: (a) By induction on p, the number of wffs among $A_1, A_2, \ldots, A_n, B$ which fail to be in conjunctive normal form, and (b) when $p = 0$, by induction on the number of occurrences of '&' in $A_1, A_2, \ldots, A_n, B$.
Step 1: $p = 0$.
Step 1.1: There is an i such that A_i is of the form A_{i_1} & A_{i_2}. Proof similar to the proof of Case 3, Step 1.1, but with Case 5 doing duty for Case 2 and with **DI** and **DE** doing duty for **HI** and **HE**.
Step 1.2: B is of the form B_1 & B_2. Proof similar to the proof of Case 3, Step 2.2, but with Case 5 doing duty for Case 2 and with **DI** and **DE** doing duty for **HI** and **HE**.
Step 2: $p > 0$.
Step 2.1: There is an i such that A_i fails to be in conjunctive normal form. Suppose $A_1, A_2, \ldots, A_n \vdash B$ is valid. Then

$$A_1, A_2, \ldots, A_{i-1}, A_i^*, A_{i+1}, \ldots, A_n \vdash B, \tag{6.1}$$

where A_i^* is any result of putting A_i in conjunctive normal form, is bound to be valid and hence—in view of Step 1 or of the hypothesis of induction—provable by means of **S**, **DI**, **DE**, **CI**, and **CE**. But $A_1, A_2, \ldots, A_n \vdash B$ follows from (6.1) by means of the said rules. Hence T2.
Step 2.2: B fails to be in conjunctive normal form. Proof similar to the proof of Step 2.1.

Case 7: The only connective that occurs in $A_1, A_2, \ldots, A_n \vdash B$ is '≡'.
Proof: (a) By induction on p, the number of occurrences of '≡' in B, (b) when $p = 0$, by induction on q, the number of nested occurrences of '≡' in $A_1, A_2, \ldots, A_n$, and (c) when $q = 0$, by induction on the number of unnested occurrences of '≡' in $A_1, A_2, \ldots, A_n$.
Step 1: $p = 0$.
Step 1.1: $q = 0$. Suppose $A_1, A_2, \ldots, A_n \vdash B$ is valid. Then (1) there is bound to be an i such that A_i is B, in which case

$$A_1, A_2, \ldots, A_{j-1}, A_{j+1}, \ldots, A_n \vdash B, \tag{7.1}$$

where A_j ($j < i$ or $j > i$) is the left-most one of $A_1, A_2, \ldots, A_n$ to exhibit an occurrence of '≡', is valid and hence—in view of Case 1 or of the hypothesis of induction—provable by means of **S**, **BI**, and **BE**, or (2) there is bound to be an i and there is bound to be a j ($j < i$ or $j > i$) such that A_i is $A_j \equiv A_{i_2}$, in which case

$$A_1, A_2, \ldots, A_{i-1}, A_{i_2}, A_{i+1}, \ldots, A_n \vdash B \tag{7.2}$$

Proof Routines for the Propositional Calculus 313

is valid and hence—in view of Case 1 or of the hypothesis of induction—provable by means of **S**, **BI**, and **BE**, or (3) there is bound to be an i and there is bound to be a j ($j < i$ or $j > i$) such that A_i is $A_{i_1} \equiv A_j$, in which case

$$A_1, A_2, \ldots, A_{i-1}, A_{i_1}, A_{i+1}, \ldots, A_n \vdash B \tag{7.3}$$

is valid and hence—in view of Case 1 or of the hypothesis of induction—provable by means of **S**, **BI**, and **BE**.[15] But $A_1, A_2, \ldots, A_n \vdash B$ follows from (7.1) in the first case by means of **S**, from (7.2) in the second by means of **S**, **BI**, and **BE**, and from (7.3) in the third by means of **S**, **BI**, and **BE**. Hence T2.

Step 1.2: $q > 0$. Then there is bound to be an i such that A_i is of one of the two forms $(A_{i_1} \equiv A_{i_2}) \equiv A_{i_3}$ and $A_{i_1} \equiv (A_{i_2} \equiv A_{i_3})$. Now suppose $A_1, A_2, \ldots, A_n \vdash B$ is valid. Then all three of

$$A_1, A_2, \ldots, A_{i-1}, A_{i_1}, A_{i_2} \equiv A_{i_3}, A_{i+1}, \ldots, A_n \vdash B, \tag{7.4}$$

$$A_1, A_2, \ldots, A_{i-1}, A_{i_2} A_{i_1} \equiv A_{i_3}, A_{i+1}, \ldots, A_n \vdash B, \tag{7.5}$$

and

$$A_1, A_2, \ldots, A_{i-1}, A_{i_3}, A_{i_1} \equiv A_{i_2}, A_{i+1}, \ldots, A_n \vdash B \tag{7.6}$$

are bound to be valid and hence—in view of the hypothesis of induction—provable by means of **S**, **BI**, and **BE**.[16] But $A_1, A_2, \ldots, A_n \vdash B$ follows from (7.4)–(7.6) by means of the said rules. Hence T2.

Step 2: $p > 0$. Then B is bound to be of the form $B_1 \equiv B_2$. Now suppose $A_1, A_2, \ldots, A_n \vdash B$ is valid. Then both

$$A_1, A_2, \ldots, A_n, B_1 \vdash B_2 \tag{7.7}$$

and

$$A_1, A_2, \ldots, A_n B_2 \vdash B_1 \tag{7.8}$$

are bound to be valid and hence—in view of Case 1 or of the hypothesis of induction—provable by means of **S**, **BI**, and **BE**. But $A_1, A_2, \ldots, A_n \vdash B$ follows from (7.7)–(7.8) by means of the said rules. Hence T2.

Case 8: The only two connectives that occur in $A_1, A_2, \ldots, A_n \vdash B$ are '$\equiv$' and '$\supset$'.

Proof: (a) By induction on p, the number of occurrences of '$\equiv$' and '$\supset$' in B, (b) when $p = 0$, by induction on q, the number of nested occurrences on '$\equiv$' and '$\supset$' in $A_1, A_2, \ldots, A_n$, and (c) when $q = 0$, by induction on the number of unnested occurrences of '$\supset$' in $A_1, A_2, \ldots, A_n$.

Step 1: $p = 0$.
Step 1.1: $q = 0$. Then there is bound to be an i such that A_i is of the form $A_{i_1} \supset A_{i_2}$. Now suppose $A_1, A_2, \ldots, A_n \vdash B$ is valid. Then both

314   Part 3: Provability

$$A_1, A_2, \ldots, A_{i-1}, A_{i_1} \equiv A_{i_2}, A_{i+1}, \ldots, A_n \vdash B \qquad (8.1)$$

and

$$A_1, A_2, \ldots, A_{i-1}, A_{i_2}, A_{i+1}, \ldots, A_n \vdash B \qquad (8.2)$$

are bound to be valid and hence—in view of Case 7 or of the hypothesis of induction—provable by means of **S, BI, BE, CI,** and **CE**.[17] But $A_1, A_2, \ldots, A_n \vdash B$ follows from (8.1)–(8.2) by means of the said rules. Hence T2.

Step 1.2: $q > 0$. Then there is bound to be an i such that A_i is of one of the eight forms $(A_{i_1} \equiv A_{i_2}) \equiv A_{i_3}$, $A_{i_1} \equiv (A_{i_2} \equiv A_{i_3})$, $(A_{i_1} \supset A_{i_2}) \supset A_{i_3}$, $A_{i_1} \supset (A_{i_2} \supset A_{i_3})$, $(A_{i_1} \supset A_{i_2}) \equiv A_{i_3}$, $A_{i_1} \equiv (A_{i_2} \supset A_{i_2})$, $(A_{i_0} \equiv A_{i_2}) \supset A_{i_3}$, and $A_{i_1} \supset (A_{i_2} \equiv A_{i_3})$, where in the last case A_{i_1} is a propositional variable.

Step 1.2.1: A_i is of one of the first two forms listed. Proof similar to the proof of Case 7, Step 1.2, but with **S, BI, BE, HI,** and **HE** doing duty for **S, BI,** and **BE**.

Step 1.2.2: A_i is of one of the next two forms listed. Proof similar to the proof of Case 2, Step 1.2, but with **S, BI, BE, HI,** and **HE** doing duty for **S, HI,** and **HE**.

Step 1.2.3: A_i is of the form $(A_{i_1} \supset A_{i_2}) \equiv A_{i_3}$. Suppose $A_1, A_2, \ldots, A_n \vdash B$ is valid. Then both

$$A_1, A_2, \ldots, A_{i-1}, A_{i_1}, A_{i_2} \equiv A_{i_1}, A_{i+1}, \ldots, A_n \vdash B \qquad (8.3)$$

and

$$A_1, A_2, \ldots, A_{i-1}, A_{i_1} \supset A_{i_2}, A_{i_3}, A_{i+1}, \ldots, A_n \vdash B \qquad (8.4)$$

are bound to be valid and hence—in view of Case 7 or of the hypothesis of induction—provable by means of **S, BI, BE, HI,** and **HE**.[18] But $A_1, A_2, \ldots, A_n \vdash B$ follows from (8.3)–(8.4) by means of the said rules. Hence T2.

Step 1.2.4: A_i is of the form $A_{i_1} \equiv (A_{i_2} \supset A_{i_3})$. Proof similar to the proof of Step 1.2.3, but with A_{i_1} doing duty for A_{i_3}, A_{i_2} doing duty for A_{i_1}, and A_{i_3} doing duty for A_{i_2}.

Step 1.2.5: A_i is of the form $(A_{i_1} \equiv A_{i_2}) \supset A_{i_3}$. Suppose $A_1, A_2, \ldots, A_n \vdash B$ is valid. Then all three of

$$A_1, A_2, \ldots, A_{i-1}, A_{i_1}, A_{i_2} \supset A_{i_3}, A_{i+1}, \ldots, A_n \vdash B, \qquad (8.5)$$

$$A_1, A_2, \ldots, A_{i-1}, A_{i_2}, A_{i_1} \supset A_{i_3}, A_{i+1}, \ldots, A_n \vdash B, \qquad (8.6)$$

and

$$A_1, A_2, \ldots, A_{i-1}, A_{i_3}, A_{i+1}, \ldots, A_n \vdash B \qquad (8.7)$$

are bound to be valid and hence—in view of Case 7 or of the hypothesis of induction—provable by means of **S**, **BI**, **BE**, **HI**, and **HE**.[19] But A_1, A_2, ..., $A_n \vdash B$ follows from (8.5)–(8.7) by means of the said rules. Hence T2.

Step 1.2.6: $A_{i_1} \supset (A_{i_2} \equiv A_{i_3})$, where A_{i_1} is a propositional variable. Suppose $A_1, A_2, \ldots, A_n \vdash B$ is valid. Then both

$$A_1, A_2, \ldots, A_{i-1}, A_{i_1} \supset A_{i_2}, A_{i_1} \supset A_{i_3}, A_{i+1}, \ldots, A_n \vdash B \quad (8.8)$$

and

$$A_1, A_2, \ldots, A_{i-1}, A_{i_2} \equiv A_{i_3}, A_{i+1}, \ldots, A_n \vdash B \quad (8.9)$$

are bound to be valid and hence—in view of Case 7 or of the hypothesis of induction—provable by means of **S**, **BI**, **BE**, **HI**, and **HE**.[20] But A_1, A_2, ..., $A_n \vdash B$ follows from (8.8)–(8.9) by means of the said rules. Hence T2.

Step 2: $p > 0$. Then B is bound to be one of the two forms $B_1 \equiv B_2$ and $B_1 \supset B_2$.

Step 2.1: B is of the form $B_1 \equiv B_2$. Proof similar to the proof of Case 7, Step 2, but minus the reference to Case 1 and with **S**, **BI**, **BE**, **HI**, and **HE** doing duty for **S**, **BI**, and **BE**.

Step 2.2: B is of the form $B_1 \supset B_2$. Proof similar to the proof of Case 2, Step 2, but with Case 7 doing duty for Case 1 and with **S**, **BI**, **BE**, **HI**, and **HE** doing duty for **S**, **BI**, and **BE**.

Case 9: The only two connectives that occur in $A_1, A_2, \ldots, A_n \vdash B$ are '≡' and '&'.

Proof: (a) By induction on p, the number of occurrences of '≡' and '&' in B, (b) when $p = 0$, by induction on q, the number of nested occurrences of '≡' and '&' in $A_1, A_2, \ldots, A_n$, and (c) when $q = 0$, by induction on the number of unnested occurrences of '&' in $A_1, A_2, \ldots, A_n$.

Step 1: $p = 0$.

Step 1.1: $q = 0$. Then there is bound to be an i such that A_i is of the form A_{i_1} & A_{i_2}, in which case T2 by the same reasoning as in Case 3, Step 1.1, but with Case 7 doing duty for Case 2 and with **BI** and **BE** doing duty for **HI** and **HE**.

Step 1.2: $q > 0$. Then there is bound to be an i such that A_i is of one of the eight forms $(A_{i_1} \equiv A_{i_2}) \equiv A_{i_3}$, $A_{i_1} \equiv (A_{i_2} \equiv A_{i_3})$, $(A_{i_1}$ & $A_{i_2})$ & A_{i_3}, A_{i_1} & $(A_{i_2}$ & $A_{i_3})$, $(A_{i_1} \equiv A_{i_2})$ & A_{i_3}, A_{i_1} & $(A_{i_2} \equiv A_{i_3})$, $(A_{i_1}$ & $A_{i_2}) \equiv A_{i_3}$, and $A_{i_1} \equiv (A_{i_2}$ & $A_{i_3})$, where A_{i_3} in the seventh case and A_{i_1} in the eighth case are propositional variables.

Step 1.2.1: A_i is of one of the first two forms listed. Proof similar to the proof of Case 7, Step 1.2, but with **S**, **BI**, **BE**, **CI**, and **CE** doing duty for **S**, **BI**, and **BE**.

Step 1.2.2: A_i is of one of the next four forms listed. Proof similar to the proof of Step 1.1.

Step 1.2.3: A_i is of the form $(A_{i_1}$ & $A_{i_2}) \equiv A_{i_3}$, where A_{i_3} is a propositional variable. Suppose $A_1, A_2, \ldots, A_n \vdash B$ is valid. Then all three of

$$A_1, A_2, \ldots, A_{i-1}, A_{i_1} \equiv A_{i_3}, A_{i_2}, A_{i+1}, \ldots, A_n \vdash B, \quad (9.1)$$

$$A_1, A_2, \ldots, A_{i-1}, A_{i_2} \equiv A_{i_3}, A_{i_1}, A_{i+1}, \ldots, A_n \vdash B, \quad (9.2)$$

and

$$A_1, A_2, \ldots, A_{i-1}, A_{i_1} \equiv A_{i_3}, A_{i_2} \equiv A_{i_3}, A_{i+1}, \ldots, A_n \vdash B \quad (9.3)$$

are bound to be valid and hence—in view of Case 7 or of the hypothesis of induction—provable by means of **S, BI, BE, CI,** and **CE**.[21] But $A_1, A_2, \ldots, A_n \vdash B$ follows from (9.1)–(9.3) by means of the said rules. Hence T2.

Step 1.2.4: A_i is of the form $A_{i_1} \equiv (A_{i_2} \& A_{i_3})$, where A_{i_1} is a propositional variable. Proof similar to the proof of Step 1.2.3, but with A_{i_1} doing duty for A_{i_3}, A_{i_2} doing duty for A_{i_1}, and A_{i_3} doing duty for $A_{i_{3_2}}$.

Step 2: $p > 0$. Then B is bound to be of one of the two forms $B_1 \equiv B_2$ and $B_1 \& B_2$.

Step 2.1: B is of the form $B_1 \equiv B_2$. Proof similar to the proof of Case 7, Step 2, but minus the reference to Case 1 and with **S, BI, BE, CI,** and **CE** doing duty for **S, BI,** and **BE**.

Step 2.2: B is of the form $B_1 \& B_2$. Proof similar to the proof of Case 3, Step 2.2, but with Case 7 doing duty for Case 2 and with **BI** and **BE** doing duty for **HI** and **HE**.

Case 10: The only two connectives that occur in $A_1, A_2, \ldots, A_n \vdash B$ are '$\equiv$' and '$\vee$'.

Proof: (a) By induction on p, the number of occurrences of '$\equiv$' and '$\vee$' in B, (b) when $p = 0$, by induction on q, the number of nested occurrences of '$\equiv$' and '$\vee$' in $A_1, A_2, \ldots, A_n$, and (c) when $q = 0$, by induction on the number of unnested occurrences of '$\vee$' in $A_1, A_2, \ldots, A_n$.

Step 1: $p = 0$.

Step 1.1: $q = 0$. Then there is bound to be an i such that A_i is of the form $A_{i_1} \vee A_{i_2}$, in which case T2 by the same reasoning as in Case 5, Step 2, but with Case 7 doing duty for Case 1 and with **S, BI, BE, DI,** and **DE** doing duty for **S, DI,** and **DE**.

Step 1.2: $q > 0$. Then there is bound to be an i such that A_i is of one of the eight forms $(A_{i_1} \equiv A_{i_2}) \equiv A_{i_3}$, $A_{i_1} \equiv (A_{i_2} \equiv A_{i_3})$, $(A_{i_1} \vee A_{i_2}) \vee A_{i_3}$, $A_{i_1} \vee (A_{i_2} \vee A_{i_3})$, $(A_{i_1} \equiv A_{i_2}) \vee A_{i_3}$, $A_{i_1} \vee (A_{i_2} \equiv A_{i_3})$, $(A_{i_1} \vee A_{i_2}) \equiv A_{i_3}$, and $A_{i_1} \equiv (A_{i_2} \vee A_{i_3})$, where A_{i_3} in the seventh case and A_{i_1} in the eighth case are propositional variables.

Step 1.2.1: A_i is of one of the first two forms listed. Proof similar to the proof of Case 7, Step 1.2, but with **S, BI, DI,** and **DE** doing duty for **S, BI,** and **BE**.

Step 1.2.2: A_i is of one of the next four forms listed. Proof similar to the proof of Step 1.1.
Step 1.2.3: A_i is of the form $(A_{i_1} \lor A_{i_2}) \equiv A_{i_3}$, where A_{i_3} is a propositional variable. Suppose $A_1, A_2, \ldots, A_n \vdash B$ is valid. Then all three of

$$A_1, A_2, \ldots, A_{i-1}, A_{i_1}, A_{i_3}, A_{i+1}, \ldots, A_n \vdash B, \quad (10.1)$$

$$A_1, A_2, \ldots, A_{i-1}, A_{i_2}, A_{i_3}, A_{i+1}, \ldots, A_n \vdash B, \quad (10.2)$$

and

$$A_1, A_2, \ldots, A_{i-1}, A_{i_1} \equiv A_{i_3}, A_{i_2} \equiv A_{i_3}, A_{i+1}, \ldots, A_n \vdash B \quad (10.3)$$

are bound to be valid and hence—in view of Case 7 or of the hypothesis of induction—provable by means of **S, BI, BE, DI,** and **DE**.[22] But $A_1, A_2, \ldots, A_n \vdash B$ follows from (10.1)–(10.3) by means of the said rules. Hence T2.
Step 1.2.4: A_i is of the form $A_{i_1} \equiv (A_{i_2} \lor A_{i_3})$, where A_{i_1} is a propositional variable. Proof similar to the proof of Step 1.2.3, but with A_{i_1} doing duty for A_{i_3}, A_{i_2} doing duty for A_{i_1}, and A_{i_3} doing duty for A_{i_2}.
Step 2: $p > 0$. Then B is bound to be of one of the forms $B_1 \equiv B_2$ and $B_1 \lor B_2$.
Step 2.1: B is of the form $B_1 \equiv B_2$. Proof similar to the proof of Case 7. Step 2, but minus the reference to Case 1 and with **S, BI, BE, DI,** and **DE** doing duty for **S, BI,** and **BE**.
Step 2.2: B is of the form $B_1 \lor B_2$. Suppose $A_1, A_2, \ldots, A_n \vdash B$ is valid. Then

$$A_1, A_2, \ldots, A_n, B_1 \equiv B_2 \vdash B_1 \quad (10.4)$$

is bound to be valid and hence—in view of Case 7 or of the hypothesis of induction—provable by means of **S, BI, BE, DI,** and **DE**.[23] But $A_1, A_2, \ldots, A_n \vdash B$ follows from (10.4) by means of the said rules. Hence T2.

Case 11: The only two connectives that occur in $A_1, A_2, \ldots, A_n \vdash B$ are '$\supset$' and '$\lor$'.
Proof by induction on the number of occurrences of '$\lor$' in $A_1, A_2, \ldots, A_n, B$.
Step 1: B is of the form $B_1 \lor B_2$, where B_2 does not exhibit any '$\lor$'. Suppose $A_1, A_2, \ldots, A_n \vdash B$ is valid. Then

$$A_1, A_2, \ldots, A_n \vdash (B_1 \supset B_2) \supset B_2 \quad (11.1)$$

is bound to be valid and hence—in view of Case 2 or of the hypothesis of induction—provable by means of **S, HI, HE, DI,** and **DE**.[24] But $A_1, A_2, \ldots, A_n \vdash B$ follows from (11.1) by means of the said rules. Hence T2.
Step 2: B has a component of the form $B_j \lor B_k$, where B_k does not exhibit any

'∨'. Suppose $A_1, A_2, \ldots, A_n \vdash B$ is valid. Then

$$A_1, A_2, \ldots, A_n \vdash B, \qquad (11.2)$$

where B' is like B except for exhibiting $((B_j \supset B_k) \supset B_k) \supset B_l$ where B exhibits $(B_j \vee B_k) \supset B_l$ or for exhibiting $B_j \supset ((B_j \supset B_k) \supset B_k)$ where B exhibits $B_i \supset (B_j \vee B_k)$, is bound to be valid and hence—in view of Case 2 or of the hypothesis of induction—provable by means of **S**, **HI**, **HE**, **DI**, and **DE**. But $A_1, A_2, \ldots, A_n \vdash B$ follows from (11.2) by means of the said rules. Hence T2.

Step 3: There is an i such that A_i is of the form $A_{i_1} \vee A_{i_2}$, where A_{i_2} does not exhibit any '∨'. Proof similar to the proof of Step 1.

Step 4: There is an i such that A_i has a component of the form $A_{i_j} \vee A_{i_k}$, where A_{i_k} does not exhibit any '∨'. Proof similar to the proof of Step 2.

Cases 12–16 are provable along similar lines. Appended is a table (Table 2b) of the various cases to which they reduce and of the transformations—effected for illustration's sake on $B_1 \supset B_2$, $B_1 \& B_2$, $B_1 \vee B_2$, and $B_1 \equiv B_2$—which ensure those reductions. A key to the abbreviations used in Table 2b is supplied in Table 2a, where '$\rightarrow$' is to be read 'is short for'.

TABLE 2a

T1: $B_1 \supset B_2 \rightarrow (B_1 \& B_2) \equiv B_1$

T2: $B_1 \supset B_2 \rightarrow (B_1 \vee B_2) \equiv B_2$[25]

T3: $B_1 \& B_2 \rightarrow ((B_1 \supset B_2) \supset B_2) \equiv (B_1 \equiv B_2)$

T4: $B_1 \& B_2 \rightarrow (B_1 \vee B_2) \equiv (B_1 \equiv B_2)$

T5: $B_1 \vee B_2 \rightarrow (B_1 \supset B_2) \supset B_2$

T6: $B_1 \vee B_2 \rightarrow (B_1 \& B_2) \equiv (B_1 \equiv B_2)$

T7: $B_1 \equiv B_2 \rightarrow (B_1 \supset B_2) \& (B_2 \supset B_1)$

TABLE 2b

Cases	Reducible to Cases	By means of
12: '⊃', '&', and '∨'	3	T5
13: '⊃', '&', and '≡'	3	T7
	8	T3
14: '⊃', '∨', and '≡'	8	T5
	10	T2
15: '&', '∨', and '≡'	9	T6
	10	T4

16: '⊃', '&', 'V', $\begin{cases} 3 & \text{T5 and T7} \\ 8 & \text{T3 and T5} \\ 9 & \text{T1 and T6} \\ 10 & \text{T2 and T4} \end{cases}$
  and '≡'

3. I complete in this section the proof of T2 by solving the case where A_1, A_2, ..., $A_n \vdash$ exhibits only '~' (Case 17) and reducing to Case 17 the fifteen cases where $A_1, A_2, \ldots, A_n \vdash B$ exhibits besides '~' any one, any two, any three, or all four of '⊃', '&', 'V', and '≡'.

Case 17: The only connective that occurs in $A_1, A_2, \ldots, A_n \vdash B$ is '~'.
Proof by induction on p, the number of wffs among $A_1, A_2, \ldots, A_n, B$ which consist of two or more occurrences of '~' followed by a propositional variable.
Step 1: $p = 0$. Suppose $A_1, A_2, \ldots, A_n \vdash B$ is valid. Then (1) there is bound to be an i such that A_i is B, in which case $A_1, A_2, \ldots, A_n \vdash B$ follows from $B \vdash B$ (= **R**) by means of **E** and **P**, or (2) there is bound to be an i and there is bound to be a j ($j < i$ or $j > i$) such that A_i is $\sim A_j$, in which case $A_1, A_2, \ldots, A_n \vdash B$ follows from $A_j \vdash A_j$ and $\sim A_j \vdash \sim A_j$ (= **R**) by means of **T**, **P**, **NI**, and **NE**.[26] Hence T2.
Step 2: $p > 0$. Then there is bound to be an i such that A_i is of the form $\underbrace{\sim\sim \ldots \sim}_{k \text{ times}} A_i^*$, where $k \geq 2$ and A_i^* is a propositional variable, or B is bound to be of the form $\underbrace{\sim\sim \ldots \sim}_{k \text{ times}} B^*$, where $k \geq 2$ and B^* is a propositional variable.
Step 2.1: A_i is of the form $\underbrace{\sim\sim \ldots \sim}_{k \text{ times}} A_i^*$. Suppose $A_1, A_2, \ldots, A_n \vdash B$ is valid and k is even. Then

$$A_1, A_2, \ldots, A_{i-1}, A_i^*, A_{i+1}, \ldots, A_n \vdash B \qquad (17.1)$$

is bound to be valid and hence—in view of Step 1 or of the hypothesis of induction—provable by means of **S**, **NI**, and **NE**.[27] Or suppose $A_1, A_2, \ldots, A_n \vdash B$ is valid and k is odd. Then

$$\cdot A_1, A_2, \ldots, A_{i-1}, \sim A_i^*, A_{i+1}, \ldots, A_n \vdash B \qquad (17.2)$$

is bound to be valid and hence—in view of Step 1 or of the hypothesis of induction—provable by means of **S**, **NI**, and **NE**.[28] But $A_1, A_2, \ldots, A_n \vdash B$ follows from (17.1) in one case and from (17.2) in the other by means of the said rules. Hence T2.
Step 2.2: B is of the form $\underbrace{\sim\sim \ldots \sim}_{k \text{ times}} B^*$. Proof similar to the proof of Step 2.1.

Case 18: The only two connectives that occur in $A_1, A_2, \ldots, A_n \vdash B$ are '$\sim$' and '$\supset$'.
Proof by induction on the number of occurrences of '$\supset$' in $A_1, A_2, \ldots, A_n, B$.
Step 1: There is an i such that A_i is of the form $\underbrace{\sim\sim \ldots \sim}_{k \text{ times}}(A_{i_1} \supset A_{i_2})$ where $k \geq 0$.
Step 1.1: k equals 0 or k is even. Suppose $A_1, A_2, \ldots, A_n \vdash B$ is valid. Then both

$$A_1, A_2, \ldots, A_{i-1}, \sim A_{i_1}, A_{i+1}, \ldots, A_n \vdash B \qquad (18.1)$$

and

$$A_1, A_2, \ldots, A_{i-1}, A_{i_2}, A_{i+1}, \ldots, A_n \vdash B \qquad (18.2)$$

are bound to be valid and hence—in view of Case 17 or of the hypothesis of induction—provable by means of **S, NI, NE, HI,** and **HE**.[29] But $A_1, A_2, \ldots, A_n \vdash B$ follows from (18.1)–(18.2) by means of the said rules. Hence T2.
Step 1.2: k is odd. Suppose $A_1, A_2, \ldots, A_n \vdash B$ is valid. Then

$$A_1, A_2, \ldots, A_{i_1}, \sim A_{i_2}, A_{i+1}, \ldots, A_n \vdash B \qquad (18.3)$$

is bound to be valid and hence—in view of Case 17 or of the hypothesis of induction—provable by means of **S, NI, NE, HI,** and **HE**.[30] But $A_1, A_2, \ldots, A_n \vdash B$ follows from (18.3) by means of the said rules. Hence T2.
Step 2: B is of the form $\underbrace{\sim\sim \ldots \sim}_{k \text{ times}}(B_1 \supset B_2)$, where $k \geq 0$.
Step 2.1: k equals 0 or k is even. Suppose $A_1, A_2, \ldots, A_n \vdash B$ is valid. Then

$$A_1, A_2, \ldots, A_n, B_1, \vdash B_2 \qquad (18.4)$$

is bound to be valid and hence—in view of Case 17 or of the hypothesis of induction—provable by means of **S, NI, NE, HI,** and **HE**.[31] But $A_1, A_2, \ldots, A_n \vdash B$ follows from (18.4) by means of the said rules. Hence T2.
Step 2.2: k is odd. Suppose $A_1, A_2, \ldots, A_n \vdash B$ is valid. Then both

$$A_1, A_2, \ldots, A_n \vdash B_1 \qquad (18.5)$$

and

$$A_1, A_2, \ldots, A_n \vdash \sim B_2 \qquad (18.6)$$

are bound to be valid and hence—in view of Case 17 or of the hypothesis of induction—provable by means of **S, NI, NE, HI,** and **HE**.[32] But $A_1, A_2, \ldots, A_n \vdash B$ follows from (18.5)–(18.6) by means of the said rules. Hence T2.

Case 19: The only two connectives that occur in $A_1, A_2, \ldots, A_n \vdash B$ are '$\sim$' and '&'.

Proof similar to the proof of Case 18, but with '&' doing duty for '⊃', **CI** and **CE** doing duty for **HI** and **HE**,

$$A_1, A_2, \ldots, A_{i-1}, A_{i_1}, A_{i_2}, A_{i+1}, \ldots, A_n \vdash B$$

doing duty for (18.1)–(18.2),

$$A_1, A_2, \ldots, A_{i-1}, {\sim}A_{i_1}, A_{i+1}, \ldots, A_n \vdash B$$

and

$$A_1, A_2, \ldots, A_{i-1}, {\sim}A_{i_2}, A_{i+1}, \ldots, A_n \vdash B$$

doing duty for (18.3),

$$A_1, A_2, \ldots, A_n \vdash B_1$$

and

$$A_1, A_2, \ldots, A_n \vdash B_2$$

doing duty for (18.4), and

$$A_1, A_2, \ldots, A_n, B_1 \vdash {\sim}B_2$$

doing duty for (18.5)–(18.6).

Case 20: The only two connectives that occur in $A_1, A_2, \ldots, A_n \vdash B$ are '${\sim}$' and '$\vee$'.

Proof similar to the proof of Case 18, but with '$\vee$' doing duty for '⊃', **DI** and **DE** doing duty for **HI** and **HE**,

$$A_1, A_2, \ldots, A_{i-1}, A_{i_1}, A_{i+1}, \ldots, A_n \vdash B$$

and

$$A_1, A_2, \ldots, A_{i-1}, A_{i_2}, A_{i+1}, \ldots, A_n \vdash B$$

doing duty for (18.1)–(18.2),

$$A_1, A_2, \ldots, A_{i-1}, {\sim}A_{i_1}, {\sim}A_{i_2}, A_{i+1}, \ldots, A_n \vdash B$$

doing duty for (18.3),

$$A_1, A_2, \ldots, A_n, {\sim}B_1 \vdash B_2$$

doing duty for (18.4), and

$$A_1, A_2, \ldots, A_n \vdash {\sim}B_1$$

and

$$A_1, A_2, \ldots, A_n \vdash {\sim}B_2$$

doing duty for (18.5)–(18.6).

Case 21: The only two connectives that occur in $A_1, A_2, \ldots, A_n \vdash B$ are '${\sim}$' and '$\equiv$'.

Proof similar to the proof of Case 18, but with '≡' doing duty for '⊃', **BI** and **BE** doing duty for **HI** and **HE**,

$$A_1, A_2, \ldots, A_{i-1}, A_{i_1}, A_{i_2}, A_{i+1}, \ldots, A_n \vdash B$$

and

$$A_1, A_2, \ldots, A_{i-1}, {\sim}A_{i_1}, {\sim}A_{i_2}, A_{i+1}, \ldots, A_n \vdash B$$

doing duty for (18.1)–(18.2),

$$A_1, A_2, \ldots, A_{i-1}, A_{i_1}, {\sim}A_{i_2}, A_{i+1}, \ldots, A_n \vdash B$$

and

$$A_1, A_2, \ldots, A_{i-1}, {\sim}A_{i_1}, A_{i_2}, A_{i+1}, \ldots, A_n \vdash B$$

doing duty for (18.3),

$$A_1, A_2, \ldots, A_n, B_1 \vdash B_2$$

and

$$A_1, A_2, \ldots, A_n, B_2 \vdash B_1$$

doing duty for (18.4), and

$$A_1, A_2, \ldots, A_n, {\sim}B_1 \vdash B_2$$

and

$$A_1, A_2, \ldots, A_n, {\sim}B_2 \vdash B_1$$

doing duty for (18.5)–(18.6).

Cases 22–32 are provable in the same manner as Case 11. Appended is a table (Table 3b) of the various cases to which they reduce and of the transformations—effected for illustration's sake on $B_1 \supset B_2$, $B_1 \,\&\, B_2$, $B_1 \lor B_2$, and $B_1 = B_2$—which insure those reductions. A key to the abbreviations used in Table 3b is supplied in Table 3a.

TABLE 3a

T1: $B_1 \supset B_2 \rightarrow {\sim}(B_1 \,\&\, {\sim}B_2)$

T2: $B_1 \supset B_2 \rightarrow {\sim}B_1 \lor B_2$

T3: $B_1 \,\&\, B_2 \rightarrow {\sim}(B_1 \supset {\sim}B_2)$

T4: $B_1 \,\&\, B_2 \rightarrow {\sim}({\sim}B_1 \lor {\sim}B_2)$

T5: $B_1 \lor B_2 \rightarrow {\sim}B_1 \supset B_2$

T6: $B_1 \lor B_2 \rightarrow {\sim}({\sim}B_1 \,\&\, {\sim}B_2)$

T7: $B_1 \equiv B_2 \rightarrow {\sim}((B_1 \supset B_2) \supset {\sim}(B_2 \supset B_1))$

Proof Routines for the Propositional Calculus 323

T8: $B_1 \equiv B_2 \rightarrow \sim(B_1 \& \sim B_2) \& \sim(B_2 \& \sim B_1)$

T9: $B_1 \equiv B_2 \rightarrow \sim(\sim(\sim B_1 \vee B_2) \vee \sim(\sim B_2 \vee B_1))$

TABLE 3b

Cases	Reducible to Cases	By means of
22: '$\sim$', '$\supset$', and '&'	18 19	T3 T1
23: '$\sim$', '$\supset$', and '$\vee$'	18 20	T5 T2
24: '$\sim$', '$\supset$', and '$\equiv$'	18	T7
25: '$\sim$', '&', and '$\vee$'	19 20	T6 T4
26: '$\sim$', '&', and '$\equiv$'	19	T8
27: '$\sim$', '$\vee$', and '$\equiv$'	20	T9
28: '$\sim$', '$\supset$', '&' and '$\vee$'	18 19 20	T3 and T5 T1 and T6 T2 and T4
29: '$\sim$', '$\supset$', '&', and '$\equiv$'	18 19	T3 and T7 T1 and T8
30: '$\sim$', '$\supset$', '$\vee$', and '$\equiv$'	18 20	T5 and T7 T2 and T9
31: '$\sim$', '&', '$\vee$', and '$\equiv$'	19 20	T6 and T8 T4 and T9
32: '$\sim$', '$\supset$', '&', '$\vee$', and '$\equiv$'	18 19 20	T3, T5, and T7 T1, T6, and T8 T2, T4, and T9

4. My main theorem, T2, fails, as I remarked in Section 2, when the elimination rules for '$\supset$' and '$\equiv$' are respectively made to read like **HE**$'$ and **BE**$'$. $p \supset q$, $(p \supset r) \supset q \vdash q$, for example, though classically valid, is not intuitionistically valid; **R, T, P, HI**, and **HE**$'$, on the other hand, are all intuitionistically sound; $p \supset q$, $(p \supset r) \supset q \vdash q$ is therefore not provable by means of **R, T, P, HI**, and **HE**$'$.[33] Similarly, p, $(r \equiv p) \equiv (r \equiv q) \vdash q$ and p, $(r \equiv q) \equiv (r \equiv p) \vdash q$, though classically valid, are not intuitionistically valid; **R, T, P, BI**, and **BE**$'$, on the other hand, are all intuitionistically sound; neither p, $(r \equiv p) \equiv (r \equiv q) \vdash q$ nor p, $(r \equiv q) \equiv (r \equiv p) \vdash q$ is therefore provable by means of **R, T, P, BI**, and **BE**$'$.

It should, nonetheless, be noted that **HE** follows from **HE'** by means of **R, T, P, HI, NI**, and **NE** or by means of **R, T, P, HI, BI**, and **BE**, and hence may occasionally give way to **HE'**. Similarly, **BE** follows from **BE'** by means of **R, T, P, BI, HI**, and **HE** or by means of **R, T, P, BI, NI**, and **NE**, and hence may occasionally give way to **BE'**. Finally, **NE** follows from the intuitionist elimination rule for '$\sim$', namely:

NE': *If* (1) $A_1, A_2, \ldots, A_n \vdash B$ *and* (2) $A_1, A_2, \ldots, A_n \vdash \sim B$, *then* $A_1, A_2, \ldots, A_n \vdash C$,

by means of **R, T, P, NI, HI**, and **HE** or by means of **R, T, P, NI, BI**, and **BE**, and hence may occasionally give way to **NE'**.[34]

Now for my second conjecture. Suppose $A_1, A_2, \ldots, A_n \vdash B$ exhibits no connective or exhibits no connective other than '&' and '∨'. It follows from T1 and T2 that if $A_1, A_2, \ldots, A_n \vdash B$ is provable or, as I shall now put it, classically provable, then $A_1, A_2, \ldots, A_n \vdash B$ is provable by means of **R, T, P, CI, CE, DI**, and **DE**. But all seven of those rules—I just noted—are intuitionistically sound. Hence if $A_1, A_2, \ldots, A_n \vdash B$ is classically provable, then $A_1, A_2, \ldots, A_n \vdash B$ is intuitionistically provable as well.[35] I conjectured that in view of this result one cannot convert a set of structural and intelim rules fit for PC$_I$, the intuitionist variant of PC, into one fit for PC by altering the intelim rules for '&' or '∨'.[36] The surmise is of some interest since we have long known how to bridge the gap between PC$_I$ and PC by altering the intelim rules for '$\sim$' and have recently learned how to bridge that gap by altering the intelim rules for '⊃' or those for '≡'. Proof of it is now available, but must be saved for another occasion.[37]

Notes

1. See [5] pp. 56–66, where I offered the conjecture for a slightly different, but equivalent, set of structural and intelim rules. Four cases of my conjecture (Cases 1, 4, 5, and 6) have been studied independently by Nuel D. Belnap, Jr. and R. H. Thomason; see Note 2.

2. In view of T1 and T2 a T-statement T, when provable at all, is bound to be provable by means of **S** and the intelim rules for such of the connectives '$\sim$', '⊃', '&', '∨', and '≡' as occur in T. Now let the following structural rule:

C: *If* (1) $A_1, A_2, \ldots, A_n, B \vdash C$ *and* (2) $A_1, A_2, \ldots, A_n \vdash B$, *then* $A_1, A_2, \ldots, A_n \vdash C$,

be appended in Table 1 to **R, T**, and **P**; let a T-statement T be rated derivable from n ($n \geq 0$) T-statements $T_1, T_2, \ldots, T_n$ if T is the last entry in a finite column of T-statements each one of which is a T_i, or is of the form **R** in Table 1, or follows from one or more previous T-statements in the column by application of one of the remaining rules in Table 1; and let the same T-statement T be rated derivable from the same T-statements $T_1, T_2, \ldots, T_n$ by means of **S** and zero or more of the intelim rules in Table 1 if T is the last entry in a finite column of T-statements each one of which is a T_i, or is of the form **R** in Table 1, or follows from one or more previous T-statements in the column by application of **T, P, C**, or one of the intelim rules in question. Belnap and Thomason have recently proved of any $n+1$ T-statements $T, T_1, T_2, \ldots, T_n$, which exhibit no connective or exhibit no connective other than '&' and '∨' that T, when derivable at all from $T_1, T_2, \ldots T_n$, is derivable from them by means of **S** and the intelim rules for such of the connectives '&' and '∨' as

Proof Routines for the Propositional Calculus 325

occur in T, T_1, T_2, ..., T_n; see [2]. I would conjecture, to generalize upon this result, that a T-statement T, when derivable at all from n T-statements T_1, T_2, ..., T_n, is derivable from them by means of **S** and the intelim rules for such of the connectives '$\sim$', '$\supset$', '&', '$\vee$', and '$\equiv$' as occur in T, T_1, T_2, ..., T_n. Rule **C**, by the way, is redundant in the presence of the intelim rules for any one of the connectives '$\sim$', '$\supset$', '&', '$\vee$', and '$\equiv$'.

3. Version **HE** of the elimination rule for '$\supset$' was suggested to me by Stig Kanger. As later discovered, **BE** can be simplified to read "If A_1, A_2, ..., $A_n \vdash B$ and A_1, A_2, ..., $A_n \vdash (D \equiv B) \equiv (D \equiv C)$, then A_1, A_2, ..., $A_n \vdash C$. See [6], Note 14, on the matter.

4. Note that if there were no i such that A_i is B, then A_1, A_2, ..., $A_n \vdash B$ would come out false when the truth-value **T** is assigned to every one of A_1, A_2, ..., and A_n and the truth-value **F** is assigned to B.

5. Note that if there were no i such that A_i is B and there were no two i and j such that A_i is $A_j \supset A_{i_2}$, then A_1, A_2, ..., $A_n \vdash B$ would come out false when **F** is assigned to B, **F** is assigned to the left-hand component of every conditional among A_1, A_2, ..., and A_n whose right-hand component is assigned **F**, and **T** is assigned to every other propositional variable that may occur in A_1, A_2, ..., and A_n. Note also that $(A_j \& (A_j \supset A_{i_2})) \equiv (A_j \& A_{i_2})$ is valid.

6. Note that $((A_{i_1} \supset A_{i_2}) \supset A_{i_3}) \equiv ((A_{i_1} \& (A_{i_2} \supset A_{i_3})) \vee A_{i_3})$ is valid, a point which was brought to my attention by Henry Hiz and Nuel D. Belnap and proved crucial to the solution of Case 2.

7. Note that $(A_{i_1} \supset (A_{i_2} \supset A_{i_3})) \equiv ((A_{i_1} \supset A_{i_3}) \vee (A_{i_2} \supset A_{i_3}))$ is valid.

8. Case 2 could be proved somewhat more simply if I modified it to read: "The only connective (if any) that occurs in A_1, A_2, ..., $A_n \vdash B$ is '$\supset$'," and did not insist on reducing it to Case 1. The same holds true of a few other cases in this section.

9. Note that when A_i is a conditional, then the A_i in question is of the first form listed, and when A_i is a conjunction, then the A_i in question is of the seventh form listed. That the eight forms listed (and like ones in the proofs of Cases 8–10) are exhaustive was pointed out to me by Belnap and proved crucial to the solution of Case 3.

10. Note that $((A_{i_1} \& A_{i_2}) \supset A_{i_3}) \equiv ((A_{i_1} \supset A_{i_3}) \vee (A_{i_2} \supset A_{i_3}))$ is valid.

11. Note that $(A_{i_1} \supset (A_{i_2} \& A_{i_3})) \equiv ((A_{i_1} \supset A_{i_2}) \& (A_{i_1} \supset A_{i_3}))$ is valid; note also that, so long as A_{i_1} is a propositional variable, $A_{i_1} \supset A_{i_2}$ and $A_{i_1} \supset A_{i_3}$ jointly exhibit one nested occurrence of '$\supset$' and '&' less than $A_{i_1} \supset (A_{i_2} \& A_{i_3})$ does.

12. The above proof of Step 1, presupposing as it does rule **C** of note 2, no longer goes through when the elimination rule for '&' is phrased in the more traditional fashion:

CE′: If A_1, A_2, ..., $A_n \vdash B \& C$, then (1) A_1, A_2, ..., $A_n \vdash B$ and (2) A_1, A_2, ..., $A_n \vdash C$,

since **CE′** does not yield **C**. Belnap has obtained a proof of Step 1 which eschews **CE** in favor of **CE′**. The proof, however, does not suit my declared strategy of reducing all of Cases 2–16 to Case 1. In view of the conjecture of Note 2, I also prefer of two elimination rules the one which yields **C**. **CE** was suggested to me as a substitute for **CE′** by Belnap.

13. Note that if there were no i such that A_i is or occurs in B_1 or B_2, then A_1, A_2, ..., $A_n \vdash B$ would come out false when **T** is assigned to every one of A_1, A_2, ..., A_n, and **F** is assigned to every propositional variable that occurs in B.

14. The above proof of Case 5 still goes through when the elimination rule for '$\vee$' is phrased in the more traditional fashion:

DE′: If (1) A_1, A_2, ..., A_n, $B \vdash D$ and (2) A_1, A_2, ..., A_n, $C \vdash D$, then A_1, A_2, ..., A_n, $B \vee C \vdash D$.

In view, however, of the conjecture of Note 2, I prefer **DE**, which yields rule **C** of that note, to **DE′**, which does not. **DE** was suggested to me as a substitute for **DE′** by Belnap.

15. Note that if there were no i such that A_i is B and there were no two i and j such that A_i is $A_j \equiv A_{i_2}$ or $A_{i_1} \equiv A_j$, then A_1, A_2, ..., $A_n \vdash B$ would come out false when **F** is assigned to B, **F** is assigned to the left-hand (right-hand) component of every biconditional among A_1, A_2, ..., and

A_n whose right-hand (left-hand) component is assigned **F**, and **T** is assigned to every other propositional variable that may occur in $A_1, A_2, \ldots, A_n$. Note also that $(A_j \mathbin{\&} (A_j \equiv A_{i_2})) \equiv (A_j \mathbin{\&} A_{i_2})$ is valid.

16. Note that $((A_{i_1} \equiv A_{i_2}) \equiv A_{i_3}) \equiv (((A_{i_1} \mathbin{\&} (A_{i_2} \equiv A_{i_3})) \lor (A_{i_1} \mathbin{\&} (A_{i_1} \equiv A_{i_3}))) \lor (A_{i_3} \mathbin{\&} (A_{i_1} \equiv A_{i_2})))$ is valid, a point which was brought to my attention by Belnap and proved crucial to the solution of Case 7.

17. Note that $(A_{i_1} \supset A_{i_2}) \equiv ((A_{i_1} \equiv A_{i_2}) \lor A_{i_2})$ is valid.
18. Note that $((A_{i_1} \supset A_{i_2}) \equiv A_{i_3}) \equiv ((A_{i_1} \mathbin{\&} (A_{i_2} \equiv A_{i_3})) \lor ((A_{i_1} \supset A_{i_2}) \mathbin{\&} A_{i_3}))$ is valid.
19. Note that $((A_{i_1} \equiv A_{i_2}) \supset A_{i_3}) \equiv (((A_{i_1} \mathbin{\&} (A_{i_2} \supset A_{i_3})) \lor (A_{i_2} \mathbin{\&} (A_{i_1} \supset A_{i_3}))) \lor A_{i_3})$ is valid.
20. Note that $(A_{i_1} \supset (A_{i_2} \equiv A_{i_3})) \equiv (((A_{i_1} \supset A_{i_2}) \mathbin{\&} (A_{i_1} \supset A_{i_3})) \lor (A_{i_2} \equiv A_{i_3}))$ is valid.
21. Note that $((A_{i_1} \mathbin{\&} A_{i_2}) \equiv A_{i_3}) \equiv ((((A_{i_1} \equiv A_{i_3}) \mathbin{\&} A_{i_2}) \lor ((A_{i_2} \equiv A_{i_3}) \mathbin{\&} A_{i_1})) \lor ((A_{i_1} \equiv A_{i_3}) \mathbin{\&} (A_{i_2} \equiv A_{i_3})))$ is valid.
22. Note that $((A_{i_1} \lor A_{i_2}) \equiv A_{i_3}) \equiv (((A_{i_1} \mathbin{\&} A_{i_3}) \lor (A_{i_2} \mathbin{\&} A_{i_3})) \lor ((A_{i_1} \equiv A_{i_3}) \mathbin{\&} (A_{i_2} \equiv A_{i_3})))$ is valid.
23. Note that $(B_1 \lor B_2) \equiv ((B_1 \equiv B_2) \supset B_2)$ is valid.
24. Note that $(B_1 \lor B_2) \equiv ((B_1 \supset B_2) \supset B_2)$ is valid. The need for the restriction "where B_2 does not exhibit any '$\lor$'" (and like ones on Steps 2–4) was pointed out to me by Belnap.
25. Or, less familiarly, $(B_1 \equiv B_2) \lor B_2$.
26. Note that if there were no i such that A_i is B and there were no two i and j such that A_i is $\sim A_j$, then $A_1, A_2, \ldots, A_n \vdash B$ would come out false when **F** is assigned to every propositional variable that is prefaced in $A_1, A_2, \ldots,$ and A_n by '$\sim$', **T** is assigned to every other propositional variable that may occur in $A_1, A_2, \ldots,$ and A_n, and **T** or **F** is assigned to the propositional variable that occurs in B according as that variable is prefaced or not by '$\sim$'.

27. Note that, where k is even, $\underbrace{\sim\sim\ldots\sim}_{k\text{ times}} A_i^* \equiv A_i^*$ is valid.

28. Note that, where k is odd, $\underbrace{\sim\sim\ldots\sim}_{k\text{ times}} A_i^* \equiv \sim A_i^*$ is valid.

29. Note that, where k is 0 or even, $\underbrace{\sim\sim\ldots\sim}_{k\text{ times}}(A_{i_1} \supset A_{i_2}) \equiv (\sim A_{i_1} \lor A_{i_2})$ is valid.

30. Note that, where k is odd, $\underbrace{\sim\sim\ldots\sim}_{k\text{ times}}(A_{i_1} \supset A_{i_2}) \equiv (A_{i_1} \mathbin{\&} \sim A_{i_2})$ is valid.

31. Note that, where k is 0 or even, $\underbrace{\sim\sim\ldots\sim}_{k\text{ times}}(B_1 \supset B_2) \equiv (B_1 \supset B_2)$ is valid.

32. Note that, where k is odd, $\underbrace{\sim\sim\ldots\sim}_{k\text{ times}}(B_1 \supset B_2) \equiv (B_1 \mathbin{\&} B_2)$ is valid.

33. **HE**, by the way, is nothing but a combined version of **HE'** and Peirce's Law.
34. For proofs of some of those results, see [3], [7], and [5].
35. Similarly, $A_1, A_2, \ldots, A_n \vdash B$, when classically valid, is intuitionistically valid as well, so long as $A_1, A_2, \ldots, A_n \vdash B$ exhibits no connective or exhibits no connective other than '&' and '$\lor$'.
36. See [5].
37. See [1]. R. E. Vesley's disproof of the conjecture in [8] uses an intelim rule for '$\lor$' which violates the requirements implicitly placed here upon an intelim rule. Weak forms of the conjecture have already been proved by D. H. J. de Jongh in [4] and by Belnap and Thomason in [2].

References

[1] Belnap, N. D., Jr., Leblanc, H., and Thomason, R. H. 1963. "On *Not* Strengthening Intuitionistic Logic." *Notre Dame Journal of Formal Logic* (hereafter *NDJFL*) 4: 310–20 (#29 in this volume).

[2] Belnap, N. D., Jr., and Thomason, R. H. 1963. "A Rule-Completeness Theorem." *NDJFL* 4: 39–43.

[3] Beth, E. W., and Leblanc, H. 1960. "A Note on the Intuitionist and the Classical Propositional Calculus." *Logique et Analyse* 11–12: 174–75 (#27 in this volume).

[4] de Jongh, D. H. J. 1961. "Recherches sur les I-valuations." *Compte-Rendu des Travaux Effectués par l'Université d'Amsterdam dans le Cadre du Contrat Euratom*, pp. 173–78.

[5] Leblanc, H. 1962. "Etudes sur les Règles d'Inférence dites Règles de Gentzen, Première Partie," *Dialogue* 1: 56–66.

[6] ———. 1966. "Two Separation Theorems for Natural Deduction." *NDJFL* 7: 159–80 (#24 in this volume).

[7] Leblanc, H., and Belnap, N. D., Jr. 1962. "Intuitionism Reconsidered." *NDJFL* 3: 79–82 (#28 in this volume).

[8] Vesley, R. E. 1963. "On Strengthening Intuitionistic Logic." *NDJFL* 4: 80.

24

Two Separation Theorems
for Natural Deduction

Extending a result of mine in [8], I shall first establish that a Gentzen sequent of the sort

$$A_1, A_2, \ldots, A_n \to B,$$

where $A_1, A_2, \ldots, A_n$ ($n \geq 0$), and B are wffs of the first-order quantificational calculus (QC), is invariably provable—when intuitionistically valid—by means of the four structural rules **R**, **T**, **P**, and **C** in Table 1 below and the intelim rules of that table for such (and only such) of the seven operators '$\sim$', '$\supset$', '&', '$\vee$', '$\equiv$', '$\forall$', and '$\exists$' as occur in the sequent. I shall then establish that, save when in $\{\vee, \forall\}$, $\{\vee, \&, \forall\}$, $\{\vee, \forall, \exists\}$, or $\{\vee, \&, \forall, \exists\}$, a sequent of the selfsame sort is provable—when classically valid—by means of **R**, **T**, **P**, **C**, and the intelim rules of Table 3 below for such (and only such) of the seven operators '$\sim$', '$\supset$', '&', '$\vee$', '$\equiv$', '$\forall$', and '$\exists$' as occur in the sequent. The two results have interesting corollaries: one to the effect that a wff A of QC, when intuitionistically implied by a set S of wffs of QC, is invariably deducible from S by means of rule **GR'** in Table 6 below and the intelim rules of that table for such (and only such) of the seven operators '$\sim$', '$\supset$', '&', '$\vee$', '$\equiv$', '$\forall$', and '$\exists$' as occur in a member of S or in A; another to the effect that A, when classically implied by S, is in all but four cases deducible from S by means of **GR'** and the intelim rules of Table 7 below for such (and only such) of the seven operators in question as occur in a member of S or in A.

1. With all seven of '$\sim$', '$\supset$', '&', '$\vee$', '$\equiv$', '$\forall$', and '$\exists$' understood to serve as primitive signs of QC, let an expression of the sort

$$A_1, A_2, \ldots, A_n \to B_1, B_2, \ldots, B_m,$$

where $A_1, A_2, \ldots, A_n$ ($n \geq 0$), $B_1, B_2, \ldots, B_m$ ($m > 0$ if $n = 0$, otherwise $m \geq 0$) are wffs of QC, count as an *L-sequent*, and—when $m = 1$—as an *N-sequent* as well.[1] Let the sequent be said to be in α, where α is a (possibly empty) subset of $\{\sim, \supset, \&, \vee, \equiv, \forall, \exists\}$, if every operator that occurs in the sequent belongs to α and vice-versa. And let it be declared *intuitionistically valid* or, for short, I-*valid* [*classically valid*, or, for short, C-*valid*] if: (i) in the case that $n = 0$, the wff (...$(B_1 \vee B_2) \vee$ ...) $\vee B_m$ is I-valid [C-valid], (ii) in the case that $m = 0$, the wff ((...$(A_1 \& A_2) \&$ ...) & $A_{n-1}) \supset \sim A_n$ is I-valid [C-valid], and (iii) in the case that $n > 0$ and $m > 0$, the wff ((...$(A_1 \& A_2)$ & ...) & $A_n) \supset ((...(B_1 \vee B_2) \vee$ ...) $\vee B_m)$ is I-valid [C-valid].[2] Next, let a finite column of L-sequents [N-sequents] count as a *proof* of an L-sequent [N-sequent] S by means of a set Φ of rules of inference if the column closes with S and every entry in the column follows from p ($p \geq 0$) entries preceding the entry by application of a member of Φ.[3] Finally, let an L-sequent [N-sequent] S be declared *provable* by means of a set Φ of rules of inference if there is a proof of S by means of Φ.

It is readily shown that every N-sequent provable by means of the following rules of inference is I-valid, and hence that the said rules are *intuitionistically sound*:[4]

TABLE 1

Structural rules:

R(eiteration): $\quad A \to A$

T(hinning): $\quad \dfrac{K \to A}{B, K \to A}$

P(ermutation): $\quad \dfrac{K, A, B, L \to C}{K, B, A, L \to C}$

C(ontraction): $\quad \dfrac{A, A, K \to B}{A, K \to B}$

Intelim rules:

For '$\sim$':

NE$_I$: $\quad \dfrac{K \to \sim A \text{ and } K \to \sim\sim A}{K \to A}$

$\dfrac{K, A \to B \text{ and } K, A \to B}{K \to \sim A}$

For '$\supset$':

HE$_I$: $\quad \dfrac{K \to A \text{ and } K \to A \supset B}{K \to B}$

HI: $\quad \dfrac{K, A \to B}{K \to A \supset B}$

For '&':

CE:
$$\frac{K \to A \mathbin{\&} B \text{ and } K, A, B \to C}{K \to C}$$

CI:
$$\frac{K \to A \text{ and } K \to B}{K \to A \mathbin{\&} B}$$

For '$\vee$':

DE:
$$\frac{(i)\ K \to A \vee B,\ (ii)\ K, A \to C,\ \text{and}\ (iii)\ K, B \to C}{K \to C}$$

DI:
$$\frac{K \to A \text{ or } K \to B}{K \to A \vee B}$$

For '$\equiv$':

BE$_\mathrm{I}$:
$$\frac{(i)\ K \to A \text{ and } (ii)\ K \to A \equiv B \text{ or } K \to B \equiv A}{K \to B}$$

BI:
$$\frac{K, A \to B \text{ and } K, B \to A}{K \to A \equiv B}$$

For '$\forall$':

$\forall$E:
$$\frac{K \to (\forall X)A \text{ and } K, A' \to B}{K \to B}$$

$\forall$I:
$$\frac{K \to A'}{K \to (\forall X)A}$$

For '$\exists$':

$\exists$E:
$$\frac{K \to (\exists X)A \text{ and } K, A' \to B}{K \to B}$$

$\exists$I:
$$\frac{K \to A'}{K \to (\exists X)A}$$

Notes: (a) Throughout the above rules K and L are to be finite (and possibly empty) sequences of wffs separated by commas. (b) In the last four rules A' is to be like A except for exhibiting free occurrences of some individual variable X' (not necessarily distinct from X) wherever A exhibits free occurrences of X. In $\forall$I X' is not to occur free in $K \to (\forall X)A$. (d) In $\exists$E X' is not to occur free in $K \to (\exists X)A$.

Leaving that matter of soundness to the reader, I shall restrict myself to proving—as earlier announced—the following so-called *Separation Theorem*:[5]

Theorem 1. *Let α be any subset of $\{\sim, \supset, \mathbin{\&}, \vee, \equiv, \forall, \exists\}$; S be any N-sequent in α; and Φ_α consist of rules* **R**, **T**, **P**, *and* **C** *in Table 1 and the intelim rules of that table for such (and only such) operators as belong to α. If S is* **I**-*valid, then S is provable by means of Φ_α.*

I shall make use, when proving Theorem 1, of a result of Gentzen's to the effect that every **I**-valid L-sequent of the sort

$$A_1, A_2, \ldots, A_n \to$$

or the sort

$$A_1, A_2, \ldots, A_n \to B$$

in which no individual variable occurs both bound and free, is provable by means of the following rules (and vice-versa):[6]

TABLE 2

Structural rules:

Reiteration (**R**): $\qquad A \to A$

Thinning:

  to the left (**Tl**)   to the right (**Tr**)

$$\frac{K \to L^*}{A, K \to L^*} \qquad\qquad \frac{K \to}{K \to A}$$

Permutation to the left (**Pl**):

$$\frac{K, A, B, K' \to L^*}{K, B, A, K' \to L^*}$$

Contraction to the left (**Cl**):

$$\frac{A, A, K \to L^*}{A, K \to L^*}$$

Introduction rules:

For '∼':

  to the left (**Nll**)   to the right (**Nlr**):

$$\frac{K \to A}{\sim A, K \to} \qquad\qquad \frac{A, K \to}{K \to \sim A}$$

For '⊃':

  to the left (**Hll**):   to the right (**Hlr**):

$$\frac{K \to A \text{ and } B, K' \to L^*}{A \supset B, K, K' \to L^*} \qquad\qquad \frac{A, K \to B}{K \to A \supset B}$$

For '&':

  to the left (**Cll**):   to the right (**Clr**):

$$\frac{A, K \to L^* \text{ or } B, K \to L^*}{A \mathbin{\&} B, K \to L^*} \qquad\qquad \frac{K \to A \text{ and } K \to B}{K \to A \mathbin{\&} B}$$

For '∨':

  to the left (**Dll**):   to the right (**Dlr**):

$$\frac{A,\ K \to L^* \text{ and } B,\ K \to L^*}{A \lor B,\ K \to L^*} \qquad \frac{K \to A \text{ or } K \to B}{K \to A \lor B}$$

For '≡':

  to the left (**Bll**):

$$\frac{(i)\ K' \to A \text{ and } B,\ K' \to L^* \text{ or } (ii)\ K' \to B \text{ and } A,\ K' \to L^*}{A \equiv B,\ K,\ K' \to L^*}$$

  to the right (**Blr**):

$$\frac{A,\ K \to B \text{ and } B,\ K \to A}{K \to A \equiv B}$$

For '∀':

  to the left (**∀ll**):   to the right (**∀lr**):

$$\frac{A',\ K \to L^*}{(\forall X)A,\ K \to L^*} \qquad \frac{K \to A'}{K \to (\forall X)A}$$

For '∃':

  to the left (**∃ll**):   to the right (**∃lr**):

$$\frac{A',\ K \to L^*}{(\exists X)A,\ K \to L^*} \qquad \frac{K \to A'}{K \to (\forall \exists)A}$$

Notes: (a) Throughout the above rules K and K' are to be finite (and possibly empty) sequences of wff separated by commas, and L^* is to be a sequence of at most one wff. (b) In the last four rules A' is to be as in Note (b) under Table 1. (c) In **∀lr** X' is not to occur free in $K \to (\forall X)A$. (d) In ∃ll X' is not to occur free in $(\exists X)A,\ K \to L^*$.

Gentzen's result can be put more sharply. Consider indeed a column of L-sequents that qualifies as a proof by means of rules from Table 2 of an L-sequent S of the sort $A_1, A_2, \ldots, A_n \to$ or the sort $A_1, A_2, \ldots, A_n \to B$; suppose S is in a subset α of $\{\sim, \supset, \&, \lor, \equiv, \forall, \exists\}$; and suppose a given operator, call it O, does not belong to α. Any L-sequent that follows from one or two other L-sequents by application of a rule from Table 2 is sure—as the reader may verify—to exhibit O if the one L-sequent from which it follows or at least one of the two L-sequents from which it follows exhibits O. But if so, then any entry in the column under consideration that exhibits O is otiose, and hence can be lopped off. Hence:

Lemma 1. *Let α be any subset of $\{\sim, \supset, \&, \lor, \equiv, \forall, \exists\}$, and S be any L-sequent in α of the sort $A_1, A_2, \ldots, A_n \to$ or the sort $A_1, A_2, \ldots, A_n \to B$*

in which no individual variable occurs both bound and free. If S is **I**-valid, then S is susceptible of a proof in which every entry follows from previous entries in the proof by application of a structural rule in Table 2 or an introduction rule of that table for a member of α.

2. Suppose for proof of Theorem 1 that S is an **I**-valid N-sequent—and, hence, an **I**-valid L-sequent—in which no individual variable occurs both bound and free, and suppose S is in a subset α of $\{\supset, \&, \vee, \equiv, \forall, \exists\}$ (Cases 1–64). Because of Lemma 1 S is susceptible of a proof in which every entry (i) follows from previous entries in the proof by application of a structural rule in Table 2 or an introduction rule of that table for a member of α, and hence (ii) is of the sort $A_1, A_2, \ldots, A_n \to B$.[7] But it is readily shown that: (a) if an L-sequent S_j of the sort $A_1, A_2, \ldots, A_n \to B$ follows from another L-sequent S_i of the same sort by application of a structural rule in Table 2 or a one-premise rule of that table for a member of the aforementioned α, then S_j is sure to be provable by means of Φ_α if S_i is,[8] and (b) if an L-sequent S_j of the sort $A_1, A_2, \ldots, A_n \to B$ follows from two other L-sequents S_h and S_i of the same sort by application of a two-premise rule of Table 2 for a member of the aforementioned α, then S_j is sure to be provable by means of Φ_α if both S_h and S_i are. Hence every entry in the aforementioned proof of S is sure to be provable by means of Φ_α. Hence so is S.

To verify points (a)–(b),[9] suppose an L-sequent follows by application of **HII** from two L-sequents $K \to A$ and $B, K' \to C$, and hence reads $A \supset B, K, K' \to C$; and suppose $K \to A$ and $B, K' \to C$ are both provable by means of Φ_α.[10] Then $A \supset B, K, K', B \to C$, which follows from $B, K' \to C$ by application of **T** and **P**, is sure to be provable by means of Φ_α. Hence so is $A \supset B, K, K' \to B \supset C$, which follows from $A \supset B, K, K', B \to C$ by application of **HI**. But $A \supset B, K, K' \to A$, which follows from $K \to A$ by application of **T** and **P**, is sure to be provable by means of Φ_α; $A \supset B, K, K' \to A \supset B$ is provable by means of **R**, **T**, **P**; and hence $A \supset B, K, K' \to B$, which follows from $A \supset B, K, K' \to A$ and $A \supset B, K, K' \to A \supset B$ by application of HE_I, is sure to be provable by means of Φ_α. Hence $A \supset B, K, K' \to C$, which follows from $A \supset B, K, K' \to B \supset C$ and $A \supset B, K, K' \to B$ by application of HE_I, is sure to be provable by means of Φ_α.

Or suppose an L-sequent follows by application of **CII** from another L-sequent $A, K \to C$ or $B, K \to C$, and hence reads $A \& B, K \to C$; and suppose $A, K \to C$ or $B, K \to C$ is provable by means of Φ_α. Then $A \& B, K, A, B \to C$, which follows from either one of $A, K \to C$ and $B, K \to C$ by application of **T** and **P**, is sure to be provable by means of Φ_α. But $A \& B, K \to A \& B$ is provable by means of **R**, **T**, and **P**. Hence $A \& B, K \to C$, which follows from $A \& B, K \to A \& B$ and $A \& B, K, A, B \to C$ by application of **CE**, is sure to be provable by means of Φ_α.

Or suppose an L-sequent follows by application of **DII** from two L-sequents $A, K \to C$ and $B, K \to C$, and hence reads $A \vee B, K \to C$; and suppose A, K

→ C and B, $K \to C$ are both provable by means of Φ_α. Then $A \lor B$, K, $A \to C$ and $A \lor B$, K, $B \to C$, which respectively follow from A, $K \to C$ and B, $K \to C$ by application of **T** and **P**, are sure to be provable by means of Φ_α. But $A \lor B$, $K \to A \lor B$ is provable by means of **R**, **T**, and **P**. Hence $A \lor B$, $K \to C$, which follows from $A \lor B$, K, $A \to C$, $A \lor B$, K, $B \to C$, and $A \lor B$, $K \to A \lor B$ by application of **DE**, is sure to be provable by means of Φ_α.

Or suppose an L-sequent follows by application of **BII** from two L-sequents $K \to A$ and B, $K' \to C$, and hence reads $A \equiv B$, K, $K' \to C$; and suppose $K \to A$ and B, $K' \to C$ are both provable by means of Φ_α. Then $A \equiv B$, K, $K' \to A$, which follows from $K \to A$ by application of **T** and **P** is sure to be provable by means of Φ_α. But $A \equiv B$, K, $K' \to A \equiv B$ is provable by means of **R**, **T**, and **P**. Hence $A \equiv B$, K, $K' \to B$, which follows from $A \equiv B$, K, $K' \to A$ and $A \equiv B$, K, $K' \to A \equiv B$ by application of $\textbf{BE}_\textbf{I}$, is sure to be provable by means of Φ_α. Hence so is $A \equiv B$, K, K', $C \to B$, which follows from $A \equiv B$, K, $K' \to B$ by application of **T** and **P**. But $A \equiv B$, K, K', $B \to C$, which follows from B, $K' \to C$ by application of **T** and **P**, is sure to be provable by means of Φ_α. Hence so is $A \equiv B$, K, $K' \to B \equiv C$, which follows from $A \equiv B$, K, K', $B \to C$ and $A \equiv B$, K, K', $C \to B$ by application of **BI**. Hence so is $A \equiv B$, K, $K' \to C$, which follows from $A \equiv B$, K, $K' \to B \equiv C$ and $A \equiv B$, K, $K' \to B$ by application of $\textbf{BE}_\textbf{I}$. Suppose then the L-sequent follows by application of **BII** from $K \to B$ and A, $K' \to C$. By a similar reasoning $A \equiv B$, K, $K' \to C$ is sure to be provable by means of Φ_α if $K \to B$ and A, $K' \to C$ both are.

Or suppose an L-sequent follows by application of **∀II** from another L-sequent A', $K \to B$, where A' is as required, and hence reads $(\forall X)A$, $K \to B$; and suppose A', $K \to B$ is provable by means of Φ_α. Then $(\forall X)A$, K, $A' \to B$ is sure to be provable by means of α_α. But $(\forall X)A$, $K \to (\forall X)A$ is provable by means of **R**, **T**, and **P**. Hence $(\forall X)A$, $K \to B$, which follows from $(\forall X)A$, $K \to (\forall X)A$ and $(\forall X)A$, K, $A' \to B$ by application of **∀E**, is sure to be provable by means of Φ_α.

Or suppose an L-sequent follows by application of **∀Ir** from another L-sequent $K \to A'$, where A' and X' are as required, and hence reads $K \to (\forall X)A$; and suppose $K \to A'$ is provable by means of Φ_α. If X' is distinct from X (and hence does not occur free in A), then (i) A is sure to be like A' except for exhibiting free occurrences of X wherever A' exhibits free occurrences of X', and (ii) X is sure not to occur free in A'. Hence, whether or not X' is the same as X, $K \to (\forall X)A$ follows from $K \to A'$ by application of **∀I**. Hence $K \to (\forall X)A$ is sure to be provable by means of Φ_α.

Or suppose an L-sequent follows by application of **∃II** from another L-sequent A', $K \to B$, where A' and X' are as required, and hence reads $(\exists X)A$, $K \to B$; and suppose A', $K \to B$ is provable by means of Φ_α. Then $(\exists X)A$, K, $A' \to B$ is sure to be provable by means of Φ_α. But $(\exists X)A$, $K \to (\exists X)A$ is provable by means of **R**, **T**, and **P**, and $(\exists X)A$, $K \to B$ follows (again whether or not X' is the same as X) from $(\exists X)A$, $K \to (\exists X)A$ and $(\exists X)A$, K, $A' \to B$ by application of **∃E**. Hence $(\exists X)A$, $K \to B$ is sure to be provable by means of Φ_α.

Two Separation Theorems for Natural Deduction   335

Take then S to be in a subset α of $\{\sim, \supset, \&, \vee, \equiv, \forall, \exists\}$ to which belongs the connective '$\sim$' (Cases 65–128). In view of Lemma 1 S is susceptible of a proof in which every entry: (i) follows from previous entries in the proof by application of a structural rule in Table 2 or an introduction rule of that table for a member of α, and hence (ii) is of the sort $A_1, A_2, \ldots, A_n \to$ or the sort $A_1, A_2, \ldots, A_n \to B$.[11] Now let an L-sequent of the former sort have the N-sequent $A_1, A_2, \ldots, A_{n-1} \to \sim A_n$ as its N-*counterpart*, and one of the sort $A_1, A_2, \ldots, A_n \to B$ have itself as its N-*counterpart*. It is readily shown that: (a) if an L-sequent S_j of the sort $A_1, A_2, \ldots, A_n \to$ or the sort $A_1, A_2, \ldots, A_n \to B$ follows from another L-sequent S_i of either sort by application of a structural rule in Table 2 or a one-premiss rule in that table for a member of the aforementioned α, then the N-counterpart of S_j is sure to be provable by means of Φ_α if the N-counterpart of S_i is, and (b) if an L-sequent S_j of the sort $A_1, A_2, \ldots, A_n \to$ or the sort $A_1, A_2, \ldots, A_n \to B$ follows from two other L-sequents S_h and S_i of either sort by application of a two-premiss rule in Table 2 for a member of the aforementioned α, then the N-counterpart of S_j is sure to be provable by means of Φ_α if the N-counterpart of each one of S_h and S_i is. Hence the N-counterpart of every entry in the aforementioned proof of S is sure to be provable by means of Φ_α. Hence so is the N-counterpart of S. Hence so is S.

To verify points (a)–(b),[12] suppose an L-sequent follows by application of **Tr** from another L-sequent $A_1, A_2, \ldots, A_n \to$, and hence reads $A_1, A_2, \ldots, A_n \to B$; and suppose the N-counterpart $A_1, A_2, \ldots, A_n \to \sim A_n$ of $A_1, A_2, \ldots, A_n \to$ is provable by means of Φ_α. Then $A_1, A_2, \ldots, A_n, B \to \sim A_n$ is sure to be provable by means of Φ_α. But $A_1, A_2, \ldots, A_n, B \to A_n$ is provable by means of **R**, **T**, and **P**. Hence $A_1, A_2, \ldots, A_n \to \sim B$, which follows from $A_1, A_2, \ldots, A_n, B \to A_n$ and $A_1, A_2, \ldots, A_n, B \to \sim A_n$ by application of **NI**, is sure to be provable by means of Φ_α. Hence by the same reasoning so is $A_1, A_2, \ldots, A_n \to \sim\sim B$. Hence so is the (N-counterpart of) $A_1, A_2, \ldots, A_n \to B$, which follows from $A_1, A_2, \ldots, A_n \to \sim B$ and $A_1, A_2, \ldots, A_n \to \sim\sim B$ by application of **NE**$_1$.

Or suppose an L-sequent follows by application of **NII** from another L-sequent $\to B$, and hence reads $\sim B \to$; and suppose (the N-counterpart of) $\to B$ is provable by means of Φ_α. Then $\sim B \to B$ is sure to be provable by means of Φ_α. But $\sim B \to \sim B$ is provable by means of **R**. Hence the N-counterpart $\to \sim\sim B$ of $\sim B \to$, which follows from $\sim B \to B$ and $\sim B \to \sim B$ by application of **NI**, is sure to be provable by means of Φ_α. Suppose then the L-sequent follows by application of **NII** from $A_1, A_2, \ldots, A_n \to B$, where $n > 0$, and hence reads $\sim B, A_1, A_2, \ldots, A_n \to$; and suppose (the N-counterpart of) $A_1, A_2, \ldots, A_n \to B$ is provable by means of Φ_α. Then $\sim B, A_1, A_2, \ldots, A_n \to B$ is sure to be provable by means of Φ_α. But $\sim B, A_1, A_2, \ldots, A_n \to \sim B$ is provable by means of **R**, **T**, and **P**. Hence the N-counterpart $\sim B, A_1, A_2, \ldots, A_{n-1} \to \sim A_n$ of $\sim B, A_1, A_2, \ldots, A_n \to$, which follows from $\sim B, A_1, A_2, \ldots, A_n \to B$ and $\sim B, A_1, A_2, \ldots, A_n \to \sim B$ by application of **NI**, is sure to be provable by means of Φ_α.

Or suppose an L-sequent follows by application of **NIr** from another L-sequent $B, A_1, A_2, \ldots, A_n \to$, where $n > 0$, and hence reads $A_1, A_2, \ldots, A_n \to \sim B$; and suppose the N-counterpart $B, A_1, A_2, \ldots, A_{n-1} \to \sim A_n$ of $B, A_1, A_2, \ldots, A_n \to$ is provable by means of Φ_α. Then $A_1, A_2, \ldots, A_n, B \to \sim A_n$ is sure to be provable by means of Φ_α. But $A_1, A_2, \ldots, A_n, B \to A_n$ is provable by means of **R**, **T**, and **P**. Hence (the N-counterpart of) $A_1, A_2, \ldots, A_n \to \sim B$, which follows from $A_1, A_2, \ldots, A_n, B \to A_n$ and $A_1, A_2, \ldots, A_n, B \to \sim A_n$ by application of **NI**, is sure to be provable by means of Φ_α.

Or suppose an L-sequent follows by application of **HII** from two other L-sequents $\to A$ and $B \to$, and hence reads $A \supset B \to$; and suppose the N-counterparts $\to A$ and $\to \sim B$ of $\to A$ and $B \to$ are both provable by means of Φ_α. Then $A \supset B \to A$ and $A \supset B \to \sim B$ are sure to be provable by means of Φ_α. But $A \supset B \to A \supset B$ is provable by means of **R**. Hence $A \supset B \to B$, which follows from $A \supset B \to A$ and $A \supset B \to A \supset B$ by application of **HE**$_1$, is sure to be provable by means of Φ_α. Hence so is the N-counterpart $\to \sim(A \supset B)$ of $A \supset B \to$, which follows from $A \supset B \to B$ and $A \supset B \to \sim B$ by application of **NI**. Suppose then the L-sequent follows by application of **HII** from two other L-sequents $A_1, A_2, \ldots, A_n \to A$, where $n > 0$, and $B \to$, and hence reads $A \supset B, A_1, A_2, \ldots, A_n \to$; and suppose the N-counterparts $A_1, A_2, \ldots, A_n \to A$ and $\to \sim B$ of $A_1, A_2, \ldots, A_n \to A$ and $B \to$ are both provable by means of Φ_α. Then $A \supset B, A_1, A_2, \ldots, A_n \to A$ and $A \supset B, A_1, A_2, \ldots, A_n \to \sim B$ are sure to be provable by means of Φ_α. But $A \supset B, A_1, A_2, \ldots, A_n \to A \supset B$ is provable by means of **R**, **T**, and **P**. Hence $A \supset B, A_1, A_2, \ldots, A_n \to B$, which follows from $A \supset B, A_1, A_2, \ldots, A_n \to A$ and $A \supset B, A_1, A_2, \ldots, A_n \to A \supset B$ by application of **HE**$_1$, is sure to be provable by means of Φ_α. Hence so is the N-counterpart $A \supset B, A_1, A_2, \ldots, A_{n-1} \to \sim A_n$ of $A \supset B, A_1, A_2, \ldots, A_n \to$, which follows from $A \supset B, A_1, A_2, \ldots, A_n \to B$ and $A \supset B, A_1, A_2, \ldots, A_n \to \sim B$ by application of **NI**.[13]

Or suppose an L-sequent follows by application of **CII** from another L-sequent $A \to$ or $B \to$, and hence reads $A \& B \to$; and suppose the N-counterpart $\to \sim A$ of $A \to$ or the N-counterpart $\to \sim B$ of $B \to$ is provable by means of Φ_α. Then $A \& B \to \sim A$ or $A \& B \to \sim B$ is sure to be provable by means of Φ_α. But $A \& B \to A \& B$ is provable by means of **R**; $A \& B, A, B \to A$ provable by means of **R**, **T**, and **P**; and $A \& B, A, B \to B$ provable by means of **R** and **E**. Hence $A \& B \to A$, which follows from $A \& B \to A \& B$ and $A \& B, A, B \to A$ by application of **CE**, and $A \& B \to B$, which follows from $A \& B \to A \& B$ and $A \& B, A, B \to B$ by application of **CE**, are sure to be provable by means of Φ_α. Hence so is the N-counterpart $\to \sim(A \& B)$ of $A \& B \to$, which follows from $A \& B \to A$ and $A \& B \to \sim A$ or from $A \& B \to B$ and $A \& B \to \sim B$ by application of **NI**.

Or suppose an L-sequent follows by application of **DII** from other two L-sequents $A \to$ and $B \to$, and hence reads $A \vee B \to$; and suppose the N-counterparts $\to \sim A$ and $\to \sim B$ of $A \to$ and $B \to$ are both provable by means of Φ_α. Then $A \vee B, A, A \vee B \to \sim A$ and $A \vee B, B, A \vee B \to \sim B$ are both

Two Separation Theorems for Natural Deduction   337

provable by means of **R**, **T**, and **P**. Hence $A \lor B$, $A \to \sim(A \lor B)$, which follows from $A \lor B$, A, $A \lor B \to A$ and $A \lor B$, A, $A \lor B \to \sim A$ by application of **NI**, and $A \lor B$, $B \to \sim(A \lor B)$, which follows from $A \lor B$, B, $A \lor B \to B$ and $A \lor B$, B, $A \lor B \to \sim B$ by application of **NI**, are sure to be provable by means of Φ_α. But $A \lor B \to A \lor B$ is provable by means of **R**. Hence $A \lor B \to \sim(A \lor B)$, which follows from $A \lor B \to A \lor B$, $A \lor B$, $A \to \sim(A \lor B)$, and $A \lor B$, $B \to \sim(A \lor B)$ by application of **DE**, is sure to be provable by means of Φ_α. Hence so is the N-counterpart $\to \sim(A \lor B)$ of $A \lor B \to$, which follows from $A \lor B \to A \lor B$ and $A \lor B \to \sim(A \lor B)$ by application of **NI**.

Or suppose an L-sequent follows by application of **BII** from two other L-sequents $\to A$ and $B \to$, and hence reads $A \equiv B \to$; and suppose the N-counterparts $\to A$ and $\to \sim B$ of $\to A$ and $B \to$ are both provable by means of Φ_α. Then $A \equiv B \to A$ and $A \equiv B \to \sim B$ are sure to be provable by means of Φ_α. But $A \equiv B \to A \equiv B$ is provable by means of **R**. Hence $A \equiv B \to B$, which follows from $A \equiv B \to A \equiv B$ and $A \equiv B \to A$ by application of **BE**$_1$, is sure to be provable by means of Φ_α. Hence so is the N-counterpart $\to \sim(A \equiv B)$ of $A \equiv B \to$, which follows from $A \equiv B \to B$ and $A \equiv B \to \sim B$ by application of **NI**. Suppose then the L-sequent follows by application of **BII** from two other L-sequents $\to B$ and $A \to$, and hence reads again $A \equiv B \to$; and suppose the N-counterparts $\to B$ and $\to \sim A$ of $\to B$ and $A \to$ are both provable by means of Φ_α. Then $A \equiv B \to B$ and $A \equiv B \to \sim A$ are sure to be provable by means of Φ_α. But $A \equiv B \to A \equiv B$ is provable by means of **R**. Hence $A \equiv B \to A$, which follows from $A \equiv B \to A \equiv B$ and $A \equiv B \to B$ by application of **BE**$_1$, is sure to be provable by means of Φ_α. Hence so is the N-counterpart $\to \sim(A \equiv B)$ of $A \equiv B \to$, which follows from $A \equiv B \to A$ and $A \equiv B \to \sim A$ by application of **NI**. Suppose then the L-sequent follows by application of **BII** from two other L-sequents $A_1, A_2, \ldots, A_n \to A$, where $n > 0$, and $B \to$, and hence reads $A \equiv B, A_1, A_2, \ldots, A_n \to$; and suppose the N-counterparts $A_1, A_2, \ldots, A_n \to A$ and $\to \sim B$ of $A_1, A_2, \ldots, A_n \to A$ and $B \to$ are both provable by means of Φ_α. Then $A \equiv B, A_1, A_2, \ldots, A_2 \to A$ and $A \equiv B$, $A_1, A_2, \ldots, A_n \to \sim B$ are sure to be provable by means of Φ_α. But $A \equiv B$, $A_1, A_2, \ldots, A_n \to A \equiv B$ is provable by means of **R**, **T**, and **P**. Hence $A \equiv B, A_1, A_2, \ldots, A_n \to B$, which follows from $A \equiv B, A_1, A_2, \ldots, A_n \to A$ and $A \equiv B, A_1, A_2, \ldots, A_n \to A \equiv B$ by application of **BE**$_1$, is sure to be provable by means of Φ_α. Hence so is the N-counterpart $A \equiv B, A_1, A_2, \ldots, A_{n-1} \to \sim A_n$ of $A \equiv B, A_1, A_2, \ldots, A_n \to$, which follows from $A \equiv B, A_1, A_2, \ldots, A_n \to B$ and $A \equiv B, A_1, A_2, \ldots, A_n \to \sim B$ by application of **NI**. Suppose then the L-sequent follows by application of **BII** from $A_1, A_2, \ldots, A_n \to B$, where $n > 0$, and $A \to$, and hence reads $A \equiv B, A_1, A_2, \ldots, A_n \to$. By a similar reasoning the N-counterpart of $A \equiv B, A_1, A_2, \ldots, A_n \to$ is sure to be provable by means of Φ_α if the N-counterparts of $A_1, A_2, \ldots, A_n \to B$ and $A \to$ both are.

Or suppose an L-sequent follows by application of **VII** from another L-sequent $A' \to$, where A' is as required, and hence reads $(\forall X)A \to$; and suppose the N-counterpart $\to \sim A'$ of $A' \to$ is provable by means of Φ_α. Then

$(\forall X)A \to \sim A'$ is sure to be provable by means of Φ_α. But $(\forall X)A \to (\forall X)A$ is provable by means of **R**, and $(\forall X)A, A' \to A'$ provable by means of **R** and **T**. Hence $(\forall X)A \to A'$, which follows from $(\forall X)A \to (\forall X)A$ and $(\forall X)A, A' \to A'$ by application of **∀E**, is provable by means of Φ_α. Hence so is the N-counterpart $\to \sim(\forall X)A$ of $(\forall X)A \to$, which follows from $(\forall X)A \to A'$ and $(\forall X)A \to \sim A'$ by application of **NI**.

Or suppose an L-sequent follows by application of **∃II** from another L-sequent $A' \to$, where A' and X' are as required, and hence reads $(\exists X)A \to$; and suppose the N-counterpart $\to \sim A'$ of $A' \to$ is provable by means of Φ_α. Then $(\exists X)A, A', (\exists X)A \to \sim A'$ is sure to be provable by means of Φ_α. But $(\exists X)A, A', (\exists X)A \to A'$ is provable by means of **R**, **T**, and **P**. Hence $(\exists X)A, A' \to \sim(\exists X)A$, which follows from $(\exists X)A, A', (\exists X)A \to A'$ and $(\exists X)A, A', (\exists X)A \to \sim A'$ by application of **NI**, is sure to be provable by means of Φ_α. But $(\exists X)A \to (\exists X)A$ is provable by means of **R**. Hence $(\exists X)A \to \sim(\exists X)A$, which follows (whether or not X' is the same as X) from $(\exists X)A \to (\exists X)A$ and $(\exists X)A, A' \to \sim(\exists X)A$ by application of **∃E**, is sure to be provable by means of Φ_α. Hence so is the N-counterpart $\to \sim(\exists X)A$ of $(\exists X)A \to$, which follows from $(\exists X)A \to \sim(\exists X)A$ and $(\exists X)A \to (\exists X)A$ by application of **NI**.

We have restricted ourselves so far to N-sequents in which no individual variable occurs both bound and free. Suppose, however, one or more individual variables, say, $X_1, X_2, \ldots, X_k$, occur both bound and free in the N-sequent S of Theorem 1; suppose S' is like S except for exhibiting bound occurrences of k individual variables foreign to S at those and only those places where S exhibits bound occurrences of $X_1, X_2, \ldots, X_k$, respectively; and suppose S is **I**-valid. Then S' is sure to be **I**-valid as well, and hence provable by means of Φ_α. But if S' is provable by means of Φ_α, then so is S, as a long—but elementary enough—argument will show. Hence S, if **I**-valid, is sure to be provable by means of Φ_α.

3. Now for **C**-valid N-sequents. It is readily shown that every N-sequent provable by means of the following rules of inference is **C**-valid, and hence that the said rules are *classically sound*:[14]

TABLE 3

Structural rules: Same as in Table 1
Intelim rules:

For '&', '∨', '∀', and '∃': Same as in Table 1

For '∼':

NE:
$$\frac{K \to \sim\sim A}{K \to A}$$

NI: Same as in Table 1

For '⊃':

HE: $$\frac{K \to A \supset B \text{ and } K \to (A \supset C) \supset A}{K \to B}$$

HI: Same as in Table 1

For '≡':

BE: $$\frac{K \to A \text{ and } K \to (B \equiv A) \equiv (B \equiv C)}{K \to C}$$

BI: Same as in Table 1

Leaving that matter to the reader, I shall prove in outline form the following separation theorem:

Theorem 2. *Let α be any subset of $\{\sim, \supset, \&, \vee, \equiv, \forall, \exists\}$ other than $\{\vee, \forall\}$, $\{\&, \vee, \forall\}$, $\{\vee, \forall, \exists\}$, and $\{\&, \vee, \forall\exists\}$; S be any N-sequent in α; and Ψ_α consist of rules **R**, **T**, **P**, and **C** in Table 3 and the intelim rules of that table for such (and only such) operators as belong to α. If S is **C**-valid, then S is provable by means of Ψ_α.*

I shall make use, when proving Theorem 1, of yet another result of Gentzen's:

Lemma 2. *Let α be any subset of $\{\sim, \supset, \&, \vee, \equiv, \forall, \exists\}$, and S be any L-sequent in α in which no individual variable occurs both bound and free. If S is **C**-valid, then S is susceptible of a proof in which every entry follows from previous entries in the proof by application of a structural rule in Table 4 or an introduction rule of that table for a member of α.*[15]

TABLE 4

Structural rules:

Reiteration (**R**): $A \to A$

Thinning:

to the left (**Tl**)

$$\frac{K \to L}{A, K \to L}$$

to the right (**Tr**)

$$\frac{K \to L}{K \to L, A}$$

Permutation:

to the left (**Pl**)

$$\frac{K, A, B, L \to M}{K, B, A, L \to M}$$

to the right (**Pr**)

$$\frac{K \to L, A, B, M}{K \to L, B, A, M}$$

Contraction:

   to the left (**Cl**)   to the right (**Cr**)

$$\frac{A,\ A,\ K \to L}{A,\ K \to L} \qquad\qquad \frac{K \to L,\ A,\ A}{K \to L,\ A}$$

Introduction rules:

For '∼':

   to the left (**Nll**)   to the right (**Nlr**)

$$\frac{K \to L,\ A}{\sim A,\ K \to L} \qquad\qquad \frac{A,\ K \to L}{K \to L,\ \sim A}$$

For '⊃':

   to the left (**Hll**)   to the right (**Hlr**)

$$\frac{K \to M,\ A\ \text{and}\ B,\ L > N}{A \supset B,\ K,\ L \to M,\ N} \qquad\qquad \frac{A,\ K \to L,\ B}{K \to L,\ A \supset B}$$

For '&':

   to the left (**Cll**)   to the right (**Clr**)

$$\frac{A,\ K \to L\ \text{or}\ B,\ K \to L}{A\ \&\ B,\ K \to L} \qquad\qquad \frac{K \to L,\ A\ \text{and}\ K \to L,\ B}{K \to L,\ A\ \&\ B}$$

For '∨':

   to the left (**Dll**)   to the right (**Dlr**)

$$\frac{A,\ K \to L\ \text{and}\ B,\ K \to L}{A \vee B,\ K \to L} \qquad\qquad \frac{K \to L,\ A\ \text{or}\ K \to L,\ B}{K \to L,\ A \vee B}$$

For '≡':

   to the left (**Bll**)

$$\frac{(i)\ K \to M,\ A\ \text{and}\ B,\ L \to N\ \text{or}\ (ii)\ K \to M,\ B\ \text{and}\ A,\ L \to N}{A \equiv B,\ K,\ L \to M,\ N}$$

   to the right (**Blr**)

$$\frac{A,\ K \to L,\ B\ \text{and}\ B,\ K \to L,\ A}{K \to L,\ A \equiv B}$$

For '∀':

   to the left (**∀ll**)   to the right (**∀lr**)

$$\frac{A',\ K \to L}{(\forall X)A,\ K \to L} \qquad\qquad \frac{K \to L,\ A'}{K \to L,\ (\forall X)A}$$

For '∃':

to the left (∃⊦)   to the right (∃⊦)

$\dfrac{A', K \to L}{(\exists X)A, K \to L}$ $\dfrac{K \to L, A'}{K \to L, (\exists X)A}$

Notes: (a) Throughout the above rules, K, L, M, and N are to be finite (and possibly empty) sequences of wffs separated by commas. (b) In the last four rules A' is to be as in Note (b) under Table I. (c) In ∀⊦r is not to occur free in $K \to L$, $(\forall X)A$. (d) In ∃⊦l X' is not to occur free in $(\exists X)A, K \to L$.

I shall also make use of the following result, due to R. H. Thomason and myself:[16]

Lemma 3. *Let α be any subset of $\{\&, \forall, \exists\}$; let S be any L-sequent in α in which no individual variable occurs both bound and free; and let χ_α consist of the structural rules in Table 4 and the introduction rules of that table for such (and only such) operators as belong to α. Then S is provable by means of χ_α if and only if S is provable by means of χ_α minus rule* **Cr** *(Contraction to the right).*

4. Suppose for proof of Theorem 2 that S is a **C**-valid N-sequent, and hence a **C**-valid L-sequent; suppose, as we indeed may without loss of generality, that no individual variable occurs both bound and free in S; and suppose S is in a subset α of $\{\sim, \supset, \&, \vee, \equiv, \forall, \exists\}$ to which belongs at least one of '$\sim$', '$\vee$', '$\supset$', and '$\equiv$'. Because of Lemma 2 S is susceptible of a proof in which every entry follows from previous entries in the proof by application of a structural rule in Table 4 or an introduction rule of that table for a member of α, and— save when '$\sim$' belongs to α—is of the sort $A_1, A_2, \ldots, A_n \to B_1, B_2, \ldots, B_m$, where $m \geq 1$. Now (i) in the case that '$\sim$' belongs to α, let an L-sequent of the sort $A_1, A_2, \ldots, A_n \to$ have the N-sequent $A_1, A_2, \ldots, A_{n-1} \to \sim A_n$ as its N-counterpart, one of the sort $A_1, A_2, \ldots, A_n \to B$ have itself as its N-counterpart, and one of the sort $A_1, A_2, \ldots, A_n \to B_1, B_2, \ldots, B_m$, where $m > 1$, have the N-sequent $A_1, A_2, \ldots, A_n, \sim B_1, \sim B_2, \ldots, \sim B_{m-1} \to B_m$ as its N-counterpart; (ii) in the case that '$\sim$' does not belong to α, but '$\vee$' does, let an L-sequent of the sort $A_1, A_2, \ldots, A_n \to B$ have itself as its N-counterpart, and one of the sort $A_1, A_2, \ldots, A_n \to B_1, B_2, \ldots, B_m$, where $m > 1$, have the N-sequent $A_1, A_2, \ldots, A_n \to (\ldots (B_1 \vee B_2) \vee \ldots) \vee B_m$ as its N-counterpart; (iii) in the case that neither one of '$\sim$' and '$\vee$' belongs to α, but '$\supset$' does, let an L-sequent of the sort $A_1, A_2, \ldots, A_n \to B$ have itself as its N-counterpart, and one of the sort $A_1, A_2, \ldots, A_n \to B_1, B_2, \ldots, B_m$, where $m > 1$, have the N-sequent $A_1, A_2, \ldots, A_n, B_1 \supset B_m, B_2 \supset B_m, \ldots, B_{m-1} \supset B_m \to B_m$ as its N-counterpart; and (iv) in the case that none of '$\sim$', '$\vee$', and '$\supset$' belongs to α, but '$\equiv$' does, let an L-sequent of the sort $A_1, A_2, \ldots, A_n \to B$ have itself as its N-counterpart, and one of the

sort $A_1, A_2, \ldots, A_n \to B_1, B_2, \ldots, B_m$, where $m > 1$, have the N-sequent $A_1, A_2, \ldots, A_n, B_1 \equiv B_m, B_2 \equiv B_m, \ldots, B_{m-1} \equiv B_m \to B_m$ as its N-counterpart. It can be shown—readily in some cases, by dint of hard labor in others—that: (a) if an L-sequent S_j follows from another L-sequent S_i by application of a structural rule in Table 4 or a one-premise rule of that table for a member of the aforementioned α, then the N-counterpart of S_j is sure to be provable by means of Ψ_α if the N-counterpart of S_i is, and (b) if an L-sequent S_j follows from two other L-sequents S_h and S_i by application of a two-premise rule of Table 4 for a member of the aforementioned α, then the N-counterpart of S_j is sure to be provable by means of Ψ_α if the N-counterpart of each one of S_h and S_j is. But if so, then S is sure to be provable by means of Ψ_α.

The argument accounts for 116 out of the 124 cases covered by Theorem 2.

Suppose then S to be in a subset of α of $\{\&, \forall, \exists\}$. In view of Lemmas 2 and 3 S is susceptible of a proof in which every entry follows from previous entries in the proof by application of one of rules **R**, **Tl**, **Tr**, **Pl**, **Pr**, and **Cl** in Table 4 or an introduction rule of that table for a member of α. But if so, then S is susceptible of a proof in which every entry follows from previous entries in the proof by application of one of rules **R**, **T**, **P**, and **C** in Table 1 or an introduction rule of Table 5 for a member of α.

TABLE 5

For '&':

to the left	to the right
$\dfrac{A, K \to C \text{ or } B, K \to C}{A \& B \to C}$	Like **Cl** in Table 1

For '$\forall$':

to the left	to the right
$\dfrac{A', K \to B}{(\forall X)A, K \to B}$	Like $\forall$**I** in Table 1

For '$\exists$':

to the left	to the right
$\dfrac{A', K \to B}{(\exists X)A, K \to B}$	Like $\exists$**I** in Table 1

Notes: (a) In the introduction rule for '$\forall$' to the left A' is to be as in Note (b) under Table 1 (b) In the introduction rule for '$\exists$' to the left X' is to be any individual variable that does not occur free in $(\exists X)A, K \to B$.

But any L-sequent that is provable by means of the said rules is sure—as the reader may verify—to be **l**-valid. Hence S is sure to be **l**-valid. Hence in view of Theorem 1 S is sure to be provable by means of Ψ_α.

The argument accounts for the remaining 8 of the 124 cases covered by Theorem 2.[17]

In view of Theorem 1, Theorem 2 also holds true of such N-sequents in $\{\vee, \forall\}$, $\{\&, \vee, \forall\}$, $\{\vee, \forall\ \exists\}$, or $\{\&, \vee, \forall\ \exists\}$ as happens to be both **C**-valid and **I**-valid. It does not hold true, however, of those which, though **C**-valid, are not **I**-valid as well.[18] And this for a simple reason: any N-sequent provable by means of **R, T, P, NI, HI, CE, CI, DE, DI, BI, ∀E, ∀I, ∃E**, or **∃I** is sure— as we remarked earlier—to be **I**-valid. The argument of pages 338–341 is thus bound to falter for the four subsets $\{\vee, \forall\}$, $\{\&, \vee, \forall\}$, $\{\vee, \forall, \exists\}$, and $\{\&, \vee, \forall, \exists\}$ of $\{\supset, \&, \vee, \equiv, \forall, \exists\}$. It does go through, however, if the following rule, to be called $\forall I_v$, is enlisted as an extra intelim rule for '$\forall$':

$$\frac{K \to A' \vee B}{K \to (\forall X) A \vee B}$$

where A' is like A except for exhibiting free occurrences of X' wherever A exhibits free occurrences of some individual variable X (not necessarily distinct from X'), and X' is not to occur free in $K \to (\forall X)A \vee B$.

Hence:

Theorem 3. *Let α be any one of the four subsets $\{\vee, \forall\}$, $\{\&, \vee, \forall\}$, $\{\vee, \forall, \exists\}$, and $\{\&, \vee, \forall, \exists\}$ of $\{\sim, \supset, \&, \vee, \equiv, \forall, \exists\}$; S be any **C**-valid N-sequent in α; and Ψ_α consist of rules **R, T, P**, and **C** in Table 3 and the intelim rules of Table 3 for such and only such operators as belong to α.*
(a) *If S is I-valid, then S is provable by means of Ψ_α.*
(b) *If S is not I-valid, then S is provable by means of Ψ_α and rule $\forall I_v$.*

Since any N-sequent that is provable by means of $\forall I_v$ is provable by means of: (i) **DE, DI, ∀E, ∀I, NE**, and **NI**, (ii) **DE, DI, ∀E, ∀I, HE**, and **HI**, and (iii) **DE, DI, ∀E, ∀I, BE**, and **BI**, we also have:

Theorem 4. *Let α, S, and Ψ_a be as in Theorem 3.*
(a) *If S is I-valid, then S is provable by means of Ψ_a.*
(b) *If S is not I-valid, then S is provable by means of Ψ_a plus rules **NE** and **NI**, or rules **HE** and **HI**, or rules **BE** and **BI**.*

When **R** is generalized to read:

GR: $K, A, L \to A$,

the remaining three structural rules of Table 1 are expendable. Proof that the first two, **T** and **P**, are, will be found in [9]. Suppose then there is a proof of $A, A, K \to B$ by means of **GR** and zero or more intelim rules from Table 1 [Table 3], and suppose some entry in the proof of $A, A, K \to B$ does not open with A, A, K. The result of lopping off that entry is sure—as the reader may verify—to constitute a proof of $A, A, K \to B$ by means of **GR** and the intelim rules in question. Suppose then the proof of $A, A, K \to B$ runs:

$$A, A, K, L_1 \rightarrow B_1$$
$$A, A, K, L_2 \rightarrow B_2$$
$$\vdots$$
$$A, A, K, L_{p-1} \rightarrow B_{p-1}$$
$$A, A, K \rightarrow B_p (= B),$$

where for each i from 1 to $p-1$ L_i consists of zero or more wffs separated by commas. The parallel column

$$A, K, L_1 \rightarrow B_1$$
$$A, K, L_2 \rightarrow B_2$$
$$\vdots$$
$$A, K, L_{p-1} \rightarrow B_{p-1}$$
$$A, K \rightarrow B_p (= B)$$

is sure—as the reader may verify—to constitute a proof of A, $K \rightarrow B$ by means of **GR** and the intelim rules in question.

Hence the following corollaries of Theorems 1–3:

Theorem 5. *Let α be any subset of $\{\sim, \supset, \&, \vee, \equiv, \forall, \exists\}$; let S be any N-sequent in α; and let Φ'_α consist of rule **GR** and the intelim rules of Table 1 for such (and only such) operators as belong to α. If S is **I**-valid, then S is provable by means of Φ'_α.*

Theorem 6. *Let α be any subset of $\{\sim, \supset, \&, \vee, \equiv, \forall, \exists\}$ other than $\{\vee, \forall\}$, $\{\&, \vee, \forall\}$, $\{\vee, \forall, \exists\}$, and $\{\&, \vee, \forall, \exists\}$; let S be any N-sequent in α; and let Ψ'_α consist of rule **GR** and the intelim rules of Table 3 for such (and only such) operators as belong to α. If S is **C**-valid, then S is provable by means of Ψ'_α.*

Theorem 7. *Let α be any one of the four subsets $\{\vee, \forall\}$, $\{\&, \vee, \forall\}$, $\{\vee, \forall, \exists\}$, and $\{\&, \vee, \forall, \exists\}$; $\{\sim, \supset, \&, \vee, \equiv, \forall, \exists\}$ let S be any **C**-valid N-sequent in α; and let Ψ'_α be as in Theorem 6.*
(a) *If S is **I**-valid, then S is provable by means of Ψ'_α.*
(b) *If S is not **I**-valid, then S is provable by means of Ψ'_α and rule $\forall I_v$.*

Now consider the following two sets of rules for conducting so-called *natural deductions* in Heyting's first-order quantificational calculus (Table 6) and in the classical first-order quantificational calculus (Table 7):

Two Separation Theorems for Natural Deduction   345

TABLE 6

Generalized Reiteration: From a set $\{A_1,A_2, \ldots ,A_n\}$ of premises one may deduce any one of $A_1, A_2, \ldots , A_n$ as a conclusion (**GR**)

Intelim rules for '~': (a) If from a set $\{A_1,A_2, \ldots ,A_n\}$ of premises one may deduce each one of two conclusions ~B and ~~B, then from the same set $\{A_1,A_2, \ldots ,A_n\}$ one may deduce B as a conclusion;
(b) If from a set $\{A_1,A_2, \ldots ,A_n\} \cup \{B\}$ of premises one may deduce each one of two conclusions C and ~C, then from the subset $\{A_1,A_2, \ldots ,A_n\}$ of the original set $\{A_1,A_2, \ldots ,A_n\} \cup \{B\}$ one may deduce ~B as a conclusion.

Intelim rules for '⊃': (a) If from a set $\{A_1,A_2, \ldots ,A_n\}$ of premises one may deduce each one of two conclusions B and $B \supset C$, then from the same set $\{A_1,A_2, \ldots ,A_n\}$ one may deduce C as a conclusion;
(b) If from a set $\{A_1,A_2, \ldots ,A_n\} \cup \{B\}$ of premises one may deduce a conclusion C, then from the subset $\{A_1,A_2, \ldots ,A_n\}$ of the original set $\{A_1,A_2, \ldots ,A_n\} \cup \{B\}$ one may deduce $B \supset C$ as a conclusion.

Intelim rules for '&': (a) If from a set $\{A_1,A_2, \ldots ,A_n\}$ of premises one may deduce a conclusion B & C and from the superset $\{A_1,A_2, \ldots ,A_n\} \cup \{B,C\}$ of $\{A_1,A_2, \ldots ,A_n\}$ deduce a conclusion D, then from the original set $\{A_1,A_2, \ldots ,A_n\}$ one may deduce D as a conclusion;
(b) If from a set $\{A_1,A_2, \ldots ,A_n\}$ of premises one may deduce each one of two conclusions B and C, then from the same set $\{A_1,A_2, \ldots ,A_n\}$ one may deduce B & C as a conclusion.

Intelim rules for '∨': (a) If from a set $\{A_1,A_2, \ldots ,A_n\}$ of premises one may deduce a conclusion $B \vee C$ and from each one of the two supersets $\{A_1, A_2, \ldots ,A_n\} \cup \{B\}$ and $\{A_1,A_2, \ldots ,A_n\} \cup \{C\}$ of $\{A_1,A_2, \ldots ,A_n\}$ deduce a conclusion D, then from the original set $\{A_1,A_2, \ldots ,A_n\}$ one may deduce D as a conclusion;
(b) If from a set $\{A_1,A_2, \ldots ,A_n\}$ of premises one may deduce a conclusion B, then from the same set $\{A_1,A_2, \ldots ,A_n\}$ one may deduce either one of $B \vee C$ and $C \vee B$ as a conclusion.

Intelim rules for '≡': (a) If from a set $\{A_1,A_2, \ldots ,A_n\}$ of premises one may deduce each one of two conclusions B and $B \equiv C$ or B and $C \equiv B$, then from the same set $\{A_1,A_2, \ldots ,A_n\}$ one may deduce C as a conclusion;
(b) If from a set $\{A_1,A_2, \ldots ,A_n\} \cup \{B\}$ of premises one may deduce a conclusion C and from the set $\{A_1,A_2, \ldots ,A_n\} \cup \{C\}$ deduce B as a conclusion, then from the subset $\{A_1,A_2, \ldots ,A_n\}$ of the two sets $\{A_1,A_2, \ldots ,A_n\} \cup \{B\}$ and $\{A_1,A_2, \ldots ,A_n\} \cup \{C\}$ one may deduce $B \equiv C$ as a conclusion.

Intelim rules for '∀': Let B' be like B except for exhibiting free occurrences of an individual variable X' wherever A exhibits free occurrences of an individual variable X.
(a) If from a set $\{A_1,A_2, \ldots ,A_n\}$ of premises one may deduce a conclusion

($\forall X$)B and from the superset $\{A_1,A_2, \ldots ,A_n\} \cup \{B'\}$ of $\{A_1,A_2, \ldots ,A_n\}$ deduce a conclusion C, then from the original set $\{A_1,A_2, \ldots ,A_n\}$ one may deduce C as a conclusion;
(b) If from a set $\{A_1,A_2, \ldots ,A_n\}$ of premises one may deduce a conclusion B', then from the same set $\{A_1,A_2, \ldots ,A_n\}$ one may deduce ($\forall X$)B a conclusion, so long as X' does not occur free in any one of $A_1, A_2, \ldots , A_n$, ($\forall X$)B.

Intelim rules for '$\exists$': Let B' be as in the previous rules.
(a) If from a set $\{A_1,A_2, \ldots ,A_n\}$ of premises one may deduce a conclusion ($\exists X$)B and from the superset $\{A_1,A_2, \ldots ,A_n\} \cup \{B'\}$ of $\{A_1,A_2, \ldots ,A_n\}$ deduce a conclusion C, then from the original set $\{A_1,A_2, \ldots ,A_n\}$ one may deduce C as a conclusion, so long as X' does not occur free in any one of $A_1, A_2, \ldots , A_n, B$, and C.
(b) If from a set $\{A_1,A_2, \ldots ,A_n\}$ of premises one may deduce a conclusion B', then from the same set $\{A_1,A_2, \ldots ,A_n\}$ one may deduce ($\exists X$)B as a conclusion.

TABLE 7

GR': Same as in Table 6.

Intelim rules for '&', '$\vee$', '$\forall$', and '$\exists$': Same as in Table 6.

Intelim rules for '$\sim$': (a) If from a set $\{A_1,A_2, \ldots ,A_n\}$ of premises one may deduce a conclusion $\sim\sim B$, then from the same set $\{A_1,A_2, \ldots ,A_n\}$ one may deduce B as a conclusion;
(b) As in Table 6.

Intelim rules for '$\supset$': (a) If from a set $\{A_1,A_2, \ldots ,A_n\}$ of premises one may deduce each one of two conclusions $B \supset C$ and $(B \supset D) \supset B$, then from the same set $\{A_1,A_2, \ldots ,A_n\}$ one may deduce C as a conclusion;
(b) As in Table 6.

Intelim rules for '$\equiv$': (a) If from a set $\{A_1,A_2, \ldots ,A_n\}$ of premises one may deduce each one of two conclusions B and $(C \equiv B) \equiv (C \equiv D)$, then from the same set $\{A_1,A_2, \ldots ,A_n\}$ one may deduce D as a conclusion.
(b) As in Table 6.

It is readily shown that if an N-sequent $A_1, A_2, \ldots , A_n \to B$ in α is provable by means of rule **GR** and the intelim rules of Table 1 [Table 3] for such (and only such) operators as belong to α, then B is deducible from $\{A_1,A_2, \ldots ,A_n\}$ by means of rule **GR'** in Table 6 [Table 7] and the intelim rules of Table 6 [Table 7] for such and only such operators as belong to α.[19] Suppose then that B is held to be **I**-implied [**C**-implied] by $\{A_1,A_2, \ldots ,A_n\}$ if $A_1, A_2, \ldots , A_n \to B$ is **I**-valid [**C**-valid]. We will have the following two corollaries of Theorems 5–6 (and, hence, of Theorems 1–2):

Theorem 8. *Let* $A_1, A_2, \ldots , A_n$ $(n \geq 0)$, *and* B *be wffs of* QC, *and* α

consist of those among the operators '∼', '⊃', '&', '∨', '≡', '∀', *and* '∃' *that occur in* $A_1, A_2, \ldots, A_n$, *and* B. *If* B *is* **I**-*implied by* $\{A_1, A_2, \ldots, A_n\}$, *then* B *is deducible from* $\{A_1, A_2, \ldots, A_n\}$ *by means of rule* **GR**' *in Table 6 and the intelim rules of that table for such (and only such) operators as belong to* α.

Theorem 9. *Let* $A_1, A_2, \ldots, A_n$, B, *and* α *be as in Theorem 8. If* α *is other than* $\{\vee, \forall\}$, $\{\&, \vee, \forall\}$, $\{\vee, \forall, \exists\}$, *and* $\{\&, \vee, \forall, \exists\}$, *and* B *is* **C**-*implied by* $\{A_1, A_2, \ldots, A_n\}$, *then* B *is deducible from* $\{A_1, A_2, \ldots, A_n\}$ *by means of rule* **GR**' *in Table 7 and the intelim rules of that table for such (and only such) operators as belong to* α.

With a wff A held to be: (i) **I**-implied [**C**-implied] by an infinite set S of wffs of A is **I**-implied [**C**-implied] by a finite subset of S,[20] and (ii) deducible from S by means of **GR**' and zero or more intelim rules from Table 6 [Table 7] if A is deducible from a finite subset of S by means of those rules, Theorems 7–8 readily generalize into:

Theorem 10. *Let* A *be a wff of* QC, S *be a set of wffs of* QC, *and* α *consist of those among the operators* '∼', '⊃', '&', '∨', '≡', '∀', *and* '∃' *which occur in a member of* S *or in* A. *If* A *is* **I**-*implied by* S, *then* A *is deducible from* S *by means of rule* **GR**' *in Table 6 and the intelim rules of that table for such (and only such) operators as belong to* α.

Theorem 11. *Let* A, S, *and* α *be as in Theorem 10. If* A *is* **C**-*implied by* S *and* α *is other than* $\{\vee, \forall\}$, $\{\&, \vee, \forall\}$, $\{\vee, \forall, \exists\}$, *and* $\{\&, \vee, \forall, \exists\}$, *then* A *is deducible from* S *by means of rule* **GR**' *in Table 7 and the intelim rules of that table for such (and only such) operators as belong to* α.

A like-minded corollary of Theorem 7 (and, hence, of Theorem 3) holds true, with rule $\forall I'_v$ understood to be the following analogue of $\forall I_v$: "Let B' be like B except for exhibiting free occurrences of X' wherever B exhibits free occurrences of some individual variable X (not necessarily distinct from X'). If from a set $\{A_1, A_2, \ldots, A_n\}$ of premises one may deduce a conclusion $B' \vee C$, then from the same set $\}A_1, A_2, \ldots, A_n\}$ one may deduce $(\forall X)B \vee C$ as a conclusion, so long as X' does not occur free in any one of $A_1, A_2, \ldots, A_n, B, C$."[21]

Theorem 12. *Let* A, S, *and* α *be as in Theorem 10; let* A *be* **C**-*implied by* S; *and let* α *be one of* $\{\vee, \forall\}$, $\{\&, \vee, \forall\}$, $\{\vee, \forall, \exists\}$, *and* $\{\&, \vee, \forall, \exists\}$.
(a) *If* A *is* **I**-*implied by* S, *then* A *is deducible from* S *by means of rule* **GR**' *in Table 7 and the intelim rules of that table for such (and only such) operators as belong to* α.
(b) *If* A *is not* **I**-*implied by* S, *then* A *is deducible from* S *by means of rule* **GR**' *in Table 7, the intelim rules of that table for such (and only such) operators as belong to* α, *and rule* $\forall I'_v$.[22]

Notes

1. The letter 'N', which along with the letter 'L' comes from [5], is short for 'natural' in the phrase 'natural deduction'. The relationship between the rules of Tables 1 and 3 and the familiar ones for conducting so-called *natural deductions* is studied in the fifth section of this paper.

2. For an account of intuitionist validity, see [7].

3. When $p = 0$, the member of Φ in question is more commonly called an *axiom schema*. When $p = 1$, I shall occasionally refer to the member of Φ in question as a *one-premise rule*; when $p = 2$, as a *two-premise rule*.

4. Except for **NE$_I$**, **CE**, **BE$_I$**, **BI**, and **∀E**, the rules in question all turn up in [6]. **CE** was suggested to me by Nuel D. Belnap, Jr. **NE$_I$** is due to Paul Bernays, who offered it in [1] as an alternative to the more familiar rule:

$$\frac{K \to A \text{ and } K \to {\sim}A}{K \to B}$$

The appellation 'intelim', coined by F. B. Fitch in [4], is short of course for 'introduction-elimination'. The 'I' in '**NI**', '**HI**', '**CI**', and so on, is short for 'Introduction'; and the '**E**' in '**NE$_I$**', '**HE$_I$**', '**CE**', and so on, short for 'Elimination'. I write '**NE$_I$**', '**HE$_I$**', and '**BE$_I$**', with the subscript 'I' short for 'intuitionist', to distinguish the three rules from their counterparts in Table 3.

5. I borrow the phrase 'Separation Theorem' from [3].

6. See [5]. Gentzen treats $A \equiv B$ as short for $(A \supset B) \& (B \supset A)$, and hence does without introduction rules for '$\equiv$'. That the result quoted in the text still holds true when '$\equiv$' serves as a primitive connective and rules of the sorts **BII** and **BIr** in Table 2 serve as introduction rules for '$\equiv$', has independently been noted by Bernays in [2]. The 'I' in '**EI**', '**PI**', '**CI**', and so on, is short for 'to the left'; the 'r' in '**Er**', '**Pr**', '**Cr**', and so on, is short for 'to the right'.

7. Note for proof of (ii) that '${\sim}$' does not belong to any of the subsets of $\{{\sim}, \supset, \&, \vee, \equiv, \forall, \exists\}$ under consideration here. Hence no entry in the proof of S can be had by application of **NII**. Hence none can be of the sort $A_1, A_2, \ldots, A_n \to$. But no L-sequent of the sort $A_1, A_2, \ldots, A_n \to B$, $B_2, \ldots, B_m$, where $m > 1$, can be had by application of a rule from Table 2. Hence (ii).

8. Φ_α, the reader may recall, consists of **R**, **T**, **P**, **C**, and the intelim rules of Table 1 for such (and only such) operators as belong to α.

9. That (a) holds true when S_j follows from S_i by application of **TI**, **PI**, **CI** (in view of (ii) **Tr** does not enter into account here), **HIr**, **DIr**, or **∃Ir**, and (b) holds true when S_j follows from S_h and S_i by application of **CIr** or **BIr**, needs no proof.

10. Note here that '$\supset$' is sure to belong to α, and hence **HE$_I$** and **HI**—two rules we make use of a few lines hence—sure to belong to Φ_α. Like remarks apply throughout this section.

11. Recall for proof of (ii) that no L-sequent of the sort $A_1, A_2, \ldots, A_n \to B_1, B_2, \ldots, B_m$, where $m > 1$, can be had by application of a rule from Table 2.

12. That (a) holds true when S_j follows from S_i by application of **EI**, **PI**, **CI**, **HIr**, **DIr**, **∀Ir**, or **∃Ir**, and (b) holds true when S_j follows from S_h and S_i by application of **CIr** or **BIr**, needs no proof.

13. The case where the L-sequent in question follows from $A_1, A_2, \ldots, A_n \to A$, where $n \geq 0$, and $B, A_{n+1}, A_{n+2}, \ldots, A_{n+k} \to C$, where $k > 0$, has already been treated; and so—by implication—has been the one where the L-sequent follows from $A_1, A_2, \ldots, A_n \to A$, where $n \geq 0$, and $B, A_{n+1}, A_{n+2}, \ldots, A_{n+k} \to$, where $k > 0$, since the N-counterparts of $B, A_{n+1}, A_{n+2}, \ldots, A_{n+k} \to$ and $A \supset B, A_1, A_2, \ldots, A_{n+k} \to$ are $B, A_{n+1}, A_{n+2}, \ldots, A_{n+k-1} \to {\sim}A_{n+k}$ and $A \supset B, A_1, A_2, \ldots, A_{n+k-1} \to {\sim}A_{n+k}$. Like remarks apply throughout the balance of the section.

14. Rule HE was suggested to me by Stig Kanger. Rule **BE** is due to Paul Bernays, who offered it in [1] as an alternative to the introduction rule for '$\equiv$' that I used in [8], to wit:

$$\frac{K \to A \text{ and either } K \to (B \equiv A) \equiv (B \equiv C) \text{ or } K \to (B \equiv C) \equiv (B \equiv A)}{K \to C}$$

15. Gentzen again has no rules for '$\equiv$', but his original result easily generalizes into Lemma 2.

Incidentally, it follows from results of S. Maehara and M. Ohnishi (see [11]) that *so long as rules* **Nlr**, **Hlr**, **Blr**, *and* **∀lr** *in Table 4 are weakened to read like their counterparts in Table 2*, every L-sequent provable by means of the rules of Table 4 is **I**-valid, and vice-versa.

16. See [10].
17. For a different proof of Theorem 2 for the thirty-two cases where α is a subset of $\{\sim, \supset, \&, \vee, \equiv\}$, and an algorithm for proving S (when **C**-valid) in each one of those thirty-two cases, see [8].
18. Cases in point are '$(\forall x)(f(x) \vee p) \to (\forall x)f(x) \vee p$', '$(\forall x)(f(x) \vee (p \& p)) \to (\forall x)f(x) \vee (p \& p)$', '$(\forall x)(f(x) \vee (\exists x)p) \to (\forall x)f(x) \vee (\exists x)p$', and '$(\forall x)(f(x) \vee (\exists x)(p \& p)) \to (\forall x)f(x) \vee (\exists x)(p \& p)$'.
19. For proof see [9].
20. A may also be said to be **C**-implied by S if $S \cup \{\sim A\}$ is not simultaneously satisfiable. That A is **C**-implied by S if and only if A is **C**-implied by a finite subset of S then follows from the so-called *Compactness Theorem* (to the effect that a set of wffs of **QC** is simultaneously satisfiable if and only if every finite subset of the set is).
21. A congener of rule $\forall I'_v$ appears in [4].
22. My thanks go to Paul Bernays, Michael D. Resnik, and Richmond H. Thomason, who read a first draft of this paper.

References

[1] Bernays, P. 1962. Review of H. Leblanc's "Etudes sur les règles d'inférence dites règles de Gentzen." *The Journal of Symbolic Logic* (hereafter *JSL*) 27: 248–49.

[2] ———. 1965. "Betrachtungen zum Sequenzen-Kalkul." *Contributions to Logic and Methodology in Honor of J. M. Bochenski*. Amsterdam: North-Holland.

[3] Curry, H. B. 1963. *Foundations of Mathematical Logic*. New York: McGraw-Hill.

[4] Fitch, F. B. 1952. *Symbolic Logic: An Introduction*. New York: Ronald Press.

[5] Gentzen, G. 1934. "Untersuchungen über das logische Schliessen." *Mathematische Zeitschrift* 39: 176–210, 403–31.

[6] ———. 1936. "Die Widerspruchsfreiheit der reinen Zahlentheorie." *Mathematische Annalen* 112: 493–565.

[7] Kripke, S. A. 1965. "Semantical Analysis of Intuitionistic Logic I." *Formal Systems and Recursive Functions*, pp. 92–130. Amsterdam: North-Holland.

[8] Leblanc, H. 1963. "Proof Routines for the Propositional Calculus." *Notre Dame Journal of Formal Logic* 4: 81–104 (#23 in this volume).

[9] ———. 1966. *Techniques of Deductive Inference*. Englewood Cliffs: Prentice-Hall.

[10] Leblanc, H., and Thomason, R. H. 1966. "The Demarcation Line between Intuitionist Logic and Classical Logic." *Zeitschrift fur mathematische Logik und Grundlagen der Mathematik* 12: 257–62 (#30 in this volume).

[11] Umezawa, T. 1959. "On Intermediate Propositional Logics." *JSL* 24: 20–26.

25
Two Shortcomings of Natural Deduction

1. Whereas logic primers written in the twenties, the thirties, and occasionally well into the forties dealt mostly with the proving of valid formulas, recent ones take as their main order of business the deducing of formulas from sets of same,[1] and—following the example set by Cooley, Fitch, Quine, and others—carry out deductions by the *natural deduction* or *subordinate proof* method.[2]

The method in question makes for deductions in which all lines are obtained by one or another of a handful of rules and, hence, dispenses entirely with axioms. Some of the rules are pretty classic, like Modus Ponens (**HE** in Table 1 below), which goes back to the Stoics. Others are of newer vintage, and the method owes them one of the names it goes by. I have in mind Conditionalization (**HI** in Table 1), which allows one—should a subordinate deduction headed by the premises $A_1, A_2, \ldots, A_n$, and B close with a line C—to deduce $B \supset C$ from $A_1, A_2, \ldots,$ and A_n alone; also Reductio ad Absurdum (**NI** in Table 1), which allows one—should a first subordinate deduction headed by the premises $A_1, A_2, \ldots, A_n$, and B close with a line C, and a second subordinate deduction headed by the same premises close with the line $\sim C$—to deduce $\sim B$ from $A_1, A_2, \ldots,$ and A_n alone.

All primers carry a rule for dropping the universal quantifier that may preface a given line, hence in effect for eliminating the quantifier letter '∀' from that line; one for prefacing a given line with a universal quantifier, hence in effect for introducing '∀' into that line; one for eliminating the quantifier letter '∃'; and one for introducing '∃'. Since Modus Ponens can be thought of as a rule for eliminating the connective '⊃', and Conditionalization as one for introducing '⊃', they also carry a pair of so-called *intelim rules* (i.e., introduction-elimination rules) for '⊃'. Anxious to handle all seven of '∼', '⊃', '&', '∨', '≡', '∀' and '∃' by means of separate rules, some primers go four better, so to speak, and also enlist intelim rules for '∼', '&', '∨', and '≡'.

Fairly typical of this approach to deduction are the following rules, one a rule for reiterating in the course of a deduction any premise one may wish, the remaining fourteen intelim rules of the sort just mentioned.

350

TABLE 1

Reiteration: From a set S of premises one may deduce any member of S as a conclusion.[3] **(R)**

Intelim rules for '~': (a) If from a set S of premises one may deduce a conclusion $\sim\sim A$, then from the same set S one may deduce A as a conclusion. **(NE)**[4]

(b) If from a set $S \cup \{A\}$ of premises one may deduce each one of two conclusions B and $\sim B$, then from the subset S of the original set $S \cup \{A\}$ one may deduce $\sim A$ as a conclusion. **(NI)**

Intelim rules for '⊃': (a) If from a set S of premises one may deduce each one of two conclusions A and $A \supset B$, then from the same set S one may deduce B as a conclusion. **(HE)**

(b) If from a set $S \cup \{A\}$ of premises one may deduce a conclusion B, then from the subset S of the original set $S \cup \{A\}$ one may deduce $A \supset B$ as a conclusion. **(HI)**

Intelim rules for '&': (a) If from a set S of premises one may deduce a conclusion $A \& B$, then from the same set S one may deduce either one of A and B as a conclusion.[5] **(CE)**

(b) If from a set S of premises one may deduce each one of two conclusions A and B, then from the same set S one may deduce $A \& B$ as a conclusion. **(CI)**

Intelim rules for '∨': (a) If from a set S of premises one may deduce a conclusion $A \vee B$ and from each one of the two supersets $S \cup \{A\}$ and $S \cup \{B\}$ of S deduce a conclusion C, then from the original set S one may deduce C as a conclusion.[6] **(DE)**

(b) If from a set S of premises one may deduce a conclusion A, then from the same set S one may deduce either one of $A \vee B$ and $B \vee A$ as a conclusion. **(DI)**

Intelim rules for '≡': (a) If from a set S of premises one may deduce each one of two conclusions A and $A \equiv B$ or each one of two conclusions A and $B \equiv A$, then from the same set S one may deduce B as a conclusion **(BE)**

(b) If from a set $S \cup \{A\}$ of premises one may deduce a conclusion B and from the set $S \cup \{B\}$ deduce A as a conclusion, then from the subset S of the original sets $S \cup \{A\}$ and $S \cup \{B\}$ one may deduce $A \equiv B$ as a conclusion. **(BI)**

Intelim rules for '∀': (a) Let $A(X'/X)$ be like A except for exhibiting free occurrences of some individual variable X' wherever A exhibits free occurrences of some individual variables X. If from a set S of premises one may deduce the conclusion $(\forall X)A$, then from the same set S one may deduce $A(X'/X)$ as a conclusion.[7] **(∀E)**

(b) If from a set S of premises one may deduce a conclusion A, then from the same set S one may deduce $(\forall X)A$ as a conclusion, so long as X does not occur fre in any member of S. **(∀I)**

Intelim rules for '∃': (a) If from a set S of premises one may deduce a conclusion $(\exists X)A$ and from the superset $S \cup \{A\}$ of S deduce a conclusion B, then from the original set S one may deduce B as a conclusion, so long as X does not occur free in any member of S, nor in B.[8] **(∃E)**

(b) Let $A(X'/X)$ be as in ∀E. If from a set S of premises one may deduce the conclusion $A(X'/X)$, then from the same set S one may deduce $(\exists X)A$ as a conclusion. **(∃I)**

It is my sorry duty to report that the rules of Table 1, and by rebound a great many of their analogues in current handbooks of logic, have two shortcomings.

2. Supposing a finite set S of premises, say, $\{B_1, B_2, \ldots, B_n\}$ ($n \geq 0$), to imply a conclusion A if the conditional

$$B_1 \supset (B_2 \supset (\ldots (B_n \supset A) \ldots))$$

is valid,[9] and an infinite set S to imply A if a finite subset of S does,[10] one can readily show that A is not deducible from S by the rules of Table 1 unless A is implied by S. It follows, however, from a result of Montague and Henkin that (i) the conclusion '$(\forall x)f(x)$', though implied by the set of premises $\{f(x), (\forall y)f(y)\}$, is not deducible from $\{f(x), (\forall y)f(y)\}$ by the rules of Table 1, nor (ii) is the conclusion '$\sim(\exists x)\sim f(x)$', though implied by the set of premises $\{f(x), \sim(\exists y)\sim f(y)\}$, deducible by them from $\{f(x), \sim(\exists y)\sim f(y)\}$.[11]

Proof of (i) and (ii) is as follows. Let A be a formula and X an individual variable. If A is atomic, declare it to be positive with respect to X or, for short, X-positive; if A is of the form $\sim B$, declare it to be X-positive if B is X-negative, otherwise declare it X-negative; if A is of the form $B \supset C$, declare it to be X-positive if B is X-negative or if C is X-positive, otherwise declare it X-negative; if A is of the form $B \& C$, declare it X-positive if both B and C are X-positive, otherwise declare it X-negative; if A is of the form $B \lor C$, declare it X-positive if at least one of B and C is X-positive, otherwise declare it X-negative; if A is of the form $B \equiv C$, declare it X-positive if both B and C are X-positive or both are X-negative, otherwise declare it X-negative; if A is of the form $(\forall X)B$, declare it to be X-negative; if A is of the form $(\exists X)B$, declare it to be X-positive; and if A is of the form $(\forall Y)B$ or the form $(\exists Y)B$, where Y is distinct from X, declare it to be X-positive if B is X-positive, otherwise declare it X-negative.

It is easily verified that if a conclusion A is deducible from a set S of premises by the rules of Table 1, then for every individual variable X that occurs free in at least one member of S, A is bound to be X-positive if every member of S is X-positive. It is easily verified also that: (i') though '$f(x)$' and '$(\forall y)f(y)$' are both x-positive, '$(\forall x)f(x)$' is not, and (ii') though '$f(x)$' and '$\sim(\exists y)\sim f(y)$' are both x-positive, '$\sim(\exists x)\sim f(x)$' is not. (i) and (ii) thus hold true, and the rules of Table 1, though sound, are therefore not complete, a serious enough shortcoming.

Things can fortunately be put to rights in a number of ways, among them:

Alternative One: Enlist an extra rule, to read: "If from a set S of premises one may deduce a conclusion A, then one may deduce A from any superset of S."[12]

Alternative Two: Amend ∀I and ∃E to read, respectively:

∀I': If from a set S' of premises one may deduce a conclusion A, then from any superset S of the original set S' one may deduce $(\forall X)A$ as a conclusion, so long as X does not occur free in any member of S'.

∃E': If from a set S of premises one may deduce a conclusion $(\exists X)A$ and from a subset $S' \cup \{A\}$ of the set $S \cup \{A\}$ one may deduce a conclusion B, then from the original set S one may deduce B as a conclusion, so long as X does not occur free in any member of S', nor in B.[13]

Alternative Three: Amend ∀I and ∃E to read, respectively:

Two Shortcomings of Natural Deduction   353

∀I'': If from the null set ∅ of premises one may deduce a conclusion A, then from any set S of premises one may deduce $(\forall X)A$ as a conclusion.

∃E'': If from a set S of premises one may deduce a conclusion $(\exists X)A$ and from the set $\{A\}$ one may deduce a conclusion B, then from the original set S one may deduce B as a conclusion, so long as X does not occur free in B.[14]

Alternative Four: Amend ∀I and ∃E to read, respectively, like ∀I''' and ∃E''' below, restrict S in the remaining thirteen rules to be finite, and take a conclusion A to be deducible from a infinite set S of premises if A is deducible from a finite subset of S;

∀I''': Let $A(X'/X)$ be as in ∀E. If from a finite set S of premises one may deduce the conclusion A, then from the same set S one may deduce $(\forall X')A(X'/X)$ as a conclusion, so long as X and X'—should they occur free in A—do not occur free in any member of S.

∃E''': Let $A(X'/X)$ be as in ∀E. If from a finite set S of premises one may deduce the conclusion $(\exists X')A(X'/X)$ and from the superset $S \cup \{A\}$ of S one may deduce a conclusion B, then from the original set S one may deduce B as a conclusion, so long as X and X'—should they occur free in A—do not occur free in any member of S, nor in B.

Of these alternatives the last one proves from a practical point of view to be considerably handier than the first three.

Note: A variant of Alternatives Four may be worth listing: Amend ∀I and ∃E to read, respectively, like ∀I'''' and ∃E'''' below, in the remaining thirteen rules restrict S to being finite, and take a conclusion A to be deducible from an infinite set S of premises if A is deducible from a finite subset of S:

∀I'''': Let $A(X'/X)$ be as in ∀E. If from a finite set S of premises one may deduce $A(X'/X)$ as a conclusion, then from the same set S one may deduce $(\forall X)A$ as a conclusion, so long as X' does not occur free in any member of S, nor in $(\forall X)A$.

∃E'''': Let $A(X'/X)$ be as in ∀E. If from a finite set S of premises one may deduce $(\exists X)A$ as a conclusion and from the superset $S \cup \{A(X'/X)\}$ of S deduce a conclusion B, then from the original set S one may deduce B as a conclusion, so long as X' does not occur free in any member of S, nor in $(\exists X)A$, nor in B.[15]

3. Even when amended along the above lines, the rules of natural deduction still have a shortcoming. Consider indeed '$(p \supset q) \supset p$', a premise that exhibits no occurrences of '$\sim$', and 'p', a conclusion that exhibits no occurrence of '$\sim$' either. 'p', though deducible from $\{(p \supset q) \supset p\}$ by **R, HE, HI, NE**, and **NI**, is not deducible from $\{(p \supset q) \supset p\}$ by the first three of these rules, and that for a simple reason. Any conclusion A that is deducible from a set S of premises by **R, HE**, and **HI**, is bound to be implied by S according to intuitionist standards, or, for short, to be I-implied by S.[16] But 'p' is not I-implied by $\{(p \supset q) \supset p\}$. Hence, '$p$' cannot be deduced from $\{(p \supset q) \supset p\}$ by **R, HE**, and **HI** alone. Or consider 'p' and '$(r \equiv p) \equiv (r \equiv q)$', two premises that exhibit no occurrence of '$\sim$', and 'q', a conclusion that exhibits no occurrence of '$\sim$' either. 'q', though deducible from $\{p, (r \equiv p) \equiv (r \equiv q)\}$ by means of **R, BE, BI, NE**, and **NI**, is not deducible from $\{p, (r \equiv p) \equiv (r \equiv q)\}$ by the first three of these rules, and that for a like reason. Any conclusion A that is deducible from a set S of premises by **R, BE**, and **BI**, is bound to be I-implied by S. But 'q' is not I-implied by $\{p, (r \equiv p) \equiv (r \equiv q)\}$,[17] and so cannot be deduced from $\{p, (r \equiv p) \equiv (r \equiv q)\}$ by **R, BE**, and **BI**

alone. Or consider '$(\forall x)(f(x) \lor p)$', a premise that exhibits no occurrence of '$\sim$', and '$(\forall x)f(x) \lor p$', a conclusion that exhibits no occurrence of '$\sim$' either. '$(\forall x)f(x) \lor p$', though deducible from $\{(\forall x)(f(x) \lor p)\}$ by **R, DE, DI, ∀E, ∀I''''**, **NE**, and **NI**, is not deducible from $\{(\forall x)(f(x) \lor p)\}$ by the first five of these rules, and that for a like reason. Any conclusion A that is deducible from a set S of premises by **R, DE, DI, ∀E,** and **∀I'''**, is bound to be I-implied by S. But '$(\forall x)f(x) \lor (p)$ is not I-implied by $\{(\forall x)(f(x) \lor p)\}$. Hence '$(\forall x)f(x) \lor p$' is not deducible from $\{(\forall x)(f(x) \lor p)\}$ by **R, DE, DI, ∀E,** and **∀I'''** alone.[18]

To generalize matters, let a well-formed formula A of QC be said to be *in K*, where K is a (possibly empty) subset of

$$\{\sim, \supset, \&, \lor, \equiv, \forall\exists\},$$

if every operator (i.e., connective or quantifier letter) that occurs in A belongs to K, and every operator that belongs to K occurs in A. It can be shown that in 76 out of 128 cases a conclusion A in K, when implied by a set S of premises in K, is invariably deducible from S by R and the intelim rules of Table 1[19] *for only such operators as belong to K*. In the remaining 52 cases, however, to wit: the 48 cases where at least one of '$\supset$' and '$\equiv$' belongs to K, but '$\sim$' does not, and the four cases where K consists of '$\lor$' and '$\forall$' (Case 125), of '$\&$', '$\lor$', and '$\forall$' (Case 126), of '$\lor$', '$\forall$', and '$\exists$' (Case 127), or of '$\&$', '$\lor$', '$\forall$', and '$\exists$' (Case 128), recourse to **NE** and **NI** proves ineluctable whenever A is not I-implied by S.[20]

Things can be put to rights in the first 48 of those 52 cases. It can indeed be shown that if **HE** and **BE** are amended to read, respectively, like **HE'** and **BE'** below, then in all but four cases a conclusion A in K, when implied by a set S of premises in K, is invariably deducible from S by **R** and the intelim rules of Table 1 for only such operators as belongs to K:

HE': If from a (finite) set S of premises one may deduce each of two conclusions $(A \supset C) \supset A$ and $A \supset B$, then from the same set S one may deduce B as a conclusion.

BE': If from a (finite) set S of premises one may deduce each of two conclusions A and $(C \equiv A) \equiv (C \equiv B)$, then from the same set S one may deduce B as a conclusion.[21]

As a result, 'p', though not deducible from $\{(p \supset q) \supset p\}$ by **R, HE,** and **HI**, is nonetheless deducible from $\{(p \supset q) \supset p\}$ by **R** and two bona fide rules for '$\supset$', namely: **HE'** and **HI**; and 'q', though not deducible from $\{p, (r \equiv p) \equiv (r \equiv q)\}$ by **R, BE,** and **BI**, is nonetheless deducible from $\{p, (r \equiv p) \equiv (r \equiv q)\}$ by **R** and two bona fide rules for '$\equiv$', namely: **BE'** and **BI**.

The four outstanding cases are of course Cases 125–128, and they prove quite recalcitrant. It can indeed be shown of any conclusion A and set S of premises that if A is deducible from S by **R** and rules for '$\&$', '$\lor$', '$\forall$', or '$\exists$' that meet standard specifications, then A is bound to be I-implied by S.[22] So there is no hope of our ever deducing '$(\forall x)f(x) \lor p$' from $\{(\forall x)(f(x) \lor p)\}$ by **R** and congeners of **DE, DI, ∀E,** and **∀I'''**, or from $\{(\forall x)(f(x) \lor (p \& p))\}$ by **R** and congeners of **CE, CI, DE, DI, ∀E,** and **∀I''', ∃E''',** and **∃I** or from

Two Shortcomings of Natural Deduction   355

$\{(\forall x)(f(x) \lor (\exists x)p)\}$ by **R** and congeners of **DE**, **DI**, $\forall$**E**, $\forall$**I'''**, $\exists$**E'''**, and $\exists$**I**, or from $\{(\forall x)(f(x) \lor (\exists x)(p \& p))\}$ by **R** and congeners of **CE**, **CI**, **DE**, **DI**, $\forall$**E**, $\forall$**I'''**, $\exists$**'''**, and $\exists$**I**.

Cases 125–128 will fall in line if one is willing to use—alongside rules for single operators such as **DE**, **DI**, $\forall$**E**, and $\forall$**I'''**, and so on—such as a rule for the pair of operators $<\lor, \forall>$, say:

$\forall$**I**$_v$: If from a (finite) set S of premises one may deduce a conclusion $A \lor B$, then from the same set S one may deduce $(\forall X)A \lor B$ as a conclusion, so long as X does not occur free in any member of S, nor in B.

or, to stick more closely to the wording of $\forall$**I'''**,

$\forall$**I**$_v$**'''**: Let $A(X'/X)$ be as in $\forall$**E**. If from a (finite) set S of premises one may deduce a conclusion $A \lor B$, then from the same set S one may deduce $(\forall X')A(X'/X) \lor B$ as a conclusion, so long as X and X'—should they occur in A—do not occur free in any member of S, nor in B.

It can indeed be shown that a conclusion A in $\{\lor, \forall\}$, when implied by a set S of premises in $\{\lor, \forall\}$, is invariably deducible from S by **R**, **DE**, **DI**, $\forall$**E**, $\forall$**I'''**, and $\forall$**I**$_v$**'''**; a conclusion A in $\{\lor, \&\forall\}$, when implied by a set S of premises in $\{\lor, \&, \forall\}$, is invariably deducible from S by **R**, **DE**, **DI**, **CE**, **CI**, $\forall$**E**, $\forall$**I**$_v$**'''**; a conclusion A in $\{\lor, \forall, \exists\}$, when implied by a set S of premises in $\{\lor, \forall\exists\}$, is invariably deducible from S by **R**, **DE**, **DI**, $\forall$**E**, $\forall$**I'''**, $\forall$**I**$_v$**'''**, $\exists$**E'''**, and $\exists$**I**; and a conclusion A in $\{\lor, \&, \forall, \exists\}$, when implied by a set S of premises in $\{\lor, \&, \forall, \exists\}$, is invariably deducible from S by **R**, **DE**, **DI**, **CE**, **CI**, $\forall$**E**, $\forall$**I'''**, $\forall$**I**$_v$**'''** $\exists$**E'''**, and $\exists$**I**.[23]

$\forall$**I**$_v$**'''** can be thought of as a rule for introducing the quantifier letter '$\forall$' into the special context $A \lor B$, and, hence, as an intelim rule of a sort. It is, however, at variance with the kind of rules that most handbooks of natural deduction favor.[24]

Notes

1. Or, equivalently, of sentences from sets of sentences.

2. J. C. Cooley probably deserves in this connection more than alphabetical priority. So far as I know, [4], published in 1942, is the first one to employ the natural deduction method (devised, incidentally, by Jaśkowski and Gentzen in 1934).

3. All premises and conclusions mentioned in the rules of Table 1 are presumed to be formulas of the first-order predicate calculus. In rule **R** S of course has to be non-empty. In the remaining rules S may be empty, and in all fifteen S may be infinite as well as finite.

4. Throughout, '**E**' is for 'Elimination' and '**I**' for 'Introduction'. As for '**N**', '**H**', '**C**', '**D**', and '**B**', they are short, respectively, for 'Negation', 'Horseshoe', 'Conjunction', 'Disjunction', and 'Biconditional'.

5. Or, to ensure more symmetry between the rules for '&' and those for our remaining connectives: "If from a set S of premises one may deduce a conclusion $A \& B$ and from the superset $S \cup \{A, B\}$ of S deduce a conclusion C, then from the original set S one may deduce C as a conclusion." One set is understood to be a superset of another if the latter set is a subset of the former.

6. Concerning the notion of a superset, see Note 5.

7. Or, to ensure more symmetry between our various rules: "Let $A(X'/X)$ be like A except for exhibiting free occurrences of the individual variable X' wherever A exhibits free occurrences of the individual variable X. If from a set S of premises one may deduce the conclusion $(\forall X)A$ and from

356   Part 3: Provability

the superset $S \cup \{A(X'/X)\}$ of S one may deduce a conclusion B, then from the original set S one may deduce B as a conclusion.'' In much of the literature ∀E goes by the name 'UI' (for 'Universal Instantiation'), ∀I below by the name 'UG' (for 'Universal Generalization'), ∃E below (and counterparts of ∃E like ∃E* in Note 8) by the name 'EI', and ∃I below by the name 'EG'.

8. Quite a few textbooks rather have it at this point that if from a set S of premises one may deduce a conclusion $(\exists X)A$ (better, $(\exists X')A(X'/X)$, where $A(X'/X)$ is as in ∀E), then from the same set S one may deduce A as a conclusion, so long as X meets (X and X' meet) a restriction for which we have no space here. The rule in question, call it ∃E*, has a drawback which—in my opinion—far outweighs its undeniable merits. Whereas indeed a conclusion A deduced from a set S of premises by means of ∃E is invariably implied by S, a conclusion deduced from S by means of ∃E* is occasionally not implied by S, and the occasions on which A is not implied by S must be spelled out in a postscript to ∃E*. Note also that, when ∃E* is enlisted as elimination rule for '∃', a further restriction must be placed upon the individual variable X of ∀I (or, if ∀I''' below is enlisted as introduction rule for '∀', upon the two individual variables X and X' of ∀I'''). The restriction in question is incorrectly put in a surprisingly large number of textbooks.

9. Hence, in the event that $n = 0$, if A is valid.

10. Under this understanding of things, A proves to be implied by finite or infinite S if (and only if) the set $S \cup \{\sim A\}$ is not simultaneously satisfiable, a criterion that could do duty for the one in the text and is often used in the literature.

11. See [11].

12. The rule in question goes by various names in the literature, among them 'Thinning', 'Weakening', and 'Expansion'.

13. Note that amending only one of ∀I and ∃E will not do. With ∀I made to read like ∀I', but ∃E kept as originally stated, (ii) still holds true; and with ∃E made to read like ∃E', but ∀I kept as originally stated, (i) still holds true. For proof in the first case, let $(\forall X)B$ be X-positive or X-negative according as B is, but let $(\exists X)B$ be invariably X-positive; in the second case, let $(\exists X)B$ be X-positive or X-negative according as B is, but let $(\forall X)B$ be invariably X-negative.

14. Alternative Three is due in effect to Montague and Henkin; see [11]. The authors report on a proposal of S. C. Kleene in [6], pp. 94–98, which constitutes yet another way of putting things to rights here.

15. Proof that each one of the above alternatives permits deduction of A from S whenever A is implied by S will be found in [9]. For further and more up-to-date information on this whole matter, see the last paper in this volume.

16. A conclusion A is taken here to be I-*implied by a finite set S of premises*, say, $\{B_1, B_2, \ldots, B_n\}$, if the conditional $B_1 \supset (B_2 \supset (\ldots (B_n \supset A) \ldots))$ is valid in the sense of [7] (for short, if the conditional in question is I-valid), and to be I-*implied by an infinite set S* if A is I-implied by a finite subset of S. Since $B_1 \supset (B_2 \supset (\ldots (B_n \supset A) \ldots))$ may be valid according to classical standards without being I-valid, a conclusion A may be implied according to classical standards by a set S of premises without being I-implied by S. For proof that 'p' is not I-implied by $\{(p \supset q) \supset p\}$, see Exercise 26.10 in [3].

17. For proof that 'q' is not I-implied by $\{p, (r \equiv p) \equiv (r \equiv q)\}$, see again Exercise 26.10 in [3].

18. For proof that '$(\forall x)f(x) \lor p$' is not I-implied by $\{(\forall x)(f(x) \lor p)\}$, see pp. [6], 487–90. Note in this connection that entry (10) in Exercise 38.8 of [3] p. 208, first printing, is in error, and should run as in the 1962 printing: $A \lor (a)B \supset (a)(A \lor B)$, if a is not free in A.

19. As amended in Section 2 of this paper.

20. Intuitionist logic fares much better on this score than classical logic. Let NE be weakened to read, as suggsted by P. Bernays in [2]. "If from a (finite) set S of premises one may deduce each one of two conclusions $\sim A$ and $\sim \sim A$, then from the same set S one may deduce A as a conclusion." It can then be shown that—no matter which subset of $\{\sim, \supset, \&, \lor, \equiv, \forall, \exists\}$ K may be—a conclusion A in K, when I-implied by a set S of premises in K, is invariably deducible from S by R and the intelim rules of Table 1 (as amended in Section 2 of this paper) for only such operators as belong to K. Proof of the fact is supplied in [10].

21. Proof of the fact that for the thirty-two cases where neither '∀' nor '∃' belongs to K can be obtained from [8]; proof of the fact for the remaining ninety-two cases is outlined in [10]. I make

use in the first of these two papers of a different elimination rule for '≡', **BE''**: "If from a (finite) set S of premises one may deduce each one of two conclusions A and $(C \equiv A) \equiv (C \equiv B)$ or each one of two conclusions A and $(C \equiv B) \equiv (C \equiv A)$, then from the same set S one may deduce B as a conclusion." That **BE'** can do duty for **BE''** was noted by Bernays in [2]. **HE'** is due to S. Kanger.

22. For proof of part of the result, see [1].
23. See [10].
24. A rule similar to $\forall I_v$, namely: "If from a set S of premises one may deduce a conclusion $(\forall X)(A \lor B)$, then from the same set S one may deduce $A \lor (\forall X)B$ as a conclusion, so long as X does not occur free in any member of S nor in A," appears in [5], p. 141, where it is dubbed an "elimination rule relating universal quantification and disjunction." My thanks go to R. H. Thomason and W. A. Wisdom, who read an earlier version of the paper.

References

[1] Belnap, N. D., Jr., Leblanc, H., and Thomason, R. H. 1963. "On *Not* Strengthening Intuitionistic Logic," *Notre Dame Journal of Formal Logic* (hereafter *NDJFL*) 4: 313–20 (#29 in this volume).
[2] Bernays, P. 1962. Review of H. Leblanc's "Etudes sur les règles d'inference dites règles de Gentzen." *The Journal of Symbolic Logic* (hereafter *JSL*) 27: 248–49.
[3] Church, A. 1956. *Introduction to Mathematical Logic,* Vol. I. Princeton: Princeton University Press.
[4] Cooley, J. C. 1942. *Primer of Formal Logic.* New York: Macmillan.
[5] Fitch, F. B. 1952. *Symbolic Logic.* New York: Ronald Press.
[6] Kleene, S. C. 1952. *Introduction to Metamathematics.* Princeton: van Nostrand.
[7] Kripke, S. A. 1965. "Semantical Analysis of Intuitionistic Logic I." *Formal Systems and Recursive Functions,* pp. 92–130. Amsterdam: North-Holland.
[8] Leblanc, H. 1963. "Proof Routines for the Propositional Calculus." *NDJFL* 4: 81–104 (#23 in this volume).
[9] ———. 1966. *Techniques of Deductive Inference.* Englewood Cliffs: Prentice-Hall.
[10] ———. 1966. "Two Separation Theorems for Natural Deduction." *NDJFL* 7: 159–80 (#24 in this volume).
[11] Montague, R., and Henkin, L. 1956. "On the Definition of 'Formal Deduction'." *JSL* 21: 129–36.

26

Subformula Theorems for N-Sequents

With all seven of '$\sim$', '$\supset$', '&', '$\vee$', '$\equiv$', '$\forall$', and '$\exists$' understood to serve as primitive signs, let an expression of the sort

$$A_1, A_2, \ldots, A_n \to B_1, B_2, \ldots, B_m,$$

where $A_1, A_2, \ldots, A_n$ ($n \geq 0$), $B_1, B_2, \ldots,$ and B_m ($m > 0$ if $n = 0$, otherwise $m \geq 0$) are wffs of the first-order quantificational calculus (QC), count as an L-*sequent* of QC; let an L-sequent of QC of the sort

$$A_1, A_2, \ldots, A_n \to B$$

count as an N-*sequent* of QC;[1] and let an L-sequent S of QC count as a *Gentzen L-sequent* of QC if no individual variable of QC occurs both bound and free in S. When $m = 0$, let $\sim((\ldots(A_1 \& A_2) \& \ldots) \& A_n)$ count as the *wff-associate* of $A_1, A_2, \ldots, A_n \to B_1, B_2, \ldots, B_m$; when $m > 0$ and $n = 0$, let $(\ldots(B_1 \vee B_2) \vee \ldots) \vee B_m$ count as its wff-associate; and, when $m > 0$ and $n > 0$, let

$$((\ldots(A_1 \& A_2) \& \ldots) \& A_n) \supset ((\ldots(B_1 \vee B_2) \vee \ldots) \vee (B_m))$$

count as its wff-associate. Let an L-sequent S of QC be declared *classically valid* (C-valid, for short) when the wff-associate of S is C-valid; and let S be declared *intuitionistically valid* (I-valid, for short) when its wff-associate is I-valid.[2]

Next, where S is an L-sequent of QC and Φ is a set of rules of inference, let a finite column of L-sequents of QC count as a *proof* of S by means of Φ if: (i) the column closes with S, and (ii) every entry in the column holds by application of a premiseless rule in Φ or follows from p ($p \geq 1$) previous entries in the column by application of a p-premise rule in Φ; let the column count as an N-*proof* of S if every entry in the column is an N-sequent of QC; and let Φ be said to *permit proof* [N-*proof*] of S if there exists a proof [N-proof] of S.

Finally, let each one of $A_1, A_2, \ldots, A_n$ count as an *antecedent formula*, and each one of $B_1, B_2, \ldots, B_m$ count as a *succedent formula*, of $A_1, A_2, \ldots, A_n \to B_1, B_2, \ldots, B_m$. Where A and B are wffs of QC, let A count as a subformula of B if: (i) A and B are the same, (ii) B is of the sort $\sim C$ and A counts as a subformula of C, (iii) B is of one of the four sorts $C \supset D$, $C \& D$, $C \vee D$, and $C \equiv D$, and A counts as a subformula of C and/or D, or (iv) B is of one of the two sorts $(\forall X)C$ and $(\exists X)C$, and A counts for some individual variable Y of QC as a subformula of $C(Y/X)$, where $C(Y/X)$ is like C except for containing free occurrences of Y wherever C contains free occurrences of X. Where S is an L-sequent of QC and Φ is a set of rules of inference, let a proof of S by means of Φ count as a *subformula-minded proof* of S by means of Φ if each antecedent and each succedent formula of each entry in the said proof counts as a subformula of some antecedent or some succedent formula of S. And let Φ be said to *permit subformula-minded proof* of S if there exists a subformula-minded proof of S by means of Φ.

At the beginning of [2] Gentzen stated (in effect) that congeners of the rules of Table 5 for '$\sim$', '$\supset$', '&', '$\vee$', '$\forall$', and '$\exists$' permit subformula-minded deduction of every I-valid wff of QC that contains no '$\equiv$' and in which no individual variable of QC occurs both bound and free.[3] In response to that aside of his, we shall establish here that rule **R** in Table 1, and the rules of that table for '$\sim$', '$\supset$', '&', '$\vee$', '$\equiv$', '$\forall$', and '$\exists$', permit subformula-minded proof (and, hence, subformula-minded N-proof)[4] of every Gentzen N-sequent of QC that is I-valid (*Theorem 1*.) We shall then establish that rules **GR** and **GCut** in Table 3, and the rules of that table for '$\sim$', '$\supset$', '&', '$\vee$', '$\equiv$', '$\forall$', and '$\exists$', permit subformula-minded proof (though not necessarily subformula-minded N-proof) of every Gentzen N-sequent of QC that is C-valid (*Theorem 2*). The results are somewhat intriguing, since seven of the rules for '$\sim$', '$\supset$', '&', '$\vee$', '$\equiv$', '$\forall$', and '$\exists$' in Table 1, and seven of the rules for those connectives and quantifier letters in Table 3, are so-called "elimination" rules, and rule **GCut** in Table 3 is a special case of Gentzen's *Schnitt*.[5] And they may be welcome to devotees of *natural deduction*, who insist on each one of '$\sim$', '$\supset$', '&', '$\vee$', '$\equiv$', '$\forall$', and '$\exists$' obeying two rules: one an introduction rule, the other an *elimination* rule.

1. To prove Theorem 1, we first call on another set of rules, the rules in Table 2,[6] and show that, where S is an N-sequent of QC,

Lemma 1. *Any proof of S by means of rules from Table 2 converts into a subformula-minded proof of S by means of rules from Table 1.*

We then show that, where S is again an N-sequent of QC,

Lemma 2. *Any subformula-minded proof of S by means of rules from Table 1 converts into a subformula-minded proof of S by means of the same rules minus* **P, C, T,** *and* **Cut.**

Since the rules in Table 2 permit—in view of a result of Gentzen's in [2]— proof of every Gentzen N-sequent of QC that is I-valid,[7] it will follow from

Lemmas 1 and 2 that rule **R** in Table 1, and the rules of that table for '~', '⊃', '&', '∨', '≡', '∀', and '∃', permit subformula-minded proof of every such N-sequent.

For proof of Lemma 1, consider first an N-sequent S of QC that contains no '~'; suppose there exists a proof of S by means of rules from Table 2; and suppose, as one may without loss of generality, that the proof in question is subformula-minded.[8] Then the proof is sure to consist of q ($q \geq 1$) N-sequents $S_1, S_2, \ldots, S_q$, that hold by rule **SR** or follow from previous N-sequents in the proof by application of a rule other than **Tr**, **NIl**, and **NIr**. But, if so, then the result of substituting the entries supplied in Cases 1–9 below for any entry S_i that follows from previous entries in the proof by application of **HIl**, **HIr**, **CIl**, **DIl**, **BIl**, **BIr**, **∀Il**, or **∃Il**, is sure to count as a subformula-minded proof of S by means of rules from Table 1.[9]

Case 1: S_i is the sort $A \supset B, K, K' \to L^*$, and follows from $K \to A$ ($= S_g$) and $B, K' \to L^*$ ($= S_h$) by application of **HIl**.

i.1	$A \supset B, K', K \to A$	$(\mathbf{T}, g)^{10}$
i.2	$A \supset B, K, K' \to A$	$(\mathbf{P}, \text{i.1})^{11}$
i.3	$A \supset B, K, K' \to A \supset B$	$(\mathbf{R})$
i.4	$A \supset B, K, K' \to B$	$(\mathbf{HE}, \text{i.2}, \text{i.3})$
i.5	$A \supset B, K, B, K' \to L^*$	$(\mathbf{T}, h)$
i.6	$A \supset B, K, K', B \to L^*$	$(\mathbf{P}, \text{i.5})$
i.7	$A \supset B, K, K' \to L^*$	$(\mathbf{Cut}, \text{i.4}, \text{i.6})$.

Case 2: S_i is of the sort $K \to A \supset B$, and follows from $A, K \to B$ ($= S_h$) by application of **HIr**.

i.1	$K, A \to B$	$(\mathbf{P}, h)$
i.2	$K \to A \supset B$	$(\mathbf{HI}, \text{i.1})$.

Case 3: S_i is of the sort $A \& B, K \to L^*$, and follows from $A, K \to L^*$ or $B, K \to L^*$ ($= S_h$) by application of **CIl**.

i.1	$A \& B, B, A, K \to L^*$ or $A \& B, A, B, K \to L^*$	$(\mathbf{T}, h)$
i.2	$A \& B, K, A, B \to L^*$	$(\mathbf{P}, \text{i.1})$
i.3	$A \& B, K, A \to A \& B$	$(\mathbf{R})$
i.4	$A \& B, K, A \to B$	$(\mathbf{CE}, \text{i.3})$
i.5	$A \& B, K, A \to L^*$	$(\mathbf{Cut}, \text{i.2}, \text{i.4})$
i.6	$A \& B, K \to A \& B$	$(\mathbf{R})$

i.7 $A \mathbin{\&} B, K \to A$ (**CE**, i.6)

i.8 $A \mathbin{\&} B, K \to L^*$ (**Cut**, i.5, i.7).

Case 4: S_i is of the sort $A \lor B, K \to L^*$, and follows from $A, K \to L^*$ ($= S_g$) and $B, K \to L^*$ ($= S_h$) by application of **D**II.

i.1 $A \lor B, A, K \to L^*$ (**T**, g)

i.2 $A \lor B, K, A \to L^*$ (**P**, i.1)

i.3 $A \lor B, B, K \to L^*$ (**T**, h)

i.4 $A \lor B, K, B \to L^*$ (**P**, i.3)

i.5 $A \lor B, K \to A \lor B$ (**R**)

i.6 $A \lor B, K \to L^*$ (**DE**, i.2, i.4, i.5).

Case 5: S_i is of the sort $A \equiv B, K, K' \to L^*$, and follows from $K \to A$ ($= S_g$) and $B, K' \to L^*$ ($= S_h$) by application of **B**II. Same entries as in Case 1, but with every occurrence of $A \supset B$ made into one of $A \equiv B$, and with **BE** doing duty for **HE** in the credentials of entry i.4.

Case 6: S_i is of the sort $A \equiv B, K, K' \to L^*$, and follows from $K \to B$ ($= S_g$) and $A, K' \to L^*$ ($= S_h$) by application of **B**II. Same entries as in Case 1, but with every occurrence of $A \supset B$ made into one of $A \equiv B$, the last occurrence of A in i.1–i.2 made into one of B, etc.

Case 7: S_i is of the sort $K \to A \equiv B$, and follows from $A, K \to B$ ($= S_g$) and $B, K \to A$ ($= S_h$) by application of **BI**r.

i.1 $K, A \to B$ (**P**, g)

i.2 $K, B \to A$ (**P**, h)

i.3 $K \to A \equiv B$ (**BI**, i.1, i.2).

Case 8: S_i is of the sort $(\forall X)A, K \to L^*$, and follows for some individual variable Y of QC from $A(Y/X), K \to L^*$ ($= S_h$) by application of $\forall$II.

i.1 $(\forall X)A, K \to (\forall X)A$ (**R**)

i.2 $(\forall X)A, K \to A(Y/X)$ ($\forall$**E**, i.1)

i.3 $(\forall X)A, A(Y/X), K \to L^*$ (**T**, h)

i.4 $(\forall X)A, K, A(Y/X) \to L^*$ (**P**, i.3)

i.5 $(\forall X)A, K \to L^*$ (**Cut**, i.2, i.4).

Case 9: S_i is of the sort $(\exists X)A, K \to L^*$, and follows for some individual variable Y of QC that does not occur free in $(\exists X)A, K \to L^*$ from $A(Y/X), K \to L^*$ ($= S_h$) by application $\exists$II.

i.1 $(\exists X)A,\ K \to (\exists X)A$ **(R)**

i.2 $(\exists X)A,\ A(Y/X),\ K \to L^*$ **(T,** h**)**

i.3 $(\exists X)A,\ K,\ A(Y/X) \to L^*$ **(P,** i.2**)**

i.4 $(\exists X)A,\ K \to L^*$ $(\exists$**E,** i.1, i.3).

Consider then an N-sequent S of QC that contains at least one '~'; suppose there exists a proof of S by means of rules from Table 2; suppose the proof of S is subformula-minded; and suppose, as one may without loss of generality, that if any entry S_i in the proof of S follows from a previous entry by application of $\exists$**II**, then at least one existentialization variable for S_i in the proof of S does not occur free in S.[12] Unlike the proof on p. 360, this one may contain one or more entries of the sort $K \to$ (this, of course, because of rule **NII**). In such a case, $\sim\!A'$ being any wff of the sort $\sim\!A$ that occurs in some antecedent or some succedent formula of S, (i) replace every entry of the sort $K \to$ by the two entries $K \to A'$ and $K \to \sim\!A'$, to be known as the *stand-ins* of $K \to$; (ii) if any entry S_i of the sort $K \to$ follows in the proof of S from a previous entry $K' \to B$ by application of **NII** (and hence is of the sort $\sim\!B,\ K' \to$), insert between the two stand-ins of S_i and whichever entry precedes them, the following two entries:

$$\sim\! B,\ K' \to B$$

$$\sim\! B,\ K' \to \sim\! B,$$

the first one of which follows from $K' \to B$ by application of **T**, the second one of which holds by application of **R**, and the two of which yield the two stand-ins $\sim\! B,\ K' \to A'$ and $\sim\! B,\ K' \to \sim\! A'$ of S_i by application of **NE**; and (iii) if any entry S_i follows in the proof of S from a previous entry $B,\ K' \to$ by application of **NIr** (and hence is of the sort $K' \to \sim\! B$), insert between S_i and whichever entry precedes it, the following two entries:

$$K',\ B \to A'$$

$$K',\ B \to \sim\! A',$$

the two of which respectively follow from the stand-ins $B,\ K' \to A'$ and $B,\ K' \to \sim\! A'$ of $B,\ K' \to$ by application of **P**, and yield S_i by application of **NI**.[13] The resulting column of N-sequents then converts, like the one on p. 360, into a subformula-minded proof of S by means of rules from Table 1.[14]

Now for Lemma 2. Suppose there exists a subformula-minded proof of an N-sequent S of QC by means of rules from Table 1; and suppose at least one entry in the proof in question follows from previous entries in the proof by application of **P, C, T,** or **Cut**. Then the proof is easily turned into (a subformula-minded) one (by means of rules from Table 1) in which one entry less follows from previous entries in the proof by application of **P, C, T,** or **Cut**. For let S_i be the first entry in the proof of S that follows from previous entries in the proof by application of **P, C, T,** or **Cut**.

Case 1: S_i follows from a previous entry $K, A, B, L \to C$ ($= S_h$) by application of **P**, and hence is of the sort $K, B, A, L \to C$. Among the columns made up of one or more of the first h entries in the proof of S, any one that counts as a subformula-minded proof of S_h by means of rules from Table 1 other than **P, C, T,** and **Cut**, may without loss of generality be presumed to be of the sort

$K, A, B, L, M_1 \to C_1$

$K, A, B, L, M_2 \to C_2$

.
.
.

$K, A, B, L, M_{q-1} \to C_{q-1}$

$K, A, B, L \to C_q \, (= C)$,

where for each j from 1 to $q - 1$ M_j consist of zero or more wffs of QC. But, if so, then the column

$K, B, A, L, M_1 \to C_1$

$K, B, A, L, M_2 \to C_2$

.
.
.

$K, B, A, L, M_{q-1} \to C_{q-1}$

$K, B, A, L \to C_q$

counts as a subformula-minded proof of S_i by means of rules from Table 1 other than **P, C, T,** and **Cut**, and—when substituted for S_i in the proof of S—makes for a subformula-minded proof of S by means of rules from Table 1 in which one entry less follows from previous entries by application of **P, C, T,** and **Cut**.

Case 2: S_i follows from a previous entry $A, A, K \to B$ ($= S_h$) by application of **C**, and hence is of the sort $A, K \to B$. Proof similar to that of Case 1, but with the following two columns doing duty for those in Case 1:

$A, A, K, M_1 \to B_1$ and $A, K, M_1 \to B_1$

$A, A, K, M_2 \to B_2$ $A, K, M_2 \to B_2$

.   .
.   .
.   .

$A, A, K, M_{q-1} \to B_{q-1}$ $A, K, M_{q-1} \to B_{q-1}$

$A, A, K \to B_q \, (= B)$ $A, K \to B_q$.

Case 3: S_i follows from a previous entry $K \to A$ ($= S_h$) by application of **T**, and hence is of the sort $B, K \to A$. Among the columns made up of one or more of the first h entries in the proof of S, any one that counts as a subformula-minded proof of S_h by means of rules from Table 1 other than **P, C, T**, and **Cut**, may without loss of generality be presumed, first, to be of the sort

$K, M_1 \to A_1$

$K, M_2 \to A_2$

.

.

.

$K, M_{q-1} \to A_{q-1}$

$K \to A_q \, (= A),$

and, second, to be such that, if any entry S_d in the column follows from a previous entry by application of **∀I** or from two previous entries by application of **∃E**, then at least one of the universalization or deëxistentialization variables for S_d in the column does not occur free in B.[15] But, if so, then the column

$B, K, M_1 \to A_1$

$B, K, M_2 \to A_2$

.

.

.

$B, K, M_{q-1} \to A_{q-1}$

$B, K \to A_q$

counts as a subformula-minded proof of S_i by means of rules from Table 1 other than **P, C, T**, and **Cut**, and—when substituted for S_i in the proof of S—makes for a subformula-minded proof of S by means of rules from Table 1 in which one entry less follows from previous entries by application of **P, C, T**, or **Cut**.

Case 4: S_i follows from two previous entries $K, A \to B$ ($= S_g$) and $K \to A$ ($= S_h$) by application of **Cut**, and hence is of the sort $K \to B$. Among the columns made up of one or more of the first g entries in the proof of S, any one that counts as a subformula-minded proof of S_g by means of rules from Table 1 other than **P, C, T**, and **Cut**, may without loss of generality be presumed to be of the sort

$K, A, M_1 \to B_1$

$K, A, M_2 \to B_2$

.

.

.

$K, A, M_{q-1} \to B_{q-1}$

$K, A \to B_q (=B)$.

But, if so, then the column

$K, M_1 \to B_1$

$K, M_2 \to B_2$

.

.

.

$K, M_{q-1} \to B_{q-1}$

$K \to B_q$

either counts or can be so added onto that it will count as a subformula-minded proof of S_i by means of rules from Table 1 other than **P, C, T,** and **Cut**, and— when substituted for S_i in the proof of S—makes for a subformula-minded proof of S by means of rules from Table 1 in which one entry less follows from previous entries by application of **P, C, T,** or **Cut**. For suppose in particular that entry $K, A, M_k \to B_k$ in the first-displayed column holds by application of **R**, and that B_k and A are the same. Among the columns made up of one or more of the first h entries in the proof of S, any one that counts as a subformula-minded proof of $K \to A$ by means of rules from Table 1 other than **P, C, T,** and **Cut**, can in view of Cases 3 and 1 be turned into a subformula-minded proof of $K, M_k \to A(=B_k)$ by means of the same rules. Hence inserting that proof of $K, M_k \to A$ minus its last entry between $K, M_{k-1} \to B_{k-1}$ and $K, M_k \to B_k$, should account for the presence of $K, M_k \to B_k$ in the second-displayed column.[16]

2. To prove Theorem 2, we call on yet another set of rules, those in Table 4,[17] and show that, where S is an L-sequent of QC,

Lemma 3. *Any proof of S by means of rules from Table 4 converts into a subformula-minded proof of S by means of rules from Table 3.*

We then show that, where S is again an L-sequent of QC,

Lemma 4. *Any subformula-minded proof of S by means of rules from Table 3 converts into a subformula-minded proof of S by means of the same rules minus* **GPl** *and* **GTl**.

Since the rules in Table 4 permit—in view of a result of Kanger's in [4]—[18] proof of every Gentzen L-sequent, and hence of every Gentzen N-sequent, of QC that is C-valid, it will follow from Lemmas 3 and 4 that rules **GR** and

GCut in Table 3, and the rules of that table for '~', '⊃', '&', '∨', '≡', '∀', and '∃', permit subformula-minded proof of every such N-sequent.

For proof of Lemma 3, consider a proof by means of rules from Table 4 of an L-sequent S of QC; and suppose, as one may without loss of generality, that the proof in question is subformula-minded. The result of substituting the entries supplied in Cases 1–12 below for any entry S_i that follows from previous entries in the proof by application of **GNIl**, **GNIr**, **GHIl**, **GHIr**, **GCIl**, **GDIl**, **GDIr**, **GBIl**, **GBIl**, **G∀Il**, **G∃Il**, or **G∃Ir**, is sure to count as a subformula-minded proof of S by means of rules from Table 3.[19]

Case 1: S_i is of the sort $K, \sim A, L \to M$, and follows from $K, L \to A, M$ ($= S_h$) by application of **GNIl**.

i.1 $\sim A, K, L \to A, M$ (**GTI**, h)

i.2 $K, \sim A, L \to A, M$ (**GPI**, i.1)

i.3 $K, \sim A, L \to \sim A, M$ (**GR**)

i.4 $K, \sim A, L \to M$ (**GNE** i. 2, i. 3).

Case 2: S_i is of the sort $K \to L, \sim A, M$, and follows from $A, K \to L, M$ ($= S_h$) by application of **GNIr**.

i.1 $K, A \to L, M$ (**GPI**, h)

i.2 $K \to L, \sim A, M$ (**GNI**, i.1).

Case 3: S_i is of the sort $K, A \supset B, L \to M$, and follows from $K, L \to A, M$ ($= S_g$) and $K, B, L \to M$ ($= S_h$) by application of **GHIl**.

i.1 $A \supset B, K, L \to A, M$ (**GTI**, g)

i.2. $K, A \supset B, L \to A, M$ (**GPI**, i.1)

i.3 $K, A \supset B, L \to A \supset B, M$ (**GR**)

i.4 $K, A \supset B, L \to B, M$ (**GHE**, i.2- i.3)

i.5 $A \supset B, K, B, L \to M$ (**GTI**, h)

i.6 $K, A \supset B, L, B \to M$ (**GPI**, i.5)

i.7 $K, A \supset B, L \to M$ (**GCut**, i.4, i.6).

Case 4: S_i is of the sort $K \to L, A \supset B, M$, and follows from $A, K \to L, B, M$ ($= S_h$) by application of **GHIr**.

i.1 $K, A \to L, B, M$ (**GPI**, h)

i.2 $K \to L, A \supset B, M$ (**GHI**, i.1).

Case 5: S_i is of the sort $K, A \& B, L \to M$, and follows from $K, A, B, L \to M$ ($= S_h$) by application of **GCIl**.

Subformula Theorems for N-Sequents   367

i.1 $A \mathbin{\&} B, K, A, B, L \to M$ (GTI, h)

i.2 $K, A \mathbin{\&} B, L, A, B \to M$ (GPI, i.1)

i.3 $K, A \mathbin{\&} B, L, A \to A \mathbin{\&} B, M$ (GR)

i.4 $K, A \mathbin{\&} B, L, A \to B, M$ (GCE, i.3)

i.5 $K, A \mathbin{\&} B, L, A \to M$ (GCut, i.2, i.4)

i.6 $K, A \mathbin{\&} B, L \to A \mathbin{\&} B, M$ (GR)

i.7 $K, A \mathbin{\&} B, L \to A, M$ (GCE, i.6)

i.8 $K, A \mathbin{\&} B, L \to M$ (GCut, i.5, i.7).

Case 6: S_i is of the sort $K, A \lor B, L \to M$, and follows from $K, A, L \to M$ ($= S_g$) and $K, B, L \to M$ ($= S_h$) by application of **GDIl**.

i.1 $A \lor B, K, A, L \to M$ (GTI, g)

i.2 $K, A \lor B, L, A \to M$ (GPI, i.1)

i.3 $A \lor B, K, B, L \to M$ (GTI, h)

i.4 $K, A \lor B, L, B \to M$ (GPI, i.3)

i.5 $K, A \lor B, L \to A \lor B, M$ (GR)

i.6 $K, A \lor B, L \to M$ (GDE, i.2, i.4, i.5).

Case 7: S_i is of the sort $K \to L, A \lor B, M$, and follows from $K \to L, A, B, M$ ($= S_h$) by application of **GDIr**.

i.1 $K \to L, A \lor B, B, M$ (GDI, h)

i.2 $K \to L, A \lor B, A \lor B, M$ (GDI, i.1)

i.3 $K, A \to L, A, M$ (GR)

i.4 $K, A \to L, A \lor B, M$ (GDI, i.3)

i.5 $K, B \to L, B, M$ (GR)

i.6 $K, B \to L, A \lor B, M$ (GDI, i.5)

i.7 $K \to L, A \lor B, M$ (GDE, i.2, i.4, i.6).

Case 8: S_i is of the sort $K, A \equiv B, L \to M$, and follows from $K, A, B, L \to M$ ($= S_g$) and $K, L \to A, B, M$ ($= S_h$) by application of **GBIl**.

i.1 $A \equiv B, K, L \to A, B, M$ (GTI, h)

i.2 $K, A \equiv B, L \to A, B, M$ (GPI, i.1)

i.3 $K, A \equiv B, L, A \to A, M$ (GR)

i.4 $K, A \equiv B, L, A \to A \equiv B, M$ (GR)

i.5 $K, A \equiv B, L, A \to B, M$ (**GBE**, i.3, i.4)

i.6 $K, A \equiv B, L \to B, M$ (**GCut**, i.2, i.5)

i.7 $A \equiv B, K, A, B, L \to M$ (**GTI**, g)

i.8 $K, A \equiv B, L, B, A \to M$ (**GPI**, i.7)

i.9 $K, A \equiv B, L, B \to B, M$ (**GR**)

i.10 $K, A \equiv B, L, B \to A \equiv B, M$)   **GR**)

i.11 $K, A \equiv B, L, B \to A, M$ (**GBE**, i.9, i.10)

i.12 $K, A \equiv B, L, B \to M$ (**GCut**, i.8, i.11)

i.13 $K, A \equiv B, L \to M$ (**GCut**, i. 6, i.12).

Case 9: S_i is of the sort $K \to L, A \equiv B, M$, and follows from $A, K \to L, B, M$ ($= S_g$) and $B, K \to L, A, M$ ($= S_h$) by application of **GBIr**.

i.1 $K, A \to L, B, M$ (**GPI**, g)

i.2 $K, B \to L, A, M$ (**GPI**, h)

i.3 $K \to L, A \equiv B, M$ (**GBI**, i.1, i.2).

Case 10: S_i is of the sort $K, (\forall X)A, L \to M$, and follows for some individual variable Y of QC from $K, A(Y/X), (\forall X)A, L \to M$ ($= S_h$) by application of **G∀Il**.

i.1 $K, (\forall X)A, L \to (\forall X)A, M$ (**GR**)

i.2 $K, (\forall X)A, L \to A(Y/X), M$ (**G∀E**, i.1)

i.3 $K, (\forall X)A, L, A(Y/X) \to M$ (**GPI**, h)

i.4 $K, (\forall X)A, L \to M$ (**GCut**, i.2, i.3).

Case 11: S_i is of the sort $K, (\exists X)A, L \to M$, and follows for some individual variable Y of QC that does not occur free in $K, (\exists X)A, L \to M$ from $K, A(Y/X), L \to M$ ($= S_h$) by application of **G∃Il**.

i.1 $K, (\exists X)A, L \to (\exists X)A, M$ (**GR**)

i.2 $(\exists X)A, K, A(Y/X), L \to M$ (**GTI**, h)

i.3 $K, (\exists X)A, L, A(Y/X) \to M$ (**GPI**, i.2)

i.4 $K, (\exists X)A, L \to M$ (**G∃E**, i.1, i.3),

where Z is any individual variable of QC that does not occur free in $K \to L$ $(\exists X)A, M$.

Case 12: S_i is of the sort $K \to L, (\exists X)A, M$ and follows for some individual variable Y of QC from $K \to L, A(Y/X), (\exists X)A, M$ ($= S_h$) by application of **G∃Ir**.

i.1 $K \to L, (\exists X)A, (\exists X)A, M$ (G∃I, h)

i.2 $K, A(Z/X) \to L, A(Z/X), M$ (GR)

i.3 $K, A(Z/X) \to L, (\exists X)A, M$ (G∃I, i.2)

i.4 $K \to L, (\exists X)A, M$ (G∃E, i.1, i.3).

Now for Lemma 4. Suppose there exists a subformula-minded proof of an L-sequent S of QC by means of rules from Table 3. Then by the same reasoning as on p. 363 (Case 1) and p. 364 (Case 3) there is sure to be a subformula-minded proof of S by means of the same rules minus **GPI** and **GTI**.[20]

3. Of the two proofs of S mentioned in Lemma 3, call the one by means of rules from Table 4 *the first-stage proof of S*, and call the other (by means of rules from Table 3) *the second-stage proof of S*. When S does not contain any '~', the second-stage proof of S is sure to contain no entry of the sort $K \to$, if—as may be assumed without loss of generality—the first-stage proof of S is subformula-minded. On the other hand, when S contains at least one '~', then the second-stage proof of S may contain one or more entries of the sort $K \to$. Suppose, however, as may be done without loss of generality, that if any entry in the (second-stage) proof of S follows from a previous entry by application of **G∀I** or from two previous entries by application of **G∃E**, then at least one of the universalization or deëxistentialization variables for S_i in the (second-stage) proof of S does not occur free in S. Then the result of: (i) replacing every entry of the sort $K \to$ in the (second-stage) proof of S by the two entries $K \to A'$ and $K \to \sim A'$, where $\sim A'$ is any wff of the sort $\sim A$ that occurs in some antecedent or some succedent formula of S, (ii) if a given entry S_i in the (second-stage) proof of S follows from a previous entry $K', B \to$ by application of **GNI** (and hence is of the sort $K' \to \sim B$), inserting between $K' \to \sim B$ and whichever entry precedes it, the two entries $K' \to A'$, $\sim B$ and $K' \to \sim A'$, $\sim B$,[21] (iii) if a given entry S_i is of the sort $K \to$ and follows from two previous entries $K, B \to$ and $K \to B$ by application of **GCut**, inserting between $K \to B$ and whichever entry follows it proofs of $K \to B, A'$ and $K \to B, \sim A'$ (see Case 3 of Lemma 2 for hints on the matter), (iv) if a given entry S_i is of the sort $K \to$ and follows from three previous entries $K, B \to$, $K, C \to$, and $K \to B \lor C$ by application of **GDE**, inserting between $K \to B \lor C$ and whichever entry follows it proofs of $K \to B \lor C, A'$ and $K \to B \lor C, \sim A'$, and (v) if a given entry S_i is of the sort $K \to$ and follows from two previous entries $K \to (\exists X)B$ and $K, B(Y/X) \to$ by application of **G∃E**, inserting between $K \to (\exists X)B$ and whichever entry precedes it proofs of $K \to (\exists X)B, A'$ and $K \to (\exists X)B, \sim A'$, will count as a subformula-minded proof of S (by means of rules from Table 3) in which no entry is of the sort $K \to$.

As a result, Theorem 2 can be sharpened some, the rules from Table 3 listed therein making not only for a subformula-minded proof of S, but also for one in which every entry boasts at least one succedent formula.

Theorem 1 and Theorem 2 in its sharper form, have interesting applications so far as the teaching of elementary logic goes.

Let a deduction of the sort conducted in §§1.2 and 2.2 of [6] count as a Fitch-deduction (of a wff of QC from a finite set of wffs of QC), and one that runs like a Fitch-deduction but in which any entry other than a premiss may consist of more than one wff, count as a generalized Fitch-deduction (of a non-empty sequence of wffs of QC from a finite set of wffs of QC). Next, let the rules in Table 5 [Table 6] be said to permit subformula-minded deduction of a wff B of QC from a set $\{A_1, A_2, \ldots, A_n\}$ ($n \geq 0$) of wffs of QC if: (i) there exists a Fitch-deduction [generalized Fitch-deduction] of B from $\{A_1, A_2, \ldots, A_n\}$ by means of rules from that table, and (ii) every entry [every wff in every entry] in the deduction counts as a subformula of one or more of $A_1, A_2, \ldots, A_n, B$. Lastly, let B be said to be classically implied (C-implied, for short) by $\{A_1, A_2, \ldots, A_n\}$ if the N-sequent $A_1, A_2, \ldots, A_n \to B$ is C-valid, and to be intuitionistically implied (I-implied, for short) by $\{A_1, A_2, \ldots, A_n\}$ if $A_1, A_2, \ldots, A_n \to B$ is I-valid.

Since any subformula-minded proof of $A_1, A_2, \ldots, A_n \to B$ by means of rule **R** in Table 1 and the rules of that table for '∼', '⊃', '&', '∨', '≡', '∀', and '∃' automatically converts into a subformula-minded (Fitch-) deduction of B from $\{A_1, A_2, \ldots, A_n\}$ by means of rules from Table 5,[22] then in view of Theorem 1 the rules of Table 5 are sure to permit subformula-minded deduction of B from $\{A_1, A_2, \ldots, A_n\}$ whenever B is I-implied by $\{A_1, A_2, \ldots, A_n\}$ and $A_1, A_2, \ldots, A_n \to B$ counts as a Gentzen N-sequent.[23] Similarly, since any subformula-minded proof of $A_1, A_2, \ldots, A_n \to B$ by means of rules **GR** and **GCut** in Table 3, and the rules of that table for '∼', '⊃', '&', '∨', '≡' '∀', and '∃', automatically converts into a subformula-minded (generalized Fitch-) deduction of B from $\{A_1, A_2, \ldots, A_n\}$ by means of rules from Table 6, then in view of Theorem 2 (as we sharpened it three paragraphs back) the rules of Table 6 are sure to permit subformula-minded deduction of B from $\{A_1, A_2, \ldots, A_n\}$ whenever B is C-implied by $\{A_1, A_2, \ldots, A_n\}$ and $A_1, A_2, \ldots, A_n \to B$ counts as a Gentzen N-sequent.

APPENDIX

Note: Unless otherwise indicated, K, L, and M in the tables that follow are to consist of zero or more wffs of QC (separated, when there are more than one, by commas); and $A(Y/X)$ is to stand to A as $C(Y/X)$ does to C on p. 359.

TABLE 1

Structural rules:

Reiteration (**R**):	$K, A, L \to A$
Thinning (**T**):	$\dfrac{K \to A}{B, K \to A}$

Permutation (**P**): $$\dfrac{K, A, B, L \to C}{K, B, A, L \to C}$$

Contraction (**C**): $$\dfrac{A, A, K \to B}{A, K \to B}$$

Cut: $$\dfrac{K, A \to B \text{ and } K \to A}{K \to B}$$

Introduction-elimination rules for '~', '⊃', '&', '∨', '≡', '∀', and '∃':

(1) For '~':

NI: $$\dfrac{K, A \to B \text{ and } K, A \to \sim B}{K \to \sim A}$$

NE: $$\dfrac{K \to A \text{ and } K \to \sim A}{K \to B}$$

(2) For '⊃':

HI: $$\dfrac{K, A \to B}{K \to A \supset B}$$

HE: $$\dfrac{K \to A \text{ and } K \to A \supset B}{K \to B}$$

(3) For '&':

CI: $$\dfrac{K \to A \text{ and } K \to B}{K \to A \& B}$$

CE: $$\dfrac{K \to A \& B \text{ or } K \to B \& A}{K \to A}$$

(4) For '∨':

DI: $$\dfrac{K \to A \text{ or } K \to B}{K \to A \vee B}$$

DE: $$\dfrac{\text{(i) } K \to A \vee B, \text{ (ii) } K, A \to C, \text{ and (iii) } K, B \to C}{K \to C}$$

(5) For '≡':

BI: $$\dfrac{K, A \to B \text{ and } K, B \to A}{K \to A \equiv B}$$

BE: $$\dfrac{\text{(i) } K \to A \text{ and (ii) } K \to A \equiv B \text{ or } K \to B \equiv A}{K \to B}$$

(6) For '∀':

∀I: $$\dfrac{K \to A(Y/X)}{K \to (\forall X)A}$$

∀E:
$$\frac{K \to (\forall X)A}{K \to A(Y/X)}$$

(7) For '∃':

∃I:
$$\frac{K \to A(Y/X)}{K \to (\exists X)A}$$

∃E:
$$\frac{K \to (\exists X)A \text{ and } K, A(Y/X) \to B}{K \to B}$$

Restrictions: In ∀I the individual variable Y is not to occur free in $K \to (\forall X)A$; in ∃E it is not to occur free in $K \to (\exists X)A$ nor in B.

Convention: (i) Let $K \to (\forall X)A$ ($= S_i$) follow in a proof of an N-sequent S from a previous entry by application of ∀I, and let $K \to A(Y/X)$ be any entry previous to S_i from which S_i follows by application of ∀I; then Y is to count as a *universalization variable* for S_i in the proof of S. (ii) Let $K \to B$ ($= S_i$) follow in a proof of an N-sequent S from two previous entries by application of ∃E, and let $K \to (\exists X)A$ and $K, A(Y/X) \to B$ be any pair of entries previous to S_i from which S_i follows by application of ∃E; then Y is to count as a *deëxistentialization variable* for S_i in the proof of S.

TABLE 2

Note: In this table L^* is to consist of at most one wff.

Structural rules:
Specialized Reiteration (**SR**): $A \to A$.

Thinning: to the left (**Tl**): $\qquad\qquad\qquad$ to the right (**Tr**):

$$\frac{K \to L^*}{A, K \to L^*} \qquad\qquad \frac{K \to}{K \to A}.$$

Permutation to the left (**Pl**):

$$\frac{K, A, B, K' \to L^*}{K, B, A, K' \to L^*}.$$

Contraction to the left (**Cl**):

$$\frac{A, A, K \to L^*}{A, K \to L^*}.$$

Introduction rules:

(1) For '~':

$\qquad\qquad$ to the left (**Nll**): $\qquad\qquad\qquad$ to the right (**Nlr**):

$$\frac{K \to A}{\sim A, K \to} \qquad\qquad \frac{A, K \to}{K \to \sim A}$$

(2) For '⊃':

to the left (**HIl**):

$$\frac{K \to A \text{ and } B, K' \to L^*}{A \supset B, K, K' \to L^*}$$

to the right (**HIr**):

$$\frac{A, K \to B}{K \to A \supset B} \, .$$

(3) For '&':

to the left (**CIl**):

$$\frac{A, K \to L^* \text{ or } B, K \to L^*}{A \& B, K \to L^*}$$

to the right (**CIr**):

$$\frac{K \to A \text{ and } K \to B}{K \to A \& B} \, .$$

(4) For '∨':

to the left (**DIl**):

$$\frac{A, K \to L^* \text{ and } B, K \to L^*}{A \lor B, K \to L^*}$$

to the right (**DIr**):

$$\frac{K \to A \text{ or } K \to B}{K \to A \lor B} \, .$$

(5) For '≡':

to the left (**BIl**):

$$\frac{\text{(i) } K \to A \text{ and } B, K' \to L^* \text{ or (ii) } K \to B \text{ and } A, K' \to L^*}{A \equiv B, K, K' \to L^*} \, .$$

to the right (**BIr**):

$$\frac{A, K \to B \text{ and } B, K \to A}{K \to A \equiv B} \, .$$

(6) For '∀':

to the left (**∀Il**):

$$\frac{A(Y/X), K \to L^*}{(\forall X)A, K \to L^*}$$

to the right (**∀Ir**):

$$\frac{K \to A(Y/X)}{K \to (\forall X)A} \, .$$

(7) For '∃':

to the left (**∃Il**):

$$\frac{A(Y/X), K \to L^*}{(\exists X)A, K \to L^*}$$

to the right (**∃Ir**):

$$\frac{K \to A(Y/X)}{K \to (\exists X)A} \, .$$

Restrictions: In **∀Ir** the individual variable Y is not to occur free in $K \to (\forall X)A$; in **∃Il** it is not to occur free in $(\exists X)A, K \to L^*$.

Convention: Let $(\exists X)A, K \to L^*$ follow in a proof of an N-sequent S from a previous entry by application of **∃Il**, and let $A(Y/X), K \to L^*$ be any entry previous to S_i from which S_i follows by application of **∃Il**; then Y is to count as an existentialization variable for S_i in the proof of S.

TABLE 3

Note: In this table, the next, and the last, '**G**' is short for 'Generalized'.
Structural rules:

GR: $\qquad K, A, L \to M, A, N.$

GTI: $\qquad \dfrac{K \to L}{A, K \to L}$.

GPI: $\qquad \dfrac{K, A, B, L \to M}{K, B, A, L \to M}$.

GCut: $\qquad \dfrac{K, A \to L \text{ and } K \to A, L}{K \to L}$.

Introduction-elimination rules:

(1) For '~':

GNI: $\qquad \dfrac{K, A \to L, M}{K \to L, \sim A, M}$

GNE: $\qquad \dfrac{K \to L, A, M \text{ and } K \to L, \sim A, M}{K \to L, M}$.

(2) For '⊃':

GHI: $\qquad \dfrac{K, A \to L, B, M}{K \to L, A \supset B, M}$.

GHE: $\qquad \dfrac{K \to L, A, M \text{ and } K \to L, A \supset B, M}{K \to L, B, M}$.

(3) For '&':

GCI: $\qquad \dfrac{K \to L, A, M \text{ and } K \to L, B, M}{K \to L, A \,\&\, B, M}$.

GCE: $\qquad \dfrac{K \to L, A \,\&\, B, M \text{ or } K \to L, B \,\&\, A, M}{K \to L, A, M}$.

(4) For '∨':

GDI: $\qquad \dfrac{K \to L, A, M \text{ or } K \to L, B, M}{K \to L, A \lor B, M}$.

GDE: $\dfrac{\text{(i) } K \to L, A \lor B, M, \text{ (ii) } K, A \to L, M, \text{ and (iii) } K, B \to L, M}{K \to L, M}$.

(5) For '≡':

GBI: $\qquad \dfrac{K, A \to L, B, M \text{ and } K, B \to L, A, M}{K \to L, A \equiv B, M}$.

GBE: $\dfrac{\text{(i) } K \to L, A, M \text{ and (ii) } K \to L, A \equiv B, M \text{ or } K \to L, B \equiv A, M}{K \to L, B, M}$.

(6) For '$\forall$':

$\quad$ **G$\forall$I:** $\qquad\qquad\qquad\qquad$ **G$\forall$E:**

$\quad \dfrac{K \to L, A(Y/X), M}{K \to L, (\forall X)A, M} \qquad\qquad \dfrac{K \to L, (\forall X)A, M}{K \to L, A(Y/X), M}$.

(7) For '$\exists$':

$\quad$ **G$\exists$I:** $\qquad\qquad\qquad\qquad$ **G$\exists$E:**

$\quad \dfrac{K \to L, A(Y/X), M}{K \to L, (\exists X)A, M} \qquad \dfrac{K \to L, (\exists X)A, M \text{ and } K, A(Y/X) \to L, M}{K \to L, M}$.

Restrictions: In **G$\forall$I** the individual variable Y is not to occur free in $K \to L$, $(\forall X)A, M$; in **G$\exists$E** it is not to occur free in $K \to L, (\exists X)A, M$.
Convention: (i) Let $K \to L, (\forall X)A, M$ ($= S_i$) follow in a proof of an N-sequent S from a previous entry by application of **G$\forall$I**, and let $K \to L$, $A(Y/X), M$ be any entry previous to S_i from which S_i follows by application of **G$\forall$I**; then Y is to count as a universalization variable for S_i in the proof of S. (ii) Let $K \to L, M$ ($= S_i$) follow in a proof of an N-sequent S from two previous entries by application of **G$\exists$E**, and let $K \to L, (\exists X)A, M$ and $K, A(Y/X) \to L, M$ be any pair of entries previous to S_i from which S_i follows by application of **G$\exists$E**; then Y is to count as a deëxistentialization variable for S_i in the proof of S.

TABLE 4

Structural rules:

GR: $\qquad\qquad K, A, L \to M, A, N$.

Introduction rules:

(1) For '$\sim$', '$\supset$', '&', and '$\vee$': Same as *9 (rechristened **GNII**), *8 ($=$ **GNIr**), *3 ($=$ **GHII**), *2 ($=$ **GHIr**), *5 ($=$ **GCII**), *4 ($=$ **GCIr**), *7 ($=$ **GDII**), and *6 ($=$ **GDIr**) on p. 17 of [4], but minus such (Greek) letters as are declared superfluous on p. 18.
(2) For '$\equiv$':

GBII: $\qquad \dfrac{K, A, B, L \to M \text{ and } K, L \to A, B, M}{K, A \equiv B, L \to M}$.

GBIr: $\qquad \dfrac{A, K \to L, B, M \text{ and } B, K \to L, A, M}{K \to L, A \equiv B, M}$.

(3) For '∀':

G∀Il: $\dfrac{K, A(Y/X), (\forall X)A, L \to M}{K, (\forall X)A, L \to M}$.

G∀Ir: $\dfrac{K \to L, A(Y/X), M}{K \to L, (\forall X)A, M}$.

(4) For '∃':

G∃Il: $\dfrac{K, A(Y/X), L \to M}{K, (\exists X)A, L \to M}$.

G∃Ir: $\dfrac{K \to L, A(Y/X), (\exists X)A, M}{K \to L, (\exists X)A, M}$.

Restrictions: In **G∀Ir** the individual variable Y is not to occur free in $K \to L$, $(\forall X)A, M$; and in **G∃Il** it is not to occur free in $K, (\exists X)A, L \to M$.

TABLE 5

The table is to consist of **R** on p. 354 of [7], ⊃**E** and ⊃**I** (called here **HE** and **HI**) on p. 354, ~**I** (called here **NI**) on p. 354, &**E** and &**I** (called here **CE** and **CI**) on p. 355, ∨**E** and ∨**I** (called here (**DE** and **DI**) on p. 344, ≡**E** and ≡**I** (called here **BE** and **BI**) on p. 356, plus the following five rules:

NE:
```
1 | A₁
2 | A₂
⋮ | ⋮
n | Aₙ
⋮ | ⋮
p | B
⋮ | ⋮
q | ~B
⋮ | ⋮
r | C   (NE, p, q)
```

∀I:
```
1 | A₁
2 | A₂
⋮ | ⋮
n | Aₙ
⋮ | ⋮
p | B(Y/X)
⋮ | ⋮
q | (∀X)B   (∀I, p)
```

∀E:
```
1 | A₁
2 | A₂
⋮ | ⋮
n | Aₙ
⋮ | ⋮
p | (∀X)B
⋮ | ⋮
q | B(Y/X)   (∀E, p)
```

∃I: 1 | A_1 ∃E: 1 | A_1
     2 | A_2 2 | A_2
     ⋮ | ⋮   ⋮ | ⋮
     n | A_n n | A_n
     ⋮ | ⋮   ⋮ | ⋮
     p | $B(Y/X)$ p | $(\exists X)B$
     ⋮ | ⋮   ⋮ |
     q | $(\exists X)B$ (∃I, p)   q | | $B(Y/X)$
                                          | | ⋮
                                        r | | C
                                    r + 1 | C (∃E, p, q, r)

Restrictions: In ∀I the individual variable Y is not to occur free in any one of $A_1, A_2, \ldots, A_n$, $(\forall X)B$; in ∃E it is not to occur free in any one of $A_1, A_2, \ldots, A_n$, $(\exists X)B$, C.

TABLE 6

Note: In rule **GCut** of this table K is to consist of one or more wffs; in rules **GNI**, **GNE**, **GDE**, and **G∃E** K or L is to consist of one or more wffs.

GR: 1 | A_1 GCut: 1 | A_1
     2 | A_2 2 | A_2
     ⋮ | ⋮   ⋮ | ⋮
     n | A_n n | A_n
     ⋮ | ⋮   ⋮ | ⋮
     p | K, A_i, L (**GR**, i)   p | B, K
                                        ⋮ |
                                        q | | B
                                          | | ⋮
                                        r | | K
                                    r + 1 | K (**GCut**, p, q, r)

GNI: 1 | A_1 GNE: 1 | A_1
     2 | A_2 2 | A_2
     ⋮ | ⋮   ⋮ | ⋮
     n | A_n n | A_n
     ⋮ | ⋮   ⋮ | ⋮
     p | | B p | K, B, L
     ⋮ | | ⋮   q | $K, \sim B, L$
     q | | K, L ⋮ | ⋮
 q + 1 | $K, \sim B, L$ (**GNI**, p, q) r | K, L (**GNE**, p, q)

378   Part 3: Provability

GHI:
$$
\begin{array}{l|l}
1 & A_1 \\
2 & A_2 \\
\vdots & \vdots \\
n & A_n \\
\hline
\vdots & \vdots \\
p & \quad\begin{array}{l|l} & B \\ & \vdots \\ & K, C, L \end{array} \\
\vdots \\
q \\
q+1 & K, B \supset C, L \quad (\textbf{GHI}, p, q)
\end{array}
$$

GHE:
$$
\begin{array}{l|l}
1 & A_1 \\
2 & A_2 \\
\vdots & \vdots \\
n & A_n \\
\hline
\vdots & \vdots \\
p & K, B, L \\
\vdots & \vdots \\
q & K, B \supset C, L \\
\vdots & \vdots \\
r & K, C, L \quad (\textbf{GHE}, p, q)
\end{array}
$$

GCI:
$$
\begin{array}{l|l}
1 & A_1 \\
2 & A_2 \\
\vdots & \vdots \\
n & A_n \\
\hline
\vdots & \vdots \\
p & K, B, L \\
\vdots & \vdots \\
q & K, C, L \\
\vdots & \vdots \\
r & K, B \,\&\, C, L \quad (\textbf{GCI}, p, q)
\end{array}
$$

GCE:
$$
\begin{array}{l|l}
1 & A_1 \\
2 & A_2 \\
\vdots & \vdots \\
n & A_n \\
\hline
\vdots & \vdots \\
p & K, B \,\&\, C, L \text{ or } K, C \,\&\, B, L \\
\vdots & \vdots \\
q & K, B, L \quad (\textbf{GCE}, p)
\end{array}
$$

GDI:
$$
\begin{array}{l|l}
1 & A_1 \\
2 & A_2 \\
\vdots & \vdots \\
n & A_n \\
\hline
\vdots & \vdots \\
p & K, B, L, \text{ or } K, C, L \\
\vdots & \vdots \\
q & K, B \vee C, L \quad (\textbf{GDI}, p)
\end{array}
$$

GDE:
$$
\begin{array}{l|l}
1 & A_1 \\
2 & A_2 \\
\vdots & \vdots \\
n & A_n \\
\hline
\vdots & \vdots \\
p & K, B \vee C, L \\
q & \quad\begin{array}{l|l} & B \\ & \vdots \\ & K, L \end{array} \\
\vdots \\
r \\
r+1 & \quad\begin{array}{l|l} & C \\ & \vdots \\ & K, L \end{array} \\
\vdots \\
s \\
s+1 & K, L \quad (\textbf{GDE}, p, q, r, r+1,
\end{array}
$$

GBI:
$$\begin{array}{c|l}
1 & A_1 \\
2 & A_2 \\
\vdots & \vdots \\
n & A_n \\
\hline
\vdots & \vdots \\
p & \quad\;\; B \\
\vdots & \vdots \\
q & \quad\;\; K, C, L \\
q+1 & \quad\;\; C \\
\vdots & \vdots \\
r & \quad\;\; K, B, L \\
r+1 & K, B \equiv C, L \quad (\textbf{GBI}, p, q, q+1, r)
\end{array}$$

GBE:
$$\begin{array}{c|l}
1 & A_1 \\
2 & A_2 \\
\vdots & \vdots \\
n & A_n \\
\hline
\vdots & \vdots \\
p & K, B, L \\
\vdots & \vdots \\
q & K, B \equiv C, L \text{ or } K, C \equiv B, L \\
\vdots & \vdots \\
r & K, C, L \quad (\textbf{GBE}, p, q)
\end{array}$$

G∀I:
$$\begin{array}{c|l}
1 & A_1 \\
2 & A_2 \\
\vdots & \vdots \\
n & A_n \\
\hline
\vdots & \vdots \\
p & K, B(Y/X), L \\
\vdots & \vdots \\
q & K, (\forall X)B, L \quad (\textbf{G}\forall\textbf{I}, p)
\end{array}$$

G∀E:
$$\begin{array}{c|l}
1 & A_1 \\
2 & A_2 \\
\vdots & \vdots \\
n & A_n \\
\hline
\vdots & \vdots \\
p & K, (\forall X)B, L \\
\vdots & \vdots \\
q & K, B(Y/X), L \quad (\textbf{G}\forall\textbf{E}, p)
\end{array}$$

G∃I:
$$\begin{array}{c|l}
1 & A_1 \\
2 & A_2 \\
\vdots & \vdots \\
n & A_n \\
\hline
\vdots & \vdots \\
p & K, B(Y/X), L \\
\vdots & \vdots \\
q & K, (\exists X)B, L \quad (\textbf{G}\exists\textbf{I}, p)
\end{array}$$

G∃E:
$$\begin{array}{c|l}
1 & A_1 \\
2 & A_2 \\
\vdots & \vdots \\
n & A_n \\
\hline
\vdots & \vdots \\
p & K, (\exists X)B, L \\
\vdots & \vdots \\
q & \quad\;\; B(Y/X) \\
\vdots & \vdots \\
r & \quad\;\; K, L \\
r+1 & K, L \quad (\textbf{G}\exists\textbf{E}, p, q, r)
\end{array}$$

Restrictions: In **G∀I** the individual variable Y is not to occur free in any one of $A_1, A_2, \ldots, A_n$, nor in $K, (\forall X)B, L$; in **G∃E** it is not to occur free in any one of $A_1, A_2, \ldots,$ and A_n, nor in $K, (\exists X)B, L$.

380   *Part 3: Provability*

Notes

1. L-sequents were first introduced by Gentzen in [2]. As L-sequents of a sort, N-sequents ('N' as in 'Natural Deduction') already figure in [2]; their first solo appearance, however, is in [3].

2. For an account of intuitionistic validity, see [5].

3. Tables 1 to 6 will be found in the Appendix. For Gentzen's account of a deduction see [2]. A subformula-minded deduction of a wff A is one in which every wff in every branch of the deduction is a subformula of A. Gentzen explicitly bars an individual variable from appearing both bound and free in the same formula; as a result, the restriction "in which no individual variable of QC occurs both bound and free" is omitted in [2].

4. As one glance at the rules in Table 1 will reveal, any proof of an N-sequent S of QC by means of these rules is sure to count as an N-proof of S. The rules in Table 1 are in large part adapted from rules in [3], and those in Table 3 are in large part straightforward generalizations of their counterparts in Table 1. Some occurrences of 'L', and some of 'M', in Table 3 (and Table 6) are superfluous, but they make for simpler proofs of Lemmas 3 and 4 below.

5. Needing the label '**Cut**' in Table 1 and the label '**GCut**' in Table 3, we refer to Gentzen's own Cut rule by its German name.

6. Except **BIl** and **BIr** (Gentzen treats a wff of the sort $A \equiv B$ as short for one of the sort $(A \supset B) \& (B \supset A)$), the rules in Table 2 come from [2].

7. Gentzen's original result does not cover N-sequents that contain '$\equiv$'. It is easily extended, though, to cover them as well (a point noted in [1]), once **BIl** and **BIr** (or equivalents thereof) are drafted as introduction rules for '$\equiv$'. Since Gentzen tacitly bars an individual variable from occurring both bound and free in the same N-sequent, he talks of (N-)sequents where I talk of Gentzen N-sequents.

8. As the reader may verify, deleting from a proof of S (by means of rules from Table 2) any entry with an antecedent or a succedent formula that does not count as a subformula of any antecedent or any succedent formula of S, is sure to make for a subformula-minded proof of S (by means of rules from Table 2).

9. Note that rules **CIr**, **DIr**, **∀Ir**, and **∃Ir** in Table 2 respectively coincide with rules **CI**, **DI**, **∀I**, and **∃I** in Table 1 and that under the circumstances obtaining here rules **Pl** and **Cl** in Table 2 respectively coincide with rules **P** and **C** in Table 1.

10. In case K' consists of a non-zero number, say, p, of wffs, then entry i.1 has to be understood as short for $p + 1$ entries, each one following from the previous one by application of **T**. A like remark applies at many subsequent points.

11. In case either one of K and K' consists of zero wffs, then entry i.2 is redundant; in case both K and K' consist of a non-zero number of wffs, p in one case and q in the other, then entry i.2 has to be understood as short for $p \times q$ entries.

12. In case every existentialization variable for S_i in the proof of S occurs free in S, select any previous entry $A(Y/X)$, $K \to L^*$ ($= S_h$) from which S_i follows by application of **∃Il**, select among the columns made up of one or more of the first h entries in the proof of S any one that counts as a subformula-minded proof of S_h by means of rules from Table 2, and—Z being any individual variable of QC that is foreign to the proof of S—replace by an occurrence of Z every free occurrence of Y in the column. Inserting the resulting column between, say, S_{i-1} and S_i is sure to make for a subformula-minded proof of S by means of rules from Table 2 such that at least one universalization variable for S_i does not occur free in S.

13. Note that if a given entry S_i follows in the proof of S by application of **Tr** from a previous entry $K \to$, and hence is of the sort $K \to B$, then the two stand-ins $K \to A'$ and $K \to \sim A'$ of $K \to$ automatically yield S_i by application of **NI**. Hence only applications of **NIl** and **NIr** in the proof of S call for special attention here.

14. Note indeed that if a given entry of the sort $(\exists X)B$, $K \to$ follows in the proof of S from a previous entry by application of **∃Il**, there is sure to be a previous entry $B(Y/X)$, $K \to$ such that Y does not occur free in $\sim A'$, and hence $(\exists X)B$, $K \to A'$ and $(\exists X)B$, $K \to \sim A'$ are sure to follow from $B(Y/X)$, $K \to A'$ and $B(Y/X), K \to \sim A'$, respectively, by application of **∃Il**. This because at

least one existentialization variable for $B(Y/X)$, $K \to$ is presumed not to occur free in S (nor, as a result, in $\sim A'$).

15. See in this connection Note 12, which is easily extended to suit the present case.

16. Where S is an N-sequent of QC and $S(Y/X)$ is like S except for containing free occurrences of Y wherever S contains free occurrences of X, let $S(Y/X)$ be said to follow from S by application of rule **S** ('S' for 'Substitution'). It is readily checked that, if S is an I-valid N-sequent of QC not of the Gentzen sort, then there exists an N-sequent S' of QC of the Gentzen sort such that: (i) rule **R** in Table 1, and the rules of that table for '$\sim$', '$\supset$', '&', '$\vee$', '$\equiv$', '$\forall$', and '$\exists$', permit subformula-minded proof of S' (this of course because of Theorem 1, and (ii) S follows from S' by repeated applications of rule **S**.

17. Except **GBII** and **GRIr** (to be found in [1]), the rules in Table 4 come from [4].

18. Kanger's result does not cover L-sequents that contain occurrences of '$\equiv$'. It is easily extended, though, to cover them as well, once **GBII** and **GBIr** (or equivalents thereof) are drafted as introduction rules for '$\equiv$'. Since Kanger explicitly bars an individual variable from occurring both bound and free in the same L-sequent (individual constants, which in Kanger play one of the roles played here by individual variables, may occur in an L-sequent of [4], but they are never quantified, of course), he talks of (L-)sequents where I talk of Gentzen L-sequents.

19. Note that rules **GCIr** and **G$\forall$Ir** in Table 4 respectively coincide with rules **GCI** and **G$\forall$I** in Table 3.

20. It is readily checked that, if S is a C-valid N-sequent of QC not of the Gentzen sort, then there exists an N-sequent S' of QC of the Gentzen sort such that: (i) rules **GR** and **GCut** in Table 3, and the rules of that table for '$\sim$', '$\supset$', '&', '$\vee$', '$\equiv$', '$\forall$', and '$\exists$', permit subformula-minded proof of S' (this because of Theorem 2), and (ii) S follows from S' by repeated applications of rule **S** in Note 16. The reasoning employed on p. 364–65 to eliminate applications of **Cut** does not extend to applications of **GCut**. Whether **GCut** can be struck from the list of rules in Theorem 2 is an open question.

21. Note that $K' \to A'$, $\sim B$ and $K' \to \sim A'$, $\sim B$ follow from the two stand-ins K', $B \to A'$ and K', $B \to \sim A'$ of K', $B \to$ by application of **GNI**, and yield $K' \to \sim B$ by application of **GNE**.

22. See [6], pp. 31–32 and p. 114, for examples.

23. A like result will be found in [8] for the case where $A_1, A_2, \ldots, A_n, B$ contain no '$\sim$' nor '$\equiv$' (Prawitz, who covers the case where at least one of $A_1, A_2, \ldots, A_n, B$ contains the propositional constant 'f', treats $\sim A$ as short for $A \supset$ f and $A \equiv B$ as short for $(A \supset B) \& (B \supset A)$). Prawitz' proof (a more direct one than mine, incidentally, whereby any (Fitch-) deduction of B from $\{A_1, A_2, \ldots, A_n\}$ by means of the rules on p. 20 of [7] is made subformula-minded) is easily extended to cover the missing cases, once suitable rules for '$\sim$' and '$\equiv$' are supplied.

References

[1] Bernays, P. 1965. "Betrachtungen zum Sequenzen-Kalkul." *Contributions to Logic and Methodology in Honor of J. M. Bochenski*, pp. 1–44. Amsterdam: North-Holland.

[2] Gentzen, G. 1934. "Untersuchungen über das logische Schliessen." *Mathematische Zeitschrift* 39: 176–210, 403–31.

[3] ———. 1936. "Die Widerspruchsfreiheit des reinen Zahlentheorie." *Mathematische Annalen* 112: 493–565.

[4] Kanger, S. 1957. *Provability in Logic*. Stockholm: Almquist and Wiksell.

[5] Kripke, S. A. 1965. "Semantical Analysis of Intuitionistic Logic I." *Formal Systems and Recursive Functions*, pp. 92–130. Amsterdam: North-Holland.

[6] Leblanc, H. 1966. *Techniques of Deductive Inference*. Englewood Cliffs: Prentice-Hall.

[7] Leblanc, H. and Wisdom, W. A. 1972. *Deductive Logic*. Boston: Allyn and Bacon.

[8] Prawitz, D. 1965. *Natural Deduction, A Proof-Theoretical Study*. Stockholm: Almquist and Wiksell.

27

A Note on the Intuitionist and the Classical Propositional Calculus

E. W. Beth, coauthor

Consider the following version of PC, the propositional calculus:
(a) The primitive signs of PC are to be: a denumerably infinite list of propositional variables, the two connectives '$\sim$' and '$\supset$', and the two parentheses '(' and ')';
(b) The formulas of PC, referred to hereafter by means of 'A', 'B', 'C', and 'D', are to be all infinite sequences of primitive signs of PC;
(c) The well-formed formulas (wffs) of PC are to be: all propositional variables, all formulas of the form $\sim A$, where A is a wff of PC, and all formulas of the form $(A \supset B)$, where A and B are wffs of PC.

It is known that all the wffs of PC which are intuitionistically valid can be obtained by means of the following rules, the first four of which are structural rules, the last four elimination and introduction rules:

R1. $A \vdash A$ (Reflexivity);

R2. If $A_1, A_2, \ldots, A_n \vdash B$, then $A_1, A_2, \ldots, A_{n+1} \vdash B$ (Thinning);

R3. If $A_1, A_2, \ldots, A_n \vdash B$, then $A_i, A_2, \ldots, A_{i-1}, A_1, A_{i+1}, \ldots, A_n \vdash B$ (Permutation);

R4. If $A_1, A_2, \ldots, A_n \vdash A_{n+1}$ and $A_1, A_2, \ldots, A_{n+1} \vdash B$, then $A_1, A_2, \ldots, A_n \vdash B$ (Cut);

R5. $A, \sim A \vdash B$ (Weak elimination rule for '$\sim$');

R6. If $A_1, A_2, \ldots, A_{n+1} \vdash B$ and $A_1, A_2, \ldots, A_{n+1} \vdash \sim B$, then $A_1, A_2, \ldots, A_n \vdash \sim A_{n+1}$ (Introduction rule for '$\sim$');

R7. $A, A \supset B \vdash B$ (Weak elimination rule for '$\supset$');

R8. If $A_1, A_2, \ldots, A_{n+1} \vdash B$, then $A_1, A_2, \ldots, A_n \vdash A_{n+1} \supset B$ (Introduction rule for '$\supset$').[1]

It is also known that all the wffs of PC which are classically valid can be obtained by means of **R1–R4, R6–R8**, and the following elimination rule for '∼':

R5. ∼∼A ⊢ A (Strong elimination rule for '∼').

We wish to prove here that the self-same wffs, that is, the wffs of PC which are classically valid, can be obtained by means of **R1–R6, R8**, and the following elimination rule for '⊃':

R7'. A ⊃ B, (A ⊃ C) ⊃ A ⊢ B (Strong elimination rule for '⊃').[2]

We first prove that **R7** follows from **R1–R6, R7'**, and **R8**.

R7. A, A ⊃ B ⊢ B.

(1) A, A ⊃ B, A ⊃ B ⊢ A	(R1, R2)
(2) A, A ⊃ B ⊢ (A ⊃ B) ⊃ A	(R8, 1)
(3) A, A ⊃ B, (A ⊃ B) ⊃ A ⊢ B	(R7', R2, R3)
(4) A, A ⊃ B ⊢ B	(R4, 2, 3)[3]

We next prove that **R5'** follow from **R1–R6, R7'**, and **R8**.

R5'. ∼∼A ⊢ A.

(1) A ⊃ ∼A, A ⊢ A	(R1, R2, R3)
(2) A ⊃ ∼A, A ⊢ ∼A	(R7, R3)[4]
(3) A ⊃ ∼A ⊢ ∼A	(R6, 1, 2)
(4) ∼∼A, A ⊃ ∼A ⊢ ∼A	(R2, R3, 3)
(5) ∼∼A, A ⊃ ∼A ⊢ ∼∼A	(R1, R2)
(6) ∼∼A ⊢ ∼(A ⊃ ∼A)	(R6, 4, 5)
(7) ∼∼A, A ⊃ ∼A ⊢ ∼(A ⊃ ∼A)	(R2, 6)
(8) ∼∼A, A ⊃ ∼A, ∼(A ⊃ ∼A) ⊢ A	(R5, R2, R3)
(9) ∼∼A, A ⊃ ∼A ⊢ A	(R4, 7, 8)
(10) ∼∼A ⊢ (A ⊃ ∼A) ⊃ A	(R8, 9)
(11) ∼∼A, (A ⊃ ∼A) ⊃ A, A ⊃ A ⊢ A	(R7', R2, R3)
(12) ∼∼A, (A ⊃ ∼A) ⊃ A ⊢ A ⊃ A	(R1, R8, R2, R3)
(13) ∼∼A, (A ⊃ ∼A) ⊃ A ⊢ A	(R4, 11, 12)
(14) ∼∼A ⊢ A	(R4, 10, 13)

The result we have just obtained may throw additional light on the relationship between the classical propositional calculus and the intuitionist one.

384   *Part 3: Provability*

The classical propositional calculus has frequently been described as an intuitionist propositional calculus with a strengthened elimination rule for '∼'. In view of our result the classical propositional calculus may likewise be described as an intuitionist propositional calculus with a strengthened elimination rule for '⊃'.

Notes

1. Throughout the above rules n may of course be equal to 0 as well as larger than 0.
2. **R7'** was suggested to me by Stig Kanger. For additional information concerning the rule, see papers 21, 23, 24, and 25 in this volume.
3. The above proof of **R7** was suggested to me by Stig Kanger.
4. Use of **R7** is legitimate here, as **R7** has already been shown to follow from **R1–R6, R7'**, and **R8**.

28
Intuitionism Reconsidered
N. D. Belnap, Jr., coauthor

It has long been known that standard Gentzen rules of inference for PC_I, the intuitionist propositional calculus, will do for PC_C, the classical propositional calculus, once the intuitionist elimination rule for '$\sim$', namely:

NE_I: $A, \sim A \vdash B$,

is strengthened to read:

NE_C: $\sim\sim A \vdash A$.

It has recently been shown that the said rules will also do for PC_C once the intuitionist elimination rule for '$\supset$', namely:

HE_I: $A, A \supset B \vdash B$,

is strengthened to read:

HE_C: $A \supset B, (A \supset C) \supset A \vdash B$.[1]

We shall now show that the said rules will finally do for PC_C once the intuitionist elimination rule for '$\equiv$', namely:

BE_I: (a) $A, A \equiv B \vdash B$

  (b) $A, B \equiv A \vdash B$,

is strengthened to read:

BE_C: (a) $A, (C \equiv A) \equiv (C \equiv B) \vdash B$

  (b) $A, (C \equiv B) \equiv (C \equiv A) \vdash B$.

The debate between intuitionist logic and classical logic, a debate which originally centered around '$\sim$' and has more recently come to center around '$\supset$', can thus be made to center around '$\equiv$' as well. Details are as follows.

Let all five of '$\supset$', '$\sim$', '&', '$\vee$', and '$\equiv$' serve as primitive connectives of PC_C; let 'A', 'B', and 'C' range over the well-formed formulas of PC_C; let 'A_1, $A_2, \ldots, A_n \vdash B$', where $n > 0$, be short for 'B is deducible in PC_C from the

385

sequence made up of the wffs $A_1, A_2, \ldots$, and A_n in that order'; let '⊢ A' be short for 'A is deducible in PC_C from the null sequence of wffs'; and, finally, let '⊢' obey the following rules, where $n \geq 0$.

Structural Rules

R: $A \vdash A$ (Reflexivity);

P: If $A_1, A_2, \ldots, A_{i-1}, A_i, A_{i+1}, A_{i+2}, \ldots, A_n, A_{n+1}, A_{n+2} \vdash B$, then $A_1, A_2, \ldots, A_{i-1}, A_{i+1}, A_i, A_{i+2}, \ldots, A_n, A_{n+1}, A_{n+2} \vdash B$, where $i \leq n+1$ (Permutation);

T: If $A_1, A_2, \ldots, A_n \vdash B$, then $A_{n+1}, A_1, A_2, \ldots, A_n \vdash B$ (Thinning);

C: If $A_1, A_2, \ldots, A_n, A_{n+1} \vdash B$ and $A_1, A_2, \ldots, A_n \vdash A_{n+1}$, then $A_1, A_2, \ldots, A_n \vdash B$ (Cut).

Elimination and Introduction Rules

HE$_I$: $A, A \supset B \vdash B$ (Intuitionist elimination rule for '$\supset$');

HI: If $A_1, A_2, \ldots, A_n, A_{n+1} \vdash B$, then $A_1, A_2, \ldots, A_n \vdash A_{n+1} \supset B$ (Introduction rule for '$\supset$');

NE$_I$: $A, \sim A \vdash B$ (Intuitionist elimination rule for '$\sim$');

NI: If $A_1, A_2, \ldots, A_n, A_{n+1} \vdash B$ and $A_1, A_2, \ldots, A_n, A_{n+1} \vdash \sim B$, then $A_1, A_2, \ldots, A_n \vdash \sim A_{n+1}$ (Introduction rule for '$\sim$');

CE: (a) $A \& B \vdash A$, (b) $A \& B \vdash B$ (Elimination rule for '&');

CI: If $A_1, A_2, \ldots, A_n \vdash B$ and $A_1, A_2, \ldots, A_n \vdash C$, then $A_1, A_2, \ldots, A_n \vdash B \& C$ (Introduction rule for '&');

DE: If $A_1, A_2, \ldots, A_n, A_{n+1} \vdash B$ and $A_1, A_2, \ldots, A_n, A_{n+2} \vdash B$, then $A_1, A_2, \ldots, A_n, A_{n+1} \lor A_{n+2} \vdash B$ (Elimination rule for '$\lor$');

DI: (a) $A \vdash A \lor B$, (b) $B \vdash A \lor B$ (Introduction rule for '$\lor$');

BE$_C$: (a) $A, (C \equiv A) \equiv (C \equiv B) \vdash B$, (b) $A, (C \equiv B) \equiv (C \equiv A) \vdash B$ (Elimination rule for '$\equiv$');

BI: If $A_1, A_2, \ldots, A_n, B \vdash C$ and $A_1, A_2, \ldots, A_n, C \vdash B$, then $A_1, A_2, \ldots, A_n \vdash B \equiv C$ (Introduction rule for '$\equiv$').

The following lemmas are then provable:

Lemma 1. $A, A \equiv B \vdash B$ (**BE$_I$**(a)).

1	$A \vdash A$	(**R**)
2	$\vdash A \equiv A$	(**BI**, 1, 1)
3	$A \equiv B \vdash A \equiv A$	(**T**, 2)

4	$A \equiv B, A \equiv B \vdash A \equiv A$	(T, 3)
5	$A \equiv B \vdash A \equiv B$	(R)
6	$A \equiv A, A \equiv B \vdash A \equiv B$	(T, 5)
7	$A \equiv B, A \equiv A \vdash A \equiv B$	(P, 6)
8	$A \equiv B \vdash (A \equiv A) \equiv (A \equiv B)$	(BI, 4, 7)
9	$A, A \equiv B \vdash (A \equiv A) \equiv (A \equiv B)$	(T, 8)
10	$A, (A \equiv A) \equiv (A \equiv B) \vdash B$	(BE_C(a))
11	$A \equiv B, A, (A \equiv A) \equiv (A \equiv B) \vdash B$	(T, 10)
12	$A, A \equiv B, (A \equiv A) \equiv (A \equiv B) \vdash B$	(P, 11)
13	$A, A \equiv B \vdash B$	(C, 9, 12)

Lemma 2. $A, B \equiv A \vdash B$ (BE_I(b)).

Similar proof, but using BE_C(b) instead of BE_C(a).

Lemma 3. *If* $A_1, A_2, \ldots, A_n \vdash B$ *and* $A_1, A_2, \ldots, A_n \vdash B \equiv C$, *then* $A_1, A_2, \ldots, A_n \vdash C$.

1	$B, B \equiv C \vdash C$	(Lemma 1)
2	$A_1, A_2, \ldots, A_n, B, B \equiv C \vdash C$	(T, 1)
3	$A_1, A_2, \ldots, A_n \vdash B \equiv C$	(Given)
4	$B, A_1, A_2, \ldots, A_n \vdash B \equiv C$	(T, 3)
5	$A_1, A_2, \ldots, A_n, B \vdash B \equiv C$	(P, 4)
6	$A_1, A_2, \ldots, A_n, B \vdash C$	(C, 2, 5)
7	$A_1, A_2, \ldots, A_n \vdash B$	(Given)
8	$A_1, A_2, \ldots, A_n \vdash C$	(C, 6, 7)

Lemma 4. *If* $A_1, A_2, \ldots, A_n \vdash B$ *and* $A_1, A_2, \ldots, A_n \vdash C \equiv B$, *then* $A_1, A_2, \ldots, A_n \vdash C$.

Similar proof, but using Lemma 2 instead of Lemma 1.

Lemma 5. *If* $A_1, A_2, \ldots, A_n \vdash B$ *and* $A_1, A_2, \ldots, A_n \vdash {\sim}B$, *then* $A_1, A_2, \ldots, A_n \vdash C$.

Similar proof, but using NE_I instead of Lemma 1.

Lemma 6. $\vdash (\sim A \equiv \sim\sim A) \equiv (\sim A \equiv A)$.

1	$A, \sim A \equiv A \vdash \sim A$	(Lemma 2)
2	$\sim A \equiv A, A \vdash \sim A$	(P, 1)
3	$A \vdash A$	(R)
4	$\sim A \equiv A, A \vdash A$	(T, 3)
5	$\sim A \equiv A \vdash \sim A$	(NI, 2, 4)
6	$\sim A \equiv A \vdash \sim A \equiv A$	(R)
7	$\sim A \equiv A \vdash A$	(Lemma 3, 5, 6)
8	$\sim A \equiv A \vdash \sim A \equiv \sim\sim A$	(Lemma 5, 5, 7)
9	$\sim A, \sim A \equiv \sim\sim A \vdash \sim\sim A$	(Lemma 1)
10	$\sim A \equiv \sim\sim A, \sim A \vdash \sim\sim A$	(P, 9)
11	$\sim A \vdash \sim A$	(R)
12	$\sim A \equiv \sim\sim A, \sim A \vdash \sim A$	(T, 11)
13	$\sim A \equiv \sim\sim A \vdash \sim\sim A$	(NI, 10, 12)
14	$\sim A \equiv \sim\sim A \vdash \sim A \equiv \sim\sim A$	(R)
15	$\sim A \equiv \sim\sim A \vdash \sim A$	(Lemma 4, 13, 14)
16	$\sim A \equiv \sim\sim A \vdash \sim A \equiv A$	(Lemma 5, 13, 15)
17	$\vdash (\sim A \equiv \sim\sim A) \equiv (\sim A \equiv A)$	(BI, 8, 16)

Lemma 6, plus the three rules **T**, **BE$_C$**, and **C**, now lead to the promised result:

Theorem 1. $\sim\sim A \vdash A$ (**NE$_C$**).

1	$\vdash (\sim A \equiv \sim\sim A) \equiv (\sim A \equiv A)$	(Lemma 6)
2	$\sim\sim A \vdash (\sim A \equiv \sim\sim A) \equiv (\sim A \equiv A)$	(T, 1)
3	$\sim\sim A, (\sim A \equiv \sim\sim A) \equiv (\sim A \equiv A) \vdash A$	(BE$_C$)
4	$\sim\sim A \vdash A$	(C, 2, 3)

The fourteen rules **R, P, T, C, HE$_I$, NI, NE$_I$, NI, CE, CI, DE, DI, BE$_I$**, and **BI** provide for all valid inferences in PC$_I$.[2] The self-same rules with NE$_C$ in place of NE$_I$ provide, on the other hand, for all valid inferences in PC$_C$.[3] We thus conclude in the light of Theorem 1 (and Lemmas 1 and 2) that standard Gentzen rules of inference for PC$_I$ will do for PC$_C$ once the intuitionist elimination rule for '≡' is strengthened to read like BE$_C$. We also conjecture, by the way, that any structural rule which holds in PC_C also holds in PC_I, that any elimination or introduction rule for '&' and '∨' which holds in PC_C also holds in PC_I, and hence that the only way of turning standard Gentzen rules of inference for PC_I into rules for PC_C is to strengthen the elimination or introduction rules for '∼', or those for '⊃', or those for '≡'. We cannot, however, address ourselves to that problem here.[4]

Notes

1. See [2]. Rule HE_C was suggested to me by Stig Kanger.
2. That the rules in question provide for all valid inferences in PC_I can be shown by matching them against the axioms and rules of inference of P_S^i in [3], pp. 141–42.
3. That the rules in question provide for all valid inferences in PC_C can be shown by matching them against the axioms and rules of inference of P_H in [3], pp. 140–41.
4. For proofs of these various conjectures, see [1]. As was discovered after the writing of this paper, rule $BE_C(b)$ can be dispensed with. See [4], Note 14, on the matter.

References

[1] Belnap, N. D., Jr., Leblanc, H., and Thomason, R. H. 1963. "On Not Strengthening Intuitionistic Logic." *Notre Dame Journal of Formal Logic* (hereafter *NDJFL*) 4: 310–20 (#29 in this volume).
[2] Beth, E. W., and Leblanc, H. 1960. "A Note on the Intuitionist and the Classical Propositional Calculus." *Logique et Analyse* 11–12: 174–75 (#27 in this volume).
[3] Church, A. 1956. *Introduction to Mathematical Logic, Volume I*. Princeton: Princeton University Press.
[4] Leblanc, H. 1966. "Two Separation Theorems for Natural Deduction." *NDJFL* 7: 159–80 (#24 in this volume).

29

On Not Strengthening Intuitionistic Logic

N. D. Belnap, Jr., and R. H. Thomason, coauthors

We wish to reexamine—in the wake of [9]—the question of converting so-called *structural* and *intelim rules* for PC_I, the intuitionistic propositional calculus, into rules for PC_C, the classical one. Use will be made throughout of so-called *turnstile statements*, i.e., of expressions of the form $A_1, A_2, \ldots, A_n \vdash B$, where $A_1, A_2, \ldots, A_n$ ($n \geq 0$), and B are wffs consisting of propositional variables, zero or more of the connectives '&', 'V', '~', '⊃', and '≡', and zero or more parentheses.[1]

One can pass from PC_I to PC_C by amending the intelim rules for '~', a result of long standing, or by amending the intelim rules for either one of '⊃' and '≡', a more recent find.[2] In a talk at Yale University in 1961, however, Leblanc conjectured that amending the intelim rules for either one of '&' and 'V' will not do the trick. The point, mentioned in [6], appears as follows in [8]:

We also conjecture, by the way, that any structural rule which holds in PC_C also holds in PC_I, that any elimination or introduction rule for '&' and 'V' which holds in PC_C also holds in PC_I, and hence that the only way of turning Gentzen-like rules of inference for PC_I into rules for PC_C is to strengthen the elimination or introduction rules for '~' or those for '⊃', or those for '≡'.

Leblanc's conjecture, to which we devote the rest of this paper, has had a rather checkered career: proved true at one time or another by three different writers in two different ways, it has also been proved false once.[3] To resolve this seeming contradiction and sort out what has been proved true and what false, we shall have another look at some of the key terms in the above quotation. It will turn out that the readings of Leblanc's conjecture in [1], [4], and [9] are not quite apposite, and that of two fresh ones which we consider here one is unrestrictedly true (= Theorem 1 below), while the other holds under a slight restriction (= Theorem 2 below).

1. To simplify our analysis of the conjecture, we shall ignore the distinction between introduction and elimination rules and concentrate, for the time being, on so-called *rules for* 'V'. Under these provisos the conjecture comes to read:

Any rule for '∨' which holds in PC_C also holds in PC_I.

What, however, are we to understand by *a rule for* '∨' and what by a rule for '∨' *holding in* PC_C, PC_I, *or any calculus C*.

Two interpretations of *holding in a calculus C* suggest themselves. (i) A rule *R* might be said to hold in a calculus *C* if the conclusion of *R* is obtainable by means of the axioms and primitive rules of *C* from the premises of *R* or, to put it more briefly, if *R* is provable in *C*. (ii) A rule *R* might also be said to hold in a calculus *C* if the premises of *R* cannot be theorems of *C* without the conclusion of *R* being also a theorem of *C* or, to borrow Lorenzen's term, if *R* is *admissible* in *C*. We thus wind up with two possible readings of Leblanc's conjecture:

(1) Any rule for '∨' which is provable in PC_C is also provable in PC_I

and

(2) Any rule for '∨' which is admissible in PC_C is also admissible in PC_I.

At least three interpretations of *a rule for* '∨' come to mind. (i′) A rule *R* might be said to qualify as a rule for '∨' if *R*, thought of as a wholesale metastatement, exhibits no connective but '∨'. According to this interpretation Vesley's rule in [9] to wit:

R1: *From ⊢ A* and A,P ⊢ Q to infer ⊢ A ∨ P, where P and Q are distinct propositional variables, A contains no propositional variable but P, and A* is obtainable from A by substitution,*

counts as a rule for '∨' and is disproof of (2), as Vesley has shown. **R1**, of course, is no disproof of (1), since it is not provable in PC_C.[4] Other rules which also count as rules for '∨' according to interpretation (i′) are, however, disproofs of (1), among them:

R2: *From A ⊢ A to infer ⊢ A ∨ B, where A is a propositional variable and B consists of A and one extra sign.*[5]

Since rules such as **R1** and **R2** were definitely not contemplated by Leblanc, interpretation (i′) is out of the question and hence Vesley's reading of (2) is inapposite.

According to a second interpretation, (ii′) a rule *R* might be said to qualify as a rule for '∨' if no inference condoned by *R* exhibits any connective but '∨'. With *a rule for* '∨' thus understood, not only do **R1** and **R2** fail to pass as rules for '∨', but both (1) and (2) hold true. Proof of (1) is to be found in [1] and [4]. As for (2), it follows from a theorem of Leblanc's in [7] to the effect that any turnstile statement $A_1, A_2, \ldots, A_n \vdash B$ which exhibits no connective but '∨' is provable in PC_I if provable in PC_C.

Interpretation (ii′), however, is much too limiting, and hence the reading of

(1) in [1] and [4] is also inapposite. Consider indeed the following Gentzen-like rule for '∨'

R3: *From* $A_1, A_2, \ldots, A_n \vdash B$ *to infer* $A_1, A_2, \ldots, A_n \vdash B \vee C$ *(or $C \vee B$)*.

The rule was meant to condone such inferences as $p \vdash q \vee r$ from $p \vdash q$, which exhibit no connective but '∨'. But it was also meant to condone such inferences as $p \vdash (q \& r) \vee s$ from $p \vdash q \& r$, which, though exhibiting a connective other than '∨', exhibit it—so to speak—*inessentially*.

A third and more attractive interpretation is available, however, to wit: (iii') A rule *R* is to qualify as a rule for '∨' if every inference condoned by *R* can be gotten by substitution from some inference condoned by *R* that exhibits no connective but '∨'. With *a rule for* '∨' thus understood, **R2** (as well as **R1**) fails again to count as a rule for '∨',[6] and (1) proves to be true, as we shall demonstrate below (see Conjecture Ic). (2), on the other hand, is false. Consider indeed the rule which condones only the following two inferences:

R4: (a) *From* $\vdash p$ *to infer* $\vdash p \vee r$;
(b) *From* $\vdash p \supset p$ *to infer* $\vdash p \vee {\sim}p$.

R4 counts as a rule for '∨' according to interpretation (iii'); it is admissible in PC_C; and yet it is not admissible in PC_I.

Though false of some of the rules which according to interpretation (iii') count as rules for '∨', (2) is nonetheless true of all those *closed under substitution*, that is, of all those which condone any inference gotten by substitution from some inference already condoned by them. As a matter of fact, not only can it be shown that

(2') Any rule for '∨' which is closed under substitution and is admissible in PC_C is admissible in PC_I;

it can even be shown (see Conjecture IIc below) that

(2'') Any rule for '∨' which is closed under substitution and is admissible in PC_C is provable in PC_I.

Vesley's rule, by the way, is not closed under substitution,[7] whereas all rules stemming from [3] are.

One final word before we tackle our new readings of Leblanc's conjecture. As the above attests, the inferences which a rule condones may matter more than the metaterms in which it is couched. We shall accordingly identify a rule with the set of all the inferences it condones or—to put it more briefly—with the set of all its instances. We shall also treat an instance of a rule as an ordered pair $<\Sigma, T>$, Σ consisting of all the turnstile statements which for the occasion do duty as premises and *T* being the turnstile statement which does duty as conclusion. This departure from customary ways of thinking about a rule has further advantages into which we cannot go here.

On Not Strengthening Intuitionist Logic 393

2. A number of definitions are first in order, which we rehearse in five batches.

By a *well-formed formula* (wff) we shall understand any propositional variable, any expression of the form $\sim A$, where A is a wff, and any expression of one of the forms $(A \ \& \ B)$, $(A \lor B)$, $(A \supset B)$, and $(A \equiv B)$, where A and B are wffs. By a *turnstile statement* (⊢-statement) we shall understand any expression of the form $A_1, A_2, \ldots, A_n \vdash B$, where $A_1, A_2, \ldots, A_n$ ($n \geq 0$), and B are wffs. And by *the wff-associate of a* ⊢-statement $A_1, A_2, \ldots, A_n \vdash B$ we shall understand the wff B or the wff $(A_1 \ \& \ A_2 \ \& \ \ldots \ \& A_n) \supset B$, according as $n = 0$ or $n > 0$.

Our next batch of definitions has to do with the notion of a rule. By a *premises-conclusion pair* we shall understand any ordered pair $<\Sigma, T>$, where Σ is a finite (and possibly empty) set of ⊢-statements and T is a ⊢-statement. By a *rule* we shall understand any set of premises-conclusion pairs, and by an *instance of a rule* any member of a rule. Given two premises-conclusion pairs $<\Sigma, T>$ and $<\Sigma', T'>$, we shall say that $<\Sigma, T>$ *yields* $<\Sigma', T'>$ (or, equivalently, $<\Sigma', T'>$ *is obtainable from* $<\Sigma, T>$ *by substitution* if $v_1, v_2, \ldots,$ and v_p being all the propositional variables that occur in $<\Sigma, T>$ and $A_1, A_2, \ldots, A_p$ being (not necessarily distinct) wffs, $<\Sigma', T'>$ is like $<\Sigma, T>$ except for exhibiting, for each i from 1 through p, A_i wherever $<\Sigma, T>$ exhibits v_i. We shall say that R is *a rule for K*, where K is a (possibly empty) subset of $\{\&, \lor, \sim, \supset, \equiv\}$, if every instance of R is obtainable by substitution from some instance of R which exhibits only connectives in K.[8] And we shall say that a rule R is *closed under substitution* if every premises-conclusion pair obtainable by substitution from some instance of R is an instance of R.

Our third batch of definitions has to do with the semantical notion of validity. We shall say that a ⊢-statement T is *classically valid* or, for short, C-*valid* (*intuitionistically valid* or, for short, I-*valid*) if the wff-associate of T is C-valid (I-valid).[9] We shall say that a premises-conclusion pair $<\{T_1, T_2, \ldots, T_n\}, T>$ ($n \geq 0$) is C-valid (I-valid) if the T-statement $T_1^*, T_2^*, \ldots, T_n^*, \vdash T^*$, where $T_1^*, T_2^*, \ldots, T_n^*,$ and T^* are the wff-associates of $T_1, T_2, \ldots, T_n,$ and T, respectively, is C-valid (I-valid). We shall say that a rule R is C-valid (I-valid) if every instance of R is C-valid (I-valid). And we shall say that a rule R is *weakly* C-*valid* (*weakly* I-*valid*) if for every instance $<\Sigma, T>$ of R either some member of Σ is not C-valid (I-valid) or else T is C-valid (I-valid).

Our fourth batch of definitions has to do with the syntactical notions of provability and admissibility. We shall say that a premises-conclusion pair $<\Sigma, T>$ is *provable by means of a set S of rules* if T is the last entry in a column of ⊢-statements $T_1, T_2, \ldots, T$, such that, for each i from 1 through T_i belongs to Σ or is preceded in the column by s ($s \geq 0$) ⊢-statements $T_{i_1}, T_{i_2}, \ldots, T_{i_s}$ such that $<\{T_{i_1}, T_{i_2}, \ldots, T_{i_s}\}, T_i >$ is an instance of a rule in S.[10] We shall say that a ⊢-statement T is *provable by means of a set S of rules* if $<\emptyset, T>$ is so provable. We shall say that a rule R is provable by means of a set S of rules if every instance of R is so provable. We shall say that a premises-conclusion pair, a ⊢-statement, or a rule is *provable in* PC_C (PC_I) if it is provable by means of the set of rules for PC_C (PC_I) in [8]. And we shall say that a rule R is *admissible in* PC_C (PC_I) if for every instance $<\Sigma, T>$ of R either some member of Σ is not provable in PC_C (PC_I) or else T is provable in PC_C (PC_I).

Turning, lastly, to a syntactico-semantical notion, we shall say that the rules in a set S are *intuitionistically rule-complete* if every I-valid rule is provable by means of S.

With these definitions out of the way, we next proceed to formulate our conjectures. For expository reasons we offer four equivalent versions of each.

Conjecture Ia. Any C-valid rule for $\{\&, \vee\}$ is provable in PC_I.
Conjecture Ib. Any C-valid rule for $\{\&, \vee\}$ is I-valid.
Conjecture Ic. Any rule for $\{\&, \vee\}$ which is provable in PC_C is provable in PC_I.
Conjecture Id. Let the rules in S be intuitionistically rule-complete, and let R be a C-valid rule for $\{\&, \vee\}$. Then any rule (and hence any ⊢-statement) provable by means of S and R is provable by means of S alone.
Conjecture IIa. Any weakly C-valid rule for $\{\&, \vee\}$ which is closed under substitution is provable in PC_I (and hence admissible in PC_I).
Conjecture IIb. Any weakly C-valid rule for $\{\&, \vee\}$ which is closed under substitution is I-valid (and hence weakly I-valid).
Conjecture IIc. Any rule for $\{\&, \vee\}$ which is closed under substitution and is admissible in PC_C is provable in PC_I (and hence admissible in PC_I).
Conjecture IId. Let the rules in S be intuitionistically rule-complete, and let R be a weakly C-valid rule for $\{\&, \vee\}$ which is closed under substitution. Then any rule (and hence any ⊢-statement) provable by means of S and R is provable by means of S alone.

Of the foregoing, Ib (IIb) follows from Ia (IIa) and the fact that any rule provable in PC_I is I-valid; Ic follows from Ia and the fact that any rule provable in PC_C is C-valid; IIc follows from IIa and the fact that any rule admissible in PC_C is weakly C-valid; and Id (IId) follows from Ia (IIa) and the fact that any rule provable in PC_I is provable by means of the set S of rules mentioned in Id (IId). We accordingly restrict ourselves to proving Ia and IIa, the latter via a rather interesting lemma concerning classical validity.

Theorem 1. *Any C-valid rule for* $\{\&, \vee\}$ *is provable in* PC_I. (= Conjecture Ia)

Proof: Let R be a C-valid rule for $\{\&, \vee\}$ and $<\Sigma, T>$ be an instance of R. Then there is bound to be a premises-conclusion pair $<\Sigma', T'>$ which is an instance of R, exhibits only connectives in $\{\&, \vee\}$, and yields $<\Sigma, T>$ by substitution. But if $<\Sigma', T'>$ is an instance of R, then $<\Sigma', T'>$ is bound to be C-valid; if $<\Sigma', T'>$ is C-valid and exhibits only connectives in $\{\&, \vee\}$, then $<\Sigma', T'>$ is bound by a result of Belnap and Thomason's in [1] to be provable in PC_I;[11] and if $<\Sigma', T'>$ is provable in PC_I and yields $<\Sigma, T>$ by substitution, then $<\Sigma, T>$ is also bound to be provable in PC_I, since substitution is provability-preserving. Hence R is bound to be provable in PC_I.

Lemma 1. *Any weakly C-valid rule which is closed under substitution is C-valid.*

Proof: Suppose R is closed under substitution and is not C-valid. Then there is bound to be an instance of R, say $<\Sigma, T>$, which is not C-valid, and hence there is bound to be an assignment of truth-values to the propositional variables in $<\Sigma, T>$ which satisfies every member of Σ but fails to satisfy T. Now consider the result $<\Sigma', T'>$ of substituting '$p \lor \sim p$' for every propositional variable in $<\Sigma, T>$ which is assigned the truth-value **T** in the said assignment and '$p \ \& \sim p$' for every one which is assigned the truth-value **F**. Every member of Σ' is bound to be C-valid, while T' is not. Hence $<\Sigma', T'>$ is not weakly C-valid. But $<\Sigma', T'>$ is bound to be an instance of R, since R is closed under substitution. Hence R is not weakly C-valid.

Theorem 2. *Any weakly C-valid rule for* $\{\&, \lor\}$ *which is closed under substitution is provable in* PC_I. (= Conjecture IIa)
Proof by Theorem 1 and Lemma 1.

It should now be clear that any structural rule, any rule for '&', and any rule for '$\lor$' which holds in PC_C in the sense of being provable in PC_C also holds in PC_I, and that any structural rule, any rule for '&', and any rule for '$\lor$' which holds in PC_C in the sense of being admissible in PC_C also holds in PC_I, so long in the latter case as the rule is closed under substitution. It should likewise be clear that the only way of turning Gentzen-like rules for PC_I into rules for PC_C or, to be more explicit about it, of so amending the former rules as to permit proof of any C-valid rule and ⊢-statement, is to strengthen the rules for '$\sim$', or those for '$\supset$', or those for '$\equiv$'.

Notes

1. Concerning turnstile statements generally, see p. 287.
2. See [2] and [8].
3. See [1] and [4] for proofs of the conjecture, [9] for a disproof of it.
4. **R1** condones such an inference as ⊢ $p \lor p$ from ⊢ $p \supset p$ and $p, p \vdash q$, even though ⊢ $p \lor p$ is not obtainable from ⊢ $p \supset p$ and $p, p \vdash q$ by means of the axioms and primitive rules of PC_C. **R1** is therefore not provable in PC_C.
5. Because of the wording of **R2**, B has to be $\sim A$, where A is a propositional variable, say 'p'. But ⊢ $p \lor \sim p$, though obtainable from $p \vdash p$ by means of the axioms and primitive rules of PC_C, is not obtainable from $p \vdash p$ by means of the axioms and primitive rules of PC_I. Though provable in PC_C, **R2** is therefore not provable in PC_I.
6. **R2** fails to count as a rule for '$\lor$' according to interpretation (iii') because such an inference as ⊢ $p \lor \sim p$ from $p \vdash p$, though condoned by **R2**, cannot be gotten by substitution from any inference condoned by **R2** that exhibits no connective but '$\lor$'. Similarly, **R1** fails to count as a rule for '$\lor$' according to interpretation (iii'), because such an inference as ⊢ $\sim p \lor \sim p$ from ⊢ $\sim p$ and $\sim p, p \vdash q$, though condoned by **R1**, cannot be gotten by substitution from any inference condoned by **R2** that exhibits no connective but '$\lor$'.
7. Note for proof that such an inference as ⊢ $q \lor \sim q$ from ⊢ $\sim q$ and $\sim q, q \vdash q$, though gotten by substitution from an inference condoned by **R1**, is not itself condoned by **R1**.

8. Note that what we called above a *structural rule* proves under the present terminology to be a rule for any subset of $\{\&, \vee, \sim, \supset, \equiv\}$ and hence for $\{\&, \vee\}$, and that what we called a *rule for* '&' or a *rule for* '∨' proves under the present terminology to be a rule for $\{\&, \vee\}$.

9. For an account of intuitionistic validity, see [5].

10. Axiom schemata can be viewed as rules with instances of the form $<\varnothing, \mathbf{T}>$ and hence do not call here for separate mention.

11. The rules that figure in [1], though different from the Leblanc-Belnap ones in [8], are provable in PC_I, as the reader may verify on his own.

References

[1] Belnap, N. D., Jr., and Thomason, R. H. 1963. "A Rule-Completeness Theorem." *Notre Dame Journal of Formal Logic* (hereafter *NDJFL*) 4: 39–43.

[2] Beth, E. W., and Leblanc, H. 1960. "A Note on the Intuitionist and the Classical Propositional Calculus." *Logique et Analyse* 11–12: 174–76. (#27 in this volume).

[3] Gentzen, G. 1934–35. "Untersuchungen über das logische Schliessen." *Mathematische Zeitschrift* 39: 176–210, 405–31.

[4] de Jongh, D. H. J. 1961. "Recherches sur les I-Valuations." *Compte-Rendu des Travaux Effectués par l'Université d'Amsterdam dans le Cadre du Contrat Euratom*, pp. 173–78.

[5] Kripke, S. A. 1965. "Semantical Analysis of Intuitionistic Logic I." *Formal Systems and Recursive Functions*, pp. 92–130. Amsterdam: North-Holland.

[6] Leblanc, H. 1962. "Etudes sur les Règles d'Inférence dites Règles de Gentzen, Première Partie." *Dialogue* 1: 56–66.

[7] ———. 1963. "Proof Routines for the Propositional Calculus." *NDJFL* 4: 81–104 (#23 in this volume).

[8] Leblanc, H., and Belnap, N. D., Jr. 1962. "Intuitionism Reconsidered." *NDJFL* 3: 79–82 (#28 in this volume).

[9] Vesley, R. E. 1963. "On Strengthening Intuitionistic Logic." *NDJFL* 4: 80.

30
The Demarcation Line Between Intuitionist Logic and Classical Logic
R. H. Thomason, coauthor

In an effort to sharpen the demarcation line between intuitionist logic and classical logic, we shall sort out the sequents of the form

$$A_1, A_2, \ldots, A_n \to B_1, B_2, \ldots, B_m,$$

where $m \geq 0$, and then those of the more special form $A_1, A_2, \ldots, A_n \to B$, that are sure—if classically valid—to be intuitionistically valid as well.

1. Let an expression of the form

$$A_1, A_2, \ldots, A_n \to B_1, B_2, \ldots, B_m,$$

where $A_1, A_2, \ldots, A_n$ ($n \geq 0$), $B_1, B_2, \ldots$, and B_m ($m > 0$ if $n = 0$, otherwise $m \geq 0$) are well-formed formulas (wffs) of the first-order quantificational calculus, count as an *L-sequent*, and let an L-sequent of the form

$$A_1, A_2, \ldots, A_n \to B$$

count as an *N-sequent*.[1] Let an L-sequent $A_1, A_2, \ldots, A_n \to B_1, B_2, \ldots, B_m$ be said to be *in* α, where α is a (possibly empty) subset of the set of operators $\{\sim, \supset, \&, \vee \equiv, \forall, \exists\}^2$ if every operator that occurs in $A_1, A_2, \ldots, A_n$, $B_1, B_2, \ldots$, or B_m belongs to α. When m equals 0, let $\sim((\ldots(A_1 \& A_2) \& \ldots) \& A_n)$ count as the *wff-associate* of $A_1, A_2, \ldots, A_n \to B_1, B_2, \ldots, B_m$; when n equals 0, let $(\ldots (B_1 \vee B_2) \vee \ldots) \vee B_m)$ serve as the *wff-associate* of the L-sequent; and when neither m nor n equals 0, let $((\ldots A_1 \& A_2) \& \ldots) \& A_n) \supset ((\ldots (B_1 \vee B_2) \vee \ldots) \vee B_m)$ serve as its *wff-associate*. Let an L-sequent be rated *classically valid* (C-valid) if its wff-associate is C-valid, and *intuitionistically valid* (I-valid) if its wff-associate is I-valid.[3] Finally, let an L-sequent S be said to be *provable* by a (possibly empty) set R of rules if S turns up last in a finite column of L-sequents[4] each one of which is of the form $A \to A$, where A is an atomic wff, or follows from previous entries in the column by application of a member of R.

Gentzen showed in [1] that every C-valid L-sequent in $\{\vee, \&, \exists\}$ is provable by the following rules, where K, L, M, and N are finite (and possibly empty) sequences of wffs and commas:[5]

TABLE 1

Structural rules:

Thinning to the left:
$$\frac{K \to L}{A, K \to L}$$

Thinning to the right:
$$\frac{K \to L}{K \to L, A}$$

Permutation to the left:
$$\frac{K, A, B, L \to M}{K, B, A, L \to M}$$

Permutation to the right:
$$\frac{K \to L, A, B, M}{K \to L, B, A, M}$$

Contraction to the left:
$$\frac{A, A, K \to L}{A, K \to L}$$

Contraction to the right:
$$\frac{K \to L, A, A}{K \to L, A}$$

Cut:
$$\frac{A, K \to M \text{ and } L \to N, A}{K, L \to M, N}$$

Introduction rules:

For '&' to the left:
$$\frac{A, K \to L \text{ or } B, K \to L}{A \& B, K \to L}$$

For '&' to the right:
$$\frac{K \to L, A \text{ and } K \to L, B}{K \to L, A \& B}$$

For '$\vee$' to the left:
$$\frac{A, K \to L \text{ and } B, K \to L}{A \vee B, K \to L}$$

For '$\vee$' to the right:
$$\frac{K \to L, A \text{ or } K \to L, B}{K \to L, A \vee B}$$

For '$\forall$' to the left:
$$\frac{A', K \to L}{(\forall X)A, K \to L}$$

For '$\forall$' to the right:
$$\frac{K \to L, A'}{K \to L, (\forall X)A}$$

For '$\exists$' to the left:
$$\frac{A', K \to L}{(\exists X)A, K \to L}$$

For '$\exists$' to the right:
$$\frac{K \to L, A'}{K \to L, (\exists X)A}$$

Note: In the last four rules A' is to be like A except for exhibiting free occurrences of some individual variable X' wherever A exhibits free occurrences of X; in the introduction rule for '$\forall$' to the right and for '$\exists$' to the left X' is not to occur free in any wff in K, in any wff in L, in $(\forall X)A$, or in $(\exists X)A$.

It is clear that, where α is any subset of $\{\&, \forall, \exists\}$, any L-sequent in α that is provable by the rules of Table 1 is sure to be provable by the seven structural

The Demarcation Line Between Intuitionist Logic and Classical Logic   399

rules in Table 1 and the introduction rules of that table for only such operators as belong to α. But any L-sequent that is provable by the seven structural rules in Table 1 and the introduction rules of that table for '&', '∨', and '∃' is sure—as the reader can verify—to be I-valid. We thus have:

Theorem 1. *Let S be an L-sequent in {&,∨,∃}. If S is C-valid, then S is I-valid (and vice-versa).*

The result cannot be improved upon: none indeed of the C-valid L-sequents '~~$p \to p$', '$(p \supset q) \supset p \to p$', '$p$, $(r \equiv p) \equiv (r \equiv q) \to q$', and '$(\forall x)(f(x) \lor p) \to\to (\forall x)f(x) \lor p$' is I-*valid*. Exactly eight varieties of L-sequents are thus sure to be I-valid if C-valid, to wit: those that exhibit no connective or quantifier letter, those that exhibit only '&', those that exhibit only '∨', those that exhibit only '∃', those that exhibit only '&' and '∨', those that exhibit only '&' and '∃', those that exhibit only '∨' and '∃', and those that exhibit only '&', '∨', and '∃'.

Theorem 1, holding as it does of every L-sequent in {&,∨,∃}, yields:

Theorem 2. *Let S be an N-sequent in {&,∨,∃}. If S is C-valid, then S is I-valid (and vice-versa).*

The result can be improved upon, as we shall now show.

2. Besides being provable by the seven structural rules of Table 1 and the introduction rules of that table for '&', '∀', and '∃', a C-valid L-sequent in {&,∀,∃} is also provable by the same rules minus Contraction to the right. We arrive at the result after three lemmas.

Lemma 1. *Let R consist of Thinning to the left, Thinning to the right, Permutation to the left, Permutation to the right, Contraction to the left, Cut, and the introduction rules of Table 1 for '&', '∀', and '∃'; and let S be an L-sequent in {&,∀,∃} of the form $K \to B_1, B_2, \ldots, B_m$, where $m \geq 1$. If S is provable by R, then so is $K \to B_i$ for some i from 1 to m.*
Proof by mathematical induction on the number k of entries in the proof of S.
Basis: $k = 1$. Then S is an axiom, and hence is of the form $B_1 \to B_1$. But if so, then $K \to B_i$ is provable by **R** for some i from 1 through m.
Induction Step (sample cases):
Case 1: S follows from a previous entry in the proof of S by Thinning to the left. Then S is of the form $A, K' \to B_1, B_2, \ldots, B_m$, and the entry from which S follows is $K' \to B_1, B_2, \ldots, B_m$. But if $K' \to B_1, B_2, \ldots, B_m$ turns up in the proof of S, then $K' \to B_1, B_2, \ldots, B_m$ is provable by **R**. Hence by the hypothesis of the induction $K' \to B_i$ is provable by **R** for some i from 1 through m. Hence so is $K \to B_i$, which follows from $K' \to B_i$ by Thinning to the left.

Case 2: S follows from a previous entry in the proof of S by Thinning to the right. Then the entry from which S follows is $K \rightarrow B_1, B_2, \ldots, B_{m-1}$. But if $K \rightarrow B_1, B_2, \ldots, B_{m-1}$ turns up in the proof of S, then $K \rightarrow B_1, B_2, \ldots, B_{m-1}$ is provable by $\boldsymbol{R}$. Hence by the hypothesis of the induction $K \rightarrow B_i$ is provable by $\boldsymbol{R}$ for some i from 1 through $m - 1$. Hence so is $K \rightarrow B_i$ for some i from 1 through m.[6]

Case 6: S follows from two previous entries in the proof of S by Cut. Then S is of the form $K', K'' \rightarrow B_1, B_2, \ldots, B_{j-1}, B_j, B_{j+1}, \ldots, B_m$ ($j \leq m$), and the entries from which S follows are $A, K' \rightarrow B_1, B_2, \ldots, B_j$ and $K'' \rightarrow B_{j+1}, B_{j+2}, \ldots, B_m, A$ for some wff A or other. But if $A, K' \rightarrow B_1, B_2, \ldots, B_j$ and $K'' \rightarrow B_{j+1}, B_{j+2}, \ldots, B_m, A$ turn up in the proof of S, then $A, K' \rightarrow B_1, B_2, \ldots, B_j$ and $K'' \rightarrow B_{j+1}, B_{j+2}, \ldots, B_m, A$ are provable by $\boldsymbol{R}$. Hence by the hypothesis of the induction $A, K' \rightarrow B_{i'}$ ($i' \leq j$) and either $K'' \rightarrow B_{i''}$ ($j + 1 \leq i'' \leq m$) or $K'' \rightarrow A$ are provable by $\boldsymbol{R}$. Now suppose $K'' \rightarrow B_{i''}$ is provable by $\boldsymbol{R}$. Then so is $K \rightarrow B_{i''}$, which follows from $K'' \rightarrow B_{i''}$ by Thinning to the left. Or suppose $A, K' \rightarrow B_{i'}$ and $K'' \rightarrow A$ are provable by $\boldsymbol{R}$. Then so is $K \rightarrow B_{i'}$, which follows from $A, K' \rightarrow B_{i'}$ and $K'' \rightarrow A$ by Cut. In either case, therefore, $K \rightarrow B_i$ is provable by $\boldsymbol{R}$ for some i from 1 through m.

Case 8: S follows from two previous entries in the proof of S by the introduction rule for '&' to the right. Then S is of the form $K \rightarrow B_1, B_2, \ldots, B_{m-1}, B_{m_1} \& B_{m_2}$, and the entries from which S follows are $K \rightarrow B_1, B_2, \ldots, B_{m-1}, B_{m_1}$ and $K \rightarrow B_1, B_2, \ldots, B_{m-1}, B_{m_2}$. But if $K \rightarrow B_1, B_2, \ldots, B_{m-1}, B_{m_1}$ and $K \rightarrow B_1, B_2, \ldots, B_{m-1}, B_{m_2}$ turn up in the proof of S, then $K \rightarrow B_1, B_2, \ldots, B_{m-1}, B_{m_1}$ and $K \rightarrow B_1, B_2, \ldots, B_{m-1}, B_{m_2}$ are provable by $\boldsymbol{R}$. Hence by the hypothesis of the induction either $K \rightarrow B_i$ is provable by $\boldsymbol{R}$ for some i from 1 through $m - 1$, or else both $K \rightarrow B_{m_1}$ and $K \rightarrow B_{m_2}$ are provable by $\boldsymbol{R}$, in which case $K \rightarrow B_m$—which follows from $K \rightarrow B_{m_1}$ and $K \rightarrow B_{m_2}$ by the introduction rule for '&' to the right—is provable by $\boldsymbol{R}$. In either case, therefore, $K \rightarrow B_i$ is provable by $\boldsymbol{R}$ for some i from 1 through m.

Lemma 2. *Let $\boldsymbol{R}$ and S be as in Lemma 1. Then S is provable by $\boldsymbol{R}$ if and only if $K \rightarrow B_i$ is provable by $\boldsymbol{R}$ for some i from 1 through m.*
Proof: Suppose $K \rightarrow B_i$ is provable by $\boldsymbol{R}$ for some i from 1 through m. Then so is S, which follows from $K \rightarrow B_i$ by Thinning to the right and (possibly) Permutation to the right. Hence Lemma 2 by Lemma 1.

Lemma 3. *Let $\boldsymbol{R}$ be as in Lemma 1, and $K \rightarrow L, A, A$ be an L-sequent in $\{\&, \forall, \exists\}$. Then $K \rightarrow L, A, A$ is provable by $\boldsymbol{R}$ if and only if $K \rightarrow L, A$ is.*
Proof: Let L be $B_1, B_2, \ldots, B_m$, where $m \geq 0$. In view of Lemma 2 $K \rightarrow L, A, A$ is provable by $\boldsymbol{R}$ if and only if $K \rightarrow B_i$ for some i from 1 through m or $K \rightarrow A$ is provable by $\boldsymbol{R}$. But in view of Lemma 2 again $K \rightarrow L, A$ is provable

by R if and only if $K \to B_i$ for some i and 1 through m or $K \to A$ is provable by R. Hence Lemma 3.

Theorem 3. *Let R be as in Lemma 1, and S be an L-sequent in $\{\&,\forall,\exists\}$. If S is provable by R plus Contraction to the right, then S is provable by R alone.*[7]
Proof: Let

$$(1)\ K_1 \to L_1, A_1\ (2)\ K_2 \to L_2, A_2 \ldots (p)\ K_p \to L_p, A_p$$

be the p ($p \geq 1$) entries in the proof of S that follow from a previous entry in the proof by Contraction to the right, and for each i from 1 through p let $K_i \to L_i, A_i, A_i$ be the entry from which $K_i \to L_i, A_i$ follows. Since $K_i \to L_i, A_i, A_i$ turns up in the proof of S, then $K_i \to L_i, A_i, A_i$ is provable by R plus Contraction to the right, and hence in view of Lemma 3 there is a proof of $K_i \to L_i, A_i$ by R alone. But if so, then the result of substituting for the two entries $K_i \to L_i, A_i, A_i$ and $K_i \to L_i, A_i$ in the proof of S the said proof of $K_i \to L_i A_i$ by R alone constitutes a proof of S by R alone.

Since—as we already remarked—any L-sequent in α that is provable by the rules of Table 1 is sure to be provable by Thinning, Permutation, Contraction, Cut, and the introduction rules of Table 1 for only such operators as belong to α, we have, in view of Gentzen's 1934 result and Theorem 3:

Theorem 4. *Let R be as in Lemma 1 and S be an N-sequent in $\{\lor,\forall,\exists\}$. If S is C-valid, then S is provable by R.*

But any N-sequent that is provable by the twelve rules listed in Lemma 1 is sure to be provable by the following special cases of ten of those rules:[8]

TABLE 2

Structural rules:

Thinning to the left: Permutation to the left: Contraction to the left:

$$\frac{K \to A}{B, K \to A}\qquad \frac{K, A, B, L \to C}{K, B, A, L \to C}\qquad \frac{A, A, K \to B}{A, K \to B}$$

Cut: $\dfrac{A, K \to B \text{ and } L \to A}{K, L \to B}$

Introduction rules:

For '&' to the left: For '&' to the right:

$$\frac{A, K \to C \text{ or } B, K \to C}{A\ \&\ B, K \to C}\qquad \frac{K \to A \text{ and } K \to B}{K \to A\ \&\ B}$$

402   Part 3: Provability

For '∀' to the left:

$$\frac{A', K \to B}{(\forall X)A, K \to B}$$

For '∀' to the right:

$$\frac{K \to A'}{K \to (\forall X)A}$$

For '∃' to the left:

$$\frac{A', K \to B}{(\exists X)A, K \to B}$$

For '∃' to the right:

$$\frac{K \to A'}{K \to (\exists X)A}$$

Hence so is the N-sequent S of Theorem 4. But any N-sequent that is provable by the rules of Table 2 is sure—as the reader may verify—to be I-valid. Hence:

Theorem 5. *Let S be an N-sequent in {&,∀,∃} or in {&,∀,∃}. If S is C-valid, then S is I-valid (and vice-versa).*

The result cannot be improved upon. Exactly twelve varieties of N-sequents are thus sure to be I-valid if C-valid, those already listed under Theorem 1, those that exhibit only '∀', those that exhibit only '&' and '∀', those that exhibit only '∀' and '∃', and those that exhibit only '&', '∀', and '∃'.

3. Theorems 1 and 5 may dispel certain popular misconceptions about disjunction and existence in intuitionist logic. In view of Theorem 1 the intuitionist connective '∨' and the classical one cannot be told apart in four varieties of L-sequents (and hence of N-sequents): those that exhibit only '∨', those that exhibit only '∨' and '&', those that exhibit only '∨' and '∃', and those that exhibit only '∨', '&', and '∃'. In view of Theorem 1 again the intuitionist quantifier letter '∃' and the classical one cannot be told apart in four varieties of L-sequents (and hence of N-sequents): those that exhibit only '∨', those that exhibit only '∨' and '&', those that exhibit only '∨' and '∃', and those that exhibit only '∨', '&', and '∃'. In view of Theorem 1 again, the intuitionist quantifier letter '∃' and the classical one cannot be told apart in four varieties of L-sequents (and hence of N-sequents): those that exhibit only '∃', those that exhibit only '∃', and '&', those that exhibit only '∃' and '∨', and those that exhibit only '∃', '&', and '∨'. And in view of Theorem 5 the two quantifier letters in question cannot be told apart either in two extra varieties of N-sequents: those that exhibit only '∃' and '∀', and those that exhibit only '∃', '&', and '∀'. On some—though admittedly not on a majority of—occasions, the intuitionist's handling of '∨' and '∃' thus coincides with the classicist's.

Notes

1. L-sequents were systematically studied by Gentzen in [1], whereas N-sequents appear for the first time in [2].
2. All seven of the operators in question are understood here to be primitive.
3. For an account of intuitionist validity, see [3].
4. The column in question will occasionally be referred to as a *proof* of S by α.

5. Gentzen's full result is to the effect that any C-valid L-sequent in $\{\sim, \supset, \&, \vee, \forall, \exists\}$ is provable by the rules of Table 1 plus the following four introduction rules:

For '$\sim$' to the left:

$$\frac{K \to L, A}{\sim A, K \to L}$$

For '$\sim$' to the right:

$$\frac{A, K \to L}{K \to L, \sim A}$$

For '$\supset$' to the left:

$$\frac{K \to M, A \text{ and } B, L \to N}{A \supset B, K, L \to M, N}$$

For '$\supset$' to the right:

$$\frac{A, K \to L, B}{K \to L, A \supset B}$$

It can be shown—as Bernays independently noted—that any C-valid L-sequent in $\{\sim, \supset, \&, \vee, \equiv, \forall, \exists\}$ is provable by those rules plus the following two introduction rules:

For '$\equiv$' to the left:

$$\frac{\text{(i) } K \to M, A \text{ and } B, L \to N \text{ or (ii) } K \to M, B \text{ and } A, L \to N}{A \equiv B, K, L \to M, N}$$

For '$\equiv$' to the right:

$$\frac{A, K \to L, B \text{ and } B, K \to L, A}{K \to L, A \equiv B}$$

It can also be shown that once L in the introduction rules for '$\sim$', '$\supset$', '$\equiv$', and '$\forall$' is required to be empty, then an L-sequent is provable by the resulting twenty rules if and only if I-valid.

6. In [1] only a special case of Thinning to the right, namely:

$$\frac{K \to}{K \to A}$$

is employed for intuitionist purposes. This may have obscured the fact that Thinning to the right holds in intuitionist as well as in classical logic.

7. In view of Gentzen's *Hauptsatz* in [1] any L-sequent in which no individual variable occurs both bound and free is provable by the rules of Table 1 *minus* Cut, if provable by the rule of Table 1. Hence, in view of Theorem 3, any such sequent, if provable by the rules of Table 1, is provable by the rule of Table *minus* Cut and Contraction to the right. The result is made use of in [4].

8. Note indeed that in the absence of Contraction to the right any entry in the proof of an L-sequent S that exhibits on the right-hand side more commas than S does—and hence any entry in the proof of an N-sequent that exhibits any comma at all–can be discarded without prejudice to the proof.

References

[1] Gentzen, G. 1934–35. "Untersuchungen über das logische Schliessen." *Mathematische Zeitschrift* 39: 176–210 and 405–31.
[2] ———. 1935–36. "Die Widerspruchsfreiheit der reinen Zahlentheorie." *Mathematische Annalen* 112: 493–565.
[3] Kripke, S. A. 1965. "Semantical Analysis of Intuitiontistic Logic I." *Formal Systems and Recursive Functions*, pp. 92–130. Amsterdam: North-Holland.
[4] Leblanc, H. 1966. "Two Separation Theorems for Natural Deduction." *Notre Dame Journal of Formal Logic* 7: 159–80 (#24 in this volume).

31
Boolean Algebra and the Propositional Calculus

Manuals of logic often comment on the kinship between Boolean Algebra (BA) and the Propositional Calculus (PC). Some mention, in particular, that the propositional rewrite of any theorem of BA, that is, the result of writing '∼' for '−', '∨' for '∪', and '≡' for '=', for example, in any theorem of BA,[1] is a tautology and hence a theorem of PC. None, however, shows how to turn the propositional rewrites of standard axioms (or axiom schemata) and rules of inference for BA into a complete set of axioms (or axiom schemata) and rules of inference for PC. Instructions to that effect are offered here.

(1) Let BA be cast in the following form: (a) The primitive signs of BA are to be a denumerably infinite list of (class) variables, the two operators '−' and '∪', the predicate '=', and the two parentheses '(' and ')'; (b) The terms of BA are to be all variables, all expressions of the form $-\alpha$, where α is a term of BA, and all expressions of the form $(\alpha \cup \beta)$, where α and β are terms of BA; (c) The sentences of BA are to be all expressions of the form $\alpha = \beta$, where α and β are terms of BA; (d) $(\alpha \cap \beta)$ is to be short for $-(-\alpha \cup -\beta)$; (e) The axioms of BA are to be all sentences of BA of any of the following four forms:

BA1. $(\alpha \cup \beta) = (\beta \cup \alpha)$

BA2. $((\alpha \cup \beta) \cup \gamma) = (\alpha \cup (\beta \cup \gamma))$

BA3. $((\alpha \cap \beta) \cup (\alpha \cap -\beta)) = \alpha$

BA4. $\alpha = \alpha$.

(f) The rules of inference of BA are to be:

BA5. From $\alpha = \beta$ to infer $\beta = \alpha$

BA6. From $\alpha = \beta$ and $\beta = \gamma$ to infer $\alpha = \gamma$

BA7. From $\alpha = \alpha'$ to infer $\beta = \beta'$, where β' is like β except for containing occurrences of α' at one or more places where β contains occurrences of α.[2]

Note: As the reader undoubtedly knows, **BA7** may be replaced by three of its own subcases, to wit:

BA7.1. From $\alpha = \beta$ to infer $-\alpha = -\beta$

BA7.2. From $\alpha = \beta$ to infer $(\alpha \cup \gamma) = (\beta \cup \gamma)$

BA7.3. From $\alpha = \beta$ to infer $(\gamma \cup \alpha) = (\gamma \cup \beta)$.

A similar remark applies, mutatis mutandis, to **PC7** below.

(2) Let PC be cast in the following form: (a) The primitive signs of PC are to be a denumerably infinite list of (propositional) variables, the two connectives '~' and 'V', and the two parentheses '(' and ')'; (b) The sentences of PC are to be all variables, all expressions of the form ~A, where A is a sentence of PC, and all expressions of the form $(A \lor B)$, where A and B are sentences of PC; (c) $(A \mathbin{\&} B)$ is to be short for ~$(\sim\!A \lor \sim\!B)$, $(A \supset B)$ short for $(\sim\!A \lor B)$, and $(A \equiv B)$ short for $((A \supset B) \mathbin{\&} (B \supset A))$;[3] (d) The axioms of PC are to be all sentences of any one of the following four forms:

PC1. $(A \lor B) \equiv (B \lor A)$

PC2. $((A \lor B) \lor C) \equiv (A \lor (B \lor C))$

PC3. $((A \mathbin{\&} B) \lor (A \mathbin{\&} \sim\!B)) \equiv A$

PC4. $A \equiv A$

(e) The rules of inference of PC are to be, *for the time being*:

PC5. From $A \equiv B$ to infer $B \equiv A$

PC6. From $A \equiv B$ and $B \equiv C$ to infer $A \equiv C$

PC7. From $A \equiv A'$ to infer $B \equiv B'$, where B' is like B except for containing occurrences of A' at one or more places where B contains occurrences of A.

(3) **PC1–PC7**, the propositional rewrites of **BA1–BA7** only yield tautologies of the form $A \equiv B$ as theorems.[4] **PC1–PC7** *plus* the following rule of inference:

PC8. From A and $A \equiv B$ to infer B

constitute, however, a complete set of axiom schemata and rules of inference for PC. Proof is as follows.

Note first that

$$(A \equiv A) \equiv ((A \lor A) \supset A)$$

$$(A \equiv A) \equiv (A \supset (A \lor B))$$

$$(A \equiv A) \equiv ((A \supset B) \supset ((C \lor A) \supset (B \lor C)))$$

are short for propositional rewrites of theorems of BA and hence are theorems of PC. But by **PC4** $A \equiv A$ is a theorem of PC. Hence by **PC8**

$$(A \lor A) \supset A \tag{1}$$
$$A \supset (A \lor B) \tag{2}$$
$$(A \supset B) \supset ((C \lor A) \supset (B \lor C)) \tag{3}$$

are theorems of PC (Step one). Note also that Modus Ponens, to wit:

If A and $A \supset B$ are theorems of PC, then B is a theorem of PC,

is available here as a derived rule of inference. Let indeed A and $A \supset B$ be theorems of PC. $(A \supset B) \equiv (A \equiv (A \ \& \ B))$ is short for the propositional rewrite of a theorem of BA and hence is a theorem of PC. Hence by **PC8** $A \equiv (A \ \& \ B)$ is a theorem of PC and hence by **PC8** again $A \ \& \ B$ is a theorem of PC. But $A \equiv (A \equiv (A \equiv A))$ is short for the propositional rewrite of a theorem of BA and hence is a theorem of PC. Hence by **PC8** $A \equiv (A \equiv A)$ is a theorem of PC and hence by **PC7** $(A \equiv A) \ \& \ B$ is a theorem of PC. But $((A \equiv A) \ \& \ B) \equiv B$ is short for the propositional rewrite of a theorem of BA and hence is a theorem of PC. Hence by **PC8** B is a theorem of PC (Step two). Note finally that (1)–(3) and Modus Ponens yield all tautologies as theorems (Step three).[5] By steps one, two, and three **PC1–PC8** must therefore constitute a complete set of axiom schemata and rules of inference for PC. Q. E. D.

Note: In the first draft of [3] I remarked that **PC1–PC7**, Modus Ponens and either of

PC9. From $A \equiv (A \ \& \ B)$ to infer $A \supset B$

PC10. From $B \equiv (A \lor B)$ to infer $A \supset B$

constitute a complete set of axiom schemata and rules of inference for PC. A few months later I learned from a referee for *The Journal of Symbolic Logic* that **PC1–PC8** and Modus Ponens will do the trick.[6] Neither one of us, however, realized at the time that Modus Ponens is redundant in the presence of **PC8** and hence may be dispensed with. In the summer of 1960 J. Porte finally informed me that **PC1–PC7** *plus* any one of **PC8, PC11, PC12,** and **PC13,** where the latter rules of inference respectively read:

PC11. From $A \equiv B$, where B is any one of **PC1–PC3**, to infer A

PC12. From $A \equiv (B \equiv B)$, where B is any sentence of PC, to infer A

PC13. From $A \equiv (A \equiv A)$ to infer A

should constitute a complete set of axiom schemata and rules of inference for PC.[7] The proof offered here that **PC1–PC8** constitute such a set is believed to be new.

(4) The above set of axiom schemata and rules of inference may be simplified in two ways.

First, **PC5** and **PC6** are redundant in the presence of **PC8** and hence may be dispensed with. Note indeed that by **PC1** $(\sim(A \supset B) \lor \sim(B \supset A)) \equiv (\sim(B \supset$

A) $\vee \sim(A \supset B)$) is a theorem of PC and hence by **PC7** $(A \equiv B) \equiv (B \equiv A)$ is a theorem of PC. Hence if $A \equiv B$ is a theorem of PC, then by **PC8** $B \equiv A$ is a theorem of PC. Note also that if $A \equiv B$ is a theorem of PC, then by the same reasoning $B \equiv A$ is a theorem of PC, and hence by **PC7** $(B \equiv C) \equiv (A \equiv C)$ is a theorem of PC. Hence if $A \equiv B$ and $B \equiv C$ are theorems of PC, then by **PC8** $A \equiv C$ is a theorem of PC.

Second, **PC7** and **PC8** may be replaced by a single rule of inference, namely:

PC9. From $A \equiv A'$ and B to infer B', where B' is like B except for containing occurrences of A' at one or more places where B contains occurrences of A.

That **PC7** and **PC8**, on one hand, yield **PC9** can be seen as follows. If $A \equiv A'$ is a theorem of PC, then by **PC7** $B \equiv B'$ is a theorem of PC. But if B and $B \equiv B'$ are theorems of PC, then by **PC8** B' is a theorem of PC. Hence if $A \equiv A'$ and B are theorems of PC, then B' is a theorem of PC. That **PC9** on the other hand, yields **PC7** and **PC8** can be seen as follows. **PC8** is a mere subcase of **PC9** with B for A', A for B, and B for B'. As for **PC7**, by **PC4** $B \equiv B$ is a theorem of PC. But $B \equiv B'$ is like $B \equiv B$ except for containing occurrences of A' at one or more places where $B \equiv B$ contains occurrences of A. Hence, if $A \equiv A'$ is a theorem of PC, then by **PC9** $B \equiv B'$ is a theorem of PC.

PC1–PC4, **PC7**, and **PC8**, on one hand, **PC1–PC4** and **PC9**, on the other, thus constitute complete sets of axiom schemata and rules of inference for PC.

Notes

1. And, of course, treating the class variables in the theorem as propositional variables.
2. **BA1–BA7** make up Huntington's "fourth set" in [2].
3. From now on a few easily restored parentheses are omitted.
4. The point was brought to my attention by R. McNaughton.
5. See [1] and [4].
6. Both points are made in Note 8 of [3].
7. That **PC13** can substitute for **PC8** follows, Porte tells me, from a theorem mentioned by Tarski in his Paris lectures of 1955.

References

[1] Gotlind, E. 1947. "Ett Axiomsystem for Utsagokalkylen." *Norsk Matematisk Tidsskrift* (hereafter *NMT*) 29: 1–4.
[2] Huntington, E. V. 1933. "New Sets of Independent Postulates for the Algebra of Logic, with Special Reference to Whitehead and Russell's *Principia Mathematica.*" *Transactions of the American Mathematical Society* 35: 274–304.
[3] Leblanc, H. 1960. "On Requirements for Conditional Probability Functions." *The Journal of Symbolic Logic* 25: 238–42.
[4] Rasiowa, H. 1949. "Sur un Certain Système d'Axiomes du Calcul des Propositions." *NMT* 31: 1–3.

32

The Algebra of Logic and the Theory of Deduction

Whitehead's earliest love was algebra, and it may be by way of algebra, the so-called *algebra of logic* in particular, that he came to logic. It is thus surprising to find *Principia Mathematica* so reticent on the twinship between the algebra of logic and the theory of deduction, or, as we might put it today, the (Boolean) class calculus and the propositional calculus. Whitehead and Russell note that "the properties of negation, addition, multiplication and inclusion [for classes] . . . are, with certain exceptions, analogous to the properties of negation, addition, multiplication and implication for propositions."[1] This, however, is about as far as they carry the matter. I should therefore like to study here two ways of converting postulates for the (Boolean) Algebra of Classes (BA, for short) into full-fledged postulates for the Propositional Calculus (PC, for short) and thus elaborate somewhat on the above-quoted remark.

1. That the properties of negation, addition, multiplication, and inclusion for classes are *analogous* to the properties of negation, addition, multiplication, and implication for propositions can be dramatically enough illustrated. Let the primitive signs of BA be a denumerably infinite list of variables, the negation (or, better, complement) sign '−', the addition (or, better, union) sign '∪', the identity predicate '=', and the two parentheses '(' and ')'; let the metaaxioms of BA be as in [3]:

BA1. $(\alpha \cup \beta) = (\beta \cup \alpha)$

BA2. $((\alpha \cup \beta) \cup \gamma) = (\alpha \cup (\beta \cup \gamma))$

BA3. $(-(-\alpha \cup -\beta) \cup -(-\alpha \cup \beta)) = \alpha$

BA4. $\alpha = \alpha$;

and let the rules of inference of BA be:

BA5. From $\alpha = \beta$ to infer $\beta = \alpha$

408

BA6. From $\alpha = \beta$ and $\beta = \gamma$ to infer $\alpha = \gamma$

BA7. From $\alpha = \alpha'$ to infer $\beta = \beta'$, where β' is like β except for containing occurrences of α' at one or more places where β contain occurrences of α.[2]

The results (call them **PC1–PC4**) of substituting '$\sim$' for '$-$', '$\vee$' for '$\cup$', and '$\equiv$' for '$=$' in **BA1–BA4** will all be tautologies and, hence, be fit to appear among the axioms or theorems of PC; the results (call them **PC5–PC7**) of performing the same substitutions in **BA5–BA7** will, on the other hand, preserve tautologies and, hence, be fit to appear among the primitive or derived rules of inference of PC.

That the properties of negation, addition, multiplication, and inclusion for classes are, *with certain exceptions*, analogous to the properties of negation, addition, multiplication, and implication for propositions can likewise be dramatically illustrated. Whereas **BA1–BA7** yield as theorems all the valid formulas of BA, **PC1–PC7** (in which, by the way, '$\sim$' and '$\vee$' may be treated as primitive connectives and '$\equiv$' as a defined one)[3] yield as theorems only such tautologies as are of the form $\alpha \equiv \beta$.

Whitehead and Russell nowhere suggest how to strengthen the axioms and rules of inference of [3] if all tautologies are to be forthcoming as theorems. The problem, to my knowledge, was first tackled by C. I. Lewis in [5], pp. 80–83, and in [6], pp. 222–24. In the first passage Lewis suggests that a further axiom (or, as I would have it here, metaaxiom) be enlisted, namely: $\alpha = (\alpha = 1)$, where '$=$' must clearly be understood as '$\equiv$' and '1' as some tautology or other if the formulas collectively referred to by means of '$\alpha = (\alpha = 1)$' are to be formulas of PC. The suggestion, however, is idle, since the formulas in question are already provable as theorems of PC by means of **PC1–PC7**. In the second passage Lewis makes a similar and equally idle suggestion, $(\alpha = 0) \equiv \sim\alpha$ doing duty this time for $\alpha = (\alpha = 1)$. Before laying down this new metaaxiom, Lewis notes, however, that $\alpha = 0$ and $\sim\alpha$, on the one hand, and $\alpha = 1$ and α, on the other, are henceforth to be interchangeable. This offhand remark of his constitutes a first solution to the problem, for **PC1–PC7** *plus* the following rule of inference:

PC8. From $\alpha \equiv (\alpha \equiv \alpha)$ to infer α,

yield all tautologies as theorems.[4] A second solution to the problem is offered in [4] where **PC1–PC7** *plus* the following rule of inference:

PC9. From α and $\alpha \equiv \beta$ to infer β,

are also shown to yield all tautologies as theorems. Other rules of inference likewise fill the bill:

PC10. From $\alpha \equiv (\beta \equiv \beta)$, where β is any formula of PC, to infer α

PC11. From $\alpha \equiv \beta$, where β is any one of **PC1–PC3**, to infer α

PC12. From $\alpha \equiv (\alpha \,\&\, \beta)$ to infer $\alpha \supset \beta$

PC13. From $\beta \equiv (\beta \vee \alpha)$ to infer $\alpha \supset \beta$,

the first two of which were suggested to me by J. Porte.

That **PC1–PC7** *plus* **PC8** yield all tautologies as theorems can be demonstrated as follows. Let α be any tautology and let α^* be the formula of BA of which α is the propositional rewrite. Since **BA1–BA7** yield as theorems all the valid formulas of BA, they yield as a theorem the following valid formula of BA:

$$\alpha^* = -(-(-\alpha^* \cup \alpha^*) \cup -(-\alpha^* \cup \alpha^*)).$$

Hence **PC1–PC7** yield as a theorem the following tautology:

$$\alpha \equiv \sim(\sim(\sim\alpha \vee \alpha) \vee \sim(\sim\alpha \vee \alpha)),$$

or, for short, $\alpha \equiv (\alpha \equiv \alpha)$. Hence, by virtue of **PC8**, α is a theorem of PC.[5] That **PC1–PC7** *plus* **PC9** also yield all tautologies as theorems can be demonstrated as follows. If $\alpha \equiv \alpha$ and $(\alpha \equiv \alpha) \equiv \alpha$ are theorems of PC, then, by virtue of **PC9**, so is α. But, by virtue of **PC4**, $\alpha \equiv \alpha$ is a theorem of PC. Hence, if $(\alpha \equiv \alpha) \equiv \alpha$ is a theorem of PC, then so is α. Hence, by about the same reasoning as before, if α is a tautology, then α is a theorem of PC.[6]

2. Of the two extra rules just considered, the first might have appealed to Whitehead less than the second. When **PC8** rather than **PC9** is thrown in with **PC1–PC7**, Modus Ponens, the one rule of inference for PC officially acknowledged in *Principia Mathematica*, holds indeed in only one of its two guises. The same sort of thing happens with other sets of metaaxioms and rules of inference for PC recently offered in the literature and hence may be worth reviewing in detail.[7]

A finite sequence of formulas of PC is said to be a proof in PC if each formula in the sequence is an axiom of PC or follows from previous formulas in the sequence by application of a (primitive) rule of inference of PC; a formula of PC is next said to be provable in PC or to be a theorem of PC if it is the last formula of a proof in PC; a finite sequence of formulas of PC is then said to be a derivation in PC with n ($n \geq 0$) formulas $\alpha_1, \alpha_2, \ldots, \alpha_n$ of PC as assumption formulas if each formula in the sequence is one of $\alpha_1, \alpha_2, \ldots, \alpha_n$, or is an axiom of PC, or follows from previous formulas in the sequence by application of a (primitive) rule of inference of PC; a formula of PC is finally said to be derivable in PC from n ($n \geq 0$) formulas $\alpha_1, \alpha_2, \ldots, \alpha_n$ of PC as assumption formulas if it is the last formula of a derivation in PC with $\alpha_1, \alpha_2, \ldots, \alpha_n$ as assumption formulas.

Writing '$\alpha_1, \alpha_2, \ldots, \alpha_n \vdash \beta$,' where $n \geq 0$, for 'β is derivable in PC from $\alpha_1, \alpha_2, \ldots, \alpha_n$ as assumption formulas', and '$\vdash \alpha$' for 'α is a theorem of PC,' we are accordingly led to distinguish between two versions of Modus Ponens the so-called *provability* version, which reads

The Algebra of Logic and the Theory of Deduction 411

If ⊢ α *and* ⊢ α ⊃ β, *then* ⊢ β

and is to be referred to here as **MP1**, and the so-called *derivability* version, which reads

α, α ⊃ β ⊢ β

and is to be referred to here as **MP2**.

Whether both versions of Modus Ponens are forthcoming as rules of inference of PC depends on the metaaxioms and rules of inference PC is fitted with, as the following should show. To simplify matters I shall presume that the metaaxioms and rules of inference in question are such that

(a) If α is a theorem of PC, then α is a tautology,

and

(b) If α is a tautology, then α can effectively be shown to be a theorem of PC—that is, instructions can be supplied for constructing a finite sequence of formulas of PC of which α is the last formula.

Conditions (a) and (b) are met by **PC1–PC7** and **PC8**, by **PC1–PC7** and **PC9**, by Whitehead and Russell's own metaaxioms and rules of inference for PC, and by the recent sets of metaaxioms and rules of inference alluded to at the opening of Section 2.

(1) When, as in the case with *Principia Mathematica*, a rule reading: "From α and α ⊃ β to infer β," appears among the (primitive) rules of inference of PC, both versions of Modus Ponens are of course forthcoming as rules of inference of PC.

(2) In all other cases **MP1** is provable as follows as a metatheorem of PC: If two formulas α and α ⊃ β of PC are theorems of PC, then, by condition (a) above, α and α ⊃ β are tautologies; hence, by the definition of a tautology and the truth table for '⊃' β is a tautology; and hence, by condition (b) above, β can effectively be shown to be a theorem of PC. The foregoing proof of **MP1** is effective.

(3) In the same cases as under (2), **MP2** sometimes fails for some pairs of formulas α and β of PC and hence is sometimes not provable, whether effectively or not, as a metatheorem of PC.

(4) **MP1** and **MP2** qualify as derived rules of inference of PC, that is, as licenses for passing from two formulas α and α ⊃ β of PC to β itself when and only when effectively provable as metatheorems of PC. In the same cases as under (2), therefore, **MP1** is always forthcoming as a derived rule of inference of PC; **MP2**, on the other hand, is not always so forthcoming.

It comes as a surprise that PC may be fitted with such metaaxioms and rules of inference that **MP2** is not forthcoming as a derived rule of inference of PC. **PC1–PC7** and **PC8**, however, are a case in point, as Porte recently pointed out to me. Consider the two formulas 'p' and '$p \supset q$' of PC, where 'p' and 'q' are two propositional variables of PC. If any formula of PC, 'q', for example, is to be obtained from one or two other formulas of PC by application of **PC5**, **PC6**, **PC7**, or **PC8**, the one or two other formulas in question must be biconditionals. 'p' and '$p \supset q$,' however, are not biconditionals. Hence 'q' cannot be obtained from 'p' and '$p \supset q$' by application of **PC5**, **PC6**, **PC7**, or **PC8**. **MP2** is therefore not provable as a metatheorem of PC when **PC1–PC7** and **PC8** are elected to serve as metaaxioms and rules of inference for PC.[8]

The situation, however, changes drastically when **PC1–PC7** and **PC9** are elected to serve in that capacity: **MP2** is then effectively provable as a metatheorem of PC, and hence both **MP1** and **MP2** are forthcoming as derived rules of inference of PC. Proof of **MP2** is as follows. $\alpha \equiv (\alpha \equiv (\alpha \equiv \alpha))$ is effectively provable as a theorem of PC by means of **PC1–PC7**. Hence, by means of **PC9**, $\alpha \equiv (\alpha \equiv \alpha)$ is derivable in PC from α and $\alpha \supset \beta$ as assumption formulas. But $(\alpha \supset \beta) \equiv (\alpha \equiv (\alpha \& \beta))$ is effectively provable as a theorem of PC by means of **PC1–PC7**. Hence, by means of **PC9**, $\alpha \equiv (\alpha \& \beta)$; hence, by means of **PC9** again, $\alpha \& \beta$; and hence, by means of **PC7**, $(\alpha \equiv \alpha) \& \beta$, are successively derivable in PC from α and $\alpha \supset \beta$ as assumption formulas. But $((\alpha \equiv \alpha) \& \beta) \equiv \beta$ is effectively provable as a theorem of PC by means of **PC1–PC9**. Hence, by means of **PC9**, β is derivable in PC from α and $\alpha \supset \beta$ as assumption formulas. The foregoing proof of **MP2** is effective.[9]

In view of the results just arrived at, Whitehead might have preferred **PC9** over **PC8** as a way of converting postulates for BA into full-fledged postulates for PC.

Notes

1. See [8], p. 89.
2. See [3], pp. 274–304. **BA1–BA3** appear in the paper as Postulates 4.3, 4.4, and 4.6 on p. 280, **BA4–BA7** as Postulates **A**, **B**, **C**, and **D** on the same page.
3. To be more explicit, $\alpha \supset \beta$ may—as in *Principia Mathematica*—be short for $\sim\alpha \vee \beta$, $\alpha \& \beta$ short for $\sim(\sim\alpha \vee \sim\beta)$, and $\alpha \equiv \beta$ short for $(\alpha \supset \beta) \& (\beta \supset \alpha)$ (and, hence, for $\sim(\sim\alpha \vee \beta) \vee \sim(\sim\beta \vee \alpha)$)).
4. This result, as Jean Porte informs me, is a corollary of a theorem mentioned by Tarski in the course of his Paris lectures of 1955.
5. The argument offered in the text is a simplification of one due to Porte.
6. For another proof that **PC1–PC7** and **PC9** yield all tautologies as theorems, see [4]. Note when perusing [4] that **PC8–PC13** here appear in [4] as **PC13**, **PC8**, **PC12**, **PC11**, **PC9**, and **PC10**, respectively.
7. See [1], [2], and [7].
8. The same result holds true with **PC10** or **PC11** in place of **PC8**.
9. The same result holds true with **PC12** or **PC13** in place of **PC9**.

References

[1] Anderson, A. R., and Belnap, N. D., Jr. 1959. "A Simple Treatment of Truth Functions." *The Journal of Symbolic Logic* (hereafter *JSL*) 24: 301–02.
[2] Hiz, H. 1959. "Extendible Sentential Calculus." *JSL* 24: 193–202.
[3] Huntington, E. V. 1933. "New Sets of Independent Postulates for the Algebra of Logic, with

Special Reference to Whitehead and Russell's *Principia Mathematica*." *Transactions of the American Mathematical Society* 35: 274–304.
[4] Leblanc, H. 1962. "Boolean Algebra and the Propositional Calculus." *Mind* 71: 383–86 (#31 in this volume).
[5] Lewis, C. I. 1918. *A Survey of Symbolic Logic*. Berkeley: University of California Press.
[6] Lewis, C. I., and Langford, C. H. 1932. *Symbolic Logic*. New York: Dover.
[7] Porte, J. 1960. "Un Système pour le Calcul des Propositions où la Règle de Détachement n'est pas Valable." *Comptes-Rendus des Séances de l'Académie des Sciences*. 251: 188–89.
[8] Whitehead, A. N., and Russell, B. 1910–13. *Principia Mathematica*. Cambridge: Cambridge University Press.

33

All or None: A Novel Choice of Primitives for Elementary Logic

R. H. Thomason, coauthor

In [1] Ludwik Borkowski takes a quantifier symbol 'Q_i' (e.g., the familiar '$\forall$') to permit definition of another quantifier symbol 'Q_j' if, 'f' being a singulary predicate variable, there exists a formula A of QC_i—a first-order quantificational calculus with 'Q_i' as its one primitive quantifier symbol[1]—such that: (1) under the intended interpretations of 'Q_i' and 'Q_j' the biconditional $(Q_j X) f(X) \equiv A$ is valid, (2) no individual variable occurs free in A, and (3) A contains no propositional variable, nor any predicate variable other than 'f'.

It is clear that by means of negation, implication, and universal quantification at most eight pairwise non-equivalent formulas[2] can be constructed satisfying (1)–(3). So, under Borkowski's understanding of things, '$\forall$' permits definition of exactly eight non-equivalent quantifier symbols, and hence of exactly eight non-equivalent quantifications, namely:[3]

$(Q_1 X)B$: $(\forall X)B$ (i.e., For all X, B)

$(Q_2 X)B$: $(\forall X) \sim B$ (i.e., For no X, B)

$(Q_3 X)B$: $\sim(\forall X)B$ (i.e., Not for all X, B)

$(Q_4 X)B$: $\sim(\forall X)\sim B$ (i.e., For some X, B)

$(Q_5 X)B$: $(\forall X)B \lor (\forall X)\sim B$ (i.e., For all or no X, B)

$(Q_6 X)B$: $\sim(\forall X)\sim B$ & $\sim(\forall X)B$ (i.e., For some, but not all X, B)

$(Q_7 X)B$: $(\forall X)B \lor \sim(\forall X)B$ (i.e., For all or not all X, B)

$(Q_8 X)B$: $(\forall X)B$ & $\sim(\forall X)B$ (i.e., For all and not all X, B).

The quantifier symbols 'Q_2', 'Q_3', and 'Q_4' likewise permit definition of these eight. 'Q_5' and 'Q_6', on the other hand, permit definition of only four of the eight quantifier symbols: namely, of 'Q_5', 'Q_6', 'Q_7', and 'Q_8'. Finally, 'Q_7' and 'Q_8' permit definition of only two of them: namely, of 'Q_7' and 'Q_8'.

Condition (3) above is easily seen to be redundant. For if a formula A of QC_i

All or None: A Novel Choice of Primitives for Elementary Logic   415

exists satisfying (1) and (2) but not (3), let B be the result of replacing all components of A of the kind P by $(Q_iX)f(X)$, and all those of the kind $G(X_1, \ldots, X_n)$, where G differs from 'f', by $f(X_1)$ & . . . & $f(X_n)$. Clearly, B will satisfy (1), (2), and (3). On the other hand, condition (2) is not redundant. Indeed, suppose that this condition is dropped, a move we defend at the close of the paper. Since the biconditionals $(\forall X)A \equiv ((Q_5X)A \ \& \ A)$ and $(\forall X)A \equiv (\sim(Q_6X)A \ \& \ A)$ are both valid, each one of 'Q_5' and 'Q_6' will permit definition of '$\forall$', and hence of all eight of the quantifier symbols 'Q_1'–'Q_8'. The intended definitions, of course, are

$$(Q_1X)A =_{df} (Q_5X)A \ \& \ A$$

and

$$(Q_1X)A =_{df} \sim(Q_6X)A \ \& \ A.^4$$

Availing ourselves of this fact, we submit here a novel version, QC_5, of the first-order quantificational calculus which is readily shown equivalent to standard formulations.

The primitive signs of QC_5 are to be the customary propositional, predicate, and individual variables, the five connectives '$\sim$', '$\supset$', '&', '$\vee$', and '$\equiv$', the one quantifier symbol 'Q_5', the comma, and the two parentheses '(' and ')'.[5] The formulas of QC_5, and bondage and freedom of occurrences of individual variables in formulas, are characterized in the usual way. An individual variable X will be said to occur bound [free] in a formula A of QC_5 if at least one occurrence of X in A is bound [free].

Besides formulas of QC_5 that with the aid of rule **R1** below permit proof of all tautologies of QC_5 (and which, of course, are themselves tautologies), the axioms of QC_5 are to include all formulas of QC_5 of the sort

AQ₅. $(Q_5X)A \supset (A' \supset A'')$,

where, X' and X'' being individual variables not necessarily distinct from one another nor from X, A' and A'' are to be like A except for exhibiting free occurrences of X' and X'', respectively, wherever A exhibits free occurrences of X.[6]

The primitive rules of inference of QC_5 are to be:

R1. From A and $A \supset B$ to infer B;
R2'. From either one of $A \supset B$ and $A \supset \sim B$ to infer $A \supset (Q_5X)B$, so long as X does not occur free in A.[7]

A finite column of formulas of QC_5 is to constitute a proof in QC_5 of a formula A of QC_5 if the column closes with A and every entry in the column is an axiom of QC_5 or follows from previous entries by application of **R1** or **R2'**. And a formula A of QC_5 will be said to be provable in QC_5 if there is a proof in QC_5 of A.

Finally, the quantifier sign '$\forall$' is to be defined in QC_5 by means of the definition announced above:

D1′. $(\forall X)A =_{df} (Q_5 X)A \mathbin{\&} A$,

whereby a formula $(Q_5 X)A \mathbin{\&} A$ of QC_5 may be abridged as $(\forall X)A$.

The standard first-order quantificational calculus, called here QC_1, against which we match QC_5, will have '$\forall$' as its one primitive quantifier symbol, and hence formulas of the sort $(\forall X)A$ (rather than $(Q_5 X)A$) as its quantifications. Besides tautologous axioms, analogous to those of QC_5, its axioms are to include all formulas of the sort

AQ$_1$. $(\forall X)A \supset A'$,

where A' is like A except for exhibiting free occurrences of some individual variable X' (not necessarily distinct from X) wherever A exhibits free occurrences of X. Its two primitive rules of inference are to be **R1**, above, *plus* the following rule:

R2. From $A \supset B$ to infer $A \supset (\forall X)B$, so long as X does not occur free in A.

Finally, the quantifier symbol 'Q_5' is to be defined in QC_1 by means of the following definition:

D1. $(Q_5 X)A =_{df} (\forall X)A \lor (\forall X)\sim A$

whereby a formula $(\forall X)A \lor (\forall X)\sim A$ may be abridged as $(Q_5 X)A$.

Every formula A of QC_5 expands by way of **D1** into a unique formula of QC_1, to be known hereafter as the QC_1-*counterpart* of A; and every formula A of QC_1 expands by way of **D1′** into a unique formula of QC_5, to be known hereafter as the QC_5-*counterpart* of A. We will establish the equivalence of QC_1 and QC_5 by showing that a formula A of QC_1 is provable in QC_1 if and only if its QC_5-counterpart—$\tau_5(A)$, for short—is provable in QC_5 (Theorem 1), and that a formula A of QC_5 is provable in QC_5 if and only if its QC_1-counterpart—$\tau_1(A)$, for short—is provable in QC_1 (Theorem 2).[8] The lemmas below will be useful in connection with our two theorems. Proof of Lemma 3, a rule for QC_5 of substitutivity of equivalence, proceeds like that of *342 in [2], but with Lemma 2 doing duty for Church's *334.

Lemma 1. *Every formula of QC_5 of the sort $(Q_5 X')B' \supset (Q_5 X)B$, where X' is an individual variable foreign to B, and B' exhibits occurrences of X' wherever B exhibits free occurrences of X, is provable in QC_5.*

Proof: In case X' is the same as X, Lemma 1 holds by propositional means (for short, by **P**). So suppose X' is distinct from X. Then the column

1 $(Q_5 X')B' \supset (B \supset B')$	$(\mathbf{AQ_5})$[9]
2 $((Q_5 X')B' \mathbin{\&} \sim B') \supset \sim B$	$(\mathbf{P}, 1)$
3 $((Q_5 X')B' \mathbin{\&} \sim B') \supset (Q_5 X)B$	$(\mathbf{R2'}, 2)$[10]
4 $(Q_5 X')B' \supset (B' \supset B)$	$(\mathbf{AQ_5})$
5 $((Q_5 X')B' \mathbin{\&} B') \supset B$	$(\mathbf{P}, 4)$

6 $((Q_5X')B' \mathbin{\&} B') \supset (Q_5X)B)$ (**R2′**, 5)[11]

7 $(Q_5X')B' \supset (\forall X)B$ (**P**, 3, 6)

can be so augmented as to constitute a proof in QC_5 of entry 7. Hence Lemma 1.[12]

Lemma 2. *Every formula of* QC_5 *of the sort* $(Q_5X)(A \equiv B) \supset ((Q_5X)A \equiv (Q_5X)B)$ *is provable in* QC_5.

Proof: Let X' be an individual variable foreign to A and B, and let A' and B' be like A and B, respectively, except for exhibiting occurrences of X' wherever A and B exhibit free occurrences of X. Then the following column:

1 $(Q_5X)A \supset (A \supset A')$ (**AQ₅**)

2 $(Q_5X)A \supset (A' \supset A)$ (**AQ₅**)

3 $((Q_5X)(A \equiv B) \mathbin{\&} (Q_5X)A) \supset (A \equiv A')$ (**P**, 1–2)

4 $((Q_5X)(A \equiv B) \mathbin{\&} (Q_5X)A) \supset ((A \equiv B) \equiv (A' \equiv B'))$ (Steps similar to 1–3)

5 $(((Q_5X)(A \equiv B) \mathbin{\&} (Q_5X)A) \mathbin{\&} B) \supset B'$ (**P**, 3–4)

6 $(((Q_5X)(A \equiv B) \mathbin{\&} (Q_5X)A) \mathbin{\&} B) \supset (Q_5X')B'$ (**R2′**, 5)

7 $(Q_5X')B' \supset (Q_5X)B$ (Lemma 1)

8 $(((Q_5X)(A \equiv B) \mathbin{\&} (Q_5X)A) \mathbin{\&} B) \supset (Q_5X)B$ (**P**, 6–7)

9 $(((Q_5X)(A \equiv B) \mathbin{\&} (Q_5X)A) \mathbin{\&} \sim(Q_5X)B) \supset \sim B$ (**P**, 8)

10 $(((Q_5X)(A \equiv B) \mathbin{\&} (Q_5X)A) \mathbin{\&} \sim(Q_5X)B) \supset (Q_5X)B$ (**R2′**, 9)

11 $((Q_5X)(A \equiv B) \mathbin{\&} (Q_5X)A) \supset (Q_5X)B$ (**P**, 10)

12 $((Q_5X)(A \equiv B) \mathbin{\&} (Q_5X)B) \supset (Q_5X)A$ (Steps similar to 1–11)

13 $(Q_5X)(A \equiv B) \supset ((Q_5X)A \equiv (Q_5X)B)$ (**P**, 11–12)

can be so augmented as to constitute a proof in QC_5 of entry 11. Hence Lemma 2.

Lemma 3. *If* A *and* $B \equiv B'$ *are provable in* QC_5, *then so is* A', *where* A' *is like* A *except for exhibiting* B' *at one or more places where* A *exhibits* B.

Lemma 4. *Let* A *be a formula of* QC_5, *and let* A' *be like* A *except for exhibiting free occurrences of some individual variable* X' *wherever* A *exhibits free occurrences of* X. *Then* $((Q_5X)A \mathbin{\&} A) \equiv ((Q_5X)A \mathbin{\&} A')$ *is provable in* QC_5.
Proof by **AQ₅** and **P**.

Lemma 5. *Let* A *be a formula of* QC_5, *and* B *be a result of replacing various components of* A *of the sort* $(Q_5X)C \mathbin{\&} C$ *by ones of the sort* $(Q_5X)C \mathbin{\&} C'$, *where* C' *is like* C *except for exhibiting free occurrences of some individual*

variable X' wherever C exhibits free occurrences of X. Then $A \equiv B$ is provable in QC_5.
Proof by Lemmas 3–4.

Lemma 6. *Every formula of* QC_5 *of the sort*

$$(((Q_5X)A \ \& \ A) \lor ((Q_5X){\sim}A \ \& \ {\sim}A)) \equiv (Q_5X)A$$

is provable in QC_5.

Proof: Let X' be an individual variable foreign to A, and A' be like A except for exhibiting occurrences of X' wherever A exhibits free occurrences of X. Then the following column:

1 $(Q_5X)A \supset (A \supset A')$	$(\mathbf{AQ_5})$
2 $((Q_5X)A \ \& \ {\sim}A') \supset {\sim}A$	$(\mathbf{P}, 1)$
3 $((Q_5X)A \ \& \ {\sim}A') \supset (Q_5X){\sim}A$	$(\mathbf{R2'}, 2)$
4 $((Q_5X)A \ \& \ {\sim}(Q_5X){\sim}A) \supset {\sim}{\sim}A'$	$(\mathbf{P}, 3)$
5 $((Q_5X)A \ \& \ {\sim}(Q_5X){\sim}A) \supset (Q_5X){\sim}A$	$(\mathbf{R2'}, 4)$
6 $(Q_5X)A \supset (Q_5X){\sim}A$	$(\mathbf{P}, 5)$
7 $(Q_5X){\sim}A \supset (Q_5X)A$	(Steps similar to 1–6)
8 $(((Q_5X)A \ \& \ A) \lor ((Q_5X){\sim}A)) \equiv (Q_5X)A$	$(\mathbf{P}, 6\text{–}7)$

can be so augmented as to constitute a proof of entry 8 in QC_5. Hence Lemma 6.

Theorem 1. *Let A be a formula of* QC_1. *Then A is provable in* QC_1 *if and only if $\tau_5(A)$ is provable in* QC_5.
Proof:
Part one: Suppose the column made up of the p formulas $A_1, A_2, \ldots, A_p$ of QC_1 constitutes a proof of A in QC_1; and suppose A_i ($i = 1, 2, \ldots,$ or p) is one of the propositional axioms of QC_1. Then $\tau_5(A_i)$ is an axiom of QC_5, and hence is provable in QC_5 (*Case 1*). Or suppose A_i is of the sort $(\forall X)B \supset B'$, where B' is like B except for exhibiting free occurrences of some individual variable X' wherever B exhibits free occurrences of X; suppose that C is $\tau_5(B)$, that C' is like C except for exhibiting occurrences of X' wherever C exhibits free occurrences of X, and that D is $\tau_5(B')$. Since C' clearly will exhibit *free* occurrences of X' wherever C exhibits free occurrences of X, then $(Q_5X)C \supset (C \supset C')$ is of the sort $\mathbf{AQ_5}$, and so is provable in QC_5. But, by Lemma 5, $C' \equiv D$ is provable in QC_5. Hence, by $\mathbf{P}$, $((Q_5X)C \ \& \ C) \supset D$ is provable in QC_5. But $((Q_5X)C \ \& \ C) \supset D$ is $\tau_5(A_i)$. Hence $\tau_5(A_i)$ is provable in QC_5 (*Case 2*). Or suppose that A_i follows from two previous entries A_h and $A_h \supset A_i$ by application of $\mathbf{R1}$. Since $\tau_5(A_h \supset A_i)$ is the same as $\tau_5(A_h) \supset \tau_5(A_i)$, $\tau_5(A_i)$ follows from $\tau_5(A_h)$ and $\tau_5(A_h \supset A_i)$ by application of $\mathbf{R1}$ and hence is provable in

All or None: A Novel Choice of Primitives for Elementary Logic   419

QC_5 if $\tau_5(A_h)$ and $\tau_5(A_h \supset A_i)$ are (*Case 3*). Or suppose A_i is of the sort $B \supset (\forall X)C$, where X does not occur free in B, and follows from a previous entry A_h (namely, $B \supset C$) by application of **R2**; suppose that D is $\tau_5(B)$, that D' is like D except for exhibiting occurrences of some individual variable foreign to D wherever D exhibits free occurrences of X, and that E is $\tau_5(C)$. By Lemma 5, $D \equiv D'$ is provable in QC_5. Hence, by **P**, $D' \supset E$ is provable in QC_5 if $D \supset E$ is. But X does not occur free in D'; hence $D' \supset (Q_5X)E$ follows from $D \supset E$ by application of **R2'**. Thus by **P**, $D \supset ((Q_5X)E \& E)$ is provable in QC_5 if $D \supset E$ is. But $D \supset E$ is $\tau_5(A_h)$, and $D \supset ((Q_5X)E \& E)$ is $\tau_5(A_i)$. Hence $\tau_5(A_i)$ is provable in QC_5 if $\tau_5(A_h)$ is (*Case 4*). It follows by course-of-values induction on i that $\tau_5(A_i)$ is provable in QC_5 for every i from 1 to p. Thus $\tau_5(A)$ must be provable in QC_5 if A is provable in QC_1.
Part two: Suppose $\tau_5(A)$ is provable in QC_5. Then clearly, $\tau_5(A)$ is valid, and hence so is A. But then, by the semantical completeness of QC_1, A is provable in QC_1. Hence A is provable in QC_1 if $\tau_5(A)$ is provable in QC_5.

Theorem 2.   *Let A be a formula of QC_5. Then A is provable in QC_5 if and only if $\tau_5(A)$ is provable in QC_1.*
Proof:
Part one: Suppose that A is provable in QC_5. Then clearly A is valid, and hence so is $\tau_1(A)$. But then, by the semantical completeness of QC_1, $\tau_1(A)$ is provable in QC_1. Hence $\tau_1(A)$ is provable in QC_1 if A is provable in QC_5.
Part two: Suppose $\tau_1(A)$ is provable in QC_1. Then, by Part One of Theorem 1 above, $\tau_5(\tau_1(A))$ is provable in QC_5. But A results from $\tau_5(\tau_1(A))$ by a sequence of interchanges whereby components of $\tau_5(\tau_1(A))$ of the sort $((Q_5X)B \& B) \lor ((Q_5X){\sim}B \& {\sim}B)$ are turned in for components of the sort $(Q_5X)B$. Hence, by Lemmas 3 and 6, A must be provable in QC_5.

Our two theorems yield as corollaries analogues for QC_5 of various metamathematical results concerning QC_1: in particular, Gödel's completeness theorem, Löwenheim's theorem and Skolem's generalization thereof, and Church's undecidability theorem. The Craig-Lyndon interpolation theorem, however, fails for QC_5; a counterexample is provided by our introductory remarks.[13] Although, e.g., $((Q_5X)f(X) \& f(X)) \supset f(X')$ is provable in QC_5 (where X and X' differ), there is no *closed formula* A, with 'f' its sole predicate variable (and without propositional variables), such that both $((Q_5X)f(X) \& f(X)) \supset A$ and $A \supset f(X')$ are provable in QC_5—since A would then count as a definition in Borkowski's sense of 'Q_1' in terms of 'Q_5'.

This last example highlights the fact that **D1'** is *not* a definition in Borkowski's sense of 'Q_1' in terms of 'Q_5'. And doubtless, some readers will balk at **D1'** on the ground that X, when it occurs free in A, occurs free in $(Q_5X)A \& A$, the definiens we enlisted in QC_5 for $(\forall X)A$. Note, however, that $(Q_5X)A \& A$ is (semantically) equivalent to infinitely many formulas of QC_5 in which X does not occur free, and hence that X, when it occurs free in A, does so for form's sake only. In [5], an individual variable X occurring in a formula

A of QC_1, QC_5, or any other first-order quantificational calculus, is said to occur *semantically* (as opposed to *syntactically*) bound in A if A is semantically equivalent to any formula like A except for exhibiting some individual variable foreign to A wherever A exhibits X; and that X is said to occur *semantically* (as opposed to *syntactically*) free in A if X does not occur semantically bound in A.[14] Now, so long as the symbol 'Q_j' in clause (1) of Borkowski's definition is semantically interpreted as a quantifier (say, in the sense of [6]), any formula A satisfying clause (1) must also satisfy the condition: (2') *X does not occur semantically free in A*. But this more liberal clause (2') seems entirely in the spirit of Borkowski's definition, which must have been intended to rule out only those cases in which A semantically depends on the individual variable X. It therefore appears that clause (2) is an overrestrictive addition to clause (1). But, if so, then $(Q_5X)A$ & A strikes us as a perfectly suitable definiens for $(\forall X)A$ in QC_5.[15]

Notes

1. '=' is presumed throughout not to figure among the primitive signs of QC_i. See Note 3 on the matter.
2. As in much of the literature we take A to be (semantically) equivalent to B if $A \equiv B$ is valid.
3. The situation changes drastically when '=' is available as a primitive sign: '$\forall$' then permits definition of infinitely many quantifier symbols. See [6] in this connection.
4. Like-minded definitions of $\Box A$ are feasible in modal logic. Let 'C' be short for 'It is contingent that' (i.e., 'It is possible, but not necessary, that') and '$\bar{C}$' be short for 'It is not contengent that'. $\Box A$ can then be defined as $\bar{C}A$ & A.
5. Though we could dispense with some of our primitive signs, we prefer to keep the number of defined signs of QC_5 (and of QC_1, below) to a minimum.
6. The present formulation of QC_5 owes some to a referee for *The Journal of Symbolic Logic*. At present it is not known whether $(Q_5X)A \supset (A \supset A')$ (or $(Q_5X)A \supset (A' \supset A)$), with A' understood as in $\mathbf{AQ_5}$, could substitute for $\mathbf{AQ_5}$. Together, these special cases of $\mathbf{AQ_5}$ would deliver all the theorems of QC_5; but we conjecture that, alone, neither would. (Given a strengthened version of **R2'**—one which permits inference of $B \supset (Q_5X)A$ from either of $B \supset A'$ and $B \supset \sim A'$, where A' is as in $\mathbf{AQ_5}$ and X' does not occur free in $B \supset (Q_5X)A$—either of these two special cases would do the trick. But the amended rule departs further from **R2** below than our **R2'** does.)
7. Introduction rules for 'Q_5' in a Gentzen-like version of QC_5 that acknowledges sequents of the sort $A_1, A_2, \ldots, A_n \to B_1, B_2, \ldots, B_m$ ($n \geq 0$ and $m > 0$) are as follows:

$Q_5 \to$ $\to Q_5$

$$\frac{A', \Gamma \to \Delta \text{ and } \Gamma \to \Delta, A''}{(Q_5X)A, \Gamma \to \Delta} \qquad \frac{\Theta \to \Xi, A' \text{ or } A', \Theta \to \Xi}{\Theta \to \Xi, (Q_5X)A}$$

where A' and A'' are as in $\mathbf{AQ_5}$, and X' is not to occur free in any formula in Θ or in Σ, nor—should X' be distinct from X—in A. See [3], pp. 442–43.

8. Our proofs below of Part One of Theorem 1 and of Part Two of Theorem 2 provide effective means of turning a proof in QC_1 of a formula A into a proof of QC_5 of $\tau_5(A)$ and of turning a proof in QC_5 of a formula $\tau_1(A)$ into a proof in QC_5 of A. On the other hand, our proofs of Part Two of Theorem 1 and of Part One of Theorem 2, depending as they do on the semantical completeness of QC_1, do not provide effective means of turning a proof in QC_5 of a formula $\tau_5(A)$ into a proof in QC_1 of A, nor of turning a proof in QX_1 of a formula A into a proof in QC_5 of $\tau_1(A)$. We leave to the reader the straightforward task of finding alternative proofs which provide solutions to the latter two problems.

9. Since (i) B' is like B except for exhibiting free occurrences of X' wherever B exhibits free occurrences of X and (ii) X' is foreign to B, B is sure to be like B' except for exhibiting free occurrences of X and wherever B' exhibits free occurrences of X'. So $(Q_5X')B' \supset (B \supset B')$ is of the sort $\mathbf{AQ_5}$.

10. Since (i) B' is like B except for exhibiting free occurrences of X' wherever B exhibits free occurrences of X and (ii) X' is distinct in this case from X, X is sure not to occur free in $(Q_5X')B'$ & $\sim B'$. So the appeal to $\mathbf{R2'}$ is justified.

11. For the same reasons as in Note 10, X is sure not to occur free in $(Q_5X')B'$ & B'.

12. The proof of Lemma 1 in the original version of this paper was incorrect, as Yashuhara pointed out in [7].

13. Concerning the Craig-Lyndon interpolation theorem, see [4], Section 56.

14. Some readers may feel that the notion of semantical freedom is unsuited to syntactical uses, since it is not clear that the notion is effective. On the other hand, it is not known—so far as we are aware—that semantical freedom is *not* effective. Certainly, the question should be settled one way or another before extensive syntactical applications of the notion are made.

15. Thanks are due to Mostowski for bringing to our attention the problem discussed here, and to Yasuhara for spotting errors and misprints in the original version of the paper.

References

[1] Borkowski, L. 1958. "On Proper Quantifiers I." *Studia Logica* 8: 65–130.

[2] Church, A. 1956. *Introduction to Mathematical Logic, Volume I*. Princeton: Princeton University Press.

[3] Kleene, S. C. 1952. *Introduction to Metamathematics*. New York: van Nostrand.

[4] ———. 1967. *Mathematical Logic*. New York: Wiley.

[5] Leblanc, H. 1968. "Syntactically Free, Semantically Bound: A Note on Variables." *Notre Dame Journal of Formal Logic* 9: 167–70.

[6] Mostowski, A. 1957. "On a Generalization of Quantifiers." *Fundamenta Mathematicae* 44: 12–36.

[7] Yasuhara, M. 1979. Review of original version of present paper. *The Journal of Symbolic Logic* 34: 124–25.

34

Matters of Separation

R. K. Meyer, coauthor

1. Extending in some respects, sharpening in others, results in the literature, we establish here that:

(1) *Every classically valid wff A of* $QC_=$, *the first-order quantificational calculus with identity, is provable by means of axiom schemata* **A1–A3** *and rule* **R1** *in Table 1, plus the axiom schemata and rules of that table for only such of the logical symbols* '~', '&', '∨', '≡', '∀', '∃', *and* '=' *as occur in A, and*

(2) *Every intuitionistically valid wff A of* $QC_=$ *is provable by means of axiom schemata* **A1–A2** *and rule* **R1** *in Table 1, plus the axiom schemata and the seven rules of that table for only such of the logical symbols in question as occur in A.*

In the first of our two theorems **R2** is to serve as rule for '∀'; in the second, **R2** or **R2′** according as '&' occurs or not in *A*.

TABLE 1

Axiom schemata:

For '⊃': **A1.** $A \supset (B \supset A)$
 A2. $(A \supset (B \supset C)) \supset ((A \supset B) \supset (A \supset C))$
 A3. $((A \supset B) \supset A) \supset A$

For '~': **A4.** $(A \supset B) \supset (\sim B \supset \sim A)$
 A5. $A \supset \sim\sim A$
 A6. $\sim\sim A \supset (\sim A \supset B)$

For '&': **A7.** $(A \& B) \supset A$
 A8. $(A \& B) \supset B$
 A9. $A \supset (B \supset (A \& B))$

For '∨': **A10.** $A \supset (A \vee B)$
 A11. $B \supset (A \vee B)$
 A12. $(A \supset C) \supset ((B \supset C) \supset ((A \vee B) \supset C))$

For '≡': **A13.** $A \supset ((A \equiv B) \supset B)$
A14. $A \supset ((B \equiv A) \supset B)$
A15. $(A \supset B) \supset ((B \supset A) \supset (A \equiv B))$

For '∀': **A16.** $(\forall X)A \supset A(Y/X)$

For '∃': **A17.** $A(Y/X) \supset (\exists X)A$

For '=': **A18.** $X = X$
A19. $X = Y \supset (A \supset A(Y/X))$, where A is an atomic wff of $QC_=$.

Attendant substitution conventions: (i) In **A16–A17** $A(Y/X)$ is to be like A except for containing free Y wherever A contains free X. (ii) In **A19** $A(Y/X)$ is to be like A except for containing (free) Y at zero or more places where A contains (free) X.

Rules:

For '⊃': **R1.** *From A and $A \supset B$ to infer B.*

For '∀': **R2.** *From $A \supset B$ to infer $A \supset (\forall X)B$, so long as X does not occur free in A.*
R2'. *From $A \supset (B \supset C)$ to infer $A \supset (B \supset (\forall X)C)$, so long as X does not occur free in either one of A and B.*

For '∃': **R3.** *From $A \supset B$ to infer $(\exists X)A \supset B$, so long as X does not occur free in B.*

The earliest forerunner of (2) is probably a result of Curry's in [1], which differs from (2) in only three minor respects: (i) A is restricted throughout to be a wff of QC, the first-order quantificational calculus without identity, (ii) '≡' is ignored, being treated as a defined sign, and (iii) **R2** serves in all cases as rule for '∀', the extra axiom schema

B1. $(\forall X)(A \supset B) \supset (A \supset (\forall X)B)$, where X does not occur free in A,

being thrown in when '&' does not occur in A.[1] The earliest anticipation of (1) that we know of is a theorem of Kleene's in [4], p. 459, to the effect that if a wff A of QC is classically valid, then A is provable by means of axiom schemata **A1–A2**, the following two axiom schemata (for '∼'):

B2. $(A \supset B) \supset ((A \supset \sim B) \supset \sim A)$

B3. $\sim\sim A \supset A$,

rule **R1**, plus the axiom schemata and rules of Table 1 for only such of the four logical symbols '&', '∨', '∀', and '∃' as occur in A. Like Curry, Kleene ignores '≡', uses **R2** as his one rule for '∀', and calls on axiom schema **B1** when '&' does not occur in A. A partial forerunner of (1) and (2) is of course [3], in which Kanger proves both theorems for the case where A is a wff of SC, the sentential calculus.[2]

2. For proof of (1) consider first the case where A contains no occurrence of '$=$' and hence is a wff of QC. It is shown in [5] that every classically valid sequent of the sort

$$A_1, A_2, \ldots, A_n \to B,$$

where $A_1, A_2, \ldots, A_n (n \geq 0)$, and B are wffs of QC, is provable by means of the axiom schema

$$K, A, L \to A \qquad\qquad (\mathbf{Ax})$$

and the intelim rules of Table 2 for only such of the seven logical symbols '$\supset$', '$\sim$', '$\&$', '$\vee$', '$\equiv$', '$\forall$', and '$\exists$' as occur in the sequent.[3]

TABLE 2

Introduction rules	Elimination rules

For '$\supset$':

$$\dfrac{K, A \to B}{K \to A \supset B} \qquad\qquad \dfrac{K \to A \supset B \quad K \to (A \supset C) \supset A}{K \to B}$$

For '$\sim$':

$$\dfrac{K, A \to B \quad K, A \to \sim B}{K \to \sim A} \qquad\qquad \dfrac{K \to \sim\sim A}{K \to A}$$

For '$\&$':

$$\dfrac{K \to A \quad K \to B}{K \to A \& B} \qquad\qquad \dfrac{K \to A \& B}{K \to A} \quad \dfrac{K \to A \& B}{K \to B}$$

For '$\vee$':

$$\dfrac{K \to A}{K \to A \vee B} \quad \dfrac{K \to B}{K \to A \vee B} \qquad\qquad \dfrac{K, A \to C \quad K, B \to C \quad K \to A \vee B}{K \to C}$$

For '$\equiv$':

$$\dfrac{K, A \to B \quad K, B \to A}{K \to B \equiv B} \qquad\qquad \dfrac{K \to A \quad K \to (C \equiv A) \equiv (C \equiv B)}{K \to B}$$

For '$\forall$':

$$\dfrac{K \to A}{K, L \to (\forall X)A} \qquad\qquad \dfrac{K \to (\forall X)A}{K \to A(Y/X)}$$

For '$\exists$':

$$\dfrac{K \to A(Y/X)}{K \to (\exists X)A} \qquad\qquad \dfrac{K, L \to (\exists X)A \quad K, A \to B}{K, L \to B}$$

For '∀' and '∨':

$$\frac{K \to A \lor B}{K, L \to (\forall X)A \lor B}$$

Attendant restrictions: (i) In the introduction rule for '∀' the variable X is not to occur free in any wff in K. (ii) In the elimination rule for '∃' and the introduction rule for '∀' and '∨', X is not to occur free in any wff in K nor in B.

Now let the *wff-associate* of a sequent of the sort $\to B$ be B, that of a sequent of the sort $A_1 \to B$ be $A_1 \supset B$, that of a sequent of the sort $A_1, A_2 \to B$ be $A_1 \supset (A_2 \supset B)$, and so on. It is easily verified that the wff-associate of any sequent of the above sort $K, A, L \to A$ is provable by means of **A1–A2** and **R1**. It can also be verified (see Section 4 for three sample cases) that (i) if a sequent S follows from another sequent S_1, or two other sequents S_1 and S_2, or three other sequents S_1, S_2, and S_3 by application of an intelim rule of Table 2 for one or (as in the case of the introduction rule for '∀' and '∨') two of the logical symbols '⊃', '∼', '&', '∨', '≡', '∀', and '∃', and (ii) the wff-associate of S_1, or the wff-associates of S_1 and S_2, or the wff-associates of S_1, S_2, and S_3 are provable by means of a set α of axiom schemata and rules for Table 1, then the wff-associate of S is provable by means of α, **A1–A3, R1**, and the axiom schemata and rules of Table 1 for the one symbol or the two symbols in question.

Take then the wff A of (1) on p. 422. Since A is presumed to be classically valid, the corresponding sequent $\to A$ is sure to be classically valid as well. Hence there is sure to be a proof of $\to A$ by means of the one axiom schema and the intelim rules of Table 2 for only such of the logical symbols '⊃', '∼', '&', '∨', '≡', '∀', and '∃' as occur in $\to A$. Hence there is sure to be for each entry $K_i \to B_i$ in the proof in question of $\to A$ a proof of the wff-associate of $K_i \to B_i$ by means of **A1–A3, R1**, and the axiom schemata and rules of Table 1 for only such of the logical symbols '∼', '&', '∨', '≡', '∀', and '∃' as occur in $\to A$. Hence, in particular, there is sure to be a proof of A (the wff-associate of $\to A$) by means of **A1–A3, R1**, and the axiom schemata and rules of Table 1 for only such of the logical symbols '∼', '&', '∨', '≡', '∀', and '∃' as occur in $\to A$ and hence in A.[4]

3. Consider then the case where A contains at least one occurrence of '='. Since A is presumed to be classically valid and since the axiom schemata and rules of Table 1 permit proof of every classically valid wff of $QC_=$, there is sure to be a column of wffs of $QC_=$ that closes with A and counts as a proof of A by means of the axiom schemata and rules of Table 1. Now let $B_1, B_2, \ldots, B_n$ ($n \geq 0$) be in any order all the entries in the column in question that are of the sort **A18** or the sort **A19** in Table 1. By virtue of the Deduction Theorem

$$B_1 \supset (B_2 \supset (\ldots \supset (B_n \supset A) \ldots))$$

is sure to be provable by means of the axiom schemata and rules of Table 1 minus **A18–A19**. Hence so is the result

$$B'_1 \supset (B'_2 \supset (\ldots \supset B'_n \supset A') \ldots))$$

of turning in every component of $B_1 \supset (B_2 \supset (\ldots \supset (B_n \supset A) \ldots))$ of the sort $X = Y$ for one of the sort $F(X,Y)$, where F is any two-place predicate variable of QC that is foreign to $B_1 \supset (B_2 \supset (\ldots \supset (B_n \supset A) \ldots))$. But $B'_1 \supset (B'_2 \supset (\ldots \supset (B'_n \supset A') \ldots))$ is a wff of QC, and—being provable by means of the axiom schemata and rules of Table 1 minus **A18–A19**—is sure to be classically valid. Hence, by the case covered in Section 2, $B'_1 \supset (B'_2 \supset (\ldots \supset (B'_n \supset A') \ldots))$ is sure to be provable by means of **A1–A3, R1**, and the axiom schemata and rules of Table 1 for only such of the logical symbols '$\sim$', '&', '$\vee$', '$\equiv$', '$\forall$', and '$\exists$' as occur in $B'_1 \supset (B'_2 \supset (\ldots \supset (B'_n \supset A') \ldots))$. Hence clearly $B_1 \supset (B_2 \supset (\ldots \supset (B_n \supset A) \ldots))$ is sure to be provable by means of **A1–A3, R1**, and the axiom schemata and rules of Table 1 for only such of the symbols in question as occur in $B_1 \supset (B_2 \supset (\ldots \supset (B_n \supset A) \ldots))$. Hence A is sure to be provable by means of **A1–A3, A18–A19, R1**, and the axiom schemata and rules of Table 1 for only such of the symbols in question as occur in one or more of $B_1, B_2, \ldots, B_n, A$. But none of '$\sim$', '&', '$\vee$', '$\equiv$', '$\forall$', and '$\exists$' occurs in anyone of $B_1, B_2, \ldots, B_n$; and '$=$', which does occur in each one of $B_1, B_2, \ldots, B_n$, is presumed to occur in A. Hence A is sure to be provable by means of **A1–A3, R1**, and the axiom schemata and rules of Table 2 for only such of the logical symbols '$\sim$', '&', '$\vee$', '$\equiv$', '$\forall$', '$\exists$', and '$=$' as occur in A.[5]

4. The three sample cases that we promised to work out in detail are the introduction rule for '$\forall$' ($= \forall$I), the introduction rule for '$\forall$' and '$\vee$' ($= \forall_\vee$), and the elimination rule for '$\exists$' ($= \exists$E). Throughout α is to be an arbitrary set of axiom schemata and rules from Table 1.

Lemma 1. $((A \supset B) \supset B) \supset ((A \supset (\forall X)B) \supset B)$ *is provable by means of* **A1–A2, A16,** *and* **R1**.
Proof: $(\forall X)B \supset B$ is provable by means of **A16**. Hence Lemma 1.

Lemma 2. *If* $A \supset (B \supset C)$ *is provable by means of* α, *then* $A \supset (B \supset (\forall X)C)$ *is provable by means of* α, **A1–A3, A16, R1,** *and* **R2,** *so long as* X *does not occur free in either one of* A *and* B.
Proof: Suppose $A \supset (B \supset C)$ is provable by means of α. Since $(A \supset (B \supset C)) \supset (((A \supset (B \supset (\forall X)C)) \supset C) \supset C)$ is provable by means of **A1–A3** and **R1**, then $((A \supset (B \supset (\forall X)C)) \supset C) \supset C$ is provable by means of α, **A1–A3,** and **R1**. Hence in view of Lemma 1 $((A \supset (B \supset (\forall X)C)) \supset (\forall X)C) \supset C$ is provable by means of α, **A1–A3, A16,** and **R1**. Suppose next that X does not occur free in either one of A and B. Then $((A \supset (B \supset (\forall X)C)) \supset (\forall X)C) \supset (\forall X)C$, which follows from $((A \supset (B \supset (\forall X)C)) \supset (\forall X)C) \supset C$ by application of

Matters of Separation 427

R2, is provable by means of α, **A1–A3, A16, R1,** and **R2**. But $(((A \supset (B \supset (\forall X)C)) \supset (\forall X)C) \supset (\forall X)C) \supset (A \supset (B \supset (\forall X)C))$ is provable by means of **A1–A3** and **R1**. Hence Lemma 2.[6]

Lemma 3. $(\forall X)(A \supset B) \supset (A \supset (\forall X)B)$, *where X does not occur free in A, is provable by means of* **A1–A3, A16, R1,** *and* **R2**.
Proof: $(\forall X)(A \supset B) \supset (A \supset B)$ is provable by means of **A16**. Hence Lemma 3 by Lemma 2.

Theorem 1. *If the wff-associate* $B_1 \supset (B_2 \supset (\ldots \supset (B_m \supset A) \ldots))$ *of* B_1, $B_2, \ldots, B_m \to A$ *is provable by means of* α, *then the wff-associate* $B_1 \supset (B_2 \supset (\ldots \supset (B_m \supset (C_1 \supset (C_2 \supset (\ldots \supset (C_n \supset (\forall X)A) \ldots)))) \ldots))$ *of* B_1, $B_2, \ldots, B_m, C_1, C_2, \ldots, C_n \to (\forall X)A$ *is provable by means of* α, **A1–A3, A16, R1,** *and* **R2**, *so long as X does not occur free in any one of* $B_1, B_2, \ldots, B_m$. (∀I)
Proof by mathematical induction on m.
Basis: Suppose A is provable by means of α. Then $(p \supset p) \supset A$ is provable by means of α, **A1–A2**, and **R1**. Hence $(p \supset p) \supset (\forall X)A$, which follows from $(p \supset p) \supset A$ by application of **R2**, is provable by means of α, **A1–A2, R1,** and **R2**. Hence so is $C_1 \supset (C_2 \supset (\ldots \supset (C_n \supset (\forall X)A) \ldots))$.
Inductive Step: Suppose $B_1 \supset (B_2 \supset (\ldots \supset (B_m \supset A) \ldots))$ is provable by means of α, and X does not occur free in anyone of $B_1, B_2, \ldots$, and B_m. Then by the hypothesis of the induction (with n equal to 0) $B_1 \supset (B_2 \supset (\ldots \supset (\forall X)(B_m \supset A) \ldots))$ is provable by means of α, **A1–A3, A16, R1,** and **R2**. But in view of Lemma 3 $(B_1 \supset (B_2 \supset (\ldots \supset (\forall X)(B_m \supset A) \ldots))) \supset (B_1 \supset (B_2 \supset (\ldots \supset (B_m \supset (\forall X)A) \ldots)))$ is provable by means of **A1–A3, A16, R1,** and **R2**. Hence $B_1 \supset (B_2 \supset (\ldots \supset (B_m \supset (\forall X)A) \ldots))$ is provable by means of α, **A1–A3, A16, R1,** and **R2**. Hence so is $B_1 \supset (B_2 \supset (\ldots \supset (B_m \supset (C_1 \supset (C_2 \supset (\ldots \supset (C_n \supset (\forall X)A) \ldots)))) \ldots))$.

Lemma 4. $(\forall X)(A \lor B) \supset ((\forall X)A \lor B)$, *where X does not occur free in B, is provable by means of* **A1–A3, A10–A12, A16, R1,** *and* **R2**.
Proof: $(\forall X)(A \lor B) \supset (A \lor B)$ is provable by means of **A16**, and $(A \lor B) \supset ((B \supset A) \supset A)$ provable by means of **A1–A3, A10–A12,** and **R1**. Hence $(\forall X)A \lor B) \supset ((B \supset A) \supset A)$ is provable by means of **A1–A3, A10–A12, A16, R1,** and **R2**. Hence in view of Lemma 1 so is $(\forall X)(A \lor B) \supset ((B \supset (\forall X)A) \supset A)$. Hence so is $(\forall X)(A \lor B) \supset ((B \supset (\forall X)A) \supset (\forall X)A)$, which follows from $(\forall X)(A \lor B) \supset ((B \supset (\forall X)A) \supset A)$ by application of **R2**. But $((B \supset (\forall X)A) \supset (\forall X)A) \supset ((\forall X)A \lor B)$ is provable by means of **A1–A3, A10–A12,** and **R1**. Hence Lemma 4.

Theorem 2. *If the wff-associate* $C_1 \supset (C_2 \supset (\ldots \supset (C_m \supset (A \lor B)) \ldots))$ *of* $C_1, C_2, \ldots, C_m \to A \lor B$ *is provable by means of* α, *then the wff-associate* $C_1 \supset (C_2 \supset (\ldots \supset (C_m \supset (D_1 \supset (D_2 \supset (\ldots \supset (D_n \supset ((\forall X)A \lor B)) \ldots)))) \ldots))$ *of* $C_1, C_2, \ldots, C_m, D_1, D_2, \ldots, D_n \to (\forall X)A \lor B$ *is* *provable by means of* α, **A1–A3, A10–A12, A16, R1,** *and* **R2**, *so long as X does not occur free in anyone of* C_1, C_2, ..., C_m, *and B.* ($\forall I_V$)

Proof: Suppose $C_1 \supset (C_2 \supset (\ldots (C_m \supset (A \lor B)) \ldots))$ is provable by means of α, and X does not occur free in anyone of C_1, C_2, ..., and C_m. Then, in view of Theorem 1, $C_1 \supset (C_2 \supset (\ldots \supset (C_m \supset (\forall X) (A \lor B)) \ldots))$ is provable by means of α, **A1–A3, A16, R1,** and **R2**. Suppose next that X does not occur free in B. Then, in view of Lemma 4, $C_1 \supset (C_2 \supset (\ldots \supset (C_m \supset ((\forall X)A \lor B)) \ldots))$ is provable by means of α, **A1–A3, A10–A12, A16, R1,** and **R2**. Hence so is $C_1 \supset (C_2 \supset (\ldots \supset (C_m \supset (D_1 \supset (D_2 \supset (\ldots \supset (D_n \supset ((\forall X)A \lor B)) \ldots)))) \ldots))$.

Theorem 3. *If the wff-associates* $C_1 \supset (C_2 \supset (\ldots \supset (C_m \supset (D_1 \supset (D_2 \supset (\ldots \supset (D_n \supset (\exists X)A) \ldots)))) \ldots))$ *and* $C_1 \supset (C_2 \supset (\ldots \supset (C_m \supset (A \supset B)) \ldots))$ *of* C_1, C_2, ..., C_m, D_1, D_2, ..., $D_m \rightarrow (\exists X)A$ *and* C_1, C_2, ..., C_m, $A \rightarrow B$ *are provable by means of* α, *then the wff-associate* $C_1 \supset (C_2 \supset (\ldots \supset (C_m \supset (D_1 \supset (D_2 \supset (\ldots \supset (D_n \supset B) \ldots)))) \ldots))$ *of* C_1, C_2, ..., C_m, D_1, D_2, ..., $D_n \rightarrow B$ *is provable by means of* α, **A1–A2, R1,** *and* **R3**, *so long as X does not occur free in anyone of* C_1, C_2, ..., C_m, *and B.* ($\exists E$)

Proof: Suppose $C_1 \supset (C_2 \supset (\ldots \supset (C_m \supset (A \supset B)) \ldots))$ is provable by means of α. Then $A \supset (C_1 \supset (C_2 \supset (\ldots \supset (C_m \supset B) \ldots)))$ is provable by means of α, **A1–A2,** and **R1**. Suppose next that X does not occur free in anyone of C_1, C_2, ..., C_m, and B. Then $(\exists X)A \supset (C_1 \supset (C_2 \supset (\ldots \supset (C_m \supset B) \ldots)))$, which follows from $A \supset (C_1 \supset (C_2 \supset (\ldots \supset (C_m \supset B) \ldots)))$ by application of **R3**, is provable by means of α, **A1–A2, R1,** and **R3**. Hence so is $(C_1 \supset (C_2 \supset (\ldots \supset (C_m \supset (D_1 \supset (D_2 \supset (\ldots \supset (D_n \supset (\exists X)A) \ldots)))) \ldots))) \supset (C_1 \supset (C_2 \supset (\ldots \supset (C_m \supset (D_1 \supset (D_2 \supset (\ldots \supset (D_n \supset B) \ldots)))) \ldots)))$. Hence Theorem 3.

5. Proof of (2) on p. 422 is essentially like that of (1), except for using another result from [5], this one to the effect that every intuitionistically valid sequent of the sort $A_1, A_2, \ldots, A_n \rightarrow B$ is provable by means of the axiom schema K, A, L → A and the intelim rules of Table 3 for only such of the seven logical symbols '⊃', '~', '&', '∨', '≡', '∀', and '∃' as occur in the sequent.

TABLE 3

Introduction rules: Same as in Table 1 *minus* $\forall I_V$.
Elimination rules:

For '&', '∨', '∀', and '∃': Same as in Table 2.

For '⊃':
$$\frac{K \rightarrow A \quad K \rightarrow A \supset B}{K \rightarrow B}$$

For '∼': $$\frac{K \to \sim A \quad K \to \sim\sim A}{K \to A}$$

For '≡': $$\frac{K \to A \quad K \to A \equiv B}{K \to B} \qquad \frac{K \to A \quad K \to B \equiv A}{K \to B}$$

To restrict ourselves again to quantificational matters, ∃E can be handled as in Section 4. ∀I, on the other hand, calls for fresh treatment, since our proof of **B1** in Section 4 (see Lemma 3) makes use of **A3**. Proof of **B1** by means of **A1–A2, A7–A9, A16, R1**, and **R2** is readily had. We do not know, however, of any proof of **B1** by means of **A1–A2, A16, R1**, and **R2** alone, nor for that matter of any proof of **B1** by means of **A1–A2, A16, R1, R2**, and the axiom schemata and rules of Table 1 for anyone of '∼', '∨', '≡', and '∃'; and hence, in every case in which the wff A of (2) contains no '&', resort to **R2′**, which of course delivers **B1** at a stroke.

Lemma 5. (a) **B1** *is provable by means of* **A1–A2, A7–A9, A16, R1**, *and* **R2**. (b) **B1** *is provable by means of* **A16** *and* **R2′**.
Proof: (a) $(\forall X)A \supset B) \supset (A \supset B)$ is provable by means of **A16**. But $((\forall X)(A \supset B) \supset (A \supset B)) \supset (((\forall X)(A \supset B) \,\&\, A) \supset B)$ is provable by means of **A1–A2, A7–A9,** and **R1**. Hence $((\forall X)(A \supset B) \,\&\, A) \supset B$ is provable by means of **A1–A2, A7–A9, A16,** and **R1**. Hence $((\forall X)(A \supset B) \,\&\, A) \supset (\forall X)B$, which follows from $((\forall X)A \supset B) \,\&\, A) \supset B$ by application of **R2**, is provable by means of **A1–A2, A7–A9, A16, R1,** and **R2**. But $(((\forall X)(A \supset B) \,\&\, A) \supset (\forall X)B) \supset ((\forall X)(A \supset B) \supset (A \supset (\forall X)B))$ is provable by means of **A1–A2, A7–A9,** and **R1**. Hence $(\forall X)(A \supset B) \supset (A \supset (\forall X)B)$ is provable by means **A1–A2, A7–A9, A16, R1,** and **R2**.
(b) $(\forall X)A \supset B) \supset (A \supset B)$, from which $(\forall X)(A \supset B) \supset (A \supset (\forall X)B)$ follows by application of **R2′**, is provable by means of **A16**. Hence (b).

Theorem 4. *If the wff-associate of* $B_1, B_2, \ldots, B_m \to A$ *is provable by means of* α, *then the wff-associate of* $B_1, B_2, \ldots, B_m, C_1, C_2, \ldots, C_n \to (\forall X)A$, *where X does not occur free in any one of* $B_1, B_2, \ldots, B_m$, *is provable by means of* α, **A1–A2, A16, R1**, *and* **R2** *when* **A7–A9** *belongs to* α, *otherwise by means of* α, **A16**, *and* **R2′**. (∀I)

Notes

1. The last note on p. 288 of [1] suggests that **B1′** $(\forall X)(A \supset B) \supset ((\exists X)A \supset B)$, where X does not occur free in B, is also needed in the absence of '&', but this is probably unintended since **B1′** is provable by means of **A1–A2, A16, R1**, and **R3**.
2. Except **A9**, borrowed from [6], **A1–A12** are the very axiom schemata that Kanger uses in [3]. Robinson notes in [6] that $(A \supset \sim B) \supset (B \supset \sim A)$ and $\sim A \supset (A \supset B)$ can do duty for all three of **A4–A6**.
3. In four out of five cases the quantificational rules of Table 1 are simplifications (suggested by rules of Fitch's in [2]) of their counterparts in [5]. As the reader may wish to verify, they permit proof of exactly the same sequents as their counterparts in [5] do.

4. The argument is reminiscent of arguments in [1], [3], [4], and [5].

5. A like argument obviously goes through for any predicate constant other than '=' whose axiom schemata are all of the sort $A_1 \supset (A_2 \supset (\ldots \supset (A_n \supset B) \ldots))$, where $A_1, A_2, \ldots, A_n$ ($n \geq 0$), B are atomic.

6. The two conditions $(A \supset (B \supset C)) \supset (((A \supset (B \supset (\forall X)C)) \supset C) \supset C)$ and $(((A \supset (B \supset (\forall X)C)) \supset (\forall X)C) \supset (A \supset (B \supset (\forall X)C))$, though provable by means of **A1–A3** and **R2**, are not provable by means of **A1–A2** and **R1** alone. Hence **B1** (see Lemma 3) will call for a fresh proof in Section 5.

References

[1] Curry, H. B. 1939. "A Note on the Reduction of Gentzen's Calculus LJ." *Bulletin of the American Mathematical Society* 45: 288–93.

[2] Fitch, F. B. 1952. *Symbolic Logic*. New York: The Ronald Press.

[3] Kanger, S. 1955. "A Note on Partial Postulate Sets for Propositional Logic." *Theoria* 21: 99–104.

[4] Kleene, S. C. 1952. *Introduction to Metamathematics*. New York: van Nostrand.

[5] Leblanc, H. 1966. "Two Separation Theorems for Natural Deduction." *Notre Dame Journal of Formal Logic* 7: 159–80 (#24 in this volume).

[6] Robinson, T. T. 1968. "Independence of Two Nice Sets of Axioms for the Propositional Calculus." *The Journal of Symbolic Logic* 33: 265–70.

35
Generalization in First-Order Logic

Dealing initially with QC, the standard quantificational calculus of order one, I shall comment on a shortcoming, reported in 1956 by Montague and Henkin, in Church's 1944 account of *a proof from hypotheses*, and sketch three ways of righting things. The third, which exploits a trick of Fitch's and for this reason will be called *Fitch's account*, is the simplest of the three. I shall investigate it some, supplying fresh proof of **UGT**, the *Universal Generalization Theorem*. The proof holds good, it will turn out, as one passes from QC to QC*, the presupposition-free variant of QC. Turning next to $QC_=$, the standard quantificational calculus of order one with identity, and to the presupposition-free variant $QC^*_=$ of $QC_=$, I shall establish the lemmas needed there to obtain **UGT**. That given Fitch's account of a proof from hypotheses **UGT** holds for $QC^*_=$ was argued in my recent *Truth-Value Semantics*, but the argument is circular, as Robert J. Cosgrove found out to my dismay.

The results submitted here are elementary, to be sure; but the difficulty that Montague and Henkin reported was quite a serious one, and ways of meeting it accordingly deserve attention. The results, by the way, are readily adapted to suit most (if not all) logics with quantifiers.

1. In most treatments of the calculus, QC has as its *primitive signs*:
 (a) For each d from 0 on, $\aleph_0$ predicate variables of degree d (to be referred to by means of 'F^d'),[1]
 (b) $\aleph_0$ individual variables, say, 'x', 'y', 'z', 'x'', 'y'', 'z'', etc. (to be referred to by means of 'X' and 'Y',
 (c) the three logical operators '$\sim$', '$\supset$', and '$\forall$',
and
 (d) '(', ')', and ','.
It has as its *formulas* all finite sequences of primitive signs of QC (said sequences to be referred to by means of 'A', 'B', and 'C'). And it has as its *well-formed formulas* (wffs) all formulas of QC of any of the following four sorts:
 (i) $F^d(X_1, X_2, \ldots, X_d)$, where $d \geq 0$,
 (ii) $\sim A$, in case A is a wff of QC,

(iii) $(A \supset B)$, in case A and B are wffs of QC,[2] and

(iv) $(\forall X)A$, in case A is a wff of QC.

Further, any wff of QC counts as a *well-formed part* of itself; A counts as a well-formed part of the wffs $\sim A$ and $(\forall X)A$; A and B count as well-formed parts of the wff $A \supset B$; and any well-formed part of a well-formed part of a wff A counts as a well-formed part of A. An *occurrence* O of an individual variable X of QC in a wff A of QC is said to be *bound* if O is in a well-formed part of A of the sort $(\forall X)B$; O is said to be *free* in A if O is not bound in A; and the variable X itself is said to *occur free* in A if at least one occurrence of X in A is free. And I shall refer by means of '$A(Y/X)$' to A itself when at least one free occurrence of X in A is in a well-formed part of A of the sort $(\forall Y)B$, otherwise to the result of replacing every free occurrence of X in A by an occurrence of Y.

So much (at this point) for the primitive vocabulary and the grammar of QC. There are numerous axiomatizations of QC in the literature. An especially serviceable one reckons as the *axioms* of QC all wffs of QC of any of the following six sorts:

A1. $A \supset (B \supset A)$

A2. $(A \supset (B \supset C)) \supset ((A \supset B) \supset (A \supset C))$

A3. $(\sim A \supset \sim B) \supset (B \supset A)$

A4. $(\forall X)(A \supset B) \supset ((\forall X)A \supset (\forall X)B)$

A5. $A \supset (\forall X)A$

A6. $(\forall X)A \supset A(Y/X)$.

where in the fifth case X does not occur free in A.

Given some such axiomatization, the pre-1956 literature would generally[3] own as a *proof in* QC *from a finite set* S *of wffs of* QC any column

$$A_1$$
$$A_2$$
$$\vdots$$
$$A_p$$

of wffs of QC such that, for each i from 1 through p, (i) A_i belongs to S, or (ii) A_i is an axiom of QC, or (iii) A_i is preceded by a wff $A_g \supset A_i$ for some g smaller than i, in which case A_i is said to *follow from* A_g *and* $A_g \supset A_i$ *by* **MP** (= Modus Ponens), or (iv) A_i is of the sort $(\forall X)A_h$ for some h smaller than i and some individual variable X of QC that does not occur free in any member of S, in which case A_i is said to *follow from* A_h *by* **UG** (= Universal Generalization) and X is said to be *(universally) generalized upon.*

A wff A of QC would then be declared (a) *provable in* QC *from a finite set* S *of wffs of* QC if there is a proof $\mathfrak{P}$ in QC from S such that the last entry in $\mathfrak{P}$ is A, (b) *provable in* QC *from an infinite set* S *of wffs of* QC if A is provable in

QC from at least one finite subset of S, and (c) *provable in* QC if A is provable in QC from $\varnothing$.

The account stems from a 1944 publication of Church's [2], and so will be called *Church's account of a proof from hypotheses*.[4] As mentioned on p. 431, it has a serious shortcoming. Indeed, Montague and Henkin have shown in [18] that—given Church's account—the wff '$(\forall y)(g(y) \supset g(y))$', though a semantic consequence of the set $\{g(y)\}$, is *not* provable in QC from $\{g(y)\}$.[5] So the following result, known of course as the *Strong Completeness Theorem for* QC and in which '$S \vdash A$' is to be understood as short for 'A is provable in QC from S':

(A) *If a wff A of* QC *is a semantic consequence of a set S of wffs of* QC, *then $S \vdash A$.*

cannot be had in [2].

It is easy to spot, incidentally, where (current versions of) Henkin's 1949 proof of **(A)** would break down in [2].[6] Having constructed an infinite array S_0, S_1, S_2, etc. of sets of wffs of QC, one goes on to show that $\sum_{i=0} S_i$ is sure to be syntactically consistent if each one of S_0, S_1, S_2, etc. is; and one does so by arguing that if $\sum_{i=0} S_i$ were syntactically inconsistent, then so would be some finite subset of $\sum_{i=0} S_i$, hence so would be some finite subset of one of S_0, S_1, S_2, etc., and hence so would be one of S_0, S_1, S_2, etc. Now this last step appeals to a familiar result:

(B) *If $S \vdash A$, then $S' \vdash A$ for any superset S' of S,*

which cannot be had in [2]. For proof, consider again the Montague-Henkin wff '$(\forall y)(g(y) \supset g(y))$'. Given Church's account of a proof from hypothese '$(\forall y)(g(y) \supset g(y))$' is provable in QC (= provable in QC from $\varnothing$). Yet, as Montague and Henkin showed, the wff is not provable in QC from the superset $\{g(y)\}$ of $\varnothing$.

Now for three solutions to this difficulty.[7]

There is a new (and welcome) trend in logic writings: (1) using for each type of variables one array of letters as *bound* variables and another array as *free* variables, and (2) reserving the label 'variables' for the letters that serve as bound variables and calling the other letters *parameters*.[8]

Under this convention, *which we henceforth heed*, several changes must be brought to the material on pp. 431–432:

first, clause (a) on p. 431 must be edited to read

(a) for each d from 0 on, $\aleph_0$ predicate parameters of degree d (to be referred to by means of '$F^{d'}$');

second, clause (b) on p. 431 must give way to the double clause

(b1) $\aleph_0$ individual variables, say, 'x', 'y', 'z', 'x'', 'y'', 'z'', etc. (to be referred to by means of 'X' and 'Y'),

(b2) $\aleph_0$ individual parameters, say, 'a', 'b', 'c', 'a'', 'b'', 'c'', etc. (to be referred to by means of 'P');

third, clause (i) on p. 431 must be edited to read

(i) $F^d(P_1, P_2, \ldots, P_d)$, where $d \geq 0$;

fourth, clause (iv) on p. 432 must be edited to read

(iv) $(\forall X)A$, in case the result $A(P/X)$ of putting an individual parameter P of QC everywhere for X in A is a wff of QC;[9]

fifth, the paragraph on p. 432 that deals with the well-formed parts of a wff and with bound and free (occurrences of) individual variables is needless;

sixth, the restriction on the individual variable X of axiom schema **A5** on p. 432 is similarly needless; and

seventh, axiom schema **A6** on p. 432 must be edited to read

A6. $(\forall X)A \supset A(P/X)$.

Using two arrays of individual signs disposes of the Montague-Henkin difficulty. First, draft the letter '*I*' to refer to the individual signs (i.e., the individual variables and the individual parameters) of QC; and then, generalizing the '$A(P/X)$' twice used above, draft '$[(A)(I'/I)]$' (when no ambiguity threatens, '$[A(I'/I)]$', '$(A)(I'/I)$', or plain '$A(I'/I)$') to refer to the result of putting (individual sign) I' everywhere for (individual sign) I in (formula)A. This done, edit clause (iv) on p. 432 as the distinction between variables and parameters requires:

(iv) A_i is of the sort $(\forall X)[A(X/P)]$ for some h smaller than i and some individual parameter P of QC that is foreign to each member of S,[10] in which case A_i is said to *follow from* A_h *by* **UG** and P to be *quasi-generalized upon* and the Montague-Henkin problem is solved. Proof that **(B)** holds true given this account of things can indeed be retrieved from [13], a text published some ten years after [18] and in which I used only one array of individual signs but met the Montague-Henkin difficulty in essentially the same manner as above.[11]

I have grown dissatisfied with the account, though. Deviating in this from Church, I would rather characterize provability from sets of hypotheses *at a stroke* rather than distinguish as [3] and [13] do between finite sets and infinite ones. Unfortunately, if you delete the qualifier 'finite' from the twenty-sixth line on p. 432, edit clause (iv) on that page to read as in the previous paragraph, and take a wff A of QC to be *provable in QC from a set S (be S finite or infinite) of wffs of* QC if there is a proof $\mathfrak{B}$ in QC from S such that the last entry in $\mathfrak{B}$ is A, then **(B)** no longer holds true. Indeed, a slight adaptation of the Montague-Henkin argument in [17] will show that '$(\forall y)(g(y) \supset g(y))$', though provable in QC from $\varnothing$, is no longer provable from the infinite superset $\{g(a), g(b), g(c), g(a'), g(b'), g(c'), \ldots\}$ of $\varnothing$.[12]

Another account, one which handles provability from hypotheses at a stroke, can be retrieved from pp. 94–98 of [10], which—Kleene tells me—were written up by 1942. Kleene's account is complicated, however, and Montague and Henkin accordingly devised a substitute one, to which I restrict myself.[13] To quote almost verbatim from [18], "where $\mathfrak{C}$ and $\mathfrak{C}'$ are columns of wffs of QC, call $\mathfrak{C}$ a *subcolumn of* $\mathfrak{C}'$ if and only if the wffs of $\mathfrak{C}$ appear among those of $\mathfrak{C}'$ in the same order which they have in $\mathfrak{C}$. (It is not required that two consecutive

Generalization in First-Order Logic 435

wffs in $\mathfrak{C}$ appear consecutively in $\mathfrak{C}'$.)" Next, tailoring matters to suit the distinction drawn here between variables and parameters, you understand

(1) by a *proof in* QC any finite column $\mathfrak{C}$ of wffs of QC such that, for any wff A in $\mathfrak{C}$, A is an axiom of QC, or follows by **MP** from two earlier entries in $\mathfrak{C}$, or follows by **UG** (reading as on p. 432) from an earlier entry in $\mathfrak{C}$ and

(2) by a *proof in* QC *from a set S of wffs of* QC any finite column $\mathfrak{C}$ of wffs of QC such that, for any wff A in $\mathfrak{C}$, A belongs to S, or is an axiom of QC, or follows by **MP** from two earlier wffs in $\mathfrak{C}$, or is of the sort $(\forall X)[B(X/P)]$, where B is the last entry in a subcolumn of $\mathfrak{C}$ that qualifies as a proof in QC. A wff A of QC is then declared *provable in* QC *from a set S of wffs of* QC if there is a proof $\mathfrak{P}$ in QC from S such that A is the last entry in $\mathfrak{P}$.

That **(B)** holds true given this second account of things is immediately evident.

As for Fitch's account, it stems from [5], a paper published in 1948 and hence antedating [18] by eight years. (Fitch, by the way, was unaware in 1948 of the difficulty eventually reported by Montague and Henkin,[14] and the latter were unaware in 1956 of Fitch's paper.) The account, tailored here to suit our distinction between variables and parameters, is of the simplest. You identify the *axioms* of QC *recursively*, first declaring any wff of QC of any of the sorts **A1–A6**, for example, an axiom of QC and next declaring any wff of QC of the sort $(\forall X)[A(X/P)]$ an axiom of QC and if A itself is one.[15] You then acknowledge as a *proof of* QC *from a set S of wffs of* QC any finite column $\mathfrak{C}$ of wffs of QC such that, for any wff A in $\mathfrak{C}$, A belongs to S, or is an axiom of QC (in the sense just defined), or follows by **MP** from two earlier entries in $\mathfrak{C}$; and you declare a wff A of QC *provable in* QC *from a set S of wffs of* QC if there is a proof $\mathfrak{P}$ in QC from S such that A is the last entry in $\mathfrak{P}$.[16]

That **(B)** holds true given this third account of things is immediately evident.

Proof of **(A)**, the Strong Completeness Theorem for QC, calls for a number of lemmas besides **(B)**. One of them is the Universal Generalization Theorem mentioned on p. 431. It runs:

(C) *If* $S \vdash A$, *then* $S \vdash (\forall X)[A(X/P)]$, *so long as X is foreign to A and P is foreign to S*,

and helps to show that if any one of the sets S_0, S_1, S_2, etc. on p. 433, say, set S_n, were syntactically inconsistent, then so would set S_{n-1} be.

That **(C)** holds true given Leblanc's account of a proof from hypotheses is immediately evident. That it holds true given Montague and Henkin's account is shown in [18], pp. 133–34. And that it holds true given Fitch's account readily follows from (3.7.12) on pp. 336–37 of [17].

As perusal of [13], [18], and [17] will show, further lemmas needed to prove **(A)** and the various lemmas needed to prove the converse of **(A)**:

(A′) *If* $S \vdash A$, *where S is a set of wffs and A is a wff of* QC, *then A is a semantic consequence of S,* (= *the Strong Soundness Theorem for* QC) all hold true given Leblanc's account, given Montague and Henkin's, and given Fitch's. Each of our three accounts thus puts things to rights.

These preliminaries over with, I limit myself henceforth to Fitch's account, and with an eye to further results prove (**C**) anew.

2. I first establish (**C**) for the case where X is foreign to S (= Theorem 1), and obtain as a corollary that if $A(P/X)$ is provable in QC, then $(\forall X)A$ is sure to be (= Theorem 2). With Theorem 1 on hand, I then establish (**C**) for the general case (= Theorem 3). The resulting demonstration of (**C**) is admittedly longer than that of (3.7.12) in [17]. But *the portion of it that yields Theorem 1 (and hence Theorem 2) does without axiom schema* **A6**. In the lemmas and theorems that follow '$S \vdash A$' is to be understood as 'A is provable in QC from S (in Fitch's sense)', and '$\vdash A$' as 'A is provable in QC (in Fitch's sense)'.

Lemma 1. (a) *If A is an axiom of* QC, *then so is $A(Y/X)$, so long as Y is foreign to A.*
(b) *If A belongs to S or is an axiom of* QC, *then $S \vdash A$.*
(c) *If $S \vdash A$ and $S \vdash A \supset B$, then $S \vdash B$.*
(d) *If $S \vdash A$, then there is a finite subset S' of S such that $S' \vdash A$.*
(e) *If $S \vdash A$, then $S' \vdash A$ for any superset S' of S.*
(f) *If $S \vdash (\forall X)(A \supset B)$, then $S \vdash (\forall X)A \supset (\forall X)B$.*
(g) *If $S \vdash (\forall X)(A \supset B)$ and $S \vdash (\forall X)A$, then $S \vdash (\forall X)B$.*
(h) *If $S \vdash A$, then $S \vdash (\forall X)A$, so long as X is foreign to A.*
Proof: (a) Proof of A is by cases. It uses three easily verified facts: (i) $(\sim A)(Y/X)$ is the same as $\sim[A(Y/X)]$; (ii) $(A \supset B)(Y/X)$ is the same as $A(Y/X) \supset B(Y/X)$; (iii) $((\forall X)A)(Y/X)$ is the same as $(\forall Y)[A(Y/X)]$; and (iv) if A is a wff of QC, then so is $A(Y/X)$, so long as Y is foreign to A.
(b)–(h) Proofs of these, when not immediate, are routine.

Lemma 2. *Let X be foreign to S and to A. If there is a proof in QC from S whose last entry is A, then there is one to which X is foreign.*
Proof: Let the column made up of $B_1, B_2, \ldots, B_p$ constitute a proof in QC from S whose last entry is A, and let Y be an individual variable of QC foreign to all of $B_1, B_2, \ldots, B_p$. (i) A routine induction shows that the column made up of $B_1(Y/X), B_2(Y/X), \ldots, B_p(Y/X)$ constitutes a proof in QC from S whose last entry is $B_p(Y/X)$. For suppose B_i ($1 \leq i \leq p$) belongs to S. With X foreign to S, $B_i(Y/X)$ is sure to be the same as B_i and hence to belong to S. Or suppose B_i is an axiom of QC. With Y foreign to B_i, $B_i(Y/X)$ is sure by L1(a) to be an axiom of QC as well. Or suppose B_i is the ponential of, say, B_g and B_h, where B_h is $B_g \supset B_i$. Since $B_h(Y/X)$ and $B_g(Y/X) \supset B_i(Y/X)$ are the same, $B_i(Y/X)$ is sure to be the ponential of $B_g(Y/X)$ and $B_h(Y/X)$. (ii) Since X is foreign to $B_1(Y/X), B_2(Y/X), \ldots, B_p(Y/X)$, there is sure in view of (i) to be a proof in QC from S whose last entry is $B_p(Y/X)$ and to which X is foreign. But,

with X foreign to A ($= B_p$), $B_p(Y/X)$ is sure to be the same as B_p and hence as A. Hence there is sure to be a proof in QC from S whose last entry is A and to which X is foreign. Hence L2.

Theorem 1. *Let X be foreign to S and A, and P be foreign to S. If $S \vdash A$, then $S \vdash (\forall X)[A(X/P)]$. (UGT for QC, Special Case)*
Proof: Suppose $S \vdash A$. Since X is foreign to S and A, there is sure by L2 to be a proof in QC from S whose last entry is A and to which X is foreign. Let the column made up of $B_1, B_2, \ldots, B_p$ constitute then such a proof. A routine induction shows that $S \vdash (\forall X)[B_i(X/P)]$ ($1 \leq i \leq p$), and hence that $S \vdash (\forall X)[B_p(X/P)]$ ($= (\forall X)[A(X/P)]$). For suppose that B_i belongs to S and hence by L1(b) that $S \vdash B_i$. Since X is foreign to B_i, $S \vdash (\forall X)B_i$ by L1(h). But, with P foreign to S, B_i and $B_i(X/P)$ are sure to be the same. Hence $S \vdash (\forall X)[B_i(X/P)]$. Or suppose B_i is an axiom of QC. Since X is foreign to B_i, $(\forall X)[B_i(X/P)]$ is sure to be well-formed, and hence by the inductive clause in Fitch's account of an axiom of QC to qualify as an axiom of QC. Hence $S \vdash (\forall X)[B_i(X/P)]$ by L1(b). Or suppose B_i is the ponential of, say, B_g and B_h, where B_h is $B_g \supset B_i$. By the hypothesis of the induction $S \vdash (\forall X)[B_g(X/P)]$ and $S \vdash (\forall X)[(B_g \supset B_i)(X/P)]$. But $(\forall X)[(B_g \supset B_i)(X/P)]$ and $(\forall X)B_g(X/P) \supset B_i(X/P))$ are the same. Hence $S \vdash (\forall X)(B_g(X/P) \supset B_i(X/P))$, and hence $S \vdash (\forall X)[B_i(X/P)]$ by L1(g).

Theorem 2. *Let X be foreign to A. If $\vdash A$, then $\vdash (\forall X)[A(X/P)]$.*
Proof by T1, with $\emptyset$ serving as S.

The reader will have noticed that, as promised, the foregoing proof of Theorem 1 (and hence that of Theorem 2) does without **A6**.

Lemma 3. $\vdash (\forall Y)((\forall X)A \supset A(Y/X))$.
Proof: Let P be an individual parameter of QC foreign to A. $(\forall X)A \supset A(P/X)$ counts as an axiom of QC. But, with $(\forall Y)((\forall X)A \supset A(Y/X))$ presumed to be well-formed, $(\forall Y)[((\forall X)A \supset A(P/X))(Y/P)]$ is likewise sure to be well-formed. Hence, by the inductive clause in Fitch's account of an axiom of QC, $(\forall Y)[((\forall X)A \supset A(P/X))(Y/P)]$ counts as an axiom of QC. But, with P foreign to A, $((\forall X)A \supset A(P/X))(Y/P)$ and $(\forall X)A \supset A(Y/X)$ are sure to be the same. Hence $(\forall Y)((\forall X)A \supset A(Y/X))$ counts as an axiom of QC. Hence L3 by L1(b).

Lemma 4. *Let Y be foreign to $(\forall X)A$. If $S \vdash (\forall X)A$, then $S \vdash (\forall Y)[A(Y/X)]$.*
Proof: Suppose $S \vdash (\forall X)A$. Then $(\forall X)A$ is sure to be well-formed. But, with $(\forall X)A$ well-formed and Y foreign to $(\forall X)A$, $(\forall Y)((\forall X)A \supset A(Y/X))$ is likewise sure to be well-formed. Hence $\vdash (\forall Y)((\forall X)A \supset A(Y/X))$ by L3, hence $\vdash (\forall X)(\forall X)A \supset (\forall Y)[A(Y/X)]$ by L1(f), and hence $S \vdash (\forall Y)(\forall X)A \supset (\forall Y)[A(Y/X)]$ by L1(e). But since $S \vdash (\forall X)A$ and Y is foreign to $(\forall X)A$, $S \vdash (\forall Y)(\forall X)A$ by L1(h). Hence $S \vdash (\forall Y)[A(Y/X)]$ by L1(c). Hence L4.

Theorem 3. *Let X be foreign to A, and P be foreign to S. If S ⊢ A, then S ⊢ (∀X)[A(X/P)]. (**UGT** for QC, General Case)*
Proof: Suppose that $S \vdash A$, and hence by L1(d) that $S' \vdash A$ for some finite subset S' of S; and let Y be an individual variable of QC distinct from X and foreign to S' and A. Then $S' \vdash (\forall Y)[A(Y/P)]$ by T1, and hence $S \vdash (\forall Y)[A(Y/P)]$ by L1(e). But, with X foreign to A and Y distinct from X, X is sure to be foreign to $(\forall Y)[A(Y/P)]$. Hence $S \vdash (\forall X)[(A(Y/P))(X/Y)]$ by L4. But, with Y foreign to A, $(A(Y/P))(X/Y)$ and $A(X/P)$ are sure to be the same. Hence $S \vdash (\forall X)[A(X/P)]$. Hence T3.

The reader will have noticed that, though the proof of Lemma 3 resorts to **A6**, that of Lemma 4 and hence that of Theorem 3 do not. They merely presuppose that $(\forall Y)((\forall X)A \supset A(Y/X))$, when well-formed, is provable in QC. The point will prove crucial further on.[17]

A version of Theorem 2 and one of Theorem 3 can be had which are closer to the intelim rule **∀I** of Natural Deduction. Proof of Lemma 5 is immediate.

Lemma 5. *Let P be foreign to A. Then A and (A(P/X))(X/P) are the same.*

Theorem 4. (a) *Let P be foreign to (∀X)A. If ⊢ A(P/X), then ⊢ (∀X)A.*
(b) *Let P be foreign to S and to (∀X)A. If S ⊢ A(P/X), then S ⊢ (∀X)A. (**∀I** for QC)*
Proof: (a) Suppose $\vdash A(P/X)$. Since X is foreign to $A(P/X)$, $\vdash (\forall X)[A(P/X))(X/P)]$ by T2. But, being presumed to be foreign to $(\forall X) A$, P is sure to be foreign to A. Hence $\vdash (\forall X)A$ by L5. Hence (a).
(b) Proof like that of (a), but using T3 in lieu of T2.

The foregoing proof of Theorem 4(a), the reader will have noticed, does without **A6**; and that of Theorem 4(b) merely presupposes that $(\forall Y)((\forall X)A \supset A(Y/X))$, when well-formed, is provable in QC.

Now for QC*, the subcalculus of QC that grew out of [15] and [8], and is commonly known as *free logic (without identity)*. Space prevents me from supplying a full-fledged semantics for QC*. From a model-theoretic stance, suffice it to note that (i) ∅ counts in QC* as a domain and (ii) when the domain is non-empty, the individual parameters 'a', 'b', 'c', etc. may go in QC* without values.[18] A Strong Soundness Theorem for QC* and (as established in [14], pp. 136–45) a Strong Completeness one can be had if **A6** on p. 434 is weakened to read

A6*. $(\forall Y)((\forall X)A \supset A(Y/X))$.[19]

and the *Commutation Law for Universal Quantifiers*, to wit:

A7*. $(\forall X)(\forall Y)A \supset (\forall Y)(\forall X)A$,

is adopted as an extra axiom schema.[20]
Wffs of QC* of the sort $(\forall Y)((\forall X)A \supset A(Y/X))$, once made into axioms of

Generalization in First-Order Logic 439

QC*, are sure of course to be provable in QC*. So, as announced on p. 431, the foregoing demonstration of Theorem 3 (and hence that of Theorem 4 as well) holds good for QC*; and, starring '⊢' to signal that the calculus at issue is QC*, I conclude:

Theorem 5. (a) *Let X be foreign to A, and P be foreign to S. If S ⊢* A, then S ⊢* ($\forall X$)[A(X/P)]*. (**UGT** *for* QC*)
(b) *Let P be foreign to S and to* ($\forall X$)A. *If S ⊢* A(P/X), then S ⊢* ($\forall X$)A.* ($\forall$**I** *for* QC*)

Fitch's account of a proof from hypotheses thus yields **UGT** (and $\forall$**I**) for both QC and QC*.[21]

3. $QC_=$, the (standard) quantificational calculus of order one with identity, has the same *primitive signs* as QC, *plus* of course the identity predicate '='. Its *formulas* are all finite sequences of primitive signs of $QC_=$. Under our convention regarding variables and parameters, its *well-formed formulas* (wffs) are all formulas of the sort (i) on p. 434, *plus* all those of the sort ($P = P'$),[22] *plus* all those of either of the sorts (ii)–(iii) on pp. 431–32 (with '$QC_=$' substituting there for 'QC'), *plus* all those of the sort (iv) on p. 434 (with '$QC_=$' substituting there for 'QC'). And its *atomic wffs* are all those of the sort (i) on p. 434, *plus* all those of the sort $P = P'$ above. (For brevity's sake I shall write '($A \equiv B$)' in lieu of '$\sim((A \supset B) \supset \sim(B \supset A))$', and '($\exists X$)A' in lieu of '$\sim(\forall X)\sim A$'.)

Among the numerous axiomatizations of $QC_=$, three—retouched to suit the distinction between variables and parameters—rate mention at this point. The oldest and best known of them would own as the *axioms* of $QC_=$ all wffs of any of the sorts **A1–A5** on p. 432, *plus* all those of the sort **A6** on p. 434, *plus* all those of the sort

$$P = P \qquad (1)$$

or the sort

$$P = P' \supset (A \supset A(P'//P)), \qquad (2)$$

where $A(P'//P)$ is like A except for exhibiting P' *at zero or more places* where A exhibits P. Another, supplied by Tarski in [21], dispenses with **A6**, uses in lieu of (1) the axiom schema

$$(\exists X)(X = P),$$

and uses in lieu of (2) the axiom schema

$$P = P' \supset (A \supset A(P'/_1 P)), \qquad (3)$$

where (i) A is atomic and (ii) $A(P'/_1 P)$ is like A except for exhibiting P' *at exactly one place* where A exhibits P.[23] And yet another, exploiting a suggestion of van Fraassen's,[24] is like the second, but uses in lieu of (3) the following two axiom schemata:

$$P = P' \supset (A \supset A(P'/P))$$

and

$$P = P' \supset (A(P'/P) \supset A),$$

where in either case A is presumed to be atomic.[25]

Given any of these axiomatizations, the pre-1956 literature would generally understand proofs from hypotheses in the manner of Church,[26] which of course blocks the *Strong Completeness Theorem for* $QC_=$:

(**D**) *If a wff A of* $QC_=$ *is a semantic consequence of a set S of wffs of* $QC_=$, *then $S \vdash A$.*

Here as in QC things can be mended in at least three different ways: Leblanc's way, Montague and Henkin's, and Fitch's. Opting again for Fitch's, I shall acknowledge as the *axioms* of $QC_=$ all wffs of any of the five sorts **A1–A5** on p. 432, all those of any of the following three sorts:

B1. $(\exists X)(X = P)$,

B2. $P = P' \supset (A \supset A(P'/P))$, where A is atomic,

B3. $P = P' \supset (A(P'/P) \supset P)$, where A is atomic,

and all those of the sort $(\forall X)[A(X/P)]$, where A is an axiom of $QC_=$; and I shall understand proofs from hypotheses as in lines 21–24, p. 435 (with '$QC_=$' substituting there for 'QC').

Here as in QC my concern is with **UGT**, one of the main lemmas needed to obtain (**D**). Following Tarski's precedent in [22], I shall first establish

$$P = P' \supset (A \supset A(P'/P))$$

for any wff A of $QC_=$, atomic or not. Borrowing from [15] and [22],[27] I shall then establish

$$(\exists X)(X = P) \supset ((\forall X)A \supset A(P/X)),$$

and get therefrom the counterpart for $QC_=$ of L3 in Section 2:

$$(\forall Y)((\forall X)A \supset A(Y/X)).$$

Since the proof of T3 in Section 2 uses only L3 and axioms whose counterparts for $QC_=$ are available here, the way will be clear for **UGT**. Proofs of the other lemmas needed to obtain (**D**) will be found in [15].

In what follows I write '$\vdash_=$' to signal that the calculus at issue in $QC_=$.

Lemma 6. (a) $\vdash_= A \supset ((A \supset B) \supset B)$.
(b) *If* $\vdash_= A \supset B$ *and* $\vdash_= B \supset C$, *then* $\vdash_= A \supset C$.
(c) *If* $\vdash_= A \supset (B \supset C)$, *then* $\vdash_= B \supset (A \supset C)$.

Generalization in First-Order Logic 441

(d) If $\vdash_= A \supset (B \supset C)$ and $\vdash_= C \supset C'$, then $\vdash_= A \supset (B \supset C')$.
(e) If $\vdash_= A \supset (B \equiv C)$, then $\vdash_= A \supset (B \supset C)$ and $\vdash_= A \supset (C \supset B)$.
(f) If $\vdash_= A \supset (B \supset C)$ and $\vdash_= A \supset (C \supset B)$, then $\vdash_= A \supset (B \equiv C)$.
(g) If $\vdash_= A \supset (B \equiv B')$ and $\vdash_= A \supset (C \equiv C')$, then $\vdash_= A \supset ((B \supset C) \equiv (B' \supset C'))$.
(h) $\vdash_= (A \supset B) \supset (\sim B \supset \sim A)$.
(i) If $\vdash_= \sim A \supset B$, then $\vdash_= \sim B \supset A$.
(j) If $\vdash_= A \supset (B \equiv C)$, then $\vdash_= A \supset (\sim B \equiv \sim C)$.
Proof left to the reader.

Lemma 7. (a) If $\vdash_= A(P/X) \supset B(P/X)$, then $\vdash_= (\forall X)A \supset (\forall X)B$, so long as P is foreign to $(\forall X)A$ and to $(\forall X)B$.
(b) If $\vdash_= A \supset (\forall X)(B \supset C)$, then $\vdash_= A \supset ((\forall X)B \supset (\forall X)C)$.
(c) If $\vdash_= A \supset (B(P/X) \supset C(P/X))$, then $\vdash_= A \supset ((\forall X)B \supset (\forall X)C)$, so long as P is foreign to A, $(\forall X)B$, and $(\forall X)C$, and X is foreign to A.
(d) If $\vdash_= A \supset (B(P/X) \equiv C(P/X))$, then $\vdash_= A \supset ((\forall X)B \equiv (\forall X)C)$, so long as P and X are as in (c).
(e) $\vdash_= (\forall X)(A \supset B) \supset ((\exists X)A \supset (\exists X)B)$.
(f) If $\vdash_= A(P/X) \supset B(P/X)$, then $\vdash_= (\exists X)A \supset (\exists X)B$, so long as P is foreign to $(\exists X)A$ and to $(\exists X)B$.
(g) $\vdash_= (\exists X)A \supset A$.
(h) $\vdash_= (\exists X)(A \supset B) \supset ((\forall X)A \supset B)$, so long as X is foreign to B.
Proof:
(a) Suppose $\vdash_= A(P/X) \supset B(P/X)$, and hence $\vdash_= (A \supset B)(P/X)$. Suppose further that P is foreign to $(\forall X)A$ and to $(\forall X)B$, and hence to $(\forall X)(A \supset B)$ as well. Then $\vdash_= (\forall X)(A \supset B)$ by T4(a), and hence $\vdash_= (\forall X)A \supset (\forall X)B$ by L1(f). Hence (a).

(b) Suppose $\vdash_= A \supset (\forall X)(B \supset C)$. With $(\forall X)(B \supset C)$ presumed here to be well-formed, $(\forall X)(B \supset C) \supset ((\forall X)B \supset (\forall X)C)$ is sure to be well-formed and hence to count as an axiom of $QC_=$. Hence $\vdash_= (\forall X)(B \supset C) \supset ((\forall X)B \supset (\forall X)C)$ by L1(b). Hence $\vdash_= A \supset ((\forall X)B \supset (\forall X)C)$ by L6(b). Hence (b).

(c) Suppose $\vdash_= A \supset (B(P/X) \supset C(P/X))$, and hence $\vdash_= A \supset (B \supset C)(P/X)$. Suppose further that X is foreign to A. Then A and $A(P/X)$ are the same, and hence $\vdash_= A(P/X) \supset (B \supset C)(P/X)$. Suppose finally that P is foreign to A, $(\forall X)B$, and $(\forall X)C$. Then P is sure to be foreign to $(\forall X)A$ and to $(\forall X)B \supset C$. Hence $\vdash_= (\forall X)A \supset (\forall X)(B \supset C)$ by (a). But, with A presumed here to be well-formed and with X foreign to A, $A \supset (\forall X)A$ is sure to be well-formed and hence to count as an axiom of $QC_=$. Hence $\vdash_= A \supset (\forall X)A$ by L1(b), hence $\vdash_= A \supset (\forall X)(B \supset C)$ by L6(b), and hence $\vdash_= A \supset ((\forall X)B \supset (\forall X)C)$ by (b).

(d) Suppose $\vdash_= A \supset (B(P/X) \equiv C(P/X))$. Then $\vdash_= A \supset (B(P/X) \supset C(P/X))$ by L6(e). Suppose further that P is foreign to A, $(\forall X)B$, and $(\forall X)C$, and X is foreign to A. Then $\vdash_= A \supset ((\forall X)B \supset (\forall X)C)$. But by the same reasoning and under the same assumptions $\vdash_= A \supset ((\forall X)C \supset (\forall X)B)$. Hence $\vdash_= A \supset ((\forall X)B \equiv (\forall X)C)$ by L6(f).

(e) Let P be an individual parameter of $QC_=$ foreign to $(\forall X)(A \supset B)$ and to

442   Part 3: Provability

$(\forall X)(\sim B \supset \sim A)$. $\vdash_= (C(P/X) \supset B(P/X)) \supset (\sim[B(P/X)] \supset \sim[C(P/X)])$ by L6(h). But $(A(P/X) \supset B(P/X)) \supset (\sim[B(P/X)] \supset \sim[A(P/X)])$ and $(A \supset B)(P/X) \supset (B \supset \sim A)(P/X)$ are the same. Hence $\vdash_= (A \supset B)(P/X) \supset (\sim B \supset \sim A)(P/X)$, hence $\vdash_= (\forall X)(A \supset B) \supset (\forall X)(\sim B \supset \sim A)$ by (a), and hence $\vdash_= (\forall X)(A \supset B) \supset ((\forall X)\sim B \supset (\forall X)\sim A)$ by (b). But $\vdash ((\forall X)\sim B \supset (\forall X)\sim A) \supset ((\exists X)A \supset (\exists X)B)$ by L6(h). Hence (e) by L6(b).

(f) Suppose $\vdash_= A(P/X) \supset B(P/X)$, and hence $\vdash_= (A \supset B)(P/X)$; suppose further that P is foreign to $(\exists X)A$ and to $(\exists X)B$, and hence to $(\forall X)(A \supset B)$. Then $\vdash_= (\forall X)(A \supset B)$ by T4(a). Hence $\vdash_= (\exists X)A \supset (\exists X)B$ by (e) and L1(c). Hence (f).

(g) With $(\exists X)A \supset A$ presumed here to be well-formed, $\sim A \supset (\forall X)\sim A$ is sure to be well-formed and hence to count as an axiom of $QC_=$. Hence $\vdash_= \sim A \supset (\forall X)\sim A$ by L1(b), and hence $\vdash_= (\exists X)A \supset A$ by L6(i).

(h) Let P be an individual parameter of $QC_=$ foreign to $(\forall X)A$ and to $(\forall X)((A \supset B) \supset B)$. $\vdash_= A(P/X) \supset ((A(P/X) \supset B(P/X)) \supset B(P/X))$ by L6(a). But $(A(P/X) \supset B(P/X)) \supset B(P/X)$ and $((A \supset B) \supset B)(P/X)$ are the same. Hence $\vdash_= A(P/X) \supset ((A \supset B) \supset B)(P/X)$, and hence $\vdash_= (\forall X)A \supset (\forall X)((A \supset B) \supset B)$ by (a). But $\vdash_= (\forall X)((A \supset B) \supset B) \supset ((\exists X)(A \supset B) \supset (\exists X)B)$ by (e). Hence $\vdash_= (\forall X)A \supset ((\exists X)(A \supset B) \supset (\exists X)B)$ by L6(b), and hence $\vdash_= (\exists X)(A \supset B) \supset ((\forall X)A \supset (\exists X)B)$ by L6(c). Suppose further that X is foreign to B. Since B is presumed here to be well-formed, $(\exists X)B \supset B$ is sure to be well-formed, and hence $\vdash_= (\exists X)B \supset B$ by (g). Hence (h) by L6(d).

Lemma 8. (a) $\vdash_= P = P' \supset (A \equiv A(P'/P))$.
(b) $\vdash_= P = P' \supset (A \supset A(P'/P))$.
(c) $\vdash_= P = P' \supset (A(P/X) \supset A(P'/X))$, *so long as P is foreign to A.*
Proof:

(a) Proof of (a) is by mathematical induction on the number n of logical operators in A.
Basis: $n = 0$, in which case A is atomic. Then $P = P' \supset (A \supset A(P'/P))$ and $P = P' \supset (A(P'/P) \supset A)$, being presumed here to be well-formed, count as axioms of $QC_=$. Hence (a) by L1(b) and L6(f).
Inductive Step: $n > 0$.
Case 1: A is a negation $\sim B$, and hence $A(P'/P)$ is $(\sim B)(P'/P)$. $\vdash_= P = P' \supset (B \equiv B(P'/P))$ by the hypothesis of the induction, and hence $\vdash_= P = P' \supset (\sim B \equiv \sim[B(P'/P)])$ by L6(j). But $\sim[B(P'/P)]$ and $(\sim B)P'/P)$ are the same. Hence $\vdash_= P = P' \supset (\sim B \equiv (\sim B)(P'/P))$.
Case 2: A is a conditional $B \supset C$, and hence $A(P'/P)$ is $(B \supset C)(P'/P)$. $\vdash_= P = P' \supset (B \equiv B(P'/P))$ and $\vdash_= P = P' \supset (C \equiv C(P'/P))$ by the hypothesis of the induction, and hence $\vdash_= P = P' \supset ((B \supset C) \equiv (B(P'/P) \supset C(P'/P)))$ by L6(g). But $B(P'/P) \supset C(P'/P)$ and $(B \supset C)(P'/P)$ are the same. Hence $\vdash_= P = P' \supset ((B \supset C) \equiv (B \supset C)(P'/P))$.
Case 3: A is a quantification $(\forall X)B$, and hence $A(P'/P)$ is $((\forall X)B)(P'/P)$. Let P'' be an individual parameter of $QC_=$ distinct from each of P and P', and foreign to $(\forall X)B$. $\vdash_= P = P' \supset (B(P''/X) \equiv (B(P''/X))(P'/P))$ by the hypoth-

esis of the induction. But, with P'' distinct from each of P and P', $(B(P''/X))(P'/P)$ and $(B(P'/P))(P''/X)$ are the same. Hence $\vdash_= P = P' \supset (B(P''/X) \equiv (B(P'/P))(P''/X))$. But P'' is sure to be foreign to $P = P'$, $(\forall X)B$, and $(\forall X)[B(P'/P)]$, and X is of course foreign to $P = P'$. Hence $\vdash_= P = P' \supset ((\forall X)B \equiv (\forall X) [B(P'/P)])$ by L7(d). But $(\forall X)[B(P'/P)]$ and $((\forall X)B)(P'/P)$ are the same. Hence $\vdash_= P = P' \supset ((\forall X)B \equiv ((\forall X)B)(P'/P))$.
(b) By (a) and L6(e).
(c) $\vdash_= P = P' \supset (A(P/X) \supset (A(P/X))(P'/P))$ by (b). Now suppose P to be foreign to A. Then $(A(P/X))(P'/P)$ and $A(P'/X)$ are sure to be the same. Hence (c)

Lemma 9. (a) $\vdash_= (\exists X)(X = P) \supset ((\forall X)A \supset A(P/X))$.
(b) $\vdash_= (\forall Y)(\exists X)(X = Y) \supset (\forall Y)((\forall X)A \supset A(Y/X))$.
Proof:
(a) Let P' be an individual parameter of QC$_=$ distinct from P and foreign to $(\forall X)A$. $\vdash_= P = P' \supset (A(P'/X) \supset A(P/X))$ by L8(c). But, with P' distinct from P and foreign to $(\forall X)A$ (and hence to A), $P' = P$ and $(X = P)(P'/X)$ are sure to be the same, and so are $A(P'/X) \supset A(P/X)$ and $(A \supset A(P/X))(P'/X)$. Hence $\vdash_= (X = P)(P'/X) \supset (A \supset A(P/X))(P'/X)$, and hence $\vdash_= (\exists X)(X = P) \supset (\exists X)(A \supset A(P/X))$ by L7(f). But, as X is foreign to $A(P/X)$, $\vdash_= (\exists X)(A \supset A(P/X)) \supset ((\forall X)) \supset ((\forall X)A \supset A(P/X))$ by L7(h). Hence (a) L6(b).
(b) Let P be an individual parameter of QC$_=$ foreign to A. $\vdash_= (\exists X)(X = P) \supset ((\forall X)A \supset A(P/X))$ by (a). But with $(\forall Y)(\exists X)(X = Y)$ presumed here to be well-formed, Y is sure to be distinct from X, and hence $(\exists X)(X = P)$ and $((\exists X)(X = Y))(P/Y)$ to be the same. Hence $\vdash_= ((\exists X)(X = Y))(P/Y) \supset ((\forall X)A \supset A(P/X))$. But, with $(\forall Y)((\forall X)A \supset A(Y/X))$ presumed here to be well-formed, Y is sure be foreign to A, and hence $(\forall X)A \supset A(P/X)$ and $((\forall X)A \supset A(Y/X))(P/Y)$ to be the same. Hence $\vdash_= ((\exists X)(X = Y))(P/Y) \supset ((\forall X)A \supset A(Y/X))(P/Y)$. But, being foreign to A, P is sure to be foreign to $(\forall Y)(\exists X)(X = Y)$ and to $(\forall Y)((\forall X)A \supset A(Y/X))$. Hence (b) by L7(a).

Lemma 10. (a) $\vdash_= (\forall Y)(\exists X)(X = Y)$.
(b) $\vdash_= (\forall Y)((\forall X)A \supset A(Y/X))$.
Proof:
(a) Let P be an individual parameter of QC$_=$. $(\exists X)(X = P)$ counts as an axiom of QC$_=$. Hence $\vdash_= (\exists X)(X = P)$ by L1(b). But, with $(\forall Y)(\exists X)(X = Y)$ presumed here to be well-formed, Y is sure to be distinct from X, and hence $(\exists X)(X = P)$ and $((\exists X)(X = Y))(P/Y)$ to be the same. Hence $\vdash_= ((\exists X)(X = Y))(P/Y)$, and hence (a) by T4(a).
(b) By (a), L9(b), and L1(c).

Hence:

Theorem 6. (a) *Let X be foreign to A, and P be foreign to S. If $S \vdash_= A$, then $S \vdash_= (\forall X)[A(X/P)]$.* (UGT *for* QC$_=$).

(b) Let P be foreign to S and to $(\forall X)A$. If $S \vdash_= A(P/X)$, then $S \vdash_= (\forall X)A$. ($\forall$I for $QC_=$).

Proof:
(a) Proof like that of T3, but using L10(b) in lieu of L3.
(b) Proof like that of T4(b), but using (a) in lieu of T3.

The reader will have noticed that, though the proof of L10(a) resorts to **B1**, that of L10(b) and hence that of T6 does not. They merely presuppose that $(\forall Y)(\exists X)(X = Y)$, when well-formed, is provable in $QC_=$.[28]

Now for $QC_=^*$, the presupposition-free quantificational calculus of order one with identity, and proof there of **UGT**. A Strong Soundness Theorem for $QC_=^*$ and (as established in [14], pp. 146–49) a Strong Completeness one can be had if **B1** on p. 440 is weakened to read

B1*. $(\forall Y)(\exists X)(X = Y)$,

and the Law of Reflexivity for ' = ', to wit:

B4*. $P = P$

is adopted as an extra axiom schema.[29]

Wffs of $QC_=^*$ of the sort $(\forall Y)(\exists X)(X = Y)$, once made into axioms of $QC_=^*$, are sure to be provable in $QC_=^*$. So the foregoing demonstration of T6 holds good for $QC_=^*$; and, writing '$\vdash_=^*$' to signal that the calculus at issue here is $QC_=^*$, I conclude:

Theorem 7. (a) Let X be foreign to A, and P be foreign to S. If $S \vdash_=^* A$, then $S \vdash_=^* (\forall X)[A(X/P)]$. (**UGT** for $QC_=^*$)
(b) Let P be foreign to S and to $(\forall X)A$. If $S \vdash_=^* A(P/X)$, then $S \vdash_=^* (\forall X)A$. ($\forall$I for $QC_=^*$).

Fitch's account of a proof from hypotheses thus yields **UGT** (and $\forall$I) for $QC_=^*$ as well as for $QC_=$,[30] and the error detected by Cosgrove in [14] stands corrected.[31]

The results in Section 2 hold *mutatis mutandis* for most logics with quantifiers. Consider, for example, QC^2, the quantificational calculus of order two. QC^2 has as its primitive signs the signs in (b1)–(b2) on p. 433, *plus* those in (c)–(d) on p. 431, *plus* for each d from $\aleph_0$ on $\aleph_0$ predicate variables and $\aleph_0$ predicate parameters of degree d. Predicate variables of degree d are referred to by means of 'F^d', individual variables by means of 'X', variables in general (i.e., predicate variables and individual ones) by means of 'V', and parameters in general (i.e., predicate parameters and individual ones) by means of 'P'. $[(A)(P/V)]$ is to be the result of putting P everywhere for V in A, where (i) in case V is a predicate variable, P is a predicate parameter of the same degree as V, and (ii) in case V is an individual variable, P is an individual parameter;

and $[(A)\ (V/P)]$ is to be understood in a like manner, but with 'P' and 'V' and interchanged throughout.

The formulas of QC^2 are all finite sequences of primitive signs of QC^2. Its wffs are all formulas of QC^2 of the sort (i) on p. 434, *plus* all those of either of the sorts (ii)–(iii) on pp. 431–32 (with 'QC^2' there for 'QC'), *plus* all those of the sort $(\forall V)A$, where for some parameter P of QC^2 $A(P/V)$ is a wff of QC^2. And its axioms are all those of the sorts **A1–A3** on p. 432, *plus* all those of the sorts

B1$_2$. $(\forall V)(A \supset B) \supset ((\forall V)A \supset (\forall V)B)$

B2$_2$. $A \supset (\forall V)A$

B3$_2$. $(\forall V)A \supset A(P/V)$,

plus all those of the sort

B4$_2$. $(\exists F^d)(\forall X_1)(\forall X_2) \ldots (\forall X_d)(F^d(X_1, X_2, \ldots, X_d) \equiv A)$,

where the predicate variable F^d is foreign to A,[32] *plus* all those of the sort $(\forall V)[A(V/P)]$, where A is an axiom of QC^2.

Given Fitch's account of a proof from hypotheses, the counterparts for QC^2 of L1–2 in Section 2 clearly hold true. So we may conclude as in Section 2:

Theorem 8. *Let V be foreign to S and A, and P be foreign to S. If $S \vdash A$, then $S \vdash (\forall V)[A(V/P)]$.*

But the counterparts for QC^2 of L3–4 also hold true, the counterpart of L3 reading

$$\vdash (\forall V')((\forall V)A \supset A(V'/V)),$$

where V and V' are either two predicate variables of the same degree or two individual variables, and $A(V'/V)$ is the result of putting V' everywhere for V in A,
and the counterpart of L4 reading

If $S \vdash (\forall V)A$, then $S \vdash (\forall V')[A(V'/V)]$, so long as V' is foreign to $(\forall V)A$,

where V, V', and $A(V'/V)$ are as on lines 22–24.
So we may conclude as in Section 2:

Theorem 9. *Let V be foreign to A, and P be foreign to S. If $S \vdash A$, then $S \vdash (\forall V)[A(V/P)]$.* (**UGT** *for* QC^2)

Since the proof of Theorem 9 merely presupposes that $(\forall V')((\forall V)A \supset A(V'/V))$, when well-formed, is provable in QC^2, the theorem is also sure to hold true for the presupposition-free variant of QC^2, a calculus gotten from QC^2 by dropping axiom schema **B3$_2$** in favor of

B3$_2^*$. $(\forall V')((\forall V)A \supset A(V'/V))$,

dropping axiom schema **B4$_2$**, and adopting the Commutation Law for Universal Quantifiers

B5$_2^*$. $(\forall V)(\forall V')A \supset (\forall V')(\forall V)A$

as an extra axiom schema. So,

Theorem 10. *Let V be foreign to A, and P be foreign to S. If $S \vdash A$, then $S \vdash^*$ $(\forall V)[A(V/P)]$. (**UGT** for the presupposition-free variant of QC^2)*

APPENDIX

1. To accommodate the many who have no access to [13], I supply proof of (**B**) for QC given Leblanc's account of a proof from hypotheses. I understand $[(A)(I_1'/I_1)]$ as on p. 434, and—generalizing matters—understand $[(A)(I_1', I_2', \ldots, I_n'/I_1, I_2, \ldots, I_n)]$ as $[([(A)(I_1', I_2', \ldots, I_{n-1}'/I_1, I_2, \ldots, I_{n-1}])(I_n'/I_n)]$. For the occasion '$S \vdash A$' is of course short for 'A is provable in QC from S (in Leblanc's sense)'.

Lemma 11. *Let S be finite. If $S \vdash A$, then $S \cup \{B\} \vdash A$.*

Proof: Suppose $S \vdash A$; let the column made up of $A_1, A_2, \ldots, A_p$ constitute a proof in QC from S whose last entry is A; let $P_1, P_2, \ldots, P_k$ ($k \geq 0$) be all the individual parameters of QC that are quasi-generalized upon in the column in question and occur in B; let $P_1', P_2', \ldots, P_k'$ be k individual parameters of QC that are distinct from $P_1, P_2, \ldots, P_k$ and are foreign to $A_1, A_2, \ldots, A_p$ and $S \cup \{B\}$; and let $X_1, X_2, \ldots, X_k$ be k individual variables of QC foreign to $A_1, A_2, \ldots, A_p$. Then the column

1	$A_1(P_1', P_2', \ldots, P_k'/P_1, P_2, \ldots, P_k)$	
2	$A_2(P_1', P_2', \ldots, P_k'/P_1, P_2, \ldots, P_k)$	
⋮	⋮	
p	$A_p(P_1', P_2', \ldots, P_k'/P_1, P_2, \ldots, P_k)$	
$p + 1$	$(\forall X_k)[A_p(P_1', P_2', \ldots, P_{k-1}', X_k/P_1, P_2, \ldots, P_k)]$	(**UG**, p)
$p + 2$	$(\forall X_{k-1})(\forall X_k)[A_p(P_1', P_2', \ldots, P_{k-2}', X_{k-1}, X_k/P_1, P_2, \ldots, P_k)]$	(**UG**, $p + 1$)
⋮	⋮	
$p + k$	$(\forall X_1)(\forall X_2) \ldots (\forall X_k) [A_p(X_1, X_2, \ldots, X_k/P_1, P_2, \ldots, P_k)]$	(**UG**, $p + k - 1$)
$p + k + 1$	$p + k \supset (\forall X_2)(\forall X_3) \ldots (\forall X_k)[A_p(X_2, X_3, \ldots, X_k/P_2, P_3, \ldots, P_k)]$	(**A6**)
$p + k + 2$	$(\forall X_2)(\forall X_3) \ldots (\forall X_k) [A_p(A_p(X_2, X_3, \ldots, X_k/P_2, P_3, \ldots, P_k)]$	
		(**MP**, $p + k, p + k + 1$)
$p + k + 3$	$p + k + 2 \supset (\forall X_3)(\forall X_4) \ldots (\forall X_k)[A_p(P_3, P_4, \ldots, P_k)]$	(**A6**)
$p + k + 4$	$(\forall X_3)(\forall X_4) \ldots (\forall X_k)[A_p(X_3, X_4, \ldots, X_k/P_3, P_4, \ldots, P_k)]$	
		(**MP**, $p + k + 2, p + k + 3$)
⋮	⋮	
$p + 3k - 2$	$(\forall X_k)[A_p(X_k/P_k)]$	(**MP**, $p + 3k - 4, p + 3k - 3$)
$p + 3k - 1$	$p + 3k - 2 \supset A_p$	(**A6**)
$p + 3k$	A_p	(**MP**, $p + 3k - 2, p + 3k - 1$)

is sure to constitute a proof in QC from $S \cup \{B\}$ with A_p ($= A$) as its last entry. For suppose A_i ($1 \leq i \leq p$) belongs to S. Since $P_1, P_2, \ldots, P_k$ are quasi-generalized upon in the original proof, they are sure to be foreign to S and hence to A_i. So $A_i(P_1', P_2', \ldots, P_k'/P_1, P_2, \ldots, P_k)$ is sure to be the same as A_i, and hence to belong to S. Or suppose A_i is an axiom of QC. Then by the same argument as on pp. 33–35 in [14] $A_i(P_1', P_2', \ldots, P_k'/P_1, P_2, \ldots, P_k)$ is sure to be an axiom of QC. Or suppose A_i follows from A_g and A_h by **MP**, and hence A_h, say, is of the sort $A_g \supset A_i$. Since $A_h(P_1', P_2', \ldots, P_k'/P_1, P_2, \ldots, P_k)$ and $A_g(P_1', P_2', \ldots, P_k'/P_1, P_2, \ldots, P_k) \supset A_i(P_1', P_2', \ldots, P_k'/P_1, P_2, \ldots, P_k)$ are the same, $A_i(P_1', P_2', \ldots, P_k'/P_1, P_2, \ldots, P_k)$ is sure to follow from $A_g(P_1', P_2', \ldots, P_k'/P_1, P_2, \ldots, P_k)$ and $A_h(P_1', P_2', \ldots, P_k'/P_1, P_2, \ldots, P_k)$ by **MP**. Or suppose A_i follows from A_h by **UG**, and hence is of the sort $(\forall X)[A_h(X/P)]$ for some individual parameter P of QC foreign to S; and suppose first that P is foreign to B. Since $((\forall X)[A_h(X/P)])(P_1', P_2', \ldots, P_k'/P_1, P_2, \ldots, P_k)$ and $(\forall X)[(A_h(P_1', P_2', \ldots, P_k'/P_1, P_2, \ldots, P_k))(X/P)]$ are the same and since P is sure to be foreign to $S \cup \{B\}$, $A_i(P_1', P_2', \ldots, P_k'/P_1, P_2, \ldots, P_k)$ is sure to follow from $A_h(P_1', P_2', \ldots, P_k'/P_1, P_2, \ldots, P_k)$ by **UG**. Suppose next that P occurs in B, and hence is one of $P_1, P_2, \ldots,$ and P_k, say P_j. Since $((\forall X)[A_h(X/P_j)])(P_1', P_2', \ldots, P_k'/P_1, P_2, \ldots, P_k)$ and $(\forall X)[(A_h(P_1', P_2', \ldots, P_k'/P_1, P_2, \ldots, P_k))(X/P_j')]$ are the same, and since—P_j' being sure to be foreign to $S \cup \{B\}$—$(\forall X)[(A_h(P_1', P_2', \ldots, P_k'/P_1, P_2, \ldots, P_k))(X/P_j')]$ follows from $A_h(P_1', P_2', \ldots, P_k'/P_1, P_2, \ldots, P_k)$ by **UG**, $((\forall X)[A_h(X/P_j)])(P_1', P_2', \ldots, P_k'/P_1, P_2, \ldots, P_k)$ is sure to follow from $A_h(P_1', P_2', \ldots, P_k'/P_1, P_2, \ldots, P_k)$ by **UG**. Hence $S \cup \{B\} \vdash A$.

Theorem 11. *If $S \vdash A$, then $S' \vdash A$ for any superset S' of S.*
Proof: Let S' be an arbitrary superset of S.
Case 1: S' is finite, and hence is of the sort $S \cup \{B_1, B_2, \ldots, B_n\}$ for some n larger than 0. Then S is sure to be finite as well, and hence T11 by n applications of L11.
Case 2.1: S' is infinite, but S is finite. Then T11 by definition.
Case 2.2: Both S' and S are infinite. Suppose $S \vdash A$. Then by definition $S'' \vdash A$ for some finite subset S'' of S. But S'' is bound to be a finite subset of S' as well. Hence $S' \vdash A$ by definition.

2. I next establish that wffs of $QC\underline{*}$ of the sort $(\forall X)(\forall Y)A \supset (\forall Y)(\forall X)A$ are provable in $QC\underline{*}$ (given the axiomatization of $QC\underline{*}$ in Section 3 and Fitch's account of a proof from hypotheses). The result follows of course from the Completeness Theorem in [14], but because of the difficulties attending $(\forall X)(\forall Y)A \supset (\forall Y)(\forall X)A$ in QC and QC*, the demonstration that follows may be welcome. For brevity's sake I write '$(A \& B)$' in lieu of '$\sim(A \supset \sim B)$'.

Lemma 12. (a) *If $\vdash\underline{*} A \supset (B \supset C)$ and $\vdash\underline{*} A' \supset (C \supset C')$, then $\vdash\underline{*} A \supset (A' \supset (B \supset C'))$.*

448   Part 3: Provability

(b) If $\vdash\underline{*} A \supset (B \supset (C \supset C'))$, then $\vdash\underline{*} (B \& C) \supset (A \supset C')$.
(c) If $\vdash\underline{*} (A \& B) \supset (C \supset C')$, then $\vdash\underline{*} C \supset (A \supset (B \supset C'))$.
(d) If $\vdash\underline{*} A(P/X) \supset (B \supset C(P/X))$, then $\vdash\underline{*} (\forall X)A \supset (B \supset (\forall X)C)$, so long as (i) P is foreign to $(\forall X)A$, B, and $(\forall X)C$, and (ii) X is foreign to B.
(e) If $\vdash\underline{*} A(P/X) \supset (B \supset (C \supset C'(P/X)))$, then $\vdash\underline{*} (\forall X)A \supset (B \supset (C \supset (\forall X)C'))$, so long as (i) P is foreign to $(\forall X)A$, B, C, and $(\forall X)C$, and (ii) X is foreign to B and C.
(f) $\vdash\underline{*} (\forall Y)[A(Y/X)] \supset (\forall X)A$.
(g) If $\vdash\underline{*} A \supset (\forall Y)[B(Y/X)]$, then $\vdash\underline{*} A \supset (\forall X)B$.
(h) If $\vdash\underline{*} A \supset (B \supset (\forall Y)[C(Y/X)])$, then $\vdash\underline{*} A \supset (B \supset (\forall X)C)$.

Proof:
(a)–(c) Proofs left to the reader.

(d) Suppose $\vdash\underline{*} A(P/X) \supset (B \supset C(P/X))$, suppose P is as in (i), and suppose X is as in (ii). Then $\vdash\underline{*} B \supset (A(P/X) \supset C(P/X))$ by L6(c), hence $\vdash\underline{*} B \supset ((\forall X)A \supset (\forall X)C)$ by L7(c), and hence $\vdash\underline{*} (\forall X)A \supset (B \supset (\forall X)C)$ by L6(c).

(e) Suppose $\vdash\underline{*} A(P/X) \supset (B \supset (C \supset C'(P/X)))$, suppose P is as in (i), and suppose X is as in (ii). Then $\vdash\underline{*} (B \& C) \supset (A(P/X) \supset C'(P/X))$ by (b), hence $\vdash\underline{*} (B \& C) \supset ((\forall X)A \supset (\forall X)C')$ by L7(c), and hence $\vdash\underline{*} (\forall X)A \supset (B \supset (C \supset (\forall X)C'))$ by (c).

(f) In case X and Y are the same, proof of (f) is routine. So suppose X and Y are distinct from each other. Then $(\forall X)((\forall Y)[A(Y/X)] \supset (A(Y/X))(X/Y))$ is sure to be well-formed. Hence $\vdash\underline{*} (\forall X)((\forall Y)[A(Y/X)] \supset (A(Y/X))(X/Y))$ by L10(b), hence $\vdash\underline{*} (\forall X)((\forall Y)[A(Y/X)] \supset A)$, and hence $\vdash\underline{*} (\forall Y)[A(Y/X)] \supset (\forall X)A$ by L1(f).

(g) Proof by L12(g) and L6(b).
(h) Proof by L12(g) and L6(d).

Theorem 12. $\vdash\underline{*} (\forall X)(\forall Y)A \supset (\forall Y)(\forall X)A$.

Proof: Let P and P' be individual parameters of QC$\underline{*}$ distinct from each other and foreign to $(\forall X)(\forall Y)A$, and let Z be an individual variable of QC$\underline{*}$ foreign to $(\forall X)(\forall Y)A$. $\vdash\underline{*} (\exists X)(X = P) \supset ((\forall X)(\forall Y)A \supset ((\forall Y)A)(P/X))$ by L9(a), and hence $\vdash\underline{*} (\exists X)(X = P) \supset ((\forall X)(\forall Y)A \supset (\forall Y)[A(P/X)])$. Similarly, $\vdash\underline{*} (\exists Y)(Y = P') \supset ((\forall Y)[A(P/X)] \supset (A(P/X))(P'/Y))$ by L9(a), and hence $\vdash\underline{*} (\exists Y)(Y = P') \supset ((\forall Y)[A(P/X)] \supset (A(P'/Y))(P/X))$. So, $\vdash\underline{*} (\exists X)(X = P) \supset ((\exists Y)(Y = P') \supset ((\forall X)(\forall Y)A \supset (A(P'/Y))(P/X)))$ by L12(a), hence $\vdash\underline{*} ((\exists X)(X = Z))(P/Z) \supset ((\exists Y)(Y = P') \supset ((\forall X)(\forall Y)A \supset ((A(P'/Y))(Z/X))(P/Z)))$, and hence $\vdash\underline{*} (\forall Z)(\exists X)(X = Z) \supset ((\exists Y)(Y = P') \supset ((\forall X)(\forall Y)A \supset (\forall Z)[(A(P'/Y))(Z/X)]))$ by L12(e). But, since $(\forall Z)(\exists X)(X = Z)$ counts as an axiom of QC$\underline{*}$, $\vdash\underline{*} (\forall Z)(\exists X)(X = Z)$ by L1(b). Hence $\vdash\underline{*} (\exists Y)(Y = P') \supset ((\forall X)(\forall Y)A \supset (\forall Z)[A(P'/Y))(Z/X)])$ by L1(c), hence $\vdash\underline{*} (\exists Y)(Y = P') \supset ((\forall X)(\forall Y)A \supset (\forall X)[A(P'/Y)])$ by L12(h), hence $\vdash\underline{*} ((\exists Y)(Y = Z)) (P'/Z) \supset ((\forall X)(\forall Y)A \supset ((\forall X)[A(Z/Y)])(P'/Z))$, and hence $\vdash\underline{*} (\forall Z)(\exists Y)(Y = Z) \supset ((\forall X)(\forall Y)A \supset (\forall Z)(\forall X)[A(Z/Y)])$ by L12(d). But, since $(\forall Z)(\exists Y)(Y = Z)$ counts as an axiom of QC$\underline{*}$, $\vdash\underline{*} (\forall Z)(\exists Y)(Y = Z)$ by L1(b). Hence $\vdash\underline{*}

$(\forall X)(\forall Y)A \supset (\forall Z)(\forall X)[A(Z/Y)]$ by L1(c), hence $\vdash_{\underline{*}} (\forall X)(\forall Y)A \supset (\forall Z)[((\forall X)A)(Z/Y)]$, and hence $\vdash_{\underline{*}} (\forall X)(\forall Y)A \supset (\forall Y)(\forall X)A$ by L12(g).[33]

Notes

1. Predicate variables of degree 0 are of course sentence variables.
2. When no ambiguity threatens, I shall write '$A \supset B$' in lieu of '$(A \supset B)$'.
3. Generally, *but not without fail*: the Kleene account mentioned on p. 434 appeared in 1952.
4. See p. 45 of [2]. Church limits himself there to the case where S is finite. However, in [3], p. 310, he takes a wff A of QC^2 (the quantificational calculus of order two) to be provable in QC^2 from an infinite set S of wffs of QC^2 if A is provable in QC^2 from a finite subset of S. So the account in the text is close enough to Church's intentions to be attributed to Church.
5. Their proof, retouched to suit our axiomatization of QC, is of utmost simplicity. To each wff A of QC assign a value $v(A)$ as follows: (a) in case A is of the sort (i) on p. 431, $v(A) = 1$; (b) in case A is of the sort $\sim B$, $v(A) = 1 - v(B)$; (c) in case A is of the sort $B \supset C$, $v(A) = 1$ if $v(B) = 0$ or $v(C) = 1$, otherwise $v(A) = 0$; (d) in case A is of the sort $(\forall X)B$ and X is distinct from 'y' or foreign to B, $v(A) = v(B)$, otherwise $v(A) = 0$. A routine induction shows that if the column

$$A_1$$
$$A_2$$
$$\vdots$$
$$A_p$$

constitutes a proof in QC from a finite set S of wffs of the sort (i) on p. 431 and 'y' occurs free in at least one member of S, then $v(A_i) = 1$ for each i from 1 through p. (Note in particular that, with 'y' occurring free in at least one member of S, no entry in the column that follows from an earlier entry by **UG** can be of the sort $(\forall y)B$.) But $v('(\forall y)(g(y) \supset g(y))') = 0$. So there can be no proof in QC from $\{g(y)\}$ with '$(\forall y)(g(y) \supset g(y))$' as its last entry.
6. For a recent version of Henkin's proof, see [17], pp. 285–93. The original version is of course in [6].
7. Church's account in [3] of a proof in QC from a finite set of wffs of QC differ from that in [2]. Using three extra rules of inference (Alphabetic Change of Bound Variables, Substitution for Individual Variables, and Substitution for Predicate Variables), it yields (**B**) for finite S and S' (= *362 on pp. 199–200). It is, however, too intricate for review here.

In some presentations of QC only *closed* wffs (i.e., only wffs in which there occur no free individual variables) can count as axioms, only proofs from sets of closed wffs can count as proofs, and hence only closed wffs are provable (be it from $\emptyset$ or from a non-empty set of wffs). In such presentations the Montague-Henkin difficulty does not arise, and an account of a proof from hypotheses for which (**B**) (and, as a corollary of Henkin's proof, (**A**)) holds true is easily had: adopt the axioms in either edition of [19] as your axioms and drop (iv) on p. 432. However, open wffs matter as much—I believe—as closed ones, and the presentations of QC considered here strike me as unduly restricted.
8. Meyer and I used this terminology in [16] in connection with individual variables, and I have since used it regularly in connection with all types of variables.
9. Under the present wording of clause (iv), identical quantifiers can no longer overlap in a wff of QC. So, for example, when a conditional of the sort $A \supset (\forall X)A$ is well-formed, the individual variable X is sure to be foreign to the antecedent A, a point to bear in mind when coming to change number six.
10. Henceforth I shall abridge 'foreign to each member of S' as 'foreign to S'.
11. The proof, tailored to suit the present context, is reproduced in the Appendix.
12. Let $v(A)$ be defined as in Note 5 (but with clause (i) understood as on p. 434 rather than p. 431). A routine induction will show that if the column

450   Part 3: Provability

$$A_1$$
$$A_2$$
$$\vdots$$
$$A_p$$

constitutes a proof in QC from $\{g(a), g(b), g(c), g(a'), g(b'), g(c'), \ldots\}$, then $v(A_i) = 1$ for each i from 1 through p. (Note in particular that, with each individual parameter of QC occurring in $\{g(a), g(b), g(c), g(a'), g(b'), g(c'), \ldots\}$, no entry in the column can follow from an earlier entry by **UG**.) But $v('(\forall y)(g(y) \supset g(y))') = 0$, as before. Hence the conclusion in the text.

13. In [11], a 1967 publication of Kleene's, simplifications are brought to the account in [10], but the Montague-Henkin account still remains the easier one.

14. And remained unaware of it until the writer brought it to his attention in the early sixties.

15. Or, as [17] has it on p. 328, declaring any wff of QC of the sort $(\forall X)A$ an axiom of QC if, for some individual parameter P of QC foreign to $(\forall X)A$, $A(P/X)$ is an axiom of QC. The two characterizations amount to the same. For suppose, on one hand, that $A(P/X)$ is an axiom of QC, and hence by the characterization in the text that so is $(\forall X)[(A(P/X))(X/P)]$. If P is foreign to $(\forall X)A$ and hence to A, then $(A(P/X))(X/P)$ and A are sure to be the same, and hence $(\forall X)A$ is sure to be an axiom of QC (as the characterization in [17] would have it). Suppose, on the other hand, that A is an axiom of QC. With A and $(\forall X)[A(X/P)]$ both presumed here to be well-formed, X is sure to be foreign to A, and hence A and $(A(X/P))(P/X)$ have to be the same. So $(A(X/P))(P/X)$ is sure to be an axiom of QC, and hence by the characterization in [17] $(\forall X)[A(X/P)]$ is sure to be one as well (as the characterization in the text would have it).

16. In Montague and Henkin's account and in Fitch's I implicitly take a wff A of QC to be *provable* in QC if A is provable in QC from $\emptyset$. Fitch in [5] merely deals with provability, and the calculus he is concerned with is a modal extension of QC. But the account owes enough to Fitch to be credited to him.

17. The reader will also have noticed that *the above proof of* **UGT** *makes no use of axiom schemata* **A1-A3**, *and hence holds no matter one's axiom schemata for* '$\sim$' *and* '$\supset$'. It thus holds for a variety of first order quantificational calculi.

18. A semantics for QC* of the truth-value sort will be found in [14], pp. 135–36, and one of the model-theoretic sort can be gotten from [24]. The model-theoretic semantics in the original version of [16] is defective, as Shipley established in [20] (as is the correction offered in [14], p. 161, Note 62). See p. 72 for a fresh revision of [16] and a sketch of Shipley's own semantics.

19. So far as I know, **A6*** made its first appearance in [12]. Though axiomatizations of QC* (see pp. 439–40) go back to 1959, the first axiomatization of QC* is probably to be found in [12].

20. In [16] Meyer and I assumed without further ado that $(\forall X)(\forall Y)A \supset (\forall Y)(\forall X)A$ was provable in QC*. However, Trew questioned this in [23], and as all attempts to prove the Commutation Law in question have so far failed, we now incline to think with Trew that **A7*** is independent. The reader will recall the difficulties that Quine experienced with $(\forall X)(\forall Y)A \supset (\forall Y)(\forall X)A$ in [19]. With the closure $()[A]$ of a wff A defined as in that edition of *Mathematical Logic*, he could not prove $()[(\forall X)(\forall Y)A \supset (\forall Y)(\forall X)A]$ and hence adopted it as an extra axiom schema. Fitch showed in 1941 that proof of $()[(\forall X)(\forall Y)A \supset (\forall Y)(\forall X)A]$ can be had if the definition of $()[A]$ is amended; and, using yet another definition of $()[A]$, so did Berry the very same year (see [4] and [1]). However, whether given Quine's original notion of a closure $()[(\forall X)(\forall Y)A \supset (\forall Y)(\forall X)A]$ is independent in [19] and, in particular, whether $(\forall X)(\forall Y)A \supset (\forall Y)(\forall X)A$ itself is, remain open questions.

21. The point made in Note 17 regarding **A1-A3** holds here as in QC.

22. When no ambiguity threatens, I shall write '$P = P'$' in lieu of '$(P = P')$'.

23. Tarski had an additional axiom schema: $(\forall X)A \supset A$, but Kalish and Montague showed it redundant in [9]. Note that, as Tarski uses but one run of individual variables, X may occur free in the consequent of his axiom schema.

24. The suggestion was in a letter than van Fraassen wrote to the author in early 1966.

25. That $P = P$ is provable in QC$_=$ given the last two axiomatizations will be shown in Note 28. The proof there is essentially Tarski's in [22].

26. As would much of the post-1956 literature: surprisingly enough, the Montague-Henkin paper received little notice. There are exceptions, of course: [10] among pre-1956 publications and [13] among post-1956 ones.

27. That $(\exists X)(X = Y) \supset ((\forall X)A \supset A(Y/X))$ follows from $X = Y \supset (A \supset A(Y/_{t}X))$ (and $(\forall X)A \supset A$) was announced in [21], a 1951 abstract, but proof of the fact was supplied only in [22], a 1965 paper. I was unaware of [21] when I offered proof of $(\exists X)(X = P) \supset ((\forall X)A \supset A(P/X))$ from $P = P' \supset (A \supset A(P'/P))$ in [15], a 1959 paper; and Tarski was of course unaware of [15] when he elaborated [21] into [22].

28. Unlike the proof of Theorem 3, that of Theorem 6 makes recourse to **A1–A3**. This could of course be avoided by drafting, say, $(\forall Y)((\forall X)A \supset A(Y/X))$ as an extra axiom schema, but the resulting axiomatization of QC$_=$ would be of little interest.

That $P = P$ is provable in QC$_=$ (given our axiomatization of QC$_=$ on p. 440 or its Tarski forebear) can be shown as follows. Let P' be an individual parameter of QC$_=$ distinct from P. $\vdash_= P' = P \supset (P' = P \supset P = P)$ by L1(b); hence $\vdash_= P' = P \supset P = P$ by routine steps; hence $\vdash_= (X = P)(P'/X) \supset (P = P)(P'/X)$; hence $\vdash_= (\exists X)(X = P) \supset (\exists X)(P = P)$ by L7(f); and hence $\vdash_= (\exists X)(X = P) \supset P = P$ by L7(g) and L6(b). (That $(\exists X)(X = P) \supset P = P$ is provable in QC$_=$, and provable in QC$_=$ without recourse to **B1**, will be recalled in Note 30.) But $\vdash_= (\exists X)(X = P)$ by L1(b). Hence $\vdash_= P = P$ by L1(c).

29. It is easily seen that **B4***, shown in Note 28 to be provable in QC$_=$, is independent of **A1–A5**, **B1***, and **B2–B3**. Let $v(P = P) = 0$ for any individual parameter P of QC$^*_=$; let $v(A) = 1$ for any other atomic wff A of QC$^*_=$; let $v(\sim A) = 1 - v(A)$; let $v(A \supset B) = 1$ unless $v(A) = 1$ and $v(B) = 0$, in which case $v(A \supset B) = 0$; and let $v((\forall X)A) = 1$. As the reader may wish to verify, wffs of QC$^*_=$ of any of the sorts **A1–A5**, **B1***, and **B2–B3** all evaluate to 1; wffs of the sort **B4***, on the other hand, evaluate to 0. (For further comments on **B4***, see Note 30). And, adapting an argument of Ermanno A. Bencivenga's, it is easily seen that **B1*** is independent of **A1–A5**, **B2–B3**, and **B4***. First, by a *Bencivenga sequence for* QC$^*_=$ understand any (infinite) sequence of the sort $<\Sigma_1, \Sigma_2, \Sigma_3, \ldots>$, where Σ_1, Σ_2, Σ_3, etc. are (possibly empty) sets of individual parameters of QC$^*_=$. Then, *Seq* being a Bencivenga sequence for QC$^*_=$, take $P = P$ to be true on *Seq* for any individual parameter P of QC$^*_=$; take any other atomic wff of QC$^*_=$ to be false on *Seq*; take $\sim A$ to be true on *Seq* if and only if A is false on *Seq*; take $A \supset B$ to be true on *Seq* if and only if A is false on *Seq* or B is true on *Seq*; and take $(\forall X)A$ to be true on *Seq* if and only if (i) $A(P/X)$ is true on *Seq* for every member P of Σ_1 in case X is 'x', (ii) $A(P/X)$ is true on *Seq* for every member P of Σ_2 in case X is 'y', (iii) $A(P/X)$ is true on *Seq* for every member P of Σ_3 in case X is 'z', etc. As the reader may wish to verify, wffs of QC$^*_=$ of any of the sorts **A1–A5**, **B2–B3**, and **B4*** are all true on any Bencivenga sequence in which Σ_1 is non-empty but Σ_2 is; wffs of the sort **B1***, on the other hand, are false on any such sequence.

30. The reader will notice that the proof of Theorem 7 makes no use of **B4***, which was drafted as an axiom schema of QC$^*_=$ only for completeness' sake. Under any alternative treatment of identity $P = P$ could be weakened to read $P = P \supset (\exists X)(X = P)$. Since $(\exists X)(X = P) \supset P = P$ is already provable in QC$^*_=$ (see Note 28), one would obtain $(\exists X)(X = P) \equiv P = P$, the counterpart in QC$^*_=$ of a familiar theorem of *Principia Mathematica*.

31. The error occurs in the proof of **T5.3.15**, which presupposes $(\forall Y)((\forall X)A \supset A(Y/X))$ and yet is used to prove $(\forall Y)((\forall X)A \supset A(Y/X))$ in **T5.3.16**.

32. **B4**$_2$ is of course the *Axiom of Comprehension*. The axiomatization of QC^2 used here stems from [7].

33. Thanks are due to Robert J. Cosgrove, Michael J. Duffy, and Myles McNally for reading and spotting errors in an earlier draft of the paper.

References

[1] Berry, G. D. W. 1941. "On Quine's Axioms of Quantification." *The Journal of Symbolic Logic* (hereafter *JSL*) 6: 23–27.

[2] Church, A. 1944. *Introduction to Mathematical Logic, Part I*. Princeton: Princeton University Press.

452   Part 3: Provability

[3] _____ . 1956. *Introduction to Mathematical Logic*, Vol. I. Princeton: Princeton University Press.
[4] Fitch, F. B. 1941. "Closure and Quine's *101." *JSL* 6: 18–22.
[5] _____ . 1948. "Intuitionistic Modal Logic with Quantifiers." *Portugaliae Mathematica* 17: 113–18.
[6] Henkin, L. 1949. "The Completeness of the First-Order Functional Calculus." *JSL* 14: 159–66.
[7] _____ . 1950. "Banishing the Rule of Substitution for Functional Variables." *JSL* 15: 81–91.
[8] Hintikka, J. 1959. "Existential Presuppositions and Existential Commitments." *The Journal of Philosophy* 56: 125–37.
[9] Kalish, D., and Montague. R. 1965. "On Tarski's Formalization of Predicate Logic with Identity." *Archiv für mathematische Logik und Grundlagenforschung* (hereafter *AMLG*) 7: 81–101.
[10] Kleene, S. C. 1952. *Introduction to Metamathematics*. Amsterdam: North-Holland.
[11] _____ . 1967. *Mathematical Logic*. New York: Wiley.
[12] Lambert, K. 1963. "Existential Import Revisited." *Notre Dame Journal of Formal Logic* 4: 288–92.
[13] Leblanc, H. 1966. *Techniques of Deductive Inference*. Englewood Cliffs: Prentice-Hall.
[14] _____ . 1976. *Truth-Value Semantics*. Amsterdam: North-Holland.
[15] Leblanc, H., and Hailperin, T., 1959. "Non-Designating Singular Terms." *The Philosophical Review*. 68: 239–43 (#1 in this volume).
[16] Leblanc, H., and Meyer, R. K. 1970. "On Prefacing $(\forall X)A \supset A(Y/X)$ with $(\forall Y)$: A Free Quantification Theory without Identity." *Zeitschrift für mathematische Logik und Grundlagen der Mathematik* (hereafter *ZMLGM*) 16: 447–72 (#3 in this volume).
[17] Leblanc, H., and Wisdom, W. A. 1976. *Deductive Logic*, second edition. Boston: Allyn and Bacon.
[18] Montague, R., and Henkin, L. 1956. "On the Definition of 'Formal Deduction'." *JSL* 21: 129–36.
[19] Quine, W. V. 1940. *Mathematical Logic*, first edition. New York: Norton.
[20] Shipley, C. T. 1972. "A Semantical Theory and Several Deductive Systems for Universally Free Logic." Ph.D. dissertation, University of Nebraska.
[21] Tarski, A. 1951. "Remarks on the Formalization of the Predicate Calculus (Abstract)." *Bulletin of the American Mathematical Society* 57: 81–82.
[22] _____ . 1965. "A Simplified Formalization of Predicate Logic with Identity." *AMLG* 7: 61–79.
[23] Trew, A. 1970. "Non-Standard Theories of Quantification and Identity." *JSL* 35: 267–94.
[24] van Fraassen, B. C. 1966. "The Completeness of Free Logic." *ZMLGM* 12: 219–34.

H. Leblanc: A Bibliography

Books

An Introduction to Deductive Logic. 1955. New York: John Wiley and Sons, Inc.
Logica Matematica (J. M. Ferrater Mora, coauthor). 1955, second revised edition 1962. Mexico: Fondo de Cultura Economica.
Statistical and Inductive Probabilities. 1962. Englewood Cliffs, NJ: Prentice-Hall, Inc.
Techniques of Deductive Inference. 1966. Englewood Cliffs, NJ: Prentice-Hall, Inc.
Deductive Logic (W. A. Wisdom, coauthor), 1972, second revised edition 1976. Boston: Allyn and Bacon, Inc. (*Exercise Solutions.* 1972. Boston: Allyn and Bacon, Inc.)
Truth, Syntax and Modality (H. Leblanc, editor). 1973. Amsterdam: North-Holland Publishing Co.
Truth-Value Semantics. 1976. Amsterdam: North-Holland Publishing Co.
Existence, Truth, and Provability. 1982. Albany: State University of New York Press.
Essays in Epistemology and Semantics (H. Leblanc, coeditor). In preparation. Haven Publishing Corporation.
Probabilistic Semantics. In preparation. Dordrecht: Reidel Publishing Co.

Articles

"The Semiotic Function of Predicates." 1949. *The Journal of Philosophy* 46: 838–4.
"A Modernistic Approach to Hume's Theory of Induction and Causation." 1949. *Bulletin of the Eastern Division of the American Philosophical Association* 13–44.
"On Definitions." 1950. *Philosophy of Science* 17: 302–309.
"Positions and Propositions on Universals." 1951. *Philosophy and Phenomenological Research* 42: 95–104.
"Evidence Logique et Degré de Confirmation." 1954. *Revue Philosophique de Louvain* 52: 619–25.
"Three Types of Scientific Explanation." 1955. *The Journal of Symbolic Logic* 20: 93.
"Two Probability Concepts." 1956. *The Journal of Philosophy* 53: 679–88.
"On Logically False Evidence Statements." 1957. *The Journal of Symbolic Logic* 22: 345–49.
"The Contemporary Logic of Statements." 1958. *Readings in Logic,* R. Houde, ed., Dubuque, IA: William C. Brown Co. 243–75 and 301–02.
"Nondesignating Singular Terms" (T. Hailperin, coauthor). 1959. *The Philosophical Review* 68: 239–43 (#1 in this volume).
"Report on Grant No. 2131." 1959. *Year Book 1958,* Philadelphia: The American Philosophical Society 345.

"On Chances and Estimated Chances of Being True." 1959. *Revue Philosophique de Louvain* 57: 225–39.
"Professor Darlington and the Confirmation of Laws." 1959. *Philosophy of Science* 24: 364–66.
"On Requirements for Conditional Probability Functions." 1960. *The Journal of Symbolic Logic* 25: 238–42. Abstract of same in *The Journal of Symbolic Logic*, 1959, 24: 318.
"On a Recent Allotment of Probabilities to Open and Closed Sentences." 1960. *Notre Dame Journal of Formal Logic* 1: 171–75. Abstract of same in *Abstracts of Contributed Papers, International Congress for Logic, Methodology, and Philosophy of Science*, Stanford University. 84–85.
"A Note on the Intuitionist and the Classical Propositional Calculus" (E. W. Beth, coauthor). 1960. *Logique et Analyse* 11–12: 174–76 (#27 in this volume).
"On So-Called Degrees of Confirmation." 1960. *The British Journal for the Philosophy of Science* 10: 312–15.
"A New Interpretation of c(h,e)." 1961. *Philosophy and Phenomenological Research* 21: 373–76.
"An Extension of the Equivalence Calculus." 1961. *Zeitschrift für mathematische Logik und Grundlagen der Mathematik* 7: 104–05.
"Probabilities as Truth-Value Estimates." 1961. *Philosophy of Science* 28: 414–17.
"The Algebra of Logic and the Theory of Deduction." 1961. *The Journal of Philosophy* 58: 553–58 (#32 in this volume).
"Boolean Algebra and the Propositional Calculus." 1962. *Mind* 71: 383–86 (#31 in this volume).
"Etudes sur les Règles d'Inférence dites Règles de Gentzen, Première Partie." 1962. *Dialogue* 1: 56–66.
"Intuitionism Reconsidered" (N. D. Belnap, Jr., coauthor). 1962. *Notre Dame Journal of Formal Logic* 3: 79–82 (#28 in this volume).
"Structural Rules of Inference." 1962. *Notre Dame Journal of Formal Logic* 3: 201–05 (#22 in this volume).
"Proof Routines for the Propositional Calculus." 1963. *Notre Dame Journal of Formal Logic* 4: 355–67 (#23 in this volume).
"A Revised Version of Goodman's Paradox on Confirmation." 1963. *Philosophical Studies* 14: 49–51.
"Statistical and Inductive Probabilities." 1963. *Induction: Some Current Issues*, H. E. Kyburg, Jr., and Nagel, E., eds., Middletown, Wesleyan University Press, 3–26.
"That Positive Instances are No Help." 1963. *The Journal of Philosophy* 60: 453–62.
"Etudes sur les Règles d'Inférence dites Règles de Gentzen. Deuxième Partie." 1963. *Dialogue* 1: 355–67.
"On Not Strengthening Intuitionistic Logic" (N. D. Belnap, Jr., and R. H. Thomason, coauthors). 1963. *Notre Dame Journal of Formal Logic* 4: 310–20 (#29 in this volume). Abstract of same in *The Journal of Symbolic Logic*, 1963, 28: 297.
"On the Definition of 'Formal Deduction'." 1964. *The Journal of Symbolic Logic* 29: 150.
"Marginalia on Gentzen's Sequenzen-Kalkule." 1965. *Contributions to Logic and Methodology in Honor of J. M. Bochenski*, A. T. Tymieniecka, ed. Amsterdam: North-Holland Publishing Co., 73–83 (#21 in this volume).
"Minding one's X's and Y's." 1965. *Logique et Analyse* 18: 209–10.
"The Demarcation Line between Intuitionist Logic and Classical Logic" (R. H. Thomason, coauthor). 1966. *Zeitschrift für mathematische Logik und Grundlagen der Mathematik* 12: 257–62 (#30 in this volume).
"Two Separation Theorems for Natural Deduction." 1966. *Notre Dame Journal of Formal Logic* 7: 159–80 (#24 in this volume).
"Two Shortcomings of Natural Deduction." 1966. *The Journal of Philosophy* 68: 29–37 (#25 in this volume). Abstract of same in *The Review of Metaphysics*, 1966, 19: 835.
"All or None: A Novel Choice of Primitives for Elementary Logic" (R. H. Thomason, coauthor). 1967. *The Journal of Symbolic Logic* 32: 345–51 (#33 in this volume). Abstract of same in *The Journal of Symbolic Logic*, 1968, 31: 683.
"Completeness Theorems for Some Presuppositions-Free Logics" (R. H. Thomason, coauthor). 1968. *Fundamenta Mathematicae* 62: 125–64 (#2 in this volume). Abstract of same in *The Journal of Philosophy*, 1966, 21: 699–700.

Bibliography 455

"Subformula Theorems for N-Sequents." 1968. *The Journal of Symbolic Logic* 33: 161–79 (*#26* in this volume). Abstract of same in *The Journal of Symbolic Logic*, 1966, 31: 693–95.

"A Simplified Account of Validity and Implication for Quantificational Logic." 1968. *The Journal of Symbolic Logic* 33: 231–35 (*#8* in this volume).

"On Meyer and Lambert's Quantificational Calculus FQ." 1968. *The Journal of Symbolic Logic* 33: 275–80.

"Syntactically Free, Semantically Bound: A Note on Variables." 1968. *Notre Dame Journal of Formal Logic* 9: 167–70.

"A Rationale for Analogical Inference." 1969. *Philosophical Studies* 20: 29–31.

"A Simplified Strong Completeness Theorem for $QC_=$." 1969. *Akten des xiv. Internationalen Kongresses für Philosophie*. 3: 83–95 (*#9* in this volume).

"Open Formulas and the Empty Domain" (R. K. Meyer, coauthor). 1969. *Archiv für mathematische Logik und Grundlagenforschung* 12: 78–84 (*#5* in this volume).

"Three Generalizations of a Theorem of Beth's." 1969. *Logique et Analyse* 47: 205–20 (*#11* in this volume). Abstract of same in *The Journal of Symbolic Logic*, 1969, 34: 155.

"A Liberated Version of S5" (K. Lambert and R. K. Meyer, coauthors). 1969. *Archiv für mathematische Logik und Grundlagenforschung* 12: 151–54 (*#6* in this volume).

"Truth-Value Semantics for the Theory of Types" (R. K. Meyer, coauthor). 1970. *Philosophical Problems in Logic: Some Recent Developments*, K. Lambert, ed., Dordrecht: D. Reidel Publishing Co. (*#12* in this volume). Abstract of same in *The Journal of Symbolic Logic*, 1969, 34: 181.

"A Semantical Completeness Result for Relevant Quantification Theories" (R. K. Meyer, coauthor). 1970. *The Journal of Symbolic Logic* 34: 181.

"On Prefacing $(\forall X)A \supset A(Y/X)$ with $(\forall Y)$: A Free Quantification Theory Without Identity" (R. K. Meyer, coauthor). 1971. *Zeitschrift für mathematische Logik und Grundlagen der Mathematik* 12: 153–68 (*#3* in this volume). Abstract of same in *The Journal of Symbolic Logic*, 1970, 34: 180.

"Truth-Value Semantics for a Logic of Existence." 1971. *Notre Dame Journal of Formal Logic* 12: 153–68 (*#4* in this volume).

"Truth-Value Semantics for the Modal Logics QM, QS4, and QS5." 1971. *The Journal of Symbolic Logic* 36: 581–82.

"Matters of Separation" (R. K. Meyer, coauthor). 1972. *Notre Dame Journal of Formal Logic* 13: 229–36 (*#34* in this volume).

"Duals of Smullyan Trees" (D. P. Snyder, coauthor). 1972. *Notre Dame Journal of Formal Logic* 13: 387–93.

"Wittgenstein and the Truth-Functionality Thesis." 1972. *American Philosophical Quarterly* 9: 271–74 (*#13* in this volume). Abstract of same in *The Review of Metaphysics*, 1972, 26: 183.

"Matters of Relevance." 1972. *Journal of Philosophical Logic* 1: 269–86 (*#14* in this volume). Also appeared in *Exact Philosophy: Problems, Tools, and Goals*, M. Bunge, ed., Dordrecht: D. Reidel Publishing Co., 1973, 3–20.

"Semantic Deviations." 1973. *Truth, Syntax and Modality*, H. Leblanc, ed., Amsterdam: North-Holland Publishing Co. (*#20* in this volume).

"Truth-Functionality and the Ramified Theory of Types" (G. Weaver, coauthor), 1973. *Truth, Syntax and Modality*, H. Leblanc, ed., Amsterdam: North-Holland Publishing Co. (*#15* in this volume).

"On Dispensing with Things and Worlds." 1973. *Logic and Ontology: Studies in Contemporary Philosophy*, M. K. Munitz, ed., New York: New York University Press (*#7* in this volume).

"Deux Rêves de Leibniz: Réflections sur une Lecture de Skolem et de Gödel." 1973. *La Communication, Actes du XV Congrès de l'Association des Sociétés de Philosophie de Langue Française*. Montréal, 2: 119–39.

"Completeness of Relevant Quantification Theories" (R. K. Meyer and J. M. Dunn, coauthors). 1974. *Notre Dame Journal of Formal Logic* 15: 97–121.

"A Strong Completeness Theorem for 3-Valued Logic" (H. Goldberg and G. Weaver, coauthors). 1974. *Notre Dame Journal of Formal Logic* 15: 325–30 (*#17* in this volume).

"That *Principia Mathematica*, First Edition, is Predicative After All." 1975. *Journal of Philosophical Logic* 4: 67–71 (#16 in this volume).

"A Henkin-Type Completeness Proof for 3–Valued Logic with Quantifiers." 1975. *Proceedings of the 1975 International Symposium of Multiple-Valued Logic*. Long Beach: IEEE Computer Society, 388–98. A corrected version of the paper has appeared as:

"A Strong Completeness Proof for 3–Valued Logic. Part II." 1977. *Notre Dame Journal of Formal Logic* 17: 107–16 (#18 in this volume).

"Queries on Truth Conditions." 1975. *Dialogue* 14: 410–19.

"A Completeness Result for Quantificational Tense Logic" (R. P. McArthur, coauthor). 1976. *Zeitschrift für mathematische Logik und Grundlagen der Mathematik* 22: 89–96 (#19 in this volume).

"Rules of Deduction and Truth-Tables" (J. A. Paulos and G. Weaver, coauthors). 1977. *Reports in Mathematical Logic* 8: 71–79.

"Truth-Value Assignments and Their Cardinality." 1977. *Philosophia* 7: 305–16 (#10 in this volume).

"Generalization in First-Order Logic." 1979. *Notre Dame Journal of Formal Logic* 20:835–57 (#35 in this volume).

"A Note on Popper and Carnap Probability Functions" (B. C. van Fraassen, coauthor), 1979. *The Journal of Symbolic Logic*. 44:369–73.

"Probabilistic Foundations for First-Order Logic." 1979. *Zeitschrift für mathematische Logik und Grundlagen der Mathematik* 25: 497–509.

"Probabilistic Semantics: An Overview." 1980. *Philosophia* 8: 231–49. An expanded version of the paper is to appear in *Essays in Epistemology and Semantics*, Haven Publishing Corporation.

Preface to R. D. Gumb's *Evolving Theories*, 1980, Haven Publishing Corp.

"Soundness and Completeness Proofs for Three Brands of Intuitionistic Logic" (R. D. Gumb, coauthor). To appear in *Essays in Epistemology and Semantics*. Abstract of same in *The Journal of Symbolic Logic*, 1981, 46: 201–02.

"What Price Substitutivity? A Note on Probability Theory." 1981. *Philosophy of Science* 48: 317–22.

"Free Intuitionistic Logic: A Formal Sketch." 1981. *Scientific Philosophy Today: Essays in Honor of Mario Bunge*. R. S. Cohen and Agassi, J., eds., Dordrecht: Reidel Publishing Co., 123–38.

"On Characterizing Popper and Carnap Probability Functions" (W. L. Harper and B. C. van Fraassen, coauthors). To appear in *Essays in Epistemology and Semantics*.

"Satisfiability in Probabilistic Semantics" (C. G. Morgan, coauthor). To appear in *Essays in Epistemology and Semantics*.

"Identify-Elimination in Various Free Quantificational Logics" (R. F. Barnes, Jr., coauthor). To appear in *Essays in Epistemology and Semantics*.

"Probabilistic Semantics for Intuitionistic Logic" (C. G. Morgan, coauthor). To appear in *Notre Dame Journal of Formal Logic*.

"Probability Theory, Intuitionism, and Semantics" (C. G. Morgan, coauthor). To appear in *Notre Dame Journal of Formal Logic*.

Index of Proper Names

Anderson, A. R., 131, 412

Barcan, R. *See* Marcus, R. B.
Barnes, R. F., Jr., 116, 118, 131, 137, 258
Belnap, N. D., Jr., 85, 88, 89, 128–30, 131, 136, 137, 154, 155, 196, 234, 235, 268, 271, 280, 290, 300, 305, 324, 325, 326, 327, 348, 357, 385–89, 390–96, 412
Benacerraf, P., 203
Bencivenga, E., 13, 15, 451
Bernays, P., 285, 291, 292, 348, 349, 356, 357, 380, 381, 403
Berry, G. D. W., 450, 451
Beth, E. W., 11, 15, 76, 77, 85, 88, 89, 126–27, 128, 129, 130, 131, 137, 139, 141–42, 143, 145, 155, 156, 166–76, 183, 196, 220, 234, 235, 268, 269–71, 275, 277, 279, 290, 327, 382–84, 395, 396
Borkowski, L., 292, 413–21

Carnap, R., 111, 118, 124–25, 135, 137, 268, 270, 275, 279
Chellas, B., 205, 215, 218
Church, A., 14, 15, 68, 71–72, 74, 91, 98, 137, 155, 175, 196, 198, 200, 203, 233–34, 235, 238, 273, 277–78, 279, 280, 285, 287, 291, 292, 304, 305, 356, 389, 416, 419, 421, 433, 434, 440, 449, 451, 452
Cocchiarella, N. B., 4, 15, 58, 75, 258, 266
Cooley, J. C., 350, 355, 357
Corcoran, J., 196
Cosgrove, R. J., 117, 431, 444, 451
Craig, W., 419, 421
Cresswell, M. J., 117, 118
Curry, H. B., 292, 348, 349, 423, 429, 430

de Jong, D. H. J., 326, 327, 395, 396
Dubislav, W., 292
Duffy, M. J., 451
Dunn, J. M., 85, 88, 89, 104, 116, 118, 128–30, 131, 136, 137, 154, 155, 234, 235, 271, 280

Feys, R., 102
Field, H., 132
Fisk, M., 102
Fitch, F. B., 74–75, 88, 89, 155, 169, 175, 196, 285, 291, 348, 349, 350, 357, 370, 381, 429, 430, 431, 435, 436, 440, 444, 445, 450, 452
Fujimura, T., 21

Gentzen, G., 6, 14, 15, 133, 270, 280, 284–92, 293–300, 328–57, 358–81, 388–89, 395, 396, 397–403, 420
Gödel, K., 22, 42, 47, 48, 49, 55, 56, 57, 118, 136, 137, 140, 155, 177, 196, 279, 419
Goldberg, J., 131, 240–46
Gotlind, E., 407
Gumb, R. D., 116, 118, 131, 137, 234, 238, 258

Haack, S, 13, 15
Hailperin, T., 3, 4, 5, 7, 9, 10, 11, 14, 15, 17, 18–21, 50, 55, 56, 57, 58, 73, 75, 78, 87, 89, 91, 98, 143, 438, 440, 451
Harper, W. L., 132
Hasenjaeger, G., 76, 89, 126, 137, 155
Henkin, L., 11, 12, 13, 15, 22, 23, 42, 47, 48, 49, 55, 56, 57, 74, 75, 76, 89, 97, 98, 106, 108, 109, 118, 124, 126–27, 128, 130, 132, 136, 137, 144, 145, 155, 156, 157, 159, 165, 166, 167, 169, 172, 174, 175, 176, 177, 178–79, 183, 184,

457

458 Index of Proper Names

Henkin, L. (continued)
185–87, 196, 209, 218, 227, 231–32, 234, 235, 238, 245, 258, 265, 266, 269, 270, 273, 276, 277, 279, 280, 285, 292, 356, 357, 431, 433, 434, 435, 436, 440, 449, 451, 452
Heyting, A., 344
Hilbert, D., 124, 135
Hintikka, J., 2, 5, 7, 9, 10, 14, 15, 55, 57, 58, 73, 75, 85, 88, 89, 118, 125–26, 127, 128–29, 137, 139, 141, 144, 145, 155, 161, 165, 174, 177, 178, 196, 268, 269, 271, 275, 276, 279, 280, 438, 452
Hiz, H., 57, 304, 305, 325, 412
Hobbes, T., 278
Hughes, G. E., 117, 118
Hume, D., 275
Huntington, E. V., 407, 409, 412–13

Jaśkowski, S., 3, 6, 15, 55, 57, 73, 75, 284, 285, 291, 292, 304, 305, 355

Kalish, D., 14, 15, 91, 98, 450, 452
Kanger, S., 128, 137, 285, 291, 348, 357, 381, 384, 389, 423, 429, 430
Kaplan, D., 157, 279
Kearns, J. T., 89
Kemeny, J. G., 155
Kleene, S. C., 356, 357, 420, 421, 423, 430, 434, 449, 450, 451
Kripke, S., 11, 12, 13, 14, 15, 99, 102, 104, 111–117, 118, 136, 137, 206, 212–16, 218, 274, 275, 280, 289, 292, 300, 348, 349, 357, 380, 381, 396, 402, 403
Kuratowski, C., 195

Lambert, K., 4, 7, 8, 10, 13, 14, 15, 57, 58, 59, 72, 73, 74, 75, 77, 78, 88, 89, 90, 98, 99–102, 103, 104, 107, 108, 116, 118, 130, 450, 452
Langford, C. H., 15, 409, 413
Leibnitz, G. W., 103
Leonard, H. S., 4, 7, 10, 15, 17, 21, 58, 59
Lesniewski, S., 124, 130
Lewis, C. I., 13, 15, 274, 290, 292, 409, 413
Löwenheim, L., 76, 85, 88, 90, 157, 161, 163, 419
Łukasiewicz, J., 102, 137, 245
Lyndon, R. C., 419, 421

Makinson, D. C., 116, 118, 212, 213, 216, 219, 266
Marcus, R. B., 13, 104, 111, 117, 118, 205, 208, 268, 279, 280
Massey, G. J., 102
McArthur, R. P., 131, 137, 205, 215, 216, 218, 258–66
McNally, M., 451
McNaughton, R., 407
Meyer, R. K., 4, 8, 11, 12, 13, 15, 58–75, 78,

Meyer, R. K. (continued)
87, 88, 89, 90, 91–98, 99–102, 116, 118, 130, 131, 134, 137, 155, 167, 175, 176, 177–97, 201, 203, 205, 210, 218, 219, 220, 234, 235, 237, 239, 274, 422–30, 449, 450, 452
Montague, R., 14, 15, 57, 91, 97, 98, 169, 176, 218, 219, 285, 292, 356, 357, 431, 433, 434, 435, 436, 440, 449, 450, 451, 452
Moore, G. E., 123, 124, 137, 203, 204
Morgan, C. G., 13, 15, 102
Mostowski, A., 3, 4, 9, 15, 50, 55, 56, 57, 58, 59, 73, 75, 91, 97, 98, 420, 421

Nakhnikian, G., 4, 7, 15

Popper, K., 132, 304, 305
Porte, J., 407, 410, 412, 413
Prawitz, D., 90, 292, 300, 381

Quine, W. V., 3, 4, 12, 13, 14, 15, 17, 21, 23, 55, 56, 57, 58, 59, 67–70, 73, 75, 91, 96, 97, 98, 102, 116, 123, 124, 125, 135, 137, 194, 195, 197, 268, 271, 277, 350, 450, 452

Ramsey, F. P., 124, 128, 135, 137, 268, 274, 280
Rasiowa, H., 407
Rescher, N., 4, 7, 14, 16
Resnik, M. D., 349
Robinson, A., 125, 137, 268, 271, 280
Robinson, T. T., 429, 430
Rosser, J. B., 131, 137, 245, 251, 256, 257
Routley, R., 131, 138
Russell, B., 3, 4, 11, 14, 16, 17, 21, 58, 59, 75, 77, 123, 124, 128, 130, 134, 138, 198, 200, 201, 202, 203, 204, 220–35, 236–39, 277, 408–13, 451

Salmon, W. C., 4, 7, 15
Schneider, H. H., 23, 55, 56, 57, 91, 98
Schock, R., 13, 16, 73, 75
Schütte, K., 88, 90, 126, 127–28, 130, 131, 136, 138, 154, 155, 156, 167, 177, 195, 197, 220, 234, 235, 268, 269–71, 273, 274, 275, 277, 280
Shipley, C. T., 12, 16, 72–73, 74, 75, 450, 452
Shoenfield, J. R., 125, 138, 268, 280
Skolem, T., 85, 88, 89, 90, 217, 419
Słupecki, J., 244, 245, 246
Smullyan, R. M., 89, 90, 265, 266
Snyder, D. P., 118, 119

Takeuti, G., 127, 137
Tarski, A., 14, 55, 132, 140, 181, 261, 267–68, 278–79, 280, 407, 412, 439, 440, 450, 451, 452

Index of Proper Names 459

Thomason, R. H., 11, 22–57, 58, 70, 71, 73, 75, 85, 89, 90, 91, 98, 116, 117, 118, 119, 143, 155, 174, 290, 300, 324, 325, 327, 349, 357, 389, 390–96, 397–403, 414–21
Trew, A., 12, 16, 74, 75, 450, 452
Turquette, A. R., 131, 245, 251, 256, 257

Ullian, J. S., 55
Umezawa, T., 349

van Fraassen, B. C., 4, 9, 10, 11, 12, 16, 22, 23, 55, 56, 57, 58, 74, 75, 89, 119, 130, 142, 143, 155, 174, 430, 450, 452
Vesley, R. E., 290, 292, 326–27, 390–96
von Wright, G., 274

Wajsberg, M., 240, 241, 245, 246
Weaver, G., 131, 201, 203, 205, 210, 215, 218, 219, 220–35, 238, 239, 240–46, 257, 274
Whitehead, A. N., 16, 21, 123, 124, 128, 130, 134, 138, 204, 235, 236–39, 408–13, 451
Wiener, N., 195
Wisdom, W. A., 117, 118, 165, 249–57, 191, 292, 357, 381, 436, 449, 450, 452
Wittgenstein, L, 88, 123, 124, 128, 133, 134, 135, 138, 198–204, 268, 276, 280
Woods, J., 13, 16

Yasuhara, M., 121

Index of Subject Matters

All or none, 290, 414–21
 as a quantifier, 414
 definability of singulary quantifiers in terms
  of, 414, 419–20
 Gentzen introduction rules for, 420
 quantificational logic based on, 415–19
Axiom of Reducibility, 130, 134, 198,
  200, 201, 203, 274
Axiom of Specification, 13, 26–28, 59, 91–
  97, 103, 106, 112, 133–34, 208,
  217, 218

Barcan formula(s), 13, 104, 112, 117, 131,
  205, 208, 265, 279
Beth's regular functions, 126
Beth's Theorem, 76–77, 85, 126, 166, 174
 corollaries of, 166
 generalizations of, 166–176
Boolean algebra, 290
 axioms and rules for, 404–405, 408–409
 propositional calculus and, 290, 404–407,
  408–13
 propositional rewrites of Boolean
  identities, 404

Carnap's semantics, 124–25, 270
Comprehension Axiom, 134, 137, 236–38

Deductions, Part 3 passim
 axiomatic, 283–84
 natural. *See* Natural deduction
 proofs as, 291 (*see also* Proofs from
  hypotheses)
Descriptions (Russell's theory of), 7–8, 14, 17
Domains
 countable, 124–25
 empty, 3–5, 22–23, 91–98

Domains (*continued*)
 inner and outer, 11, 22–23, 36–40,
  70–72, 117
 standard, 105
 systems of, 217
 See also Free Logic

Existence
 definition of, 6–7, 14, 17–18, 77
 logic of, 7–9, 76–90
 predicate, 7–9, 76–90
 premises, 6–8
 presuppositions in modal logic, 13, 99–102
 presuppositions in standard logic, 3–5,
  6–8, 17, 22–23, 55, 58–59, 77, 91, 103
 See also Free Logic

f-images, 179
Free logic, Part 1 passim
 axioms and rules of inference for, 5–6, 8–9,
  26–29, 60, 74, 79, 100, 107, 438
 Compactness Theorem for, 89
 Completeness Theorems for, 12, 42–49, 56,
  64–67, 80–85, 100–102
 domains in, 3–5, 11, 22–23, 36–40, 70–72,
  91–98, 117
 existence presuppositions in, 3–5, 6–8, 13,
  17, 22–23, 55, 58
 Fundamental Theorem of, 7–8, 14, 19–20,
  29, 451
 generalizations in, 431, 438–39
 inclusive quantification theory and, 12, 15,
  67–70, 91–98, 103
 modal logic, 13, 99–102, 103–104, 111–16
 non-designating terms in, 4–5, 6–8, 17, 21,
  22–23, 55–56
 open formulas in, 3–4, 58, 91–98

461

462 Index of Subject Matters

Free logic *(continued)*
  Permutation Axiom in, 12, 74, 107, 447–49, 450
  rationale for, 3–5, 13, 17, 22–23, 58–59, 76–77, 103, 106–107
  rules of natural deduction for, 5–6, 18
  semantics for. *See* Semantics for free logic
  Soundness Theorems for, 12, 63–64, 80–85
  Specification Axiom in, 4–5, 7–9, 12, 13, 14, 19–20, 26–28, 117
  Substitution Theorem for, 12, 59, 67–70
  truth-value gaps and, 9–11, 23
  vacuous quantification in, 3–4, 50–52, 56, 58, 73
  valuations and supervaluations for, 9–10
  with existence predicate, 7–9, 76–90
  with identity predicate, 1–57

Generalization (rule of), 27, 56, 74, 88–89, 97, 117, 174, 175, 285, 291, 304, 352–53, 356, 431–52
  Church's treatment of, 431, 432
  Fitch's treatment of, 169, 431, 435, 450
  Leblanc's treatment of, 434
  Montague-Henkin's treatment of, 431, 434–35, 449, 450
  the Universal Generalization Theorem, 431, 435–39, 440–41, 450
  See also Intelim rules of inference, ∀I

Henkin's Completeness Proof, 108–109, 126–27, 433
Henkin's interpretations and models, 108–109, 124, 126–27, 132, 156–61, 177, 231–33, 269
Hintikka's semantics, 118, 222–26, 269–70, 274

Identity
  as defining existence, 7–8, 17–18, 451
  free logic with, 1–57 passim, 431, 444, 447–49
  standard logic with, 1–57 passim, 422–30, 439–44, 451
Inclusive Quantification Theory
  axioms and rules of inference for, 92–93, 95–97, 106
  Completeness Theorem for, 92–94
  Modus Ponens in, 91
  open formulas in, 3–4, 58, 91–98
  Quine's validity test for, 4, 91, 97
  rules of natural deduction for, 5–6, 94–95
  semantics for, 3–4, 9, 15, 50, 55–59, 93, 97
  Specification Axiom in, 91–97, 103, 106
  Substitution Theorem for, 12, 67–70
  vacuous quantification in, 3–4, 73, 95–97
  See also Free logic
Intelim rules of inference
  lists and tables of, 285–87, 294, 301, 304, 307, 329–30, 338–39, 345–46, 351,

Intelim rules of inference *(continued)*
  371–72, 376–77, 382–83, 401–402, 424–25, 429
  BI, 307
  CI, 307, 390–95
  DI, 307, 390–95
  HI, 284–85, 307
  NI, 284–85, 307
  ∀I, 285, 304, 352–53, 356, 426–27, 429, 439–444 (*see also* Generalization)
  ∀I$_v$, 285, 298, 343, 357, 426–27
  ∃I, 351
  BE, 285, 290–91, 307, 325, 339, 348, 353–54, 357, 385
  CE, 307, 325, 348, 355, 390–95
  DE, 307, 325, 355, 390–95
  HE, 284–85, 290, 291, 298, 304, 325, 326, 338, 353–54, 357, 382–83, 385 (*see also* Modus Ponens)
  NE, 284–85, 290, 338, 348, 382–83, 385
  ∀E, 304, 355–56
  ∃E, 285, 352–53, 356, 427–28
Interpretation of quantifiers,
  standard (= objectual), 123
  substitutional, *see* Truth-value semantics, substitution interpretation of quantifiers and
Interpretations, 36–37, 53, 124, 267
  C-exhaustive, 37
  Henkin. *See* Henkin interpretations and models
  X-variants of, 37
Interpretations of languages and logics, 132–33
  predicative, 236–39
  truth-functional, 220, 224, 225, 230
  strictly truth-functional, 220–21, 224–25
Introduction rules of inference, 289, 295
  tables of, 295, 331–32, 339–41, 342, 372–73, 374–75, 375–76, 376–79, 398, 403, 420
Intuitionistic logic
  axioms and rules for, 422–23
  conversion of intuitionistic rules into classical ones, 289–90, 382–84, 385–87, 390–96
  demarcation line between intuitionistic and classical logic, 289–90, 397, 402
  entailment and validity in, 285, 300
  natural deduction rules for, 382–84, 389–90
  separation theorems for, 288–89, 290, 353–54, 356, 428–30
  subformula theorems for, 288–89
  See also L-sequents; N-sequents

Kripke's semantics, 13, 99–102, 112–18

Languages (first-order, modal, impredicative second-order, predicative second-order), 205–206
L-sequents, 285, 288–89, 293–94, 380–81
  axioms for, 289, 295
  classical validity of, 289, 296, 329, 358, 397

Index of Subject Matters 463

L-sequents (continued)
Gentzen's Haupsatz for, 297, 359, 403
Gentzen, 358, 380, 381
in a set of operators, 397
intuitionistic validity of, 296, 329, 358, 397
LJ, 288–89, 299
LK, 288–89, 293, 295, 296–97
natural deductions and, 295
rules for. See Introduction rules of inference; Structural rules of inference
separation theorems for, 288–289, 332–39
subformulas of, 288, 289
subformula theorems for, 289
Löwenheim and Löwenheim-Skolem Theorems, 76, 85, 88, 132, 157–65, 216

M-images (= M-rewrites), 146, 155, 248, 259, 271
Modal logic(s)
axioms and rules of inference for, 100, 111–12, 208–209
characteristic formulas of, 208
Barcan formula(s) in, 13, 104, 112, 117, 131
definition of modalities, 420
existential presuppositions in, 13, 99–102
free, 13, 99–102, 103–104, 111–16
monadic quantification theory and, 100, 102
possible worlds and, 99–102, 103, 112–19
semantics for, 99–100, 102, 103, 112–19, 131, 212–16, 274–75
Specification Axiom in, 13, 112
truth-functionality of, 212–16
Models, 106, 108
cardinality of, 156–165
finite, 157–65, 271–72
general, 134–35, 136, 218
Henkin, 108, 132, 156–61, 269
infinite, 157–65
standard (= normal), 136, 218
truth-value counterparts of, 108
Modus Ponens
in free logic, 26–28
in inclusive quantification theory, 91
provability and derivability versions of, 410–12
See also Intelim rules of inference, **HE**

Natural deduction, 5–6, 284–95
(generalized) Fitch-deductions, 370, 376–79
for free logic with identity, 5–6, 16
for inclusive quantification theory, 94–95
history of, 284, 350
implication in, 349, 356, 370
rules for. See Intelim rules of inference; Structural rules of inference
shortcomings (two) of, 351–57
separation theorems for, 285, 287–88, 328–49, 353–55, 356
subformula theorems for, 288, 370

N-sequents, 285, 287, 289, 293–94, 300, 380, 381
axioms for, 294, 297
classical validity of, 329, 358, 397–402
intuitionistic validity of, 329, 358, 397–402
natural deductions and, 285
N-counterparts of L-sequents, 341–42
NJ, 289, 299
NK, 289, 293, 294, 296–99
separation theorems for, 287–89, 297, 328–49
subformula theorems for, 289, 359–81
T-statements and, 287, 289, 300
Non-designating terms (= constants), 4–5, 17–21, 22–23, 55–56, 70–72
inferences involving, 4–5, 17–21

Parameters, 8, 14, 59, 104–105, 117, 125, 129, 135, 175, 199, 203, 206, 216–17, 268, 433–34
Parametric (= term) extensions, 85, 128, 130, 136, 188
PC. See Propositional Calculus
Permutation Axiom, 12, 74, 107, 447–49
Predicative second-order logic, 130, 133, 205–19, 273–74, 277
Axiom of Specification in, 133, 208
axioms and rules for, 208–209
relevance matters, 135
(strict) truth-functionality, 133–34, 273–74
substitution instances in, 134
truth-value functions for, 210–11, 273–74
truth-value semantics for, 133–34, 276–77
Presupposition-free logic. See Free logic
Principia Mathematica. See Ramified theory of types; Simple theory of types
Probabilistic semantics, 132, 137
Proofs
N-proofs, 358
operator-preserving (-minded), 288, 292, 296–99 (*see also* separation theorems)
subformula-preserving (-minded), 288–89, 292, 296–99, 359, 390 (*see also* Subformula theorems)
variable-preserving (-minded), 297
Proofs from hypotheses, 431–52
Church's treatment of, 431, 432–33, 449
Fitch's treatment of, 435
Kleene's treatment of, 434
Montague-Henkin treatment of, 434–35
Propositional Calculus
Boolean Algebra and, 290, 404–407, 408–13
axioms and rules for, 405–407, 409–13
completeness theorems for, 405–407, 409–10
Modus Ponens in, 410–12
proof routines for, 306–27
separation theorems for, 306–27
(strict) truth-functionality of, 133, 198–99
Provability, Part 3 passim

464   Index of Subject Matters

QC. See Quantificational logic
QC*. See Free logic
QC!. See Free logic with existence predicate
QC$_=$. See Quantificational logic with identity
QC$^*_=$. See Free logic with identity predicate
QC^2. See Second-order logic
QC$^{2!}$. See Predicative second-order logic
QC$^{2/\infty}$. See Ramified second-order logic
QC$^{\infty/\infty}$. See Ramified theory of types
QC$^\infty$. See Simple theory of types
QC$_3$. See Three-valued logic
QC$_5$. See All or none
QK$_t$. See Tense logic
Quantificational logic, 22–57 passim
  all or none version of, 414–21
  axioms and rules of inference for, 92, 106, 146, 208–209, 422–23
  Beth's Theroem for, 76–77, 85, 126, 166–69
  completeness theorem for, 92, 108–109, 126–27, 147–53, 167–68, 433
  free. See Free logic
  generalization in. See Generalization (rule of)
  relevance theorem for, 210
  semantics for, 25–57 passim, 103–104, 105–106, 108–109, 139–43, 268–71, 269–80
  soundness theorem for, 435
  separation theorems for, 290, 422–30
  (strict) truth-functionality of, 133, 199, 210–11
  valuations for, 61–62, 105–106, 267
  with identity, 1–57 passim, 128–29, 141–42, 147–53, 422–30, 431, 439–44, 450–51
Quantifiers
  definability of, 290, 292, 414–21
  interpretation of. See Interpretation of quantifiers
  nature and number of, 290, 414
  substitution instances of, 77–78, 88, 134–35, 199–200, 202, 222–23, 224

Ramified second-order logic, 130, 132, 134, 199–204, 220–35, 274
  Axiom of Reducibility in, 130, 220, 223, 225, 227–28, 274
  axioms and rules for, 223–24
  Comprehension Axiom in, 227, 239
  Henkin interpretations, 231–33
  instances of quantifications in, 222–23
  intended interpretation of, 225
  levels of predicates, variables, and formulas, 221, 222
  reduction to second-order logic, 130, 227–30
  standard semantics for, 231
  (strict) truth-functionality, 133–34, 200–201, 220, 225–27, 230, 233, 234, 273–79
  truth-functionality theorems for, 225, 230
  truth-value functions for, 223–25, 233–34
  truth-value semantics for, 233–34, 274

Ramified theory of types, 130–31, 220–35, 276–77
  Axiom of Reducibility for, 130, 134
  predicative interpretation of, 238
  (strict) truth-functionality of, 199, 201–202, 220–21
  See also Ramified second-order logic
Relevance matters, 129, 135, 205–19
  definition of relevance, 210, 212, 213–14
  relevance theorems, 205, 210–16
Rules, 285, 390–96
  admissible, 391, 394
  classically valid, 393
  closed under substitution, 392–96
  completeness of, 394
  derivable, 305
  derivability and provability versions of, 410–11
  for sets of connectives, 394
  instances of, 305, 391, 393–94
  intelim, 285 (see also Intelim rules of inference)
  introduction, 289 (see also Introduction rules of inference)
  intuitionistically valid, 393
  premises-conclusion pairs, 393–94
  requirements placed on, 290, 300, 326, 390–96
  structural, 285 (see also Structural rules of inference)

Satisfaction (simultaneous and otherwise), 37–39, 53–54
SC and Sentential Calculus. See Propositional Calculus
SC$_3$. See Three-valued logic
Second-order logic, 199–200, 220–35, 236–39, 273–74, 277
  Axiom of Reducibility in, 130, 170, 208–209
  Axiom of Specification in, 133
  axioms and rules for, 170, 208–209, 238, 445
  Beth's theorems for, 169–75
  completeness theorems for, 170–74, 173–74
  Comprehension Axiom in, 134, 236–38
  consistency* and consistency**, 166–67
  derivability* and derivability**, 170–73
  free, 445–46
  generalization in, 445
  Henkin's versions F* and F** of, 166–67
  impredicative formulas, 236
  impredicative interpretation of, 236–37
  levels of predicates and formulas of, 199–200
  predicative. See Predicative second-order logic
  predicative formulas of, 236
  predicative interpretation of, 134–35, 236–38, 279
  provability* and provability**, 130, 166–67
  ramified. See Ramified second-order logic

Index of Subject Matters   465

relevance matters in, 135
substitution instances of, 134, 135
(strict) truth-functionality of, 133–34, 273–74
truth-value assignments for, 170
truth-value functions for, 130, 172, 173, 209, 236–37, 273–74
truth-value semantics for, 133–34, 166, 273–74, 276, 277–78
validity (general, secondary, standard), 130, 136, 137
validity* and validity**, 172, 174
Semantics. *See* Carnap's; Hintikka's; Kripke's; Semantics for free logic; Standard; Truth-value
Semantics for free logic
  Kripke, 13, 99–102, 112–18
  Lambert-Leblanc-Meyer, 99–102
  Leblanc, 10, 12–13, 20, 77–80
  Leblanc-Meyer, 11–12, 60–63, 106–108
  Leblanc-Thomason, 11, 22–23, 36–42, 49–50, 51–55, 70–72
  Mostowski, 3–4, 9, 15, 50, 55–59, 73, 97
  Shipley, 12, 72–73
  truth-value. *See* Truth-value semantics
  van Fraassen, 9–11, 15–23
Separation matters, 285, 287–90, 292, 306, 323, 353–55, 422–30, 428–29
Sequents, 6, 285, 288–89, 293–94 (*see also* L- and N-sequents)
  antecedent formulas of, 293–94, 358
  as inference forms, 293
  arrow in, 288, 293
  formula (wff) associates of, 296, 358, 397, 425
  rules for. *See* Structural rules of inference; Intelim rules of inference; Introduction rules of inference
  soundness of rules for, 296
  succedent (= consequent) formulas, 293–94, 358
  validity, 293, 296, 329, 358, 397
Sets
  categorical, 273
  complete, 272–73
  equivalent, 272–73
  infinitely extendible (= of Type I), 79–87, 145, 147–53, 167, 171, 179, 213, 248
  isomorphic, 86, 129, 136, 141, 179, 271
  maximally consistent, 117, 135
  model, 118, 125–27, 269–70
  truth, 136, 273
  ω-complete, 117, 135–36
Simple theory of types, 130, 177–97, 236–39
  Axiom of Comprehension in, 181, 195
  axioms and rules for, 180–81
  completeness and soundness theorems for, 184, 196
  general truth-value functions for, 177, 181
  general truth-value semantics for, 181, 184–85

Simple theory of types (*continued*)
  general validity in, 181
  general verifiability in, 181
  Gödel's incompleteness theorem for, 177
  Henkin standard model-theoretic semantics for, 186
  Schütte's (strict) provability in, 327
  standard model-theoretic semantics for, 185
  standard truth-value semantics for, 188
  truth-functionality of, 193–195
  truth-value functions for, 189
Standard semantics
  for first-order quantificational logic, 25–57 passim, 105–106, 164, 268–69, 278–79
State-descriptions, 124–25, 270
Structural rules of inference, 285, 288, 289, 294, 301–305
  Contraction (**C, Cl, Cr**), 294–95, 307, 331, 341, 401, 403
  Cut, 295, 297, 299, 304, 324–25, 359
  Permutation (**P, Pl, Pr**), 288, 294, 299, 301, 307, 331
  Reiteration (**R, GR, SR**), 284–85, 287, 288, 291, 301, 307, 343–47
  Thinning (**T, Tl, Tr**), 288, 294–95, 299, 301–305, 307, 331
  Tables of structural rules, 294, 295, 301, 329, 331, 339–40, 370–71, 372, 374, 377, 382, 398, 401
Subformulas, 133, 137, 153–154, 164, 207, 270, 296, 358–59
Substitution conventions, 139, 167, 169–70, 172–73, 175, 200, 201–202, 206, 207–208, 221, 222, 238

Tarski's Convention T, 132
Tense logic, 131, 258–66
Term (= parametric) extensions, 85, 128, 130, 136
Theories, 207–19
Three-valued logic, 130–31, 240–57
Truth-functionality, 130–35, 198–203, 273–74
  strict (= strong), 130–37, 273–75
  theorems, 225–234
  See also interpretations of languages and logics
Truth-value assignments, 79–80, 108–109, 126
  cardinality of, 132, 156–65, 271–72
  identity-normal, 128–29, 142–43, 147, 162
  indexed, 259
  isomorphisms of, 168, 272
  model-theoretic counterparts of, 158–61, 272
  null, 80, 87–88
  standard, 80, 87–88
  to atomic statements, 205, 211–12
  to atomic subformulas, 205
  to statements, 209
  truth-value pairs and triples, 259–60

466 Index of Subject Matters

Truth-value functions, 133–34, 136, 209, 236–38
   general, 130, 177, 181, 236, 273–74
   predicative, 236–38
Truth-value semantics, Part 2 passim
   for free logic, 142
   for the logic of existence, 12–13, 76–78, 79–80, 85–88
   for modal logic, 99–102, 115–16, 274–75
   for quantificational logic, 103–104, 108–109, 139–43, 269–80
   for quantificational logic with identity, 128–29, 141–42
   for second-order logic, 133–34, 273–74, 276–78
   for tense logic, 258–66
   for the ramified theory of types, 127–28, 130, 136
   for the simple theory of types, 127–28, 130, 136, 177–197
   for three-valued logic, 240–57
   history of, 123–37, 144–45, 265–80
   isomorphisms, 86, 129, 136, 141, 271
   problem of implication and satisfaction in, 85–87, 110–11, 140–41
   rationale for, 123–37, 144–45, 267–80
   substitution instances, 123–37
   substitution interpretation of quantifiers and, 77–78, 88, 123–37, 198–203, 267–68, 270–71
   term extension in. *See* Term extensions
   truth-value categoricity, 273
   truth-value assignments in. *See* Truth-value assignments

Truth-value semantics (*continued*)
   truth-value functions in. *See* Truth-value functions
   truth-value verifiability, 80, 127–28
T-statements (= turnstile statements), 287, 390–96
   antecedent formulas of, 287
   derivations and proofs of, 301, 302
   formula associates of, 393
   N-sequents and, 287, 289, 300
   proof routines for, 287, 306–27
   rules for. *See* Intelim and Structural rules of inference
   separation theorems for, 287–88, 306–27
   succedent formula of, 287
   tables of rules for, 287, 301, 307
   true, 291
   turnstile, 300
   valid, 287, 291, 306

Valuations (and supervaluations)
   for free logic, 9–10, 70–72, 106–107
   for quantificational logic, 61–62, 105–106, 267
   Kripke's, 112–18
   P-variants of, 269
   relativized, 107
   Schütte's, 127–28, 130, 177
   Tarski's, 278–79
   van Fraassen's, 9–10
   X-variants of, 105, 267
Variables, 419–20
   semantical versus syntactical freedom of, 419–20